D1568663

# MEN
## OF
# TERROR

# MEN
# OF
# TERROR

*A Comprehensive Analysis of Viking Combat*

**WILLIAM R. SHORT and REYNIR A. ÓSKARSON**

WESTHOLME
Yardley

*Facing title page*: A stone carving from Lindisfarne, thought to be a gravestone depicting a Viking attack on the site. Photo: Historic England Archive.

Westholme Publishing, LLC
904 Edgewood Road
Yardley, Pennsylvania 19067
Visit our Web site at www.westholmepublishing.com

ISBN: 978-1-59416-360-9
Also available as an eBook.

Printed in the United States of America.

# CONTENTS

# PREFACE

Sometime near the end of the tenth century, a man named Fraði died in Sweden. His kinsmen raised a granite runestone in his memory in Denmark. Although the message carved into the stone is hard to interpret, it appears to tell us that Fraði was the first among all Vikings and that he was the terror of men.[1]

What did Fraði do in his lifetime that made him so admired by his kin that they raised a runestone in his honor as the first among Vikings, yet at the same time made him the terror of men? In this book, we tell the story of men like Fraði, not only about their weapons and battle-related activities but also about the inner thoughts and mindset of Viking warriors that caused them to venerate and praise activities that today we consider horrific. Along the way, we will see that Fraði achieved the ultimate goal to which all Vikings aspired: orðstírr (word-glory), that his name would be remembered and spoken after his death.

Viking society was a warrior society, with violence and the threat of violence a common thread shaping society and everyday life. Violence touched nearly every aspect of Viking culture.

Their myths and religious beliefs are so intertwined with violence that there would scarcely be any myths if there had been no violence. Men yearned for leaving this world after death and going to a paradise called Valhalla where they joined the elite warriors Einherjar in constant battles every day. Men were buried with their weapons, since even in death, they did not want to be far from them. The destiny of the gods is Ragnarök, an enormous battle between the giants and the gods, which is foretold to end in the destruction of the world.

Nearly all of their stories, the sagas, are written figuratively in blood. Most, if not all, have a feud or other ongoing violent dispute as a central plot element. The surviving law codes have extensive sections on what forms of violence are permissible and what forms are forbidden. Their imagery, such as the many picture stones in Scandinavia, most often show acts of violence and men with their weapons raised ready to strike. Viking poetry used paraphrases (kennings) often based on violence and arms. Their ships, one of the great technological triumphs of the Viking age, were optimized for speed and stealth in combat, allowing for quick landings where they were least expected and for quick getaways following a raid. Even their house architecture is aligned with the likelihood of violence in and around the home, sited for strategic advantage and featuring defensive structures, hidden doors, and secret escape tunnels.

The foreign sources that chronicle the Vikings most often tell of the violence inflicted by them on the lands they visited. While these raiders were feared because they were men of terror, like Fraði, they were sometimes cherished as mercenary troops because they could be loyal like a dog, and they were sometimes admired for their courage in adversity.

This book provides an understanding of Fraði and his people, based on the results of twenty years of research by our organization, Hurstwic. Our goal has been to advance the state of knowledge about Viking-related topics through rigorous testing and the use of the scientific method.

After introducing our research methods and sources, we have divided the book into several groups of chapters, each of which builds on what came before. The first group discusses topics that we believe are the underpinnings of Viking combat. Without a basic knowledge of these fundamentals, it will be hard to understand Viking people and their use of combat. These topics include mindset, empty-hand fighting, and a general introduction to the weapons of the Vikings and the place of those weapons in society.

We then move to a group of chapters that focuses on each weapon individually. They provide a more detailed look at the weapons of the Vikings and how these weapons were used: the prestigious sword; the iconic axe; the spear, the chosen weapon of Óðinn, the highest of the gods; the bow, an essential weapon of mass battles on land and sea, and others. Our discussion will also include the defensive tools of the Vikings.

The last group of chapters delves deeper into the nature of Viking combat: mass battles on land and sea, tactics, dueling, and raiding.

We use the controversial word *Vikings* to describe these people, who lived in Scandinavia and moved throughout other northern European lands in the early medieval period. We make this choice for numerous reasons, but the primary one is that the alternative terms are longer, less concise, and more awkward ways to refer to these northern Europeans living in the period named for them: the Viking age, circa 800–1100 CE.

Yet there are other factors at play as well. The meaning of words drifts with time, and the word *Viking* is no exception. In contemporary sources and in later medieval sources, the Old Norse word *víkingr* was reserved for seafaring men who harried and otherwise posed a threat to society, a topic discussed at length in this book. Later, the meaning drifted and was used for those deemed unworthy criminals: the bad guys of the story. Still later, the word came to mean all the Nordic people of the Viking age, and it is this sense of the word that we use in the book.

There are a number of words from the ancient Old Norse language that do not have a direct equivalent in modern English. In the text, we leave many of these words in the old language, rather than attempting to shoehorn them into an inappropriate English equivalent. Similarly, we leave place-names and personal names in the old language, using the old spelling.

The Old Norse language has several additional consonants compared to modern English, notably þ (*thorn*, pronounced like *th* in *Thor*) and ð (*edh*, pronounced like *th* in *father*). The language has many additional vowels, indicated with accents, umlauts, and ligatures. A pronunciation guide is included with the glossary. The old language is highly inflected, and we have chosen to keep the nouns in the nominative case and verbs in the infinitive for ease of understanding.

When alphabetizing personal names from lands and times that do not use family names, such as Iceland, we follow the custom of indexing using the given name and not the patronymic that follows. Accordingly, Grettir Ásmundarson falls under "G" and not "A."

In the interest of brevity, we cite only title and chapter (or verse, as appropriate) when we cite the core works of Old Norse literature, such as the sagas and the eddas. Print and online editions and translations are readily available for these works, and we do not wish to tie the reader to the version used by the authors in preparing this book. Chapter and verse numbers are not always consistent, and we have used the numbering from the Íslenzk fornrit editions where available.

# METHODOLOGY

## SCIENTIFIC APPROACH

Over a period of many centuries, the scientific approach has proven itself to be an effective route to discerning the truth and to advancing thinking and knowledge. In general, any scientific approach can be described as a method of acquiring knowledge through experimentation. The key steps are formulating a hypothesis or an idea about what is true; testing the idea through experiments and observations, often by testing a prediction made based on the hypothesis; and then refining the hypothesis based on the experimental findings and observations.

The approach has been clearly outlined by bioarchaeologist Alan Outran.[1] The process begins with the creation of a hypothesis, which the researcher tries to falsify. If the researcher can show that the hypothesis cannot be true, then the researcher discards it and seeks a new hypothesis and then repeats the test.

## THE HYPOTHESIS

Based on our idea, we create a hypothesis that can be tested. The hypothesis is a statement of fact based on our idea. An example of a hypothesis is, "Vikings wore helmets with horns." Our goal as researchers is to put the validity of the statement to the test.

## FALSIFY A HYPOTHESIS

If the hypothesis resists our attempts to falsify it and seems to be supported by available evidence, then the researcher accepts it as valid.

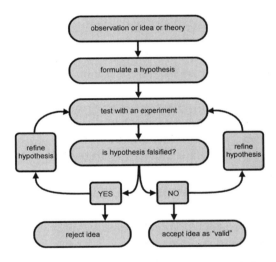

Hurstwic's research flow chart: the path we follow when using the scientific method to validate or falsify an idea. Illustration: William R. Short.

Importantly, valid is not the same as true. Valid merely means that the hypothesis has been conditionally accepted and will continue to be used to advance the research (and thus, continue to be tested) until it is falsified. This simple approach allows the researcher to make deductive leaps rather than being tied down to inductive extrapolation of existing knowledge.

## TESTING

Accordingly, we design and conduct tests based on our hypotheses. If scientific testing were represented with a flow chart, as shown in the illustration, the testing box would be large and complex inside, with many possible paths and many considerations, which we will discuss in a moment. For now, all that matters is that the output of the box has only two options. Our hypothesis exits testing bearing one of two labels: falsified or not falsified.

If, in our testing, we can prove the hypothesis wrong—falsify it—there is no need for more. The idea has been shown to be invalid. Sometimes a single, simple test, such as a thought experiment, falsifies an idea early in the testing. If testing breaks the idea in any way, it is finished. As careful researchers, we might refine our hypothesis and test again, but it is done. We don't have to discard it, but at the very least we need to set it aside until we have more or better information to allow us to do a better test.

If, in our testing, we cannot prove the hypothesis wrong, we almost certainly will want to test it again, multiple times, using various tests, probing potential weak spots.

If we cannot falsify a hypothesis after repeated tests, we label it as valid. We are, however, quick to reject an idea previously accepted as valid when new evidence comes to light that casts doubt on its validity.

## LAYERED SOURCES

We realize that no one source will provide all the answers, and so we strive to use many sources, layering one on top of the other. Can we place the literary sources on top of the archaeological sources, and then can we place pictorial sources on top of that while maintaining a solid premise? Does the idea violate the laws of the Vikings, or their moral compass, or their religious beliefs? Does it fit with their material culture and their way of life?

If we are testing a fighting move that we saw described in the literary sources, does the move fit with these other sources? Does it fit with what we know about their weapons, and with what we see of combat in picture stones, and with what we know about their sporting activities, and with what we know about the mindset?

## PHYSICAL/MATERIAL TESTING

If the hypothesis cannot be falsified with layered sources, we try physical testing or material testing. This testing may take many forms.

Some testing involves instrumenting the weapons, the targets, and the human test subjects in order to gather data we can analyze to learn about weapon use, weapon capabilities, and weapon efficacy.

If we are studying a martial move, we go to our research lab and test the idea. Is the move physically possible? We take the move through a series of pressure tests, increasing the adversarial role of the research partner.

If the move passes all these tests, we look at the idea through the lens of a force-on-force test: a test in a simulated combative setting where each side applies force, intensity, and intent to (on one side) make the idea work and (on the other side) to make the idea fail. If it is a move or a tactic, does it work against a combative training partner doing everything in his power to make it fail, while simultaneously trying to make attacks to the test subject? If it works in one round, does it work in many other rounds, with many other combatants?

Throughout all of this testing, we are constantly probing other possibilities, adding more layers to our investigation. We seek to identify any differences between how the move is performed in the research lab and how it might have been performed in Viking combat. We know there will always be differences; when performed correctly, these moves cause death or mutilation, which are not acceptable outcomes today. We work to understand and compensate for any differences imposed by modern considerations of safety and morality.

## NARROW SOURCES

Another way we keep the integrity of our research is narrow sources. Our goal is to learn how Viking people fought and used their weapons. Accordingly, we restrict ourselves to sources focused only on Viking people, such as literature about Viking people set in the Viking times, or artifacts from Viking lands in Scandinavia dated to Viking times.

Measurements of a spear thrust to a shield in the Hurstwic research lab. Photo: ©NAEPHOTO.

We are averse to using sources from outside these Viking domains, both place and time. We are adverse to using sources not focused on Vikings. It is only when there are no other sources of information that we turn our sights to other places and other times. Even though there may be good sources and artifacts found outside Scandinavia, we would rather err on the side of caution and reject these sources, if at all possible, using them only to confirm sources from within Viking times and lands.

Importantly, we do not cherry pick from those sources. All sources that fit our criteria are considered. We avoid allowing preconceived notions about the outcome of the test to affect our choice of sources.

### THE COIN TOSS

Again and again as we study the Viking people, we find there is a shortage of reliable information. For example, while there are many fragments, there is only a single mail shirt and a single helmet from Nordic lands in Viking times. Likewise, when we consider the literary sources, there is sometimes only a single mention of an important aspect of Viking combat, such as a wrestling throw or an obscure weapon. Drawing conclusions based on such a small sample size is dangerous.

The situation shares similarities with, for example, studying the outcome of a fair coin toss, but only testing it three times. If we throw a coin only three times, the chances are not insignificant that the coin will come up heads all three times. This test poorly characterizes the actual situation. When we have few examples, we must be careful with drawing inferences from them. We cannot, without additional information, claim that a single surviving mail shirt is representative of typical Viking-age mail shirts in much the same way that we cannot conclude that a tossed coin always comes up heads when thrown based on our test using three throws.

### THE MODERN MINDSET

Another possible source of bias that may skew our tightly focused research is the influence of a modern, twenty-first-century mindset on our thinking and on our analyses. None of us, neither the authors nor any of our readers, are actual Vikings. Our society is different from Viking society. Our laws are different from Viking laws. Our upbringings are different from Viking upbringings. If you are reading this book, written using twenty-first-century English, printed in lines that run from left to right using the Roman alphabet, then you are doing something a Viking never did.

This seemingly insignificant statement that we are not Vikings is crucial to our understanding and research of Vikings, as there is an enormous difference between our modern mindset and the mindset of the Vikings. That difference can skew our thinking, as we will discuss in more detail in chapter 1.

Simulated combat testing in the Hurstwic research lab. Photo: William R. Short.

An example of that difference is how we categorize information. Modern researchers tend to categorize, organize, and place things into neat boxes. These boxes, in many cases, did not exist in the Viking world; it was not how Vikings categorized their ideas.

For example, the Viking categorization of paranormal beings is very broad, open, and fluid, with the same word applied to many kinds of supernatural entities.[2] Beings such as *draugar* (zombies), *tröll* (trolls), *jötnar* (giants), and *blámenn* (blue men) are all fearsome creatures that gods and men battled against and interacted with during the Viking age. Later scholars of folklore categorized these entities in the modern age, slotting them into a few narrow categories and shoehorning them where they didn't exactly fit.

THE COMMON THREAD

For a modern researcher taking a scientific approach, this fluidity adds difficulty to the quest for knowledge. We resolve the conflict by seeking not the clear and universal truth, for it seems there isn't one from the Viking age, but rather the common thread. Instead of trying to impose a uniformity and trying to slot everything into a category, we seek the common thread that runs through the aspect of Viking culture under study: the Viking way of combat.

EFFECTIVENESS IN COMBAT

An additional trap for the unwary in the study of Viking combat is characterized by the notion of effectiveness. A researcher who is not aware of his modern mindset might seek the efficient or the effective way to use a Viking weapon. Our goal is not to find the efficient way to wield a Viking weapon but rather the Viking way to wield a Viking weapon. Simply

because a move is possible today in a training room or in a research lab does not imply it was a move used by Viking warriors in battle.

For example, did Vikings punch or kick when they fought? They both are effective ways to fight, yet as we will discuss later, they do not seem to have been the Viking way to fight.

Theories on edged-weapon combat tend to be actively tested using nonlethal combat, governed by a set of rules. Researchers exploring this field use a platform on which they build. That platform is a box that constrains them. It is possible to make groundbreaking discoveries within that platform, but they remain confined by the platform. And so, we must use numerous and novel testing approaches to avoid these constraints and to avoid permitting our modern thoughts to infect our results.

THE SEARCH FOR KNOWLEDGE

Throughout this book, the research guidelines discussed here will be our polestar in our quest for knowledge about Viking combat. We will refer to these guidelines frequently in the book, using shorthand phrases for brevity, such as "coin-toss problem" to remind the reader of the difficulty of inferring any conclusion based on a small sample size.

Like Óðinn, we constantly seek knowledge for its own sake. At the same time, we accept this simple truth: we will never know for sure.

# SOURCES

As we research Viking combat, there are many sources we can use. What we quickly find is that there is no single source of information that gives us a complete picture. At times we find significant discrepancies between sources, with one suggesting something diametrically opposed to another. Our main sources are archaeological, literary, pictorial, and miscellaneous. Here we limit ourselves to sources focused on Viking people and Viking times.

A significant limitation to all our sources is the matter of interpretation. How do we interpret the ancient excavated artifact we hold in our hand when it has been imperfectly preserved, or when its original function is not known? How do we interpret a medieval text? When it was composed, was it intended to be fantasy? History? Mockery?

ARCHAEOLOGY

Archaeology forms the bedrock of our research. For a society such as the Vikings, who lacked a written culture, archaeology is one of the few contemporary sources of information. Archaeologists study past human activities through the material remains left behind, either left intentionally (such as grave goods) or inadvertently (such as lost or discarded items). The materials could include man-made objects, such as tools, clothing, or weapons, as well as natural materials such as bones or pollen. An ancient artifact, excavated with the context of the find preserved, can be inter-preted to teach us about aspects of Viking-age life and society not available from other sources. These aspects range from dress and adornment to crops and livestock and even to cult rituals.

One major source of excavated artifacts from the Viking age is grave goods—items buried with the dead. During the early part of the Viking age, most people were heathens, and the typical practice after death was to bury the body with a few of the things the dead person used in everyday life.

Weapons were often a part of these grave goods, as evidenced by the numerous graves found with weapons in archaeological excavations. As examples, 61 percent of the graves in one cemetery in Norway contained at least one weapon,[1] and 37 percent of the graves found in Iceland have at least one edged weapon (axe, sword, or spear).[2] Additionally, burials with weapons are mentioned in the literary sources.

Yet it is not usual for these weapons to survive. In the ground, wood and leather rot, and iron rusts away. So only under unusual conditions do weapons or parts of weapons survive.

Often, excavated weapons are heavily eroded and in poor condition. The acute angles and edges erode more quickly than flat or rounded portions, and so points and edges of weapons have been more severely impacted. Some are little more than lacey remnants of the original robust blade.

An archaeological dig site at Auðkúla in west Iceland. The outline of the Viking-age longhouse is clearly visible. Photo: Margrét Hrönn Hallmundsdóttir.

Yet a few of these weapons survive virtually intact. From these excavated weapons, we can learn about the kinds of weapons Vikings used and about how they were made, the materials used in their construction, the damage they suffered in battle, and much more.

The interpretation of an artifact is not always easy or straightforward. An example of a striking object long misinterpreted as something mundane is the decorated iron rods from the Viking age, sometimes found in women's graves. They have long been interpreted as spits for roasting meat but more recently have been reinterpreted as the wands associated with magic, and especially with *völvur* (seeresses).[3] What was once a mere kitchen implement is now something magical and otherworldly.

Similarly, marks on human skeletal remains that have long been interpreted as injuries from weapons in battle have now been reinterpreted as the marks from shovels made during repeated disinterment and reburial of the skeletal remains.[4] What was once a hero's wound is now a careless shovel mark.

Interpretation is significantly more difficult without context: the place where an item was found and what the item was found in association with. Without context, much less can be said about an artifact's age and use, for example.

There is a wood carving of two men grappling found near Lillehammer, a find discussed later in the chapter on empty-hand fighting. It has no context. Up until a year before this text was written, the figure was dated to the eleventh century. Now it is thought more likely to be from the nineteenth or possibly twentieth century. What might have been an invaluable source of information about Viking-age fighting positions has to be downgraded to an interesting curiosity.

Closely related to archaeology is the study of human skeletal remains, the field of bioarchaeology, sometimes mistakenly called forensics. These studies tell us about the health of individuals and of population groups. From these studies, it is possible to infer details about daily life of Viking people. For example, the connections between the soft tissue and the bones tell us that these were strong people who worked hard rou-

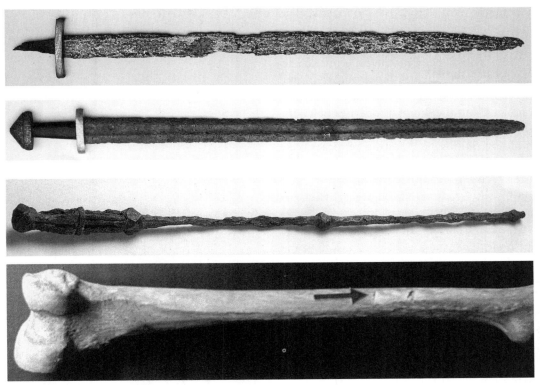

From top to bottom: An excavated Viking-age sword in a poor state of preservation. This type O sword has many losses not only along the edge but also on the faces of the blade as well. Photo: Lee A. Jones. An excavated Viking-age sword in a good state of preservation. This large type H sword has a solid, robust blade. The grip and cross-guard are modern replacements. Photo: Lee A. Jones. Is this the magical wand of a völva, or a mundane cooking tool? An iron staff from Birka grave Bj 834. Derived from Ulrik Skans, SHM 34000, Creative Commons. Is this mark on the bone due to a heroic cut from a sword, or to a careless shovel mark? A femur of an 11th century man from York, England. Photo: William R. Short.

tinely. Wear and tear of skeletal materials tell of hard work and a hard life throughout the population.[5] These robust connections imply great strength throughout much of the population and inform us of the kind of power these people could put into their weapon strikes—a common thread running through this book, as we will see. Importantly, the skeletal remains may tell us about battle injuries, including targets, weapons used, intensity and lethality of attacks, and recovery from the injuries.

An aspect of this research on skeletal remains showing battle injuries that is at first puzzling is the dearth of specimens. Surprisingly few battle injuries are found in Viking-age skeletal remains from Nordic lands. A notable example was found in Mosfell in Iceland.[6] There are not even a handful of additional examples in Iceland.[7]

Yet based on some simple assumptions, a quick comparison of the total Viking-age adult male population in Iceland compared to the number of graves excavated suggests that perhaps this small number of finds is not too far from what might be expected.[8]

EXPERIMENTAL ARCHAEOLOGY

Another important source of information in our research is experimental archaeology, a field of study in which researchers build replica artifacts that resemble those found by archaeologists and then attempt to use the replicas

XVI                                                SOURCES

for their intended purpose. Do they work as
expected? Can they be used in ways that match
what we learn from other sources?

We heavily depend on the experimental archaeological research of investigators around
the world. For example, not much would be
known about the sailing properties of Viking
ships if not for the work of the experimenters
building, sailing, and testing replica Viking
ships. Likewise, we would know little about the
use of Viking weapons without the work of
smiths who study archaeological artifacts and
build replicas.

Another example is Viking clothing. There
are few extant examples of Viking clothes, and
much has been inferred from scant evidence.
We make clothing based on the available evidence and test it to see if it works to keep the
wearer safe and reasonably comfortable in situations that resemble the northern European
climate. Do the garments work in fair weather
and foul? Do they protect from frostbite and
hypothermia? Do they wear well? Does the
clothing affect our physical activities, such as
combat? Does the clothing provide some level
of protection against weapons, as implied by
the literary sources?

When using experimental archaeology, one
must be cautious of the archaeological find
used to create the replicas for testing. It is possible to fall into the trap of creating a universe
around a single archaeological find that may
not represent typical artifacts from the Viking
age. One must be careful to avoid the coin-toss
problem in this field.

We also use experimental bioarchaeology in
our research. For example, we make test cuts
with sharp replica Viking weapons. These
sharp cutting tests are crucial to our understanding of the use of edged weapons, but we
have tested and rejected the usual test targets
as being unrepresentative of human flesh and
bone. Thus, we resorted to using an animal
carcass as a stand-in.[9]

These kinds of experiments provide deep insight into the weapons and their use. Do the
weapons cut the way we expect? Does the dam-

Top: Guðný Zoëga (bio-archaeologist) and William R.
Short examining Viking-age skeletal remains. Bottom:
Experimental bio-archaeological research at Hurstwic,
making test cuts with replica weapons to a pig carcass.
Photo: William R. Short.

age to the bones resemble what we see in
Viking-age skeletal remains? Can we inflict at
least some of the injuries often mentioned in
the sagas? Does the defensive armor protect
against damage to the body as we expect?

Yet this kind of testing is not without issues.
How well does one species stand in for another? Is the pig a good analog for a human?
Even if the species variation is acceptable, do
the tissues of a living creature respond similarly to those of a dead creature?

In addition to the problems of interpretation, there are serious moral and ethical issues
with this kind of testing. Do we want to be responsible for the death of a living creature,
solely for the purpose of cutting it up with

weapons? When our tests are completed, the scraps of the carcass are good only for feeding to animals.

We also consult with forensic experts skilled in interpreting traumatic injuries who can help us interpret material we find in other sources. These experts also help us design our experiments when we attempt to simulate battle trauma and its effects.

## LITERARY SOURCES

Most of our literary sources are Icelandic for the simple reason that far more material is available from Iceland than from any other Nordic land. It is worth spending a moment to understand how that came to be and why there is a dearth of written sources from other northern lands.

During the Viking age, the people of the north all spoke the same language, which they called *dönsk tunga* (the Danish tongue).[10] They wrote using the fuþark (the runic alphabet), and evidence suggests that many people in Viking society were literate, able to read and write the runes. Runesticks are found carrying mundane messages,[11] and the casual reading and writing of runic messages is mentioned in the sagas.[12] Public memorial stones are carved in runes.

Yet the northern people wrote only short works in runes. Longer thoughts were remembered using poetry and conveyed orally. Poets were the journalists and the historians of their day, composing verses so important events could be remembered and disseminated. They were paid handsomely by the king, and during battles they were protected within a *skjaldborg* (shield castle) so they could safely observe and report what they witnessed during the battle. For reasons not fully understood, throughout the northern lands, the Icelanders were the preeminent poets of the Viking age, composing verse for the kings of Scandinavia.

## ICELANDIC LITERARY SOURCES

When the Christian church arrived, bringing with it a written culture, it was the Icelanders who vigorously embraced this new way of re-

membering thoughts, turning out a torrent of works in their own language: Old Icelandic. They wrote histories, genealogies, and law books. They recorded in manuscript form the poems that before had been preserved only orally. And they created new literary forms.

## LAW CODES

The Icelandic law code was first written down around 1117–1118.[13] It survives in several manuscripts collectively referred to as *Grágás*, which is thought to represent the law of twelfth-century Iceland. Though it represents Christian law, the text preserves elements of pre-Christian law, such as oaths that called on heathen gods to sanctify the business of the assembly. Many of the sections on assembly procedures, homicide, penalties, and payments for injuries or death are thought to be similar to the laws practiced in Viking-age Iceland. Law codes were also recorded in Norway, such as *Frostaþingslög* and *Gulaþingslög*. These law codes show the king's role in the legal system and describe requirements not found in Icelandic law, such as the levy troops of the king, his fully equipped reserve of fighting men.

## HISTORIES

In Iceland, histories were written, such as *Landnámabók*, which tells of the discovery and settlement of Iceland in the late ninth and early tenth centuries. In addition to listing thousands of settlers and well over one thousand farms, the book relates brief but finely focused tales of the first settlers and their descendants. They tell us about the mindset of the people who chose to leave their ancestral homes in Norway to start a new life in Iceland during the Viking age.

## SAGAS OF ICELANDERS

Perhaps the most significant literary form to develop in Iceland was something new and unique: long prose works known collectively as the *Sagas of Icelanders* (*Íslendingasögur*). These stories provide a wealth of knowledge about the Viking-age people who settled and lived in Iceland. We will discuss these sagas in some detail since without them, our knowledge about the Vikings would be quite limited. For example, if we didn't have the sagas telling of the Greenlanders' voyages of exploration and settlement in that unknown western land across the Atlantic they later named Vínland,[14] would archaeologists ever have thought to look in North America for signs of Norse settlement? Even if Viking-age artifacts had been found in North America, how would they have been interpreted without knowing about the voyages from the sagas? If we didn't have the saga description of a *völva* (a magic seeress) and her equipment,[15] how could we interpret the graves of these women, laid to rest with their wands and jewels and paraphernalia?

The sagas are prose narratives written in Old Icelandic that tell stories about Icelanders during Iceland's settlement period and commonwealth period (between 850 and 1100). They were written down after the close of the Viking age, in the thirteenth century and later. The stories are probably based on oral narratives and poetry that date from the Viking age. Yet the sagas are not histories, and so they must be used with care.

There is little in the *Sagas of Icelanders* that we can confirm with certainty. Details about some of the main saga characters and important events are consistent between sagas, and some are also told in histories and genealogies describing events during the settlement of Iceland. The sagas contain anachronisms and elements of fantasy. Because they are based on oral traditions, which may be fluid, they must be used with care. We cannot blindly accept anything we read in the sagas.

The sagas are written in a dry, matter-of-fact style. Only what could be observed by a witness is reported. They are so coherent and clear that they give the sense of factual reporting of the events.

It seems likely that the sagas were not ecclesiastical but rather secular works composed by or at the request of wealthy farmers. Icelandic society differed from that of Europe during this time in that Icelandic society comprised many free, land-owning farmers. Many of

Manuscript AM 556 A, 4to, containing the oldest surviving version of *Grettis saga*. Photo: William R. Short.

these men were educated and literate, and some were ordained priests.[16] Icelandic society has always prized storytelling, and these farmers wanted stories of their ancestors, written in their own language, and compiled into books.

Many of these farmers were well acquainted with combat. Saga writing began in a turbulent period of Iceland's history known as the Sturlunga era. It was a time of nearly continuous civil war as large chieftains tried to consolidate their holds over the entire country in a long string of ceaseless battles. This period of exceptional warfare ended with the loss of Iceland's independence and the beginning of Norwegian rule.[17] Thus, it seems likely that saga authors were familiar with weapons and their use. Some of the battles in the sagas are described in fine detail.

One aspect of the *Sagas of Icelanders* that makes them so valuable is that by and large, they are about ordinary people rather than about gods or kings or trolls. We read how these Viking-age people responded to challenges, and the choices they made, and the behaviors they exhibited, and how other people responded to their behaviors. All of these descriptions help us understand more about the Viking-age people and about their mindset, discussed in greater detail in the next chapter.

Likewise, the sagas provide windows into many other aspects of Vikings' society: their beliefs and religious practices, their daily lives, and their culture. Since fights are often mentioned in the sagas, the stories also provide a window into their fighting moves, which sometimes are described in enough detail to be able to figure them out from the saga text, although sometimes the descriptions are much less clear.

At the same time Icelandic authors were writing the *Sagas of Icelanders*, they were also writing other prose works that are important sources of information in our research.

## KINGS' SAGAS

The *Kings' Sagas* (*Konungasögur*) are histories of the kings of Norway. Although Iceland was an independent country from the settlement up until the time the saga-writing age began, there was a close connection with Norway, from which many of Iceland's early settlers emigrated.

*Heimskringla* is the best known of the *Kings' Sagas* and was written by Snorri Sturluson. It tells the story of the kings of Norway from their divine origin in prehistory through to the year 1177. Snorri took great pains to find the best available sources, often depending on skaldic verses of poets who were eyewitnesses to the events about which they composed verse.

Fights are often mentioned in the *Kings' Sagas*, including large dynastic battles. The ruler of the land was determined by the outcome of these battles, which were fought on land and at sea. Thus, these sagas provide a picture of types of combat less frequently mentioned in the *Sagas of Icelanders*, and these depictions can be used to enhance our understanding of Viking combat from other written sources. Occasionally, the same battles are mentioned in both types of sagas and so can be used to crosscheck our sources. For example, the battle at Stiklarstaðir, in which King Óláfr helgi lost his life, is told in a *Kings' Saga*[18] and in a *Saga of Icelanders*.[19]

The *Kings' Sagas* show more of a society seen only dimly in the *Sagas of Icelanders*: a society run by kings, with professional fighting troops and fully equipped reserve levy troops available. While there were differences between the societies, we see there were more similarities.

## CONTEMPORARY SAGAS

Another form of history written in medieval Iceland were the contemporary sagas (*Samtíðarsögur*), which tell of events taking place in Iceland, often during the lifetimes of the authors who wrote them. *Sturlunga saga* is a collection of contemporary sagas written by different authors about events between 1117 and 1264. Often the authors were eyewitnesses to these events, and in some cases they were participants in the events they relate. As a result, the details are sometimes finely focused.

The contemporary sagas help with a vexing problem: understanding whether the authors of *Sagas of Icelanders* had knowledge of the differences in combat between their own time and the time of the events they wrote about in the sagas. The contemporary sagas help us with that understanding, since both they and the *Sagas of Icelanders* were written at about the same time,[20] and perhaps by some of the same authors. When the authors of *Sturlunga saga* show a clear understanding of the differences between customs of the Viking age and their own time, then perhaps the authors of some of the *Sagas of Icelanders*, likewise, were aware of those differences.

For example, one of the contemporary sagas is *Íslendinga saga*, written by Sturla Þórðarson. He describes battles in which he was an eyewitness, including many in which he was also a participant. In some of the battles, such as the battle of Örlygsstaðir in the year 1238, old, Viking-style weapons were being used at the same time as newer weapons.

Sturla tells of a buckler (*buklari*) being used in a way that makes sense only for the kind of small shield used in the thirteenth century, and of a shield (*skjöldr*) being used in a way that only makes sense for a large Viking-era shield.[21] He describes moves[22] that could have come directly from the I.33 sword-and-buckler training manual,[23] the earliest surviving European combat treatise, which was written at about this time.

## LEGENDARY SAGAS

Other prose works from medieval Iceland are

the legendary sagas (*Fornaldarsögur*). In these sagas, the treatment of time and of location is casual, unlike the *Sagas of Icelanders*, which often relate the time and place of the events in fine detail. To readers today, and likely to the people of the Viking age, these sagas had the impression of unreality and of fantasy. Very often, the fight descriptions are fantastic to a high degree.

Regardless, the legendary sagas can help us see a clearer picture of the hazy puzzle we are trying to assemble. An example is empty-hand fighting. The many examples of empty-hand fighting in the legendary sagas complement the smaller number of descriptions in other literary sources. Similarly, the legendary sagas fill in many of the blanks related to archery, since some of the heroes of these sagas are skilled archers to the degree that their nicknames are derived from archery, such as Örvar-Oddr (Arrow-Odd) and Án bogsveigir (Án bow-bender).

A sense of fantasy permeates these sagas, yet one can discern small details in the descriptions that can illuminate other sources in our research.

### MISCELLANEOUS ICELANDIC PROSE

Several sagas survive that do not neatly fall into any of these categories, such as *Jómsvíkinga saga* and *Færeyinga saga*, yet are valuable in our research. Additionally, there are numerous *þættir*, short works of prose that, like the sagas, tell tales of kings, of Icelanders, and of legendary heroes.

### POETRY

In addition to new works of prose, medieval Icelanders wrote down poetry that had been composed in the Viking age and conveyed orally since that time. Two significant books of poetry have survived, both called *Edda*, a word whose origin and meaning are unclear.

Two major forms of verse were in use during this period: eddic poetry and skaldic poetry. Both are complicated and difficult, but skaldic poetry was by far more convoluted. It was considered an art form, with complex rhythm, alliteration, sentence structure, and wordplay.

This complexity served to showcase the artistic abilities of the poet.

Skaldic verse was sufficiently complex that unravelling the meaning of a verse might not be possible on first hearing it. There are examples of people hearing a verse but not being able to interpret its meaning until reflecting on the verse later.[24]

Medieval Icelandic writers believed that skaldic verse was reliably preserved through the centuries since its original composition,[25] in part because of these complexities. Any error in remembering the verse would be instantly recognizable, because some aspect of the rhythm or alliteration or wordplay would fail to work.

### EDDAS

The earlier book of verse is called the *Poetic Edda* (*Eddukvæði*), a carefully curated collection of eddic poetry divided into mythological poems and heroic poems. These verses are, for the most part, preserved only in a single manuscript, the *Codex Regius*, dated to around 1270. The poems themselves are older, and at least some are thought to have been composed in the Viking age.[26] These mythological poems form the basis of much of our knowledge of the Norse myths. Knowledge of these myths helps us understand the mindset of the Viking warrior, which we will explore in depth in the next chapter.

The stories related in the poems are ancient, and some seem to predate the Viking age by centuries, with deep roots that extend well before the adoption of Christianity in the northern lands.[27] The story of the god Þórr fishing for the serpent that encircles the world is shown in an eighth-century picture stone, told in tenth-century eddic poetry and in Snorri's thirteenth-century prose summary, and illustrated in an eighteenth-century paper manuscript. This myth was well known and much loved in northern lands. It was kept alive by northern people in pictures, oral verse, and written texts for many generations.

The heroic poems in the *Poetic Edda* tell of ancient heroes and reveal the ideal of the northern people: the proper way for a praise-worthy warrior to behave. Additionally, one of the eddic poems, *Hávamál*, is a pragmatic, down-to-earth guide to proper behavior in everyday Viking-age life. We refer to the verse repeatedly in this book to understand the Viking way. It teaches the need to be prepared for a fight at all times[28] and to be cautious and wary.[29]

The later book of poetry, the *Prose Edda* (*Snorra edda*), was written by Snorri Sturluson in the early part of the thirteenth century. Even well after the Viking age, skaldic poetry was thought to be one of the highest of art forms. Snorri says in his text that he wrote the book to instruct young poets on the art of skaldic verse.[30]

In order to understand old skaldic poetry and to create new verses, poets needed to have a deep knowledge of the Norse mythology, since much of the wordplay in the verses is based on the myths. For example, kennings are a form of wordplay in which a phrase stands for a word. So "blood of Ymir" stands for "sea,"[31] but would be meaningless unless one knew the Norse creation myth that tells that when the gods created the world, they made the seas and other waters of the world from the blood of the giant Ymir.[32]

Snorri provides a prose summary of many of the myths, which otherwise would be incomprehensible from the other surviving sources. He also quotes many skaldic verses composed by Viking-age poets, most of whom are named. All of this mythic and heroic material is yet another source to help us illuminate and understand the mindset of the Viking warrior and how he saw the world.

RUNESTONES

There is a contemporary written source about Viking people found in Scandinavia: runestones, containing runic inscriptions carved into stone monuments. They usually take the form of memorials to dead friends, kinsmen, and fellow warriors. The stories are briefly told and difficult to interpret, yet they confirm the widespread travels of Viking people to distant

Runestone U 1161 depicts a moment in the story of Þórr fishing for the world serpent. Derived from: Gunnar Creutz, *Thor and the Midgard Serpent from the Altuna runestone at Altuna church, Enköpings municipality, Uppland, Sweden*. Creative Commons.

lands. Additionally, they provide a contemporary confirmation of the heroic ideal expressed in later written sources such as the *Sagas of Icelanders*.

In addition to the Nordic sources, there are literary sources from other lands and other times that may provide useful information in our search for the truth. An example is the poem *Waltharius*, written in Latin in the tenth century. It tells of battles set in Germanic lands centuries earlier, and some of the characters in the poem also appear in legendary sagas and in the Eddas.

Some of these sources tell of the interactions between Vikings and other societies from the point of view of the people on the receiving end of Viking activities.

### ANGLO-SAXON CHRONICLES

One such source is the *Anglo-Saxon Chronicles*, written in the kingdoms that eventually became England. Vikings were frequent and unwelcome visitors to these lands, and their exploits are often mentioned. These annals give a clear but at times distorted image of how these raiders were perceived by those unfamiliar with Vikings, their culture, and their code of conduct.[33] Some believe that the authors may have exaggerated the violent and barbaric acts of the Vikings. Comparisons with other medieval texts show the *Anglo-Saxon Chronicles* can be biased, perhaps altered to better fit an agenda.[34] Yet in at least a few cases, the courageous behavior of some individual Norsemen seems to have been admired.

The *Anglo-Saxon Chronicles* tell of the activities of the Viking invaders in England: the battles, the treaties and agreements, and the settlements. The *Chronicles* give us a different outlook on Vikings that is important to our research: the point of view of a society unfamiliar (at first) and adversarial with the Viking people.

Eyewitness accounts, such as the description of the Viking siege of Paris written by the monk Abbo Cernuus of Saint-Germain, likewise are valuable, yet not without their limitations. Abbo is criticized as being more interested in the theology of the siege than in events surrounding it, as we discuss in a later chapter.

### LITERATURE FROM THE SOUTH

There are also Greek and Byzantine sources that tell us about Viking people serving in the Varangian Guard, the elite troops that were the bodyguard to the Byzantine emperors. Several of these sources suggest that the two-handed axe was the preferred weapon of the guard,

Runestone Öl 28 states that Herþrúðr raised this stone in memory of her son Smiðr, a good valiant man. Derived from Berig, *Runestone at the church of Gårdby, Öland, Sweden.* Creative Commons.

who were called "axe-bearing barbarians" by the twelfth-century historian Anna Komnene, writing about the events of the eleventh century.[35] Exploits of Vikings who traveled south for military adventures, presumably with the Varangian Guard, are recorded in some of the Swedish memorial runestones, further confirming the literary sources.[36]

In their extensive travels, Viking people interacted with people from other cultures. Notably, the Arab diplomat Ibn Fadlan met a group of Rús traders while traveling on the Volga River and wrote about these people.[37] Again, there are problems with this source. It is not clear who the Rús people were. Perhaps they were Vikings from lands in or near Sweden, or perhaps they were something else. Many of their attributes reported by Ibn Fadlan do not correspond to attributes of Vikings described in Scandinavian sources.

Often, the discrepancies between Ibn Fadlan and Scandinavian sources are deep. Ibn Fadlan

An illumination depicting the Varangian Guard in the eleventh-century Madrid Skylitzes manuscript. Derived from Alonso de Mendoze, *Varangian Guardsmen, an illumination from the eleventh-century chronicle of John Skylitzes.*

reports these people to be "the filthiest of all Allah's creatures," in contrast to information in sagas,[38] the eddic poetry,[39] Anglo-Saxon sources,[40] Greek treaties dealing with the Varangian Guard,[41] and Icelandic law books,[42] all of which highlight the cleanliness and fastidiousness of the northern people.

Moorish sources tell of Viking raids in present-day Spain and Portugal.[43] They describe the tactics used by the Viking raiders and some of the responses devised by the Moors to defeat these raiders from the north.

SCANDINAVIAN SOURCES IN LATIN

Near the end of the Viking age and later, authors in other northern lands wrote in Latin about the Viking-age people. While the books are nearly contemporaneous with the Viking age, the authors sometimes wrote based on second- and third-hand material of which they had no direct knowledge, and so the texts are thought to be less than reliable.

Adam of Bremen wrote *Geste Hammaburgensis* on behalf of the Catholic Church in the last half of the eleventh century, so the events are seen from a Christian point of view. Most

of the book discusses ecclesiastical matters, but he does talk about the people and geography of the lands to the north. Despite his proximity to these lands, it does not appear that he ever visited them to obtain first-hand information. Yet despite these weaknesses, his book is one of the few contemporary accounts of heathen practices in the north.

Saxo Grammaticus completed his book *Gesta Danorum* at the beginning of the thirteenth century. The book was a history of the kings of Denmark and was written at the time the country gained dominance over the Baltic lands. The text may have been written to provide the Danish people with a national history comparable to that of older and more-established lands to the south. As a result, the author, a Danish patriot, may have altered and relocated material to meet his goal.[44] Saxo states in his preface that he relied heavily on Icelandic sources in writing his book.[45]

Yet Saxo appears to have come from a military family, and he states that both his father and grandfather served with and fought for the king.[46] Thus, Saxo's description of mass battles

Top: A reconstruction of a portion of the tapestry from the Oseberg burial. Derived from Eirik Irgens Johnsen, *Vognopptog, rekonstruksjion av billedvev fra Oseberg, Tønsberg. Akvarell ved Mary Storm.* Creative Commons. Bottom: A small portion of the Bayeux Tapestry depicting the Battle of Hastings. Detail of the Bayeux Tapestry, eleventh century, with special permission from the City of Bayeux.

may be based on personal experiences of his kinsmen in the century after the Viking age.

Using these sources composed in Latin to understand Viking combat requires additional care because of the use of classical Latin terminology by these medieval authors to describe Viking fighting practices. An example is the use of the Latin term *testudo* to describe Viking shield formations. The *testudo* (tortoise shell) is a well-known and well-understood formation used by Roman legions and recorded by Roman authors. The use by the medieval authors of this sort of terminology may have been an attempt to showcase their education and their awareness of classical knowledge by writing in the style of classical authors and by using classical terminology. We must be aware that this classical terminology may not accurately describe what Vikings used.[47]

## LATER SCANDINAVIAN SOURCES

*Konungs skuggsjá* (King's Mirror) was written in Norway in the mid-thirteenth century, well after the close of the Viking age. It is a textbook, probably written to educate the sons of the king. One section contains detailed information about the king's retainers and their duties, touching on military topics and combat. While the text is fascinating, it is not very applicable to our research. The society of medieval Norway had evolved in the centuries since the Viking age. The book is a contemporary textbook intended for its age, and it teaches about weapons and combat and courtly manners that had changed significantly in the centuries since the Viking age.

Another late Scandinavian source is *Hednalagen*,[48] thought to be a remnant of Swedish pre-Christian law that survives as a fragment in a thirteenth-century law document.[49] It provides valuable insight into the nature of duels. *Hirðskrá* is a late-thirteenth-century set of laws that applies to the king's men. Although from well after the Viking age, it provides additional information about the activities of the king's chosen warriors.

## PICTORIAL SOURCES

Related to the literary sources are the pictorial ones. The Viking people created few realistic renditions of the human figure: their pictures are generally crude, with limited details. Picture stones show Viking warriors dressed for battle, and tapestries show Viking people dressed in what may be ceremonial garb. There is usually insufficient detail to provide us with useful information.

Additionally, the pictures show an imperfect understanding of the use of perspective, an art that allows a three-dimensional object to be represented on a two-dimensional surface. This imperfect understanding can make it difficult for us to reinterpret the two-dimensional figure back to the original three-dimensional object.

Yet images from ancient picture stones provide us with a wealth of information on a number of topics, including the carry methods of weapons, the weapons more commonly used, dueling practices, shields on ships, and the antiquity of the myths.

Images from other lands contemporary with the Vikings provide more details, such as tapestries, manuscript illustrations, and carvings. For example, the Franks Casket, a magnificently carved whalebone chest dating from the eighth century, adds details of archery and shield use seen in other pictorial sources.

The Bayeux Tapestry is an embroidered cloth nearly 70 m (230 ft) long that shows the events leading to and including the Battle of Hastings in the year 1066. Since neither army depicted on the tapestry could be accurately described as Viking, extreme care must be taken in using this source to confirm or fill in small details of the much larger picture of combat. For example, the images show use of archery, details of helmet strapping, and of garments under mail that are helpful in our research.

## MATERIAL FROM OTHER LANDS

There are additional areas we consider in our research. We compare the Vikings to other contemporary cultures. As we study Viking combat, we must also keep in mind the combat used by the opponents of the Vikings. Across centuries of conflict, the Vikings and the Franks, for example, could not help but influence one another.

In a similar manner, Viking travelers and traders in eastern Europe may have seen weapons and moves that impressed them sufficiently that they may have brought them home with them. So eastern weapons and armor might be found in a Viking context, notably at Birka in Sweden, where evidence suggests a substantial presence of fighters from the east or influenced by eastern ways.

An intriguing example is the thumb ring made of bone found in south Iceland.[50] These rings were used by archers when drawing a Hunnish-style bow, a weapon from eastern European and Asian lands, as discussed in the archery chapter. Perhaps these exotic bows were in use in Viking-age Iceland.[51]

### MATERIAL FROM OTHER TIMES

We also look at material from before and after the Viking age. Earlier sources are even more limited than Viking-age material. Regardless, information we can glean from these periods gives us a clearer vision of the evolution of arms and armor, and more insight into the possible purpose of the tools and the weapons. For example, the Vendel-era sword is a magnificently decorated work of art, covered with precious metals, yet it is a crude chopping weapon. The evolution of the sword into the more plain but more versatile Viking-era sword tells us about the changes in both the use and the kinds of people who used this weapon.

### KINESIOLOGY

We also draw upon modern sciences. We use the science of kinesiology in our research, which helps us fill in gaps that none of our currently available sources can. Kinesiology is the study of the mechanics of body movement. Many human movements are, in a sense, universal.

For example, how did Vikings swing their weapons? As we will see in later chapters, we don't know with any certainty, and the Vikings left little behind to teach us. And so, our approach to swinging the weapon is based on the simplest and most logical way the body moves in more prosaic hitting activities with a tool in hand, such as the motions used in tennis, baseball, woodcutting, and others.

In some ways, we use kinesiology as one might use the blank, wild-card tile in a game of Scrabble. It helps us work out the puzzle and fit the pieces together. When a piece is missing, we go back to basics. We use kinesiology to tell us how humans move, and we use that knowledge as a placeholder to continue our research

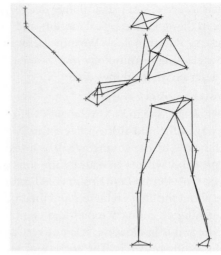

A kinesiological model used to simulate and interpret a golf swing. Illustration: Magnús Kjartan Gíslason.

until we can find the concrete information we need to fill in the missing gaps.

### ETYMOLOGY

Etymology is an important source of information in our research. The origin of the word for an object can give us strong clues about the use of an object. For example, the etymology of the word for *spjót* (spear) derives from the word for a spit,[52] the iron rod inserted through a piece of meat to cook it over a fire. This common origin suggests that the intended use of a spear is to skewer something all the way through.

### FOLK MATERIAL

Last, we look at folk material—echoes of the Viking age that still reverberate. A valuable resource in our research is the Nordic people today who grew up using the old ways of their lands. They remember many of these ways that perhaps have not changed so much from the way things were done in Nordic lands in the Viking age. These people are a valuable source of information about the old ways.

For example, there are people alive today who built and lived in turf houses in their youth. They can tell us about cutting and building with turf, the main building material in Viking-age Iceland. Turf-building practices probably did not change in any significant way between the Viking age and the twentieth century, when some of these people grew up on farms that still used turf buildings.

Another example is *glíma*, the Icelandic sport wrestling system that has its roots in the combative wrestling practiced in the Viking age, a topic discussed in detail in a later chapter. *Glíma* is the only combative activity to have survived from the Viking age that is still practiced.

A throw in a modern glíma tournament. Photo: Glímusamband Íslands.

SUMMARY

None of these sources alone tells us the full story of how Vikings fought and used their weapons. And so we use many sources as we try to reverse engineer how Vikings fought. It is not merely matching up information but rather building layer upon layer of detail from many sources, each strengthening the layers above and below. As we build, these layers become our stronghold of information, and our picture of how Vikings fought becomes more clear and solid.

Our twenty-year adventure in the study of Vikings has been thrilling, with numerous surprises and twists as we have tested and learned more about these ancient people. We invite you to join us as we share the tales of our adventures, and the details of what we have learned, beginning with the three pillars of Viking combat: mindset, empty-handed fighting, and an overview of the weapons of the Vikings. They form the foundation to an understanding of Viking combat.

# - 1 -

# THE VIKING MINDSET

Deyr fé, deyja frændr,
deyr sjálfr it sama;
en orðstírr deyr aldregi
hveim er sér góðan getr.
— *Hávamál*, v. 76

Every behavior of humans is guided by their mindset. The mindset determines everyday behavior—what one does or doesn't do. For example, how often does one take a bath? Vikings apparently bathed and groomed themselves frequently, based on archaeological finds,[1] Eddic poetry,[2] and even treaties requiring that baths be provided as often as desired.[3] Similarly, does one keep one's beard or shave it? What gift does one give to a friend?

These kinds of questions apply not only to behavior in everyday life but also to behavior in combat. How does one treat the enemy? How does one treat a defenseless foe lying wounded on the ground? How does one treat a comrade in arms?

We use an analogy to a computer system to explain the concept of mindset. The human body is the hardware. The body's operating system includes various neurological processes, such as respiration and the pain reflex. These systems are more alike than different among the human population.

What distinguishes individuals to a greater degree is their software—their mindset. Thoughts govern action, and understanding this software is fundamental to our understanding how Vikings fought.

In this chapter, we will use several sources to peel back the outer layers to illuminate the mindset of the Viking warrior lying beneath. Mindset distinguishes which tactics and actions are acceptable and which are not.

For example, in Viking society it was permissible to kill but heinous to murder. A murder, done in secret, was a horrific crime of the very worst sort, as taught in law codes such as *Gulaþingslög*.[4] *Grágás* defines murder as a killing where a man hides it, conceals the corpse, or does not admit the deed.[5] In contrast, killing, the taking of a life with full disclosure, was not only possible with impunity, there is even a legal term (*eiga vígt*) for having a legal right to kill.[6] Similarly, it was fine to rob—to take someone's belongings by force, with their knowledge—but it was heinous to steal—to take someone's belongings by stealth, without their knowledge.[7]

As we will see throughout this book, the Viking culture was a warrior culture and was infused with violence. Vikings' society and their law codes demanded that people be constantly prepared and ever vigilant against an attack, as discussed later in the chapter. The constant threat of that violence can be seen in many aspects of their culture: in their myths, in their laws, in the architecture of their homes, in their memorials to the dead, in their grave goods, and in the pictorial and literary sources they left behind.

SOURCES

It would be highly informative if we could find a Viking to bring to a psychologist for evaluation. Sadly, that option is closed to us, and so we must look for clues elsewhere.

Sources such as picture stones and tapestries show us what people of the era thought important enough to remember. Although subject to interpretation, they show climactic moments in some of the myths. They show warriors dressed for battle with weapons raised. They show slain warriors being welcomed into Valhalla.

Rune stones and similar contemporary writing tell us about the great deeds of Vikings for which they themselves wanted to be remembered: "King Haraldr who won for himself all Denmark and Norway" on a stone in Jelling,[8] and from the Gripsholm stone, "They went manfully [drengr-like] far after gold, and in the east gave food to the eagles [killed their enemies]."[9]

Archaeological finds, especially grave goods, teach us about their beliefs on the afterlife and about the objects they thought were important enough that they wanted to be buried with them. People were buried with some of the objects that defined them: a blacksmith was buried with his blacksmithing tools[10] and a völva (seeress) with her magic wand.[11] Weapons are frequently found in graves, suggesting the need to be armed and ready in whatever-may-come afterlife.

Literary sources provide an expansive window on the Vikings, with many examples of behavior that express their mindset, both directly and indirectly. Many aspects of this mindset seem consistent over a wide range of material ranging from the corpus of the sagas and eddas that were committed to writing in thirteenth- and fourteenth-century Iceland to the Viking-age runestones from Norway, Denmark, and Sweden. This self-consistency over

many Viking lands and over many centuries strengthens our confidence in these more numerous and more detailed Icelandic sources that postdate the Viking age.

The literary sources are especially valuable because they often tell us what the community thought about a person's actions, and so we see clear examples of what actions were praised and admired by the community and what was considered repugnant. As discussed later in this chapter, the community's thoughts mattered greatly.

The literary sources provide two kinds of information about mindset: direct and indirect. Sources with direct information state what the appropriate behavior should be. Perhaps the prime example is the poem Hávamál, a guide to the proper way for a Viking to behave day to day. The clear guidelines within the poem teach us about the correct mindset for a Viking, such as looking behind the door before entering a room.[12]

Sources with indirect information do not directly state the proper behavior. That behavior must be inferred by what other people say about someone's activities and by how the community responds to actions. Both the Sagas of Icelanders and Heimskringla are examples of sources with indirect information, revealing information about what the community felt was the proper way to behave.

In our search for Viking mindset and how it affected combat, all roads seem to lead to one fundamental concept: the preservation of one's good name.

YOUR GOOD NAME

The most important aspect of a Viking was his good name. His good name meant everything. A man's good name is the only thing that survives his death, as stated in the verse from Hávamál that opens this chapter:

> Cattle die, kinsmen die,
> one day you die yourself;
> but the word-glory will not die
> for the man that wins it.[13]

Vikings went to extremes to attain a good name and to expunge a blot that tarnished one, and those extremes included killing and death. Again and again, sagas record men saying they would rather die than live in a diminished state.[14]

The qualities that gave a man a good name are mentioned repeatedly in the literary sources and on the runestone memorials. Yet we have some difficulty in translating these Old Norse words into modern English, in part because the English words that most often come to mind all have Latin roots and are not at all cognate with the Old Norse words. We must tease out the equivalent English meanings through careful, step-by-step study of how the words were used.

Vikings sought a characteristic called *frægð* or *frami*, the state of being in which a man's name was often spoken. *Frægð* or *frami* was usually obtained through some kind of exploit involving a high degree of danger, and in most cases that meant combat.[15] Perhaps the closest English equivalent to *frægð* or *frami* is *fame*.

This need for fame leads to an interesting aspect of the Viking culture. For a man to have any merit or fame, his name must be spoken about, and his adventures must be discussed and communicated through society. Without people talking about one's exploits and accomplishments, there can be no fame. The exploits have no meaning, similar to a beautiful Viking ship missing its sail and rudder and without any means to guide it.

This situation suggests Viking people were early adopters of social media. Again and again in the literary sources, people greeted travelers with the question, "What is the news?"[16] Even without an internet, news spread quickly and widely in Viking lands. Unlike later medieval Europeans, Vikings traveled extensively, even those of modest social standing. Nowhere was this more true than in Iceland, where every summer, a significant percentage of the population of the land met at the Alþing national assembly, learned the news from all the districts, and took that news back to their home districts to disseminate.

It is worth distinguishing the concept of fame from that of celebrity, a common meaning of the word *fame* in modern times. Unlike these more-recent times, when popular media and the internet make it possible to discuss names because the names are famous, Viking-age people discussed names because of the deeds and accomplishments of the owners of those names. *Frægð* or *frami* derived from these actions and deeds. Men are called name-famous (*nafnfrægr*) or name-known (*nafnkunnigr*) in the literary sources because of their actions.[17] As the Viking Bósi stated in his saga, "No one becomes famous for nothing."[18]

Vikings sought to be spoken about for their deeds, not only while alive but, more importantly, in death. They sought *orðstírr*, a word that is a portmanteau of *orð* (word) and *tírr* (glory): *word-glory*. Word-glory was a desired goal, in which people said good things about a person's behavior and glorified his name and deeds. It was of the utmost importance to a Viking to attain a good *orðstírr* and to avoid and to rectify a bad one.[19] As *Hávamál* teaches, a good *orðstírr* never dies.[20]

People spoke about the *virðing* of others, meaning worth but often translated as respect. The word was also used to mean one's financial worth, often in the law codes, but as *virðing* relates to mindset, the word is taken to mean one's worth to those around him. *Virðing* was given to a man by others based on his actions or inactions. It is frequently said in the literary sources that *virðing* was laid on someone, perhaps in the way a mantle or cloak was laid on a man's shoulders, and often by a king or earl.[21] As with these other qualities, it was said to be better to die with *virðing* than to live with shame.[22]

In the literary sources, *virðing* often goes hand in hand with the quality of *sæmd*, perhaps best translated as *prestige*. One gained *virðing* and *sæmd* by facing danger, such as by raiding or dueling or some other heroic feat, usually involving combat.[23] One also gained *sæmd* by successfully prosecuting a legal case, or by obtaining compensation in some other

Kerling, a notable *drangr* (rocky pinnacle) in north Iceland. Photo: William R. Short.

way.[24] Additionally, *sæmd* could be conferred, usually by a king or an earl on someone who had provided support in a battle.[25]

One's *virðing* and *sæmd* is measured by two qualities: *drengskapr* and *níð*. The first is desirable, and the second reprehensible. They are not opposites, but rather measures of the good and bad within each person.

It is through this chain that the Viking achieves the immortal good name he seeks. This good name derives from *orðstírr*, which comes from achieving *frami* and *frægð*, which are acquired from *virðing* and *sæmd*, which are won by doing some deed in a *drengr*-like way: *drengskapr*.

### DRENGSKAPR

*Drengskapr* is the quality that lies closest to the heart of a Viking. It is the attribute that seems to be central to understanding the Viking mindset and much of what made someone a Viking. Sadly, there is no direct English translation, making discussion more difficult. *Drengskapr* is what makes a man a *drengr*, and to be a *drengr* is what a Viking aspired to. It was the pinnacle, not only for Viking men, but also for Viking women.[26]

Viking mindset was driven by the desire to be a *drengr*. Viking mindset moved people to do the things that were *drengr*-like and to avoid the things that diminished the quality of a *drengr*.

A *drengr* was quite simply a person who could be trusted: a person who could be counted on to the death, regardless of the situation, regardless of the circumstances, regardless of the odds. The word retains that meaning in modern legal usage in Icelandic law. When signing certain kinds of contracts, the signatory pledges his *drengskapr* to uphold the terms of the contract.[27] But it was more than trust alone that made someone a *drengr*; it was trust infused with honor.

The word is related to *drangr*, a rocky pinnacle,[28] which gives a picture of how a *drengr* should behave. He must stand strong and secure, even though he stands alone.[29] He must not retreat or flee, and he must be ever-present and ever-ready in fair times and foul.

A *drengr* was the person you wanted to be in your family and on your team, and in your *félag* (business partnership) and at your side when you harried. The characteristics of a *drengr* were many.

### LOYALTY

The foremost characteristic of a *drengr* was loyalty,[30] providing support for the people in his life to whom support was due, whether that be family, *félagi* (business partners), shipmates, or kings. In Viking society, a violent attack could occur at any time, and the kind of man you wanted close to you was a man you could trust to be loyal. Accordingly, the loyalty of the king's men in his *hirð* (bodyguard),[31] and of the crew on sea voyages,[32] whether for trading or for harrying, could not be at doubt, since that loyalty was likely to be tested in combat. A *drengr*, whose loyalty was unquestioned, was the kind of man required.

### NEVER GIVE UP

A *drengr* does not give up and does not give in.[33] A *drengr* was expected to go to extreme lengths to achieve his goals.[34] A *drengr* was expected to give his all,[35] fighting to the death regardless of the goal or the odds. There are numerous mentions of men fighting *drengr*-like (*drengilega*), both in defense and on the attack,[36] fighting despite all odds and not giving up. Like Asbjörn, whose runic memorial stone reads, "He did not flee at Uppsala, but slaughtered as long as he had a weapon,"[37] men fought to the bitter end.

One of the clearest examples of this *drengr*-like trait is Gisli's single-handed defense against twelve attackers, the climax of thirteen years of tracking and pursuit by his opponents. Gísli killed seven, but as the end approached, he stood, with his back at the edge of a precipice, and with his intestines hanging out from his wounds. As his opponents closed in for the kill, Gísli did not give up. He tied his intestines back into his gut with his belt, and as his dying act, he split one more of his opponents in two from head to waist.[38]

COURAGE

Other traits of a *drengr* are courage and bravery,[39] traits praised again and again in the literary sources and tested in battle and combat. A young man was supposed to test his courage by facing danger before he settled down and became a man,[40] including not only danger from combat, but danger from facing destiny head-on.

Indeed, it is this meaning of *drengr* that is retained in later literary sources,[41] such as the law codes,[42] and in the modern Scandinavian languages: a *drengr* as a boy, young and as yet untested as a man.

FAIR PLAY

A *drengr* was expected to show fair play[43] and respect for others,[44] and to have the strength to do what is right.[45] A free man who comes peacefully to the king of his own free will to resolve a dispute with the king expects the king to be *drengr*-like and to allow him to leave in peace and freedom.[46] A king is *drengr*-like when he aids people who come to him for help.[47] A merchant behaves in a *drengr*-like manner when he describes his goods honestly and doesn't attempt to cheat his customer.[48]

A man who does not show respect will not receive respect. A man might roam the land, threatening with an iron fist and gaining fear, but he does not gain respect.[49] He is not a *drengr*. A *drengr* was expected to do the right thing, even though it was not the easy choice, and even though it might cost him his life.[50]

OTHER TRAITS OF A DRENGR

Another trait that was a mark of a *drengr* was imperturbability and emotional composure,[51] even under extreme duress, both in battle and in everyday activities. It was *drengr*-like to withstand wounds and injuries well and without complaint.[52]

A *drengr* showed magnanimity[53] in battle and in legal affairs. He was humane, showing mercy to the weak.[54] And he was truthful,[55] and a man of his word.[56] We see many examples of Vikings being clever and using misdirection to achieve their aims, but to lie or to break one's word would be to destroy a man's *orðstírr*.

This aspect of Viking culture is symbolized by what is perhaps the most potent icon of the Viking: the oath ring. The law required every temple to have an oath ring: an arm ring used for the swearing of oaths that was made of silver and reddened by the blood of a sacrificial animal. The ring was worn by the *goði* (chieftain and priest) at all public assemblies.[57] It seems possible that some of the arm rings found in the archaeological records represent these oath rings. The law codes[58] and the literary sources tell of the sanctity of the oath.[59] Breaking an oath led to being cast out of society and resulted in punishment from the god Vár.[60] The word of a *drengr* was as strong and unyielding as if set in stone, something to be trusted and relied on no matter what, and the oath ring was a concrete reminder of the sanctity of these oaths to the Viking people.

Together, these qualities characterized a *drengr*. The mindset of the Viking was such as to guide his behavior to bring him to this ideal. *Hávamál* summarizes this goal: "The greatest good among men . . . is living life unblemished," and, "Good renown (*orðstírr*) will never

A modern replica of a Viking-age oath ring. Photo: William R. Short.

die for anyone who earned it."[61] This belief lasted centuries after the end of the Viking age, appearing in late works such as *Konungs skuggsjá* and *Hirðskrá*.[62]

Yet in order to reach this exalted state of *drengr*, a man's qualities needed to be tested, and many of these qualities were such that they were best tested in battle. Without the danger inherent in combat, the concept of *drengr* most likely could not exist. That this battle testing was on the path that led to the pinnacle of Viking society adds more weight to the idea that violence was a significant part of Viking society.

### ÓDRENGR

Mindset also guided a man to avoid being tarred by behaviors that were the opposite of *drengr*, called *ódrengr*.[63] Showing lack of courage, fleeing a battle, lack of emotional composure under adversity, betrayal, and withholding support for the weak[64] were not the activities of a *drengr*, and showing these behaviors diminished a man and made him an *ódrengr*.

The goal of a Viking was to achieve a good name, which derived from *orðstírr*, which came from earning *frami* and *frægð*, which were ac-

quired from *virðing* and *sæmd*, which were won by doing some deed in the manner of a *drengr*, a state of trust infused with honor that characterized the best kind of man.

### NÍÐ

The other quantity of a man that was weighed to assess his *virðing* and *sæmd* was *níð*. The desired level of *níð* was nil. The word *níð* is sometimes translated as *shame*, but that English word scarcely carries the weight of *níð* as it existed in Viking society. Not even a hint of *níð* was tolerable for any man of stature. Men sought to avoid any kind of behavior thought to be *níð*, the qualities that made a man a *níðingr*. Mindset was driven by a desire to avoid *níð* at all costs.

It is easy to believe that *níð* might in some way be the opposite of *drengskapr*: that *níð* is merely *ódrengr*. Yet *níð* contained an element of the supernatural that is absent in *drengskapr*. One could be branded a *níð* for behaviors or activities, but *níð* sometimes was invoked and placed upon a man, making it similar to a curse.

At the top of the list of behaviors causing *níð* were a breach of trust, betrayal, and treachery. That this behavior caused *níð* is stated on a runestone that bridges the centuries separating us from Vikings. It states that Sassurr betrayed his partner (*félagi*) and killed him, the work of a *níðingr*.[65] The seriousness of breaking an oath is mentioned in the literary sources[66] and in the law codes, which state that a man who violates a truce is an outcast, despised and driven off wherever the sun shines, the world is inhabited, and rivers flow to the sea.[67] Such a man cannot be trusted.

A man who failed to show up to a duel was *níðingr*, as taught in the Swedish law code *Hednalagen* and other literary sources.[68] Additional activities that branded a man as a *níðingr* included treason, disloyalty, or improper way of killing.[69] Improper ways of killing included killing kinsmen,[70] killing at night,[71] and killing defenseless people, whether they be unarmed men,[72] women and children,[73] fallen men,[74] or sleeping men.[75]

The law codes define some crimes as *níð*-crimes, such as treason, harrying in one's own land, and murder.[76] These crimes stained a man with the taint of *níð*, and they were punished with outlawry and loss of property.

Additionally, *níð* could be placed on someone, in the manner of a curse, with words or by a physical symbol. In Viking society, words had power, and *níð* expressed verbally carried weight because words, if said with enough intention, became reality. This belief is best seen in the supernatural episodes in the literary sources and in the younger legal documents from the Viking lands.[77] Some spoken insults were thought to be such a serious matter that the law permitted a man to kill someone who spoke these forms of insults.[78]

Many of the insults minimize the heroic aspects of the victim and belittle his courage and manhood at the same time. Some of the insults revolve around the idea that the man had feminine traits: that he was cowardly or weak or lacking in what was considered to be masculine traits, such as lacking a beard,[79] or that he was more familiar with women's work than men's,[80] or, even more demeaning, that he was the passive partner in a homosexual encounter.[81]

The insult was given greater strength by comparing a man to a mare[82] or saying he had the heart of a mare, implying he had no courage at all since the heart was thought to be the seat of bravery.[83] The insult appears in some of the myths[84] as well as other literary sources.[85]

Poetry was an especially potent way to express words for multiple reasons. Poetry was thought to have supernatural powers, in that it magnified the effect of the words. It made the spoken words into reality. Þorsteinn jarlsskáld recited a *níð* verse to avenge himself on Earl Hákon. As he spoke the *níð* verses to the earl, the words seemed at first to praise the earl, but as the verses continued, the earl began to itch all over his body. The hall grew dark, and the earl's beard began to rot and his hair to fall out.[86]

Another reason poetry was thought especially potent for expressing thoughts was that the nature of Viking-age poetry allowed the verse to be easily remembered and shared, so that the words reached the ears of the entire community. Poetry was thought to be a reliable way to disseminate news of events. King Óláfr placed his poets in the protection of a shield castle before a battle so that they could witness at close range, and then compose and recite verses telling of the events of the battle to inform people back home of the glorious deeds of the king and his warriors.[87] Poetry was a powerful and permanent way to gain *orðstírr*, or to be remembered as a *níðingr*, not only because the verses were remembered and the name and deeds passed from one pair of lips to the next, but because of the powerful connection of poetry with Óðinn, the highest of the gods.

In addition to being easily remembered and disseminated, some poetry was thought to be an accurate record of events. In the prologue to his history of the Norwegian kings, Snorri Sturluson wrote that he gathered most of his information from the ancient skaldic poetry, still remembered and recited in Snorri's own time. He added that he regarded as true the material in these poems that were recited before the leading men or their sons, since no one would dare tell falsehoods and fabrications to the men whose deeds were told in the verses.[88]

The god of poetry, Bragi, tells the stories of the gods in verse, further adding weight to the idea that poetry was a reliable way of remembering and communicating great deeds.[89]

All of these examples suggest that expressing an idea in verse made the idea easier to remember and disseminate. *Níð* expressed in verse guaranteed that the *níð* reached the ears of the entire community. *Grágás* states that the penalty for composing even half a stanza of poetry with defamation or mockery in it was full outlawry, and the penalty for reciting such poetry was the same as for composing it.[90]

*Níð* could also be placed on someone by erecting a physical symbol of the *níð*. Wooden effigies (*tréníð*) were raised to dishonor a man who had engaged in shameful behavior, no-

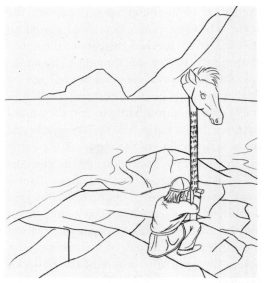

*Níðstöng*, a scorn pole. Illustration: Barbara Wechter.

tably, failing to show up to a duel. The figures took the forms of two men, one behind the other, with the implication that the *níðingr* was the submissive partner in a sexual act.[91]

The *níðstöng* (shaming-pole) was the most potent and serious of all the symbols of *níð*. This pole represents many of the ideas behind *níð*. It was not only about making someone feel ashamed and disrespected in the society using a public symbol for all to see, but it also had supernatural powers directed at the one who would receive the *níð*.

Egill's *níðstöng*, raised against the king and queen in Norway, brings all these elements of *níð* together. After a lengthy dispute, Egill raised a *níðstöng* against King Eiríkr and Queen-mother Gunnhildr. Egill set up a pole on the shore, placed a mare's head at the end of it, and recited a curse. He directed the curse at the *landvættir* (land-spirits) inhabiting the land, sending them all astray with no rest until they had driven the king and queen from the land. He drove the pole into a cleft in a rock, turned the head toward land, and carved the curse in runes into the pole.[92]

The episode makes clear the supernatural aspect of the *níð* curse and the power of *níð*. Even the land-spirits cannot rest until this *níð*-curse

is released. *Níð* is no mere slander or shame but an overarching taint that sullies a man. *Níð* must be resolved.

The power of *níð* is indicated by the number of incidents in which a man was told his intended behavior was *níð*, and he reversed course and made alternate plans to avoid such ignominy. In 43 percent of the cases where *níð* was discussed in the literary sources,[93] the perpetrator of the *níð* chose a different path, either of his own volition or by men nearby who refused to carry out any *níð* activities on his behalf. For example, when Eyjólfr ordered his men to kill the wife of Gísli, Hávarðr told the men to stand up to Eyjólfr and not do the work of a *níðingr* (*níðingsverk*).[94] They did not want to be tainted by *níð*, and they prevented Eyjólfr from carrying out his disgraceful act.

A man receiving *níð* in any form would have to take strong steps to recover his good name or else be forever diminished in the eyes of the community. The response seems to have depended on the nature of the activity that caused the *níð*, but the usual response ended in the death of the man who caused the *níð*, either through outlawry or an ambush, duel, or other attack. A man who gained *níð* by killing in an improper way was outlawed in more than half the cases reported in the literary sources.[95] A man who delivered *níð* as a curse was killed in more than half the cases.

The desire to become *drengr* and the revulsion against becoming *níðingr* were two forces that shaped the mindset of the Vikings and thus directed their behavior. In battle, a *drengr* adhered to the qualities of *drengskapr*.

In many ways, a *drengr* by your side in a fight shared many qualities with a faithful dog: both are loyal and trusting to the extreme, surrendering their life before surrendering their loyalty, and not willing to give up while giving their all to the fight. Perhaps the biggest difference is that the dog has no awareness of the fair play and magnanimity that guided a *drengr* and no awareness of the need to avoid *níð*.

Men wanted their deeds to be remembered and talked about because the deeds were

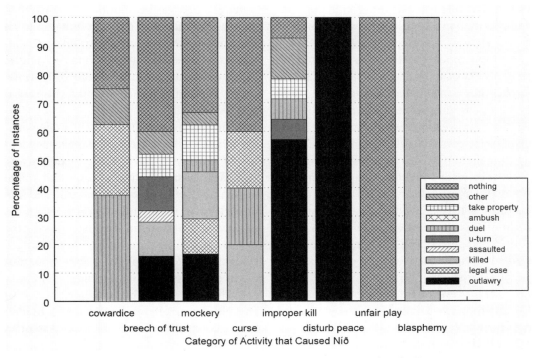

A plot of the outcome to níð for various categories of *níð* activities as reported in the literary sources.

*drengskapr* and not because they were *níð*. They craved the *virðing* and *sæmd* that came from these activities, qualities that would result in *frami* and *orðstírr* and the telling of tales that mentioned their names and their deeds long after death. It is through this chain of events that a man obtained immortality, as taught in *Hávamál*, in which a man's name was still spoken after his death. Perhaps the greatest complement to a man who exhibited *drengskapr* through his life is the prediction that his name will be remembered as long as the world is inhabited.[96]

FAMILY

The benefits that accrue from *drengskapr* and the shame that results from receiving *níð* were shared among the entire family. For example, if a man broke an oath, not only was he punished, according to the law, but his close relatives suffered the same punishment as if they, too, had broken the oath.[97] Thus, any stain on the good name of an individual was a stain on the entire family. Any attack on one family member was an attack on them all. Revenge (*hefnd*) was an accepted way to balance the scales of justice that was permitted by law.[98] Additionally, a *drengr* could not permit a stain on his family's name to go unanswered. Society demanded revenge,[99] and revenge was performed by the family in more than 80 percent of the cases described in the literary sources.[100]

What was it that Vikings considered family? Who might be involved in revenge? The meaning of family to the modern reader may be something different than its meaning to a Viking-age person. Therefore, let us explore what a family meant to the Vikings.

Although it is not clearly stated, it seems that in Icelandic law codes, families were thought to extend to four generations. We see glimpses of this in the laws about compensation for killing a man. Even the fourth cousins of the dead man are entitled to a share of the compensation.[101] So it seems that everyone who shared the same great-great-grandparents were considered family. This group includes not only blood relatives but other kinds of relations as well, including relatives by marriage, foster relations, and step relations.

A simple model based on the estimated demographics of the society in Viking-age Iceland conservatively predicts that there could be hundreds of adult males of an appropriate age to bear weapons who shared the same great-great-grandparents.[102] Any one of these adult male family members might choose to become involved with blood vengeance against not only a man who committed an offense but also against his extended family. And the usual form of this vengeance was killing, the outcome in 70 percent of the revenge attacks described in the literary sources.[103] For example, when Sámr shamed Hrafnkell, Hrafnkell did not take his revenge on Sámr, but instead, on Sámr's brother, by killing him just as he arrived home from Norway.[104]

The literary sources suggest, however, that the people involved with vengeance generally were close relatives: brothers, fathers, or sons in nearly half the cases described in the literary sources.[105] Yet there are also examples of more-distant relatives being killed to avenge the dishonorable behavior of a family member: a first cousin once removed killed by the victim's father in Gunnlaugs saga,[106] and the death of a second cousin was avenged by Gizurr on Gunnarr.[107]

There was also an appropriate timing for the revenge. Grettir commented that a slave takes revenge immediately, and a coward never.[108] The community might question the character of a man who delayed too long. When his father-in-law asked him about his plans to avenge the slander placed on him, Refr said that a man should have his plans worked out before he enters into great undertakings,[109] and ultimately his revenge was complete. The time to plan and execute revenge was in the range of weeks and months for more than half the cases reported in the literary sources.[110] Similar advice appears in the later sources, such as Hirðskrá,[111] which suggests one should not be overhasty in planning vengeance.

Yet revenge was not optional, according to custom and the law. A man felt something was left undone if revenge was not taken.[112] Gulaþingslög states that no man had the right to claim compensation more than three times unless he had taken revenge in the meantime.[113]

Family connections might hold hidden dangers, since loyalty to the family sometimes conflicted with loyalty to chieftains or supporters. In a battle, a man on the opposing side might be reminded of his family connection and find himself in serious conflict. When Snorri reminded Styr of his family connections during a battle and called him níðingr, Styr changed sides and started killing the people who, moments earlier, stood alongside him.[114] Similarly, as Kolli attacked his kinsman Björn as part of an ambush team, Björn reminded Kolli of their family connection, and Kolli at once stepped out of the fight.[115] When Hróðný learned that her brother had joined a group planning a revenge attack on her own family, she called her brother a níðingr and dissuaded him from participating in the revenge attack.[116]

Family came first. This was the complex and often dangerous familial world the Vikings lived in. It was a world with convoluted and competing loyalties, infused with the need to maintain one's own good name and the family's good name while being constantly prepared to use arms, since an attack might come against a man at any moment.[117]

LAW

Law and adherence to law was a central part of Viking society. Njáll, a prominent farmer-lawyer of Viking-age Iceland, said "with law our land shall flourish, but it will perish with lawlessness."[118] Throughout the Viking lands, people were accustomed to meeting once each year in regional legal assemblies called þing. These meetings were open to virtually all free men. In addition to regional meetings, a national þing was created in Iceland called Alþing.

Other aspects of the law differed between Iceland and other Scandinavian lands, presumably due to the presence of a central authority.

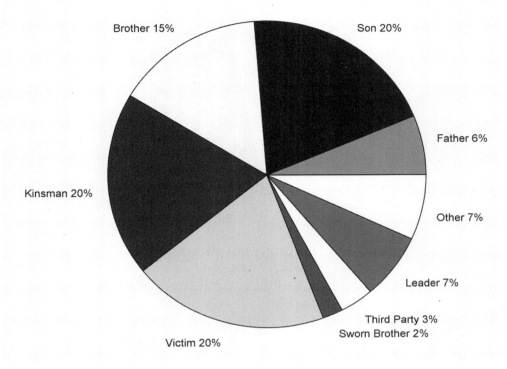

A plot of who executed the revenge as reported in the literary sources.

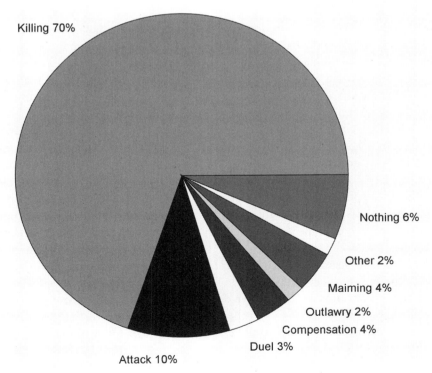

A plot of the forms of revenge taken as reported in the literary sources.

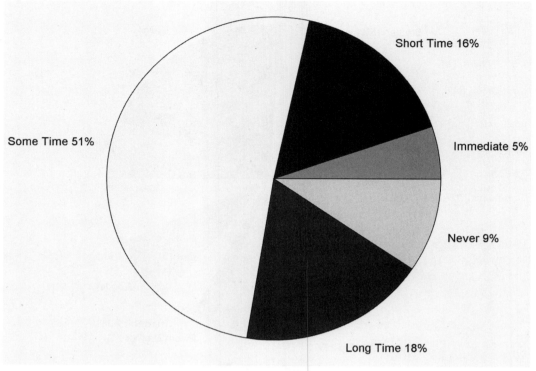

A plot of the delay in exacting revenge as reported in the literary sources.

figure, the king, in the other lands during most of the Viking age. When the Icelanders created the legal system for their new land, it seems they wanted to avoid any kind of central authority. Icelandic sources suggest that at least part of the emigration from Norway was due to King Haraldr's usurping some of the traditional freedoms and rights to which Norwegians had been accustomed,[119] so it is not surprising that Icelanders would avoid making this authority a part of their new law codes in Iceland. Adam of Bremen, writing in the eleventh century, notes of the Icelanders, "They have no king except the law."[120]

In Norway, there seem to have been four regional assemblies (lögþing) with their own law codes based on customs and legislative decisions. The laws were written down at the end of the eleventh century, and complete law codes from two of the assemblies survive: Gulaþingslög and Frostaþingslög. Various kings

modified the law codes, and by the time of King Magnús's reign in the thirteenth century, a national monarchy emerged as a sovereign power.[121] The only legal material from Denmark and Sweden significantly postdates the Viking period.

We have the most complete and detailed material from Iceland, in the form of Grágás, which survives in over one hundred forms. Portions were first written down in winter 1117–1118, and the surviving texts are thought to represent the law as it was practiced in the twelfth century.[122] While there are significant blocks of Christian laws, there are many aspects of the remaining laws that are thought to be unchanged from how the law was practiced in the Viking age before the conversion. Additionally, some of the sagas, notably Brennu-Njáls saga, follow the intricacies of legal cases so as to inform us about the workings of the legal system in some detail.

In Iceland, the power rested in the hands of the *goði* (plural *goðar*), who functioned as head of the government and head of the heathen religion. Thus, *goði* may be translated as either *priest* or *chieftain*, depending on context. This duality shows the close connection between the religion and the government. A free man's *goði* was his connection to the government, and his connection to the gods.

The *goði* was neither elected nor appointed but chosen by the free farmers of the district. A *goði* needed the support of the farmers in his district, and the farmers needed the support of the *goði*. It was part of a complex power dynamic connected to loyalty and to combat. A dispute between farmers that could not be settled one on one would generally be escalated to include the *goðar* of the two men. A *goði* needed to be able to draw on a large group of loyal armed supporters to be effective in the resolution of his supporters' disputes. Likewise, a farmer needed the loyal support of his *goði* (and his supporters) in any kind of dispute that could not be settled one on one, and so farmers looked for an effective, powerful *goði* with whom to ally. A *goði* who had insufficient supporters to successfully press his cases would find his *goðorð* (the office of *goði*) taken over forcibly by someone who felt himself better qualified for it.

The Icelandic legal system had a legislative branch to make laws and a judicial branch to try legal cases and deliver judgements. But it had no executive branch to prosecute cases or to deliver punishments decided by the court. All of these functions were private, performed by the injured party, his family, and his *goði* (and his supporters). Once the court determined guilt and set a sentence, it was up to these people to execute it. This helps explain why weapons were such a central component to Viking society. People needed weapons, or at least the threat of the use of weapons, to enforce legal decisions.

The court imposed two broad categories of punishment: outlawry and compensation. The law codes set standard compensations for a death, payable in silver, or equivalent standard merchandise, such as homespun cloth.[123]

A man condemned to outlawry was placed outside the bounds of society, and the laws no longer applied to him or protected him. His property was confiscated, and he could not be fed or sheltered. He could be killed without penalty, and many might try for the honor that ensued from killing an outlaw. Thus, in addition to the psychological terror of loneliness from being excluded from social contacts, the outlaw also faced the very real threat of lethal violence at any time. It was essentially a death sentence.

Full outlawry (*skóggangr*) was ordinarily a permanent injunction. Lesser outlawry (*fjörbaugsgarðr*) was more like a temporary banishment. Abroad, a lesser outlaw was immune from attack, and after three years, he could return home and resume his place in society.

In Iceland, outlawry was even more intense, since it was forbidden to transport a full outlaw out of Iceland. In other Scandinavian lands, an outlaw could go to a new land and start over. However, in Iceland, he was stuck on the island until he died, excluded from any social contacts.[124]

It seems that obedience to the law was, for the most part, taken seriously. As an example, the penalty for perjury was severe and swift, by law and by custom.[125] Providing false witness was punished with full outlawry.[126] Additionally, providing false witness violated a key aspect of *drengskapr*: keeping an oath. Such a man could never again be trusted.

In some cases, men chose other ways than through a court case to resolve a dispute, using duels, revenge attacks, or other forms of violence. At Gulaþing in Norway, Egill demanded to settle a court case with a duel, as was his ancient right.[127]

In some cases, a man might offer self-judgement, where he allowed his opponent to determine the case and the punishment, expecting his opponent to be magnanimous. This route required the kind of trust that came with being a *drengr*.

Taking a case to court required a level of strength and support, both to prosecute the case and to prevent it from being broken up in court by the opposing side using violence. The man prosecuting the case gathered friends, family, his *goði* and the *goði*'s supporters, and other *goðar*, in order to create alliances before the case came to court. Here is yet another example of where a *drengr* would have a sizable advantage; he would already be known and his trustworthiness well established, making him someone other people would want to support in the hopes that that support would be returned in a future case. The need for this ongoing support guided men to behave in ways that made such future support more likely and was reflected in their mindsets.

Yet a man's mindset could and did overpower the law under extreme conditions, such as Gísli's murder of his sister's husband.[128] After Gísli's brother-in-law Vésteinn was murdered in his bed while visiting Gísli, Gísli faced a difficult choice: to either murder the person responsible, a family member no less, in order to avenge the crime, or to allow the death of Vésteinn, a valiant man, to go unavenged. Gísli chose to commit a heinous crime and avenge the death rather than let the original crime stain him and his family. His choice underscores the need to keep one's name and one's family's name free of any taint, a need that could trump the rule of law.

Additionally, some men felt they were above the law. Men who had a powerful following might simply ignore the court's penalty, knowing that no one had the strength to enforce it, such as men like Gunnarr.[129] Others, like Hrafnkell, were so powerful that they boasted of never paying compensation for any of their killings.[130]

The laws provided a set of barriers to a man's behavior, barriers that prudent men observed. Yet sometimes the need to maintain their good name and that of their family overruled the need to maintain the law.

FATE

Another aspect of Viking society that affected mindset was fate. In the myths, it is written that the *Nornir* (women of destiny) shape the lives of men.[131] The text is unclear, but it appears that when a child was born, the *Nornir* chose the date of the child's death. Thus, the moment of a man's death was predetermined and nothing could change it.

Knowing that the date of a Viking's death was predetermined explains their adventurous nature. A Viking might ask himself, why not go out and do something bold? The best that can happen to me is fame, honor, and wealth, and the worst that can happen is death, which would have happened if I had stayed home in bed.

This attitude toward life is expressed in the literary sources.[132] Kolfiðr states it succinctly when talking about an upcoming duel with Búi, saying, "There are two outcomes to every danger. Either I will live or I will die."[133] There is an old saying repeated in the literary sources that there is no slaying a man destined to live.[134] With beliefs like these, why wouldn't a Viking yearn to excel, to stretch to the utmost for the achievement that brings the greatest *frami* and *orðstírr*, and the most *virðing* and *sæmd*? It is the distilled essence of what it means to be a Viking.

There seem to be examples in the literary sources where people sought to learn more about their fate and to get a glimpse of what might lie ahead. With the sources available to us, it is hard to assess whether Viking people thought that all of life was governed by fate. There does not appear to have been any belief that the date of one's death could be altered, but there does appear to have been a belief that with some knowledge of the future, better plans could be laid. It is possible that the *Nornir* not only set a date for death but also moments of destiny (*örlögþættir*) in the lives of men.[135] And so, Viking people sought to learn more about what lay ahead, and no one to a greater degree than Óðinn, who constantly pursued information about the future, as is told in the myths.[136]

It seems Vikings trusted these glimpses they saw of the future. Vikings sought out a *völva*,[137] a prophetess and a high-status member of society who was welcome at social gatherings for her insights and predictions. A detailed description of a *völva*, her rituals, and her predictions are told in *Eiríks saga rauða*.[138]

The *völva* and her place in society have not received the attention they deserve until recently. In the past, the *völva* was thought to be merely a literary tool to advance the plot of the saga in which she appears. New and revisited archaeological finds suggest that the women found in some previous excavated graves were *völvur*, based on their unusual dress, jewelry, food, drugs, and especially the iron staff often found in the grave.

Viking-age people also believed that dreams could be interpreted to predict the future. On a journey, Gunnar took a nap, and his dream predicted the ambush into which he and his brothers were riding.[139] The dream predicted the death of his brother, Hjörtr, but Hjörtr refused to leave. He knew that if it was his day to die, it did not matter if he was safe at home or fighting by his brother's side.

Perhaps the strongest example of receiving a premonition but leaving things to fate occured when Björn dreamt of his ambush and death. His wife urged him to stay home and avoid danger, but he responded, "I will not let dreams direct my movements."[140] He accepted the plans that fate held for him.

There are other examples of premonitions of death, such as weapons singing before they strike a death blow, or blood appearing on a weapon, signifying death is on the way.[141] Viking-age people believed that everyone had a *fylgja*, a protective animal spirit that accompanied them. Seeing your *fylgja* was thought to be a sure sign that death was approaching.[142]

Destiny was a universal concept that affected all beings. No matter how hard the Viking or the gods tried, destiny and death were inescapable. Life, however, was theirs for the taking. Thus, their mindset was always to be bold and adventurous, seeking riches and *frami*,

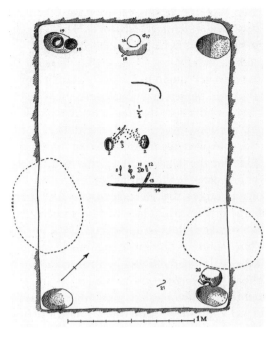

The plan of grave Bj 660 at Birka, which may be the grave of a *völva*, an interpretation based on the items found in the grave, such as the iron staff (14) laying at her waist. Derived from Holger Arbman, *Birka I. Die Gräber. Tafeln*. Creative Commons.

*virðing*, and *sæmd* whenever they could. Death was unavoidable, but the Viking mindset caused them to fight destiny for as hard and as long as they could, so they could die with *orðstírr*.

DEATH

When death arrived on its predestined day, what happened next? It seems that, to Viking people, death was more of a gray state than a black or white state.

The literary sources indicate that the dead had many states of being and many realms in which to dwell. Some people, after death, entered the realms of the gods. Warriors who fell on the battlefield might be brought to the pleasures of *Valhöll* (literally hall of the slain, and often rendered as *Valhalla* in English). These warriors became Einherjar (those who fight alone), fighting alongside Óðinn as he himself fights fate and death.[143]

Some of the fallen warriors are taken to Freyja's hall, *Fólksvangr* (Field of the Folk). When she rides to battle, half of the fallen are with her and half with Óðinn.[144] Those who drowned at sea might get caught in the net of Rán, the undertaker of the sea, and go to her realm.[145]

Many of the dead dwelled in the realm called Hel, presided over by Hel, the daughter of Loki. The place seems to have been merely an abode for the dead in the earliest sources. It was only later, in the writings of Snorri Sturluson and others, that Hel takes on the Christian characteristics of a place of punishment for oath breakers, thieves, and the like.[146]

Then there are those who spent their afterlife in the realm of the living becoming a *draugr* (ghost) or *haugbúi* (grave dweller), living on after their death on earth, sometimes in peaceful celebration,[147] sometimes guarding the treasure buried in their graves,[148] sometimes causing harm, fear, destruction, and death.[149]

Yet to the Viking people, what happened after death seems to have been far less important than what happened in life, before and during the moment of death. It is in these moments that one gained *orðstírr* that kept one's name alive. Viking mindset guided people to hold back nothing to gain *virðing* and *sæmd*. They knew that the moment of their death was not only outside of their control, it also was probably not so important because they believed something else could follow.

The details of what Viking-age people believed happened to a man after death is a hazy area that is poorly understood. What is clear is that in some way, life continued after death, either through *orðstírr* in the land of the living or with weapons in hand in places like Valhöll during the next phase of life.

LUCK, MAGIC, AND OTHER SPIRITUAL ASPECTS
Luck, magic, and other supernatural aspects of the world played a role in shaping the mindset of the Vikings.

Vikings tried their best to adhere to the correct way to treat paranormal beings of the land, such as the *landvættir* (land-spirits). These spirits could affect harvest, weather,

safety in travels, and more. The settlers in Iceland knew that this virgin land was populated by these spirits, so they sought their favor for their land taking. An early law quoted in *Landnámabók* required approaching ships to remove their dragon-head prows when approaching Iceland lest the protective land-spirits be frightened away,[150] a custom also mentioned elsewhere.[151]

The powers of this supernatural and natural world could be harnessed through the practice of magic. There are several Old Norse words for magic, such as *galdr*, derived from the phrase *to crow*, and *seiðr*, whose etymology is unclear. The practice of *seiðr* was taught by Freyja to Óðinn and others of the Æsir family of gods.[152]

Additionally, some words for magic were simply descriptive, such a *fjölkynngi*, meaning *multiknowledge*. Magic was based on knowledge, and the greatest master of magic was Óðinn, who constantly seeks knowledge.[153]

Magical acts happen in almost every literary source, and archeological finds have been connected with magic, such as the *völva* wands discussed earlier. Magic was real to the people of the Norse world, something to be feared as well as something that could aid one in battle. The use of magic by berserks and sorcerers and witches to dull blades so the weapons won't bite or cut appears not only in the sagas[154] but also in Saxo.[155]

Wise men took precautions against this kind of magic before a battle. Men intending to fight someone who was known to blunt edges would carry two swords. It seems that it was necessary to see the weapon to blunt it, so when their opponents blunted the first sword, the second sword, out of sight and thus still sharp, was put in play.[156]

In addition to blunting weapons, men used a range of magic and magical items in battle to help them achieve victory: magical weapons,[157] magical charms that prevented cuts,[158] magical garments that resisted cuts,[159] and spells that cast darkness or altered vision or changed appearances.[160]

Additionally, the Norse people strongly believed in the power of luck (*gæfa*). Men sought to ally themselves with lucky men and to possess lucky things. King Hákon, when advised to flee before King Ingi, remarked that due to his good luck, he never had to flee a battle and would not now.[161]

Conversely, men distanced themselves from unlucky men. Grettir's request to serve the king was refused because the king thought him unlucky and did not want such a man in his band of fighters.[162]

### SUMMARY AND CONCLUSIONS

The Viking belief in predestination and fate, and the strong desire to achieve immortality by attaining *orðstírr*, drove Viking-age people in directions different from most other world cultures. A Viking-age man saw no need to hold back in any of his ventures, whether they be travel, combat, or trade.

These beliefs shaped Viking mindset, and mindset shaped Viking behavior to favor taking actions thought to be *drengskapr* in everyday life and in combat. To be labeled a *drengr* was the pinnacle of excellence.

At the same time, mindset drove people to avoid behaviors called *níð*, behaviors that destroyed one's reputation and status.

These behaviors were most often tested in the crucible of battle, which implies that if violence were not such a pivotal part of Viking society, the concept of *drengr* could not exist. It was in this testing that *frami*, *sæmd*, and *virðing* were gained, leading to *orðstírr* and the immortality of a good name spoken often after a man's death.

Repeatedly, we see the central place that battle occupied in the society. Saxo's words perhaps best summarize this idea:

> In times past people believed that the supreme goal was a celebrity achieved not by dazzling riches but hard activity in war. Illustrious men once made it their concern to pick quarrels, start up old feuds, loathe ease, choose soldiering in preference to peace, be evaluated by courage rather than property, and take their greatest delight in battles, their least in banqueting.[163]

In the next chapter, we start our exploration of how Vikings fought by looking at the companion of the mental elements discussed in this chapter: the power-based and brutal empty-hand fighting methods of the Vikings.

*Hnébragð* (knee trick). Photo: ©NAEPHOTO.

# EMPTY-HAND COMBAT

Understanding the empty-hand fighting system of the Vikings has been paramount in our research on them. As we will show in this chapter, without a deep understanding of empty-hand fighting, it would be difficult to decipher the power-based ways Vikings fought.

Grappling was a central part of Viking culture. Viking-age people grappled for sport: to learn who was the strongest and most accomplished. They grappled for fun: an entertainment wherever people gathered. They grappled to humiliate others and to take them down a notch. And people turned their grappling skills into a lethal, empty-hand fighting system used in combative life-and-death situations. These examples of Viking grappling illustrate the importance of the activity to the society.

While the words *grappling* or *wrestling* are sometimes used to describe these activities, they are insufficient here because we are exploring something more than just wrestling. We call it *empty-hand fighting* because that phrase is more expansive. The term applies to all combative moves that don't directly involve weapons, even though a particular empty-hand encounter may lead to weapons being used to end the fight.

SOURCES

Grappling is the delivery system for empty-hand fighting in the Viking age. The delivery system is the fighter's preferred or chosen way to deliver the attack and the defense in combat. As with most other aspects of Viking combat, we must use many sources to reverse engineer Viking-age empty-hand fighting.

The archaeological records for empty-hand fighting are slight. There is place-name evidence suggesting that wrestling competitions took place on a site, such as *Fangabrekka* (Wrestling Slope) at Þingvellir, the outdoor meeting site of Iceland's parliament for centuries. *Víga-Glúms saga* tells us that men wrestled there during the Alþing, competing in teams.[1]

Both *Eyrbyggja saga*[2] and *Landnámabók*[3] mention the stone *Þórs steinn* (Thor's stone) on Þórsnes in west Iceland, on which men's backs were broken when they were sacrificed. Þórr was the god related to grappling, and breaking the back was a common move in wrestling, as is discussed later.

Few artifacts related to empty-hand fighting can be identified. Perhaps the most famous is a carved wooden likeness of two men grappling found near Lillehammer in Norway.[4] The arms of the men pivot. Some believe that the figures use the trouser grip discussed later in this chapter. The date of origin of the item is disputed. Until recently, it was thought to be from the eleventh century, and thus highly applicable to the study of Viking grappling. Yet our in-depth research into Viking-age wrestling

*Þórs steinn*, the stone in west Iceland upon which men's backs were broken for sacrifice, as told in the literary sources. Photo: William R. Short.

brought the date of the artifact into question, and we contacted the museum holding the artifact to inquire. Subsequently, it reevaluated the figure to a much later date,[5] and thus it was not applicable to Viking grappling. Some now suggest a date as late as the early twentieth century.[6]

Bioarchaeological studies of Viking-age human skeletal remains reveal little to help us understand Viking-age empty-hand fighting. Evidence of strong musculature in the skeletal material could be due to the hard physical labor of the period as easily as to strength gained from empty-hand fighting. We have nothing that marks one individual as a grappler and another as a nongrappler. What is often found in the study of Viking-age skeletal remains is that most individuals show signs of strong muscles and hard work.[7]

The literary evidence for Viking-age empty-hand fighting is far more abundant. The *Sagas of Icelanders* offer numerous episodes of empty-hand fighting, sometimes with enough detail to clearly visualize the moves used.

Another type of saga, the legendary sagas (*Fornaldarsögur*), are shrouded in fantasy and a sense of unreality. Yet many of the episodes involving empty-hand fighting have a clear air of realism. They offer details that help us fit together the puzzle pieces.

*Snorra edda* has an episode of empty-hand fighting. It tells of the classic wrestling match between the god Þórr and an elderly foster mother, Elli, the personification of old age.[8]

*Heimskringla* contains a few references to empty-hand fighting, but a telling example is an exchange between King Sigurðr and King Eysteinn as they compared their accomplishments and their wrestling skills.[9] The episode is discussed in more detail later in this chapter.

*Grágás* has two notable references to empty-hand fighting. The first says that a man playing in a game or a wrestling match who is injured unintentionally is himself responsible for the injury, since he is free to leave the game as he pleases.[10]

The second reference describes several categories of blows, all of which are punishable by full outlawry. A hit from the fist or the feet (a kick) that leaves a visible mark is considered a blow. Any hit that knocks a man into a daze is considered a blow.[11] *Frostaþingslög*, likewise, lays out the penalties for pushing away a man with hostile intent, or for knocking him down, or for leaping on him.[12]

Saxo tells us that a young king trained in boxing.[13] Saxo uses the Latin term *caestus*, referring to the straps on the hands and forearms used in classical competitions. Here, it seems likely Saxo used a classical term to describe a Viking empty-hand fighting, even though the competitions were quite dissimilar.[14]

In addition to literary sources, pictorial sources might be useful. Unfortunately, to our knowledge, there are few ancient images that show empty-hand fighting from Viking lands in Viking times.

Another possible source is the vestiges of Viking-age empty-hand fighting that remain in modern or near-modern sport. There may have been wrestling systems in Norway, Sweden, Denmark, and the Faroe Islands, however, those systems have all but disappeared, and insufficient traces were left behind on which to build a clear picture. There are folk-style wrestling systems in use today that are thought to have lineage to Norse Viking-age wrestling, such as Scottish backhold, Gouren, Cumberland, and Westmorland wrestling, Schwingen, and others, but the origins of them all are very unclear.

*Glíma* is the national sport of Iceland, with national competitions. It is a belt-wrestling sport and, at first glance, might seem to be an ideal source of information about Viking grappling.

Yet our research has suggested caution is needed when using modern *glíma* as a window into the world of Viking wrestling. While there are similarities, there are also differences, not only because of the drift that happened over the centuries but also because of what appears to be intentional changes to the sport that were made at times in Iceland's history.

Yet we will delve deeply into *glíma* because it is the only combative activity alive today that holds a documented, nearly unbroken line that

A carved wooden figure of two men wrestling, originally thought to be from the eleventh century, and now thought to be much more recent. Lillehammer museum SS-01506. Photo: Helge Sognli.

can be traced back to the Vikings. Thus, it is a unique source that helps us understand Viking-age empty-hand fighting.

TERMINOLOGY

Before we dig into the history of *glíma*, it will be helpful to define the terms we use in this book so there can be no confusion. In many modern sources, the word *glíma* is used to refer to a Viking-age sport, to a Viking-age combat move, and to the modern Icelandic sport.

In the Viking age, both *glíma*[15] and *fang*[16] were used for what today we would call grappling or wrestling. In some sagas, the words are used interchangeably.[17]

*Fang* is a word with many meanings related to a catching or a holding and includes variations such as an embrace.[18] One of the meanings is grappling or wrestling. An additional meaning is the area of the human body between breast and arms, which informs us about what body parts were most involved and gives us clues as to what Viking-age wrestling looked like.

Similarities and differences between modern Icelandic wrestling (*glíma*) on the left, and Viking-age wrestling (*fang*) on the right. Photo: ©NAEPHOTO.

*Glíma* likewise means wrestling.[19] While the word *fang* appears in other northern languages, ancient and modern, the word *glíma* appears only in Icelandic and Faroese.[20] Its etymology is unknown, but it is thought to be related to *glý*, meaning glee or gladness.[21] So perhaps "game of gladness" is an apt description.[22] Others dispute this interpretation and suggest the word derives from *game* or *entertainment*.[23]

There is one additional word used for wrestling mentioned in the literary sources, and that is *rjá*. Also spelled *hrjá*, it has the sense of *to struggle* or *to wrestle*.[24] In *Grettis saga*, Grettir says he has stopped doing *rjá*,[25] with no explanation of why he said that just before he agreed to wrestle.

### GLÍMA AND FANG

In a desire to reduce confusion and to ease the reader's way through the text, we will use *glíma* in this book to refer to the modern national sport of Iceland and the word *fang* to refer to the wrestling method of the Viking age.

There are a number of similarities between modern *glíma* and ancient *fang*. Many of the throws that are legal in a *glíma* competition appear to be similar to throws used in *fang* and described in the literary sources. Some of these throws even bear the same names in modern and ancient sources, such as *sniðglíma* (body drop)[26] and *hælkrókr* (heel-hook).[27]

The rules that define loss and victory seem to be the same in *glíma* and *fang*. In *glíma*, the official rule is that if thigh, butt, torso, shoulder, head, or upper arm touch the ground, it is a *bylta*, a full fall.[28] Competitive *fang* has a similar culmination, in that typically there is a clear ending with the vanquished opponent on the ground. The definition of a throw is written in the law code for combative *fang*; the punishment is full outlawry for throwing a man to the ground such that he goes down on either knee or hand or further.[29]

In *glíma*, the rules used to state that if you go down on one knee once, you can continue fighting (*hnéskítr*), but if you go down two or more times, it is a *bylta* and commonly ends the bout. The rules seem to be similar in *fang*, based on examples in the literary sources,[30] and even in the grappling match between Þórr and Elli.[31]

The differences between *glíma* and *fang* are more profound. In *glíma*, there are strict requirements for attire: a leotard, skin shoes, and a specific wrestling harness.[32] The harness was devised in the opening years of the twentieth century, and it is one of the defining aspects of *glíma* as a national wrestling style.[33] Prior to this change, *glíma* wrestlers used a trouser grip, discussed later in this chapter.[34]

In the literary sources, there is little mention of specific clothing worn for *fang*. Sometimes it is said that men stripped to their waist before wrestling.[35] The *fangastakkr* (wrestling shirt), an upper body garment worn to protect the wrestler, is discussed later in this chapter.

*Stígandi*, which literally means stepping, was a requirement added to *glíma* to ensure that the wrestling would not become static.[36] Competitors must step in a clockwise direction while attempting their throws.[37] This addition to *glíma* was added at the close of the nineteenth century.[38]

There does not seem to be any mention in the sagas of any similar requirement for movement during *fang*. In some *fang* competitions, the competitors moved all over the wrestling field.[39] Nothing in the stories suggest a required, standard stepping, but rather, it seems opponents went at it right away.[40]

*Glíma* rules require competitors to adopt a tall, upright posture during the competition.[41] It is forbidden to crouch, bend the hips, or widen the stance.[42] To do so is to *bolast*, a vile and, more importantly, an unattractive unsportsmanlike conduct.[43] This posture is very different from that of other wrestling systems worldwide, and it appears to have been adopted in the middle of the nineteenth century.[44]

Nothing like this posture is described for *fang*, and episodes in the sagas point away from this *glíma*-style posture. For Grettir to duck under and grab Glámr would seem to require him to *bolast* in the epic wrestling fight at Þórhallsstaðir.[45]

At some point in Iceland's history, the values of *glíma* changed. *Fang*, the wrestling style of the Viking age, was strength based, so much so that people were unsure of a man's strength until they had seen him wrestle.[46] In the Viking age, strength and power were valued in a wrestler, but in modern *glíma*, finesse, agility, and beauty are what is most prized.[47] *Glíma* today puts the least emphasis on that which the Vikings most praised in their wrestling.[48]

A passage from *Magnússona saga* confirms this idea for ancient grappling. In the saga, King Sigurðr and King Eysteinn compare their accomplishments. Sigurðr says he was always able to throw Eysteinn when they wrestled, but Eysteinn counters that he was better in games requiring agility.[49] The passage suggests that even kings wrestled and that skill in wrestling was prized by them. It further suggests that agility was not a primary factor for success at wrestling.

### THE EVOLUTION OF GLÍMA

How did *fang* become *glíma*? What caused these seismic changes, and when did they occur? We will probably never know with certainty, but there are very reliable clues.

During the Sturlunga era in the twelfth and thirteenth centuries, Iceland experienced something close to a civil war as *goðar* (chieftains) attempted to consolidate their rule by grabbing power and influence from less-powerful chieftains through force and political maneuvering. Violent conflict between competing chieftains was nearly continuous.[50]

This era came to an end in 1262, when the Icelanders agreed to give up their independence and become subjects of the king of Norway.[51] It is not clear why they were willing to do so; perhaps after a century of bloodshed, they thought they were buying peace.[52]

There were many changes, and perhaps some of them helped drive the evolution of *fang* to *glíma*. There was no major warfare in the land after the loss of independence.[53] Since there was less bloodshed, there was less need for ordinary farmers to be trained in combat. Perhaps that change influenced the mindset of the warrior-farmer. Before, one always needed to be prepared for combat because of the constant threat of blood vengeance as taught in *Hávamál*[54] and told in the literary sources and discussed in the mindset chapter. Could it be that *fang* as a combative method was close to obsolete?

Additionally, before the loss of independence, individual churches were under the rule of the *bóndi* (head of the household) who farmed the land around the church. After the change, the bishop claimed control over all the churches.[55] The church gained more control over the lives and customs of the Icelandic people. Perhaps the church wanted to distance itself from old ways that might have heathen influences, such as *fang*.

Perhaps these were first steps in the evolution of the combative fighting method *fang* into an educational tool called *glíma* to help young boys mature into men. But the more seismic changes seem to have occurred later, around the time that Icelanders began agitating first for home rule and then for their independence from the Danish crown, which ruled Iceland at the end of the nineteenth century.

Many fundamental changes were taking place in the society at this time. Traditional Icelandic turf houses were being replaced with modern concrete structures, using a method developed in Iceland.[56] The use of traditional runic inscriptions was dropped as being old-fashioned.[57] Fishing, one of Iceland's major industries, was being modernized and mechanized.[58] The educational system was being improved, with compulsory attendance for children in urban areas.[59] As in other lands, a prohibition movement grew,[60] and beer especially was thought to be associated with the state of Denmark and thus not a patriotic drink.[61]

An independent nation needs something unique that separates it from other nations. And perhaps *glíma* was thought to be something that could be claimed to be uniquely Icelandic. It was at this time that many big changes were made to the sport. The wrestling harness was adopted.[62] Posture changed from a traditional wrestling stance to standing tall and erect.[63] *Stígandi* was now required.[64] And *glíma* became more of an event. Spectators

dressed up for the show, and wrestlers wore less clothing that was more revealing.[65] It was around this time that the various throws and gripping methods used in the folk wrestling systems of Iceland were categorized and systemized, identifying what should be in the national sport of *glíma* and what didn't belong there.[66]

Perhaps it was at this time, at the beginning of the twentieth century, that *fang* of the ancient past truly became modern *glíma*: a tool for differentiating Iceland from other countries.[67]

It is not fully clear what factors drove *fang* to become *glíma* and whether the change happened gradually or suddenly, but the change is unmistakable. While *fang* and *glíma* have their similarities, they also have fundamental differences.

One type of wrestling that was left out of the *glíma* when it became systemized was *hryggspenna* (literally, spanning the back). It is a wrestling method in which the wrestlers grasp each other around the back in a strong embrace and from that position try to take each other down. Even though not part of *glíma*, it is still practiced. Both ancient and modern *hryggspenna* are power sports, and agility does not play a major role.[68]

VIKING-AGE FANG

What was *fang*, and why did it hold such a place of importance in Viking-age society? In part, it was a test of a man's strength in a society that placed a premium on strength. The literary evidence strongly suggests that a *fang* match was a test of strength,[69] such as the one between Þórr and Elli.[70] That strength was prized is evident by the many introductions to saga heroes that begin with a mention of the man's strength and skill with arms, such as the description of Gunnarr Hámundarson.[71]

When Kings Sigurðr and Eysteinn compared their accomplishments, Sigurðr stated that a leader (*höfðingi*) must be stronger and more skilled at arms than other men.[72] In *Finnboga saga ramma*, Þorgeirr asked Finnbogi to show him some feat of power, and Finnbogi asked

Þorgeirr if he wanted him to wrestle. Finnbogi didn't wrestle but instead lifted very heavy stones.[73] This episode demonstrates the importance of power in wrestling. Wrestling was not only compared to lifting heavy stones, it was the first thought when it came to demonstrating feats of power.

As power and strength were most important in *fang* in the human world, it makes sense that Þórr would be the god of *fang*. Þórr is not only the strongest of the gods, he is also the only god who is mentioned to have wrestled. He wrestled against Elli, the personification of old age.[74] The wrestling episode depicts Þórr as a mighty wrestler, for old age brings everyone down, but Þórr could only be brought down to one knee by this indomitable force. In addition, Þórr apparently wrestled with King Óláfr's men, whom he thought little of and found to be weaklings.[75]

Þórr seems to have been called on directly for wrestling. In *Gunnlaugs saga ormstungu*, Þórðr called on Þórr for assistance in a wrestling bout.[76]

There are other direct connections to Þórr as a god of *fang*, such as *Þórs steinn* (Thor's stone), mentioned earlier. In later centuries, after Christianity had taken over in Iceland, special wrestling magic staves were still associated with Þórr.[77] Simply put, *fang* was a test of strength and power in all realms.

A reflection on the daily activities of a Viking-age person suggests this strength would be necessary for survival. Virtually every kind of farm chore was accomplished with human labor. Bioarchaeological studies of Viking-age skeletal remains show a population of strong, robust people.[78]

Little is known about how (or even if) Viking-age men trained for combat. Perhaps *fang* competitions tested many of the same attributes that a man needed for combat, since it seems the way they wrestled for sport was similar to the way they fought in a life-and-death conflict.

Lastly, *fang* competitions were a form of entertainment. Fangbrekka, the wrestling site at

Modern day stone lifting competition at a Hurstwic feast. Photo: William R. Short.

Þingvellir, is an ideal venue for sport wrestling, with a flat area for the combatants and sloping hills for spectators to watch the bouts. At the Hegranessþing competition in which Grettir wrestled, people sat down near the booths to watch.[79]

That this kind of competition was entertainment fits with the love of Viking-age people to test, challenge, and compete, whether it be tests of skill, wit, or strength. *Fang* competitions for sport and entertainment occurred wherever people gathered with leisure time: at a *þing* assembly, in the longhouse, at game festivals, at trading centers.[80] *Fang* was also used in combative, life-or-death situations by men and women against men, as well as trolls, ghosts, and other paranormal beings, both armed and unarmed.

## COMBATIVE FANG

Many fights using *fang* were to the death. The difference between sporting *fang* and combative *fang* seems to be less about the moves used, which were similar, but rather about what happened before and after the wrestling bout.

It is possible there were differences in the starting position between combative and sporting *fang*, but the main differences seemed to be in the intent, in the end positions, and in the follow-up. For example, the ending move and the follow-up in combative *fang* was something intended to cause death: a throw made to break the back or neck,[81] or, once on the ground, to finish the fight with or without a weapon.

### THE NATURE OF FANG

What did *fang* look like? While some saga descriptions provide details of a few of the moves, the big picture is less clear. Using the available sources and the fundamentals of kinesiology of wrestling in general, we next try to make the picture more clear.

*Fang* seems to have had five phases: entering, grip, throw, ground position, and finishing. We will look at these phases separately.

### ENTERING

Entering was the start of the fight. From out of empty-hand fighting range, the fighter had to enter into a range that would allow grappling, but how he did that is uncertain. The literary sources give us clues. The words that show up most often in this entering phase of *fang* are *renna*,[82] *hlaupa*,[83] and *undir*.[84] *Renna* and *hlaupa* are associated with such concepts as running, leaping, flowing, sliding, and similar fast, forward motions. *Undir* means under or underneath.[85] The combination implies a rapid forward movement, entering swiftly and, at the same time, ducking under the opponent's arms to secure the stronger position.[86]

The most logical approach based on wrestling kinesiology and the word usage in the literary sources[87] would be an entering move similar to a wrestler's tackle in today's sport world.

One wonders if, in sporting *fang*, men started in a grip, perhaps something like *hryggspenna*, to ensure that combatants were in an equal starting position, with neither fighter having an advantage. The text describing the *fang* competition between Klaufi and Þórðr

Wrestler's tackle. Photo: William R. Short.

might be interpreted as first getting a grip and then beginning to wrestle, while the match between Grettir and Þórðr starts out of range as Þórðr runs in.[88]

In many cases, unarmed fighters entered into *fang* on an armed man because of necessity: they were caught unarmed.[89] Or, on rare occasions, their weapon didn't bite and became useless in the midst of a fight, leading to the near suicidal move of dropping the weapon to enter into *fang*.[90]

### GRIP

After entering, a combatant must secure a grip on his opponent. Several grips have been theorized by modern Viking interpreters, but only a few are mentioned in the ancient sources. Let us explore all of these grips and see which ones are the most likely.

*Brókartök* (trouser grip) is a method of securing a grip using your opponent's trousers, probably at the hips, near where the pockets would be in modern trousers, or on the waistband. In *glíma*, this is the only legal grip, and it is made on the wrestling harness at the hips. Yet gripping the trousers during *fang* is only twice mentioned in the literary sources: once for a fully clothed man (where the skirt of the tunic might interfere with getting the grip), and once for a man who has stripped to the waist.[91] After these early examples, the next mention of a trouser grip seems to have been in 1847,[92] when Iceland was pushing for independence and *glíma* was evolving from *fang*.

The trouser grip was probably not the starting grip in a wrestling match, nor was it the preferred grip in a combative situation. It is not described that way in the two saga episodes mentioned above. The literary sources suggest that the starting grip was more likely to be on the upper body, and the moves sought after that starting position also suggest an upper body grip.

*Axlatök* (shoulder grip) or *lausatök* (free grip) is a method for securing a grip using the clothing on the shoulders, although it is possible the grab was made to the material on the front of the upper garment corresponding to the lapels of a modern jacket.[93] The earliest accounts of these grips are from the younger Icelandic sources and said to be similar to Cornish wrestling.[94]

The fact that *axlatök* is most often called *lausatök* has given countless theories of what this mysterious-sounding grip might be, and some modern practitioners have given it a new life. There are few literary episodes where the shoulders are gripped that could be connected to *fang*. One simple reason for this is that *fang* was done bare-chested.[95] It goes without saying that there is little to grab on the shoulders and chest of a bare-chested man, and at least one example suggests that taking off one's shirt was expected of a wrestler.[96] When Gunnarr arrived to a *fang* competition dressed in a *hjúpr* (a loose upper body garment), the earl asked Gunnarr why he did not take off his clothes. Another example of what seems to be a specialized wrestling garment is the *fangastakkr* (wrestling shirt).[97]

These two episodes need to be analyzed to understand the nature of the clothing and why it was worn. In both episodes, the men were to wrestle a supernatural being called a *blámaðr*. All supernatural beings have a common way to fight empty handed. They squeeze with their supernatural strength such that they break bones,[98] and they rip flesh off their opponent

Top: One of the earliest known photographs of *brókartök* (trouser grip), dating from the period 1905-1920. Photo: National Museum of Iceland. Bottom: *Axlatök* (shoulder grip) is also known as *lausatök*. Photo: ©NAEPHOTO.

with their claws.[99] The *fangastakkr* and other specialized clothing was meant to protect against such superhuman *fang*, and it is described as such in the episodes.

Based on the shedding of clothes before a competition, lack of episodes in the literary sources, and the impossibility of performing the moves described in the literary sources with the *axlatök* grip, we are left to assume that *axlatök* was not the preferred grip of *fang*.

*Hálstök* (collar hold) is a method of securing a hold around the back of the neck of the opponent using one or both hands. This grip theoretically happens once in the literary sources under unique circumstances when a *draugr* (animated corpse) placed his claws in the back of the head of Hrómundr and tore the flesh from his skull.[100] Apart from this single mention, nothing similar to this hold is mentioned in the sources, and in fact, it is not mentioned in any later Icelandic sources until 1886. It may have been connected to the development of Greco-Roman wrestling,[101] or perhaps as a move against wrestlers who *bolast*, so that they would stop that habit for a more beautiful erect stance.[102] Because of the lack of sources, we must conclude that the *hálstök* hold was not a sought-after grip.

*Hryggspennutök* (back spanning grip/back hold) is what we call the grip that was sought after in *hryggspenna*. It is a grip around the opponent's waist, with the arms under the arms of the opponent and joining behind his lower back. Many clues point to this grip being the most-practiced and sought-after grip in *fang*. This grip comes up again and again in the sources,[103] and in a sense, it is the common thread flowing through most wrestling episodes in them.

*Hryggspennutök* is also the only possible grip to perform many of the throws mentioned in the literary sources, especially throws that happen frequently, such as breaking the back or raising the opponent up to the chest. Another meaning of the word *fang* is an *embrace with the chest and arms*,[104] which gives us further clues about which body parts were used in this preferred grip.

THROWS

After getting a grip, the *fang* wrestler would like to move the fight to its conclusion by throwing or taking down his opponent using a *bragð* (a trick). While other wrestling systems use words like *technique*, *throw*, *take down*, and others, the word in the literary sources is *bragð*, meaning a quick movement or a trick.[105] Whether more emphasis was on the trickiness

or quickness is hard to decipher, but both concepts are crucial to the practice of *fang* and *glíma*.

Although numerous throws are possible, only a small number appear in the literary sources. Some appear infrequently, others many times. The hip throw (*mjaðmahnykkr* or *lausamjöðm* or *mjöðm* or *loftmjöðm*) is known in many styles of grappling today, including *glíma*. It uses the thrower's hip as a pivot point over which to throw the opponent, and there are several examples in the literary sources.[106]

A body drop (*sniðglíma*) is another traditional throw using the thigh as the pivot point. This throw is used in many modern styles and in several sagas.[107]

The move of breaking the back (*brjóta á bak aptr*) seems, in the literary sources, to refer to actually breaking the spine as well as to a throw in which the thrower breaks the posture of his opponent's back. The move causes the axis of the opponent's upper body to fall backward, resulting in a loss of balance and a fall. The move is no longer legal in modern-day *glíma*, but it was the ancient move taken out of the sport most recently when *glíma* was systemized. It lingered to the degree that the belt had to be changed in 1966 just so wrestlers didn't go for this move.[108]

Breaking the back is a goal in modern-day *hryggspenna*. It seems to be one of the most frequently used takedowns used by Viking-age *fang* fighters.[109] The phrase breaking the back (*brjóta á bak aptr*), and the term *hryggspenna* (spanning the back), and the Scandinavian term *brydning* (breaking) together suggest that this takedown was very common.

There are many episodes of lifting and throwing in the literary sources where the opponent is brought in to the chest, lifted, then violently dashed to the ground.[110] This move is seen in a number of wrestling styles today. In *glíma*, there are a variety of related moves that would enhance the lift and throw to make the crash more violent, including such moves as *klofbragð* (groin trick) or *hnébragð* (knee trick). There is no way to say for sure if *fang* fighters

The *hálstök* (collar hold). Photo: ©NAEPHOTO.

*Hryggspennutök*, a grip around the lower part of the torso of the opponent. Photo: ©NAEPHOTO.

The hip throw, called *mjaðmahnykkr*, *lausamjöðm*, *mjöðm*, or *loftmjöðm*. Photo: ©NAEPHOTO.

*Sniðglíma* (body drop). Photo: ©NAEPHOTO.

used these additional tricks. The moves are not described well enough in the sagas to decipher.

The *hælkrókr* (heel hook) is a leg trip—hooking your opponent's foot with your foot and maneuvering him so he trips over your leg.[111] It is a traditional move in many wrestling styles, and it is still used in *glíma*.

Breaking the back. Photo: ©NAEPHOTO.

*Ristarbragð* (instep trick). Photo: ©NAEPHOTO.

*Klofbragð* (groin trick). Photo: ©NAEPHOTO.

*Hælkrókr* (heel hook). Photo: ©NAEPHOTO.

A few other throws and takedowns are mentioned in the sagas. Many are difficult to interpret based on the text, or can be interpreted in multiple ways. Here we give our best interpretation of a few of those throws, knowing that these interpretations may be distorted or off target and not an accurate representation of the throw as it was used in *fang*.

*Tábragð* or *ristarbragð* (toe trick or instep trick) is a takedown that is banned in *glíma*. The move involves stepping on your opponent's toes or instep and pushing him, causing him to go down.[112]

A throw that is difficult to decipher was used by Refr. He grabbed what might be interpreted as the top of his opponent's trousers (*brókarlindahald*). With the other hand between his opponent's shoulder blades, Refr threw him onto the frozen ground so he landed on his elbows and skinned them both.[113] It seems to be a scooping throw, but it is not clear from the saga text if Refr's grip on the trousers was from the front or the back, or even what he was grabbing on the trousers.

The foot sweep seems to have been used in *fang*, according to the saga, but again, the interpretation is difficult. Gunnlaugr swept both legs from under his opponent, and the fall was so great that it twisted the ankle of the foot on which Gunnlaugr was standing.[114] The description makes it seem likely that Gunnlaugr was standing on one leg and sweeping with the other, a classic example of a foot sweep.

The double-leg takedown apparently was also used. Hallfreðr grabbed both of his opponent's legs from a low position while crouching by a fire. He then rose up and threw his opponent down.[115] The move, as described in the text, seems to be a double-leg takedown. Though not legal in modern *glíma*, this move, called *grikkr* or *hnykkr*, was used until the early 1900s before *glíma* became systemized.

GROUND POSITION

While the throws were most likely intended to be debilitating or deadly,[116] *fang* fighters followed their opponent down to the ground after the throw to secure a superior position to end

Refr's throw. Photo: ©NAEPHOTO.

*Leggjarbragð* (foot sweep). Photo: ©NAEPHOTO.

*Grikkr* (double leg takedown). Photo: ©NAEPHOTO.

*Láta kné fylgja kviði* (knee ride), a superior position. Photo: ©NAEPHOTO.

the fight. From this position they could rough up their opponents, kill them (with either a weapon or empty hand), simply rest, or even discuss the situation with their opponent.[117]

A superior position in *fang* was similar to that of most wrestling systems: on top of one's opponent, securely pinning him down. In most cases these ground positions were attained immediately after the throw, but there were instances where a wrestler fought to attain the position,[118] as well as where he fought to keep the position once attained.[119]

Most of these positions are not described in detail in the literary sources, but one ground position is mentioned again and again: *láta kné fylgja kviði* (literally, to let the knee follow the belly, or perhaps more accurately, the lower abdomen).[120] Perhaps it was similar to the knee-on-belly or knee ride position of some modern-day ground wrestling systems: a controlling position capable of causing significant discomfort. This idea is supported by the literal meaning of the phrase as well as by the options available to the wrestler from this position described in the literary sources, as will be discussed later.

In the accounts of *fang* fights told in the sagas, superior positions are mentioned that

are too vaguely described to speculate on, leaving the possibility of ground positions other than knee on belly. It reminds us that much ancient knowledge has been lost.

### FINISHING THE FIGHT

Once the *fang* fighter had his opponent down and secured in a superior position during combat, he finished off his opponent with a move intended to be lethal. His choice of final step depended on what options were available to him at that moment. While there are a variety of possible moves, the three main moves mentioned in the stories all involve the neck area: strangulation,[121] biting through the neck or trachea,[122] and breaking or dislocating the neck.[123]

The description of the neck-breaking move in *Bárðar saga* fits perfectly with the hangman's fracture (seen in modern times, for example, in victims of motor-vehicle accidents), in which a hyperextension of the head and distraction of the neck results in multiple fractures of the axis (second cervical vertebra).[124]

In some cases, *fang* fighters finished off their opponents with a weapon.[125] It might not be safe to risk ground position to reach for a weapon, but sometimes a weapon was readily available, either on the person of the fighter on top or nearby. Weapons such as knives, saxes

EMPTY-HAND COMBAT 33

(short swords discussed in a later chapter), and axes[126] were used.

### ADDITIONAL MOVES

While the preferred empty-handed delivery system of the Vikings was wrestling, non-wrestling moves built on the delivery system. These additional moves were, for various reasons, rarely used by Viking fighters, despite their apparent advantage.

Two of these moves are punching and kicking, and as mentioned earlier in this chapter, *Grágás* prohibits both, with the punishment of full outlawry.[127] Punches seem to have been used only in emotional situations, where someone became so upset that he lost control and lashed out.[128] Occasionally, punches were used as a threat.[129]

The punches are often accurately focused and do what the hitter intended, so it seems that Viking-age people knew how and where to hit. Both Grettir and Þórr hit their opponents under the ear,[130] a highly effective target.

If Viking fighters knew how to throw a punch, why didn't they use it more often in their fighting? Why weren't their empty-hand sporting games based on boxing, like many other societies? We do not know, but some clues point to an explanation.

The use of weapons (or at least the credible threat of the use of weapons) was very much a part of Viking culture. A man unwilling to use weapons would quickly find himself at the bottom of society, as discussed in the mindset chapter.

The tools of Viking combat all require the warrior to be able to grip them, whether it be sword, shield, axe, or spear. If the hand is injured so it cannot grip the weapon, the ability of a Viking fighter to survive an encounter is diminished. Yet a punch risks damage to the carpal and metacarpal bones of the hand, especially when connecting to the strong, thick frontal bone of the skull. Additionally, infection is possible if the skin is broken should the hands contact the teeth.

Perhaps these risks were sufficient to cause a Viking fighter to avoid using his fists. Perhaps there were other, even more compelling reasons that have not yet surfaced.

There are few suggestions in any of the sources that Viking-age combatants used kicks in combat. When Þórr kicked a dwarf into a funeral pyre,[131] one has the sense that it was done in anger. Grettir twice used a kick in a combative situation, once when he was set upon by an overwhelming band of farmers intent on subduing him.[132] His kicks were (like the punches described earlier) effective, landing on a target that resulted in knocking out or debilitating his opponents.

Again, we must ask why a useful move was avoided. Why didn't Viking fighters kick? The law codes, and the stories in the sagas, tell us they were aware of the move and knew how to perform it.

One possible reason is that kicking did not mesh well with wrestling, the preferred delivery system for empty-hand fighting. Wrestling requires balance and a solid connection to the ground, but kicking requires at least one foot off the ground, working against solid balance. Additionally, ground surfaces in northern lands include wet grass, snow, and ice, all surfaces on which Viking shoes offer little traction or grip from which to make a kick. Further, *fang* requires a fighter to be at close-range—close enough to grab his opponent, which is not the ideal range for kicking.

So perhaps these reasons made it less likely that Viking-age fighters used kicks in combat. Perhaps, as with punches, a kick was made in an emotional situation. Perhaps it was the move made by an out-of-control man lashing out, rather than a fully-in-control warrior.

Another move sometimes related to empty-hand fighting is eye gouging, but few, if any, of the episodes of eye gouging in the literary sources can be said to occur during *fang*. Typically they take the form of punishment for an offense: an intentional mutilation.[133] The act was punishable by full outlawry, according to *Grágás*, and *Frostaþingslög* adds that not only the man who did the deed, but the two people who held down the victim were all outlawed.[134]

OTHER ASPECTS OF FANG

There is another aspect to *fang* that was common to all the the combat-related activities of the Vikings: improvisation, which Viking fighters took advantage of. Perhaps the most notable case of improvisation during *fang* is told in *Fóstbrœðra saga*, where Þormóðr and Falgeirr wrestled. Exhausted after a long fight, they fell into the sea, where Falgeirr's belt broke. Þormóðr pulled down Falgeirr's trousers so he couldn't swim, and Falgeirr drowned.[135]

In some cases, objects were intentionally placed on the wrestling field that could be used in the fight, most notably the *fanghella* (wrestling stone) over which an opponent's body could be broken or split.[136] It was probably similar to Þórs stein mentioned earlier. The stone *Hryggbrjótr* (spine breaker) is mentioned in the lost saga of the settler Hringr, and the stone still stands in Hringsdalr in west Iceland. The stone has formidable back-breaking edges, as seen in the photo, and these edges fit the descriptions of back-breaking stones in the literary sources.[137]

Men also took advantage of well-placed stones they opportunistically found in order to break their opponents, using the move when a properly shaped stone was at hand during a *fang* fight.[138]

Fighters took advantage of their environment in other ways during *fang*. There are examples of dropping an opponent onto the edge of the furniture in a house or other items to break his back,[139] dropping a man head-first into a boiling cauldron to kill him,[140] and using a rock set in the earth as a footbrace, causing the opponent to tumble backward to the ground.[141]

SUMMARY

*Fang* was important in Viking society and still is for anyone researching the ways Vikings fought, or Vikings in general. Without an understanding of *fang*, it would be impossible to decipher the combative methods of Vikings.

*Fang* gives us clues about the mindset of the Vikings in combat. Wrestlers who compete in

Top: *Hryggbrjótr* (Spine Breaker), a *fang* stone located at Hringsdalr in west Iceland, and the only known *fang* stone connected with Viking-age *fang*. Photo: Reynir A. Óskarson. Bottom: A wide stance ready to receive or to deliver a rushing attack. Photo: William R. Short.

dynamic, power-based systems need to be constantly on alert. The slightest wrong move lands a wrestler on the ground, since it gives his opponent a possibility of attaining a better

An aggressive, power-based attack with an axe. The move uses the same core concepts as empty-hand fighting. Photo: William R. Short.

position (*fangstaðr*), which he can use to advantage. When wrestlers take action, they need to take it with 100 percent determination. Anything less and the action will very likely not succeed.

The wrestler's mindset enforces being constantly on one's toes and constantly looking for ways to outsmart one's opponent. When a wrestler decides on an action, he goes full force and head on. This mindset is supported by the literary sources as well as the bioarchaeology. Men attacked with the intensity to destroy what was in front of them with a single blow.

*Fang* also gives us clues as to what was the foundation of the Viking warrior, that is, what the structure was that he moved from: his stance and body position. A warrior who has as his basis or foundation an aggressive, power-based wrestling would stand differently than a warrior who has as his basis a more technical system of wrestling or a striking art. A fighter's lowering his center of gravity and adhering strictly to the most functional way to keep his balance gives us clues as to how he would stand in a combative situation.

The countless episodes of combat in the literary source combined with modern, rigorous testing of these moves provide us with some idea of how Vikings fought. Much of this understanding would be lost if we were not familiar with *fang* and able to use it as a base on which to build.

When taken together, the sources form a picture that shows not only how Viking-age men fought empty-handed but also the importance of wrestling in Viking society and how Vikings fought in general. The sources show the differences between empty-hand fighting for sport and empty-hand fighting for combat.

The core of *fang* centered on raw power, swift movement, and cunning. The Viking fighter faced his opponent head on and up close. It was the same in sports, such as the Viking ballgame *knattleikr*. It was the same with weapons; the core was raw power, swift movement, and cunning. In the next chapter, we provide a general overview of Viking weapons and their place in Viking society.

The panoply of a Viking, showing the range of arms and armor used by Viking-age warriors. Photo: William R. Short.

# - 3 -

# INTRODUCTION TO VIKING WEAPONS

In this chapter, we provide a broad overview of Viking weapons, introducing some concepts and descriptors that are common to all weapons before taking a more detailed look at individual weapons in later chapters. We will add to the material presented in the earlier mindset chapter that demonstrates the importance of these weapons to the Viking-age people. Whatever weapon a man chose to carry, it was kept close, sharp, and prepared for instant use. It was a tool of survival.

TOOLS OF SURVIVAL

As discussed in the chapter on mindset, the nature of Viking society and Viking law meant an armed lethal attack could come at any time, in virtually any place, yet be completely in accordance with the law and with societal norms. Thus, a man's weapons made it possible for him to participate in society and the legal system in a meaningful way from a position of strength.

The Viking weapons most often mentioned were sword, spear, axe, sax, and bow and arrow. Defenses included shield, helmet, and mail. Each of these will be discussed in detail in later chapters.

Weapons were generally made of iron. Since iron making was laborious and time consuming in the Viking age, anything made of iron had value. Thus, weapons had value. Yet as a tool of survival, a weapon was not an optional thing to own. It is probable that every free man had at least one weapon.

Yet some weapons, such as swords, could be made only by specialized smiths, which added to their value. For these reasons, it is probable that a typical Viking was armed with nothing more than a single weapon, combined with a shield for defense.

Farmers who were part of the king's levy, his reserve army, were required by law to be better equipped. They were obliged to have a broad-axe or a sword, along with a spear and a shield of specified construction.[1]

A study of Viking-age burials in western Norway revealed that of the graves in which weapons were found, 61 percent contained one weapon, 24 percent contained two weapons, and only 15 percent contained three or more.[2] Of the graves that held only a single weapon, 23 percent held a sword, 29 percent a spear, and 48 percent an axe (either weapon axe or tool axe).

Weapons had greater value than merely their monetary value. Many of them were heirlooms, passed from generation to generation. They showed one's place in society. They were a visible symbol of a man's willingness to stand firm and push back against attempts to diminish or dishonor his good name. It was at the core of what it meant to be a Viking.

The loss of a prestigious weapon was catastrophic. *Laxdæla saga* tells the story of Geirmundr, who planned to abandon his wife and infant in Iceland and return to Norway. As he slept aboard his ship before his departure, his wife rowed to the ship and took his sword and left behind the infant. As she rowed away, he woke and called out for her to return the sword, saying it would be better to lose his wealth than lose the sword.[3]

As one advanced through society, one's weapons might change, or one's weapons might be reworked to indicate one's higher status. Prestigious weapons were decorated, often with precious metal, as will be described in each of the weapons chapters. Bolli Bollason left Iceland with his sword, a good but undecorated weapon. After he returned from his service with the Varangian Guard, he carried the same sword, now inlaid and bound with gold.[4]

The fact that some types of weapons are rarely found with these expensive decorations of precious metal suggests that they were considered not to be weapons of the higher classes but rather of the ordinary man.

That distinction is also reflected in the poetry. Some types of weapons have numerous *kenningar*, a form of wordplay that figured prominently in Viking-age skaldic poetry, thought to be the highest of the arts and a gift from Óðinn. A kenning uses a phrase as a substitute for a word in the verse, and the phrase often is drawn from Norse mythology. Many kennings for *sword* are recorded, but relatively few for *axe*, perhaps reflecting the difference in status between the two weapons.

Weapons, like many permanent objects of value in Viking society, were given names by their owners. Some names reflect the actions of the weapon, such as a sword named *Fótbítr* (leg biter), and the spear named *Vígr* (battle). Some names reflect the nature of the weapon, such as the axe *Rimmugýgr* (battle ogress), or the sword *Hvítingr* (shining).[5]

## BEING ARMED

The literary evidence suggests that virtually every free man was armed with a weapon in the Norse lands in the Viking age. Compared to the countless examples in the literary and pictorial sources of men being armed and ready for battle, there are few examples of men caught unarmed,[6] outside of the situations where men have put down their weapons to work, or where men were in a place where weapons were banned. There are only a few places mentioned where a Viking could not routinely carry his weapon: into a *hof* (heathen temple), before the king, and into church.[7]

Even in sleep and in death, men stayed close to their weapons, sleeping with their weapons hung on the wall over the bed[8] and buried with their weapons in their grave mounds, as told in the literary sources[9] and as found in numerous excavated graves.[10]

Archaeological evidence, such as the form of wear patterns on sword hilts, tells us that men wore their weapons not just for occasional battle but routinely, and probably handled them casually many times daily. Weapons were so much a part of the identity of a Viking man that the law code stated that a man unable to perform basic combative functions could not give witness in a legal case, essentially blocking him from the legal system.[11]

## BEING READY

These tools were not only kept close by, but they were also kept sharp and ready for use. Again and again in the literary sources, a weapon is called very sharp, with the implication that this made it an especially prized weapon.[12]

Many whetstones are found at or near house sites and in graves.[13] That men were buried with whetstones, some quite large for long-edged tools and weapons, suggests that men wished to keep their tools and weapons sharp, even in death.

The importance of a sharp edge can still be seen in modern times when butchering. A knife used for butchering or cutting meat is razor sharp, strong, and not brittle,[14] and it is kept very sharp to make the cut easier and more precise. It is no different for human flesh: a sharp blade cuts better. And so it is no surprise to find sharpening tools at Viking-age house sites, suitable for both weapons and tools.

At the house site at Hofstaðir, dozens of whetstones were found in a Viking-age context, including a rotary grindstone,[15] probably intended for fine sharpening work.[16] Other finds in the immediate vicinity suggest that repair and maintenance of edged tools and weapons made of iron was done in a particular part of the hall.[17]

It has been noted that Viking society was an agricultural society, and even high-status men were also working farmers who needed to be skilled in butchering animals. It has been suggested that these farmer/warriors might have in some way practiced and honed their combative cutting skills when they slaughtered animals. It is important to kill a bull with a single swift blow, since it is difficult and dangerous to contain an injured animal.[18]

As discussed later in the raiding chapter, Viking raiders engaged in *strandhögg*, where they drove animals to the shore to be slaughtered and butchered before being taken onto their ships, part of the booty of their raids.[19] A swift kill was essential for safe withdrawal from the raid, further suggesting the use of sharp tools, powerful cuts, and swift killing blows. When combined with the information presented in earlier chapters, it seems this same approach was used in battle as well.

The literary sources tell of professional sword sharpeners,[20] some of whom offered loaner swords[21] so no man would be without a weapon. This evidence further strengthens the idea that sharp weapons were desired.

Keeping the edge sharp and the weapon in good repair was also important to avoid rust, as well as the possibility that battle damage might propagate across the weapon, causing it to break and fail. Before an expected fight, weapons were inspected, renewed, and sharpened so they would be in tip-top condition for the conflict.[22]

Another example that shows how important it was to keep one's weapon sharp was that men turned to the supernatural to blunt the weapons of their opponents before battle,[23] rendering the weapons ineffectual.

A Viking-age whetstone found in west Iceland. Photo: William R. Short.

Lastly, when we examine well-preserved Viking swords, we can observe that even after a millennium in the earth, some of them retain evidence of having been sharp from point to cross.[24]

Together, this evidence makes clear that Viking-age farmers and warriors kept their weapons and tools extremely sharp and ready for use.

BEING TRAINED

Another aspect of being ready is physical preparation: training. Did Viking warriors train in the use of arms, and if so, how? Quite simply, no one knows. The sources are sparse.

As discussed in the sources and empty-hand chapters, bioarchaeological studies of skeletal remains show that Viking-age people were strong and robust, across the population, perhaps in large part because of the routine physical labor that was a part of everyday life in the Viking age.[25]

Literary sources tell of weapons training only occasionally. The myths tell of a young earl training with weapons: sword, shield, spears, and bows and arrows.[26] There is a mention of the king's men training with swords, cutting and parrying against one another.[27] Men went to ranges to practice their archery, as discussed in the archery chapter.[28] In the empty-hand chapter, we speculate that wrestling competitions served as training for combat. And as discussed later in this chapter, there is mention of training with projectiles.[29]

Later literary sources, such as *Konungs skuggsjá*, discuss in some detail the training of the king's men, including sword and shield, as well as various projectiles and archery.[30]

These sparse sources suggest it is possible Vikings trained in the use of arms. A few additional clues suggest they may have started their training at an early age.

The literary sources have numerous examples of children carrying and using small weapons.[31] Though few in number, these kinds of small weapons are found in the archaeological record,[32] and it has been speculated that they might have been for the use of a child.[33] Additionally, small wooden swords are found that are child-sized yet realistic enough in detail that they can be classified using standard sword typologies.[34] But we do not have information to tell us whether these finds were intended as toys, training tools, or actual weapons.

Thus we can only speculate on whether weapons training was a part of normal Viking activities. While there is tantalizing evidence that at the very least the king's men trained, there is nothing substantial enough to allow for firm conclusions.

TYPOLOGY

In studying a collection of similar things, whether it be swords or butterflies, researchers tend to categorize them, grouping like things for easier study and discussion of them. Several researchers have proposed methods of categorizing Viking weapons.

One of the first, and probably the preeminent typology of Viking weapons, was created by Jan Petersen in 1919,[35] and it is based on Viking-age weapons held by institutions in Norway. Petersen's typology remains the most frequently used, and it is the system we use in this book. His sword typology, for example, is based on the form of the hilt and ignores the form of the blade, yet it continues to be a useful method of categorizing the weapons.

Later, R. E. Mortimer Wheeler created a typology for swords from Viking-age Britain,[36] but it must be used with care since swords from Viking-age Britain seem to differ from those in Scandinavia sufficiently that the categories are not a good match. Later, this typology was expanded by R. Ewart Oakeshott.[37]

Alfred Geibig created a more complex classification system, adding material held by German institutions to the mix. His typology considers not only the form of hilt components but also the form of the blade.[38]

One reason we stay with Petersen's less complex system is that even within a given time period, there is a lot of variation in a weapon from one specimen to the next. It is hard, with all this variation, to pick up on trends and slot a particular weapon into a narrow pigeonhole. As we discussed in the sources chapter, we do not want to be misled by small sample sizes. Using fewer and broader pigeonholes makes the categories more insightful. Additionally, some weapons simply cannot be easily categorized since there are so few surviving examples. It is the coin-toss problem again; the sample size is far too small. As discussed earlier in the research chapter, it is dangerous to draw conclusions based on small sample sizes.

For some weapons, Petersen created no typology, and so for them we depend on other typologies, discussed in more detail for each weapon in the weapons chapters.

IMPROVISED WEAPONS

There is another category of weapons that needs to be explored, since this category may well contain what Vikings considered the king of Viking weapons: improvised weapons.

Vikings used what was available at the moment to succeed in their struggles, as long as it didn't conflict with the code of conduct of a *drengr*. They were not afraid to try something new—a choice that was always preferable to doing nothing and accepting the situation as it was. This improvisational nature is a key to understanding Viking mindset.

The improvised weapons Vikings used were, in some cases, not so far removed from conventional weapons: using a staff or a stick as a weapon for striking shares many similarities with using an axe. In other cases, the tools used were far removed from normal weapons, such as anvils or sled runners. The improvised

*Geirvör*, a *vígi* where Steinþórr fought Snorri goði. The place was said to be ideal for a fight because of the loose stones covering the hillside. Photo: William R. Short.

weapon that was put to use depended on what the current situation was and what objects were nearby that could be pressed into service as weapons.

In some cases, the choice was based on necessity. An unarmed man under attack had to use whatever might be in reach to increase his chances of survival. As an example, Skúta had put down his sword to repair a fallen beam used for hanging the washing. At that moment, Óláfr and Þorgautr attacked, and Skúta picked up a nearby clothes beater to defend himself from Þorgautr's axe attack[39] and ended up killing both of the would-be assassins.

In other cases, the improvised weapon might be chosen because it was better suited for the job at that moment than the conventional weapons the fighter carried. An example is told in *Eyrbyggja saga*, when Arnkell was stacking hay with his slaves. They saw a band of men coming to attack. Arnkell sent his slaves for help while he took the running blade off the hay sled and went to the top of the haystack wall. Setting down the sword and shield he carried in his hands, he used the sled runner to defend himself successfully from his many attackers. His superior position, combined with the reach of the sled runner, kept his oppo-

nents at bay better than his sword and shield could have done. When the sled runner broke, he took up his sword and shield to continue the fight.[40]

Many items were used as improvised weapons in the literary sources: whale bones, boat hooks, boat oars, manure rakes, anvils, mane shears, scythes,[41] and many others. Even gods used improvised weapons; Freyr killed a giant with the antler of a stag when his sword was unavailable.[42]

One improvised weapon is hard to consider in any other way than as the king of Viking weapons. It is not the highly valued sword. It is not Óðinn's weapon, the spear. It is not the two-handed axe most associated with Vikings. It is not one that is studied, excavated, and categorized by archaeologists nor displayed in museums by curators.

It was the humble stone. Stones are the most overlooked yet the most crucial and often-used weapon of the Vikings. Stones were free, readily available, easily accessible, and effective. Stones were used in countless episodes in the literary sources.[43] It was the weapon Vikings ran to when in danger of armed conflict, as we will see in the tactics chapter of this book where we discuss *vígi* (a superior fighting po-

The king of Viking weapons, the humble stone, in use atop a *vígi* as depicted in the film *The Final Battle of Gísli Súrsson*.

sition). Often these places are high ground where stones were readily available to use as projectiles against the enemy below.[44]

Saxo tells us that men trained by throwing stones, as does the later text *Konungs skuggsjá*.[45] Gísli proved he was more accomplished than most by throwing a stone a prodigious distance that others could not match. As he single-handedly faced down a group of opponents in a dispute, Finnbogi called his stones his *húskarlar* (farm hands), the band of "men" that would even the odds between him and his op-ponent. Gods also saw the value of throwing stones as weapons. Þórr threw a stone to stop a giantess trying to drown him.[46]

Stones were routinely thrown during naval battles.[47] Ships carried stones for ballast, but numerous times it is mentioned that before a battle, stones were brought aboard.[48] In at least one case, it is specifically mentioned that the stones were selected for throwing.[49] Rocks were also brought to fortresses to throw into or out of them.[50]

Seemingly, whenever rocks were available, they were used, and they were often available, according to the literary sources.[51]

MISCONCEPTIONS ABOUT VIKING WEAPONS
In the popular media, Viking warriors are shown using weapons for which limited or no evidence exists for their use. Here we would like to take an unbiased look at these weapons to determine the likelihood they were used by Vikings. Additionally, there are weapons men-tioned in the literary sources that seem to be unknown in the archaeological records, and these are often bundled together for conven-ience when discussing Viking weapons.

For centuries, English-language translators have used the word *halberd* for a number of unknown, long-shafted Viking weapons. These weapons include *atgeirr*, *kesja*, and others, which we discuss in the spear chapter. This choice is regrettable, since *halberd* refers to a specific weapon, unrelated to the Viking-age weapons called *halberd* by the translators. But the translation is universally used, and so we, too, will use *halberd* to describe these weapons. We distinguish between them only when we have good evidence for doing so.

The halberd was a weapon that came into prominence in the fourteenth and fifteenth centuries, long after the Viking age. It was a long-shafted weapon topped with an axe blade, a spike, and a hook or point. It was an inexpensive weapon that allowed warriors on foot to successfully engage mounted knights. It remains in use today as the ceremonial weapon of the Swiss Guard. But in the Viking age, the halberd was unknown and probably unneeded, since the Vikings did not use mounted troops. They were sea people who relied on their ships for most of their battles against other societies. Their warships were not intended for carrying horses for mounted combat. Although there are exceptions, in the cases when they did arrive for battle on horse-back, Vikings routinely dismounted and fought on foot.[52] Additionally, Viking weapons, such as the two-handed axe and the round shield, do not lend themselves to mounted combat.

Vikings certainly faced mounted troops dur-ing their travels, such as at the Battle of Stam-ford Bridge, yet it appears they did not feel at a disadvantage against cavalry. King Knútr's troops were said to be faster on their feet than horses.[53]

Fantasy sources often show a Viking with a double-edged battle-axe. There is little evidence for the use of such weapons, either in the archaeological records, pictorial sources, or literary sources. Saxo refers to an axe using the Latin term *bipennis*,[54] a double-edged axe, but it can also refer generically to a battle-axe.

War hammers and maces are crushing weapons having a heavy head on a shaft. War hammers had a hammer-like head and date from the later medieval period. Maces used a heavy head, often in the shape of a knob, sometimes having flanges, and were in use as early as Paleolithic times.

In the later medieval period, both were used to crush and to inflict damage through the plate armor used in this period. Even if the attack didn't injure the fighter wearing the plate armor, the weapons could damage the joints of the armor, limiting the wearer's mobility and reducing his capability to fight. Both weapons sometimes had spikes that could be used to penetrate the joints in plate armor.

The weapons came into more general use after the Viking age because of the "arms race" that took place in the later medieval period. As metallurgy got better, it became possible to create more-effective defenses, and weapon-smiths responded with weapons that reduced the effectiveness of the new defenses. And so, the cycle continued.

While the Norse myths tell us that Þórr used his hammer to crush the skulls of his enemies,[55] there seems to be no equivalent weapons used by Viking warriors. The literary sources tell us that warriors did occasionally improvise and use club-like sticks (*lurkr*) when nothing else was available.[56] Maces were used outside of Viking lands in the Viking era, notably to the east in Slavic lands, where mounted, armored troops were fielded, but there is little evidence for the use of maces in Viking lands. Saxo is the exception, telling of the use of maces in a mass battle.[57]

Siege engines, such as catapults and battering rams, are mentioned in contemporary literary sources from outside the Viking lands

A club-like weapon interpreted as a mace being wielded, as depicted on the Bayeux Tapestry. Detail of the Bayeux Tapestry, eleventh century, with special permission from the City of Bayeux.

but do not seem to have been in any widespread use in Viking lands during the Viking age.

In continental Europe, Abbo witnessed the siege of Paris and wrote about the events.[58] The raid took place in 885–886, when Vikings sailed up the Seine and laid siege to the city. Abbo wrote that the Danish invaders used catapults and battering rams.[59]

The text of authors like Abbo, writing in Latin and in the classical tradition, can be misleading, because the authors used classical Latin terms to approximate the Viking combat they witnessed.[60] An example is the use of *testudo*, a well-understood Roman formation, to describe a Viking shield formation that almost certainly differed in significant ways from the *testudo*.

Yet it has been suggested that Vikings copied the siege engines of their enemies, aided by de-

A speculative reconstruction of a medieval battering ram. Siege engines of this type were not the standard armament of Vikings. Photo: Adobe Stock.

serters,[61] and so it is possible they used them outside their homelands.

It is said that catapults were mounted on the stone arch over the entrance to the harbor at Jómsborg,[62] but generally, the literary sources mention the use of these siege engines within the Viking homelands only later, well after the close of the Viking age. *Konungs skuggsjá* (King's Mirror) states that a *valslönga* (catapult) was a useful weapon for defending or for attacking a castle (*kastali*),[63] a structure that probably did not exist in Viking-age Scandinavia. The weapon is also mentioned as being in use in Scandinavia in the twelfth century.[64]

When the available evidence is put together, it seems unlikely that Vikings used siege engines in their homelands during the Viking age. As discussed in the mass battle chapter, Viking fortifications differed from the castles of Europe, and especially from the larger structures existing in the time *Konungs skuggsjá* was written. It is possible that on their raids,

Vikings learned of these siege engines and constructed and used them, but the evidence is far from solid.

### SUMMARY AND CONCLUSIONS

In these last few chapters, we showed how violence occupied a pivotal position in Viking society, in its law codes, and in its mythology. Accordingly, Vikings were prepared for violence. They routinely carried a weapon, near at hand, sharp, and ready for use. It was a tool of survival, and so it was abnormal not to have one at hand. It was the primary way of causing your name to be spoken about—your *drengskapr* in the face of violent death.

Vikings praised and valued power in physical conflict. They considered their *fang* to be on par with lifting very heavy stones as a challenge. They also praised and valued power in their use of weapons. With a sharp weapon in hand, their blows were swift, powerful, and aggressive, and intended to take apart what was in front of them, similar to their method of slaughtering cattle for food. Killing efficiency was the order of the day, as long as it preserved one's good name. There was no place for flowery, highly technical moves. As with *fang* or rock throwing, the use of weapons was cunning, brutal, and swift.

Now that we have a grasp of the material in the previous three chapters, it will be easier to understand how each weapon was used, since that material forms the basis for the method Viking warriors used when operating each tool. In the next group of chapters, we will look in depth at the individual weapons that made up the panoply of a Viking warrior.

# SAX

We begin our in-depth investigation of individual weapons with what we expected to be the simplest and most straightforward weapon of the Viking warrior: the sax. Yet what appears at first to be an overgrown knife is, perhaps, not as simple as it first seems.

## INTRODUCTION

The sax is a single-edged bladed weapon that was in wide use in northern Europe well before the Viking age. The blade typically is longer than a knife and shorter than a sword, a blurry distinction we will discuss later in the chapter. As we will show, it is a weapon meant for cleaving, characteristically having simple fittings and no crossguard or pommel.

Saxes are found across Viking-age Scandinavia. Generally, they are plain, undecorated weapons with the single purpose of cleaving things in two. The literary sources tell us they were the weapon of common men, giants, and other paranormal strong men.

The exception is found at Birka, a trading town at the eastern edge of the Scandinavian lands. The town was guarded by a garrison that, based on the finds at the site, drew its troops from many eastern lands.

The saxes at Birka are typically found in the wealthier graves,[1] with decorated leather sheathes having bronze fittings and chapes. Thus, they are thought to have been a prestigious weapon.[2] Yet the Birka saxes, as with some other Birka weapons finds, are something of an outlier. The saxes found elsewhere in Scandinavia are generally unadorned: plain and simple weapons for plain and simple men.

## SOURCES

In our study of saxes, we rely on several sources, but all are sparsely populated. We rely most heavily on the archaeological records, yet saxes are not as commonly found as other weapons. Fewer saxes are found than swords, for example. The sword-to-sax ratio at Birka is about 2.4 to 1,[3] while in Iceland the ratio is 7.7 to 1,[4] and in Norway, 130 to 1.[5]

The other sources are also slim. While sax-wielding fighters are portrayed in the *Sagas of Icelanders*, only about 6 percent of the attacks in the sagas are made with saxes.[6] The sax appears only rarely or not at all in *Heimskringla*, or in the myths, or on runestones, or in poetry, or in the law codes, or in other later sources. Saxes are rarely depicted in pictorial sources. The sax is not a weapon required of the king's men in later times listed in *Hirðskrá* or *Konungs skuggsjá*.[7]

There seems to be no satisfactory answer as to why saxes are not commonly found from the Viking age. Perhaps they were not generally deposited in a grave.

A simpler and more probable explanation is that the use of the sax, an ancient weapon more commonly found in Migration period contexts, the time during and after the fall of the western Roman Empire. Perhaps the use of

From top to bottom: replica Viking-age knife, sax, and sword. Photo: William R. Short.

the sax was fading at the time of the Viking age, so that the weapon was not widely used by Viking warriors.

ETYMOLOGY

The etymology of *sax* strongly informs us about the use of the weapon. *Saxa* is the Old Icelandic word for *chop* or *hack*.[8] In the old language, *sax* referred to the weapon as well as to other domestic tools like shears, used for cutting men's hair and horses' manes,[9] a meaning retained in some modern Scandinavian languages. The word was also used to refer to the raised part of the prow of a ship that cuts the waves.[10]

The word may be at the root of the name for the Saxons, the continental people who traveled across the English Channel to settle in Britain during the fifth and sixth centuries.[11] They were known for using this weapon, notably during a mass assassination of the nobles of the Britons.[12]

*Skálm* is another word used in the literary sources for a tool that shares some characteristics with a sax. The word also has the sense of one part of a cloven thing, such as a tree branch.[13] Yet the saga sources never use *skálm* and *sax* interchangeably to refer to the same weapon, leaving the possibility that they might be different tools. The *skálm* is used as a weapon by giants,[14] as a butchering tool by men cutting up a whale,[15] and often by troll women who carry a *skálm* in one hand and a meat platter in the other.[16]

Yet the ancient poetry clearly suggests that the *skálm* was a weapon.[17] *Völuspá* tells us that as the world spirals toward Ragnarök, it will be *skálmöld* and *skeggöld*: an age of weapons, both *skálm* (sax) and *skegg* (axe).[18]

The word *scramasax*, popularly used to refer to a sax, appears even less often in the literary sources than *sax*. It is mentioned once in the early *Historia Francorum* in the sense of a *strong knife* and does not appear later.[19] How the term came to be used to refer to the Viking *sax* in modern times is not clear.

The literary sources mention several variants of the sax, including *höggsax* (hewing sax) *heftisax* (*hafted sax*),[20] and *handsax* (hand sax).[21] Other variants of sax that appear in the texts, such as *agnsax* (*bait knife*)[22] appear to be cutting tools that differ from the sax in unknown ways, based on the use in the texts.

While *sax* also refers to a variety of cutting tools, it seems to have been foremost a weapon. Some have proposed that it was an ever-ready multipurpose tool/weapon for a farmer/warrior. The literary sources do not support this use and instead describe cutting tools other than a sax being used for slaughter or for harvest.[23]

Additionally, a sax works poorly as a machete. A quick test using a replica sax to cut trees and branches standing in for a birch forest showed that the cutting abilities of the sax were limited, requiring many strikes to cut through even small branches.[24] As discussed in the previous chapter, sharp weapons were

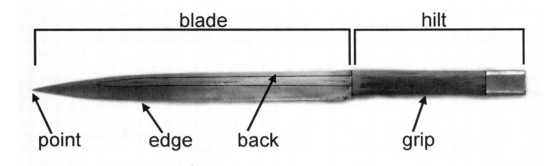

Top: Parts of the sax. Photo: William R. Short. Bottom: Decorative grooves on the blade of a Viking-axe sax. Derived from Arnold Mikkelsen, *Enægget sværd Alling Sø*. Creative Commons.

prized by Vikings. Using a sax as a cutting tool for brush would quickly dull the blade, making the sax less effective as a weapon. Together, the sources do not support the use of the sax as a general-purpose tool.

The sax is rarely mentioned in the mythology, and there seems to be little religious tone to the sax in any of the literary sources. It was not a weapon favored by the gods, unlike weapons such as the spear (Óðinn) and the sword (Freyr). Saxes appear only rarely in the myths, such as when Gunnarr said he would not be satisfied unless the heart of his brother Högni lay in his hand, cut out with a sax.[25] Perhaps the sax was merely a simple weapon for a simple man: a tool for cleaving in two whatever stood in front of you, and no more.

SALIENT FEATURES

The sax was a cutting weapon that fell between a knife and a sword in size, and sometimes the distinction among them all is unclear. It seems likely that each had a specific use, and graves containing all three weapons have been found.[26]

In essence, a sax is the large, single-edged knife of a warrior, a weapon intended for chopping and hacking. Generally, saxes have only two parts, the blade and the hilt. The sax

blade was made from iron, often with an iron body and steel edge. Some saxes were made with pattern welding, a process described in more detail later in the sword chapter. Some sax blades had one or more decorative grooves running most of the length of the blade.

The length of typical sax blades ranged from 30 to 60 cm (12 to 24 in), although there are archaeological finds categorized as saxes that are longer and shorter.[27] Small saxes might be hard to distinguish from a knife, and some large sax blades are as long as single-edged sword blades of the period.[28] Some of the moves described in the literary sources would require this kind of long sax blade, such as when Grettir cleaved Vikar in two with his sax.[29] Some weapons characterized as saxes have blades in excess of 80 cm (32 in),[30] more than long enough to accomplish the task.

Sax blades have been found in many shapes. The features that distinguish a sax generally include a single-edged blade with a thick, robust backbone; an acute sharp tip; and a broken (rather than straight) back near the point. In Scandinavia, the sharply broken back is less common than, for example, among Anglo-Saxon saxes.

Three Viking-age sax blades. Photo: William R. Short.

Petersen did not classify saxes in his landmark publication. Some researchers use O. Rygh's classification, and others have proposed alternative classification schemes, notably Georg Schmitt's typology and Anne Nørgård Jørgensen's typology.[31] Variations in sax blade length and shape can help identify their date and place of origin.

While the length and shape vary, a common element is that sax points tend to be acute and sharp, a shape that would make the weapon effective for stabbing. Yet in the literary sources, the sax is not commonly employed for stabbing, used in less than 15 percent of the sax attacks described in the sagas.[32] Cutting seems to have been the primary function of the sax, as borne out by the literary sources and the etymology.

One might wonder why have an acute point at the tip if stabbing is not a typical use of the tool? Perhaps because the longer sharp edge has advantages for cutting, or because the acute point is no more difficult to forge.

The tang was inserted into a long but simple hilt made of organic material such as wood, horn, or bone. These materials readily degrade, so little has survived to inform us about the detailed nature of the hilt. The means by which the hilt was fixed to the tang remain speculative. Rivets were generally not used; it is possible that an adhesive was.

Generally, saxes have no crossguard or pommel. The closest we see to this feature is sometimes observed on the sax type classified as the narrow sax, seen in the typology illustration opposite. Some examples of this type have a small iron plate at the front end of the grip, and an iron plate and reinforcing rivet bar or block at the butt end.[33]

The lack of a crossguard and pommel suggests that if the grip were to become slippery, the weapon could slide out of the wielder's hand, or the hand could slide past the grip onto the sharp edge of the blade. The magnitude of this problem was tested using simulated blood and simulated sweat on the wooden grip of a replica sax. In combative tests, the slippery grip required constant repositioning of the hand on the grip to keep the weapon from sliding out of the grip, or to avoid the hand sliding onto the blade.[34]

Additionally, the slippery grip reduced the effectiveness of the cut. The measured power of a sax cut delivered to a target when using a grip made slippery with simulated blood or sweat was about 40 percent less than cuts made with a dry grip.[35] Measurements of the grip in the hand showed that the slippery sax slid much farther in the hand because of the impact of the hit than a slippery sword, where the hand movement is limited by crossguard and pommel.

Compared to swords, saxes were generally more crudely fabricated. Rather than being crafted by skilled, specialized smiths, it is likely that saxes were made by smiths at a more regional level having fewer specialized skills. A single-edged blade like a sax is generally easier to forge than a double-edged blade, such as a sword.

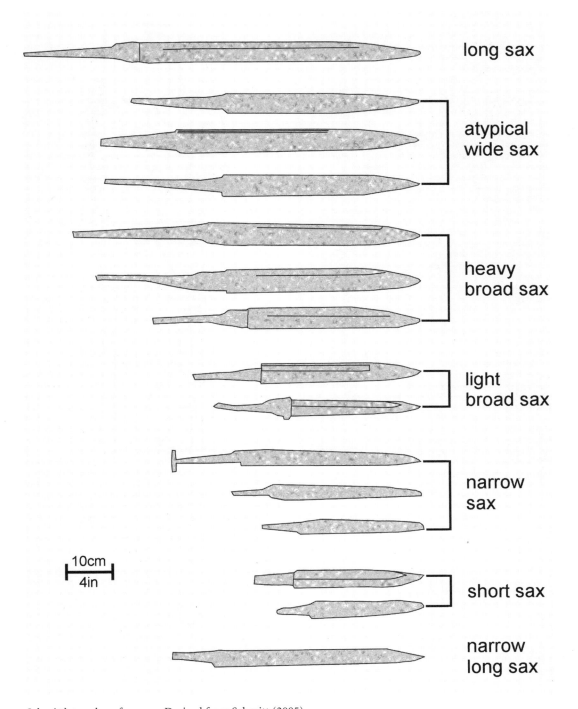

long sax

atypical
wide sax

heavy
broad sax

light
broad sax

narrow
sax

short sax

narrow
long sax

10cm
4in

Schmitt's typology for saxes. Derived from Schmitt (2005).

Pattern-welding visible in the blade of a Viking-age sax. Photo: William R. Short.

A sketch of a stone carving on a tenth-century burial cross from Yorkshire depicting a warrior carrying his sax suspended from his belt. Derived from Stefan Bollmann, *Stonecross from St. Andrew's, Middleton, Ryedale, North Yorkshire*. Creative Commons.

However, not all sax blades were crudely fabricated, and some show a high level of craftsmanship, including the use of pattern welding. The pattern welding is sometimes confined to a portion of the blade, often between the decorative grooves, or between the groove and back edge. It is thought that perhaps the grooves were placed to influence the appearance of the pattern welding, defined by the groove that edges it.[36]

Simply stated, while some saxes were treasures, according to the literary sources[37] and archaeological sources,[38] some were not. Some saxes were simply decorated using, for example, coarse twists in the pattern-welding for the thick backbone, and finer twists for the blade, creating a distinctive look to the blade.[39]

Saxes were usually carried in a leather sheath suspended horizontally from the belt, a carry method shown on a tenth-century burial cross in a churchyard in Middleton, Yorkshire.[40] The carving depicts a warrior surrounded by weapons. His sax is shown suspended from his belt in what is thought to be the typical fashion.

Longer saxes may have been carried more diagonally across the body, perhaps to reduce the width of the weapon and warrior so the sax

A speculative reconstruction of the Viking-age sax sheath from Birka found in grave Bj 834. Derived from Harald Faith-Ell in Holger Arbman, *Birka I. Die Gräber. Text*. Creative Commons.

didn't get caught by narrow openings. It has been proposed that the three rings seen on sax sheaths from Birka were used to suspend the sax from the belt in this fashion and to keep it in place as the wearer moved.[41]

Evidence suggests that saxes were carried with the edge upward, seen in the burial cross figure and in archaeological finds, where the bottom edge of the sheath mirrors the broken back shape of the sax. It has been suggested that the blade was carried this way so the sharp edge wouldn't cut through the leather sheath. The sheath generally seems to have been long enough to cover not only the blade but also most of the grip.[42]

The sheaths were formed by folding over a piece of leather around what would carry the back side of the blade and joining the leather along the sharp edge of the blade, securing it with stitching, clips, or rivets.[43] It is thought that the join was covered by decorative metal plates, as seen on the sax sheaths from Birka and elsewhere.[44] Evidence suggests that sheaths were decorated with geometric figures tooled into the leather.[45]

The literary sources by and large agree with archaeological finds and confirm that the saxes and their sheaths were intended to be routinely worn.[46] At home, sax and sheath were hung above the bed while the sax owner slept.[47]

PHYSICS OF THE SAX

Compared to other cutting weapons such as the axe and sword, the sax is generally shorter and lighter, with most of the mass distributed closer to the hand than to the tip. A computer model of the weapon shows the smaller effective mass at the contact point and the lower linear velocities at impact together result in less energy delivered to the target when cutting with a sax compared to cutting with an axe or a sword, all other things being equal.[48]

Measurements confirm the model. The energy delivered by a replica sax to a target measured about 40 percent less than the energy delivered by a replica sword,[49] not dissimilar to what the computer model predicted.

Perhaps the most significant difference between the sax and the sword is the strong backbone of the single-edged sax, making it less likely to break or fail when abused. While the literary sources tell of swords failing in battle,[50] there are few similar examples for saxes.[51] The sax was a robust, trusty weapon.

USE OF THE WEAPON

The rugged construction of the weapon, the episodes in the literary sources where the weapon was used, and even the etymology of the name of the weapon all point in the same direction: the sax was used to cleave whatever stood in front of the fighter who wielded the weapon. One saga character provides the helpful advice that when cutting with a smaller sax, you need to be more precise and aim for the joints,[52] but cleaving the target was what the sax did best.[53] Perhaps it is for this reason that saxes were the prized weapon of *jötnar* (giants),[54] ghosts,[55] and men who had the strength of a giant.[56]

Perhaps it is this use of the weapon that explains why, in the literary sources, a sax attack results in a fatality for a higher percentage of attacks than any other weapon,[57] regardless of the defensive tool used by the attacker's opponent.[58]

Some have compared a sax to a Roman *gladius* and concluded that like the Roman tool,

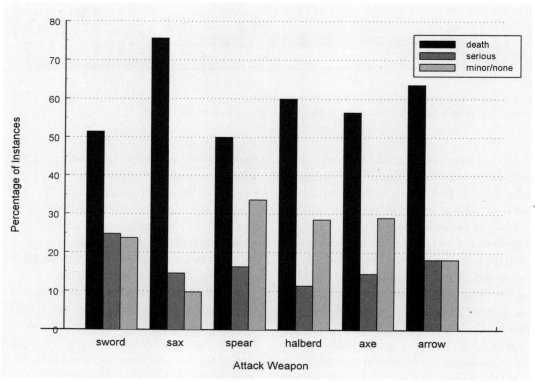

A plot of the injuries for various weapons used in attacks reported in the sagas.

the sax was a weapon for mass battle. It has been suggested that the sax was a better weapon in a mass battle than a sword or axe because of its shorter length when fighting in close order[59] and because its acute point made it suitable for stabbing. Yet there is very little mention of its use in mass battles described in any of the literary sources. Additionally, it was not a weapon required for the men of the king's levy in Norway,[60] who were called out to support the king. Perhaps at this time, the nature of mass battles rendered the sax less useful than these other weapons.

At times, the literary sources tell of a fighter using a sax in combination with another weapon,[61] yet one can not readily label it as a reserve or secondary weapon, since it is often used and mentioned above other weapons owned by the fighter using his sax.[62]

The sax seems to have been a very effective weapon, both on its own and in combination with a shield or other weapon. Perhaps being suitable for both single and dual wielding was one of the several possible reasons the weapon appealed to some Viking-age fighters.

KNIVES

The features distinguishing Viking knives from Viking saxes are hazy. The two resemble each other in many regards yet differ in their combative use. The construction of the two seems to have been similar, and often the only distinguishing feature is the length of the blade. A dividing line often used is somewhere around 20–30 cm (8–12 in); longer blades are considered saxes, while shorter blades are considered knives. This length criterion is not hard and fast but merely a convenient dividing line.

Most knives found are considerably shorter than this dividing line; the average blade length of the Viking-age knives found at York is 7.1 cm (2.8 in).[63] This distinction is a topic of some controversy among experts who try to strictly divide weapon knives (saxes) from tool knives.[64] We must be cautious of applying our modern mindset of putting things into strict categories. In the end, it seems that a knife is just a small sax, and a sax is just a big knife.

An aspect of knives that may differ from saxes is the blade shape. Knives are found with straight edges, similar to those of saxes, but knives with curved edges are also found.[65] Perhaps this difference is due to the differing needs of various household chores. For example, curved blades might be more useful for cooking chores.

Regardless, the knife and sax were used quite differently in combat. Unlike the sax, which was thought to be a weapon, the knife was an everyday tool meant for everyday jobs.[66] A man carrying only a knife was considered unarmed.[67] A knife became a weapon by necessity when no other tools were available for the task at hand,[68] an example of the improvisation skills of the Viking fighter discussed in the mindset chapter.

The knife was a constant companion. The literary sources tell of knives carried slung around the neck[69] or carried in a sheath on the belt.[70] Yet the author of *Fljótsdæla saga* notes that at the time of the saga, no one carried a knife on the belt but rather on a thong around their neck.[71] Regardless of how it was carried, a knife was an essential tool for a Viking, albeit not a combative tool unless forced by necessity.

## SUMMARY

The sax is a weapon that predates the Viking-age, fully developed and in widespread use in northern European lands by the eighth century. Perhaps the weapon is like a shark: an animal that has been on the earth unchanged for

Top: A replica Viking-age knife. Photo: William R. Short. Bottom: A knife was used in combat as a last resort. Photo: ©NAEPHOTO.

eons because it is already superb at destroying what is put in front of it. Yet it does not seem to have been much used by Viking fighters. Perhaps it was on its way out in the Viking age.

The sax seems to have been a powerful, robust cutting tool for powerful, robust fighters: a simple tool for fighters with simple needs. In their hands, according to literary sources, the sax was a weapon that delivered lethal results more often than any other weapon.

Dual wielding of an axe and a shield is depicted in the Bayeux Tapestry using both a short-hafted axe (left) and a long-hafted axe (right). Detail of the Bayeux Tapestry, eleventh century, with special permission from the City of Bayeux.

# AXE

When envisioning a Viking armed for combat, many people picture a hairy man holding a two-handed axe high at the ready. The axe is, in many ways, the iconic weapon of the Viking. Like the sax, it is a tool optimized for chopping.

## GENERAL CATEGORIES OF AXES

Viking axes came in a variety of shapes and sizes, but in the most general terms, they are divided into two broad categories: battle-axes and noncombative (tool) axes, intended primarily for working wood.

## WOOD AXE

The distinctions between the two types of axes can be blurry, but generally, a tool axe was rugged and robust to endure the wear and tear of repeated cutting of plant and wood fibers, which dull the edge more than cuts to flesh. The heads of tool axes were designed for cutting into wood fiber without getting stuck.

## BATTLE-AXE

While any of these tool axes could be pressed into service during a fight and often were,[1] a different kind of axe was intended for battle. Battle-axes were well balanced, light weight, and speedy, a consequence of their thin heads. They were intended for occasional use at the task of splitting body parts in two, rather than for everyday wood chopping, a task for which they were ill suited. They lacked the broad wedge-shaped profile needed to split wood

fibers without getting stuck, and they were in no way intended for the rigors of splitting wood.

## ONE HANDED VERSUS TWO HANDED

The distinction between one-handed and two-handed battle-axes is likewise blurry in both the archeological records and in the literary sources. A short haft might be interpreted as a one-handed axe, while a long haft might suggest two-handed use. But hafts are rarely found in the archaeological record, even though many axe-heads have been found, and the heads in isolation provide little information. The literary sources give an example of the same axe-head being hafted on different kinds of hafts,[2] suggesting the size of the axe-head is not always a good indicator of the length of the haft. Thus we are left in the dark about one-handed versus two-handed use of any particular axe-head.

Literary sources are equally vague about the distinction, with only one example of an axe specifically called two handed.[3] Only infrequently do the literary sources mention either the length of the axe haft or whether the weapon was being wielded with one hand or two. When they do make a distinction, it is usually to tell us that the haft was long (*háskeptr*)[4] or short (*skammskeptr*),[5] or that the axe was being wielded in two hands.[6]

One of the most celebrated axes in the literary sources is *Rimmugýgr* (Battle-ogress),

A comparison of one-hand and two-hand replica Viking axes. Photo: William R. Short.

which belonged to Skarpheðinn. It was sometimes wielded in one hand and sometimes in two.[7] Perhaps it was a short-hafted one-handed axe used occasionally in two hands for more power. Perhaps the haft was of intermediate length suitable for use with either one hand or two. Perhaps it was a long-hafted two-handed axe used occasionally in one hand with a shield in the other. It is a clear example of the complications of understanding the difference between one-handed and two-handed use of the axe.

There is not enough information available for us to distinguish a uniquely one-handed axe from a uniquely two-handed axe, and we will discuss the two types together. The literary sources do not give a clear picture. The archaeological sources rarely give any picture. The only sources that help us distinguish even in a small way are the pictorial sources. Accordingly, when a source strongly suggests that a

particular axe was intended for either one- or two-hand use, we will point it out.

SOURCES

In our study of Viking axes, we use many of the same sources as for other Viking weapons. The archaeological sources, such as finds of Viking-age axe-heads, teach us about the weapons and how they were made. Few axe hafts have survived, however. They can reveal length, diameter, and wood species, but we are troubled with the coin-toss problem: the sample size is too small for us to draw any solid conclusions. Archaeological evidence can even tell us about the use of axes in the cult practices of the Vikings.

Literary sources add more details to tell us something about how axes were used, both as weapons and as tools, and about the value of these weapons to society. Viking pictorial sources, such as picture stones or tapestries, infrequently show the weapon in use, but images from other contemporary cultures, such as manuscript illuminations and the Bayeux Tapestry,[8] help to fill in the gaps. As discussed in the sources chapter, our goal is to use narrow sources, so we consult these foreign sources with extreme care. By combining the sources, we gain a clearer picture of how the weapon was used.

THE AXE IN VIKING CULTURE

In a way, the axe was the iconic weapon of a Viking. The bloody axe was the nickname for Eiríkr blóðöx (blood-axe), the king of Norway. The Vikings serving in the Varangian Guard as the elite troops of the Byzantine emperor were known as axe-bearing barbarians.[9] The story of the lone Viking who prevented the English army from crossing Stamford Bridge is fondly remembered,[10] but the popularly held belief that he was armed with a two-handed axe is not recorded in the primary sources. The axe was an essential Viking tool and weapon, readily available to Viking-age fighters.

CULT OF AXES IN NORTHERN LANDS

Long before the Viking age, it appears there was a cult of axes in northern Europe. As early as Neolithic times, axes are found in the ar-

Axes were made for specific purposes, and an axe for wood differed from an axe for flesh and bone. These Viking-age axes show the range, from a weapon axe on the left to a tool axe on the right. Side and top views of each axe are shown. Photo: Lee A. Jones.

chaeological record that are unsuited for any practical use. The Alunda moose axe is a stone axe from Sweden in the shape of a moose head.[11] The hole for the haft does not even pass through the head, which suggests it was not a practical axe and may have been intended for ritual use. Bronze age stone carvings found in Scandinavia show phallic figures wielding axes[12] thought to be part of a fertility cult. From the Viking age, miniature axe amulets are found,[13] as are full-size axes with heads that are mostly open, thought to have been used for ceremonial purposes.[14]

Since axes seem to have been an important part of cult activities, one might expect them to appear in the myths. Surprisingly, the axe receives little mention in the mythology and is virtually absent in the eddas. One of the few examples is that as Ragnarök approaches, it will be an age of weapons: *skálmöld* and *skeggöld*, both *skálm* (sax) and *skegg* (axe).[15]

Snorri Sturluson writes in *Skáldskaparmál* that cutting weapons, such as swords and axes, are called *fires* or *blood* or *wounds* in poetry. He adds that axes take the names of troll women.[16]

In the skaldic poetry, axes are referred to as *troll woman of the shield, troll women of the mail shirt,* and *wolf of wounds.*[17]

ETYMOLOGY AND TYPES OF AXES

The word for *axe* is *öxi,* or occasionally *exi.* It is an ancient word, found in similar form not only in the Germanic languages but throughout the entire family of Indo-European languages, suggesting that the word for *axe* has remained the same far back into prehistory.[18] In addition, other words are used for specific axes that tell us about how the axe was intended to be used and about the nature of the axe. Sometimes the same axe is referred to by the generic word *öxi* and by the specialized word.[19] For tool axes, the words include *bolöx* (wood axe), *smíðaröx* (smithing axe), *tálgöxi* (adze), *viðaröxi* (wood axe), *taparöxi* (taper axe), *handöxi* (hand axe), and the *hálfþynna* (half-thin axe).

Likewise, battle-axes were referred to using words that distinguish them by size or shape: *breiðöxi* (broadaxe), *snaghyrnd öxi* (snaghorned axe), and *skeggexi* (bearded axe). Of these, the *skeggexi* is singled out in the literary sources as

From top to bottom: An open-head Viking axe, thought to be used for ceremonial purposes. Derived from Roberto Fortuna and Kira Ursem, *Øxse fra Ludvigshave*. Creative Commons. A Neolithic stone axe from Sweden in the shape of a moose head. Derived from Sören Hallgren, *SHM 14168*. Creative Commons. A Viking-age iron amulet in the shape of an axe. Derived from Gabriel Hildebrand, *SHM 8985*. Creative Commons.

being a common type of axe in this period,[20] and many axes of this type are seen in the archaeological record, as discussed later in the chapter.

Occasionally, the literary sources specifically describe an axe as a *litla exi* (little axe)[21] or a *mikla öxi* or *stóra öxi* (large axe).[22] Little axes are also found in the archaeological record.[23]

DANE AXE

The term *Dane axe* is popularly used today to refer to a two-handed broadaxe. The phrase does not appear in any of the ancient literary sources. One has to assume that this use of the term is a more recent invention, like so many things in the Viking lore.

HOW COMMON WERE AXES

It seems likely that every Viking-age farm had at least one axe for cutting and working wood. Without an axe, the farm could not process wood needed for buildings, tools, furniture, fuel, boats, saddles, sleds, and much more. Thus, axes must have been very common indeed in the Viking age.

Since farms required someone with basic smithing skills and a forge to maintain the farm tools on a regular basis, it seems possible that making an axe was within the capabilities of at least some farmers. Literary sources tell of a farmer forging an axe for a neighbor.[24] Yet archaeological finds of a number of rough-worked axe-heads carried together on a spruce stave[25] suggest that at least some volume production occurred at central locations, with finishing done at the regional or local level.

In the literary sources, there are numerous mentions of axes, both tool axes and weapon axes, and in some cases, axes used for both purposes. Of the weapons mentioned in the *Sagas of Icelanders*, 22 percent are axes.[26]

PHYSICS OF AN AXE

The basic physical design of the axe tells us what it was created for. It is a tool designed for splitting something in two, whether that something be a tree or a human head.

Nearly all of the mass of the weapon is at the end of a long haft, meaning the effective mass

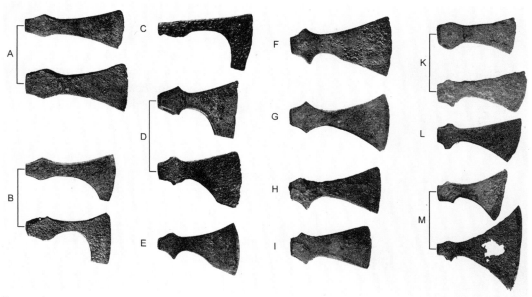

Petersen's typology for Viking-age axes. Derived from Petersen (1919).

at the point where the axe hits the target is much greater than, for example, a sword of similar total mass and length. For a two-handed axe, the effective mass is several times that of a sword, resulting in more than three times as much destructive energy delivered to the target, based on computer models.[27]

That additional effective mass in an axe means there is more energy in the weapon as it impacts the target, and more momentum, making it less likely than other weapons to be stopped by something hard like a bone. The thin, wedge-shape cross section of the head of a battle-axe allows the weapon to penetrate deep with minimal resistance, splitting the target in two. The convex shape of the edge of typical axe-heads concentrates the force to help with the cleaving action.

In some ways, the physics of the axe resembles that of a hammer. Both have a heavy head at the end of a handle. A two-handed axe is like a sledgehammer, meant to demolish what it hits, or to drive in a wedge with heavy blows. A one-handed axe is like a one-handed hammer, for a solid blow requiring more accurate hitting. It is a weapon intended for full-power

blows and complete destruction. Illugi perhaps states it most clearly when he brandishes his axe and says that it is the master key that opens every lock and every chest in the house.[28]

SALIENT FEATURES OF A VIKING AXE

Axes had two parts: the iron head and the wooden haft. Later axes sometimes had a metal buttcap to protect the far end of the haft. There is little evidence for the widespread use of buttcaps in the Viking age.

The heads came in a wide variety of sizes and shapes in the Viking age. The axe-head typology of Jan Petersen shows the variations.[29]

Based on available evidence, axe-heads were always single-edged, and almost always made of iron. The sharp bit that formed the cutting edge was typically made of steel and welded into the head, allowing the axe to hold a better edge than iron alone. Both Saxo[30] and *Cogad Gáedel re Gallaib*[31] give an example of an axe-head that might be interpreted as double-edged, but other interpretations of the words in the original Latin and Irish texts are also possible.

Smaller axes had a cutting edge ranging from 7 to 15 cm (3 to 6 in), while larger axes,

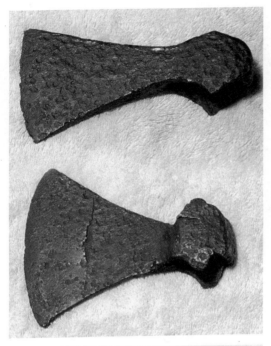

Top: A visual comparison of the type G and the type M Viking-age axe heads discussed in the text. The type G was probably intended as a tool while the type M was probably intended for battle. Bottom: The eye of a Viking axe as seen from the top. Photos: William R. Short.

such as the *breiðöxi* (broadaxe) had crescent-shaped edges as much as 45 cm (18 in) long. There are examples of these large axes mentioned in the literary sources[32] having heads 1 *ell* long, about 50 cm.

Because of the variation in the size and shape of the axe, there was likewise a wide variation in the weight. A Viking-age type M axe (approximately 11.9 cm from horn to horn, and 14.6 cm from edge to the back of the head) probably intended for battle (thickness of head is about 6 mm) weighs 362 g (0.8 lbs), while a more robust type G axe (approximately 5.7 cm from horn to horn, and 11.6 cm from edge to back of the head) probably intended as a tool

(thickness of the head is about 13 mm) weighs 524 g (1.2 lbs).[33]

Axe-heads have an eye to allow the haft to pass through the head. Generally, the eye was in the shape of an elongated "D," or of an escutcheon-style shield, and the haft was shaped to mate tightly with the eye in order to hold the head to the haft securely and to better transfer force from haft to head.

Some types of axe-heads have additional features. Most types have lugs to provide more contact area between the metal head and wooden haft, for a better, more durable fit, and for reducing stresses should sideways forces be placed on the axe. The lugs are visible in Petersen types D, E, and F, for example.

Some axe types have beards descending from the head, such as Petersen types B and C. Some axe types have acute horns, which are the points on each end of the cutting edge. These horns are quite prominent in the large Petersen type M. Rimmugýgr, the famous axe of Skarpheðinn in the sagas, is said to have had horns capable of inflicting serious damage.[34]

The back side of the axe-head, behind the eye, is called the hammer, and typically was flat.

CONSTRUCTION OF AN AXE

Axe-heads for battle characteristically had a wedge-shaped cross section and often were thin, lightweight, and elegant. These thinner axe-heads often show evidence of having been folded around what would eventually become the eye and welded together with a steel bit for the edge. In some cases the wrap was symmetrical, while in other cases it was asymmetrical, with the weld just forward of the eye. Several other variants are seen in the archaeological record, suggesting other construction methods were used.

DECORATIONS

Most axes were simple, but some elaborately decorated axe-heads are also found. The most notable is the tenth century Mammen axe-head found in Denmark, decorated on every flat surface with elaborate inlays of gold and silver.[35] The axe-head is surprisingly small,

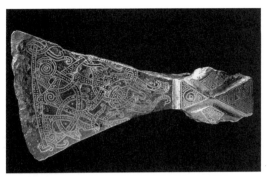

The beautifully decorated Mammen axe, buried in a grave in Denmark around the year 970. Derived from Roberto Fortuna and Kira Ursem, *Økse fra Mammen*. Creative Commons.

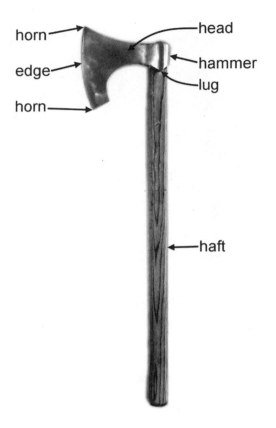

The parts of a Viking axe. Photo: William R. Short.

with a cutting edge about 10 cm (4 in) long. It seems more like an ornament than a lethal weapon.

AXE HAFTS

The haft was made of wood and fitted to mate tightly with the eye. Beyond this simple statement, there is little we can say with certainty, because so few axe hafts have been found in Viking lands. We are faced yet again with the coin-toss problem of having too small a sample size.

WOOD SPECIES

The usual wood species used for the axe hafts are not well known. One suspects that a resilient hardwood species such as ash would be best suited. The usual way to make wooden objects in the Viking age was using a process called riving, in which wood was shaved away from a radial-split section of a tree. By making radial splits, the grain follows the shape of the object, resulting in an object much less likely to break or split under stress.

A grave in Sweden provides evidence to confirm some of these speculations about haft materials and construction.[36] An axe was found whose haft had rotted away in the ground. The surviving fragments of the haft indicate it was made of maple hewn radially from a tree trunk.

Three Viking-age axes were found in a boat on the bottom of Lough Corrib in Ireland in 2013. The hafts did not survive, but fragments show that they were made of cherry.[37] Although we strive to use narrow sources, the paucity of surviving axe hafts compels us to at least consider what is found in other lands, such as these axes.

HAFT SIZE

The eyes of surviving axe-heads inform us of the cross-sectional dimensions of the axe haft, at least where it mated with the head; 35 mm x 24 mm (1.3 in x 1 in) seems typical, but of course, heads with larger and smaller eyes have been found. We have little evidence to tell us about any taper or shaping formed into the haft along its length, common features of modern axe hafts. It seems most likely that typical hafts were straight with an oval cross section throughout their length in the Viking age.

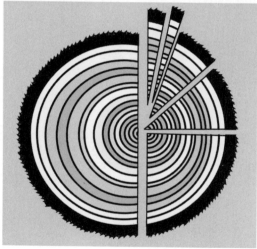

Top: One of the steps in riving an axe haft from a log. Photo: William R. Short. Bottom: Riving begins by making radial splits in the log. Illustration: William R. Short.

The available evidence does not allow us to state with any certainty typical axe haft lengths, but 70 cm seems reasonable for a one-handed axe, and 140 cm seems reasonable for a two-handed axe, as we will discuss later in the chapter.

King Óláfr helgi with a long-hafted axe depicted on a 14th century altar frontal. Derived from Wmpearl, *St. Olav alter frontal*. Creative Commons.

Perhaps the most notable surviving hafts are two tool axes with intact hafts found in the Oseberg burial, a high-status ship burial from the ninth century found in Norway. The axe hafts are 71 cm (28 in) and 78cm (31 in) long,[38] and both are uniformly straight and oval in shape.

The Swedish axe mentioned earlier provides some additional information.[39] The haft had rotted away in the ground, but the position of the head and the butt cap allow an estimation of the dimensions of the haft: about 80.5 cm (32 in) long, with a cross section of approximately 35 x 24 mm (1.3 x 1 in).

The literary sources occasionally mention axe hafts that are unusually long, but there are few details that help us determine what that length might have been.[40] *Hávarðar saga* tells us that Óláfr went in to a room, set his axe haft on the ground, and leaned on the haft,[41] suggesting it was quite tall, perhaps 130 or 140 cm (51 or 55 in), depending on Óláfr's height. Gautr ran to attack Karl with his axe and landed a blow on Karl's head, even though Karl was surrounded by a circle of men,[42] suggesting a haft long enough to reach over one man and attack another behind.

Literary sources also suggest some short-hafted axes. Axes were used as hidden or reserve weapons on occasion. Presumably, a smaller axe would be the preferred choice for this use so it could be more easily hidden. Þormóðr carried an axe that he used to kill Þorgrímr to avenge the death of his foster brother. After the killing, Þormóðr hid the axe under his cloak to make his escape.[43] Similarly, Þorgeirr held an axe behind his shield in his left hand while attacking Snorri with a spear held in his right hand. Later, when the axe became the better tool, he dropped the spear and took up the axe to split Snorri's head.[44] These examples give us clues on the lengths of shorter hafts.

The hafts of the three axes found at Lough Corrib in Ireland survive only as fragments. It is estimated that the haft of the largest of the axes was as long as 150 cm (59 in).[45] The length of the edge of this type M axe is about 25 cm (10 in).

Pictorial evidence from other times and other lands offers some additional clues and support, but since this information falls outside of our criteria for narrow sources, we must take this information with a grain of salt.

Stone carvings from the Bronze Age in Sweden show one-handed axes in use with an estimated length of 60 to 70 cm (24 to 28 in).[46] The Bayeux Tapestry has numerous depictions of men holding and fighting with two-handed axes.[47] Taking into account the typical height of men from this era suggests axe hafts as long as 140 cm (55 in).

SUBJECTIVE TESTS OF AXE HAFT LENGTHS
Subjective tests of the performance of different length hafts (60, 90, 120, and 150 cm, or 24, 36, 48, and 60 in) were conducted on axes with

Top: A stone carving of men with long-hafted axes from Bronze-age Sweden. Derived from Fred J, *Tanumshede 2005 rock carvings 5*. Bottom: Two long-hafted axes compared to the height of men holding them as depicted in the Bayeux Tapestry. Derived from Myrabella, *Tapisserie de Bayeux, Scènes 29-30-31*. Creative Commons.

different heads: a broadaxe (Petersen type M), and a bearded axe (Petersen type C). The shorter hafts gave greater accuracy, independent of head. The shorter hafts were quicker for either weight axe-head. Yet the longer haft gave more reach, and subjectively, seemed to yield more power into the target.[48] Our conclusion, based on these tests, is that any of these lengths were possible depending on what tradeoffs the warrior wielding the axe was willing to accept.

The data from these tests, combined with what we learn from literary and archaeological sources, draws us to the conclusion that a 70

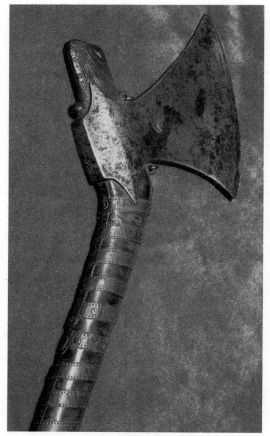

A late medieval Swedish axe that has a metal-wrapped haft. Photo: William R. Short.

cm haft length (28 in) is about right for a one-handed axe, and that a 140 cm haft length (55 in) for a two-handed axe. Yet these numbers remain pure speculation until more surviving axe hafts are found from the Viking age in Viking lands.

### METAL PARTS ON THE HAFT

The literary sources tell us that occasionally, a fighter might cut through the haft of his opponent's axe.[49] The likelihood of that move succeeding was reduced by wrapping the axe haft with something that resisted the cut, such as iron or other metal. Axe hafts of this nature from the later medieval period have survived, but not from the Viking age. However, the literary sources suggest that hafts were wrapped with iron, silver, or some unspecified material in the Viking age.[50] Skallagrímr's axe, a gift from the king, is described as being wrapped in silver.[51] Some suggest that the text implies an iron wrap decorated with silver.[52]

### MOUNTING THE HEAD ON THE HAFT

The axe was affixed to the haft in one of several ways to prevent the head from flying off the haft. One approach is to taper the eye of the axe-head and the haft so that the haft is larger than the eye above the axe-head. When the head is slid from the bottom on to the haft, it cannot fly off the haft as long as the head and haft are intact.

Additionally, it is possible that heads were fitted from above, using a haft made with a *kerf* (an open channel, like a saw cut) from front to back at the top of the haft. The head was carefully fitted from above, then a wooden wedge driven into the kerf from above to expand it inside the eye, firmly anchoring the head on the haft.

The three axes found at Lough Corrib in Ireland were mounted on the hafts in this manner, using wedges set in a kerf in the haft. Evidence suggests that the heads had been re-mounted multiple times.[53]

It is possible other fastening methods were used. But regardless of how the head was fastened to the haft, the connection was not always perfect. The literary sources say that sometimes the head flew off the haft in a fight.[54]

### CARRY METHOD

It is not clear how axes were carried when not being wielded. Axes were sharp. Our modern mindset today tells us that axes should be sheathed when not in use to protect against accidental cuts. But that is an approach we shy away from in our research. We do not want to pollute our research with modern preconceptions.

On one hand, wooden sheaths for axes are found in Sigtuna[55] in Sweden, and in Schleswig in modern-day Germany, with more found outside of Viking lands. On the other hand, the available literary evidence does not suggest that protective coverings were used with axes.

The literary sources mention knives in sheaths, saxes in sheaths, and swords in scabbards, but there seems to be no mention of spears in sheaths or axes in sheaths. Indeed, there are more than a few examples suggesting that axes could be instantly put to use without any need to prepare them by, for example, removing the sheath.[56] Additionally, there is an episode in *Íslendinga saga* of a man being wounded by his own axe as he mounted his horse to travel to a battle, suggesting no covering was in place.[57]

The episode in which Skarpheðinn's axe rang when he took it down from the wall[58] strongly suggests the axe was not sheathed while being stored. The sheaths that are found in archaeology would not permit the axe-head to ring when protecting the edge. Perhaps the practice of sheathing an axe was not a common practice in Viking times.

Regardless of the protection, it seems that axes were often carried on the shoulder[59] or in the belt,[60] according to literary sources. Archaeological evidence also suggests a belt carry. There are examples of grave finds of axes where fragments of the wooden haft are detected under the leather belt.[61]

OFFENSIVE USE OF THE AXE

Several of our sources coalesce to paint a clear picture of the use of the axe. Ancient literary and pictorial sources combine with modern biomechanical and physical considerations to spotlight the intended purpose of the tool: to sunder the enemy in two, or to remove his limb, or to split his skull.[62]

The physics show us the brutal energy levels the axe delivers to the target. The literary sources tell of episodes in which the axe splits the head in two[63] or separates the head from the neck[64] or cuts the torso in two.[65]

The axe is a tool intended for chopping, and virtually all of the axe attacks (96 percent) reported in the *Sagas of Icelanders* are chopping attacks. When the head is the target, the saga authors sometimes report that the head was split down to the shoulder.[66] That is exactly

Top: The effect of an axe cut to the head of a pig carcass, as tested by Hurstwic. The axe split the head to the shoulders, a result often mentioned in the literary sources. Photo: William R. Short. Bottom: A downward axe cut depicted in the Bayeux Tapestry. Detail of the Bayeux Tapestry, eleventh century, with special permission from the City of Bayeux.

what happened when we tested this attack using a sharp replica broadaxe on a pig carcass.[67]

The majority of the axe cuts in the sagas are made to the head, about 55 percent.[68] Of these head attacks, 76 percent resulted in death, and for 15 percent of these head attacks, the saga author states that the axe split the skull, or the axe stuck in the brain.[69] Details like these show the incredible destructive power inherent in

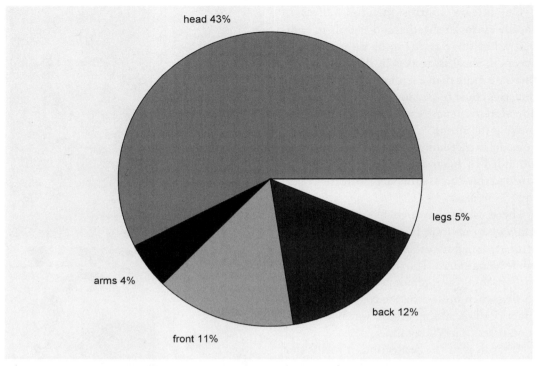

A plot of the targets of axe attacks, as reported in the *Sagas of Icelanders*.

the tool when wielded by skilled hands, power that is confirmed in our testing described later in the chapter.

Of these head attacks, at least 71 percent are described as attacks from above with the axe. It is this downward attack to the head with the axe that is being employed by most of the axemen shown on our most extensive pictorial source on axe usage, the Bayeux Tapestry.[70]

Biomechanical considerations tell us that the attack to the head from above is one of the most powerful axe attacks, combining the forces of all the strong muscles of the body from shoulders to knees together with the additional force caused by the falling body weight of the axeman as he drops his body in the attack.

THE EFFICACY OF AXE CUTS
In order to gain a sense of the capabilities of an axe blow to the head as shown in literary and pictorial sources, we turned to measurements and computer simulations, including a computer simulation of a cut to the head with

a long-hafted broadaxe compared to a cut with a short-hafted bearded axe. The broadaxe causes damage to a larger portion of the skull and brain, although realistically, either blow is likely to have had fatal consequences. Additionally, the long-hafted weapon moves with a greater linear velocity, resulting in more energy delivered to the target.[71]

Measurements confirm the simulation. We used a replica broadaxe with a 27 cm edge and a 141 cm haft (11 in and 56 in) with a total weight of 1.32 kg (2.9 lbs) and a replica bearded axe with a 15 cm edge and a 68 cm haft (6 in and 27 in) with a total weight of 0.92 kg (2.0 lbs). Averaged over multiple hits and multiple test subjects, the broadaxe delivered 2.8 times the total energy to the target compared to the bearded axe.[72]

These numbers and images show us what the Viking axe was intended to do. The energy levels predicted by the simulation are astonishing, capable of brutal damage to any part of the human body to which it is applied.

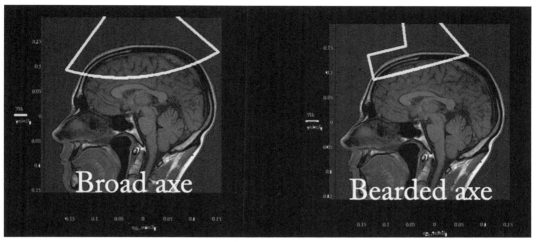

A computer simulation comparing the effects of downward cut to the head using a long-hafted broadaxe to the effects using a short-hafted bearded axe. The model predicts that the broadaxe delivers substantially more energy to the target, resulting in substantially more damage to the head.

## NONTRADITIONAL OFFENSIVE AXE USES

Additionally, other uses of the weapon are described in the literary sources. The axe was, on rare occasions, used for thrusting, utilizing the sharp horn of the axe as a point to penetrate the target.[73] Our tests against a pig carcass show that the move causes extensive internal injuries[74] because of the much greater width of the axe horn compared to, for example, a spear point or a sword point.

Likewise, when we pressure tested the move in the training room, it seemed highly effective, at least in part because the stab is so quick.[75]

But the effectiveness of the move in our testing is at odds with its infrequent use as reported in the literary and other sources. Of all the offensive attacks with an axe (or axe-like weapon) reported in the sagas, only 1 percent are a thrust with the horn.[76] If the stab is as effective as it seemed to be in our modern tests, why didn't Viking warriors use it more frequently?

No truly satisfying answer comes to mind. Perhaps, as with the sax, the axe was just simply designed for chopping, not for thrusting. Perhaps chopping with the axe was thought to be more devastating and thus a better use of the tool. Perhaps the horn was fragile, so thrusting was avoided. Perhaps the thrust sometimes unseated the head from the haft. Perhaps the horn occasionally got caught on something like a rib when withdrawing the axe. We can only speculate, with no clear answer why this seemingly effective move was so rarely used.

## AXES AS PROJECTILES

Though very popular at modern Viking festivals, the throwing of the axe happens infrequently in the literary sources. When axes were thrown, it seems to have been a move of desperation at a time when no other moves were possible.

In some cases, the axeman was already mortally wounded, so he threw his axe in the hope of avenging the wound.[77] In other cases, the axeman's wounds so limited his mobility that the only move available to him was throwing his axe at his attacker.[78] And in other cases, the attacker was too far from any possible target to make a cut, notably in mass battles. With no opportunity to close the distance, he chose to throw his axe. In these mass battles, men in the ranks farther to the rear used anything at hand as missiles, including axes, in an attempt to attack the enemy ranks that were out of

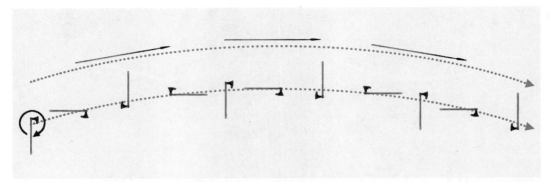

A comparison of the trajectory of a thrown spear to a thrown axe. The spear (top) is always in-line with the target as it flies and so can penetrate the target from any distance. In contrast, the axe (bottom), due to its rotation, is only in position to penetrate the target at a few discrete distances. Illustration: William R. Short

their direct reach.[79] This use of projectiles is discussed in detail in the mass battle chapter.

Unlike spears, which were intended to be thrown, using an axe as a missile is problematic due to its rotation as it flies through the air. The edge is in position to hit and penetrate the target only occasionally as it spins, meaning the throw is effective only at certain discrete distances from the target corresponding to full rotations that put the edge in line with the target. Thus, only targets at certain distances from the thrower can be hit with any expectation of penetrating the body to lethal effect.

By comparison, a spear properly thrown will have its point in line with the target until it either hits the target or drops to the ground, spent. Thus, over a wide range of throwing distances, a well-thrown spear will penetrate the target, unlike an axe.

An axe that was intended to be thrown was the *francisca*, an axe with a heavy head mounted on a short haft used notably in Frankish lands but in southern Norway as well,[80] generally in the centuries before the Viking age. The short haft of the *francisca* gives little mechanical advantage in a cutting attack, unlike a Viking axe, where the length of the haft makes powerful attacks possible. Thus, in a cut, the *francisca* is little better than a sharp stone of the same weight. But like a stone, it could be thrown to devastating effect. The *francisca* was typically thrown before a mass battle.

The unsuitability of a Viking axe for throwing becomes more clear when one compares it to the *francisca*. By design, the Viking axe is less well suited for a throw; its intended purpose was something very different. Vikings had other throwing weapons intended to be used as missiles. It seems likely the axe was used as a projectile only as a last resort.

OTHER OFFENSIVE AXE MOVES

One wonders if Vikings used their axes for hooking opponents' weapons, or body parts, or other objects. The shape of some of the axe types, notably the bearded axe, makes it seem as if they were made for this purpose. The literary sources provide only a few examples of hooking, suggesting it was not a normal use of the axe.

The literary sources mention a type of axe called *snaghyrndr öxi* (snag-horned axe).[81] Was this an axe designed for snagging and hooking? The axes called by this name are never used in this fashion in the literary sources, so there is little that can be concluded.

Some speculate that the axe was used for hooking the opponent's weapon to control it and move it to the opponent's disadvantage. When pressure tested in our combative research lab, hooking with the axe was shown to have advantages,[82] both in offense and defense. Yet there is no evidence to be found in any of the sources to support the speculation that this move was used. In this, as many other cases, our modern mindset drives us to look for something efficient, which may or may not be a move that Viking warriors used. We must guard against falling into this trap, and so the move must remain speculative.

The literary sources tell us that axes were used as a climbing tool by hooking the axe-head on to the wall of a fortification so that someone outside could pull himself up by his axe and enter the fortification over the top of the wall.[83]

The only mention in the literary sources of hooking body parts appears in *Sturlunga saga*, set after the Viking age, where Þorsteinn hooked one of Sturla's men with his axe and pulled him down under his feet, where the man was attacked.[84] When we pressure tested the move in our combative research lab,[85] we found we could make it work, but this one episode in one saga set well after the end Viking age is not sufficient to support the use of this move by Viking fighters.

The hammer, on the backside of the axe-head, was used on numerous occasions to deliver a blow that was not intended to be lethal.[86] It was used when the goal was to dishonor the opponent rather than kill him. It was an attack against an opponent unworthy of a proper blow.

DUAL WIELDING

The literary sources tell us that the axe was sometimes dual wielded, with an axe in one hand and a shield for defense in the other hand.[87] Warriors also carried an axe with another weapon, using whichever one seemed best at that moment in the fight and even using them nearly simultaneously.[88]

The Bayeux Tapestry shows fighters using an axe together with a shield in the other hand. Both short-hafted axes and long-hafted axes[89] are shown being used this way. (See page 54.)

Our tests make dual wielding a short-hafted one-handed axe quite believable, but dual wielding a long-hafted two-handed axe was hard to fathom.[90] A broadaxe and a bearded axe were tested with haft lengths of 60, 90, 120, and 150 cm (24, 36, 48, and 60 in). In one hand, the axes with longer hafts became slow,

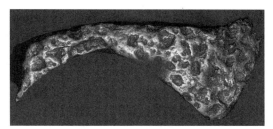

The head of a francisca, a Frankish throwing axe. Photo: William R. Short.

inaccurate, and weak compared to two-handed use of the weapon, with significantly more telegraphing of the intent and generally less control. With one-handed use, speed of the attacks increased nearly 40 percent from the longest haft to the shortest. Accuracy of the hits nearly doubled with one-handed use of the shortest haft compared to the longest haft. Shortening the haft significantly improved the performance of an axe used one-handed.

There are more than a few examples of one-handed use of long weapons in the literary sources, so there is clearly some advantage that did not emerge in our tests. Perhaps the greater range of the long-hafted weapon outweighed the disadvantages we observed. Perhaps the difference in strength between a Viking-age fighter and we moderns reduces or eliminates the differences we observed. At this time, we do not have a satisfactory explanation.

DEFENSIVE USE OF THE AXE

Our sources are mostly silent on how the axe was used for defense. The literary sources give a number of examples of the way that fighters used their axes to block the attack. Warriors parried with the axe-head,[91] moving it to block or deflect the attack. They also parried an attack with the haft of the axe, which sometimes caused the haft to break.[92] They made stop hits to their opponent, a counterattack stopping the motion of the incoming attack that could cut off the opponent's hand or cut through the haft or shaft of his weapon.[93] They struck or deflected the incoming weapon with their axe to block the attack and to throw it off line.[94]

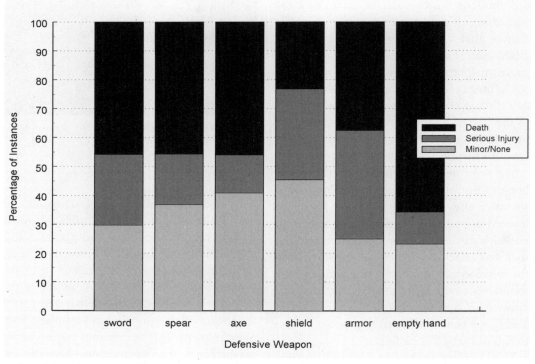

A plot of the injuries caused by an attack when defended by various weapons, as reported in the *Sagas of Icelanders*.

As a defensive tool, the axe fares about as well as a sword or a spear but not as well as a shield or armor for protecting the combatant. When an axe is used for defense, the attack is lethal in 47 percent of the attacks described in *Sagas of Icelanders*.[95]

Yet there were skilled fighters who believed that their broadaxe was the only defense they needed. Before the Battle of Stiklarstaðir, King Óláfr noticed that Þormóðr carried only his broadaxe. The king asked why he was not dressed for battle and carrying a shield like the other fighters. Þormóðr replied that his axe would serve as his shield and his mail shirt during the fight. In the battle that followed, he used his axe two-handed and was not wounded.[96]

SUMMARY AND CONCLUSIONS
The axe is one of the simpler weapons of the Viking age. It was an ageless domestic tool essential to the operation of a farm that also was modified and optimized for use as a weapon of violence. The design makes its use clear: it was intended to split body parts in two, just as it was meant to split pieces of wood in two.

The axe does not seem to have been a part of the mythological world of the Vikings. There are few kennings for an axe used in skaldic poetry.

Yet axes became the iconic weapons of the Vikings. Foreigners talked about the Viking barbarians wielding their axes, and the lone Stamford Bridge Viking was long remembered. To this day, the Viking warrior is associated with the axe. Perhaps that strong association remains because the weapon so closely matches the Viking way of fighting: brutal and powerful attacks made full force to destroy the target.

# SWORD

In the Viking age, swords were prized. They were given names and passed from generation to generation as a visible symbol of social status and prestige. They were gifts from a king or earl to his liege men. They were the technological marvels of their time, pushing the limits of available metallurgy. They were revered, even above their value in combat.

The value of a sword to a Viking-age fighter cannot be underestimated. Even beyond its martial value and its monetary value as a hard-to-fabricate iron object, a sword carried with it a level of prestige and status that was priceless: as a symbol of rank, as a unique artifact made by a skilled smith, as an heirloom passed through the family from generation to generation, and as a personal object that was prized even after it no longer had any value as a weapon. Therefore, it has been widely accepted by laymen and experts alike that swords were rare. Yet as we will see, the story is not so simple and clear-cut. Swords may have been treasured, but we will show that they were not necessarily scarce or exotic.

SOURCES

In researching swords of the Viking age, we use many of the same sources we use for other weapons. Archaeological sources tell us about the various kinds of swords that were used in the Viking age and also help inform us about how the weapons were used. Literary sources help reveal the purpose of a sword. Pictorial sources show the sword in use. Bioarchaeology, the study of skeletal remains of the people from the period, inform us about the power of the weapon to cause brutal injuries.

The sources tell us that the weapon was used to make strong cuts—the cuts required to dismember an opponent. Yet Viking swords have an important additional combative trait beyond raw power, a trait not found to the same degree in other weapons: they are capable of finesse. The literary sources tell of their quickness and agility, corroborated by physical measurements of swords.

THE PLACE OF THE SWORD IN SOCIETY

Swords were heirlooms passed from generation to generation and used for centuries. Hilts

Viking sword replica. Photo: William R. Short.

King Knútr with his hand on the hilt of his sword depicted in Stowe MS 944, an 11th century Anglo-Saxon manuscript. © The British Library Board, Stowe MS 944.

were often renewed, fixing new, more-stylish, and unworn hilts on still-serviceable blades, and swords have been found with stylistic elements that tell us the blade is centuries older than the hilt.[1]

The literary sources tend to corroborate the long life and use of many swords. For example, Grettir Ásmundarson carried a sword that had belonged to his great-grandfather, Jökull,[2] and it was already a famous sword with generations of use when Jökull owned it.[3]

Burial practices show the value of the sword to its owner. Unlike other weapons, swords were often buried touching the owner's body in the grave, rather than separated from the body as was usually the case with the spear.[4] This observation shows again that the value of a sword was more than that of a mere weapon. The sword seems to have been a part of the warrior's identity—an extension of the man—rather than a separate element.

Wear patterns on the hilts of swords suggest swords were constant companions to the own-ers, worn not just for battle but habitually, probably every day.[5] While some of this research was done with Viking swords, much of it was performed on earlier Anglo-Saxon and Scandinavian swords having more and larger nonferrous elements in the hilt, which show wear more readily than ferrous materials. Thus we apply the findings to Viking weapons with care.

*Hávamál* teaches that one should keep one's weapon close,[6] but these wear patterns suggest yet-more-intimate contact for swords. The wear patterns are consistent with the owner repeatedly putting his hand on the hilt as it hung by his side in its scabbard. We can see the hand-on-the-hilt pose in pictorial sources, notably a manuscript illumination of King Knútr, and read about it in literary sources.[7]

Literary sources also confirm that men wore their swords routinely, seldom letting them out of reach.[8] Unlike an axe or spear, a sword was easy to carry habitually, riding safe and in ready reach in its scabbard yet out of the way.

It has long been thought that swords were associated with the elite, that they were prestigious weapons for the top of society. Viking-age swords are sometimes likened to exceptional items, such as a Ferrari would be today: something exotic, expensive, and uncommon for all but the privileged. Yet as we pull together all the available evidence, our research paints a different picture.

Multiple sources suggest swords were not uncommon. Swords make up a large percentage of the weapons used in the fights described in the *Sagas of Icelanders*, about 43 percent. In some sagas, the sword is the predominant weapon used in battle. More than half the attacks described in *Vatnsdæla saga*, *Kormáks saga*, and *Þórðar saga hreðu* are made with swords. In *Heiðarvíga saga*, swords are the only weapon mentioned being used in combat.[9]

It has been suggested that this conflict between modern thought and saga examples could be explained by the observation that the sagas focus on saga heroes who are, in many cases, the more elite warriors having the family

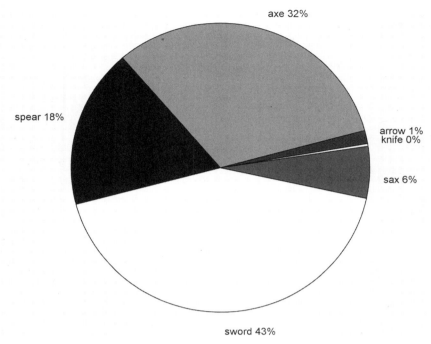

A plot of the weapons used in battle, as reported in the *Sagas of Icelanders*.

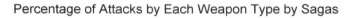

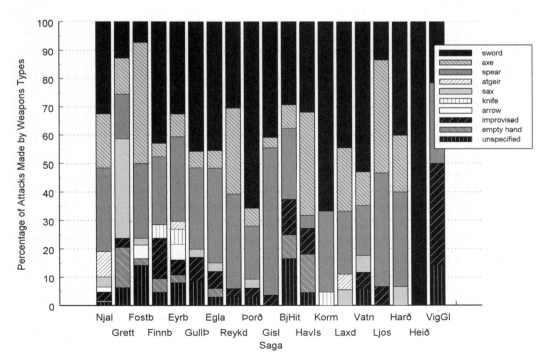

A plot of the weapons used for attacks reported in individual sagas from the *Sagas of Icelanders*.

Sigurðr slays the dragon Fáfnir with his sword Gramr, as depicted on runestone Sö 101. Derived from Ann-Sofi Cullhed, *Sigurdsristningen, Jäder, Södermanland, Sweden*. Creative Commons.

connections or the wealth or the life experiences that allow them to own and carry a prestigious weapon like a sword. Even saga heroes indelibly connected with other weapons also are said to carry and to be able to skillfully wield a sword, such as Gunnarr Hámundarson,[10] who is best known for his *atgeirr* and his bow.

Or perhaps swords were simply more common than has been previously thought, and swords were routinely carried by many Viking-age warriors across a range of social classes. A number of sources suggest this possibility.

Thousands of Viking-age swords have been found in Viking lands. Even when Petersen wrote his classic book on Viking swords at the dawn of the twentieth century, he counted more than 1,200 double-edged Viking swords from Norway alone. Irmelin Martens estimates the number of Viking swords found in Norway is now closer to three thousand.[11]

A search of Norwegian Viking-age artifacts in the archaeological database of Universitetsmuseet (University Museum in Oslo) reveals 2,366 swords, 2,687 axes, and 1,179 spears.[12] The proportion of swords to other, more mundane weapons in no way makes the sword seem like an exotic Ferrari, and these data probably underrepresent the sword as a percentage of weapons, since the counts of axes and spears likely include artifacts not intended for combat, such as wood axes or tool axes.

Swords seem to have been readily available in large numbers, at least to some. During a sea battle, King Óláfr noted his men's swords were cutting poorly, and from below his seat on his ship, he opened a chest filled with many sharp swords and handed them to his men.[13] That he had many swords in reserve under his seat on his ship does not make the sword seem like an exotic or especially rare entity.

The law code *Gulaþingslög* requires every man in the king's levy to have either a broadaxe or a sword, along with a spear and shield.[14] Since the levy was made up of ordinary farmers, it seems unlikely the law would require an out-of-the-ordinary tool for the farmers.

Picture stones from the Viking age are profoundly tilted toward swords. For example, the Stora Hammars I stone shows more than a dozen swords in the scenes depicted across its face, with scarcely any other weapon in sight.[15]

These examples do not serve to reduce the sword's prestige or value in any way, yet when taken together, they do weaken the age-old idea that the sword was rare or uncommon or out of the ordinary in Viking times. While it probably was not possible for every man to own one, the evidence suggests that many swords were in wide circulation, even among ordinary people in society.

### SWORDS IN MYTHOLOGY AND MAGIC
Swords also played a prominent role in Norse mythology. Several gods carried swords.[16] At

Ragnarök, the final battle that will destroy the world in the Norse myths, Surtr will ride at the front of the giants brandishing his sword of fire. Freyr will fall before Surtr in the battle because Freyr earlier gave up his sword in order to win the hand of his wife, Gerðr.[17] Images that depict the legend of Sigurðr using his sword to kill the dragon Fáfnir appear on a runestone and wood carvings[18] created centuries apart.

In skaldic poetry, there are a large number of kennings for *sword*, again suggesting it was a weapon that required many ways to describe its use in skaldic tales of battle. Many of these kennings use fire as an element of the kenning, suggesting the weapon was an agent of destruction: *slíðloga* (sheath flames), *sárelda* (wound fires), *hjálmelda* (helmet fires), *eldar Yggs* (the fires of Yggr [Óðinn]), *fúra fleinbraks* (the fires of spear-crash), *fúra Fjölnis* (the fires of Fjölnir [Óðinn]),[19] and many more. A number of these kennings also incorporate various names for Óðinn, which is not surprising given Óðinn's connection to warriors and battles and his role as the god who first brought war to the world.[20]

Swords were linked to magic, and some had supernatural properties. Certain warriors, notably berserks, had the ability to blunt the edge of a weapon by looking at it, or by blowing on it,[21] as discussed earlier in the mindset chapter. While the sources suggest a berserk could blunt any weapon, it was most often done to swords to take away the sword's most prized ability: to bite. The use of magic for this purpose strongly suggests that the sword's primary and most threatening function was cutting.

To ensure victory, Sigrdrífa, a valkyrie, taught Sigurðr to carve runes into the hilt of his sword. Another connection between magic and swords are the healing stones (*lyfsteinn*) carried with some swords.[22] The stone had the power to heal a wound caused by the sword, further suggesting the supernatural power of the weapon.

The sword, the most prestigious of weapons, is connected with the god most closely associated with battle and heroic warriors and magic. It is the most widespread weapon in mythology; there are more swords than either spears, axes, bows, or saxes. This connection of the sword with gods and heroes and magic in prose, poetry, and picture stones serves to emphasize the prestige of this weapon.

ETYMOLOGY

The word for sword, *sverð*, is common to the northern languages, but it is of uncertain origin. There seem to be few alternate words for swords and few other words describing variants of swords. One of the few examples of such a word is *mækir*, a word of uncertain origin.[23] In its use, in its descriptions, and in its efficacy as described in the literary sources, a *mækir* is hard to distinguish from a *sverð*.[24]

Swords are sometimes referred to using *brandr*, which more specifically means the *blade*. It is cognate with the English word *firebrand*, which suggests the destructive capability of the weapon. *Hjörr* is used in many compound words to represent *sword* but rarely as a stand-alone word for the weapon.[25]

SALIENT FEATURES OF A VIKING SWORD

Swords had two components: a blade and a hilt. The blade, with its point and edges, was the sharp business end of the weapon. At the end of the blade opposite the point, the blade narrowed to a tang to interface with the hilt. The hilt was where the swordsman gripped the weapon. The blade was permanent and unchanging, while the hilt wore out and was replaced and updated, perhaps many times during the life of a typical sword blade.[26]

Viking-age blades typically were double-edged, made from iron and/or steel, often made from multiple types of ferrous materials. The edges were nominally identical. There was a slight taper to the blade, both in width (narrowing to the point) and thickness (thinning to the point). There was a *fuller* (a central depression) down the length of both sides of the blade to reduce its weight. The point tended to be more rounded and spatulate, rather than pointed and acute, as swords later came to be.

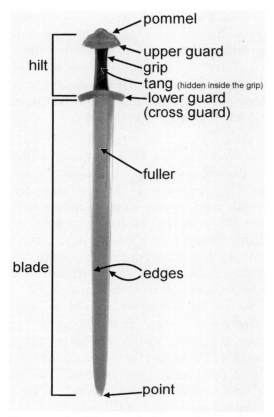

pommel

upper guard

grip

hilt

tang (hidden inside the grip)

lower guard
(cross guard)

fuller

blade

edges

point

The parts of a Viking sword. Photo: William R. Short.

Generally, the blade length of Viking swords varied between about 60 and 90 cm (24 to 36 in), with a typical blade length of 70 to 80 cm (28 to 32 in).[27] The total weight of sword was around 1 kg (2 to 3 lbs).[28]

The hilt was made up of lower guard (often called the crossguard or simply cross), grip, and upper guard and pommel. In the early part of the Viking age, the upper guard attached to the tang, and the pommel to the upper guard. In the later part of the Viking age, the pommel was simplified to eliminate the upper crossguard, and the pommel attached directly to the tang. The details of the attachment of the pommel to the sword varied, but in all cases, the tang was peened over the attachment point.

PROPERTIES OF THE BLADE

An ideal sword blade is hard and soft at the same time: hard enough that it resists bending, but soft enough that it resists breaking. This is true not only of the whole blade but also the edge. An edge that is too soft deforms on impact, resulting in an edge that dulls rapidly, but an edge that is too hard chips and breaks, creating a notch having a stress concentration that may cause the entire blade to break. Thus, the choice of material is a compromise for the bladesmith, and different materials were often used for the edge than for the rest of the blade.

Both the archaeology and the literary sources inform us that the smiths didn't always get it right. There are examples of broken blades and evidence of chipped blades in historical swords. Literary sources tell us of blades that bent in battle,[29] of blades that became so dull they no longer cut,[30] of blades that broke,[31] and of edges that picked up notches and nicks in battle.[32]

It is possible to change blade geometry to avoid some of these tendencies, but blade geometry is critical to the performance of the weapon. Modest changes in geometry have major performance costs. For example, thickening the blade to make it more rigid and less likely to bend results in a heavier, less wieldy weapon that cuts less well.[33]

Ideally, one would choose a tough, ductile material for a sword blade. Or one might use a combination of materials that together have the needed properties. Early Viking-age bladesmiths took the second route.

PATTERN WELDING

In the earlier part of the Viking age, bladesmiths were unable to make material suitable for a sword in the needed quantities and with the right combination of properties. And so smiths made blades from many lumps of stuff: different types of iron with different properties, taken from different smelts. The various materials were selected, shaped, twisted, and welded to form a composite material suitable for a sword blade. The process is called pattern welding. It was used by bladesmiths in many parts of the world, and it has its origins long before the Viking age.

Bars made of different types of iron were stacked and forge welded. The resulting stack

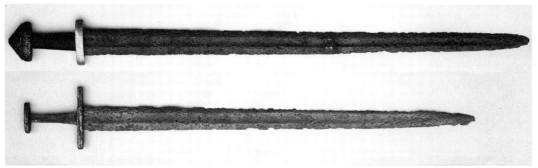

Two typical Viking-age swords representing the two most commonly encountered types of Viking-age sword hilts. Top: type H with copper and silver applied over an iron base on the hilt and cross. Bottom: type M having a simple unadorned iron crossguard and an upper guard with no pommel. Photo: Lee A. Jones.

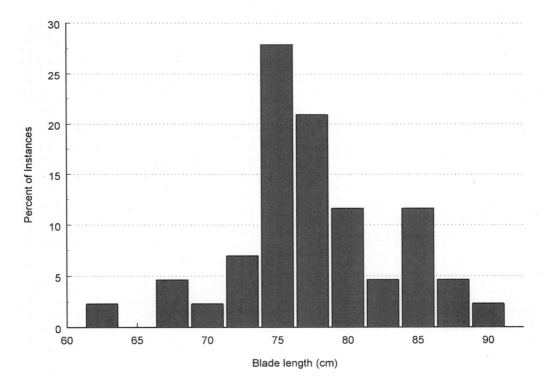

A histogram plot of blade length for a group of well-preserved Viking-age swords cataloged in Peirce (2002).

was drawn out into a long bar and then twisted. Subsequently, the twisted bar was shaped into a square cross section. Multiple twisted bars were forge welded together and shaped to form the finished blade.[34] The end result was a composite, made up of different kinds of iron that together had the necessary strength and flexibility for a sword blade.

A secondary effect of the pattern welding process is that the different types of iron create beautiful, delicate patterns visible on the surface of the blade. It seems possible that blade-smiths twisted the bars not only to create a material with the needed properties for the

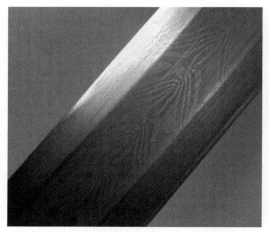

A replica pattern-welded blade showing the appearance of the pattern. Photo: William R. Short.

sword blade but also to create a visually stunning work of art. The pattern is subtle unless the surface is etched, a process used by some modern smiths, but the evidence for its use by Viking-age smiths is not strong.

The literary sources tell us that fighting men sometimes spoke of the serpent that lived in the sword blade.[35] It is easy to see how the pattern in the sword is reminiscent of a serpent. The sources tell us that men blew on the blade to call the serpent out of the blade,[36] and one can imagine that the condensation from one's breath on the cold blade might bring out the pattern, making it easier to see.

MONOSTEEL BLADES

Later in the Viking age, it became possible to create larger quantities of better material that suited the requirements for making a blade.[37] Instead of fabricating the blade from several lumps of stuff, it became possible to forge blades from a single lump of stuff, a process called monosteel fabrication. The transition to this process was not abrupt, and pattern welding continued to be used for at least some blades until near the end of the Viking age.

ULFBERHT BLADES

One type of monosteel blade that attracts much interest are those inscribed with what appears to be a maker's name. The two most

common are *Ulfberht* and *Ingelrii*. The inscriptions were made by inlaying wire into the blade to form the letters. The iron wire was often pattern welded, but there are examples of plain iron and plain steel wire used.[38] With the polishing techniques likely to have been used in the Viking age, the inlay would probably have been subtle, although some believe etchants were used to make the inlay more prominent. Often the reverse side of the blade was inlaid with geometric patterns.

Contemporary pictorial sources show the inlay. An eleventh-century Anglo-Saxon manuscript illumination shows something that closely resembles the geometric inlays seen in Ulfberht swords.[39]

Yet the early literary sources appear to be silent on the matter of these fine blades inscribed with a maker's mark. There are swords described as being ornamented (*sverð búit*),[40] but when any details of the decoration are provided, it is only the hilt that is described as being inlaid.

So many swords with these markings have been found across Europe, made over such a long period of time, that they cannot possibly be the work of two smiths named Ulfberht and Ingelrii, but rather, they are more likely the work of many generations of bladesmiths over several centuries working in established blade-making shops, most likely located along the Rhine.[41]

Because many of these blades are found widely distributed throughout the Viking lands, it is believed that the Ulfberht and Ingelrii swords were prized in the Viking age and thought to be superior to other swords. It is possible that the original Ulfberht invented a new way to fabricate a blade, using a more uniform steel having a higher carbon content than the typical monosteel blades of the period. It is further possible that he chose to identify his blades with an inlaid maker's mark.

In the decade before this book was written, the nature of Ulfberht blades has generated a good deal of breathless speculation in academic and popular publications. If we strip

Top: An Ulfberht sword blade from the Viking-age that was treated in modern times to bring out the inscription in the blade. Bottom: Geometric patterns on the reverse of an Ulfberht blade. Photos: William R. Short.

away the hyperbole, there seem to be several broad classes of blades inscribed with Ulfberht (and similar) marks.

Some of the Ulfberht swords have well-made monosteel blades using good quality, high-carbon steel. Some evidence suggests that this steel is crucible steel.[42] The process for making steel in crucibles is not thought to have been known to northern smiths in the Viking age. This steel could have come over known trade routes from middle Eastern or Asian lands, where the process was known to have been used in the Viking age.

However, the evidence for Ulfberht blade material being crucible steel is not solid at the time this book was written. More recent research suggests it is simply well-made bloomery steel created using processes known to Viking smiths. The material was folded several times to homogenize the material and remove the slag while fabricating the blade. Evidence of the process is clear in micro computer tomographical sections of several Ulfberht blades.[43] Thus the need to postulate

exotic materials to explain the Ulfberht blades is eliminated.

Some of the Ulfberht swords are inferior, being less-well designed and fabricated, using lower-quality materials. In some cases, the Ulfberht mark is poorly formed or misspelled. At least some of these blades are thought to be Viking-age counterfeits, made by smiths to capitalize on the Ulfberht name. One surviving blade is inlaid with Ulfberht on one side and Ingelrii on the other, a double counterfeit.[44]

It is likely that additional Ulfberht and Ingelrii blades remain to be identified, since the inlays are sometimes not visible to the naked eye and are revealed only by X-ray analysis or by smoothing followed by etching or metallographic staining.

Other methods were used for fabricating a sword blade as well. For example, Viking-age swords were found whose blades were made using a low-carbon core wrapped with steel.[45]

SMITHING A SWORD BLADE

Regardless of the method used, making a sword blade required a high degree of skill on

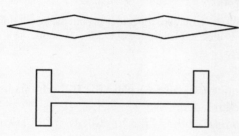

Top: A similar geometric pattern as the reverse side of the Ulfberht sword on the previous page in the sword blade as depicted in an illumination from Cotton MS Tiberius B V/1, an eleventh-century Anglo-Saxon manuscript. © The British Library Board, Cotton MS Tiberius B V/1. Bottom: The cross-sections of a Viking sword (top) and of a modern I-beam (bottom) share similarities. Both give increased strength for a given weight compared to a flat structure. Illustration: Barbara Wechter.

the part of the smith.[46] It was not a project to be undertaken by an ordinary blacksmith.

Some have speculated that Scandinavian smiths lacked the necessary skill, and that most Viking-age sword blades were made in continental Europe, in the lands now part of Germany, especially along the lower Rhine. This area has been known for its blades, both before and after the Viking age, because of the fine iron found there.[47]

The raw blades may have been shipped to Scandinavian trading towns to be finished and fitted with hilt items such as pommels and crossguards. Such fittings are found in the archaeological records of Scandinavian trading towns. Hilt parts are found rough-worked at these sites, with the flashing from the casting still attached.[48]

Yet the evidence is not so clear that sword-making in Scandinavia in the Viking age can be ruled out. Some surviving swords are thought to have been made in Norway.[49] Regardless, it seems likely that the process was limited only to a small number of skilled smiths.

The blade taper is defined by Geibig to be the width of the blade at 60 percent of the blade length relative to the width at the crossguard. The taper ranges from around 90 percent (a slight degree of tapering) for swords at the early years of the Viking age to as much as 65 percent near the end of the Viking age.[50] As we will discuss later in the chapter, tapering is one effective way of changing the sword geometry to improve the feel and apparent speed of the blade by changing the center of balance and moment of inertia.

The fuller is a thinning of the blade along its length forged into the center of both sides of the blade. It usually runs from near the point to underneath the crossguard. It allows the sword to be stronger for a given weight, in the same way that a modern steel I-beam has more strength than a rectangular beam of the same weight. This shape is used, for example, as the rail that forms railroad tracks.

The tips of Viking swords tend to be more spatulate, rather than acutely pointed. The rounded tip is less likely to break off when stressed than an acute and pointed tip. Additionally, it gives us insight into the intended use of the sword, discussed later in the chapter. The more-rounded tip suggests that thrusting was not the primary function of the weapon.

## CLASSIFICATION OF SWORDS

Various scholars have devised means for categorizing Viking swords, but perhaps the most widely used is the categorization devised by

A comparison of the points of eight Viking-age swords showing the spatulate nature of the points. Photo: Lee A. Jones.

Jan Petersen early in the twentieth century.[51] Petersen's types are succinctly defined and illustrated by Lee Jones in a more recent English-language publication.[52] The categories are based on hilt size and shape, as well as construction details. The categories allow us to group similar kinds of swords and to estimate the approximate date of the swords.

The evolution of the Viking sword is just that: evolution, rather than a revolution. In the Migration period, before the Viking age, swords shared many of the characteristics with Viking-age swords, but blade shapes and hilt details differed. While they were pattern welded like early Viking-age blades, these earlier blades generally had parallel sides with little taper. This design results in a sword that is blade heavy, making it less controllable but better suited for hacking, since it was capable of delivering more power to the target in a cut. Hilts were often ornately decorated with gold.

In the Viking age, blades became more tapered. This change brought the center of balance closer to the cross, resulting in a more maneuverable blade as will be discussed later in the chapter. Perhaps at this time, the use of the sword changed from a hacking tool to a weapon of finesse and control.

As better-quality iron and steel became available to the smith, longer blades could be made. Hilts became simpler, made of fewer pieces, and fabricated of rugged iron, rather than the more-fragile precious metals used earlier. Smaller amounts of precious metal were used for decoration, replacing inlay with inscribed geometric figures in the metal of the hilt, for example. Perhaps at this time, swords changed from being an exotic Ferrari to something more commonplace and readily available.

As the Viking age progressed, blades started to be made with a monosteel construction. Hilts had even fewer decorations, often being made from plain, undecorated iron. In part, this might be due to the need for more swords for the men of the king's levy, discussed in more detail in the mass battle chapter.

After the Viking age, blades became longer and more tapered, with a distinct point at the

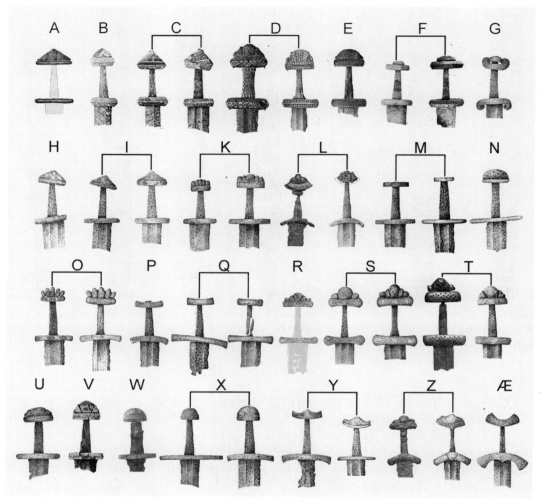

Petersen's typology for Viking-age swords. Derived from Petersen (1919).

tip. The hilts became quite minimal, reduced to a one-piece pommel and a simply formed crossguard of undecorated iron. Some of these changes were driven by the smith's ability to make better-quality materials, and some by the shifting political situation in Europe. Centralized powers were equipping centralized armies, which required plain, inexpensive gear for the king's legions of fighting men.

### SINGLE-EDGED SWORDS

While the vast majority of Viking swords are double-edged, there are a number of single-edged swords. They generally are from central and western Norway and date from early in the Viking age. The blades are typically slightly longer, on average, than double-edged swords from the same early period.[53] But when averaged over all Viking swords, the single-edged examples typically are shorter than average.[54] They generally have broad, parallel edges over most of the length, with the sharp edge tapering to the point. The unsharpened edge provides a thick, sturdy backbone. The limited taper would suggest that these single-edged swords are blade heavy, with a balance point some distance from the crossguard. Yet averaged over the set of complete, undamaged, single-edged swords described by Ian Peirce, the

A single-edge Viking-age sword from Norway. Derived from Kirsten Helgeland, *Sverd*. Creative Commons.

balance point is not dissimilar from the double-edged swords he cataloged.[55] This average may be skewed by the small number of complete single-edged swords included in that study: the coin-toss problem, again.

While most of these single-edged swords are more crudely made, some are well constructed, suggesting these were not the works of less-competent bladesmiths.[56] Presumably, this heavy chopping weapon was the intent of the smith and the preference of the fighter who wielded it.

It is thought that these single-edged swords were made by local smiths.[57] Perhaps if a smith wanted to make a sword but lacked the expertise and experience to make a double-edged one, he might start with something like a more-familiar sax and fit it with crossguard and pommel.

HILTS

The hilt of the sword is where the swordsman grips and controls his weapon. It is made up of a metallic (usually iron) pommel, upper cross, and lower cross (crossguard), together with an organic grip. Being organic, the grips do not survive well in the archaeological records, and the details remain speculative. It is possible the grip was made of wood, as used in later swords, or possibly bone, antler, or ivory. Fragments of the wood from the grip occasionally survive.[58] Grips were sometimes wrapped with leather,[59] fabric bands,[60] or wire or other metallic adornments.[61]

Bolli's sword, Fótbítr, had a hilt made of walrus ivory in the early part of the saga, but when he returned from his service in Byzantium, the hilt was gold wrapped, presumably with gold wire.[62]

Whatever the material, it was important that the hand on the sword maintain a sure grip even under adverse conditions, such as the presence of blood or sweat. A wrap over the grip helped maintain the strength of the hand's grip on the weapon. In our tests in the research lab, the energy delivered to the target by a sword with a plain wooden grip dropped when the hand became sweaty or bloody, but that decrease was reduced by about 25 percent when the grip was leather covered.[63]

The hilt was intended to be gripped one-handed and was sized accordingly. In popular publications, it is stated that Viking swords had short grips, giving rise to some theories about how the sword was gripped. Yet the vast majority of the swords found in the archaeological record seem to have grips that even a ham-handed Viking could grip easily. The mean length of the grip for 44 well-preserved Viking swords described by Peirce is 92 mm (3.6 in), with most in the range between 80 and 105 mm (3.2 to 4.1 in).[64] Petersen likewise categorized grip length for more than four hundred swords and reported a similar distribution, but there is no mention of how well preserved the individual samples were.[65]

Perhaps a possible explanation for the swords with extremely short grips is that each time the pommel is removed, some portion of the tang is likely to be lost. Accordingly, over the life of the blade, during which time the hilt may have been renewed multiple times, the tang, and thus the grip, was likely to grow shorter.[66]

The pommel served to balance the sword, bringing the center of balance closer to the grip. Without this counterweight, the sword becomes less controllable and less precise, as well as more tiring, because the sword resists the movements of the swordsman's hands. In

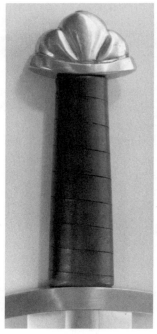

A modern replica of a leather-wrapped sword grip. Photo: William R. Short.

A historical sword grip with a wire-wrapped hilt. Derived from Ellen C. Holte, *Sverd*. Creative Commons.

A Viking sword pommel retaining traces of its silver and copper wire inlays. Photo: William R. Short.

A Viking sword pommel inscribed with geometric figures. Photo: William R. Short.

a moment, we will discuss this aspect of sword design in more depth, since this simple measurement of center of balance is only one aspect of a complex situation. These design tradeoffs are critical to the feel and function of the weapon.

The crossguard prevented the swordsman's hand from sliding off the grip and onto the sharp blade, but more importantly, it prevented the opponent's blade from sliding down the sword and onto the swordsman's hand. Additionally, it provided tactile feedback about the position of the sword in the hand.

Hilt components were sometimes decorated using techniques such as scribing and inlay. Sometimes, precious metal wire inlays were

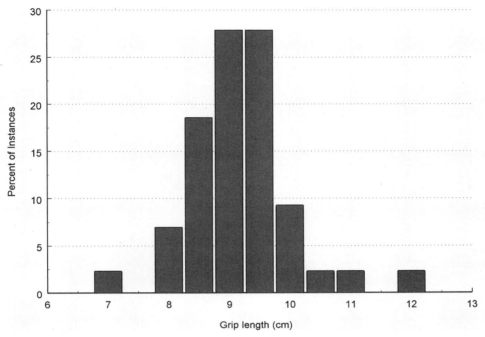

A histogram plot of grip length for a group of well-preserved Viking-age swords cataloged in Peirce (2002).

used, such as the gold, or the silver and copper inlay in the pommel of the Viking-age sword at the lower left, opposite.

In some ways, it seems the hilt, rather than the blade, identified the sword. It is the hilts that distinguished the swords in Petersen's typology. It is the hilts that are clearly depicted in pictorial sources, such as early medieval manuscripts, embroideries, stone carvings, and metallic dies.[67] And, as we will see in the next section, it was through changes to the hilt that a sword could be fine-tuned for its owner. All this evidence suggests that it was the hilt of the sword that distinguished the sword and identified its wielder to the people of the Viking age.

FEEL OF THE BLADE

Modern bladesmiths and practitioners often talk about the "feel" of the sword in the hand. This feel is often associated with a physical measure, the balance point, or center of mass: the point along the length of the blade where the sword balances. However, as we will see shortly, the feel is more complex than this simple measurement.

If the balance point is far from the grip compared to the length of the sword, the sword will feel heavy, wanting to fall toward the point. The weapon will seem unwieldy and slow in the hand. As the balance point moves closer to the grip, the sword feels faster, more controlled, and more responsive. The location of the balance point can be controlled by changing the taper of the blade and the weight of the pommel.

Making balance-point measurements on excavated Viking swords must be done with care. Excavated swords tend to have erosion, a loss of material from the blade that shifts the balance point in one direction, and at the same time, they may have a build-up of corrosion products, resulting in a gain in material and a shift in the other direction.

The balance point is often represented as a percentage of the length of the blade: the distance between the cross and the balance point relative to the total length of the blade. The mean balance point for well-preserved Viking swords cataloged in Peirce is 21 percent,[68]

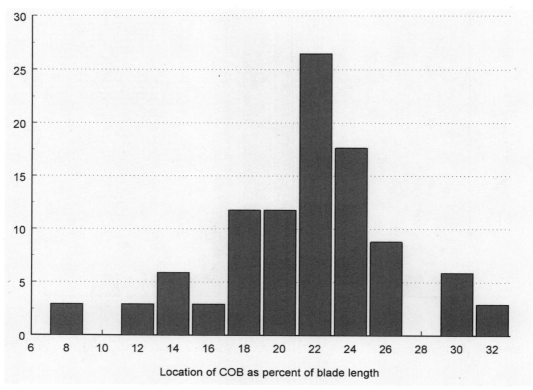

A histogram plot of center of balance as a percentage of blade length for a group of well-preserved Viking-age swords cataloged in Peirce (2002).

while the mean balance point for well-preserved Viking swords in Mikko Moilanen is 19 percent.[69]

Some very recent research, although incomplete, has shown the merits of using a sword's moment of inertia at the hand, rather than center of balance, to predict the feel of the sword in the hand.[70] The moment of inertia is the effective rotational inertia of the weapon. In the same way that an object with a small mass is easier to move in a linear direction, an object with a small moment of inertia is easier to move in a rotational direction. This measure, more than a simple center-of-balance measurement, seems to predict the feel of the weapon. Computer simulations suggest this measure will also better predict the ability of the sword to deliver destructive energy to the target than using center-of-balance measurements.

In handling historical weapons, one gets the strong sense that the swords vary significantly from example to example. Some historic Viking-age swords seem to leap into the swordsman's hand and become an extension of his arm, effortlessly moving to do the swordsman's bidding. Other fine swords seem to want only to impede the swordsman, resisting his will in every possible way.

Why the difference? Was this blade-heavy beast what the swordsman wanted? Perhaps the bladesmith was incompetent, cursed by every man who owned that sword. Or perhaps our modern preconceptions color our observations. The blade-heavy sword that seems to be a bungled mess to us moderns may have been a terrifying and effective chopping weapon in the hands of a Viking-age fighter.

The combative effectiveness of swords with various balance points was tested by making

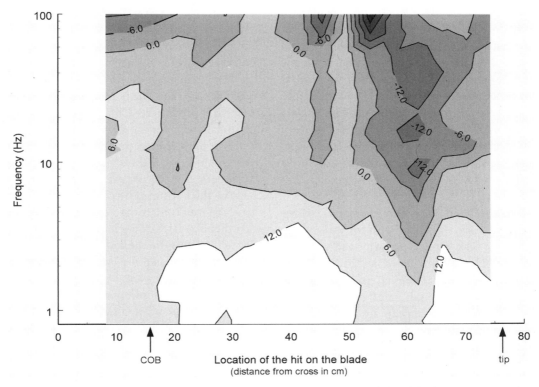

A contour plot of the spectra of the energy transmitted into the swordsman's hand for hits at various points along the blade of a replica Viking-age sword. The horizontal axis indicates the impact point on the blade where the hit was made, measured from the cross. The vertical axis indicates the frequency component being mapped. Each contour is 6dB, representing four times the energy transmitted into the hand from the hit compared to the next lower contour. The center of percussion is seen at around 60 cm, where the energy transmitted to the hand is less at all frequencies, and substantially less at high frequencies than that transmitted by hits at other blade locations.

up several swords that had nearly identical mass and dimensions but different balance points and measuring the impact of cuts with the various swords to a target. Compared to a nominal sword with a balance point at 21 percent of blade length, a sword with a balance point pushed out to 25 percent of blade length delivered about 25 percent more energy to the target.[71]

Similarly, when we did double-blind testing of swords with nearly the same mass but different balance points in simulated combat, the swords with balance points closer to the grip were characterized as fast and maneuverable with more control, while swords with balance points farther from the grip were characterized as heavy, uncompliant, but hard-hitting beasts.[72]

A fighter looking for a weapon possessing agility and speed might choose a blade balanced closer to the hilt, while a brute who wanted a powerful chopping tool might choose a blade with a center of balance closer to the point.

Other measurements help us to characterize the swords, such as the center of percussion: the point on the blade which, when struck, results in minimal vibration at the grip. A hit made at the center of percussion minimizes the transmitted shock back to the swordsman's hand.

The situation is in reality much more complicated because swords are not rigid but instead flex and vibrate when struck. Measurements of the frequency and amplitude of the vibration delivered to the swordsman's hand for hits along the length of the blade provide deeper insights into the performance of the sword. The measurements for a replica sword show the center of percussion, where the vibration delivered to the swordsman's hand is lower for all frequencies.[73]

These kinds of maps help us better understand the feel of the sword to the swordsman. The feel of higher and lower frequencies differs. A dull thud (more low frequencies) feels different than a sharp crack (more high frequencies).

Another kind of measurement shows how long the blade rings after a hit for various frequencies. The replica pattern-welded sword used for this measurement rings for a long time at 24 Hz. In comparison, a replica monosteel blade of similar length rings at a higher frequency and damps out rapidly.[74] Again, these measurements give us insight into the response of the weapon to a hit and how that energy is reflected back into the swordsman's hand.

This plot also demonstrates why Viking swords do not sing in the same way axes (for example) ring when struck. The composition and the dimensions of the sword blade create a damped structure with a low natural frequency, too low a note to be called singing.

SCABBARDS

When not in use, swords were carried in scabbards to protect the blade and to avoid unintentional injuries. Few scabbards survive, since the organic materials used for scabbards typically rot away over the centuries. But the traces of the scabbards on the surviving sword blades provide the insights needed to allow us to reconstruct the scabbards.

Most likely, the scabbard was a sandwich of several layers, holding and trapping the blade in the middle of the sandwich. The physical structure was provided by wooden slats on either side of the blade. The wood was usually lined on the inside, sometimes with fleece, so that the lanolin on the fleece helped to keep the blade from rusting. The outer layer was leather or fabric to provide the "skin" of the scabbard.

A metal fitting for the throat, the opening at the top of the scabbard, protected the scabbard in this high-wear area, as the sword was drawn and sheathed. A decorative metal or leather chape at the bottom protected the bottom of the scabbard from contact with the ground and other objects. The ancient word for chape, *döggskór*, tells its function: *dew shoe*, a protective covering to keep the dew of the ground and other detritus away from the scabbard. Since it was commonly made of nonferrous metals, the chape is often the only part of the scabbard to survive, and numerous such chapes have been found.[75]

One Viking-age scabbard that has survived relatively intact was found at Stiklarstaðir in Iceland.[76] It had a layer of linen on the inside of the wood but no fleece, and a layer of linen on the outside of the wood covered by leather. Several leather bands were placed around the scabbard to help hold things together. An iron throat near the top protected the scabbard, and the chape was made of leather.

Scabbards were often suspended from the belt, which is the carry method often depicted in pictorial sources, such as the Stora Hammars I and the Klinte Hunninge I picture stones. This kind of suspension is also clearly shown in more detail in the Bayeux Tapestry.[77]

A baldric, a leather belt over the shoulder, was used to suspend swords before and after the Viking age. Some slight literary evidence suggests that Viking-age warriors used a

A replica Viking-age scabbard. Photo: William R. Short.

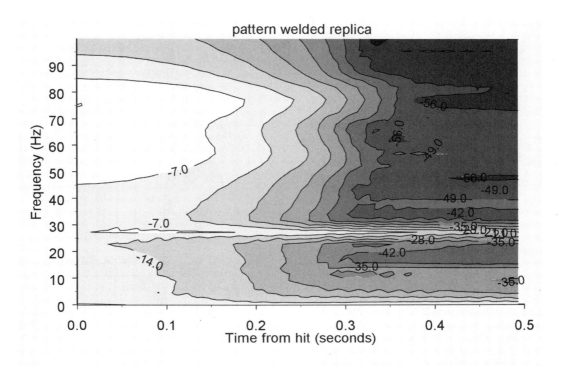

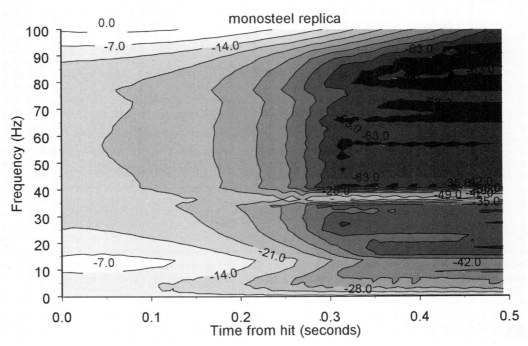

A plot of the measured energy spectrum versus time at the swordsman's hand for hits at a point on the blade near the tip, measured on two different replica Viking swords. The top plot shows the spectrum for a replica pattern-welded blade, and the bottom for a replica monosteel blade. The pattern-welded blade rings for a long time, while the monosteel blade is better damped.

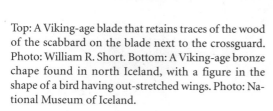

Top: A Viking-age blade that retains traces of the wood of the scabbard on the blade next to the crossguard. Photo: William R. Short. Bottom: A Viking-age bronze chape found in north Iceland, with a figure in the shape of a bird having out-stretched wings. Photo: National Museum of Iceland.

Top: Two scabbards suspended from the belt depicted in the Bayeux Tapestry. Detail of the Bayeux Tapestry, eleventh century, with special permission from the City of Bayeux. Bottom: A baldric sword suspension depicted in an illumination from Cotton MS Tiberius B V/1, an 11th century Anglo-Saxon manuscript. © The British Library Board, Cotton MS Tiberius B V/1.

baldric. Picture sources, such as the decorative Vendel-era plates, also show warriors carrying their swords with a baldric suspension.[78]

The scabbard seems to have been an essential part of a sword. A sword without a scab-bard was thought to be troublesome (*vandræða*), as in difficult to manage. King Óláfr gave a sword with no scabbard to the poet Hallfreðr, a troublesome gift for a troublesome poet.[79]

In *Harðar saga*, Indriði's wife intentionally damaged his scabbard so it would no longer hold the sword. She wanted to get the sword away from her husband so she could secretly give it to an assassin she had hired. Rather than taking a naked sword with him on a journey, Indriði left home without the weapon and its damaged scabbard.[80]

In the literary sources there are a few examples of the use of *friðbönd* (peace straps) to prevent the sword from being drawn in anger in places where its use was prohibited. While the exact nature of the straps is not known, some sources suggest they had to be unfastened or possibly untied to loosen the sword so it could be drawn.[81] There is an example in the literary sources where a man, unexpectedly needing his sword, could not unfasten the *friðbönd* quickly enough to draw the weapon.[82]

The use of peace straps informs us about Viking society. It made laws, and generally, fighting men honored these laws to keep violence in check. Rather than mindlessly resorting to violence as the first step, the use of peace straps suggests that men contemplated the law, and the need to maintain the peace was placed above the instinct of drawing the weapon without thought.

As discussed in the introduction to the weapons chapter, when their weapons were not in use, men kept them close, hung from the wall above their beds,[83] ready to be wielded in an instant.

HOW A VIKING SWORD WAS USED

Many of the aspects prized by the Viking warrior are solidified and expressed in physical form in the Viking sword. It is a speedy weapon, striking with power while permitting clever, cunning moves.

Multiple sources point to the sword being a cutting tool. Of the sword attacks described in the *Sagas of Icelanders*, 86 percent are cuts. Picture stones show warriors at the ready to make a cut. The kennings suggest its destructive powers. The physics of the blade reveal the sword's optimization for a cutting attack. The word often used to describe the sword's effect

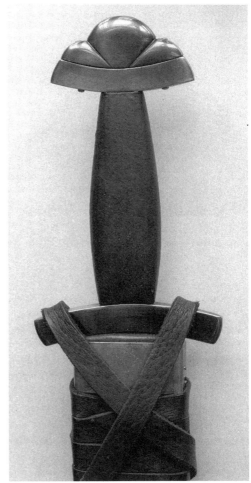

Top: Decorative bronze plates from the Vendel era depicting a baldric sword suspension. Derived from Knut Stjerna, *Hjälmar ock svärd i Beovulf* (1903). Bottom: A replica scabbard showing an interpretation of *friðbönd* (peace straps). Photo: William R. Short.

Top: The cutting capability of a Viking sword is clearly demonstrated by this 11th century skull with battle injuries. The top of the skull was nearly removed by a single percussive stroke of a sword. The clear blade shows the terminus of the stroke. Bottom: The cutting capability of a Viking sword is also demonstrated by the leg of the pig carcass that was nearly severed by a single stroke of a replica sword in this cutting test conducted by Hurstwic. It was only the sword's having been prematurely stopped by the support for the carcass that prevented the leg from being fully severed. Photos: William R. Short.

on the target is *bíta* (to bite).[84] The need for a sharp edge and the desire to use supernatural forces to dull the edge also point to the weapon as a cutting tool. The damage done to the target when a replica sword is used to cut an animal carcass only serves to hammer home the point: a sword is for cutting.

The sword is much less a thrusting tool. The blade geometry suggests that thrusting was not the main function of the weapon, and in the *Sagas of Icelanders*, fewer than 13 percent of the sword attacks were thrusts.[85]

Additionally, the sword is a biting weapon of power. It lacks the monumental power of, for example, a two-handed axe. Yet it has the power to cleave. This power can be seen in the few Viking-age skeletal remains showing sword injuries,[86] as well as in our cutting tests against animal carcasses. The sword cleanly cut through bones and muscles of the upper leg to sever the limb, and a cut across the chest cavity sliced through ribs and internal organs[87] to create the kinds of lethal injuries described in the literary sources. Sword attacks to the head or torso were lethal in over 80 percent of the incidents related in the *Sagas of Icelanders*.[88]

The literary sources tell again and again of sword cuts that severed the head from the body.[89] It is warriors preparing for this kind of full-power blow that are illustrated in contemporary picture stones, notably the Stora Hammars I stone.[90]

Even the names for swords tell us their intended use: *Hneitir* (cutter) used by King Óláfr, *Fótbítr* (leg-biter) owned by Bolli Bollason, and *Kvernbítr* (quern biter) owned by King Hákon.[91] It was the sword's cutting abilities that were prized and memorialized in the sword's name.

But the sword, unlike a weapon such as the axe, had more than raw cutting power; the sword had finesse. It had quickness and responsiveness to the swordsman's commands, allowing it to be guided to an opening while in motion. If the axe is a meteor falling from the sky to obliterate whatever it strikes, the sword is a guided missile whose trajectory can be altered while in motion to maneuver past defenses and deliver the attack with precision. The sword's maneuverability was unmatched by other weapons. When Gunnarr fought with his sword, it was so fast no eye could follow it,[92] and it appeared that there were three swords in the air at once.[93]

Physical measurements of the properties of various kinds of weapons show the sword's advantage over other weapons for quickness and maneuverability in cutting based on the physics of the tool.[94] As discussed earlier in the chapter, the moment of inertia is the equivalent mass of the tool in the hand, which is very different from the physical mass of the tool. The moment of inertia of the sword was measured to be 40 percent less than that of a one-handed axe and 80 percent less than that of a two-handed axe. Accordingly, a force from the hand on a sword delivers five times the acceleration as the same force on a two-handed axe. This difference means that the sword can be redirected, controlled, and manipulated with greater agility and quickness, and with less effort on the part of the swordsman, compared to an axe.

The literary sources tell us swords could be used to attack from every angle, taking advantage of their inherent maneuverability: straight down from above,[95] falling diagonal cuts from above, horizontal cuts across the middle,[96] and rising diagonal cuts from below.[97] It was fast enough to make quick follow-up attacks before the opponent could respond: a wounding attack followed immediately by the death blow, or a quick defense followed by death blows with the sword to other opponents one after the other.[98]

Another source that provides more details about the use of the sword is battle damage seen on some historical blades caused by impact of the sword on another weapon or shield. A study of Viking swords suggests that this damage due to battle can be distinguished from other damage by the shape of the nick and burr that is formed, and that this battle damage is confined to two places: near the center of percussion and near the hilt. As discussed earlier, the center of percussion is the best place to strike with the sword because it minimizes the impact of the hit to the swordsman, and as discussed later, near the cross is the best place to defend because it is the strongest defense.

The marks seen near the center of percussion tend to be perpendicular to the blade, and

Warriors with raised swords, ready to strike, depicted on the Stora Hammars I picture stone. Derived from Berig, *The Stora Hammars I image stone*. Creative Commons.

between 1 to 10 mm deep (0.04 to 0.4 in) deep.[99] These marks were likely made when the sword made a cut that struck the edge of the opponent's sword or shield or other defensive weapon. These are not marks made by slices or taps, but by full-power blows that impact a hard edge with power. Thus, this battle damage supports the kind of powerful sword usage seen in other sources. The marks near the hilt are discussed later, when we talk about defending with a sword.

Together, these layered sources create a picture of Viking warriors using their swords to deliver full-power cutting attacks to their opponent. As with the other weapons and even empty-hand attacks, the attacks were meant to take the opponent out of the fight: to destroy the opponent rather than to wound or injure. The maneuverability and agility of the sword added another unique and valuable capability to the swordsman's arsenal.

USE OF THE BACK EDGE

Viking swords are typically double edged. The edge that is forward when the sword is gripped in the hand is called the front edge. Which edge is in front depends solely on how the swordsman grips the sword; the two edges are nominally identical. Yet wear patterns on the pommel and grip suggest that the sword was

Front edge and back edge of the Viking sword. Which physical edge is front and which is back depends solely on the orientation of the sword in the swordsman's hand. Photo: William R. Short.

routinely carried in one particular orientation.[100] This meant one particular edge was routinely the front edge when the sword was drawn. Using the front edge is the natural way to cut, delivering a more powerful attack. Given that the same edge was consistently the edge used, what was the purpose of the other edge, the back edge?

The literary sources are, for the most part, silent, and they provide little evidence that suggests the use of the back edge. In later periods, swordsmen were taught to use the back edge for cutting,[101] as evidenced by the combat treatises for the later medieval and Renaissance periods. Yet there is little evidence from any of the Viking-age sources that suggests use of these weak, back-edge cuts, and the literary sources don't mention back-edge cuts at all.

A biomechanical analysis of the muscle groups involved suggests the weakness of a back-edge cut compared to the front-edge cut. Measurements and testing confirm the reduced power of a back-edge cut. Our measurements showed that a front-edge cut delivered

nearly six times the energy to the target as the same back-edge cut.[102]

When back-edge sword attacks were tested on an animal carcass, our cuts did not significantly penetrate the target.[103] None of these back-edge cuts resulted in anywhere near the destruction to the target that was easily obtained with a front-edge attack.

These kinds of weak, back-edge attacks do not fit with the holistic picture of Viking combat created by the sources. Every other tool was power based. It would seem odd for a Viking warrior to use a tool, such as the back edge of the sword, that did not deliver power when a more powerful tool was already in his hand: the front edge. And so we must ask: why have two edges if you only use one? A double-edged sword is likely to be harder to fabricate than a single-edged sword. A single-edged sword is likely to be a more robust weapon than a double-edged sword.

Perhaps the answer is simple: the second edge was a spare, should the preferred edge become dull or damaged during a fight. Literary sources tell us that the edges of swords grew dull in an extended fight,[104] and a nick in the edge caused a stress concentration that could lead to catastrophic failure. Having a second sharp edge available would allow the swordsman to instantly rotate in a new edge to continue his fight.

It is this use that is mentioned in the only literary example that seems to imply a back-edge attack. After Uffi killed one opponent with his sword, he feared that his sword might be damaged. To ensure the integrity of his weapon, he turned the blade around and killed the second man with the second edge.[105]

GRIPPING THE SWORD

One aspect of cutting remains controversial: how to grip the sword. Literary sources are mostly silent, and the pictorial sources have insufficient detail to teach us.

Modern practitioners have proposed a variety of grips. As we do our research and testing at Hurstwic, it is necessary for us to grip the sword in some fashion. In this, and in similar areas where we have no information, we try to be pragmatic. We use the simplest solution that accomplishes the task.

In this case, we turn to the biomechanics of how a human naturally holds a tool to deliver a blow with power. For the grip, the natural choice is the hammer grip, similar to how one holds a hammer. Until other evidence is found that breaks this conjecture, we stay with the most natural way to hold a tool used for hitting.

Another proposed grip is the handshake grip, similar to what one uses when shaking hands. Other proposed grips involve slipping at least one finger over the crossguard onto the blade, or slipping a finger on to the pommel. Both of these proposals seem to be based, at least in part, on the misconception discussed earlier that the grips of Viking-age swords were too short to allow a hammer grip.

Some of these proposed methods of gripping can be discarded as improbable when one considers the nature of the Viking sword. The crossguard was a part of the Viking sword for good reason: to protect the hand. Extending the hand past the grip would weaken the protection. Later swords that were intended to be held that way, such as the rapier of the late Renaissance, had additional guards to protect the swordsman's hand. Additionally, as discussed in the introductory weapons chapter, available evidence strongly suggests that the blade was kept very sharp from the tip to the crossguard, so there would be additional hazards involved with positioning the fingers past the crossguard and onto the blade.

In our research lab these grips were tested, measuring the energy that could be delivered to a target by a cut using a replica Viking sword. The hammer grip was capable of delivering more energy to the target than any other grip tested, ranging from 50 percent more energy to more than twice the energy of the other tested grips.[106]

Though we have no solid evidence that creates a clear picture of how Vikings held their swords, it seems likely they used what biome-

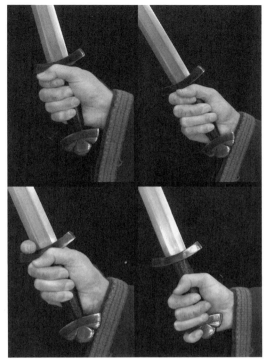

Several grips for a Viking sword proposed by modern practitioners. Clockwise from upper left: hammer grip; handshake grip; pommel grip; crossguard grip. Photo: William R. Short.

chanics and what simple measurements tell us delivered the most power: the hammer grip. Delivering power was their goal, whether it was by sword, axe, or empty hand.

### TWO-HANDED GRIP

The literary sources suggest that the usual method of wielding a sword was with a defense in the other hand, such as a shield,[107] or with a second weapon in the other hand.[108] Yet sometimes, when a fighter wanted to deliver a particularly powerful cut, perhaps because his edge wasn't biting, he would drop any other weapon he was holding and grip the sword two-handed.[109] How was this accomplished? The grip of a typical Viking-sword is not large enough to allow both hands on the grip, and the sources are silent.

In our research lab, several approaches were tested, and it was shown that a two-hand grip could increase the power delivered by the blade

A speculative method of wielding a Viking sword two-handed as depicted in the film *The Final Battle of Gísli Súrsson.*

to the target by as much as 50 percent.[110] While speculative, the measurements show that it is possible to develop substantially more power in a Viking sword cut by using two hands.

OTHER ATTACKS WITH A SWORD

Another, and less-common, use of the sword was for thrusting. Only about 13 percent of the sword attacks in the *Sagas of Icelanders* are thrusts.[111] Regardless, the literary sources tell of powerful thrusts with the weapon that penetrate the body and come out the other side.[112] Death resulted in nearly half the cases of sword thrusts reported in the sagas.[113]

The physical form of the sword suggests that thrusting with the point was a less-important use than cutting with the edge. Most surviving swords lack the acute point of, for example, a spear, which was intended for thrusting. Biomechanical considerations also give the spear the advantage in a thrust, compared to a sword, confirmed by measurements in the research lab. A spear thrust had more than twice the energy delivered to the target than a sword thrust.[114] Even when wielded one-handed, the spear thrust outperformed the sword thrust by about 40 percent.

Other parts of the sword were also used for attacks, such as the pommel. A strike with the pommel was used when the attacker didn't want to kill his opponent but merely humiliate him.[115] A pommel strike was also used when a fighter thought his opponent wasn't worthy of a proper attack.[116]

DEFENSIVE USES OF THE SWORD

Besides the obvious offensive uses of a sword, there likely were times when a sword was called on for defense. These moments seem to be extreme cases according to the literary sources, for example, when a shield was not available. When a sword was called on for defense, the fighter usually relied on body movements and stop hits for defense instead.[117]

And this brings up an area of intense interest that has not been well studied. How did Vikings block with the sword? Common sense suggests that a powerful edge-on-edge percussive contact between two swords can't be good for either blade, given the blade geometry and the metallurgy available at the time. Considering the value of a sword, a fighter might want to choose an alternative way to block, if it were at least equally effective.

A nick in a blade caused by such edge-on-edge contact is a point of weakness from which a crack can propagate across the blade, causing a complete failure. Such failures are seen in archaeological examples and described in the literary sources.[118]

Studies of historical swords clearly show nicks in the edges. The nature and location of some of the nicks make it seem likely that they were formed by defensive use of the sword. These nicks are located on the edge of the blade, closer to the hilt than the point. This part of the blade is the strongest place for blocking, regardless of the orientation of the sword, because of the better leverage obtainable from this part of the blade. Typically, nicks here are diagonal and angled to the blade. The nicks are sharp, strongly suggesting an edge-on-edge contact of two blades.[119]

Additionally, some historical swords show the evidence of nicks being removed by sharpening, resulting in a shallow arc being formed on the edge of the sword as material was removed around the nick.[120] This process is also

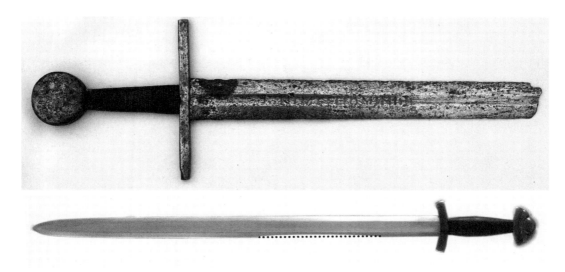

Top: An 11th century sword that most likely broke while in use. The edge shows a number of shallow cuts and cracks probably due to battle. There is an inscription inlaid into the fuller. Photo: Lee A. Jones. Bottom: Nicks in sword blades were ground out, resulting in shallow arcs in the blade that can be seen on surviving Viking swords. The depth of the arc is exaggerated in the illustration. Illustration: William R. Short.

described in the literary sources.[121] Although blade material is lost in this process, the blade is stronger because the point of weakness, the nick, has been removed, reducing the chance that a crack will form on the site and propagate across the blade.

To avoid nicking the edge, it has been suggested that Viking fighters may have used the flat of the blade to block, if a block with the sword was required. The evidence is weak. At least one historical sword shows damage to the flat of the blade consistent with a strong block with the flat, but it seems to have been an extraordinary case.[122]

Our force-on-force tests were inconclusive. In our simulated combat, blocking with the flat could be made to work, but only if the defender recognized the attack with sufficient time to respond. It could not be counted on every time; despite the desire to use the flat to defend, the edge took some abuse.[123]

This flimsy evidence does not allow us to conclude that blocking with the edge of a sword was a regularly used defense. It seems most likely that a Viking-age swordsman tried, when possible, to block with a defensive weapons such as a shield. If it wasn't possible, he used what was available, including his sword, to make the block.

CONCLUSION AND SUMMARY

The Viking sword was the technological marvel of its time, pushing the limits of available metallurgy to create a weapon of beauty, speed, power, and finesse. It was the beautiful creation of a skilled bladesmith with only a single function: cleaving body parts. In addition, the sword brought with it a level of quickness and maneuverability unmatched by other weapons.

Yet the sword was more than merely a weapon. It was also a visible symbol of status and prestige that was routinely worn, handled, and prized. It often was an heirloom that carried with it the memories of heroic deeds from the past. It was everything a Viking prized in combat: speed, power, cleverness, and cunning, all condensed into a physical form.

A rider with spear in hand on the Hunninge I picture stone. Derived from Harald Faith-Ell, *Hunninge I*. Creative Commons.

# SPEAR

The spear is an ancient weapon of deceptive simplicity. At its roots, it is a pointy stick.

Yet a spear was much more in the Viking age. It was the special weapon of Óðinn. It was a widely used weapon of Viking-age warriors from kings to commoners as well as a tool for hunting.

It is an ancient weapon; spears from the late Paleolithic era are found in Scandinavia.[1] In this chapter, we will discuss the aspects of the spear that made this simple weapon the first choice for many warriors, from the highest of the gods to the most common of men.

SOURCES

In our study of Viking-age spears, we use many of the same sources used in studying other weapons. The archaeological finds tell about the kinds of spears that were in use, and the literary sources tell us something about how the spears were used and about some of the purposes for which they were used. Pictorial sources show us images of spears in use, seen in stone carvings from as early as the Mesolithic era,[2] and in more contemporary sources such as the Oseberg Tapestry and Scandinavian picture stones. We also consult sources such as the Bayeux Tapestry and the Franks Casket with care because of our desire to use narrow sources.

ETYMOLOGY

The many words that exist for the spear suggest that many different kinds of spears were in use in the Viking age. The usual word for spear in the literary sources is *spjót*, which is cognate with the English word *spit*, the long iron rod used for roasting meat over a fire. The name suggests the intended purpose of the weapon: a tool for skewering an opponent. In verse and in personal names, *geirr* is used, an ancient word of uncertain origin.[3] There is little that suggests why one word displaced the other.

Many types of spears are mentioned in the literary sources, and it is not always clear how they relate to the spears found in the archaeological record: *fjaðurspjót* (feather spear), probably with a head shape resembling a feather; *krókaspjót* (hooked spear), having barbs or wings on the socket; *spjótsprika* (spear prick),

Modern replica spear. Photo: William R. Short.

A late Bronze-age stone carving at Litsleby in Sweden may depict an early form of Óðinn holding his spear. Derived from Sven Rosborn, *Rock carving area from the bronze age in the parish of Tanum, Bohuslän, a part of Sweden*. Creative Commons.

thought to be a thin, small spear; *snærisspjót* (stringed-spear), a spear thrown with the assistance of a string; *málaspjót* (inlaid spear), a decorated spear; and *höggspjót* (cutting spear), whose nature is speculative.

In addition, there are numerous spear-like weapons mentioned by other names in the literary sources. In some cases, the same weapon is referred to by both its specialized name and by the generic word *spjót* in the same paragraph. These include: *kesja, fleinn, heftisax, gaflak, brynþvari, brynklungr, sviða, pálstafir,* and *broddstöng*. The distinction between these variants remains unclear.

THE SPEAR IN MYTHS AND POETRY

The spear plays a large role in Norse mythology. The weapon is closely tied to Óðinn, the highest of the gods. Óðinn carried the spear

named Gungnir, and Óðinn was called the lord of spears. Gungnir, which means the swaying one, was one of the treasures of the gods made by blacksmith dwarves. The spear has runes on its point.[4]

The Litsleby Rock in Sweden is a huge stone carved with figures dating from the Bronze Age. It depicts a man wielding a spear, and the figure is 2.3 m (7.6 ft) high.[5] Some believe the figure represents an early form of Óðinn, brandishing his spear aloft.

Óðinn started the first war of the world by throwing a missile over the heads of his enemies, commonly thought to be a spear, a practice that continued in the Viking age. Viking-age warriors sometimes hurled a spear over the heads of their enemies for good luck, continuing the ancient practice.[6] In *Styrbjarnar þáttr Svíakappa*, Óðinn, in disguise, told King Eiríkr to throw a projectile over the heads of his enemies and shout, "Óðinn take you all." The implication is that by doing so, the dead were consecrated to Óðinn. Eiríkr threw the projectile which turned into a spear as it flew, blinding all his enemies, one of Óðinn's magical powers.[7]

Óðinn sacrificed himself to himself by hanging from a tree, pierced by a spear, and humans were sometimes sacrificed to Óðinn by hanging and piercing with a spear.[8]

As Óðinn's death approached, as told in the euhemerized version of the myth told by Snorri Sturluson, Óðinn had himself marked with a spear and claimed as his own all the warriors who fell in battle. Many of the Valkyries who escort fallen warriors to Óðinn in Valhöll have names that are compounds of spear (*geirr*), such as Geirahöð (spear-battle), Geiravör (spear-goddess), Geirdriful (spear-flinger), Geirönul (the one charging forward with a spear), and Geirskögull (spear-battle).[9]

In skaldic poetry, Snorri Sturluson teaches that several names can be applied to spears: for thrusts they are called *orm* (serpent) or *fiskr* (fish), and as missiles they are called *hagl* (hail) or *drífa* (snowfall) or *rota* (storm). Some of the kennings for *spear* used in verses include blood snake, corpse herring, and flying dragon of wounds.[10]

These examples show the strange position of the spear in mythology, a position not held by any other weapon. It is a weapon connected both to the gods and to battle more strongly than any other weapon. It is the chosen weapon of the highest of the gods. It is through the use of the spear that Óðinn claims the fallen warriors to join him in Valhöll, and it is spear women who escort the fallen warriors. Yet despite this strong connection with the gods, the spear is a weapon of the common man, far removed from the prestige of a sword. As we will see, it is a weapon simple in its design, fabrication, and use.

SALIENT FEATURES OF A SPEAR

Spears in the Viking age consisted of a sharp iron head fixed to a long wooden shaft, often using a socket and an iron nail to hold the head to the shaft. The Norwegian *Gulaþingslög* required every man in the king's levy to possess a spear.[11]

Spearheads were made of iron, and like sword blades, many were made with a process called pattern welding, described in detail in the sword chapter. Virtually all are socketed, using a socket whose diameter tapers toward the point. Only a few small spearheads use tangs, as is common with arrowheads. For a weapon like a spear, which is likely to be removed from a wound and used again on another enemy in a fight, the tang would not have as secure a grip on the spear shaft in the reverse direction as a socketed head fixed with a nail.

SPEAR TYPOLOGY

Spearheads are found in a wide variety of sizes and shapes, and often are categorized based on Petersen's early twentieth-century typology.[12] An alternate typology was proposed by Lena Thålin based less on appearance and more on how the spearhead was constructed.[13]

Spearheads typically have an acute, sharp tip and sharp edges, to better penetrate and open a wound through the body. Unlike the long sword blade, the shorter and more robust spearhead was better able to resist the bending and breaking forces that might damage a sharp point.

Spearhead shapes varied extensively, only partially seen in the typology illustration. Some heads have a distinct ridge along the centerline to form a strong backbone for the head. Some are relatively flat, and others have a biconvex cross section. Some heads have a rounded leaf shape, and some have an angular wedge shape. Some are slender and long, and some short and more broad. Some are broadest where the blade joins the socket, and others are broadest closer to the point. Some have long sockets relative to the blade, and some short. Some have wings on the socket, and some do not, a feature discussed in more detail later in the chapter.

The overall length varies greatly, ranging from 6 cm to 50 cm (2.5 to 20 in). An extreme example reaches 55 cm (22 in) in overall length.[14] Likewise, the width varies greatly, with some blades long and slender while others are short and wide.

The literary sources also tell of the wide variation in size, ranging from a puny *spjótsprika* (spear prick) carried by a small man to a spearhead 1 *ell* (about 50 cm or 20 in) long. An extremely long length is suggested in an example when a spear passes through the intended victim and penetrates and kills the man behind him.[15]

Occasionally, the shape of the blade is specifically mentioned in the literary sources. Þorbjörn used a broad spear to kill Atli.[16] The blade was so notable that Atli, in his dying breath, dryly commented, "Broad spears are in fashion these days." Here, and in numerous other cases, the blade of the spear is called a *fjöðr* (feather), providing some clues about the shape of the blade.[17]

It is not clear what all these variants were intended for. One can imagine that small spearheads were used for missiles. One can imagine that spears intended for thrusting would require robust heads with a strong connection to the socket that would resist bending forces.

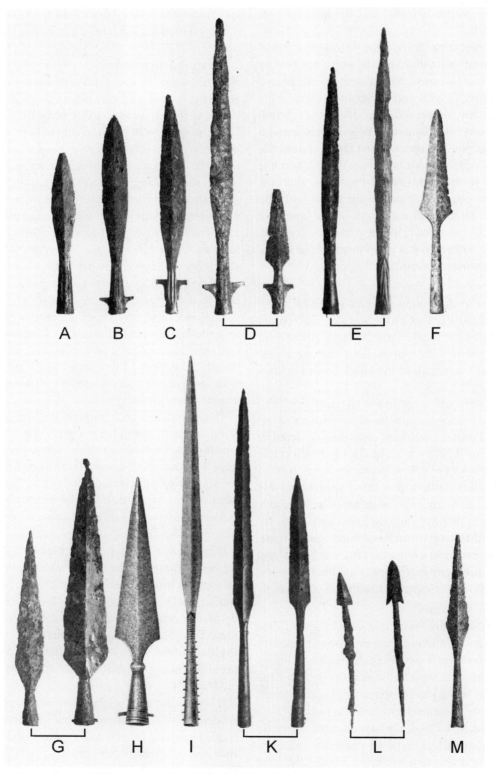

Petersen's typology for Viking-age spearheads. Derived from Petersen (1919).

Such spears were used into modern times, such as the Moro budiak spear used in the Philippines and elsewhere. This ability to resist bending would be a necessity in battle so the spear doesn't bend or break if it were to hit a solid obstacle. And one can imagine that a leaf-shaped or feather-shaped spearhead might result in a handier weapon for some kinds of moves, since it would likely be easier to pull from a wound than an angular shaped head, and thus made ready more quickly to attack the next opponent.

The sockets were round, and the internal diameter typically ranged from 2 to 3 cm (0.8 to 1.2 in), tapering toward the point. Some spears have smaller sockets, on the order of 1 cm (0.4 in). A number of these small-socketed spears have been found in Iceland[18] and other places.[19] One has to wonder if these were special-purpose spears, since a shaft small enough to mate with the socket would likely be too light-duty and too easily broken if used for thrusting.

Perhaps these small heads were optimized for throwing and for hunting. These small spears have remained in use into the modern era in some societies, including Indonesian, Filipino, and African societies, and they are used for throwing.[20] Perhaps Viking-age people used their spears in a similar way.

WINGED SPEARS

An example of a spearhead shape that is specifically mentioned in the literary sources is the *krókaspjót* (hooked spear or barbed spear). This term is thought to refer to spears with wings, seen in Petersen's types B, C, and D.

Several purposes have been proposed for the wings. A variety of wing shapes are found, not all of which are shown in Petersen's listing. A few have a curved profile, some toward the point, others away from the point,[21] which may provide clues to their intended use, discussed later.

When used for hunting, the wings limit the penetration of the spear into the animal. This is especially important for prey such as boars, which are likely to charge the hunter. Docu-

Top: A Viking-age broad spearhead. Photo: William R. Short. Bottom: A Viking-age spearhead with a small socket found in west Iceland. It is smaller in length than the broad spear shown above, having a socket inner diameter of about 18mm, as compared to the 32mm diameter of the broad spear. Photo: National Museum of Iceland.

ments describing boar hunting in northern lands date from at least the Roman times, and the practice continued into the modern era.[22] The wings prevent the animal from charging up the spear shaft once skewered.

In combat, some of the same functionality might be desired. After Özurr speared Helgi through, Helgi walked up the spear shaft to get at Özurr, a move that would not be possible with wings.[23] Additionally, the wings may have been used to prevent the spear from penetrating to the extent that it was difficult to remove the spear quickly to use against the next opponent in the fight. When Grettir thrust at two berserks with a *krókaspjót*, the spear penetrated up to the hooks (*krókr*),[24] but otherwise the use of the wings in this manner is not mentioned in the literary sources.

A move described once in the literary sources is using the wings to catch and pull a shield to open up the opponent. Askmaðr and Kýlan attacked Már, and Askmaðr used his *króksviða* (winged spear) on Már's shield to move it and create an opening for Kýlan to attack.[25] The etymology of the word for the weapon also supports this kind of move; the primary meaning of *krókr* is a hook.[26] A wing with a curved profile, seen on some archaeological examples and discussed earlier, might facilitate the move.

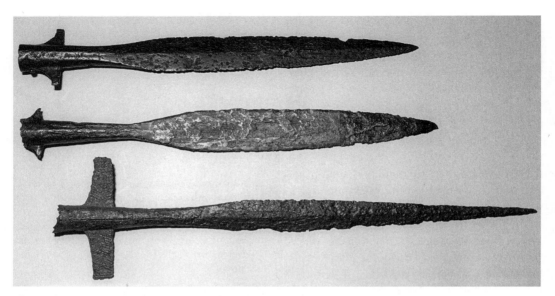

Three Viking-age spearheads with wings. Photo: William R. Short.

Another possibility is that the wings were used to trap and catch the weapons of an opponent, allowing a fighter to control his opponent's weapon. This possibility was observed during our many rounds of simulated combat with winged spears, but the move does not seem to have been mentioned in any of the sources. In our simulated combat, it happened repeatedly, even unintentionally at times, with the simplest, square-cut wings.[27]

The possibility of this use of the wings for hooking is strengthened by the observation that the wings on some surviving spearheads are nearly as narrow as the widest part of the blade,[28] making them less likely to be a design feature to limit penetration and more likely intended for some other use, such as catching.

SPEARHEAD FABRICATION

Spears were made by forging the iron blade, then drawing out the material that will be wrapped around to form the socket. Generally, the socket was welded at the join.

Spearheads were sometimes pattern welded, creating beautiful patterns in the surface of the spearhead.[29] In some examples, the center of the blade is pattern welded, while in others it is a band on either side of the rib that is pattern welded.

Some spears are decorated and ornamented in other ways, and these decorations take a number of forms. Some spears have decorative furrows along the length of the socket, such as the Petersen types B and C, or ridges, such as the Petersen type D. Some sockets are decorated with ridges and depressions that encircle the socket, such as the Petersen type F. Additionally, scribed lines were used to decorate some spearheads.

There are several examples of inlaid spears (málaspjót) in the literary sources, including the famed spear Grásíða,[30] and inlays are found in the sockets of archaeological examples. Additionally, there are examples where a number of decorative rivets stand proud of the socket of the spear, such as the Petersen type I. A beautiful example was found in Iceland, opposite, top, with twelve rivets, and inlays on the socket of silver, copper, and niello, a black alloy of sulfur with copper, silver, and lead.[31]

Another kind of spear decoration mentioned in the literary sources is *gullrekinn*, which is translated *inlaid with gold* or *gilded*.[32]

A beautifully decorated K type inlaid Viking-age spearhead found in south Iceland. Photo: National Museum of Iceland.

Many spears are so described in the literary sources,[33] although in some cases, it is the specifically the socket that is described as being gilded. Examples of spearheads gilded in gold are found in the archaeological records.[34]

A unique spearhead found in Sweden is inscribed in runes on the socket, translated to "Hrani owns this spear."[35]

### SPEAR SHAFTS

Few spear shafts have survived, and thus we are faced again with the coin-toss problem. We must be cautious of any conclusions drawn on such a small sample.

It seems likely that spear shafts were made as a straight piece of round, straight-grained wood such as ash. The diameter of the shaft likely matched the diameter of the socket, about 2 to 3 cm (0.8 to 1.2 in), tapered at the end to fit closely with the tapered socket. It is likely that the shaft was made from radial split wood for strength.

The length of the shaft is speculative. *Gísla saga* tells of a spear whose shaft was so long that a man could just reach up and touch the rivet holding the head on the shaft, suggesting this length was unusually long. Another example specifically mentions that the spear shaft being used was short,[36] suggesting the shafts were made in a variety of lengths.

Pictorial sources provide some additional clues. The Klinte Hunninge I stone shows a rider carrying a long spear, roughly the length of his horse from nose to tail. The Franks Casket shows a short spear, shorter than the height of the man holding it. The Bayeux Tapestry shows spears ranging from the height of a man to the length of a horse.[37]

Top: A Viking-age spearhead that was treated in modern times to reveal the pattern-welding in the head. Center: A Viking-age spearhead with geometric decorations inscribed into the wings. Bottom: The interior of the socket of a Viking-age spearhead. Photos: William R. Short.

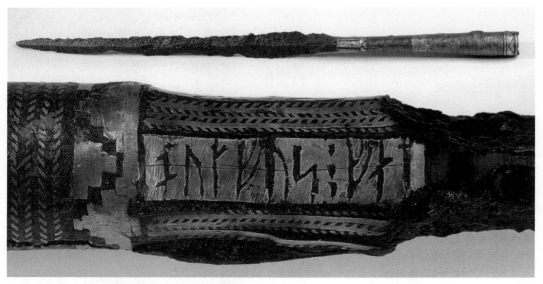

A decorated Viking-age spearhead from Gotland, inscribed in runes that read, "Hrani owns this spear . . . ." Derived from Christer Åhlin, *SHM 15928*. Creative Commons.

The best guess we can make is that the combined length of shaft and head of Viking-age spears was between 2 and 3 m long (80 to 120 in), although arguments can be made for longer and shorter shafts.

Our testing and measurements found good reasons for using longer and shorter shafts. The longer shaft allowed for more powerful attacks, both cutting and thrusting, measuring as much as twice as much energy delivered to the target in the thrusts.[38]

In force-on-force tests, this additional power was readily apparent. But the shorter shaft allowed for quicker attacks and more control. The shorter shaft made dual wielding the spear with a shield, or with a second weapon, more effective because of the increased control,[39] not surprising given the larger measured moment of inertia at the hand for the longer spear.[40]

The Lendbreen spear is a nearly intact Viking-age spear and shaft found at the edge of a glacier in Norway.[41] The shaft is 185 cm long (73 in), and the combined length of shaft and head is 230 cm (91 in). The shaft is made from birch with a diameter of 2.2 cm (0.8 in) and is thought to have shrunk slightly from its original diameter. The top 8 cm (3.1 in) of the shaft is tapered to fit the socket. This example supports conjectures based on other evidence, but with only a single example, one must be careful about drawing any conclusions.

The literary sources suggest that it was possible to break or cut the spear shaft in a number of ways, leaving the spearman holding only a stick. In multiple instances, men cut through their opponents' spear shafts with their swords or axes or saxes.[42] Even a manure rake was used to break a spear shaft when no other tool was available.[43]

This move was tested many times in our research lab in a variety of ways, and it always failed in our early tests. Wood experts we consulted thought the move unlikely, since the sharp edge of the sword might cut through the first layers of wood fiber in the shaft but would then only compress the remaining layers of fibers and fail to cut.

When the move unexpectedly succeeded during simulated combat,[44] we realized our original assessment was in error. We were forced to go back to the drawing board and revisit the problem. Further measurements and analyses allowed us to understand the physics of the move.

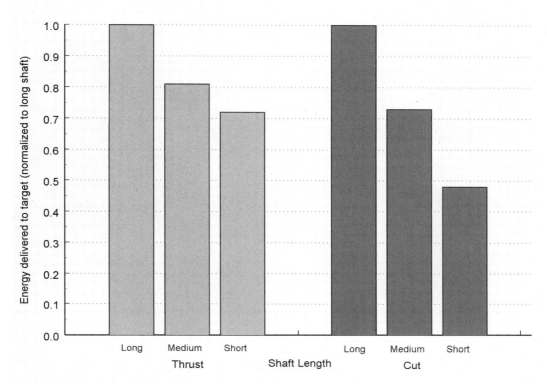

A plot of the measured relative energy delivered by a spear to a target with varying spear shaft lengths for both cuts and for thrusts.

The interaction of the inertia of the spearhead with the shaft is what makes the move possible. When hit, the wood shaft is accelerated, but the ends resist movement. The end held in the hands resists movement because of the grip on the shaft, and the end connecting to the spearhead resists movement because of the inertia of the steel head. The wood under the edge of the incoming sword is partially cut and then snaps from the acceleration imparted by the sword. Our subsequent testing shows the move not only to be possible but readily achievable.[45]

To reduce the chances of the shaft being cut, some were reinforced with iron, according to the literary sources. The reinforcements were used on conventional feather-shaped spears and on a specialized spear called at various times a *kesja*, a *spjót*, and a *brynþvari*.[46] There

seems to be little to no archaeological evidence to support this feature on the shaft in the Viking age, although this protection was used on later medieval polearms.

FIXING THE HEAD ON THE SHAFT

Evidence, both archaeological and literary, suggests that the head was held onto the shaft by a rivet. Several spears have been found with the rivet or a portion of the rivet intact. Spearheads are also found in which the hole for the rivet is clearly visible. These holes are generally small, around 2 to 3 mm (0.08 to 0.12 in) in diameter, but some are as large as 5 mm (0.2 in).[47]

The Lendbreen spear, mentioned earlier, is nearly intact.[48] The rivet is an L-shaped bit of iron with the body of the nail having a cross section of about 3 mm (0.12 in). The head of the nail was formed by bending over the iron to form the L-shape and has a smaller cross

Simulated combat testing using a spear against a two-handed axe at the Hurstwic research lab. Photo: William R. Short.

section, about 2 mm (0.08 in). Another surviving spearhead has a well-preserved rivet with a well-formed head having a diameter of 3 mm, flattening out to 6mm (0.24 in) at the socket of the spear.[49]

There are examples in the literary sources of men removing the rivet from their spear before throwing it. In one case, the intent was for the head and shaft to separate if the spear missed the target so that the spear couldn't be thrown back. In another case, the man wanted to throw only the spearhead as an insulting prank.[50] In either case, it suggests that however the rivet was fastened to the spear, it could be removed with the ordinary tools a man carried with him every day, probably his belt knife.

Not all spearheads show evidence of having been attached by rivets, so other attachment means were probably used.[51] Perhaps a tight fit between shaft and socket sufficed, although an adhesive, such as pitch, or wrapping with leather bands seems more likely. Another possible explanation is that the spears were not intended, or ever used, for combat.

CARRY METHODS

There is little evidence that clearly tells us how Viking-age fighting men carried and stored their spears when not in use, so we can only speculate. On foot, fighting men probably carried their spears in their hands,[52] perhaps resting on their shoulders. An image on a runestone and a fragment of the Oseberg Tapestry[53] show men resting the butt end of their spears on the ground.

On horseback, there is no evidence of the use of a strap over the back or a specialized stirrup to carry the weight of the weapon. A picture stone depicting a man on horseback carrying a spear shows the spear at his side at an angle, but with insufficient detail to determine the carry method.[54] A belt fitting shows a spearman on horseback holding the spear in two hands.[55] The literary sources give a few examples where they specifically state that the man rode with his spear in hand.[56]

However it was carried, either on foot or on horseback, the literary sources suggest the spear was ready for instant use. When Örn unexpectedly raised his axe at him, Guðmundr jumped off his horse and ran Örn through with his spear.[57] This kind of literary episode, combined with a lack of any solid archaeological evidence, suggest that spear sheaths were not commonly used in the Viking age.

Inside the house, spears were hung on the wall above the bed, which seems to have been the usual place for men to store their weapons. There are also examples of spears at the ready in other locations, such as by the front door, leaning against a wall.[58] These episodes suggest a spear didn't need to be unsheathed to be put to use.

OFFENSIVE USE OF THE SPEAR

All our sources lead us to the same conclusion: the spear was used for skewering something all the way through. Whether we look at the physics of the weapon, at the use as reported in the literary sources, or even at the etymology of the word for the weapon, we are drawn to this conclusion about the use of the spear, whether delivered directly or thrown through the air.

In the literary sources, the spear was used for thrusts and for throws in almost every case. Of the spear attacks described in the *Sagas of Icelanders*, 52 percent were thrusts and 45 percent were throws,[59] while only 3 percent were cuts. Regardless of how the attack was made, the spear was lethal, causing death in 50 percent of the reported spear attacks.

The physical form of the spear shows us it is intended for an attack directed along the axis of the shaft so the head hits the target point first. The physics of this attack can be modeled easily. Whether used for thrusting or used as a missile thrown through the air, the spearhead is designed to penetrate deep, piercing flesh, splitting bones, and opening a deep, bleeding wound.

THRUSTING

Again and again in the literary sources, it is this kind of devastating spear thrust that is described: a thrust that propels the spear not only into the opponent's body but through it so the

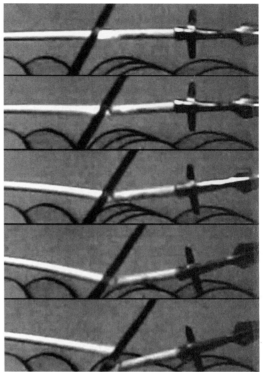

Top: Frames from a high-speed video showing the details of how a sword cuts through a spear shaft. Rather than cutting, the sword snaps the shaft. Bottom: A Viking-age spearhead, with the head of the rivet that held the spearhead to the shaft visible on the left side near the opening of the socket. Photos: William R. Short.

spearhead comes out the other side,[60] causing bleeding from deep inside the body.[61]

Our experiments with a spear thrust to an animal carcass make these results quite believable. Although the test was flawed due to the point hitting the support structure that held up the carcass, the spear penetrated one rib, splitting it in two as it cut through the organs behind the ribs.[62]

This kind of lethal result cannot come from a poking attack but rather from a powerful attack with the spearman firmly connected to the weapon with both hands to transfer the energy from his body to the point of the weapon.

## ONE-HAND USE OF THE SPEAR

Occasionally, the sagas specifically mention that the spear was used two-handed, as one would expect for a long-shafted weapon of this type.[63] Yet there are also times when the spear was double wielded with a shield[64] or other weapons,[65] which tells us that the spear was sometimes used with one hand. Picture stones, such as Klinte Hunninge 1, show a rider holding spear and shield together (see page 98), and the Ledberg stone shows a warrior holding spear and shield, with a sword on his belt.[66] The Bayeux Tapestry shows the vast majority of warriors wielding their spears one-handed.[67]

Yet a one-handed thrust is less powerful, as confirmed by measurements. Whether held overhand or underhand, a one-handed spear thrust delivered about 40 percent less energy to the target than a two-handed spear thrust.[68] In simulated combat, the sense was similar: that one-handed thrusting attacks had less power, with less control, reduced accuracy, and greater telegraphing of the attack.[69]

Even a simple model of the physical situation shows that a spear thrust with one hand will have less control and less power than with two hands. The two-handed grip creates a closed, truss-like assembly comprising the arms, shoulders, and spear shaft, creating a solid structure that resists external forces, allowing for good control over the point of the spear with little effort. In contrast, the one-handed grip is an open structure, requiring more strength to keep the point on line, while only weakly resisting external forces, such as an opponent's block or deflection.

Given the disadvantage we observed in using the spear one-handed, why did Viking warriors use it in this manner, as indicated by literary and pictorial sources? Perhaps there is an advantage that did not emerge in our tests. Perhaps the advantage of having a second weapon outweighed the disadvantages of a one-handed grip on the spear. At this time, we do not have a satisfactory explanation.

## THROWING

Using a spear as a projectile was an ancient practice for the northern people, as mentioned earlier; the myths tell us that Óðinn began the first war of the world by throwing a missile over the heads of his enemies. Some kings took pride in their throwing ability; King Óláfr was said to be able to throw two spears at once. *Kongungs skuggsjá* suggests that the king's men should train in spear throwing.[70]

As a missile, the spear was devastating, according to the literary sources. In many examples of throwing the spear, at least a portion of the spearhead exited the back side of the victim.[71]

It seems spears were thrown whenever that move best suited the situation. Most often, that arose when fighters were at too far a range to use their conventional weapons, and it was not immediately possible to close the range. Examples include naval battles before the ships met and were boarded for hand-to-hand fighting,[72] large-scale battles where the front lines were not yet in range or where men to the rear were not yet in range,[73] fights between men separated by a river or drainage ditch that couldn't easily be crossed,[74] fights against men who were protected inside a fortification,[75] fights with men who were fleeing,[76] and in general mêlée combat when a fighter saw an opponent he especially wanted to attack who wasn't yet in range of normal weapons.[77] A spear thrown from one side could wound a man in the rear of the other side, and when it happened in the fight at Geirvör, Snorri goði dryly remarked, "It's not always best to walk last."[78]

In many cases, the sagas say the spear was thrown as soon as the targeted opponent was in range, yet there are also examples of spears thrown when the men were face to face.[79]

These examples suggest spears were used as missiles even at short range, if that use seemed to be the best move for the situation.

We cannot say with any certainty that a particular spearhead was intended to be used as a projectile. A lighter weapon would have some advantages as long as the entire spear has an appropriate center of mass for throwing, yet it is desirable for the head to be robust enough to withstand an impact with an unintended target should the throw miss. As discussed earlier in this chapter, perhaps some of the puny spears found in the archaeological records are spears intended as projectiles.

It is difficult to tease out the distance a spear could fly based on the literary sources. Even in the cases where we can determine the location of a throw described in the literary sources, we cannot guarantee that the geography of the site has not changed since the saga age. As an example, most of the spear throws described in the *Sagas of Icelanders* occur in Iceland, a geologically active land.

*Reykdæla saga* tells us that Skúta shot a spear across the river ford at Eyjarvað that killed Þrándr instantly.[80] Today, the river is many tens of meters wide at this spot. A throw across the river at this point would be very nearly the distance of the current world's record for a javelin throw. We cannot say with certainty if the throw is realistic, or if it is an exaggeration, or if the site is incorrectly identified, or if the river has changed its banks.

Yet if we have an estimate of the spear velocity, a simple physical model can tell us its approximate range. World record javelin throws have a speed of about 30 m/sec (98 ft/sec).[81] The speed of a Viking spear at release must have been substantially less for several reasons, including the greater mass of the spear (more than double that of a javelin) and the lesser strength of the Viking-age people, which does not compare to that of modern athletes.

The parameters of Viking spear throws were tested in a modern setting, using throwers who ranged from competitive javelin throwers to rank beginners to Viking reenactors. The

Preparing to throw a spear. Photo: William R. Short.

measured release velocity was as high as 15 m/sec (49 ft/sec).[82] When thrown to maximize distance, with a release angle of about 45 degrees, our model predicts a flight of about 25 m (82 ft),[83] which compares favorably to the measured distances achieved by our spear throwers.

This kind of throw has the disadvantage of a long time-of flight, about 2.3 seconds, more than enough time for an aware target to move out of the way or take other defensive precautions. A more direct flight path with a lower release angle has a shorter flight time but would have a much shorter range, under 10 m (33 ft), according to our model.

Yet there are many examples, such as mass battles or naval battles or battles at a fortification, where the long time of flight wouldn't matter, since a warrior on the receiving end would be unlikely to track all the incoming spears. In numerous mass battles on land and at sea, it is said that a shower of missiles fell,[84] which suggests the intensity of the incoming projectiles in battle. Based on our simulated combat, even in a small skirmish, it can be a challenge to focus on the incoming spear flying from a distant spearman when other opponents are a threat at close range.[85]

The literary sources also suggest that in battle, combatants were unable to track all the threats. Spear throws were lethal in 51 percent

Top: A speculative reconstruction of the *snærisspjót* string (top) and throwing method (bottom). This approach resulted in greater speed, greater range, and improved accuracy compared to a conventional spear in Hurstwic's testing. Photo: William R. Short. Center: A speculative reconstruction of a *snærisspjót* throw. Even after leaving the hand, the spear continues to be accelerated by means of the throwing string, increasing the energy in the throw and imparting spin to the spear. Photo: William R. Short. Bottom: A small Viking-age spear-head found in east Iceland. Could this be the head of a *snærisspjót*? Photo: National Museum of Iceland.

of the reported cases in the *Sagas of Icelanders*, yet of those lethal spear throws, only 47 percent hit the intended target; the remainder hit and killed someone else in the enemy group, rather than the intended target. Often, the intended target simply moved out of the way while the spear was in flight, while the unintended victim was focused on some other aspect of the fight.[86]

SNÆRISSPJÓT

The literary sources tell of a spear called a *snærisspjót*, which is interpreted to be a spear with a throwing string. In these sources, a *snærisspjót* seems to be capable of greater distance and accuracy when thrown compared to a conventional spear.[87] A classic example is Helgi's use of a *snærisspjót* to kill a slave fleeing on horseback.[88]

In our research, many ideas about how to make and use a *snærisspjót* were considered. A tool often mentioned as an analog to the *snærisspjót* is the *atlatl*, a rigid lever used by numerous societies since the Stone Age to aid in throwing the spear. Yet that idea seems unlikely based on several pieces of evidence, including etymology. *Snæri* means a twisted rope,[89] suggesting that a rope plays a significant role in the use of the weapon. An *atlatl* has no twisted rope.

An approach to the *snærisspjót* that makes more sense is that of a classical amentum. This usage of the throwing string with the spear is highly effective and matches how the *snærisspjót* is used in the literary sources. Measurements show that compared to a conventional spear of the same length and mass, a thrown *snærisspjót* travels with 50 percent greater speed and delivers more than twice the energy to the target, while providing much greater accuracy.[90]

The string is attached to the spear shaft so that when it is wound around the shaft, the first two fingers of the throwing hand can be slipped into the loop as the spear shaft rests in the hand. High-speed video shows the effect of the throwing string on the motion of the spear.[91] When thrown, the string continues to

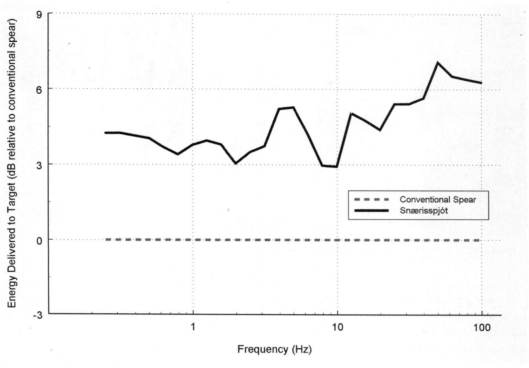

The measured energy delivered to a target by a thrown snærisspjót relative to that of a thrown spear.

accelerate the shaft after it has left the hand, increasing the speed and thus the power of the throw, and the wrap causes the spear to spiral in flight, increasing the accuracy.

An episode in a literary source says that an arrow wound was mistakenly thought to be caused by a *snærisspjót*,[92] which gives us a clue about the size of a *snærisspjót*. Perhaps some of the small spearheads seen in the archaeological records might be the head of a *snærisspjót*.[93]

RETURNING A SPEAR IN FLIGHT

A move mentioned again and again in the literary sources is catching a spear in flight and throwing it back at the opponent, often with lethal results.[94] It was considered shameful to be struck with your own weapon,[95] so the move was especially desirable, both shaming and killing the opponent in one smooth motion.

The move has been tested using several kinds of force-on-force situations in our research lab, both static situations that are one-on-one, and dynamic, chaotic situations with many-versus-many in which multiple spears may be in flight simultaneously. The move has been tested in simulated combat.[96]

Our conclusion is that the move is possible, even in a situation with multiple combatants on each side. The relatively slow flight speed of a spear gives the intended target time to prepare to pluck the weapon out of the air. When performed by someone with practice, the move requires little wind-up to send the weapon flying back to its original owner, who may not be well prepared to defend against it, having just thrown his spear. Of the lethal spear throws in the *Sagas of Icelanders*, 13 percent were spears that were plucked out of the air and thrown back to kill the person who originally threw it, or someone near him.[97]

CUTTING

Only 3 percent of the spear attacks reported in the *Sagas of Icelanders* are cuts.[98] The physics of the spear tells us that the tool is ill suited for cutting.

A spear caught in flight. Photo: William R. Short.

A cleaving tool, such as an axe, has most of its mass in the head, allowing it to cut deep into the target when swung. A spearhead's mass is not so great, compared to the mass of the shaft, so it is less well suited for cutting. A computer model tells us that the effective mass of the spear at the point of impact is nearly half that of the axe, and thus has less energy and momentum to cut deep, compared to a tool intended for cutting, like an axe.[99] The moment of inertia at the hand for a spear is several times that of an axe, making it difficult to swing to make a cut when held one-handed. Additionally, the "sweet spot"—the center of percussion—for the sword, axe, and sax is located on the blade or head near the tip, where the weapon is likely to hit the target. The calculated center of percussion of the spear is located far in front of the point and outside the physical extent of the spear.[100] As a result, any hit using the sharp edge of the head is going to kick back into the wielder's hand far more than for an axe or sword.[101]

Measurements of cuts confirm the difference. The energy delivered by a cut to the target with a replica two-handed axe measured just shy of eight times greater than the energy delivered by a cut with a spear held in two hands.[102]

Test cuts with sharp replicas further confirm the difference. A cut with a replica spear to the ribs of a pig carcass had little impact, yet a sword cut had no trouble slicing deep into the body.[103]

Thus, it is no surprise that the Viking spear was rarely used for cutting.

DEFENSIVE USE OF THE SPEAR

The literary sources say little about how the spear was used for defense. The spear shaft was used to parry attacks, diverting or deflecting or striking the incoming attack to push it off-line.[104]

When compared to other weapons used defensively, such as the sword or axe, and especially when compared to the shield, the spear was a less effective defense.[105] On a weighted basis, injuries were 20 percent more severe defending with a spear than with a sword or axe defense in the episodes described in the *Sagas of Icelanders*.

We have few other sources that can teach us any specifics of the defense. The archaeological sources and pictorial sources have little to guide us.

OTHER UNKNOWN SPEAR WEAPONS

There are several spear-like weapons mentioned in the literary sources that cannot readily be distinguished from a conventional spear in the archaeological records. One of these unknown weapons is the *höggspjót* (hewing spear), discussed earlier in the chapter. The nature of the weapon is not known, yet in some cases, the words *spjót*, *höggspjót*, and *kesja* are all used to refer to the same weapon at various times in the same chapter.[106]

The *kesja*, another unknown spear-like weapon, appears only in *Egils saga* of all the *Sagas of Icelanders*. The *kesja* is used for both thrusting and throwing. The *kesja* is mentioned in several of the *Kings' Sagas*,[107] the legendary sagas,[108] as well as in the considerably later *Sverris saga*,[109] where the *kesja* seems to have been the choice of men in mass battle on land and sea. For example, King Óláfr helgi was armed with a *kesja* as he prepared for the large-scale battle at Stiklarstaðir in which the king lost his life.[110] From these available sources, it is not clear how a *kesja* differed from a *spjót*.

Yet in one instance, a specific *kesja* is described in such clear detail that it cannot be a conventional spear. The weapon is also called a *brynþvari* (mail scraper).[111] The head is 2 ells long (98 cm, or 39 in), with a blade coming to a square point, suggesting a four-sided cross section. This is quite unlike typical spears from the archaeological record, and it is not clear what this weapon might be.

One possible explanation for multiple words being used for the same weapon is seen in other examples in the old language, where multiple words are used to represent the same concept, as discussed in the research chapter. The distinction between the words sometimes seems far more solid to us today holding a modern mindset than it appears to have been for the Viking-age people.

ATGEIRR

The *atgeirr* is another spear-like weapon mentioned numerous times in the sagas, and it is the weapon of one of the strongest fighters: Gunnarr Hámundarson. Yet again, there is little that tells us how this weapon differed from a spear. Further, the one *atgeirr* for which we have the greatest amount of information, Gunnarr's *atgeirr*, is described as being a special weapon, touched by magic. Its original owner, Hallgrímr, had a spell put on the weapon such that it was the only weapon that could kill him.[112] Thus we cannot be sure that the extraordinary properties ascribed to Gunnarr's *atgeirr* carry over to other, nonmagical *atgeirrs*. As a result, we use this source cautiously and compare it to what some of the other literary sources tell us.

The etymology of the word is also unclear. As discussed earlier, *geirr* is an early word for a spear and is of uncertain origin. The prefix *at-* is a common word having multiple possible meanings and usages, although one of the meanings is collision or a crossing of spears.[113] The available information is too vague to draw a conclusion.

Some examples of the other unknown spear-like weapons, such as *kesja*, are also referred to as *spjót*, which suggests the difference between *kesja* and *spjót* is small.[114] On the other hand, there appear to be no examples where an *atgeirr* is also referred to as a *spjót*, suggesting some fundamental difference between the two weapons. Indeed, there is a fight described in which a man with a spear fights against a man with an *atgeirr*.[115]

*Atgeirr* is used several times in kennings for warriors, such as "Baldr of the *atgeirr*" or "messengers of the *atgeirr*"[116] to refer to a warrior.

Several sources suggest that the *atgeirr* is a weapon suitable for naval battle, notably the thirteenth century Norwegian text *Konungs skuggsjá*.[117] Several users of *atgeirrs* are seamen or pirates,[118] including the original owner of Gunnarr's *atgeirr*, Hallgrímr. He is described as being a Viking and mighty fighter who must have done a lot of fighting from the deck of his warship.[119] It was his *atgeirr* he chose to use against Gunnarr.

It is not clear why an *atgeirr* would be especially suitable for naval battle. As discussed shortly, it seems likely the *atgeirr* had a long shaft, which would be helpful for providing a long reach before the opponents' ship was boarded but a major drawback during battle in the tight confines on a ship.

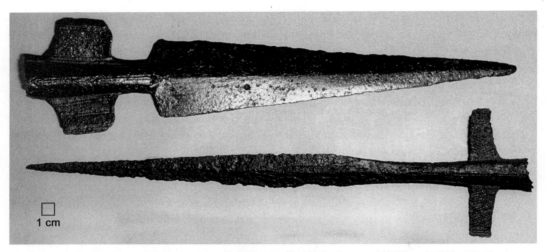

Two robust Viking-age spearheads. Could one of these be the head of an atgeirr? Photo: William R. Short.

In all the literary sources, the *atgeirr* was used primarily for thrusting. In a few cases, the *atgeirr* was thrown,[120] and it was rarely used for cutting.[121] It was an effective weapon, and when used for a thrusting attack caused death in 80 percent of the attacks reported in the *Sagas of Icelanders*.[122]

Combined, the literary sources suggest the *atgeirr* was a large, robust, spear-like tool with wings mounted on a long shaft. Little else can be said, given the lack of information. A look at the archaeological record shows that winged spearheads do exist that are long bladed with a thick, robust connection between blade and socket. Perhaps one of these might be an *atgeirr*.[123]

CUTTING SPEARS

The literary sources tell of spears having a different form that made them usable for both cutting and thrusting. For example, Refr made a spear of this kind and used it quite effectively throughout the saga for cutting, thrusting, and throwing. The spear (head) was large, but the shaft was short,[124] making the spear have some

of the physical characteristics of an axe, a weapon better suited for a cutting attack, as described earlier in the chapter. In the text, the weapon is referred to as a *spjót*.

SUMMARY AND CONCLUSIONS

The spear is a simple weapon: simple in design, construction, and use, and likely to have been readily available to all classes of men. It was required for every man in the king's levy. It was made in a vast range of shapes and sizes, and it was a tool useful not only for battle but also for domestic purposes, such as hunting.

Yet despite this simplicity, the weapon was effective; it is a long-range weapon used for throwing and thrusting that is lethal at much longer ranges that most of the other common weapons. And despite this simplicity, the weapon was the choice of kings and of the most complex of the gods, Óðinn.

It is a potent weapon, both in battle and in the mythology of the Vikings. One might say the bloody history of the Vikings was written with a spear.

# ARCHERY

Viking-age people used bow and arrow at home; on the battlefield, and at sea. In skillful hands, they could be a long-range weapon that unleashes a hailstorm of death falling from above, or a sharpshooter's weapon capable of exquisite accuracy.

In the Viking age, archery was used for domestic and martial purposes. Like a spear, it could be used for hunting and for combat. Yet unlike any other Viking weapons, archery was also used in competitions and sport, perhaps similar to wrestling. Skill in archery was prized, and competitions were arranged and held. But unlike wrestling, archery seems to have been the sport of kings and of the higher classes of Viking society.

### SOURCES

As with other weapons, we use a wide range of sources to gain an understanding about Viking-age archery. Yet the sources are sparse, and so we emphasize some sources for archery more than for other weapons.

We use literary sources, including the *Sagas of Icelanders*, histories such as *Heimskringla*, mythology from the *Eddas*, and the law codes of Iceland and of Norway. Because these sources do not provide enough detail, we also depend on material from the legendary sagas, despite their tendency toward fantasy. In the legendary sagas, archers and archery are more fully detailed than in other sources. Indeed, the title characters of two of the legendary sagas have *archer* or *arrow* as their nicknames, reflecting their prowess as archers. We also use annals from foreign lands that tell of Viking archers, such as the Moorish sources.

Not only are the literary sources scant, so are the archaeological sources. By and large, archery gear is made of organic material that does not survive well in the archaeological records. As a result, archaeology is of less help than with other weapons. Arrowheads are found made of iron, but the bows and arrow shafts and other gear are virtually unknown because so few have survived from the Viking age. Once again, we are confronted with the coin-toss problem.

Atypically, the pictorial sources give us a clearer image of archery than they do of other weapons. However, a weakness of the pictorial sources is that perspective is rarely used, as discussed in the sources chapter, and so there can be ambiguities when reinterpreting the two-dimensional figure back to the original three-dimensional object.

What the pictorial sources offer are clear examples of the tools in action. Picture stones and carvings show the bow in use, with the bows drawn and arrows stuck in targets. Some of these pictorial sources, such as the Bayeux Tapestry, fail our test for using narrow sources, and so we use them with care. An intriguing source of pictures are the illustrations of

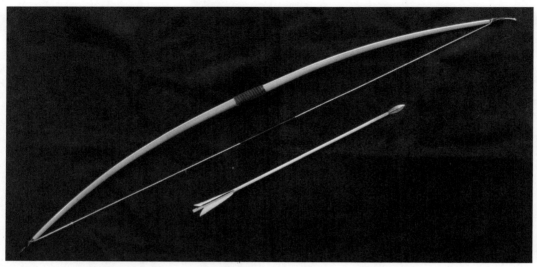

Replica Viking bow and arrow. Photo: William R. Short.

archery in Olaus Magnus's book, *Historia de Gentibus Septentrionalibus*, first published in 1555. It is much too late a work to depend on for Viking-related research, but it is interesting since it shows multiple draw methods, sometimes within the same figure.

Although the evidence is scant, we can combine all the available sources to form a hazy picture of archery gear and its use in Viking times.

BOWS

The bow is a simple device that stores energy in the wood of the bow as the archer draws the string. The energy is discharged explosively at the instant the string is released, accelerating the arrow forward to high speed. All aspects of the bow are optimized to store large amounts of energy in the wood and to release it to the arrow instantaneously.

Since few bows survive from Viking lands in the Viking era, some of the details of the bow are speculative, as one might expect when faced with the coin-toss problem. Bows were typically *longbows*, a word not used in the Viking lands. The ancient word for bow is *bogi*, meaning bowed or bent.[1]

Typical Viking-age bows were made from a single piece of straight or slightly curved wood, shaped by the bowyer to have an oval or D-shaped cross section. A string fitted from one end of the bow to the other bent the bow into an arc.

Bows were typically made of yew (*Taxus*) or elm (*Ulmus*). The yew tree produces a straight trunk in which the inner wood and outer wood have different properties, and these differences were used to advantage in the bow. The more-elastic outer wood was placed on the outside of the bow's arc, and the more-compressible inner wood on the inside,[2] allowing the bow to store more energy with less likelihood of cracking or breaking. The bows and bow fragments that have been found at Hedeby are mostly yew, with some elm.[3] Literary sources also suggest bows were made of yew,[4] and that elm bows were also used.[5]

One of the very few Viking bows to survive intact is Bow 1 found at Hedeby.[6] It is 191 cm long (75 in) with a D-shaped cross section about 40 x 53 mm (1.6 x 2.1 in) in the middle, tapering to the ends. It is slightly curved, with a 4 mm (0.16 in) deep notch across the bow at the top to hold the string. The bottom of the bow has no notch, implying that the string was tied at the bottom, as discussed later. There appears to be no grip, per se, formed into the wood, or as a separate piece that has been lost.

One of the few intact Viking-age bows, found in Hedeby. A side view, and cross-sections at several points along the bow are shown. Derived from Paulsen (1999).

Based on modern reconstructions, it is estimated that the draw weight was as much as one hundred pounds, resulting in a range of as great as 195 m (215 yds).[7] There are so few examples that one hesitates to call Bow 1 typical. But it is not atypical, based on the slight available evidence.

The size and capability of bows varied, as evidenced not only by the Viking-age bows and bow fragments that have been found but also by episodes in the literary sources.[8] When the two kings, Sigurðr and Eysteinn, were comparing their accomplishments, Sigurðr said he could draw a much heavier bow than Eysteinn, but Eysteinn countered by saying his shots were just as accurate.[9]

Einarr þambarskelfir (string-shaker) was an archer who was called better than any man with a bow. His story is told not only in the *Kings' Sagas* but also in *þættir* and legendary sagas. When his bow was broken at the battle at Svölðr, the king handed his own bow to Einarr. Einarr, a skilled archer, nocked an arrow on the king's bow and drew the arrowhead behind the string, unaccustomed to such a weak bow. He threw it down and fought with his sword.[10]

The literary sources tell us that bows could break, either from a strong archer misjudging the capability of a borrowed bow,[11] or perhaps due to wrathful gods.[12] *Hávamál* warns men not to trust a creaking bow,[13] a sign of a bow having internal weakness or damage that might cause it to unexpectedly break.

BOWSTRINGS

We know even less about bowstrings (*bogastrengir*) than about bows, since nothing defin-

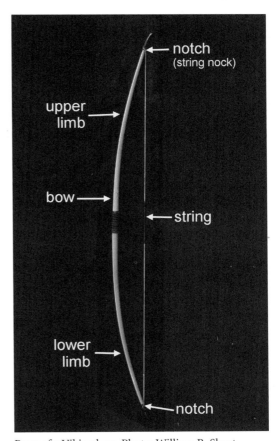

Parts of a Viking bow. Photo: William R. Short.

itive survives. Strings were likely made of plant or animal fibers twisted together. Likely candidates include flax (from which linen is woven) and hemp fibers. Linen is suggested by a kenning for arrow, "the powerful pole of the thin linen cord." Silk has also been suggested, as have animal fibers, a suggestion supported by the use of the word *þömb* (guts) to refer to a bowstring. King Óláfr's archer was named

Different methods for fastening the top and the bottom of the string to the bow are depicted in *The Life and Miracles of St. Edmund MS M.736*, a twelfth-century English manuscript. Photo: The Morgan Library & Museum, New York.

Einarr þambarskelfir (string-shaker), the best archer in Norway.[14]

Whatever material is used, it must be strong, resilient, resistant to stretching, unaffected by changes in temperature and dampness, and tough to break under the draw and release of the energy of the bow. The fibers were twisted to make a string, as suggested by episodes in the literary sources.[15] The ends of the string were twisted back on themselves to form loops, which were placed in notches at the ends of the bow, thus tensioning the bow. Some bows have notches only at one end, suggesting the string was permanently tied to the bow at the other, notchless end, a feature clearly seen in pictorial sources, such as the illustration of the martyrdom of St. Edmund by the Danes in the year 869.[16]

However the attachment of the string to the bow was accomplished, it was necessary to unstring the bow when it wasn't in use to prevent the wood from taking a set, which reduces the amount of energy it can store and deliver. Some surviving bows, such as Bow 1 from Hedeby, have a protruding nail head below the top string notch that is thought to have held the loose end of the string after the bow had been unstrung.[17]

The evidence of the size of the notch in the bow, as well as the size of the nock in the arrow shafts, discussed later, give us clues about the diameter of the bowstring. Both notch and nock are on the order of 4 mm (0.16 in), suggesting that the bowstring must have been smaller in diameter.

The literary sources tell us that bowstrings were used for other purposes, which hint at the nature of the string. On a number of occasions, and often aboard ships, bowstrings were pressed into service to bind a man's hands,[18] and, in one case, to strangle a dog that had bitten the king aboard ship.[19] These episodes suggest that the strings had substantial strength, sufficient to bind a man. They also suggest that strings, and therefore bows, were readily available aboard a ship, thus providing additional evidence that bows were commonly used in naval battles, as discussed in the mass battle chapter. Bowstrings were also used on land by archers to bind men's hands,[20] lending credence to the idea that archers carried spare bowstrings in case of breakage or other failure.

A classic example of a string failure occurred when Gunnarr defended his home at Hlíðarendi single-handedly using his bow. His enemies were able to cut his bowstring. Knowing that his enemies could never defeat him as long as he had his bow, Gunnarr asked his wife for some of her hair to twist into a bowstring.[21] She refused, so we have no indication if human hair would have worked, but Gunnarr, an accomplished archer,[22] felt it would have.

In the later medieval period into the modern period, Icelanders made cordage and yarn from both horsehair and human hair,[23] lending credence to the idea that perhaps a bowstring could be repaired using hair or even made from hair.

The feasibility of using human hair was tested in our research lab by gathering hair, twisting it into a string, and splicing it into a conventional bowstring that had been cut. Measurements showed no significant change in power delivered or accuracy of the shooting when using a string made of human hair.[24] These experiments showed the possibility of using human hair to repair a bowstring.

OTHER KINDS OF BOWS

Other types of bows are mentioned in literary sources and are even used as personal names, such as *Finnbogi* (Finnish bow) and *Húnbogi*[25] (Hunnish bow). These bows were used in other lands in Viking times. Through travel and trade, it is possible Vikings learned of these bows, yet the evidence seems slight that Vikings commonly used them.

*Finnbogi* refers to a bow that was made by gluing together two wood species, usually pine and birch, to provide the advantages of different properties of tension and compression between the inner and outer layers that yew wood provides.[26] *Finnbogi* was used in lands where yew was not readily available.

The *húnbogi*, also called a *hornbogi* (horn bow), was a composite bow made of horn, sinew, and wood to provide a more-compact yet high-power bow suited for mounted archers. Its use is well documented in eastern lands in Viking times, and Viking archers may have been exposed to these kinds of bows during their travels. When Gizurr went as a messenger to summon the invading Hunnish army to battle, Hlöðr, the leader of the Huns, ordered his men to kill the messenger. Gizurr replied, "Huns don't scare us, nor your hornbows."[27] Additionally, Vikings may have had contact with horn bows in trading towns such as Birka, where grave finds suggest the presence of Eastern mounted warriors.[28]

These bows are usually drawn with the aid of a thumb ring, and the find of an artifact in Iceland that has been interpreted as an archer's thumb ring has caused some to speculate that the *húnbogi* was used in Iceland.[29] The connec-

Top: A human-hair necklace made in the modern era demonstrates that human hair can be twisted into strong, robust strings. Photo: National Museum of Iceland. Bottom: A bowstring repaired with string twisted from human hair was tested in the Hurstwic research lab. Photo: Todd Pelletier.

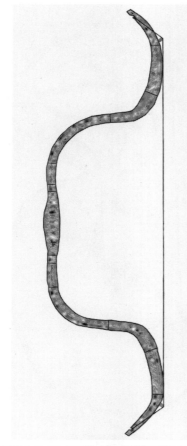

Top: An eastern-style horn bow, a composite made from layers of wood, horn, and sinew that stores more energy than wood alone. Illustration: William R. Short. Bottom: An artifact found in south Iceland which some have interpreted as an archer's thumb ring. The ring resembles those used for drawing horn bows by archers from eastern lands. Photo: National Museum of Iceland.

tions that lead one to this conclusion are tenuous, but intriguing nonetheless.

## ARROWS

An arrow consists of a head that is usually sharp and made of iron, mounted on a wooden shaft that has fletching (feathers to help achieve stable flight) near the back end of the shaft, and a nock (a slot to engage the bowstring) at the rear end of the shaft. The word for *arrow* (ör) is thought to be related to *örr* (swift).[30]

## ARROWHEADS

Arrowheads are often found in Viking graves and house sites. They are found in different shapes, intended for different purposes.

There are several typologies for arrowheads, and often, examples from Rygh's listing are used.[31] Generally, arrowheads are leaf-shaped with an acute point, double-edged, and without any barbs, similar to Rygh 539. These arrows create wide, bleeding wounds suitable for hunting, but they were suitable for combat, as well.

Yet literary sources tell us of different types of arrowheads, and archaeological examples show great variation.[32] Some arrowheads are thin, long, and narrow, often with a square cross section such as Rygh 542.[33] This design results in a light arrow that can fly far and split open a mail ring to penetrate the mail shirt. These arrows are thought to be intended for combat, where these capabilities are desired. The arrow that hit King Hákon through his mail and caused his death was called a *fleinn*, a word with multiple meanings but here thought to be a long arrowhead, perhaps of this type.[34]

Some arrows, rather than coming to a point, are bifurcated, coming to two points in a V-shape.[35] These are thought to be specialized hunting arrows.

Additionally, blunt arrowheads survive, such as the fragments found at Hedeby in which the front end of the wooden shaft expands into a flat, round terminal as large as 25 mm (1 in) in diameter.[36] Some have a distinct bevel, cre-

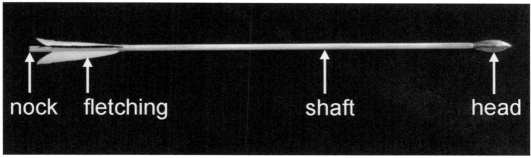

nock    fletching              shaft              head

Parts of a Viking arrow. Photo: William R. Short.

ating a blunt, point-like shape. The purpose of these arrows is not known for certain, but several show distinct marks consistent with the flattened ends hitting a hard target.

The literary sources provide an additional clue. As a demonstration of his skill as an archer, Einarr þambarskelfir could penetrate a raw oxhide hanging from a beam with a blunt arrow, called a *bakkakólfr*. The etymology of the word suggests a rounded-tip arrow intended for target practice: a combination of *kólfr* (the bulb of a plant) and *bakki*, used in compound words for an archery range,[37] a use of the bow that is discussed later in the chapter. Perhaps Einarr's feat was accomplished by an arrow similar to these archaeological finds. Additionally, it is possible that a *bakkakólfr* was an arrow used for hunting small game, such as birds,[38] which might be destroyed by a shot with a conventional arrow.

Literary sources occasionally refer to barbed arrows (*krókör*). The Gulaþing laws state that wounding a man with a barbed arrow so that the arrowhead has to be cut out is improper, with a fine of three marks. When Þormóðr pulled the arrow out lodged near his heart, the barbs, which lay on his heartstrings, pulled the fibers out. These arrows with barbs are not commonly found, although several were found at Hedeby.[39]

Viking-age arrowheads usually affixed to the shaft with a tang, a thin extension of the arrowhead that is driven into the end of the shaft. Arrowheads with sockets were used before and after the Viking age, and some sock-

eted arrowheads are found in Viking contexts.[40]

ARROW SHAFTS

Arrow shafts were made of wood. Fragments of the shaft sometimes remain attached to archaeological finds of arrows, which give us clues to the nature of the shafts. Birch (*Betula*) seems to have been the wood most commonly used for the shaft, but ash (*Fraxinus*), hazel (*Corylus*), rowan (*Sorbus*), and pine (*Pinus*) were also used.[41] The size of the shaft varied, but typical lengths were 60 to 70 cm (24 to 28 in), with a diameter of 8 to 10 mm (0.3 to 0.4 in) near the front of the shaft.[42] The diameter decreased toward the rear, widening out again at the nock. The physical and material properties of the arrow needed to be matched to the bow for optimum flight. Thus the dimensions of the arrows varied depending on the bow, with heavier draw weight bows generally requiring longer arrows.

The tang of the arrowhead was inserted into the shaft, which was reinforced with a wrapping of thread sealed with an adhesive to strengthen this high-stress connection. Birch tar seems a likely candidate for Viking-age arrows.[43] The thread was likely sinew, although arrows have been found where the thread was metallic in some high-status graves. An arrow found at Hedeby used two wraps of brass thread to reinforce the connection between head and shaft,[44] creating a strong, as well as distinctive, arrow for the archer. Likewise, the arrow used by Pálnatóki to kill the king was wrapped with gold.[45]

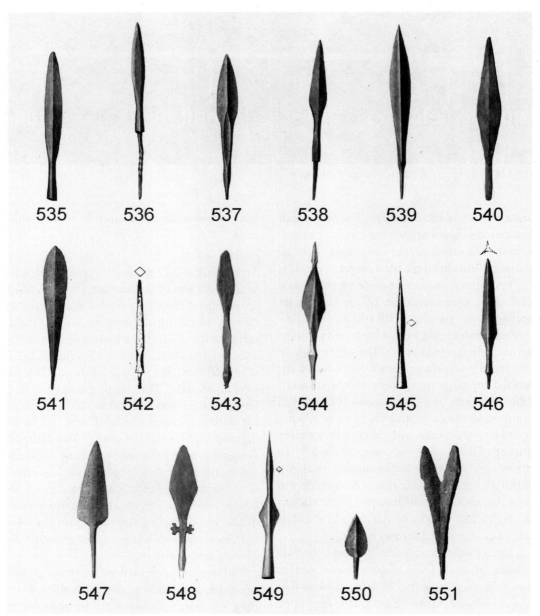

Rygh's typology for Viking-age arrowheads. Derived from Rygh (1885).

The nock, where the arrow fits to the string, was a slot made in the wood across the diameter at the rear end of the shaft. The shape of the nock in cross section was somewhere between a U-shape and a V-shape, typically about 4 mm wide and 4 mm deep (0.15 in).

Examples of brass nocks inserted into the wooden shaft have also been found with dimensions and varied shapes nearly the same as the nocks made directly into the wooden shafts.[46] Since the bowstring must fit into the nock easily, these dimensions give us some clues to the diameter of the bowstrings used, but due to the small number of finds, we face the coin-toss problem yet again.

For additional strength in this critical and highly stressed part of the arrow, the shaft widened at the end to accommodate the nock. Arrow shafts found at Hedeby widen from about 6 to 7 mm diameter (0.24 to 0.28 in) forward of the fletching to about 8 to 10 mm diameter (0.31 to 0.39 in) at the nock.[47]

The feathers that form the fletching are critical to the flight of the arrow. They add air resistance and thus reduce range, but they also stabilize the flight by causing the arrow to spin. The feathers for a given arrow must all be taken from a wing from one side of the bird so they all twist in the same direction when mounted to the arrow and work together to apply spin.

The number of fletches varied, but three was most typical. The size of the fletching likely varied as well, depending on the bow and the intended use of the arrow. Fletching was on the order of 10 cm long (4 in), but longer fletching is indicated on some arrows. The fletching was attached to the shaft with adhesive, and thread was wrapped around the shaft and the fletches all the way back to the nock, both to secure the fletches and to strengthen the shaft at the nock and prevent it from splitting.[48]

OTHER ASPECTS OF ARROWS

Arrows apparently held some special value distinct from the bow to an archer. There are examples in the literary sources of arrows that were named,[49] such as Odd's arrows called *Gusisnaut* (Gusir's gifts). In Viking society, valuable, permanent objects were often given names, including weapons such as swords, as we have seen in earlier chapters. There appears to have been no named bows in the literary sources, which suggests a lower level of importance for the weapon than for the ammunition it shot.

We have little that gives the monetary worth of a bow relative to an arrow. One of the few sources is the Norwegian Gulaþing laws, which fix the fines for missing bows or arrows aboard

An assortment of Viking-age arrowheads found in Sweden, including a barbed arrowhead (second from bottom). Derived from Yliali Asp, *SHM 15721:II:49*. Creative Commons.

a levy ship. A missing bow was fined three aurar, while missing arrows twenty-four aurar (one eyrir per arrow),[50] suggesting the value of the bundle of arrows was greater than that of the bow.

Arrows were retrieved after they were shot, or after hunting.[51] Some archers were said to be inseparable from their quiver full of arrows, always carrying them close as other men would carry their swords.[52]

Men recognized their own arrows,[53] and likewise, men were recognized by the arrows they carried.[54] Handmade arrows were probably distinctive enough to recognize, but archaeological finds tell us that arrows were marked with paint or by lines scribed into the shaft. At the judging of a hunting competition, the king identified the hunters' kills by the owners' marks in the arrows that brought down the prey. Perhaps the means of identification was similar to that recorded in the later Icelandic law code, *Jónsbók*, which states that if a whale is shot, then half of the whale goes to the man whose mark is on the missile that caused the kill.[55]

OTHER KINDS OF ARROWS

There is some evidence for other unusual forms of arrows. Perhaps the special-purpose arrow best supported by evidence is the *herör* (war arrow), which was sent out by those in command to the levy troops scattered

Archer holding additional arrows in his bow hand depicted on the Bayeux Tapestry. Detail of the Bayeux Tapestry, eleventh century, with special permission from the City of Bayeux.

throughout the district to inform the individual warriors of a threat and to order them to assemble. The Norwegian Gulaþing law states that if there are tidings of war, an iron war arrow shall be carried from landed man to landed man day and night along the coast, and that a wooden arrow was carried inland and up the fjords. Men to whom the arrow was carried were required to assemble within five days or else be outlawed.[56]

War arrows were used to call together fighting men by the king against foreign enemies[57] but also by farmers to call together fighting men against the king, in cases where the king approached to settle a grievance against the men of the district.[58]

The Norwegian law codes called for arrows to be used to assemble a þing in the district to deal with a case of homicide or serious personal injury.[59] The nature of these arrows,

whether to assemble men for war or for þing, is not known.

Some have speculated whether Vikings used arrows to deliver a payload, such as fire. A flaming arrow is mentioned in a legendary saga, created by a priest to kill a man defended by magic, and Moorish sources tell us that Viking raiders used flaming arrows to set the mosque in Seville alight during their raids in the year 845. An arrow found at Birka has been interpreted as one that might have carried burning material.[60] The evidence, when taken together, suggests that some Vikings were familiar with the concept of flaming arrows, although it seems their use was limited.

OTHER ARCHERY GEAR

Throughout history, archers have used quivers to carry their arrows and to keep them readily at hand. Viking archers, likewise, probably used quivers, called örmalr or örmælir (literally, an arrow knapsack).[61] There are several references to them in the literary sources,[62] where archers are described having a bow in the hand and a quiver on the back.[63] Oddr, an archer of such repute that his nickname was Arrow-Odd (Örvar-Oddr), carried his quiver wherever he went. When inside, men hung their quivers on a nail within easy reach.[64]

Pictorial sources are sparse, giving rise to the usual-coin toss problem. The Bayeux Tapestry, a source that must be used with care, shows quivers typically at the belt, with at least one example where the quiver appears to be at the back.[65] Olaus Magnus's Historia de Gentibus Septentrionalibus, a very late work that must be used cautiously, shows examples of belt quivers,[66] as well as examples of men apparently carrying a bundle of arrows at their back with no obvious means for containing them.[67] A few archers are shown with additional arrows in their hands, both in Olaus and in the Bayeux Tapestry,[68] yet most of the archers in the Olaus illustrations have only the arrow on their bow, with no additional arrows to be seen.

Tellingly, the word for quiver does not appear in either the Sagas of Icelanders or in Heimskringla, two lengthy collections of sagas that often mention archers and archery. We have no satisfactory explanation for that absence at this time, except that often the sagas do not mention what was considered to be the norm. When the texts tell of many arrows being shot, there is rarely any explanation of where the arrows were stored or how they were made ready to be drawn.

Gunnarr, when being ambushed, threw his arrows down on the ground, presumably so they would be in easy reach, but there is no mention of how he carried them in the moments leading up to the ambush as he was riding on horseback.[69] In the subsequent battle, he was able to wound many and kill a few, suggesting he traveled with more than a handful of arrows.

The archaeological evidence for quivers is not definitive. Leather fragments found at Hedeby have been interpreted as the remains of a quiver.[70] Regardless, bundles of arrows had to be carried by archers in some fashion, if not in a quiver.

Another puzzle is the protective gear worn by archers. Modern archers routinely wear protection on their arms and fingers against the ravages of the bowstring. There seems to be no evidence for this kind of protection being used by Viking archers, either in literary sources, pictorial sources, or archaeological sources. Perhaps Viking archers didn't need this kind of protection. Perhaps they drew their bows somewhat differently so that this protection was unnecessary, a speculation discussed later in the chapter.

WHO USED A BOW?

The literary sources make clear that archery was the activity of kings and high-status men. The poem *Rígsþula* tells of the origins of the three social classes in Nordic society, and it was the man of the highest class who was bending elm bows, twisting bowstrings, and making arrows when Rígr visited his household.[71]

During naval battles, it is mentioned that kings often fought with their bows.[72] When King Sigurðr and King Eysteinn compared their accomplishments, Sigurðr said that

archery was an accomplishment of leading men and claimed to be a stronger archer than Eysteinn.[73] These and other vignettes[74] point to archery being a skill prized by and expected of kings and leading men.

Additionally, the king's men were a part of these royal activities. Archery was said to be a sport for the king's men.[75] The descriptions of the large battles in *Heimskringla* often tell of arrows shot by the men near the king, which likely included the king's chosen men, but individual archers are rarely identified.

Similarly, the men of the king's levy likely used bows in battle. Bows and arrows were required weapons for the king's levy, with one bow and twenty-four arrows required for each pair of rowing positions on the levy ship. It is often said that in naval battles, missiles, including arrows and other projectiles, fell like hail upon the ship. It is this aspect of arrows that is featured in kennings for arrows: *hail of the bow string* and *the cutting hail of the bow*.[76]

While skill in archery was a part of the upper-class life and expected of the elite, other classes used bows as well. The king's levy was drawn from the farmers of the district. When the farmer's army fought against King Óláfr, the battle began with the farmers shooting arrows and spears at the king's army as they shouted their battle cry. As the lines advanced and met, those in the rear of the farmer's army continued to shoot arrows and to throw spears and other missiles.[77]

Gunnarr Hámundarson, the farmer at Hlíðarendi, was said to shoot with a bow better than anyone else, and it was also said that he was the archer to whom other archers were compared.[78] Yet as we will see later in this chapter, archery was probably different in Iceland than in other Viking lands.

The mythological poems tell us that gods used bows. Ullr is called the god of archery, hunting, and skiing.[79] Skaði, the daughter of a giant and the wife of a god, hunts with a bow and skis.[80]

It is not only among gods and giants that there is a connection between skiing and

Archers on skis. Derived from Olaus Magnus (1555).

archery. Among men, too, there seems to have been an association. In the literary sources, it is mentioned that several men were skilled in both archery and skiing.[81] Later pictorial sources show men on skis hunting with bows.[82] The nature of this connection between archery and skiing might offer us some clues into how Vikings actually used their bows, a topic we discuss later in this chapter.

Taken together, the evidence suggests that archery held a special place in Norse society. There was even a runic character for *bow* in the younger futhark: *ýr*, standing for yew tree and, by implication, the archer's bow.[83] It was a weapon favored by the upper classes, and as we will see in the next section, a weapon used like no other Viking weapon by the elite. Yet the bow was used by gods, farmers, and legendary heroes, as well.

### VIKING-AGE ICELAND AND ARCHERY
Viking-age Iceland differed in significant ways from other Viking lands. That difference had an impact on archery and on a number of other aspects of combat that will be discussed here and in subsequent chapters. It makes sense to pause and highlight those differences and how they impacted archery, realizing that

these differences will also impact topics in later chapters.

On one hand, the status of archery in Iceland was high, in that it was an indicator of a man's position in life. The Icelandic law code *Grágás* states that a man must be able to draw a bow if he is to bear witness.[84] A man unable to draw a bow would find it difficult to participate in governmental or legal affairs.

Yet on the other hand, the need for archery was much diminished in Iceland. Iceland was unique among Viking lands in that it had no king. As discussed in the mindset chapter, the settlers of Iceland set up a government without a central authority. Thus Iceland had no kings or earls, no *hirð* or levy, and no mass dynastic battles or naval battles. Additionally, Iceland had no elite level of society. It is among these groups and in these kinds of battles that archery played the largest role, and so Icelanders had much less use for archery in combat.

Additionally, Iceland had few game animals that could be hunted with a bow. With little to hunt, Icelanders had much less use for archery as a means for gathering food. Further, the trees best suited for making bows did not grow in any abundance in Viking-age Iceland.[85]

That is not to imply that archery had no place in Icelandic society in the Viking age, but it does suggest that it simply was a less important skill for either combat or everyday life than in other Viking lands.

Perhaps this difference explains why few arrowheads are found in Iceland, compared to other weapons. Counting up the Viking-age weapon finds in graves and house sites in Iceland, there are 0.18 arrows found for each spear found.[86] In contrast, at a cemetery of the general population in Gotland[87] and at the garrison at Birka, the ratio is about 10 arrows found for every spear.[88] This suggests a much higher prevalence of arrows among the general farmer population and among the military population in Sweden than in Iceland.

Additionally, the arrowheads found in Iceland do not include examples of the narrow one intended for martial use (Rygh 542). Instead, they are all leaf-shaped arrowheads (Rygh 539) and one bifurcated V-shaped head (Rygh 551),[89] which suggests less use of the bow for martial purposes in Iceland than in other Viking lands.

Perhaps this observation explains why Ullr, the god of archery and hunting, plays such a limited role in the mythology as recorded in the Icelandic literary sources. If archery and hunting were of less importance in Iceland than in other Scandinavian lands, it would not be surprising for the god of archery and hunting to play a lesser role in the mythology as it was recorded in written form by Icelanders.

If we look at the archers mentioned in the *Sagas of Icelanders* who use their bows in Iceland, the majority appear to be Norwegians visiting Iceland,[90] rather than Icelanders,[91] further strengthening the notion that the bow was not often used in Iceland.

A common situation in which a bow was used in Iceland was to defend one's home. Gunnarr Hámundarson shot from a window in the loft of his house, keeping many attackers at bay until his bowstring was cut. Gunnarr Hlífarson built the outer door of his house with a small opening through which he could

Top: An archer on skis thought to be the god Ullr as depicted on the Böksta stone U 855. Derived from Bengt A. Lundberg, *Detalj av runstenen, skidåkare med pilbåge*. Creative Commons. Bottom: The Ýr rune is the bent bow as stated in *Þrídeilur*, the Icelandic rune poem.

shoot, protected by the door. An unnamed archer hid in the chimney to defend the house against Hörðr and his band of outlaws.[92] Episodes like these suggest that perhaps the bow was more commonly used as a defensive weapon of the home than as a tool of combat by Viking-age Icelanders.

HOW BOWS WERE USED

Outside of Iceland, the evidence for using bows for hunting in the Viking age seems extensive. Numerous place-names based on Ullr, the god of hunting, exist in Norway and Sweden. Specialized hunting arrows are found in archaeology.[93]

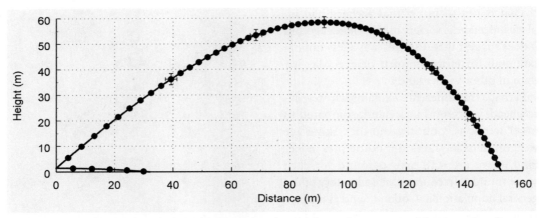

Predicted trajectory of a looped arrow shot (top: elevation=45 degrees) versus a straight arrow shot (bottom: elevation=0 degrees) using a computer model based on the Hedeby bow and arrows. Symbols along the trajectory mark the timing of the arrow flight: dots indicate 0.1 second intervals, and crosses indicate 1 second intervals.

The bow was used extensively in large-scale battles of all kinds on land and sea, a topic discussed in greater detail in a later chapter. In dynastic land battles, the fighting often began with an exchange of arrows and spears as the lines approached each other.[94] Once the lines made contact and blade fighting began, sources suggest that archers stood on high ground and shot into the mêlée.[95] This use of the bow would require excellent accuracy at directed targets, rather than a rain of arrows, to avoid hitting the fighters on the archer's side. Additionally, men in the rear ranks, out of range of their blade weapons, shot arrows and all kinds of projectiles over and into the opposing lines.[96]

In battles against armies with mounted cavalry, kings put archers on high ground to defend against mounted troops that ran in, attacked, and quickly ran back out.[97]

Notably, at the ends of battles, projectiles were often used, with arrows falling thick as snow. Yet the stories suggest some accurate and directed shooting in this chaos; King Hákon was hit with an arrow at the battle of Storð, shot by an archer who called out, "Make room for the king's slayer!" as he shot. The arrow proved fatal.[98]

As the losing side fled a mass battle, it seems likely that projectiles such as arrows would be used against them. In one case, archers from the fleeing army were ordered to high ground to provide cover for the retreat, yet they, too, fled with the rest of the army.[99] Bows were used against enemy combatants even after the battle was over, perhaps to get in one more kill before laying down arms.[100]

These examples suggest that in mass battles, archers used both a rain of arrows against the enemy host as well as shots that were accurate and carefully directed against specific targets. These different kinds of shots had distinct names in the ancient language, and they require different use of the bow, as discussed in a later section.

In battles fought around a fortification, archers shot arrows from the fortification into the attackers, taking advantage of their height to shoot down from the safety of the fort's defenses.[101] At the same time, attackers shot arrows and other missiles into the fortifications, hoping to find a vulnerable target using the only weapons available to them that were likely to hit the target.[102]

During naval battles, it is often mentioned that there were showers of missiles, including arrows.[103] King Hringr had many champions and skilled archers with him in a naval battle.[104] The archers were placed near the mast,[105] shooting over the heads of the fighters in the bow who were attempting to board the enemy vessel, as described in more detail in the mass battle chapter. The king and his elite archers often stood on the raised afterdeck at the stern, shooting arrows over the heads of the men in his ship.[106] These details give us important clues about the range of the bow, the accuracy of the shots, and the type of shots used, all of which will be discussed later in the chapter. Additionally, it says something about the skills of the archers, able to shoot over the heads of their comrades on a rocking platform and hit a specific target on a different rocking platform.

OTHER ASPECTS OF THE USE OF THE BOW

One aspect of using a bow in a battle that remains unclear is how many arrows an archer might have had available to him, whether it be a naval battle, a dynastic battle, a mêlée, or an ambush. The literary sources tell us that battles could be lengthy. During long fights, it is said that the archers were not stingy with their arrows and that the king shot arrows from his ship for a long time. In the mass battle at Brávellir, Haddr and Hróaldr specifically targeted Ubbi and put two dozen arrows into him.[107] How many arrows did an archer carry, and was that number different for an archer preparing for a mass battle or naval battle than for an archer like Gunnarr traveling from his farm?

The Gulaþing law required twenty-four arrows for each bow on the king's levy ships, which is probably the best estimate we are likely to find. *Hirðskrá* adds that a *hirð* man (part of the king's bodyguard) should have thirty-six arrows. When Gunnarr was ambushed, he was able to wound many and kill a few, suggesting he traveled with more than a handful of arrows[108] since there is no mention of any of the ambushers shooting arrows back at him that he might reuse.

One wonders how long it took a man carrying a bow to prepare it to shoot. The legendary sagas often say a man traveled with his bow and quiver on his back, or with his bow in his hand and quiver on his back, or even with bow and quiver in one hand.[109]

It seems likely that a longbow was carried unstrung, which takes the tension off the bow to prevent the wood from taking a set that reduces its ability to store energy and thus reduces its range. An expert archer states that stringing a bow, even on horseback, is a matter of mere moments.[110]

The literary sources tell of archers bending the bow (*benda upp bogann*). This phrase seems to imply the bow is being prepared to shoot. In some cases, the phrase seems to imply stringing the bow, while in others it implies laying on the arrow.

An example of the first meaning is when Gunnarr Hámundarson prepared his bow, presumably by stringing it, and then threw his arrows on the ground in easy reach to prepare for an ambush. An example of the second is when Gunnarr Þiðrandabani laid an arrow to his bow and then bent the bow to shoot and kill Þiðrandi.[111] Either way, it appears to be the work of a moment to prepare the bow to be shot.

TRAINING AND SPORT

Unlike other weapons, the bow is more technical in its use. It requires more skill than just raw power and a good swing. To use a bow, it would seem that one would need practice, and the literary sources suggest just that. Ketill practiced archery at a range (*skotbakki*), and Þórðr was said to be more skilled at archery than others and taught them archery. Grímr spent time with the king's men training archery, and the king went to a range to practice archery. Saxo tells us that men of Roller and Erik trained in archery.[112] Unlike other weapons, where there are few if any mentions of training or instruction, archery seems to be a skill that was taught and practiced in the Viking age.

The nature of the archery range is not known, but literary and archaeological sources suggest the use of blunt arrows called *bakkakólfr*.[113] The etymology of the word suggests a rounded-tip arrow,[114] a type found in archaeology, as discussed earlier.

Arrows penetrating a shield as depicted on the Franks Casket, an 8th century Anglo-Saxon chest covered with decorative carvings. ©The Trustees of the British Museum. All rights reserved.

Additionally, archery competitions were a sport, often associated with kings and their courts, where the king judged the competition and awarded the prize.[115] Archery was different from other sports in that one could be an accomplished archer even if one weren't powerful,[116] a prerequisite with most other Viking activities. With perhaps the exception of *fang*, we do not find other weapons or combatives used in sports and competition in the same way as archery.

## CAPABILITIES OF THE BOW

The available sources suggest that the bow was used in a variety of ways, and several kinds of shots are described. Both long-range and short-range shots are used in battles. Shots are described that have pinpoint accuracy, as are some where the accuracy did not much matter since the goal was to create a rain of arrows on the enemy.

## POWER

Power was valued in all combative Viking activities, and that includes archery. As we just discussed, power was not necessary; one could be a good archer even though one was not powerful. Yet the literary sources tell of powerful shots,[117] described using the word *harðskeytr*, whose literal meaning is hard missile,[118] such as Einarr's ability to shoot a blunt practice arrow through a hanging oxhide.[119]

Pictorial sources such as the Bayeux Tapestry and carvings on the Franks Casket from the eighth century show arrows whose heads have penetrated a shield.[120] In the literary sources, there are examples where the arrow penetrated the shield to the degree shown in the pictorial sources (up to where the arrowhead joins the shaft), and these shots were able to kill the man behind the shield. Saxo says the men from Gotland strung their bows so hard that their arrows could pierce a shield.[121]

Other shots described in the literary sources not involving a shield also suggest powerful shots penetrating far into the target,[122] although some of these are hard to accept as anything other than heroic exaggeration, such as Pálnatóki's arrow that entered the king's butt and exited his mouth as he leaned over a fire.[123]

RANGE

Range goes hand in hand with power. All other things being equal, a shot released with more power (and thus higher velocity leaving the bow) will travel farther, but rarely are all things equal. It is a straightforward ballistics problem, and a key factor that comes into play is the type of shot: a straight shot aimed directly at the target versus a looping shot aimed into the air.

The looping shot has greater range, reduced accuracy, and a longer time of flight. Again and again in mass battles and naval battles, we read that arrows and missiles fell on the combatants like rain or hail or snow,[124] suggesting the arrows from looped shots fell out of the sky on the combatants without a particular target in mind. It is this looping shot that is seen in the carving of the archer on the Franks Casket, as well as for the archers depicted in the Bayeux Tapestry.[125] It is a shot particularly useful in mass battle, where many targets are grouped together and hitting any particular one is less important.

A looped shot flies through the air for a long time, making it more likely to be deflected off target by wind and other variables. Additionally, the long time of flight gives the target a longer period to prepare a defense, as discussed in the spear chapter, yet in the chaos of a mass battle it is unlikely a combatant would be able to track all the incoming shots.

The best-preserved Viking bow, Hedeby Bow 1, is thought to represent a typical Viking bow. The estimated draw weight is between 82 and 102 pounds, based on a reconstruction of the bow. Using this reconstruction, light arrows flew 190 m (208 yd) and heavier arrows about 160 m (175 yd).[126]

A simple computer model of the Hedeby bow and arrow predicts a range around 150 m (164 yd),[127] similar to what a replica Hedeby bow and arrow achieved. The time of flight predicted by the model for a looped shot is 5.7 sec.

In contrast, the straight, level shot has shorter range, better accuracy, and a shorter time of flight. In a mass battle, when archers shot into the mêlée while blade fighting was occurring between both sides, it would seem that straight shooting would be required to achieve the accuracy needed to ensure the archer didn't hit someone on his own side.[128] Straight, accurate shooting is called *beinskeyttr* in the old language, literally straight missile.[129] A straight shot hits the target so soon after leaving the bow that the target, even if he is aware of the shot, will have a difficult time making a block.

The computer model of the Hedeby bow suggests a straight-level shot has a range of about 20 m (22 yd), with a time of flight of about 0.4 sec,[130] a short period for the target to prepare a defense.

The literary sources offer some additional clues to help us estimate typical ranges. At one extreme is the definition of a bowshot in the law codes. A bowshot (*ördrag*) is a legal term that defines a distance used for certain kinds of legal actions. For example, a confiscation court in which an outlaw's property is taken away must be held within a bowshot of the homefield wall of the outlaw. A late addition to *Grágás* defines a bowshot to be 240 legal fathoms, thought to be about 400 m (440 yd).[131]

This range seems improbable for a Viking bow. But the legal bowshot also seems to carry the sense that the distance defined a sanctuary (*örskotshelgr*, having the literal meaning of arrow shot sanctuary) around a home or a church, and that anyone within the distance of a bowshot was safe from an attack. A legal case against Örn gave him immunity as long as he stayed within *örskotshelgr* from his home. The sons of Önundr, wanting to avenge their father, waited until Örn left the *örskotshelgr* and killed him, and the killing was deemed to be legal.[132] So perhaps it is not surprising that the distance was overstated to maximize the protection it afforded.

The descriptions of naval battles also provide some clues to typical ranges. When Finnr shot at King Óláfr, he was shooting the combined lengths of Eiríkr jarl's ship and King Óláfr's ship, *Ormr inn langi* (Long Serpent).

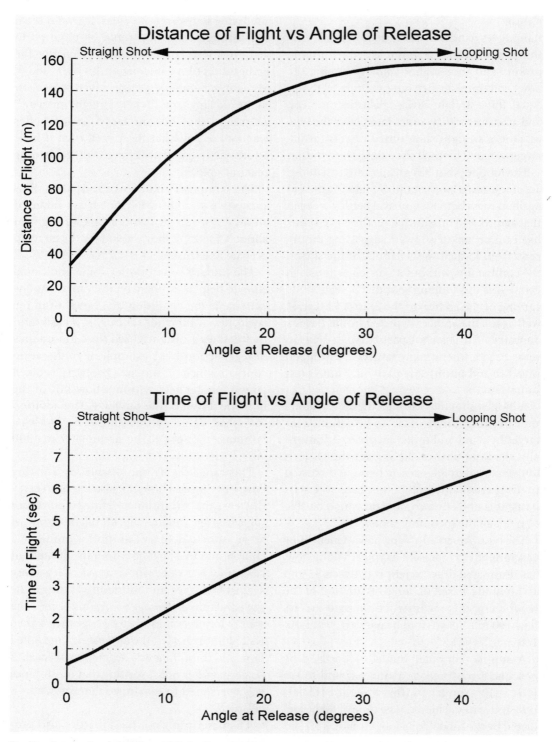

Predicted range (top) and time of flight (bottom) for an arrow shot with various elevations of the bow.

Óláfr's ship was a *dreki* with 34 *rúm*, suggesting a length well over 34 m (110 ft), as discussed later in the mass battles chapter. Eiríkr's ship is also described as being large, but it is unlikely it was as large as *Ormr inn langi*. So Finnr's accurate shot that flew over the heads of the men in each ship and hit and broke Einarr's bow out of his hands[133] was probably on the order of 50 to 60 m (55 to 65 yd).

Since many of the archers stood near the mast,[134] one might expect that many of the shots were at a shorter range, perhaps as little as 10 m (11 yds).

Another example of extremely long shots was in an archery competition. Næframaðr's final shot was a looping one that flew so far no one could see where it landed.[135]

While the bow was primarily a long-range weapon, it was also used at very short range, often when no other weapon was handy or when it was the weapon most readily at hand. When one of his men implied cowardice on the part of the king, King Óláfr threatened the man by laying an arrow on the string and aiming it at the man. Örn, outraged at a legal proceeding at the door of the house he was visiting, grabbed his bow and shot an arrow into the departing party, a distance probably no greater than a few footsteps. Men stood inside the door of their house ready to shoot arrows when unwelcome guests called.[136]

There are also examples in literary sources that suggest there was a range that was simply too short for effective use of the bow, presumably due to the situation rather than to a limitation of the bow to shoot a short distance. As the ambush against him developed, Gunnarr shot his bow as long as he could. He then dropped his bow and switched to his *atgeirr* and sword as his opponents charged him. In retelling his dream that foretold the ambush, Gunnarr says he shot the enemies in front until they came too close for him to use his bow.[137] One can imagine that as the ambushers drew closer, they started becoming more of a threat to Gunnarr with their bladed weapons, causing him to drop the bow and take up other

weapons, rather than because an arrow shot at close range from a bow was somehow less effective. Archers, like other warriors, sometimes carried other weapons with them, presumably for those times when the bow was not the best weapon for the fight.[138] At the time he was ambushed, Gunnarr was apparently carrying *atgeirr*, sword, shield, bow, and arrows.[139]

In an ambush on a frozen fjord, the sons of Þorbrandr ran over the ice to a rock standing above it, where they had good footing. Steinþórr and his men, slipping on the ice, had a difficult position. Six Norwegians with Steinþórr went away from the rock on the ice until they were in range (*skotmál*) and shot arrows at the exposed men on the rock.[140] The episode suggests there is a range that is too short for effective use of the bow.

ACCURACY

In some situations, such as mass battles, accuracy may have been less important. In a mass formation, it is just as good to hit the man standing next to the one aimed at. But other situations require accurate shooting, and the literary sources tell of some very accurate archers, suggesting that accuracy was quite important to Viking archers.[141]

Gunnarr was said to be able to hit everything he aimed at with his bow.[142] Án demonstrated some precision shooting when he saw a fire and thought someone was attacking his sheep. As he came closer, Án saw a young man who was eating meat by the fire, and he thought the man was not very wary. Án shot three arrows: the first hit the meat the man was eating, the second hit his plate, and the third hit the handle of his knife—precision shooting to teach the fellow a lesson.[143]

Literary sources suggest that very skilled archers could shoot accurately even with long, looping shots. Oddr demonstrated his skill in a hunting competition by making all his kill shots over the heads of the other competing hunters. In an archery competition, Sjólfr released a straight shot that hit the target, a gold game piece at extreme range, but Næframaðr demonstrated his superior skill by releasing a

Top: Modern-day archery, using: high draw; three finger draw; sighted shooting; sideways stance; arrow on the inside of the bow. Photo: Adobe Stock. Bottom: Archers depicted on pictures stones, such as the Hunninge I stone, rarely show enough detail to allow any interpretation of draw method. Derived from Harald Faith-Ell, *Hunninge I*. Creative Commons.

looping shot so high that it seemed to disappear from sight yet still nailed the game piece from the same extreme range.[144] These and other episodes suggest that even over long distances, skilled archers coveted accuracy,[145] which was also prized by kings.[146]

SPEED OF SHOOTING

An aspect of archery that remains a puzzle is the matter of how rapidly an archer could shoot. On one hand, as Einarr released accurate shots against Eiríkr, the earl was able to ask

a question between two shots and issue an order between the next two shots, which suggests that while Einarr was fast, he was not fantastically fast. Gunnarr, called the best archer, dropped his bow when his enemies came close, suggesting even he could not shoot fast enough to deal with close-range opponents.[147]

The literary sources do not provide additional evidence that allows us to form a clear picture of the rate of shooting of a skilled archer. The scant evidence suggests a few seconds or less between accurate, long-range shots by a Viking-age archer.

HOW THE BOW WAS DRAWN

In this section we look at the details of drawing and shooting the bow. Other Viking weapons could be used relying solely on power and a good swing, which is not the case for bow and arrow. Shooting an arrow requires technique; there are technical aspects to use of the tool. Since the available sources lack any detailed description, we enter the domain of the coin-toss problem, a domain filled with speculations.

Before beginning the discussion, we ask the reader to put aside for a moment any modern preconceptions about how a bow should be shot. In modern competitive archery, and in modern depictions of the use of a bow in popular entertainments, the bow is used in much the same way: using a high draw, with the draw hand near the face; using a three-finger draw to pull and release the string; resting the arrow on the opposite side of the bow from the draw hand; standing sideways; aiming by sighting down the arrow; and holding the string while aiming.

If we limit ourselves to narrow sources when studying how Viking-age bows were drawn, we find only two pictorial examples: the Böksta stone and the Klinte Hunninge I stone.[148] Neither image provides enough detail to form a clear picture of how the bow was drawn.

And so we must cast our net more widely to gather information: images from manuscripts and tapestries and books that are from outside the Viking lands or outside the Viking era. We expect, as with many aspects of Viking combat,

A speculative reconstruction of the Viking-age method of drawing the bow using: low-draw; two-finger draw; forward stance; arrow on the outside of the bow. Photo: William R. Short.

Low draw method of shooting the bow depicted on the Franks Casket. ©The Trustees of the British Museum. All rights reserved.

that no one draw method was universal. Accordingly, we seek the common thread that runs through the various techniques used for drawing a bow. And we see certain aspects of the technique repeatedly, albeit not exclusively.

### LOW DRAW

Pictorial sources showing archers depict the draw hand pulled back to the chest or even the belly in a low draw.[149] This position implies that the archer is not aiming using the modern method, but is more likely using instinctive shooting, relying on muscle memory gained from practice to develop the ability to shoot with accuracy to hit the target without relying on sighting.

### ARROW OUTSIDE

Most often, we see the arrow placed on the outside of the bow, on the same side of the bow as the draw hand.[150] An examination of the various illustrations suggests this position is not simply due to the artists' limited technique but rather is an attempt to show the action accurately, regardless of which side of the archer is toward the viewer and which hand is used for the draw.

Top: Arrow on the outside of the bow depicted on the Bayeux Tapestry. Detail of the Bayeux Tapestry, eleventh century, with special permission from the City of Bayeux. Bottom: Arrow on the outside of the bow re-created by a modern archer. Photo: William R. Short.

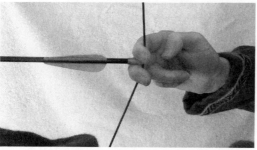

Top: Two finger draw depicted on the Bayeux Tapestry. Detail of the Bayeux Tapestry, eleventh century, with special permission from the City of Bayeux. Bottom: Two finger draw re-created by a modern archer.

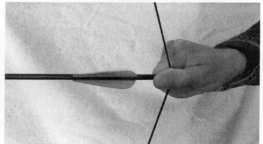

Top: Pinch grip draw as depicted in *The Life and Miracles of St. Edmund MS M.736*, a twelfth-century English manuscript. Photo: The Morgan Library & Museum, New York. Bottom: Pinch grip draw re-created by a modern archer.

### TWO-FINGER DRAW

In the cases where there is enough detail in the image to discern one draw from another, the draw most often seen uses two fingers, looped around the string above and below the arrow.[151]

Surprisingly, several images show a pinch draw, with the arrow pinched between thumb and forefinger.[152] This would seem to require tremendous grip strength to draw a heavyweight bow and would seem to slow the process of nocking and drawing, but perhaps our modern mindset is intruding. Our own testing seemed to confirm the utility of the draw.[153]

### PARALLEL STANCE AND BODY ANGLE

The images show the archer with his feet more or less parallel, and his body facing the target.[154] Support for this stance is strengthened by considering the connection between archery and skiing.

### TECHNIQUE SUMMARY

With the limited sources available, we do not think it possible to come to any final conclusion. We could speculate on additional variants; however, they would not be based on historical sources but rather modern efficiency.

Much of the research on drawing the bow outlined here was performed by Lars Andersen, a Danish artist and archer who has spent

Parallel forward focused stance depicted on the Bayeux Tapestry. Detail of the Bayeux Tapestry, eleventh century, with special permission from the City of Bayeux.

Low draw method of shooting the bow re-created by Lars Andersen. Photo: Lars Andersen.

years studying the sources and testing the approach. Andersen has demonstrated that this approach to shooting the bow, as seen in the pictorial sources, can provide the power, accuracy, and speed of shooting described in literary sources.[155]

It may simply be that there was no one standard method that Vikings used when drawing their bows. The common thread that seems to run through the sources is: a forward-focused stance, a low draw, arrow placement on the outside of the bow, and a two-finger draw.

SUMMARY

In this chapter we have summarized what is known about Viking archery. The sources are limited, but they show us that the bow was a weapon used for combat and hunting. In combat, is was capable of raining death on the enemy in mass battles on land or at sea. Yet the same weapon was also capable of precision shooting and exquisite accuracy in the hands of a skilled archer.

Unlike other weapons, it was also used for sport and competition, especially among the warrior elites, with practice ranges used for training. Skill in archery was prized by kings. And unlike other weapons, there was a god of archery.

This evidence suggests the importance of archery to the Viking-age people, an importance not reflected to the same degree in the available literary sources, perhaps because these sources almost universally were written by Icelandic authors in a land where archery was probably not much needed and not much utilized.

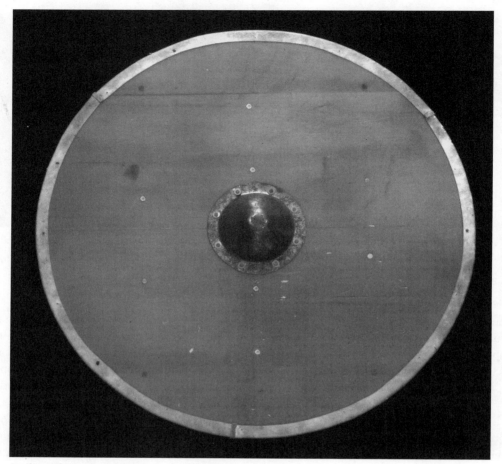

Replica Viking-age shield. Photo: William R. Short.

# SHIELD

INTRODUCTION

The shield was the primary combative defense of the Viking warrior. It was a dynamic defense, as opposed to the passive defense of armor. The literary sources strongly suggest that a man without a shield was, quite simply, defenseless.[1] Even berserks, who went into battle without armor because weapons couldn't bite them, carried shields.[2] A berserk biting the edge of his shield in preparation for combat is mentioned numerous times in the literary sources[3] and is famously depicted on a Lewis chessman, part of a carved ivory chess set from the twelfth century found in the Hebrides. [4]

Berserks are said to be the men of Óðinn, and Óðinn himself states in *Hávamál* that for defense, one should rely on a shield. The importance of being able to wield a shield is made clear in the law code *Grágás*, which states that a man must be able to wield a shield if he is to bear witness in a legal proceeding.[5] A man unable to wield a shield would find it difficult to participate in governmental or legal affairs.

It would seem that with few exceptions, every Viking had a shield and every Viking carried a shield and relied on it for defense.

SOURCES

Our study of shields is complicated. While there are many archaeological finds, they are, in virtually all cases, just fragments. We have the coin-toss problem; for many aspects of a Viking shield, the sample size is too small to draw any firm conclusions.

Pictorial sources, such as tapestries, picture stones, and jewelry figures, can offer us clues about size, shape, carry method, and usage yet require additional sources to strengthen them. Perspective is the art of representing a three-dimensional object on a two-dimensional surface, and it was an art poorly known to the Vikings. It can be difficult to reinterpret the two-dimensional figure back into three dimensions, thus deciphering the images can be challenging. The artist may have depicted using the simplest method to show a large round object without obscuring the person holding the shield, who may have been the center of the artist's creation.

Our usual literary sources tell of numerous episodes in which shields were used but offer few clear details on how it was done. The poem *Waltharius*, written in Latin in the tenth century, tells of battles set in Germanic lands centuries earlier, and some of the characters in the poem also appear in legendary sagas and in the Eddas. It is a source we turn to reluctantly because of the distance that separates the poem from Viking times and lands, yet it fills in some important missing pieces on shields and their use.

Other valuable sources include skaldic kennings, which can provide clues to the nature of shields and their use. Lastly, biomechanics aid us by informing us about how the human body performs using a Viking-age shield.

THE SHIELD IN SOCIETY

Quite simply, a Viking shield is a wooden disc with a handgrip in back and a dome-shaped iron boss in front to protect the hand. The old Icelandic word for shield is *skjöldr*, an ancient word common to all Germanic languages.[6] The origin of the word is not clear, and it has been suggested that it derives from the word for shelter, although alternatives have been suggested.

While there are numerous kennings for shields, it is not a tool much used by the principal mythological entities. Ullr is called the god of the shield, with little additional explanation. The Valkyrie Skuld carries a shield. Giants, such as Hrugnir and Hrymr, carry shields.[7] The hall of Óðinn is roofed with shields according to some sources, and has shields hung on the walls according to others.[8]

A unique group is associated with the shield: the *skjaldmær*, often literally translated as shield maiden. It is a topic discussed in more detail in the mass battle chapter. Women warriors, such as Hlegunn who led a band of warriors,[9] were called *skjaldmær*. These women have sometimes been associated with Valkyries, the paranormal women warriors who interfere with battle to lead to Óðinn the chosen warriors who were slain in battle.[10]

It seems to have been routine for a Viking to carry a shield. Without a shield, he was *berskjaldaðr*: an unshielded man. The word is a portmanteau of *bare* and *shielded*. More generally, a *berskjaldaðr* man was a vulnerable man, and the word is used in this broader sense in the literary sources.[11] In instances where a Viking had no shield, he compensated and used some other attribute as his shield. When Þormóðr prepared for the battle at Stiklarstaðir, the king saw he had no shield and asked him why he was not dressed for battle like other men and if he thought, perhaps, that his opponents did not know how to fight. Þormóðr replied that his axe would be both his shield and his armor.[12]

Literary and archaeological sources tell us that Vikings liked showy things. They dressed

to kill, both figuratively and literally. They favored bright clothing with exotic materials, and that favor also applied to their weapons, their riding gear, their jewelry, and more.

The shield was probably no exception. More than a mere survival tool, the shield was the largest surfaced item a Viking carried on his person. Numerous literary accounts tell of fine, stylish shields,[13] many colored red,[14] and some even parti-colored blue and gold,[15] some adorned with gold,[16] and some with precious stones.[17] Some shields were marked with a figure that may have identified the owner,[18] and Vikings were sometimes recognized by the shields they carried.[19]

The shield may have been the largest surface, apart from, perhaps, the battle standard, to distinguish one side from the other in a large battle. The marking of shields to identify sides in a battle does not often appear in the literary sources. One example occurs before the battle at Stiklarstaðir. King Óláfr told his men to mark *herkuml* on their helmets and shields, a war-mark in the form of the cross.[20]

Additionally, the literary sources have numerous examples of the shield serving to represent sides in a battle. When Eyvindr was accused by the king of being his enemy, Eyvindr replied that he had never played two shields: he had never served two masters. Men spoke of serving under the shield of the king, and a man who switched sides in the middle of fight was said to have switched shields.[21]

SALIENT FEATURES OF A SHIELD

The Viking-age shield is based on a simple design and is made from simple materials. It seems probable that a man competent enough to make his own house could also make a shield, and most Vikings made their own houses.

The best source of information on the physical nature of the shield is archaeology. But it is a troublesome source, in part because so few shields survive. For reasons not fully understood, far fewer defensive tools, such as shields, mail, and helmets, are found in archaeological excavations than offensive tools, such as

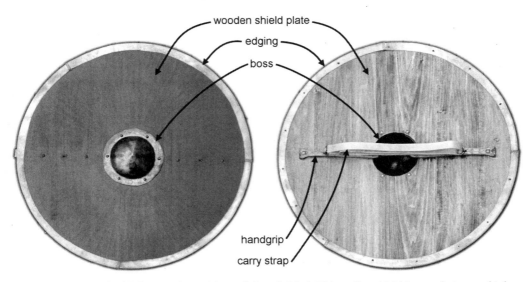

The parts of a Viking shield, front and rear (shown left and right). This replica shield has no facing, and it has a speculative reconstruction of a leather carry strap, which partially obscures the wooden handgrip crossing the back of the shield. Photo: William R. Short.

swords, axes, and spears. In Norway for example, thousands of Viking swords and fragments have been found but only a few dozens of Viking shields and fragments, and most of these are from the same Gokstad burial site in Norway.

One reason so few shields are found is that the largest part of the shield is organic, which decomposes quickly in the earth. But other factors are likely at work as well. Shields from other lands and other times are far more plentiful in the archaeological record, such as the early Anglo-Saxon society in Britain, where shields are common grave finds and where hundreds of shields have been excavated.[22]

Yet in Scandinavia, such finds are exceedingly rare. Most of the finds are fragments of shields. In only two locations have more-or-less intact shields been found: at Trelleborg in Denmark and at Gokstad. The Trelleborg shield was found outside the fortification on the site, in a water-logged area near the river, which preserved the wooden parts of the shield. The Gokstad shields were part of a high-status ship burial. Of the sixty-four shields that lined the ship when it was buried, only four survived relatively complete, pre-served by the layer of clay around the burial site.[23]

Viking-age shields possibly were not only tools for combat but also large personal items intended to be displayed: epic and beautiful symbols of the owner's accomplishments.[24] In the literary sources, there are numerous episodes of shields hanging on walls,[25] given as gifts,[26] and displayed on a ship.[27] Perhaps some of these shields were intended more for display and less for battle.

To clarify our picture of Viking shields, it is possible to examine shield finds from lands outside of Scandinavia, including lands to the east or west. However, as discussed in the sources chapter, we are strict in our use of narrow sources where possible. Using shield finds from places that may have had differences in cultures and in ways of combat may twist our understanding of Viking shields. In this chapter, we try to avoid material from other lands so as to not distort the picture, although, as we will see, achieving that goal is difficult.

Other sources that can guide us in our understanding of Viking shields include poetic references to shields. Shields are called *morðsólar* (of the war-sun), and *vígtungls* (of

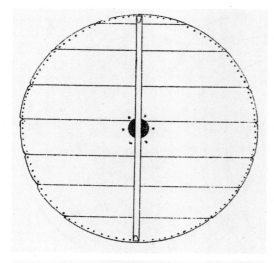

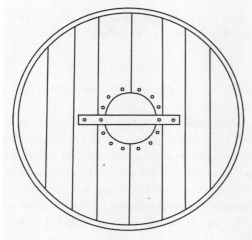

Top: Butted planks making up a Viking-age shield from the Gokstad burial. The handgrip crosses and connects to all the planks. Derived from Nicolaysen (1882). Bottom: The surviving evidence from some shields does not clearly show how the shield maintained its integrity during the rigors of combat. Structural elements such as the handgrip do not cross all of the planks, which seemingly leaves the outer two planks free floating. Illustration: Barbara Wechter.

the battle-moon), and *Svölnis salpenningi* (Óðinn's penny),[28] all suggesting the disc shape of the shield.

Many picture stones showing round shields are found, often with many shield images on each stone.[29] Figures depicted on the Oseberg Tapestry are hard to interpret, but there appear

to be several human figures bearing round shields.[30] Additionally, literary sources offer us glimpses of the physical nature of shields.

WOODEN DISC

It is clear that the body of the Viking shield was a wooden disc, sometimes called the shield plate. The tree species that made up the wooden plate varied. Generally, all that survives are fragments of wood that adhere to surviving metallic parts, such as the boss and nails.

The literary sources mention linden wood (*Tilia*, commonly known as basswood in North America), and the word *lind* (linden) is used poetically to mean shield in numerous verses.[31] Yet few shield fragments of linden wood are found. It is more commonly found in Scandinavian shields from before and after the Viking age. One of the few examples of linden wood found related to a Viking shield is a fragment detected on the underside of the boss excavated at Veiem,[32] and even this artifact may predate the Viking age.

The most common tree type found in archaeology related to shields is pine (*Pinus*), used for the Gokstad shields[33] and others.[34] Other confirmed finds include fragments of spruce (*Picea*),[35] maple (*Acer*),[36] and oak (*Quercus*).[37] Additionally, fragments of fir, rowan, and birch are suspected of being attached to some shield remains. A boss found in Iceland has traces of birch (*Betula*), rowan (*Sorbus*), and oak, suggesting that the shield was made from different species, or perhaps that the wood fragments found attached to the boss represent more than one object.[38]

This wood takes the form of wooden planks butted together to form the wooden disc. The number of planks ranges from about six to eight. The width of the planks ranges from about 10 to 15 cm (4 to 6 in). All of the Gokstad shield planks fall within this range (excepting the two thin-edge planks), with a median of 13.3 cm (5.2 in).

It is not possible to go more deeply into the specifics of the planks. As we will see many times in this chapter, we run into the coin-toss problem repeatedly in our study of shields. There is insufficient evidence to draw firm conclusions.

FIXING THE PLANKS TOGETHER

The planks were held together at least to some degree by the nails that secured the boss and the handle to the shield. Both of these items would likely cross multiple planks, so the nails that secured them also secured the planks. Yet as we will see in a moment, many surviving handles are not long enough to have crossed all the planks. If the grip and boss nails were all that secured the planks, some of them would be free floating and not fastened together to form a solid disc. Something else is needed to secure the planks.

Both the Frostaþing law and the Gulaþing law require shields to be made with three iron bands serving as braces laid on the shield.[39] This additional support would assist in keeping the shield together and add to its robustness, yet little has been found in archaeology that can be clearly confirmed as braces.

Another possibility is the use of adhesive to hold the planks together. The use of tar as an adhesive was known in Viking-age Scandinavia. Tar was used as an adhesive for the construction of arrows[40] and has been found in Viking graves.[41] The law codes set a standard price for tar and limit the amount of tar a man may make.[42] Yet finds of tar are not reported in conjunction with finds of shield components.

Younger sources from outside Viking lands provide recipes for various kinds of glues, and it is possible these were known to Vikings. Theophilus, writing in the twelfth century, provided a recipe for hide and horn glue and for cheese glue.[43] Hide glue can fail in wet conditions, but cheese glue is permanent and can be made impervious.

Regardless, little can be said with confidence about how the planks were held together to form the basic structure of the shield. Other shield components, such as rim and facing discussed later in the chapter, probably played a role to add stability and strength to the structure of the shield.

The area covered by a shield compared to a standing man. Photo: William R. Short

DIMENSIONS OF THE SHIELD

The diameter of shield finds can be measured in the case of intact shields or estimated based on the location of other finds in the grave or by the traces of the wood in the soil. Of the few shields for which a diameter can be determined, the range is from 70 to 95 cm (27.5 to 37.5 in), with a median of 90 cm (35.5 in).[44] We will see this wide range in other shield dimensions. A common thread throughout Viking shields is that one size did not fit all.

The thickness of the shield disc can be measured, for surviving shields, or estimated based on other surviving shield components, such as the nails that secure the boss or the metal clamps on the shield edge. But these estimates can be erroneous, since, for example, we can't be certain whether a nail passed through only boss and shield disc or also the grip.

Generally, we find that shield discs were shaved, such that the center was thicker than the edge. This structure reduces the weight of the shield without greatly impacting its strength, as is discussed later in the chapter.

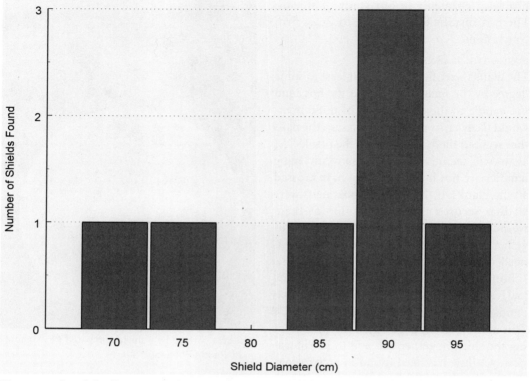

Histogram plot of the diameter of Viking-age shields for which enough evidence survives to infer or measure the diameter.

As with diameter, the thickness of shields varied. Center thickness varies from 5 to 28 mm (0.2 to 1.1 in), with a median of 12 mm (0.5 in). Edge thickness varies from 3 to 10.4 mm (0.12 to 0.4 in), with a median of 5 mm (0.2 in). Literary sources occasionally mention thick shields, yet another indication that shield dimensions varied.[45] Few shields survive such that both rim and center thickness can be measured on the same specimen. One such shield is the Trelleborg shield, which is approximately 8 mm thick at the center (0.3 in) and 5 mm thick at the edge (0.2 in).[46]

EDGING

The edge of the shield could be strengthened by securing additional material to it to form a rim. A tight, solid rim has the potential to strengthen the edge and to squeeze the shield structure more tightly together, making it more solid and more robust. On the Gokstad

and Trelleborg shields, there are small holes next to the edge equally spaced around the periphery, suggesting that some kind of edging was secured to the rim, perhaps using lacing or nails through the holes.[47] However, the evidence is far from conclusive at this time.

The most credible evidence for edging is found in the many edge clamps for shields that are found in Scandinavia. These metallic clamps fit over the edge of the shield and were nailed in place. Most are iron, but bronze clamps are also found, and some are decorated. Some remains of shields had only a few clamps, but some had dozens.[48]

The purpose of these clamps is not clear. It has been suggested that the clamps were used to repair damage to the edge of the shield, or that they fastened the facing to the shield, or that the clamps themselves served as the protective edging of the shield.

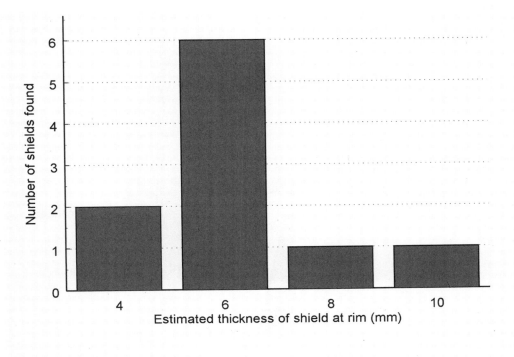

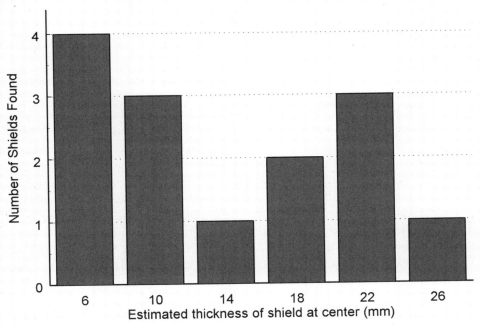

Histogram plots of the thickness of Viking-age shields for which enough evidence survives to infer or measure the thickness. The top plot shows rim thickness, and the bottom plot shows center thickness at the boss.

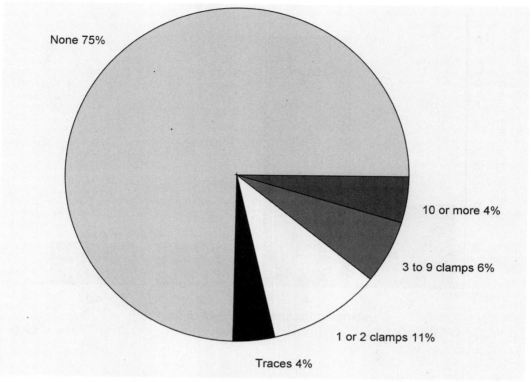

Histogram plot of the number of shield clamps found in graves that have evidence of containing a shield.

Another form of edging that seems likely is a strip of hide-based material wrapped over the edge. A material such as rawhide or leather can be attached around the edge of a shield wet, perhaps by means of the holes seen around the edge of the Gokstad shields. As the material dries, it shrinks, squeezing the structure of the shield together and strengthening it. This speculation is strengthened by the evidence seen on a shield edge clamp at Birka. Held inside the clamp are the fragments of wooden shield plate and several bits of leather. The inside surface of the clamp contains the remnants of a thick layer of hide folded around the edge of the shield plate, and separate, thinner layers of leather on each side of the shield plate held by the clamp.[49] The find could be interpreted as a layer of facing (discussed later) on the front and back of the shield plate, and a strip of edging formed around the edge from front to back and held in place by the shield clamp.

In a few cases, the literary sources mention shields that are hard to interpret as anything other than an iron-rimmed shield.[50] Perhaps this edging was formed by a nearly continuous line of metallic shield clamps around the edge discussed earlier. Some of the excavated graves have large numbers of these clamps,[51] and some of these have been interpreted as forming a continuous edge.[52] Such an edge would protect the shield plate from a cut and strengthen the shield. While solid iron shield rims are found in later periods, the evidence for their use in the Viking age is lacking.

FACING

An additional aspect of the shield plate is the possibility of a covering or facing on one or both sides of the shield. It is a material stretched over the shield plate and secured to it to add to its durability and all-around robustness. Leather and fabric facings have been suggested, and there are convincing archaeological finds of leather[53] and fabric[54] fragments stuck to the shield boss or to the edge clamps of shields. But these finds do not paint any kind of clear picture.

According to the tenth-century poem *Waltharius*, the purpose of the leather facing was to hold the shattered wood together should the shield plate break. The poet says a shield was covered with bull hide, and when a shield was shattered, the hide held the wood together.[55] This episode suggests that even though the underlying wood was damaged, the integrity of the shield was maintained by the leather facing.

The use of leather facings on shields is also suggested by the tenth-century laws of the Anglo-Saxon king Athelstan, which state that no shield maker shall cover a shield with sheepskin under penalty of a 30 shilling fine.[56] An interpretation of the law is that shields should be covered with hide, but of a more robust variety than sheepskin.

How the facing was attached to the shield remains unclear. As with the joining of the planks making up the shield plate, there are several possibilities but few certainties. Perhaps it was fixed to the shield plate with the same kinds of adhesives that might have been used for the planks. Perhaps it was sewn or otherwise attached to the plate using the holes seen around the periphery of the Gokstad shield. Perhaps the edge clamps held the facing in place. Perhaps a combination of all of these methods was used. Little can be said with certainty about the use of facing or how it was attached. But modern experiments, described later in the chapter, show the value of a firmly affixed facing in creating a strong, robust shield, especially when the wood shield plate behind it is damaged in combat.

*Tvíbyrðingr* is a word used to describe shields in the literary sources whose meaning is obscure. It is sometimes translated as twofold shield. The word is used to specify the requirements of shields used by men of the king's levy in the younger Gulaþing law, and variants appear in other sources such as the Norwegian

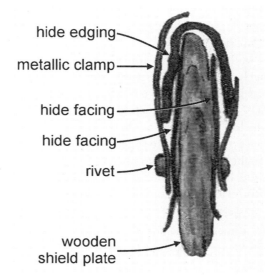

Top: Edge view of a shield clamp from Birka grave Bj 850 showing what has been interpreted as the wooden shield plate in the middle, a thin layer of facing on either side, a layer of edging folded over the edge of the shield plate, and a metallic shield clamp (only partially surviving) sandwiching it all together. Bottom: An interpretation of the many shield clamps found in Birka grave Bj 736 forming a near-continuous metal edge to the shield. Derived from Holger Arbman, *Birka I. Die Gräber. Tafeln.* Creative Commons.

law code *Bjarkeyjarréttr*. Some believe that the use of the word implies that shields were made of plywood, with multiple layers of thin wood laminated together. While this construction was used in the Roman era, there is no evidence for its use subsequently in northern or western Europe.[57]

Thus it seems unlikely that *tvíbyrðingr* refers to plywood. Another suggestion is that it refers to layers of facing, perhaps one layer in front and one behind, or even to two layers on the same side.

Multilayer shields appear in other sources, such as *Waltharius*, where the Latin words used, like the Norwegian in the law codes, have the sense of a threefold and a sevenfold shield,[58] translated as three layer and seven layer. There is little to suggest what these layers might be. Perhaps they are layers of wood, but more likely, layers of leather or fabric. There is little evidence to guide us to a clear answer.

COLORS

In numerous episodes in the literary sources, shields are said to shine or gleam.[59] The law code *Grágás* tells us that gleaming shields were an undeniable and inevitable fact of life, in the same way that the sun shone and that ships sailed.[60] It was an irrefutable truth used in an oath taken before men and gods and recorded in the laws.

Yet neither the wood plate nor a fabric or hide facing can reasonably be said to gleam. One possibility is that shields gleamed because of reflections off their metallic bosses. Or perhaps they gleamed because of their painted surfaces. It is possible that Vikings used oil-based paints as taught by Theophilus, among others, and that these paints had a glossy surface, especially if varnished[61] or oiled after the paint dried.

Archaeological evidence for painted shields exists in fragmentary form. The Gokstad shields were arrayed along the side of the ship in alternating colors of black and yellow paint, matching the color scheme of other painted parts of the ship.[62] Other shield fragments, both wooden and leather, show traces of paint.[63] Colors include red, white, black, yellow, brown, and blue. Perhaps it is these painted surfaces that caused shields to glitter, in which case, sources like the law codes would suggest shields were routinely painted.

The literary sources tell us that some shield colors had special significance. *Eiríks saga rauða* tells us that showing a red shield indicated a hostile intent,[64] while showing a white shield indicated peaceful intent.[65]

Many prominent warriors are said to carry red shields, including Óláfr, Kjartan, and Bolli, as told in *Laxdæla saga*.[66] A younger version of the Gulaþing law says shields used by the king's levy troops should be red. Rune stones commemorate men who carried red shields, and kennings for shields use the color red, such as *rauðljósa baugjörð* (the bright red ring-land).[67] The connection between the color red and the color of a shield is strong, although one can only speculate on the nature and meaning of that connection.

HANDGRIP

The handle of the shield was on the back side of the wooden plate, passing over the opening through the plate behind the boss. It was here that the shield was gripped, and several types of grips are found.

Based on archaeological, pictorial, and literary sources, there does not appear to have been any additional straps or other supports through which the hand or arm passed. While an additional arm strap was used on shields in Viking lands before and after the Viking age, there is nothing to suggest its use in Viking times. Because there was nothing to connect the arm to the shield, the shield could rotate freely from side to side around the hand. The only limit to that rotation was the strength of the shield holder's grip, and the tight fit between hand and boss in the case of a small boss.

The literary and pictorial sources are silent regarding the nature of the handgrip, but it seems to have varied, based on available fragmentary archaeological sources. Some grips were made of flat iron bars fixed to the shield across the opening to the boss. Some were not much longer then the boss opening, while others were considerably longer, nearly the full diameter of the shield.[68] Some examples have terminals for attaching the grip to the shield.[69] Some grips are decorated in bronze,[70] and elaborately decorated end terminals separate from the grip itself are also found.[71] Additionally, some of these grips are partially or fully formed into a channel to accept a wood insert, as evidenced by traces of wood being found attached to this area.[72] This arrangement places the hand farther into the boss and closer to the balance point of the shield than a flat grip would allow, resulting in a quicker and better-balanced shield, as well as a more stable and secure grip.

It has been suggested that the iron or iron-and-wood hand grips were wrapped with leather to allow a firmer grip on the shield, as was done on earlier shields, yet the evidence for this wrapping in the Viking age is slight. Some surviving handgrips have decorative elements in this area, which would seem superfluous if the grip were wrapped.[73]

Other grips that have been found are made entirely of wood. The nearly intact shields from Trelleborg and Gokstad have wooden grips. The Gokstad grips are rectangular in cross section and extend the full diameter of the shield, providing support for all the planks making up the shield plate and creating a more robust structure.[74]

In contrast, the Trelleborg grip is much shorter with a nearly round cross section. Since the grip does not contact the outer shield planks, they are not secured to anything robust, making for a weaker shield structure. The nearly round cross section means the shield holder's grip on the shield is significantly less secure against any sideways pressure or rotational forces compared to a handgrip with an oval or rectangular cross section; there is no structure to lock the handgrip securely in the hand. The relatively small diameter of the grip only serves to reinforce the idea that this shield is the odd man out. Additionally, this small, round grip is not commonly used on large, round shields used by other cultures, such as the early Anglo-Saxons.[75]

Many more iron bosses are found than iron grips in Viking-age graves, leading one to speculate whether wooden grips were more the norm for a Viking shield. Regardless, virtually all the grips found, both wood and iron, support the notion that shields were held tightly with a sideways grip, discussed later in this

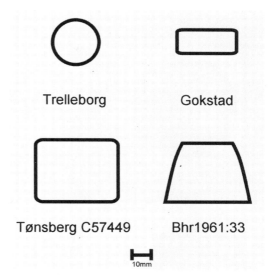

Estimated or measured cross-section of handgrips from several Viking-age shield finds. Illustration: William R. Short.

chapter. The shape is optimized for this kind of tight grip, with the longer dimension of the grip in the plane of the shield plate, where it can lie flat in the palm securely fixed to the hand when held in a sideways grip. As is stated in the poem *Waltharius*, the shield should be gripped tight with fingers fixed like glue around the handle,[76] and the handgrips found, with the exception of the grip on the Trelleborg shield, allow this kind of firm, secure grip.

### SHIELD BOSS

If we consider the physics of holding a shield, the best place for the hand to grip the shield would seem to be in the center of the shield plate, and in the plane of the shield plate. Here is where the shield is best balanced in the hand, resulting in the best control and quickest response due to the lower moment of inertia.

In order for the hand to grip the shield in this location, there must be a hole for the hand to pass through the plane of the shield plate. When gripping through the shield and around the handgrip in this location, the hand must be covered and protected from an opponent's weapons. That protection is the function of the shield boss.

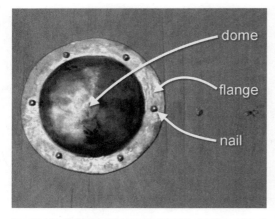

Top: Parts of a Viking shield boss. Photo: William R. Short. Center: Rygh's typology for Viking-age shield bosses. Derived from Rygh (1885). Bottom: Viking-age shield boss from Sweden which shows evidence of weapons damage. Derived from Sara Kusmin, *SHM 10347*. Creative Commons.

The boss was occasionally called a *bóla,* meaning *blister.*[77] Virtually all Viking-age shield bosses are made of iron in the shape of a half-globe, with a flange that attaches the boss to the wooden shield plate. The bosses are round and sized to fit the hand.

The most commonly used boss typology is that originally created by Rygh, which shows only four variants.[78] His type 562 is the most commonly found boss in Viking lands, a simple half-globe shape with a flange. It is likely this type was raised from a single sheet of iron. Other types, such as 564, have a neck between flange and half-globe, probably fabricated as two separate pieces and welded together. Other bosses are more conical in shape, and some have a distinct apex, such as Rygh 565. Although more commonly seen in earlier bosses, some of these Viking bosses have a stud standing proud of the apex.

The boss was affixed to the shield plate using nails through the holes in the boss flange. Generally, three to six holes and nails were used to make this connection, and the nails were usually clenched to fix the boss firmly to the shield. These clenched nails are one of our best sources of information about the thickness of the shield plate, as discussed earlier.

Some flanges were decorated by shaping the edge of the flange or by bronze embellishments. Some flanges show distinct signs of possible repair and reuse, with additional holes made in the flange to mount on a different shield plate.

The bosses themselves seem to be made of soft iron, and a number of them show clear weapons damage,[79] testimony to the ability of the weapons to cut through the thickness of the boss. This unhardened iron suggests that any hard blow to the boss might deform it, possibly injuring or trapping the hand inside.

As mentioned earlier, shield and shield components are not as commonly found in graves as weapons are. Yet hundreds of bosses and fragments have been found in Viking-age graves from Viking lands. From these finds, we can get an idea of the size and shape of typical

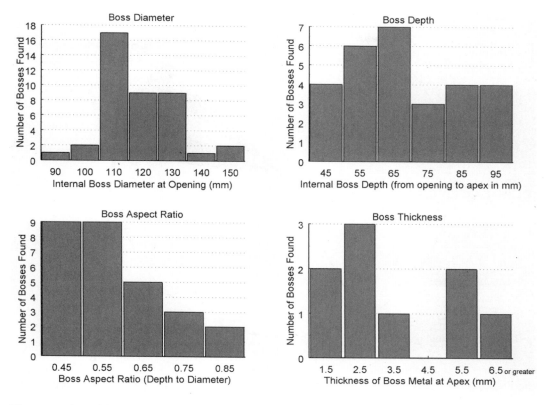

Histogram plots of shield boss dimensions tabulated from surviving Viking-age shield bosses for which enough evidence survives to infer or measure the dimensions. Top left: The internal diameter of the boss at the opening. Top right: the internal depth of the boss from opening to apex. Bottom left: The aspect ratio of the boss: the ratio of boss depth to boss diameter. An aspect ratio of 0 represents a flat boss, while an aspect ratio of 0.5 represents a half-globe. A higher aspect ratio indicates a more conical boss. Bottom right: The thickness of the boss metal sheet at the apex, neglecting any spike or dimple that stands proud of the outer surface.

bosses. The boss must be large enough to admit the hand and thick enough to protect it.

Histograms of the distribution of the internal dimensions of bosses found in Viking lands are shown in the figure above.[80] The median internal diameter of the boss at its base is 11.5 cm (4.5 in). The median internal depth of the boss, from flange to apex, is 6.5 cm (2.6 in). The aspect ratio is the ratio of the internal depth to the internal diameter and is an indication of the shape of the boss. An aspect ratio of 0 indicates a flat boss, while an aspect ratio of 0.5 represents a half-globe. A higher aspect ratio suggests a more elongated, cone-like shape. The median aspect ratio is 0.56. The median thickness of the boss at the apex is 2.6 mm (0.1 in).

These data show a wide range of boss sizes and provide more evidence that shields were not mass produced. One size does not fit all, and fighters likely chose or made the boss that best suited their needs or was available to them.

Importantly, these data provide clues on how the shield was used. Many of these bosses are small and likely would closely envelope the hand, depending on the nature of the handgrip. It suggests fighters desired a firm, tight grip on their shield so the shield did not move in the hand during use, the grip *Waltharius* called like glue between hand and handgrip.[81]

The smallest boss, from the Gokstad ship burial, is remarkably small, only 8.6 cm (3.4

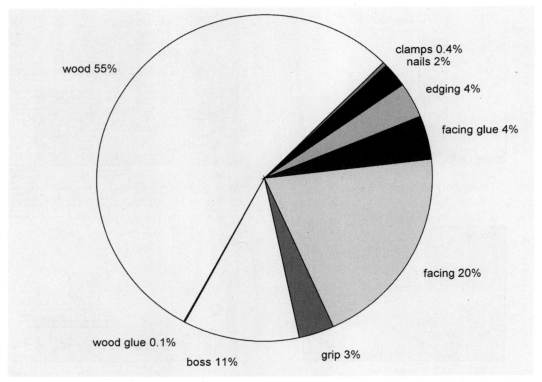

Percentage weight contribution for the various components of a Viking-age shield, based on a computer model of a shield. Assumptions: 90 cm diameter; 9 mm center thickness of shield plate; 6 mm edge thickness; half-dome iron boss having dimensions corresponding to the median of surviving bosses; leather facing on two sides; wooden handgrip; hide edging.

in) in diameter and 4.9 cm (1.9 in) deep. Such a small boss would make gripping the shield a tight fit. Yet the Gokstad boss is the exception, as seen in the histogram plots. The median boss is large enough to admit a meaty Viking fist, and the largest is almost big enough for two.

SHIELD WEIGHT

The weight of the shield depended on a multitude of factors. But none of the surviving shields are sufficiently complete to be able to use them to gauge the weight of a Viking shield. Computer modeling of Viking shields allows us to make estimates of weights for various assumptions about the nature of the shield.[82] The model shows that for any reasonable assumptions, the wood plate makes up most of the weight, even for a very thin shield. Estimated weights vary from as little as 3 kg

(6.5 lbs) for a thin, unfaced shield, to 6.5 kg (14 lbs) for a thick shield with front and rear facing. The model predicts 4 to 5 kg (9 to 11 lbs) would have been the norm based on the median shield dimensions reported earlier in the chapter.

The model also allows us to predict how the weight might vary with changes to the design, an aspect that will take on importance when we discuss the durability of the shield later in the chapter. Using the shield modeled for the plot and eliminating the shaving of the edge, for example, increases the weight by about 20 percent. Eliminating the two facings reduces the weight by about 25 percent.

In summary, little can be said about Viking shields with any degree of certainty. Shields were large, wooden discs with an iron boss in the center of the front and a handgrip behind the boss in the rear. We cannot be certain about other details, except to say that they seemed to vary from shield to shield.

SHIELD CARRY

As with other combative tools, the shield was kept within easy reach, whether at home or on the road or at sea. In the home, shields were hung on a wall.[83] When traveling and sleeping on the ground, men slept under their shields.[84]

It seems likely that shields had a leather carry strap on the back for slinging the shield on the body while traveling, leaving the hands free. Some shields are found with small iron rings, about 2.2 cm in diameter (0.9 in), fixed to a staple. These rings are thought to have been used for securing the strap to the shield.[85]

When en route, men carried their shields not on their backs, as is often thought, but at their sides. A back carry is rarely mentioned in the literary sources[86] and not much seen in the pictorial sources. Instead, our research of the pictorial[87] and literary[88] sources strongly suggests that whether a Viking was walking, standing, or riding a horse, his shield was at his side.

At sea, in popular imagination, shields lined the sides of Viking ships, hung outboard along the gunwales. This image is seen in several contemporary Viking sources, including picture stones, coins, jewelry, and graffito.[89] Archaeology supports this image; the Gokstad ship was found arrayed with 32 shields on each side.[90] Likewise, literary sources tell of ships arrayed with shields[91] and of a skipper whose shield-lined ship was so imposing that he was given the nickname Skjalda-Björn (Shield-Björn).[92]

The shield rack, which supported the shields, was a light, perforated rail attached to the upper edge of the topmost strake, sometimes on the inner surface, sometimes on the outer. Shields were supported from the rack, tied with bast cords.[93]

A portion of the shield rack survived on the Skuldelev 5 wreck, an eleventh-century warship found in Roskilde fjord in Denmark. The find gives a clear picture of one of the ways the rack supported the shields.[94] The rack, mounted on the outside, created slots between

Top: A rider carrying a shield by his side depicted on the Hunninge I picture stone. Derived from Harald Faith-Ell, *Hunninge I*. Creative Commons. Bottom: A modern rider demonstrating a side shield carry as seen in the ancient sources. Photo: @NAEPHOTO, with our thanks to Sigurður Matthíasson and Safír.

the topmost strake and the rack. Shields were dropped into the slots and tied in place, with the boss preventing the shield from falling all the way through the rack. The slots were about 3 cm wide (1.2 in) and 80 cm long (31 in), suggesting that the shields aboard the Skuldelev 5 ship were 80 to 85 cm in diameter (31 to 33 in).

It is most likely that shields were not routinely hung here while underway[95] but only when it was necessary to make the ship look especially imposing, perhaps when approach-

Top: Shields lining the side of a Viking ship as depicted on the Stora Hammars I picture stone. Derived from Berig, *The Stora Hammars I image stone*. Creative Commons. Bottom: Shields lining the side of the *Sea Stallion*, a replica of the Skuldelev 2 Viking ship. Photo: Werner Karrasch. Copyright: The Viking Ship Museum, Denmark.

ing land or approaching another ship. It is an impractical location, and several indicators suggest that hanging shields along the sides was not routine. On some surviving ships, the location of the shields overlaps the oar holes, making it impossible to row the ship with the shields in place.[96] Additionally, the shield rack, which supports the shields, is not robust on some surviving ships and would likely be unable to securely hold the shields in rough seas. On the Oseberg ship, the shield rack is described as being positively fragile.[97] More likely, shields, when not needed, were stored out of the way under the deck planks.

DURABILITY OF THE SHIELD

Compared to other Viking tools, shields were not robust, and perhaps they were even considered disposable. In episode after episode in the literary sources, the shield broke during combat in one way or another. The physics of the Viking-age shield does not permit it to survive countless heavy blows from a sharp tool, no matter what the details of its construction might be, which leads to several questions: what is the durability of a Viking-age shield, and how heavy of a blow can it survive?

Experiments have been done by modern researchers to test the durability of a shield using speculative reconstructions of authentic Viking shields, based on their best available evidence. Though we, too, have done similar testing of shields, we have opted to follow a different path, since we believe that focusing on a specific authentic shield can lead us to unreliable conclusions. We have already seen that one size does not fit all in the world of Viking shields. The robustness of a single shield does not allow us to draw conclusions about Viking shields in general. Viking shields were constructed from varying tree species, made in varying sizes, and constructed with varying materials and methods. This wide range is problematic when testing the durability of the Viking shield.

It is clear that shields broke in combat. In dueling, for example, each dueler was allowed three shields.[98] Should they all break during the duel, the fighter was expected to block with his weapons.

The literary sources give us only vague clues about the strength of the shield. Some shields were split[99] or penetrated[100] on the first strike, yet some stayed intact for a long time during a fight.[101]

We don't know the nature of the facing used on Viking-age shields with any certainty. But if facing were present, it seems likely it would increase the durability.

When a shield without facing is hit by a weapon, the weapon can penetrate the wood plate and split the wood along the grain, possibly splitting the shield. A shield that is split or broken is a less-effective defense. With facing, the hit might penetrate, but the facing holds the wood together on either side of the impact, so the shield plate does not split. The shield remains a usable and effective defense.

Tests of identical shields made with and without facing suggest that the faced shield endured six times more hits with an axe before failing than an unfaced shield.[102] The tests suggest that the facing greatly increases the abuse a shield can withstand and remain intact.

The disadvantage of the facing is that it adds weight to the shield, as discussed earlier. Addi-

Top: A replica Viking shield with no facing broke into useless fragments after two hits with a Viking axe in our tests at Hurstwic. Bottom: A replica Viking shield faced with leather was still solid and useable after six solid hits with a Viking axe. Photos: William R. Short.

tionally, there is some cost to preparing leather and fastening it to the shield.

The benefits seem significant, so why aren't all Viking shields found with traces of facing? There is no simple answer. Perhaps facing was common, and shields found without facing were intended for show or ritual. Perhaps facing wasn't used because of the expense. Perhaps Viking warriors did not see the value of adding facing to an item that was disposable. Perhaps the facing loosened and lost effectiveness when damp or wet during sea voyages. There are many possibilities and few definite answers.

## SHIELD USAGE

As we have seen, the details of the nature of the shield are unclear. Sadly, the details of the usage of the shield are equally fuzzy. It is a complex and multifaceted topic, and we must consider every conceivable angle.

In the earlier chapters, we concluded that Viking combat was based on aggression and brute power. These kinds of powerful blows would be the blows that the warrior had to defend himself against using his shield, and they are the blows that the warrior would want to deliver as he held his shield.

## A PROPOSED SHIELD POSITION

Viking-age pictorial sources offer few details. The images on the picture stones most often depict Viking warriors en route. Their shields are held in a way that might be interpreted as men on the verge of combat. The images show the shield in front of the warriors in varying ways.

Analysis of these images is further confounded by the lack of the use of perspective in the images, as discussed earlier, which makes interpreting the two-dimensional image in three-dimensional space troublesome.

The literary sources generally provide little help. The word *fyrir* is often used to describe the position of the shield in combat.[103] An example appears in *Fóstbrœðra saga*. Snorri had attacked some horses with a spear. Þorgeirr, fearing that Snorri might kill the horses, jumped off his horse, holding his shield *fyrir* himself.[104]

*Fyrir* is a troublesome word because it has multiple meanings. The primary meaning is before or in front of, but equally, it can mean in the way or between one and one's enemy.[105] Any or all of these meanings could be applied to positioning the shield.

As we consider how Viking warriors held their shields, we have to be wary about falling into a trap. We have already seen that one size does not fit all when discussing shields, and that thought also applies to holding the shield. Our modern mindset guides us to categorize and organize the evidence to create a simple,

Top: Warriors holding their shields to their sides, depicted on the Smiss picture stone. Derived from Christer Åhlin, *SHM 11521*. Creative Commons. Bottom: A modern interpretation of the sideways shield position. Photo: William R. Short.

uniform answer: the best and most efficient way to hold a Viking shield. This mindset most likely will draw us away from the truth.

Instead, we seek the common thread running through many sources, and we try not to let our modern mindset lead us astray. In many other Viking-based activities, including games, religion, and sports, complete uniformity did not exist. Similarly, there probably was no universal way to hold the shield. Accordingly, we look for the common thread among the various ways that Vikings held their shields.

In the same way that Viking warriors had to defend against powerful blows with the shields, so too did they have to deliver powerful blows with their weapon, holding the shield in the other hand. Where the shield is positioned can have a major impact on the ability of the warrior to deliver power through his weapon. If the shield is too far away from the body, it will have to be pulled back to the body in order to deliver the torque for a full-power strike. At the same time, the shield cannot be too close to the center of the body or it will get in the way of the full-body movement needed to generate a powerful strike.

Using the available evidence, combined with experiments, measurements, and simulated combat that reference that evidence, we present some speculative ideas on how the shield was held and used by Viking-age warriors.

It is likely that a range of shield positions was used. The common thread is that the shield was held sideways in front of the body to varying degrees, illustrated on the eighth century Franks Casket, the Tängelgårda picture stone, the Klinte Hunninge I stone, and the Lärbro Stora Hammars I picture stone,[106] and demonstrated in the photograph on the facing page.

These sideways positions match with the available sources. They allow the shield to be the primary defensive tool. They allow the weapon hand to deliver full-power blows without the need to change the shield position significantly. The shield can be said to be *fyrir* the shield holder.

Additionally, this sideways position allows the execution of a number of shield moves described in the literary sources. For example, fighting men sometimes hid a reserve weapon behind their shield to draw when it was better suited than their primary weapon. Þorgeirr carried a spear in his right hand, with a shield and an axe in his left hand.[107] The sideways shield position allows for a quick change from the primary weapon to secondary weapon held behind the shield.

Two-handed use of the shield is mentioned in several episodes in the literary sources.[108]

Top: Holding an axe behind a shield to use as a reserve weapon in a fight. Bottom: A speculative method of holding a Viking shield with two hands to brace against a strong attack. Photos: William R. Short.

Unlike some of the alternative shield positions, the sideways position offers a strong defense with more body mass behind the shield when gripped two handed.

A sequence depicting a speculative method of swapping sword and shield by throwing them both simultaneously in the air and catching them in opposite hands. Photo: William R. Short.

Another close match with the literary sources is the fantastic move of swapping a weapon and shield from one hand to the other in midair during a fight.[109] The sideways shield position is one of the few that allows weapon and shield to fly through the air without colliding; other shield positions don't make sense.

The move of swapping sword and shield has been tested under conditions of simulated combat.[110] It can be performed by a competent fighter. Not only is it martially effective, but it is also astounding and confounding to the fighter against which it is used.

Perhaps a good analogy might be the spinning heel hook kick in a world championship martial arts competition. It is a fantastic, unbelievable move. Yet it can be performed by a competent fighter, and if it works, it works wonders.

Another benefit of the sideways shield position is that it forms many points of contact between the shield and the warrior's body, creating a strong, unified structure of shield and body capable of absorbing the blow without throwing the shield out of position. There were no straps on the Viking shield through which the forearm passes. If the only contact

with the shield is through the hand, a powerful hit to the shield might cause the shield to flap or rotate. The sideways shield position avoids this loss of control, based on tests using simulated combat.[111]

An additional point that must be considered is biomechanics. The literary sources tell us that fights could last a long time. The sideways shield positions do not tax the body's resources, and so they can be held for a long time without tiring the arm and upper body muscles.

ANOTHER PROPOSED SHIELD POSITION

As stated earlier, there probably was no one universal shield position. Picture stones seem to show another one: warriors holding the shield low, at torso level and close to the body, with their swords raised over their head.[112]

In this position, the shield can be said to be *fyrir* the shield holder. Additional support for this position can be found in the skaldic kennings, where the shield is called *land* and the weapons *rain* or the *net of tips*,[113] suggesting that the shield was held such that the attacks landed on the flat face of the shield. The literary sources further support the idea that the flat was sometimes used to block.[114]

The front position, however, is not without some issues. The fighter must open his shield position quite a bit in order to attack with full power from this position, both to obtain full use of the hips and the power they can generate, and so that the shield is not in the way of the strike. Additionally, for some attack angles, the shield needs to move quite a bit to be in a position to defend, for example, against a downward diagonal attack from above of a two-handed axe. As a result, this position results in slower attacks and slower defenses, as confirmed in tests with simulated combat.[115] This problem is compounded by the fact that moving the shield to block these high attack angles temporarily blinds the warrior as the shield is raised above the eyeline.

The images on the picture stone suggest a solution. They show warriors using the front shield position with their swords raised over their heads as if to block an attack.[116] This solution has been suggested by some modern reenactors as well.

Yet again, we must take pains in interpreting the images. Representing the sword up high may have been the only way for the artist to place both sword and shield in the same image without obscuring other important elements when depicting this shield position.

This use of the sword as defense is problematic for other reasons, as discussed in the sword chapter. Using a sword to block exposes the weapon to the risk of serious damage. The shield was disposable; the sword was not, based on the apparent cultural and financial value assigned to the weapon. Additionally, the literary sources make clear that the shield was the primary defense. These sources do not seem to have any examples of using the sword to block when a shield was present.

A further objection to the front position arises from dueling practices. This shield position is difficult to put into play in a duel when using a shield holder, a practice discussed in the dueling chapter. When tested with simulated combat, this shield position makes little sense in a dueling situation.[117]

Top: Holding the shield low at torso level as depicted on the Stora Hammars I picture stone. Derived from Berig, *The Stora Hammars I image stone*. Creative Commons. Bottom: A modern re-creation of the low shield position. Photo: William R. Short.

Pictorial evidence suggests two possible shield positions: side and front. The other sources are silent on this matter, so there is little that can be concluded about shield position with any degree of certainty.

A modern re-creation of the problem that arises from using the low, torso-level shield position. When raising the shield to block an attack from above, the shield holder blinds himself. Photo: William R. Short.

## SHIELD MOVEMENT IN DEFENSE

Several sources tell us that shield use in defense was dynamic, and it is clear that against an incoming attack, the shield was put in motion to intercept the attack. Descriptions in the literary sources make that motion more clear. In describing the motion of a shield to defend, the words used are *bregða*, meaning to move quickly or to draw (as a sword out of a scabbard), and the word *skjóta*, meaning to shoot (with a weapon).[118] Both words have the sense of fast motion, but the descriptions in the literary sources go no further. And so we are left with little other than speculation based on generic combative biomechanics.

In general, the less movement for defense the better. Larger movements imply longer delays to position the defense for the attack and longer delays to return to its neutral defensive position for the next attack. Additionally, large movements deplete the body, an undesirable outcome in a high-stress situation like a fight, which may last for an extended period.

These ideas are based on modern thoughts on combatives and may not have much mattered to a Viking fighter. Yet a phrase used in the literary sources is *koma í opna skjöldu*.[119]

The phrase literally means to come upon someone with an open shield, and it was used when someone was surprised unpleasantly, typically when they were unprepared. The phrase suggests the better shield position is the more *en garde* shield position, leaving no openings to the body in the way that a closed door protects a house better than an open door, leaving no openings through which an attack may be made.

We cannot be certain how the shield met the incoming attack to block it, or even with what part of the shield the attack was blocked. The archaeological sources show no clear, repeated weapon damage to the few surviving shields and only some damage to the bosses. The pictorial sources are silent.

Thus, once again we are left depending on the literary sources, and they too paint a fuzzy picture. Whether the shield met the incoming attack with the edge or the flat is rarely mentioned. In the few cases where it is mentioned, the weapon is more often said to hit the flat of the shield[120] than the edge,[121] and indeed, in only one episode is it clearly stated that the weapon hit the edge of the shield.[122]

The skaldic kennings also suggest the large flat surface of the shield was the important aspect of the shield, such as *ræfri Hildar* (the roof of Hildr [Valkyrie]), and *veggjar Heðins* (of the wall of Heðinn [legendary hero]), and *gáttar gunnar* (of the door of battle). Only a few kennings refer to the edge, such as *jaðra grindar Þundar* (the edges of Óðinn's gate).[123]

Regrettably, no clear picture of shield movement forms from the available evidence. Timing and biomechanical considerations suggest less movement is better. Measurements of the ability of the shield to absorb a hit suggest a tight position is better. But the evidence is insufficient to allow us to be certain of how Vikings defended themselves with their shields.

What is more clear is how Vikings used their shields to defend others. Perhaps in the same way that men slept under their shields in the field to protect themselves,[124] so were shields

*Skjaldborg* (shield castle) defensive shield formation used to protect the king and his poets. One source tells us that the shields touched rim to rim, but another says there was a row above and another below. Illustration: Barbara Wechter.

put over dead men to protect them until they could be buried.[125] In the grave, shields were sometimes laid over the dead man's head.[126] This practice has sometimes caused confusion when iron fragments are found: are they the remains of a boss or of a helmet?[127]

Shields were also placed over wounded men to protect them from further injuries until they could be tended to. After Þórðr wounded Özurr, Þórðr pulled him out of the blood and covered him with a shield so ravens wouldn't tear him to pieces until he could be cared for.[128]

One of the most famous lines in the *Sagas of Icelanders* is "Berr er hverr á bakinu nema sér bróðir eigi." Grettir, injured to the point where he could no longer stand, said to his brother Illugi, who was defending him, "Bare is the back of a brotherless man," informing his brother of his plight.[129] Illugi threw a shield over his wounded brother to further guard him against these attacks.

In numerous other cases, men placed their own shields between an attack and a friend or kinsman to protect him during a fight.[130] Additionally during a duel, the dueler was protected by his shield holder, who held the shield for him,[131] as will be discussed in the dueling chapter.

SKJALDBORG

The *skjaldborg* is a formation mentioned numerous times in the literary sources, but the nature and the use of it seem to be widely misunderstood. Literally, it means a shield castle and is sometimes translated *shield wall*. Like a castle or a wall, it was a stationary protective formation intended to protect those inside it, made by holding up shields to form a wall. One of the few descriptions of a shield castle tells us that the edges were touching, rather than that there was significant overlap between the shields, and another suggests that there was a row of shields above and another below.[132]

Those whose survival in the battle was deemed critical were placed inside the shield castle. This group often included the king[133] and his poets.[134] The king's survival was critical to winning the battle since he led it. The poets, who were the historians and the journalists of their time, needed to witness the battle up close in order to compose poetry that recorded the events of the day for posterity. Indeed, we know what a *skjaldborg* is thanks to the verses these poets created based on their observations from inside a *skjaldborg*.

The literary sources tell us that the *skjaldborg* could form quickly, for example, to provide protection for fleeing troops after a lost battle and disband as soon as it was safe to bolt. In the literary sources, the verb *skjóta* is often used to describe the formation of a *skjaldborg*. The word means to shoot (as a weapon), emphasizing the sense of speed in creating the formation. Similar episodes in the literary sources give the sense of haste in setting up the *skjaldborg*.[135]

While in popular imagination the *skjaldborg* is a mobile formation, the literary sources suggest it was a stationary protective one.[136] *Sigrdrífumál* tells us that the Valkyrie Sigrdrífa even slept in her shield castle, fully dressed for battle.[137]

In several cases, the king studied the battle from the shield castle, then emerged from his *skjaldborg* to join the front lines of his men in the fight,[138] giving further credence to the stationary nature of the formation. Terms for the *skjaldborg* in skaldic poetry add further weight to the immobility of the formation. Snorri writes that *skjaldborg* should be referred to as hall and roof, wall and floor.[139]

The use of the *skjaldborg* on Viking raids also suggests its stationary character. Part of the band of *víkingar* formed a *skjaldborg* around their comrades to protect them while they were busy with *strandhögg*, slaughtering the animals they had seized from their victims, who were attacking the Viking raiders to prevent the livestock from being taken.[140]

Confusion about the mobility of the shield castle may occur due to the use of classical

Comparison of a Roman *scutum* (left) to a Viking shield (right). Photo: William R. Short.

Latin terminology by medieval authors writing in that language when discussing Viking fighting practices. An example is the use of the Latin term *testudo* to describe Viking fighters in sources written in medieval Latin. The *testudo* (tortoise shell) is a well-known and well-understood formation used by Roman legions and recorded by Roman authors.

The use of the word *testudo* by medieval authors to describe Viking formations may have been an attempt by the authors to showcase their education and their awareness of classical knowledge by writing in the style of classical authors and using classical terminology that may or may not accurately describe what Vikings used.[141]

Thus, when we look at the descriptions of Viking shield formations by these authors writing in Latin, care is required in interpreting their words. When Abbo writes about the use of the *testudo*, or Saxo Grammaticus, or Asser,[142] we cannot be certain what formation they are reporting on. And so we read these descriptions in Latin of Viking shield use with a healthy dose of skepticism. Additionally, because of its size and shape, the round Viking shield does not provide the protection of a Roman *scutum* shield.

It is not always clear how large the *skjaldborg* was. In some cases, a shield castle was thrown up around the king and his poets during a naval battle aboard ship,[143] suggesting it could not have been large given the limited room on a warship. Earl Eiríkr was in a *skjaldborg* in the *fyrirrúm*,[144] thought to be the space in front of the raised afterdeck of the ship, quite a confined space even aboard a large ship. On the other hand, the *skjaldborg* at the Battle of Stamford Bridge constituted most of King Haraldr's army, with his special troops inside the formation,[145] which must have formed a large castle.

### OFFENSIVE USE OF THE SHIELD

Though the shield is a defensive tool, many have speculated that it may have been used as an offensive tool as well. The evidence for such usage is sparse. Much of this speculation seems to be based on later writings, different types of shields, and different ways of fighting. Punching or bashing or binding with the shield never clearly appear in any of the sources. The rare offensive use of the shield described in the literary sources seems to come from the necessity of the situation, rather than from a calculated method.

In one case, Björn was surrounded by numerous enemies. After his arm had been cut off, he grabbed the remains of his shield by the edge and raked it across his opponent's head, killing him. In the other case, Skarpheðinn slid across the ice of a frozen river and killed Þráinn with his axe as he flew by. As he slid away to safety, Tjörvi threw his shield after Skarpheðinn to trip him, but Skarpheðinn jumped over it.[146] Apart from these two examples, there seem to be no other examples in any of the sources that give suggestions of offensive use of the shield. The shield's purpose seems to be only defensive, and not offensive.

There is, however, a shield-based tactic that falls somewhere between offensive and defensive mentioned multiple times in the literary

Testing the move of penning in an opponent with shields and sticks and staffs in order to capture him without injuring him, a test conducted in the Hurstwic research lab. Photo: William R. Short.

sources. That tactic is penning in a man using shields and other wooden objects.[147] When fighters desired to capture an opponent alive without injury, or even when the fight was going against them, they dropped their primary weapons and used shields or shafts or sticks to approach the enemy and pen him against a wall or fence so he could neither move nor fight.

This tactic has been pressure tested in simulated combat,[148] attempting to re-create as closely as possible one of the episodes described in the literary sources.[149] The results were shockingly effective. The fighter being penned in might be able to get a single strike in on one opponent, but before he has a chance for a second strike, he has been immobilized. It is a potent way to subdue a Viking who is intent on killing many of his opponents, executed by the many opponents who are just as intent on *not* killing him.

### SUMMARY

The shield was the primary defense of the Viking warrior to the degree that a man without a shield was considered defenseless. It was used in battle, in duels, and laid over the dead.

Yet more than those of any other Viking tool of war, details of the shield and its use are shrouded in mist and fog. So few shield remains are found in archaeology that we cannot be certain of its construction, and so few details of shield use are available from our sources that we cannot be certain of how it was wielded and used. Even the god of the shield, Ullr, remains an obscure figure.

Regardless, the shield was more than a tool of war. It was also a display piece to distinguish its owner, meant to be shown and to be seen on the walls of the home, along the sides of a ship, and in battle.

# ARMOR

Armor is what a warrior wears that provides passive protection from enemy attack. It provides that protection by stopping the bite of the weapon and by spreading and reducing the impact of the blow. In popular entertainments, Viking armor consists of leather and furs. In fact, most Viking warriors wore no armor, and if they wore any at all, it likely took the form of a helmet and a mail shirt.

SOURCES

Ultimately, this chapter will be disappointing for the simple reason that we have so few sources from which to draw. It is the coin-toss problem; there is nearly no Viking armor that survives in the archaeological record. Unlike Viking swords, with thousands of surviving examples, we have only one half-complete Viking helmet. How can we draw any general conclusions with a sample size of one-half? And how do we deal with the armor known to have been used outside the Viking lands and found only on the fringes of the Viking lands, such as lamellar armor? Did Vikings use it, or only warriors visiting from other lands? As discussed in the research chapter, we seek to use narrow sources and to avoid material from outside Viking lands and Viking times, using it cautiously only when nothing else survives. As we will see, so little Viking armor survives that we are reluctantly but repeatedly forced to turn to outside sources in order to gain insight into Viking armor.

The literary sources use words to describe armor whose exact nature we cannot infer. Does the usual word for personal armor, *brynja*, refer to a mail shirt, as most assume, or does it refer to something broader and more inclusive? What does it mean to *herklæðast* (dress for battle)? Dressed in clothing for war? Dressed in armor? Or something greater, such as being fully equipped for battle with weapons and armor?

Our usual literary sources, such as *Heimskringla* and the *Sagas of Icelanders* tell of armor and occasionally describe it in some detail. The Norse myths frequently mention armor but rarely provide any indication of the nature of the gear.[1]

The pictorial sources rarely show enough detail to determine what is being worn. Armor assumed to be ring mail is depicted with large circles all over the body, which might equally well represent other forms of armor.

As a result of our limited sources, when we reach the end of the chapter, we will have at least as many questions and as much uncertainty about Vikings' use of armor as we did at the start.

VIKING ARMOR

The likely form of armor in the Viking age was helmet and mail shirt. The ancient word for helmet, *hjálmr*, has as its root the word *hylja*, which means to hide or to cover.[2] The root suggests the purpose of the helmet: simply to

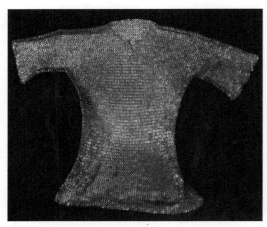

Modern replica of a Viking-age mail shirt. Photo: William R. Short.

cover the head. *Hjálmr* is also used for objects that look like a helmet, notably a hayrick: a round stack of harvested hay built in the field to promote drying of the hay.

Another word used for helmet is *stálhúfa*[3] (steel cap). It is not clear if there was a distinction between *hjálmr* and *stálhúfa*. The one example that might suggest a difference is mentioned in *Hávarðar saga*, where it is said that Vakr had a *hjálmr* on his head as he carried several *stálhúfa* in his arms.[4] Based on the limited evidence, there does not seem to be a significant distinction.

The usual word for mail is *brynja*, an ancient word whose origins are not known. Other compound words based on *brynja* were also used to designate mail shirts, such as *hringjabrynja* (ring mail) and *brynstakkr*[5] (mail shirt).

The word *herneskja* seems to apply to armor generally. The word appears only once in the *Sagas of Icelanders*, and several times in, for example, the Old Icelandic translations of classical Greek stories,[6] where the nature of the armor may have been unknown to the translator.

More difficult to interpret are the words *herklæði*[7] (war clothing) and *herklæða*[8] (to put on war clothing). In some cases, the word seems to be used for armor, and in other cases

for something more, including weapons. The implication is that *herklæði* is the gear and clothing one dons and carries for battle. To *herklæðast* oneself is to prepare for battle.

OTHER FORMS OF MAIL

In later periods, mail leggings were used, especially by mounted warriors to protect their legs while riding in the period before the use of plate armor was practical. The thirteenth century text *Konungs skuggsjá* teaches that mounted warriors should wear mail leggings, called *brynhosa* (mail hose), a word appearing in chivalric legend as well.[9] Mounted warriors are shown wearing what appears to be mail leggings in the Bayeux Tapestry.[10] Similarly, mail coifs, which protect the head and neck, often worn under a helmet, were known in later periods and are depicted on the Bayeux Tapestry.[11]

Evidence for Viking use of either of these forms of mail is scanty. Perhaps Vikings felt little need to protect their legs with mail, since they did not routinely fight from horseback, as discussed in the weapons introduction chapter. Perhaps the coif was not necessary because the combination of the nose guard and the mail curtain of some helmets provided the equivalent protection, as discussed later in the chapter.

LESS LIKELY FORMS OF VIKING ARMOR

Helmet and mail are the two forms of Viking armor that seem most solidly supported, with ample evidence from literary sources and more sparse, yet still solid, evidence from archaeological and pictorial sources. In addition, there are other forms of armor whose use by Viking warriors is even less well supported: armor that is mentioned only rarely in the literary sources, armor whose archaeological finds are from different periods or from different lands, armor for which the pictorial sources are lacking. Given the common thread that supports the Viking use of mail and helmet running through several sources but is lacking for these other forms of armor, we must assume that these other forms were not widely used, if they

Mail coifs and leggings depicted on the Bayeux Tapestry. Derived from Myrabella, *Tapisserie de Bayeux, Scènes 55 & 56*. Creative Commons.

were used at all, by Viking warriors. Since some of these forms of armor are seen in popular sources and in reenactments, we briefly review them and discuss what is known about them.

SPANGABRYNJA

The word *spangabrynja* appears in the literary sources and in one episode is made out to be something highly inferior and undesirable. The origin of the word, a portmanteau, is obscure; the root word, *spöng*, means spangle: something glittery.[12] We cannot say with certainty what the armor might have been.

It has been suggested that *spangabrynja* refers to *scale armor*, made by attaching many small, overlapping metal plates to each other and to a leather or fabric backing that forms an upper body garment. This kind of armor has been in use since antiquity by many cultures, and the individual plates may have glittered as the warrior moved. In the literary sources, there are close to one hundred references to the use of *brynja*, but fewer than a handful of references to *spangabrynja*, most from late sources not set in the Viking age.

LAMELLAR AND SPLINTED ARMOR

A related form of armor is lamellar armor, formed by metal plates laced together but unattached to a backing garment. Examples of the individual plates called *lamellae* that form the armor have been found at Birka.[13] This kind of armor was used in eastern lands, and it seems possible that Vikings may have been introduced to this form of armor through that connection. But while we find evidence of mail from multiple sources across the Viking lands, there is evidence of lamellar only from a single source at this one site. The evidence when taken together suggests that lamellar was not widely used.

Splinted armor consists of strips of metal attached to a cloth or leather backing that wraps around the limbs, providing protection to the forearms or lower legs. In popular sources, splint armor is associated with the Varangian Guard, the Viking warriors serving the Byzantine emperor. Yet there is little evidence to support the use of splint armor by the Varangians.[14] While evidence, such as Byzantine military manuals and pictorial sources, supports the use of splint armor by other Byzantine forces, notably mounted troops, the Varangian Guard fought on foot and probably was armored similarly to the lightly armored Byzantine infantry. In Scandinavia, examples of splint armor are found that date from well before the Viking age, such as that found in Valsgärde grave 8,[15] yet there is little evidence for the use of splint armor in the Viking era.

PANZARI, LEATHER, AND SKIN ARMOR

A word for armor that is occasionally used in the literary sources is *panzari*, a loan word from Latin. It is used a number of times in late sources such as *Sturlunga saga* and *Konungs skuggsjá*. The word refers to armor in the form of a jack, a sleeveless protective jacket, sometimes of leather, sometimes described as being worn over mail.[16] Its single use in the saga literature[17] is thought to be an anachronism.[18]

In popular sources, one sees Viking leather armor in abundance, yet the only other example of leather armor in the literary sources is the use of reindeer hide made invulnerable by Sami magic.[19] Leather or hide armor, magical or mundane, full-torso or bracers for the arms, does not seem to have been commonly used by Viking warriors.

One form of hide armor that is mentioned in multiple literary sources is the use of wolf-skins or bearskins as the armor of choice for berserks. Indeed, their very name implies the wearing of bearskins (*ber-* for bear and *serkr* for shirt).[20] Berserks were also called *Úlfhéðnir* (wolf skins)[21] and wore wolf skins for their armor.[22]

The nature of a *berserkr* is complex and not fully understood, as we will discuss in the mass battle chapter. In multiple sources, it is said that iron and fire could not harm the berserks. Weapons could not bite them,[23] and they needed no mail. Thus their animal skins may have been all the armor these fighters needed.

Taken together, the available evidence supports the use of helmet and mail shirt by Viking warriors. While incomplete, the evidence is consistent over several different kinds of sources. Other forms of armor, in comparison, are much less well supported by evidence. While we can say with confidence that at least some Viking fighters used helmet and mail shirt, we are on much more shaky ground when we talk about their use of these other forms of armor.

ARMOR IN VIKING SOCIETY

Several clues suggest that armor did not play as prominent a role in Viking society as weapons. There are few kennings in skaldic poetry for helmet or mail compared to the weapons: many hundreds for swords, but only sixteen kennings for helmet.[24] Whereas many weapons were named, few names are mentioned in the literary sources for armor. Some examples are King Haraldr's mail shirt named *Emma*[25] and King Hrólfr's helmet *Hildigöltr* and his mail *Finnsleif*.[26]

Helmet and mail are mentioned in the myths,[27] frequently in the same half-verse,[28] suggesting this combination of armor was typical. Yet it is heroes in the myths who wear this armor and not gods. Gods are rarely described wearing armor. Óðinn is one of the few, and one of Óðinn's names is *Hjálmberi* (helmet bearer). The myths tell us that he will wear a golden helmet and mail as he rides in front of the Einherjar and the Æsir, leading them to the final battle of Ragnarök.[29]

This panel of the Franks Casket shows multiple warriors, but only one wearing what might be as interpreted as mail, near the center of the upper row. ©The Trustees of the British Museum. All rights reserved.

## WHO USED ARMOR?

Leading from the front was the expected position in battle for the king (when not in his shield castle) and his leading men. Perhaps that explains why it was the king[30] and his chosen men[31] who were most often clad in armor. Out front, they were most at risk and thus had the greatest need for protection. The loss of the king most often implied the loss of the battle.

Armor is rarely found in graves, compared to weapons, a surprise given the importance of these elite warriors. There may be several contributing factors. The nature of armor makes it more likely to erode when in the ground compared to weapons. In addition, perhaps armor was not as much a part of the warrior's identity as his weapons and thus was less commonly buried with him.

In pictorial sources, it is much the same story. One panel of the Franks Casket shows multiple warriors but only one wearing what might be interpreted as mail.[32]

The literary sources tend to support the idea that wearing armor during battle was not routine. Of the more than three hundred battles described in the *Sagas of Icelanders*, in only 9 percent of them are one or more fighters clearly described wearing a helmet, and in only 3 percent are one or more fighters clearly described wearing mail. Even outside of battle, there are many more mentions of weapons than mail or helmets in the sagas. Swords are mentioned seven times more often than helmets and ten times more often than mail.[33]

This discrepancy is even larger in the archaeological record. In Viking lands, thousands of swords are found, yet only one partial mail shirt and one partial helmet have been found.

The literary sources can help explain the discrepancy. As mentioned above, armor was used most often by leading figures, such as kings and earls. The king's levy troops were not required to own armor.[34] It seems likely that it was the more elite warriors, such as the king's *hirð* (his bodyguards who fought in the frontmost lines) who would own and wear armor.

But armor was not reserved exclusively for the elite. The literary sources mention ordinary men having helmets[35] or mail.[36] Perhaps it was felt that armor was more necessary for an elite warrior but optional for most other warriors. It was desirable if available but not crucial if unavailable. The sources suggest that Vikings most often fought with no additional body defenses beyond their normal, everyday clothing.

HELMETS

In the Viking age, helmets took the form of a simple, round bowl of iron strapped to the top of the head. There is little evidence that suggests that Viking helmets had horns, a long-cherished popular belief. Pictorial and archaeological evidence, such as the Oseberg Tapestry, the Öland bronze plates, and the Viksø helmets[37] tell us that helmets with horns existed in Scandinavia from well before the Viking age. These ancient helmets are so thin they would not have offered much protection in combat, and their having been deposited in a bog suggests that they were used for ritual purposes. The use of horns on Viking combat helmets is almost certainly a fabrication from the modern era.

No complete Viking-age helmet has been found in Viking lands, only fragments of helmets. The most complete find is the Gjermundbu helmet, which was excavated from a rich chieftain's grave at Gjermundbu in Norway along with weapons, riding gear, and a mail shirt.[38] Less than half of the helmet has survived, but there is enough remaining for us to have a clear understanding of how it was constructed.

Top: A helmet with horns is depicted on a bronze decorative plate from the Vendel era. Derived from Knut Stjerna, *Hjälmar ock svärd i Beovulf* (1903). Bottom: The Viking-age helmet from Gjermundbu. Derived from Ove Holst, *Hjelmen fra Gjermundbu*. Creative Commons.

The helmet is a *spangenhelm*, a style made from multiple, smaller pieces of sheet iron riveted together. Viking-age smiths could not easily make large sheets of iron, which would have allowed them to make a one- or two-piece helmet. So Viking-age helmets typically were made using the *spangenhelm* construction.

The Gjermundbu helmet has one 6 cm wide (2.4 in) band circling the brow. Four additional bands (in the front, back, left, and right) rise from the brow band and curve to meet at the top. The four openings are filled with triangu-

Top: A modern replica of a Viking-age helmet having the spangenhelm style of construction. Bottom: A replica Viking helmet with cheek guards and a mail curtain to protect the neck. Photos: William R. Short.

Top: A replica Viking helmet with a nose guard. Photo: Bruce Crooks. Bottom: The Coppergate helmet, an eighth century Anglo-Saxon helmet, that has cheek guards and a mail curtain. Derived from *Coppergate helmet* York Museums Trust Staff. Creative Commons.

lar plates. The joins between the sheets are all made with rivets. The resulting iron bowl is round, with an oval-shaped opening to fit the head having a major diameter of 23.3 cm (9.1 in).[39]

The Gjermundbu helmet also features a spectacle guard attached to the brow band covering the eyes and nose and extending down to about the cheekbones. It was decorated with diagonal strips of inlaid metal, now lost.

Also found at various sites are helmet fragments identified as facial protection. These fragments are thought to be nose guards (nasals) that protect the face, rather than spectacle guards, yet the objects are so poorly preserved that they are hard to identify or distinguish.[40]

It is this nose protection that is mentioned in the literary sources and is called *nefbjörg* (nose guard).[41] The literary sources also tell of

A figure of a man wearing a helmet thought to date from the 11th or 12th century. The figure is carved from an antler. Derived from Sören Hallgren, *SHM 22044.* Creative Commons.

*kinnbjörg* (cheek guard) used on helmets.[42] They are not found in the few examples of Viking helmets that have survived.

To form a clearer picture of this kind of guard, we are forced to use a surviving helmet from a nearby land. The Coppergate helmet from York is thought to predate the Viking period by a few decades.[43] It too is of *spangenhelm* construction, with a nose guard and hinged cheek guards. The cheek guards have evidence of a point of attachment for a strap or tie under the chin to hold the helmet firmly on the head by means of the cheek guards.

The Gjermundbu helmet shows evidence of mail suspended from the back of the helmet to protect the neck. The mail curtain on the Coppergate helmet has partially survived, giving us a picture of the size of the mail protection and how it attached to the helmet. The Gjermundbu helmet also has a short spike rising from the top of the helmet, giving it a notably menacing appearance.

With so few surviving examples, there can be no typology for Viking helmets as there is for Viking swords, for example. It is the coin-toss problem; there are too few variations to study or from which we can draw conclusions.

One can only speculate about where Viking armor, such as helmets, was fabricated. It seems possible the Gjermundbu helmet was within the capabilities of Viking smiths. Yet some scholars suspect that in large part, Viking-age armor came from continental smiths. The literary sources tell of King Óláfr equipping the 120 men aboard his ship with foreign helmets, and Carolingian documents tell us the export of some kinds of armor was prohibited from Carolingian lands.[44] At this time, there seems to be little evidence that suggests where the Gjermundbu helmet was fabricated.

While the size and form of the Gjermundbu helmet can be estimated from the surviving pieces, the weight is speculative. Based on the dimensions of the surviving pieces, it appears the weight of the complete helmet (minus the mail curtain) would be in the vicinity of 2 kg (4.5 pounds).[45] The mail curtain would add some significant additional weight.

Viking-age helmets shared many features with helmets that came before and after, yet there was an evolution. Between the earlier Vendel era and the Viking era, helmets became more plain, and the solid face mask protection of the Sutton Hoo helmet evolved into the spectacle guard of the Gjermundbu helmet. In later times, as metallurgy improved and smiths could create large sheets of iron, it became possible to fabricate helmets raised from a single sheet of iron, making the *spangenhelm* construction unnecessary. Helmets became more conical and pointed at the crown, rather than round, allowing a sword blow to glance off more readily.

This conical form of helmet is seen in a figure carved from an antler that was found in Sigtuna in Sweden, thought to date from the eleventh or twelfth century.[46] It shows the head of a warrior wearing a helmet of this style with a prominent nose guard. Many of the Swedish picture stones depict warriors with rounded helmets, but the Stenkyrka Lillabjärs III stone appears to show a conical helmet.[47] An illustration of Vikings approaching Frankish lands aboard their ships appears in a manuscript on the *Life of St. Aubin* dating from around the year 1100.[48] The Vikings wear an assortment of helmets, many rounded, some more pointed, most with mail curtains in the back, and some without any nose or face protection.

Based on the limited available evidence, we cannot say with certainty what form a typical Viking-age helmet took. We have a sample size of only one: the Gjermundbu helmet. It seems probable that when a Viking warrior wore a helmet, it was a simple rounded iron *spangenhelm* with a spectacle guard or nose guard. Yet at the same time, conical shapes with nose guards and other variants cannot be ruled out, especially in the later part of the Viking age, based on evidence available at this time.

MAIL SHIRT

The other form of Viking armor for which good evidence can be found is the mail shirt. As with helmets, few examples survive in the archaeological record, and we have even fewer pictorial sources, so our knowledge is even more conjectural than with helmets.

It seems probable that mail (*brynja*) took the form of a long shirt made up of tens of thousands of interlocking iron rings. It was probably T-shaped and fell to the thighs or lower, with arms to the elbows or longer.

As with helmets, only one mail shirt has survived from Viking lands, along with fragments of many others. The most complete shirt was found in the same grave at Gjermundbu as the helmet.[49] As with the helmet, much of the shirt is missing. It was folded before being placed in the grave, and many of the folds have fused. From what survives, it is not possible to reconstruct the shirt, so the shape and length are unknown. Individual rings or groups of a few rings have been found at other sites, notably the garrison at Birka.[50]

Because there is so little material to study, there is no typology for mail. Once again, it is

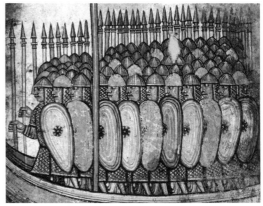

Top: A group of Vikings wearing mail and helmets depicted in *Illustrations de la vie de saint Aubin d'Angers*, an eleventh-century manuscript. Photo: Bibliothèque nationale de France. Bottom: A rider wearing a helmet depicted on the Stenkyrka Lillabjärs III stone. Derived from Gabriel Hildebrand, *Bildsten av sten*. Creative Commons.

the coin-toss problem; there are simply too few examples to compare and categorize.

The rings that form mail vary in size and construction. The rings of the Gjermundbu shirt are not uniform and vary in size. The average outer diameter is about 8 mm (0.3 in).[51] A study of surviving Viking-age mail rings shows that the Gjermundbu rings are at the small end of the range, with most mail shirt rings 9 to 11.5 mm (0.35 to 0.45 in) in diameter.[52] Generally, larger rings were made with larger diameter wire.[53]

The weave of the Gjermundbu shirt is 4-in-1, where each ring passes through its four nearest neighbors. It is the weave that is most typical for European mail from many periods.

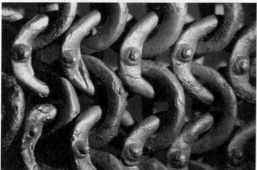

Top: A replica Viking-age mail shirt showing sleeve and skirt length thought to be typical of Viking-age mail. Photo: William R. Short. Center: A detailed view of the rings in the Gjermundbu mail shirt, showing the 4-in-1 weave typical of Viking-age mail. The Gjermundbu mail can be seen to be constructed using alternating rows of solid and riveted rings. Derived from *Brynje fra vikingtidsgraven ved Gjermundbu, C27317i.* Creative Commons. Bottom: A sample of 8-in-2 weave mail from a later period outside the Viking lands. Perhaps tvífaldr mail used a similar weave. Photo: William R. Short.

There is an aspect of mail weave that complicates the fabrication process. The mail must be shaped to fit the human form so that the shirt does not limit the warrior's mobility. Unless allowances are made, the shirt can bind, especially around the arms. So rather than being simple tubes of uniform dimensions, the dimensions of the garment vary, requiring that rows of rings have more or fewer rings than neighboring rows to form the shape of the garment. As a result, the weave is altered in places from the standard 4-in-1.

The literary sources[54] mention *tvífaldr* (doubled) mail,[55] suggesting the mail was doubled up in some manner. There are even examples of *ferfaldr* (quadrupled) mail.[56] One possibility is that the *tvífaldr* mail was simply doubled up to form two layers. Another possibility is that the mail used 8-in-2 weave, in which the rings were doubled up, with a pair of rings passing through four pairs of nearest neighbors. There are no clear archaeological examples of this weave from the Viking age, but it was used in other periods in Europe.

As the shirt was "woven" together, with rings formed around and through neighboring rings, it was necessary to make the rings solid. Viking-age iron rings that were simply bent and butted together did not have the strength to maintain their integrity during the stresses of battle when used in a mail shirt (although, as we will see later, they were used in other forms of mail). A shirt constructed of butted rings made from Viking-age iron would fall apart.

Rings were made solid in several possible ways. First, when making a shirt, half the rings could be made solid by punching them from a piece of sheet iron. This approach was used in the Gjermundbu shirt, as evidenced by the micro-details of the slag in the iron rings.[57] The remainder of the rings were riveted shut by overlapping the ends of a wire ring and setting a round rivet about 0.5 mm in diameter (20 mil) through the lap to seal it shut. There is also evidence that wire rings were made solid by welding in some ring finds.[58]

There is much that is unknown about mail construction. Even the process of making the wire to form the rings is not fully understood. Draw plates, used in later periods to draw wire to the desired size, are thought to be found among Viking-age smith's tools, such as the Mästermyr find,[59] but this identification is not without controversy.

However it was done, making mail was labor intensive, requiring skilled, delicate work to either set tiny rivets or to forge weld thin wire. It has been suggested that it would take four smiths 18 months to fabricate one mail shirt in the Viking age.[60] Additionally, the shirt required a lot of iron that carried with it some significant cost. As a result, mail shirts must have been costly and rare in the Viking age.

This discussion also raises the question of where this kind of specialized work was done. It has been suggested that mail was not routinely produced in Scandinavia in the Viking age, and that instead it was imported from the continent. Indeed, mail was one of the exports prohibited in the Carolingian empire. King Haraldr's mail was said to have come from Mikligarðr (Byzantium).[61] Yet there seems to be little evidence that rules out the production of mail in Viking homelands. At this time, the available evidence does not allow a firm conclusion about the source of mail.

Since no complete mail shirt survives from Viking lands, we must fall back on sources from other lands to speculate on the nature of the shirt. One of the best-preserved mail shirts is the mail of St. Wenceslas from Bohemia (now in the Czech Republic), thought to date from the tenth century. It is a shirt to fit a large man, with a long skirt and long sleeves. The length from the shoulder to the hem is 108 cm (42.5 in). If it were complete, it is estimated it would have eighty thousand to one hundred thousand rings,[62] which suggests a weight of 10 to 13 kg for the shirt (22 to 28 lb).[63] A similar estimate for the Gjermundbu shirt suggests its weight, if complete, would be 12 to 13 kg (26 to 28 lb).[64]

The literary sources tell us some mail shirts were long. King Haraldr's mail shirt, which was

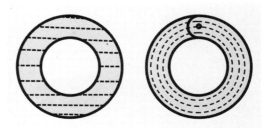

Orientation of the slag in the various rings of the Gjermundbu mail shirt is convincing proof that some rings were punched out of sheet stock, and others were formed from wire and then riveted shut. Illustration: William R. Short.

named *Emma*, reached down to his knees in some sources[65] and down to his shoes in another.[66] Pictorial sources, such as the manuscript illumination of Vikings approaching Frankish lands aboard their ships in *The Life of St. Aubin* show what appears to be mail shirts that reach to the knees.[67]

Episodes in the literary sources provide more clues. There are several examples of warriors stabbing up under the skirt of the mail shirt of their opponent.[68] These thrusts travel up into the *smáþarmar* (lower abdomen) or the *kviðr* (abdomen). For a weapon to travel up and hit the abdomen would seem to rule out a very short mail shirt, which wouldn't require the weapon to travel up to reach the abdomen, as well as ruling out a very long mail shirt, which would prevent the weapon from hitting the abdomen for any reasonable angle of thrust. This evidence would seem to suggest mid-thigh length.

Mail was used in forms other than shirts. Some helmets had a mail curtain on the back to protect the neck. Both the Gjermundbu helmet and the Coppergate helmet had mail curtains. A relatively small piece of mail can provide significant protection to the vulnerable targets at the back of the neck without interfering with mobility.

The mail on the Coppergate helmet used alternating riveted and butted rings.[69] In this application, the mail is not subject to the stresses of a mail shirt, and so butted rings could be ex-

A modern replica helmet with a mail curtain. Photo: William R. Short.

pected to survive. First, the total weight of the mail curtain is much less than that of the mail shirt, so the weight hanging from and stressing the topmost rings of a curtain is much less than for a shirt. Additionally, the vigorous motions of combat, especially around the arms and shoulders, put more stress on a shirt than the motions of head and neck place on a curtain. Thus, there is some expectation that butted rings could survive when used in a curtain.

Additionally, our cutting tests, described in more detail later in the chapter, show that butted mail hasn't the strength to withstand a sword thrust,[70] an attack much more likely to a mail shirt than to a mail curtain at the back of the neck.

HOW ARMOR WAS USED

Using armor seems to have been straightforward. Armor is passive protection. Warriors donned their armor, and it was expected to provide protection during the fight without the warrior having to do anything further. Armor reduces the risk of the edge of the weapon biting flesh, and it reduces the risk of

broken bones and other trauma by spreading out and dissipating the force of the weapon's impact.

Armor may have relied on supplemental gear to enhance its protective abilities. For example, it is necessary to lift the helmet away from the crown of the head so the impact of a blow can be dissipated and spread to protect the wearer. An iron bowl resting on the crown of the head does little to soften the impact of the blow.

The nature of the helmet suspension is highly speculative. Some have suggested a leather suspension fixed to the iron helmet. Others have suggested a cap of absorbent material worn under the helmet. Neither suggestion has strong supporting evidence, so we can say little that is definitive about what was used in the Viking age.

The helmet must be strapped or tied to the head so it doesn't shift or fall off during the extreme movements associated with combat, such as lunging forward, twisting the neck, or squatting to avoid an attack. Again, the evidence for strapping is slim, since there are so few surviving examples to study. The Coppergate helmet seems to have attachment points for a strap or tie under the chin to hold it firmly on the head.[71]

Likewise, the literary sources tell us that some helmets had these kinds of fastenings for the cheek guards. *Grágás* provides evidence that some hats used chin straps, since there were laws relating to them.[72] If chin straps were used for normal hats, it seems possible straps would be used for the more critical application of holding the helmet in place.

Pictorial sources, such as the Bayeux Tapestry, show what appears to be a helmet affixed with a strap under the chin,[73] but other interpretations are possible. The nature of this strap or tie is unknown. But taken together, these examples seem to show that a strap or tie was used to fix the helmet on the head.

An assessment was made of various straps and suspension systems for replica Viking helmets.[74] Tests were performed to determine whether the helmet was firmly fixed to the head and whether the helmet interfered with movement or balance or vision. Some of the helmet systems worked better than others, but with any of them, it was possible to make the helmet one with the head so that it didn't shift or interfere with movement. The effect on vision of the helmet's nose guard or spectacle guard varied from person to person and seemed to depend on the fit of the helmet. When the fit was secure, vision seemed unimpaired with either style guard. While these modern tests suggest possibilities, they do not prove or disprove what may have been used to suspend, pad, and secure the Viking helmet to the head of a Viking warrior.

In the case of a mail shirt, a piece of supplemental gear that is well supported is a waist belt that gathers the mail, transferring some of its weight to the hips, relieving the shoulders of the burden. The use of belts is seen in the illumination from the manuscript of St. Aubin's life.[75] In contrast, only some of the fighters wearing mail shown in the Bayeux Tapestry are clearly wearing a belt.[76] Perhaps the artists who created the tapestry chose to omit that detail for the mounted mail-clad fighters, since at least some of these figures clearly have a sword scabbard at their waist but no belt to support it.[77]

Both before and after the Viking age, evidence suggests that fighters wore a padded garment under the mail often called a *gambeson*, a later French word. The literary sources use several words that might be considered a gambeson-like garment for Viking warriors. One of these words is *vápntreyja*, which combines the word for weapon and the word *treyja*. In the *Sagas of Icelanders*, *treyja* seems to refer to a conventional fabric tunic. One of the few instances where the clothing worn under mail is described as *silkihjúpr*, a loose, silk, upper-body garment.[78]

It is in stories set later, after the Viking age, that the *treyja* and *brynja* are connected and appear together on the same warrior, notably in *Sturlunga saga* and other late sources.[79]

Vikings wearing a belt to secure their mail depicted in *Illustrations de la vie de saint Aubin d'Angers*, an eleventh-century manuscript. Photo: Bibliothèque nationale de France.

*Hirðskrá*, a late-thirteenth-century Norwegian law book, specifically states that mail or *panzari* (a jack, mentioned earlier in this chapter) should be worn over *vápntreyja*.[80] Perhaps in later periods, *vápntreyja* referred to a gambeson-like garment. Yet the support for the use of a *vápntreyja* in the Viking age is inconclusive, with evidence for and against. Nothing definitive is found in the archaeological record, and the pictorial records are not detailed enough to distinguish various kinds of armor with certainty. One can speculate about whether the various stripes and crosshatching extending beyond the sleeves of the mail-clad riders in the Bayeux Tapestry represent a *vápntreyja*, but the detail is insufficient to be able to draw any firm conclusions.

If Viking-age people did wear *vápntreyja*, it would explain why King Haraldr and his men did not wear mail at the battle of Stamford Bridge. The literary sources say the day was warm, so the king and his men left their mail aboard their ships as they prepared for the bat-

Can a mail shirt and *vápntreyja* be hidden under a Viking tunic? This modern simulation makes it seem unlikely; the added bulk is quite apparent in the photo on the right. Photo: William R. Short.

tle.[81] Mail itself, being a mesh, would not seem likely to hold in heat in a warm day. However, a padded *vápntreyja* is likely to be stifling on a warm day, holding in both heat and sweat. If wearing mail also included wearing a *vápntreyja*, it would be easy to see why these warriors chose to leave the mail behind.

The literary sources give another clue about the nature of a *vápntreyja*. There are examples of men wearing mail (or suspected of wearing mail) surreptitiously, under their tunics.[82] To determine the feasibility of the subterfuge, the ability of a normal tunic to hide underlying mail and *vápntreyja* was tested.[83] If the *vápntreyja* was heavy, like the kind of arming coat later used and worn under plate armor, then the hidden mail was readily apparent, since the wearer resembled the Michelin man. One presumes a thin *vápntreyja* with thin padding (and thus less protection) would make it easier to hide the presence of the mail under the tunic.

The effect on movement and performance when wearing mail was tested.[84] Wearing mail over normal training clothes degraded measured performance in running (a 17 percent in-crease in time), high jumping (33 percent decrease in height), and broad jumping (17 percent decrease in length). It seems safe to presume that more training while wearing mail would reduce these differences. Wearing a heavy *vápntreyja*, however, was a different story. It significantly impaired mobility while fighting in simulated combat, with or without mail.

Solid answers to the question of whether a *vápntreyja* was worn under mail remain elusive. There is little evidence from Viking-age sources that strongly suggests it, but neither is there evidence that makes its use unlikely. On the one hand, the cutting tests and the impact measurements discussed later in the chapter show that mail protects even without the use of *vápntreyja*. On the other hand, the use of the *vápntreyja* would reduce the wear and tear and filth caused by mail when worn directly over an everyday tunic. Either way, common sense suggests a padded layer can only help the mail do a better job of distributing the impact, increasing the margin of safety for the warrior wearing *vápntreyja* under mail.

WOOL CLOTHING AS ARMOR

Though unlikely intended as armor, normal woolen clothing worn by Viking-age people offered some protection against cutting attacks. While the wool is unlikely to stop a powerful cut, measurements and testing showed that it provided a surprising degree of protection against less-powerful cutting attacks and from the impact of the weapon,[85] as discussed in the next section.

PROTECTIVE ABILITIES OF ARMOR

Even though our understanding of the nature of Viking armor is far from clear, we seek to know how well it functioned to protect the warrior wearing it. We turn to the literary sources and to experimental archaeology to provide some answers.

On the one hand, there is no armor that makes the wearer invulnerable. All armor has limits to its protective ability. Despite those limits, the armor may still provide benefits that make it valuable to a Viking warrior. A layer of iron between a warrior's body and the edge of his opponent's weapon has to be a better situation than having no armor there. Our investigation looked at the limits of Viking armor.

HELMET PROTECTION

Literary sources tell us that against a cut, a helmet could provide full protection,[86] partial protection,[87] or no protection at all.[88] In one example, a fighter was surprised when his opponent's helmet held after a powerful blow,[89] while in several other examples, the blow not only split the helmet but also the skull inside.[90]

Whether splitting the helmet is an exaggeration or not, there are additional sources of injury. The energy delivered by the hit can cause internal trauma. Even if the helmet and padding spread the impact, the energy of the hit can violently accelerate the head, causing internal bleeding and trauma to the brain. It is only in recent years that the harm caused by this acceleration has come to light, since the mental impairments caused by this trauma may take a long time to reveal themselves.

The acceleration caused by the hit of a replica Viking sword to a human head wearing a replica Viking helmet was measured.[91] Even though the cut was made at a modest power level for safety, the measured rotational acceleration of the skull was over 2000 rad/sec$^2$, in excess of what is currently considered safe.

The test was insightful on several levels and generated many additional questions. Though modest, the hit to the helmet resulted in accelerations to the skull now thought likely to cause trauma to the brain. What would have happened with a full-power hit to the helmet? What if there had been no helmet to spread out and dissipate the blow? What if it had been a sharp weapon? Our cutting tests to animal carcasses show these sharp weapons cut through flesh and bone with ease. It takes little imagination to see the value of the helmet, even if the protection is not complete. More measurements are needed using accurate mannequins for safety and ethical reasons, and testing against an accurately constructed helmet

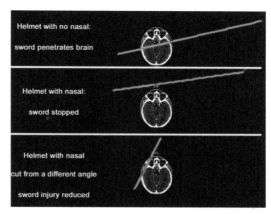

A computer simulation shows the effectiveness of the protection offered by the nose guard of a Viking helmet against a sword cut. Over a variety of angles, the nose guard blocked the weapon from entering the head.

reproduction using materials similar to Viking-age iron.

Another aspect of the protective capabilities of a Viking helmet that was measured was the degree of protection offered by the nose guard.[92] Given that the face is essentially open, surprisingly few hits reached the face or eyes during the testing. To understand how the nose guard provided that degree of protection, a computer model of the head and helmet was created.[93] The simulations showed that the nose guard provided a large degree of protection against cuts across the face from various angles, blocking the edge of the weapon from reaching anything vital. The simulation also showed that there was an optimum geometry of the guard that offered the best protection. Sadly, none of the surviving nose guards are in good enough condition to compare their geometry with what the simulation predicts to be optimal.

The literary sources suggest that a powerful cut could split the nose guard and penetrate the head,[94] yet if the nose guard held, the simulations and lab tests show that the nose guard provided a significant degree of protection.

The evidence suggests that Viking helmets have limits. They can be penetrated, according to literary sources. They do not absorb enough energy to avoid brain trauma, according to measurements. Yet it seems likely that any Viking-age warrior who had a helmet would take advantage of the protection it offered by wearing it during a fight, since there were few disadvantages to wearing one. That layer of iron could be the difference between life and death. Even outside of battle, men took advantage of the protection by wearing their helmets while traveling and even while sleeping.[95]

MAIL PROTECTION

Likewise with mail, the literary sources tell us the protection could be nil or full or something in between. Several literary examples suggest that mail could be split by weapons,[96] while one says the men in mail suffered no injuries during a long battle.[97]

Pictorial sources from outside Viking lands also suggest that mail could be split. The Bayeux Tapestry shows a number of fallen men whose mail appears to have been pierced by a spear.[98]

The ability of mail to protect against a cut was tested using sharp replica weapons, replica mail, and an animal carcass. Mail was placed on the neck and on a limb, and cuts were made to the mail.[99] In both cases, the mail provided excellent protection, with no broken bones and minimal damage to the skin, despite there being no *vápntreyja* or tunic under the mail. The mail had minor damage; the force of the impact distorted only a single ring, which was still strong enough to hold the fabric of the mail together.

That mail was difficult to penetrate is also suggested by several episodes in the literary sources. Instead of trying to go through it, fighters sometimes went around it by thrusting up under the hem of the shirt to the unprotected body underneath.[100]

Mail protects not only against the bite of the weapon but also against its impact. When making a cut with an edged weapon, the edge not only shears flesh and bone, but the weapon also delivers kinetic energy to the opponent that can break bones and damage organs and cause internal bleeding.

Top: One of several warriors depicted on the Bayeux Tapestry whose mail shirt has been penetrated by a spear. Detail of the Bayeux Tapestry, eleventh century, with special permission from the City of Bayeux. Bottom: Sword cuts caused no observable damage to a pig carcass covered with replica mail; no broken bones and no lesions to the skin could be found. Damage to the mail was minimal, with one distorted but still solid ring shown here. Photo: William R. Short.

The ability of various kinds of armor to dissipate the impact of the blow was tested with measurements using replica weapons and armor worn by a human test subject.[101] Relative to bare skin, a tunic passed 33 percent of the energy compared to the energy delivered to bare skin; *vápntreyja* alone 5.7 percent; mail alone 1.1 percent; mail with *vápntreyja* 0.5 percent; and mail with tunic 0.6 percent. Mail, whether backed by a garment or not, blocked

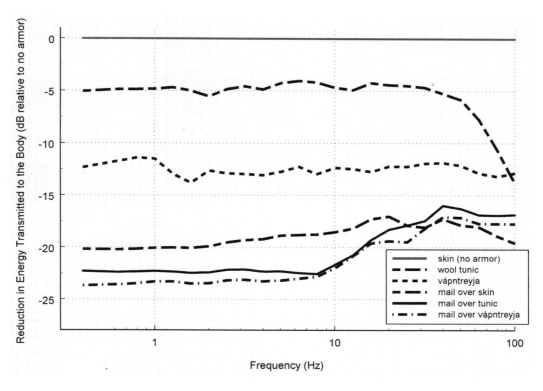

A plot of the measured ability of replica Viking-age armor to reduce the energy of a sword cut delivered to the human body which was wearing the armor. The energy reduction is plotted in the frequency domain, which helps us understand the nature of the reduction in energy, and thus, the nature of the protection.

a substantial portion of the impact of the hit from the body underneath. And surprisingly, a wool tunic alone dissipated a not-insignificant amount of the energy.

The measurements show the secondary benefit of mail. In addition to preventing the weapon from biting, mail spreads the impact of the blow, reducing the possibility of trauma that might put a warrior out of the fight. The data also show that this secondary benefit is only slightly enhanced by wearing a *vápntreyja* rather than only a tunic under the mail. Perhaps this result helps to explain why we see little evidence of a *vápntreyja* under mail in the Viking age.

SWIMMING IN MAIL

As is discussed in the next chapter, men sometimes jumped or fell overboard during naval battles while wearing mail. The literary sources suggest that some of the men drowned, and some were able to remove the shirt underwater and then swim away.[102] We were curious to test whether a man could swim while wearing mail.

The ability to swim in mail was tested using a replica mail shirt over replica Viking clothing.[103] Many people who attempted the feat sank to the bottom after only a few strokes. But two of our test subjects, who were accustomed to swimming in the cold seas of the North Atlantic, were able to swim as they pleased while wearing mail. The results show us the difficulties of swimming in mail but also suggest it might be possible. Perhaps some Viking warriors were able to swim long enough clad in mail to escape a naval battle, which explains why, during these battles, small boats sometimes were deployed to kill enemy fighters who jumped or fell overboard.[104]

A test of swimming while wearing a mail shirt. Photo: Todd Pelletier.

SUMMARY AND CONCLUSIONS

We have only limited sources that help us piece together the nature of Viking-age armor, so large portions of the picture are missing. This chapter is the perfect example of the coin-toss problem. So few examples of Viking-age armor have survived in the archaeological records that we have only a hazy picture of what the armor was, and we do not know how commonly it was used.

The available sources suggest that if a Viking fighter wore armor, it took the form of a helmet and mail shirt. This armor, like any physical material, has limits, yet despite these limits, the benefits were great enough to make wearing armor desirable for a warrior. Armor was most often used by the elite warriors whose death or injury on the battlefield might hand victory to the enemy. Armor was probably not common. Taken together, the sources lead us to the conclusion that when most Vikings fought, they did so without armor, wearing their normal, everyday clothes.

- 11 -

# MASS BATTLES

INTRODUCTION

In this chapter, we will look at the large-scale battles fought by Vikings, involving thousands, and even tens of thousands, of warriors at times. Many of these fall into the category of dynastic battles: fights in which the outcome determined who would rule the land. These large-scale mass battles would have been less likely in the early part of the Viking age, when there were no national rulers, as we will discuss in a moment.

SOURCES

As so often seems the case with Viking combat, our sources about large-scale battles are limited. The literary sources provide the most detailed information.

The *Kings' Sagas*, such as *Heimskringla*, are histories of the kings of Norway. They tell of many dynastic battles, on land and sea, from well before the Viking age to the end of the twelfth century. When writing *Heimskringla*, Snorri Sturluson relied on the skaldic verses composed by eyewitnesses to the battles, believing them to be faithfully preserved over the centuries.[1]

Sadly, we have no comparable book for the kings of Denmark or of Sweden, backed up by eyewitness accounts. Fortunately, we have some sources that show us that the nature of large-scale battle was quite similar in all Viking lands. The *Kings' Sagas* tell of battles of Nor-wegian kings, sometimes against the kings of Sweden and Denmark (such as the Battle of Svölðr),[2] and sometimes allied with them (Battle at Danavirki),[3] and warriors from all these lands fought in a similar manner.

Large parts of *Jómsvíkinga saga* tell of Danish kings and their battles during the Viking age, as do portions of *Fornkonunga saga*. The nature of these battles closely matches that of the battles related in the *Kings' Sagas*, further suggesting that mass battles shared many similarities in all Viking lands.

Additionally, the *Sagas of Icelanders* also tell of mass battles. Occasionally, the same battle is reported both in *Heimskringla*, where the focus is on the king, and in one of the *Sagas of Icelanders*, where the focus is on the Icelanders fighting for the king. The literary sources tell of numerous Icelanders who traveled for adventure as young men, and a number of them became king's men, fighting for the king.

For example, the battle at Stiklarstaðir, in which King Óláfr helgi lost his life, is reported both in *Ólafs saga helga* (where the focus is on the king) and in *Fóstbrœðra saga*[4] (where the focus is on Þormóðr Bersason). The difference in the focus of the two versions helps us better understand the nature of the large-scale battles. We see the scope of the battle where the spotlight is on the king, and we see the up-close-and-dirty combat experienced by individual warriors.

Episodes in the legendary sagas and in the *þættir* paint a similar picture of mass battle. Regrettably, these sources are less independent of one another than it might at first seem, since the authors of each likely used many of the same sources. And so we must seek additional sources that help us understand mass battles in the Viking age.

Other literary sources that discuss large-scale battles include Saxo's *Gesta Danorum*, a medieval history of Denmark completed in the thirteenth century. Saxo himself states that he used Icelandic materials to create a considerable part of his book, along with runestone inscriptions,[5] and it seems likely he used Danish sources as well.

Saxo appears to have come from a military family, stating that both his father and grandfather served with and fought for the king,[6] so perhaps Saxo was aware of the nature of mass battles, at least as they were fought during the time of his father and grandfather in the twelfth century. Yet Saxo, as well as histories such as Abbo's *De bellis Parisiacæ*, must be used with great care, especially as they relate to mass battles, due to use of Latin terms, as described in the sources chapter.

Other literary sources include later Norwegian law codes, such as *Gulaþingslög*. The law codes tell of the king's levy army and how they were called out and how they were armed. *Konungs skuggsjá*, also late, provides information about how the king's *hirð* (bodyguard and chosen men) should be armed, should train, and should conduct themselves. Because these and similar sources are late, they must be used with care.

Another literary source that can help us are the myths, which tell of mass battles among the gods, such as the first battle of the world between two families of gods, the Æsir and Vanir.[7] Additionally, runestones tell of battles and of the behavior in battle of the warrior being memorialized and his fellow warriors.

Pictorial sources, such as picture stones, show battles and hosts of fighting men but provide few clues about how the battles were conducted. Outside of Viking times and Viking lands, there are manuscript illuminations and tapestries showing large-scale battles, but they must be used with care.

Archaeological sources, such as excavations of large structures built by kings and used for battle, help create a picture of some forms of mass battle. Additionally, graves from places where warriors congregated provide insights into the kind of gear carried by warriors participating in these larger-scale battles.

Bioarchaeological examinations of skeletal remains show battle trauma, but this source is limited because there are surprisingly few examples of skeletal remains showing battle trauma from Viking lands in Viking times, as discussed in the sources chapter.

THE RISE OF VIKING KINGS

It is worth pausing for a moment to review the history of the Viking lands so the reader better understands the political changes that occurred between the time leading up to the Viking age and the end of the Viking age. These political changes transformed how large battles were conducted. It is during this time that Viking kings arose. Because of the limitations of our available sources discussed above, the focus of this review is on Norwegian kings.

In the earliest days, Norway was ruled by petty kings, earls, and other chieftains. There was no central authority for the land, and thus nothing like a large, standing military force.

That situation started changing in the reign of King Haraldr Hálfdanarson, a petty king who ascended the throne in the year 860 at age 10. His uncle took control of his *hirð*, a word sometimes translated as army, but perhaps more accurately as the armed men in his court, such as his bodyguard. Many other petty kings made incursions into Haraldr's lands, taking advantage of his weakness. Later, Haraldr asked Gyða to be his concubine, but she turned down his request as being unworthy until Haraldr ruled all of Norway independently.[8]

This feat the king largely accomplished, in battle after battle, drawing in more and more fighting men and changing the very nature of the governance of the king over his subjects. The details of Haraldr's actions as reported in *Heimskringla* may not be accurate or complete, and indeed, may be anachronistic.[9] Yet the overall picture shares similarities with that presented in other literary sources, such as *Landnámabók* and *Íslendingabók*.

King Haraldr appropriated the ancestral lands and possessions of the farmers as his own when he gained power over a district, and all were required to pay a tax to the king. An earl was appointed to collect taxes and fines. Every earl was required to have four or more *hersar* under him, high-ranking fighting men supported by a portion of the collected taxes. Each earl was required to provide sixty fighting men to the king, and each *hersir* twenty fighting men.[10]

While there are several descriptions of king's men training, as discussed in the introduction to the weapons chapter,[11] there is little that suggests these lower-level warriors received special training. Presumably the earl and the *hersir* chose the best fighters in the district to be their followers.

Thus, Haraldr set up a military structure and a means to support it, district by district, as he gained power over the land. Some believe that these actions, combined with the loss of *óðal*, the right of free farmers to own their ancestral lands, triggered the wave of emigration of many Norwegians to Iceland, although there were probably additional factors in play.[12]

It was at this time in history that there is a divergence between Norway and Iceland, based on the available sources. It seems Icelanders wanted to maintain the freedoms to which they were accustomed in Norway before Haraldr's reign. Accordingly, they set up a government with no central authority, and thus no king, a unique situation that even elicited comments from contemporary authors. Adam of Bremen wrote in the late eleventh century, "They have no king, only the law."[13] The Icelandic legal system had no executive branch and no army. Society was very flat, with only two categories of people distinguished in the law codes: free and not-free.[14]

In contrast, Norway continued on the path started by Haraldr, and the structures he put in place were strengthened by subsequent kings, leading to a feudal society with a class system supported by taxes. Land, which had formerly been ancestral, now was owned by the king and administered by his nobles, enforced by a military. Similar changes eventually arrived in Iceland during the turbulent Sturlunga era, resulting in the loss of Icelanders' independence as they agreed to become subjects of the king of Norway in 1262–1264.[15]

WARRIORS IN MASS BATTLES

Large-scale dynastic battles, pitting king against king for control of the country, used the same weapons discussed in earlier chapters and almost all of the tactics described later in the tactics chapter. What distinguished these battles from smaller-scale mêlées was the large numbers of fighters involved, as many as thousands on each side; the nature of the troops who fought, including full-time professional warriors and well-equipped reserve warriors; and the control of those troops, which seems to have been of a military nature.

As we discuss these large-scale battles, we have to look closely at the Old Icelandic words used to describe the fighters in the literary sources. The English translations must be chosen with care to avoid the implied meanings that some of these English words convey. As an example, the words *lið* and *hirð* and *herr* are often translated as army, but the military nature of the modern word *army* seems to be absent in *lið* and *herr*, which both have the sense of a host, a large group of warriors without any implication about their training, discipline, or skill. The words are also applied to nonbelligerent groups, in the sense of a people, a crew, or a household.[16]

*Hirð*, in contrast, refers to the king's personal warriors, men whose only job was to be prepared to fight for the king.[17] They formed a tight-knit group, not only among themselves but with the king. They were full-time warriors. They were his chosen men and bodyguards. Only men of unusual strength, bravery, and accomplishments were accepted into this group.[18] The king's *hirð* was filled only by heroes.[19] King Haraldr chose men from every district he ruled for this group of elite fighters, whom he supported generously. They were the fighters placed in the front lines of these large-scale battles.

We have few details about the training that the men of the *hirð* performed to maintain their readiness during the Viking age. Saxo tells us they practiced delivering and parrying blows like dueling,[20] a fighting paradigm discussed in the dueling chapter. Men went to ranges to practice their archery,[21] and they trained with other projectiles as well.[22] In the period well after the Viking age, *Konungs skuggsjá* describes the kinds of training a *hirð* man should perform: riding with shield and spear, mock combat with sword and shield, archery practice, spear throwing, and throwing stones.[23] Yet the literary sources that focus on the Viking age seem to be silent.

The king's fighting men do not seem to have been a large group. When King Óláfr helgi built a new royal residence, his *hirð* consisted of sixty men.[24] He had additional permanent staff for the house, but it seems unlikely they were called to fight for the king under normal circumstances. There were thirty *gestir* (guests), men who traveled to do the king's business on his behalf and thus were guests in many peoples' homes during their travels.[25]

The king had thirty *húskarlar* (*house men*) who were primarily servants and not warriors. They did what was necessary to provision and staff the royal residence. In addition, there were many *þrælar*—slaves and other low-status servants.

Over a century later, King Óláfr kyrri had a household staff double that of King Óláfr helgi: 120 *hirðmenn*, sixty *gestir*, and sixty *húskarlar*, and his subjects commented on the larger-than-usual numbers of household staff.[26]

THE KING'S LEVY

In addition to his permanent staff, the king had additional fighting men he could call up for service, including his earls, *hersar*, and their fighting men. Additionally, King Hákon Aðalsteinsfóstri created a levy (*leiðangur*),[27] a fully equipped reserve of fighting men. Although originally a naval-based coastal defense, the levy came to be used on land and sea for a variety of offensive and defensive purposes by the king.

Hákon made a law dividing all the districts into ship-levies (*skipreiða*).[28] The law stated how many ships of what sizes were to be available for the king's use in each district[29] and how they should be furnished, equipped, and maintained.

Typically, fighters in the levy were farmers who were equipped with the usual panoply of Viking weapons. Each free man in the levy was required to have either a broadaxe or a sword, along with a spear and a shield of specified construction. Additionally, the free farmers together were required to have one bow and twenty-four arrows for each pair of rowing positions in every levy ship.

As discussed in the sword chapter, swords became plainer and less adorned during this time. Perhaps some of these changes were driven by the need to make a larger number of swords for the use of the king's levy.

Slaves (*þrælar*) were also called to serve, and a slave who killed an enemy warrior while serving in the levy was granted his freedom.

By law, the use of the levy was reserved for times that served the public good. All free men with few exceptions (such as priests) were required to contribute to the levy, and to participate when called. To avoid disrupting the economy, only one out of every seven farmers in the district were expected to respond, leaving the others to run the farms. In times of extreme peril, more farmers were called to the levy.

The term of service for the farmers called up seems open ended, yet the farmers could not be away from their farms for an indefinite period. There are a number of examples of the levy being released and returning home when there was no longer a threat, such as when the invader left without a fight or when the battle was won and the intruder fled.[30]

To call up the levy, the king set up a system of beacons along the coast to spread the news of a threat requiring the calling up of the levy over the entire land within a week. The beacons were manned by the levy.[31]

Individual farms were informed by sending a war-arrow (*herör*) from farm to farm, a token that conflict was at hand and that men were needed to fight for the king.[32] Not only did kings send out a war-arrow, but so did farmers who were opposing the king's incursions into their district, summoning free men and slaves to defend the land.[33] While several researchers have speculated on the nature of the war-arrow, the available evidence is very slight, as discussed in the archery chapter. The Gulaþing law suggests it was made of iron.[34]

In addition to king's men and levy troops, several other types of fighters are mentioned in the historical sources. It is worth pausing to review what these sources tell us about these specialized fighters, since some of the material in popular sources can be far removed from the historical sources.

### BERSERKS

Berserks (*berserkir*) are unique but hard-to-define warriors found in all the literary sources, including the law codes, as well as in the pictorial sources. Berserks are infused with elements of magic and of the supernatural.

Even the etymology of the word is controversial, a combination of *ber-* (related to both bare and bear) and *serkr* (shirt).[35] It is said that berserks wore no armor,[36] and so some suggest the word derives from bare-shirted. It is said that berserks wore wolf skins for their armor,[37] and so others suggest the word derives from bear shirt. Indeed, berserks were called *ulfheðinn* (wolf-skin).[38]

In combat, berserks entered a state of battle frenzy (*berserksgangr*). As they entered this state, they howled like wolves or dogs and bit the edges of their shields,[39] famously depicted in the Lewis chess pieces.[40] A word used to describe entering this state is *hamask*, which

A berserk biting his shield is one of a set of 12th century chessmen carved from walrus ivory that were found on the Isle of Lewis in the Hebrides. Photo: William R. Short.

means to rage. But there is more to the meaning of the word, which is related to *hamr* (shape, or the skin of an animal). Some berserks were also called *hamrammr* (shape-changer),[41] assuming the qualities of wild animals in their fury.[42] In some examples, going berserk and changing shape are said to be equivalent.[43] Some unnaturally strong men were said not to be *einhamr* (single-shape),[44] implying they were shape changers and therefore berserks.[45]

Berserks were closely associated with heathen and magical practices. The *Grágás* law code banned going berserk under the Christian laws dealing with magic.[46] During the conversion, as a proof of the superiority of their faith, missionaries vanquished berserks.[47] Some berserks had the ability to blunt weapons through magic.[48] They were closely connected with Óðinn and were called Óðinn's men.[49] It is thought that Óðinn's name is associated with *óðr*, the fury that arises during the battle frenzy of a berserk. The connection is strengthened by Adam of Bremen, who wrote that Wodan (the Germanic name for Óðinn) was fury.[50] The links to magic and to Óðinn suggest berserks were something more than just individuals with special talents.

During their rage, berserks took on supernatural strength and courage.[51] Iron could not bite them, nor fire harm them.[52] In their rage, they attacked and killed everything in front of them, not stopping until the last man was dead.[53] Their blind animal fury occasionally caused them to attack family members.[54] Their place in battle, whether on land or at sea, was in the front of the battle, fighting for the king or other leader.[55] They were often connected with raiding and dueling.[56] In short, while in their fury, they were monstrous killing machines.

It is clear that berserks were strong, courageous warriors.[57] In a battle, it was a team of berserks that a Viking wanted by his side. Yet at home, in a domestic agricultural setting, berserks were decidedly out of place and not wanted.[58]

WOMEN WARRIORS

In the most general sense, it seems women were not supposed to fight or even bear arms in Viking society. The sources, when layered, paint a clear picture of women not routinely being a part of combat. There are countless literary sources telling of men fighting and few of women fighting. In battle, there are mentions of women being permitted to leave[59] or even being forced off the scene of a fight,[60] and the law codes ban women from carrying weapons.[61]

Conventionally, women have not been thought of as active participants in combat but rather as very influential but passive inciters to violence. Their role often was to instigate the plan that eventually led to the violence, for example, egging on their husbands or sons to make a revenge attack.[62] This seemingly clear picture of women and their separation from battle might not be so clear; it has a murky spot. The literary sources tell us that when women were forced to fight due to circumstances, they performed very well.

In *Færeyinga saga*, Þuríðr took up arms when her farm was attacked. Not only did she fight, she is said to have fought as well as any man. Similarly, when Þorbjörg encountered an armed assailant, she wrestled him down and bit out his throat to kill him.[63] How did women like Þuríðr and Þorbjörg become so capable at combat if this role was not normal or routine for their gender?

The *Grágás* law code is a product of the Christian era. While many older heathen elements remain, it is possible that under Christian laws and customs, gender roles were perhaps more solid and inflexible than in earlier times.[64]

Other clues point to that assessment as well, such as the concept of *drengr*. *Drengr* was a word used for men and women as mentioned in the mindset chapter,[65] but later it evolved and took on the meaning of a young man.[66] Women were no longer associated with *drengr*.

In the ancient heathen myths, there are a few women warriors. The giantess Skaði not only carried weapons, but when she went to avenge her father's death, all the gods became fearful of this warrior woman who was fully dressed for battle. The gods were prepared to do what was required to compensate Skaði to avoid her vengeance. Þórr, the strongest god of all, was brought down to one knee when fighting Elli, the old foster mother of a giant. She took down anyone who stepped up to her.[67]

Perhaps the strongest argument for women warriors lies in the evidence for two groups of women most notably associated with the battlefield: *skjaldmeyjar* (shield maidens)[68] and *valkyrjur* (Valkyries).

SHIELD MAIDENS

The *skjaldmeyjar* were women who took on the customs and clothing of men[69] and went to battle, most commonly as the leaders of bands of warriors.[70]

This unique group of warriors is not often mentioned in the literary sources. For example, they do not appear in the *Sagas of Icelanders* or *Heimskringla* and are only mentioned once in *Jómsvíkinga saga*, where a man is named after a *skjaldmær* (shield maiden).[71] The legendary sources and Saxo have several mentions of *skjaldmeyjar*, but even in these sources they are not common.

The word *skjaldmær* suggests that perhaps pictorial sources, such as jewelry, may provide additional clues. Figures depicting a woman carrying a shield have been found.[72] These pictorial sources and the literary descriptions are not without their interpretive flaws. While the word *skjaldmær* is associated with a shield, which the pictorial sources show, these sources do not show the woman leading from in front of her team.

Another issue is that these women are shown dressed in female clothing, unlike the description of *skjaldmær* in the literary sources, who are dressed as men. The pictures seem to have more in common with Valkyries, discussed later, than with *skjaldmær*.

The common thread of the *skjaldmær* is that these women were the daughters of earls[73] or kings[74] who, from a young age, refused to do womanly things. Instead they chose to train in arms and go to battle leading bands of men. They literally yearned for the blood of their enemies.[75] Saxo describes them best:

A silver figurine of a woman carrying a sword and a shield, thought to be a Valkyrie. Derived from John Lee, *Valkyriefigur fra Tjørnehøj, Hårby s*. Creative Commons.

There were once women in Denmark who dressed themselves to look like men and spent almost every minute cultivating soldiers' skills; they did not want the sinews of their valour to lose tautness and be infected by self-indulgence. Loathing a dainty style of living, they would harden body and mind with toil and endurance rejecting the fickle pliancy of girls and compelling their womanish spirits to act with a virile ruthlessness. They courted military celebrity so earnestly that you would have guessed they had unsexed themselves. Those especially who had forceful personalities or were tall and elegant embarked on this way of life. As if they were forgetful of their true selves, they put toughness before allure, aimed at conflicts instead of kisses, tasted blood, not lips, sought the clash of arms rather than the arm's embrace, fitted to weapons hands which should have been weaving, desired not the couch but the kill, and those they could have appeased with looks they attacked with lances.[76]

The Birka Bj 581 grave may provide evidence of women warriors in the Viking age. Its rich grave furnishings and prestigious location in the graveyard point to its being the grave of a high-status warrior,[77] and so the bones have long been assumed to be those of a man. A recent assessment shows they are the bones of a woman.[78] Multiple interpretations of this find are possible, including the possibility that this is the grave of a *skjaldmær*.

Yet this interpretation has some problems. The skeletal remains are too poorly preserved to allow any assessment of physical strength or battle trauma.[79]

The lack of sources about *skjaldmær* and the fact that most of the sources depicting them are sources set outside Scandinavia makes the concept of *skjaldmær* in the holistic picture of the Viking combat world troublesome.

## VALKYRIES

The other group of women associated with arms and armor and the battlefield is the *valkyrja* (Valkyrie).[80] *Valkyrja* is a portmanteau of *valr* (the fallen on the battlefield) and *kyrja* (the one who chooses).[81] Thus, the *valkyrja* is the one who chooses from the warriors fallen on the battlefield.

The *valkyrjur* do not often appear in the literary sources, but they appear in multiple genres of Icelandic literary sources.[82] Valkyrjur are possibly mentioned on three runic inscriptions,[83] and they likely appear on picture stones[84] and jewelry.[85]

These women are strongly associated with Óðinn.[86] Apart from serving ale to Einherjar,[87] they are said to choose the slain on the battlefield to go to Óðinn in Valhöll. Additionally, they appear to have a direct influence on the outcome of the battle.[88] They share some similarities with the goddess Freyja, who, like the *valkyrjur*, rides to the *valr* to choose from the fallen,[89] and like the *valkyrjur*, she also pours ale in Ásgarðr.[90] Neither Freyja nor the *valkyrjur* are said to do any fighting.

At the time this text was written, the very intriguing subject of women warriors in the Viking age remains unresolved, with conflicting evidence and few solid conclusions. It is a topic of intense interest, and it is being actively pursued.

Now that we have a sense for the special warriors who fought in mass battles, we turn to a study of how these mass battles were conducted. As we will see, there are more similarities than differences between mass battles on land and mass battles at sea. Naval battles might be thought of as land battles fought on floating islands. Even the nature and the names of the formations were the same, whether they be men on land or ships at sea. Yet it is worth considering each kind of battle separately.

## LAND BATTLES

Whether the battle was on land or sea, it seems that the ranks were assigned and fighters arranged on a battle-by-battle basis. At the battle at Stiklarstaðir, King Óláfr made the arrangements and gave the orders to his troops, which numbered more than 3,600 men and was considered to be a large army.[91]

## RANKS, MARKINGS, AND THE ARRANGING OF WARRIORS

In arranging his troops for the battle, the king placed his *hirð*, his best fighting men, in the front of his column. Behind them he placed his *gestir*, followed by the host of men (*lið*) who had joined the king from the Uppland and the Trondheim districts. To his right, the king placed a column led by Dagr Hringsson, a kinsman, with Dagr's standard at the head of his column of men. On his left, the king placed a third column and standard, consisting of the men sent by the king of Sweden chosen from his *hirð*, along with other fighters.[92] These columns on the sides were sometimes called *fylkingararmr*: the "arms" of the *fylking*.[93]

At Stiklarstaðir, King Óláfr ordered his men to form up in detachments (*sveitir*) and to arrange themselves in ranks (*fylkingar*).[94] As the men arranged themselves, the king conferred with his officers (*sveitarhöfðingjar*, or heads of the detachments). Óláfr told his men to maintain their lines day and night until they knew where the battle was to take place. The king added that men must know their places so that they not stray too far from their battle standard, which was placed at the front of each column.

The nature of this standard (*merki*) is speculative. It was mounted on a staff (*merkastöng*) and placed high above the heads of the fighters for all to see, since it became the pole star of the fight, the fixed point around which men fought. King Óláfr's banner at the Battle of Nesjar was white with the figure of a serpent. *Orkneyinga saga* tells of a raven standard (*hrafnsmerki*), a finely made banner embroidered with the figure of a raven; when the banner fluttered in the breeze, the raven appeared

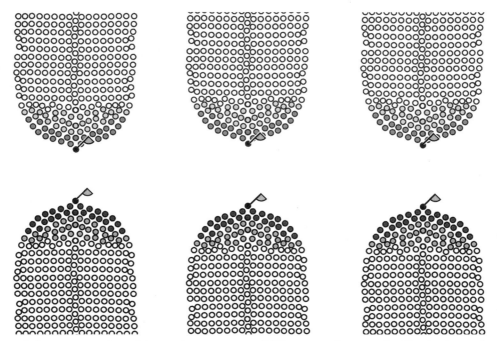

A speculative reconstruction of the usual arrangement of Viking troops in a mass land battle: three columns, each with the battle standard and standard bearer (black) in front, with the *hirð* (dark gray shading) behind him, the *gestir* (light gray shading) behind them, and the *lið* (no shading) behind them. Illustration: William R. Short.

to be flying. This kind of banner is depicted on the Bayeux Tapestry.[95]

Regardless of the nature of the standard, carrying it was considered an honor. At Stiklarstaðir, Þórðr Fólason was the standard bearer for the king, and his service is memorialized in skaldic verse.[96] When the standard bearer fell, it seems the king or earl designated someone else to take his place.[97] As Þórðr received his death blow, he jammed the pole of the battle standard into the ground so hard that it stood by itself, so it would not fall, which would have been a disgrace. The standard symbolized the king and was a visible marker of his presence. After King Haraldr's men captured Earl Hákon's battle standard and the battle seemed to have ended, a man came out of the woods, killed Haraldr's man who was holding Hákon's standard, and ran with the standard back into the woods, letting Haraldr know the earl still lived and the battle was not yet over.[98]

King Haraldr claimed that his battle standard, which he called *Landeyðan* (Land Destroyer) was his most valuable possession, since it had been foretold that anyone following that banner would be assured victory.[99]

Each column of fighters carried its own battle standard, which would allow the columns to move and be commanded independently of one another during the battle, such as when Egill brought his column to support his brother's column in the battle at Vínheiðr.[100]

The literary sources suggest that the battle arrangements were not static during the fight. When the situation changed, the king made a new plan, sounded the horn, moved his standard, and rearranged his battle lines.[101] During battles on both land and sea, it is mentioned that orders were issued with a *herblástr* (a war-blast: the sounding of a horn),[102] but the details are missing. Before the battle at Stiklarstaðir, the landed men leading the farmer's army asked the warrior-farmers to be

Top: A battle standard carried by a rider as shown in the Bayeux Tapestry. Detail of the Bayeux Tapestry, eleventh century, with special permission from the City of Bayeux. Bottom: A speculative reconstruction of a Viking battle standard. Derived from Elevatorrailfan, *Raven Banner*. Creative Commons.

alert for the sound of the horn and to be quick to respond.[103]

In these mass battles, it might have been easy for men to become confused as to who was friend and who was foe, especially in a large host of fighters.[104] It was a time when uniforms or distinctive clothing or insignia were not commonly used. At Stiklarstaðir, the king ordered that kinsmen and acquaintances stand together to better shield each other.[105] Not only were they more likely to recognize one another, reducing any confusion about friend versus foe, but they were likely to work better together as a team.

Men sometimes marked their gear with a *herkuml* (war-badge), a distinctive marking to identify sides. At the battle at Alþing, men put marks on their helmets. At Stiklarstaðir, the king ordered men to mark their shields and helmets with a cross so his men could more easily identify one another.[106] As discussed in the shield chapter, shields served to represent sides in a battle.

Before the battle, the king formed some of his fighting men into a shield-castle (*skjaldborg*), choosing the strongest and most valiant fighters.[107] The king placed several of his poets inside the protection of the shield-castle so they could witness the battle at close range and compose verses about what they witnessed, as discussed earlier in the shield chapter. Additionally, the king sometimes formed a shield castle for his own protection as he commanded his men in battle.[108]

In addition to formations of three columns of men, each behind its battle standard, a formation mentioned numerous times in the literary sources, other formations are mentioned, but only rarely. One is the battle array used by King Ingi, who ordered that the ranks (*fylking*) of his 4,800 men should be arranged very long and five deep to face the men of King Hákon, who were approaching.[109]

The other formation is the *svínfylking* (swine-array). This formation is called *caput porci* (pig's head) in ancient Latin and occasionally *rani* (snout) in Icelandic texts, and it is often rendered as boar snout in modern texts. It is a wedge-shaped formation intended to break through the opponent's ranks. The formation is mentioned being used by northern people as early as Tacitus' *Germania* in the first century through at least to *Konungs skuggsjá*[110] in the thirteenth century.

The most-detailed explanation is provided by Saxo, and it matches the general wedge-shaped formations suggested by other sources. Two men were placed in the first rank, and each subsequent rank had one more man, arranging them to form the point of a cone. Saxo even specified the age and experience of the warriors in the various parts of the wedge.[111]

While Saxo's description is detailed, it is far from precise, so it is difficult to be sure of the

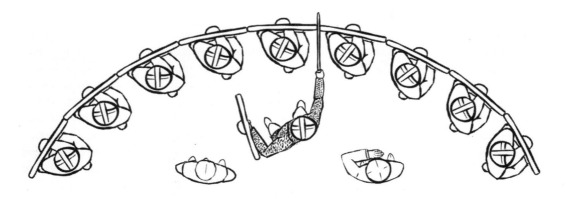

A speculative reconstruction of a *skjaldborg*, protecting the king and his poets. Illustration: Barbara Wechter.

exact formation.[112] The formation is mentioned only rarely in the sources. For example, it is not mentioned in relation to any of the battles in *Heimskringla*, nor in the *Sagas of Icelanders*. The words for this formation, *svínfylking*[113] and the apparently equivalent *fylkja hamalt*[114] and *rani*,[115] are used a few times, yet the clearest description of its use is in *Færeyinga saga*.[116] Sigmundr, while harrying in Sweden, was blocked from returning to his ships by the men of King Eiríkr. He ordered his men to form a *svínfylking*, a wedge with his kinsman Þórir in front, three men behind him, five men behind them, and so on. They formed up, ran at the Swedes, and went right through them, falling on them and killing many on their way back to their ships.

In the ancient language, the word *hamalt* was used only in the sense of this battle formation, but in later centuries the word took on additional meanings that indicate the purpose of the formation: it is a battering ram used to break through some solid structure.[117]

Curiously, the saga says the king ordered shielded men (*skjaldaðir menn*) to be placed on the wings on either side. Does this statement imply that the men in the *svínfylking* formation were unshielded, a situation that would seem to have serious consequences for the men in the *svínfylking*? Saxo tells us that the wings on either side should be ten ranks thick, with younger men in front and more-experienced

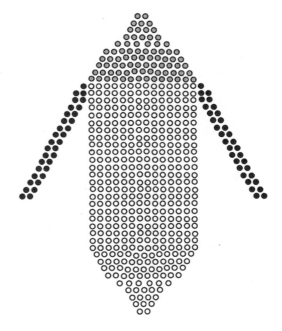

A speculative reconstruction of the *svínfylking* (boar snout) battle array based on Saxo's description. The front of the snout was made up of a group of twenty formed to make a cone (light shading). Additional groups of twenty (hatched) formed the width of the column. A similar snout was formed in the rear. Wings extended on either side (dark shading). Illustration: William R. Short.

men behind to back them up.[118] Many important details are missing in the literary sources.

A formation like *svínfylking* is stated as being used in sources from before, during, and after the Viking age. Yet the use of the formation is absent in our most detailed and extensive discussion of Viking-age mass battles, and indeed, the ancient word *svínfylking* is used only a handful of times in any of the literary sources. When Brúni saw his opponents drawn up into a *svínfylking*, he commented to the king on the strangeness of the formation,[119] suggesting it was not commonly seen in mass battle.

Based on the available sources, the *svínfylking* does not appear to be common to Viking mass battles. It seems most likely that it was used only in situations that called for it, such as when one mass of warriors wanted to break through another mass of warriors, as did Sigmundr in *Færeyinga saga*. Yet it was a formation whose value was known. In the eddic poem *Reginsmál*, Hnikarr tells Reginn that those who know how to form a wedge-shaped column (*fylkja hamalt*) get the victory.[120]

### THE FARMERS' ARMY

More than a few of the large-scale battles in the literary sources were between the king and the farmers of the district. Often these battles revolved around the religious conversion. Several of the Norwegian kings saw benefits to aligning themselves with and promoting the Christian church. Farmers in some districts resisted, preferring to maintain their ancient heathen practices, and so the king used force to push the conversion.[121]

At times, this force took the form of some very large-scale battles. It may be that the differences between the king's army and the farmers' army in skill level and experience was smaller than one might at first imagine. For many large-scale battles, a large part of the king's men were from the levy. The levy warriors were themselves farmers when not called to the levy. And so at least some of the men in the farmers' army had experience with large-scale battles, having been called up for levy duty in the past. That experience perhaps made them more used to military discipline and more aware of the strategy and planning

of a large-scale battle. Perhaps that prior service in the levy gave them experience fighting alongside other farmers in the district that made them better fighters and a better team.

What was missing from the farmers' army was the support of the king's *hirð*: solid anchors for the less-experienced fighters due to *hirð* men's leadership, training, and experience. An additional difference may have been that many of the men in the farmers' army were not experienced fighters. The group of farmers facing King Óláfr helgi at Stiklarstaðir included peasants (*þorparar*) and laborers (*verkmenn*) who probably had limited fighting skills and experience.[122] These men were unable to stay in formation, causing some parts of the line to lag behind as they moved forward into battle. Þórir and his men, experienced fighters in the farmer's army, were given the task to bring up the rear so no one was left behind and all groups in the army were in touch with one another. The dangers of having a loose formation are mentioned in the literary sources. It was easy to attack, and a loose formation resulted in the defeat of King Friðþjófr's army.[123]

Yet the farmers' *lið* at Stiklarstaðir also included landed men (*lendir menn*) like Þórir and many powerful farmers (*ríkir bændir*) who had the skill and experience to form a cohesive fighting team. The landed men were farmers who held land in the name of the king, equivalent in rank to a *hersir*. The farmers' army at Stiklarstaðir totaled 14,400 men.[124]

### RANKING AND ARRANGING OF THE FARMER-WARRIORS

With the king's troops, it was always clear who was the leader. But among the farmers, a leader had to be chosen. At Stiklarstaðir, the landed men discussed who was to be the leader of the troops, and none wanted the position, each for good reason. Kálfr, a landed man who once was King Óláfr's man, said if they could not choose a leader they should not fight and instead ask for quarter. Kálfr was appointed the leader.

Kálfr arranged his army in three columns, similar to the arrangement used by the king.

Kálfr and his standard were placed at the front of his column. In that column, Kálfr placed his *húskarlar* directly behind him. On either side in the same column, he placed two other landed men and their fighters. The farmers chosen for this column were the keenest and best-armed men, and so the center column was long and deep. On either side of the center column, two more columns of farmers from various districts were formed under their own standards.

Once the columns were arranged, Kálfr gave his instructions to his troops. He ordered them to watch their places and to stay at their proper distance from their standards. He asked them to be quick about following the orders given by sounding the horn. The farmers chose a battle cry to identify themselves and to urge each other forward.[125]

PREPARATION FOR THE BATTLE

Typically, a battlefield was a large, flat, open plain. In some cases the battle took place where the two sides happened to meet, perhaps at a strategic choke point or a fortification,[126] but in other cases, the battlefield was chosen and prepared in advance.[127] At the Battle of Rastarkálfr, King Hákon chose and marked the battlefield, and when his opponents arrived, he sent a messenger inviting them to fight on the site. *Egils saga* tells us that the battlefield at Vínheiðr was marked with poles made of hazelwood (*heslistengur*). It was said that the site had to be chosen with care to ensure it was level and large enough for the armies to gather. The use of hazel poles appears in another instance, where King Haraldr sent some of his men to his opponent, King Hringr, so that together they could mark the battlefield with hazelwood in advance of the battle.[128] Then both kings drew up their ranks and prepared for battle.

One has the sense that the intent was to provide a fair fight by ensuring that the battlefield did not give an advantage to either side, an arrangement similar to dueling sites, as described in the chapter on dueling. Yet as we will see later in this chapter, battlefields sometimes gave an advantage to one side, and some leaders found clever ways to take advantage of the terrain at the site.

Once the site was chosen, sometimes the fight started as soon as the two sides met, but it appears that at other times both armies set up camps and waited for the appointed time for the battle. This was another opportunity for misdirection and clever ruses, with one side seeking to gain an advantage over the enemy by, for example, appearing to be a much larger force than it really was.

King Aðalsteinn ordered his troops to set up the tents on some high ground, leaving every third tent empty, with small numbers of men in the other tents. Thus, to King Óláfr's scouts, it appeared to be a vast army, having such a large number of tents extending out of sight down the back side of the hill that the scouts couldn't count them all.[129]

In another example, Egill, an old, experienced fighter, took ten men and ten battle standards beyond the crest of a hill before the battle at Rastarkálfr.[130] When King Gamli Eiríksson and his men arrived at the battlefield, Egill's ten men and their battle standards appeared over the crest of the hill, and it appeared that ten large columns of enemy fighters were approaching. A large part of Gamli's men fled before the battle began.

THE BATTLE BEGINS

In large part, the use of weapons in large-scale battles was identical to that described in the individual weapons chapters earlier. The focus was on power and aggression. In the Battle at Vínheiðr, as Þórólfr led his men forward against the enemy, he hacked down men with his sword on either side until the remaining men turned and fled.[131] The battle was brutal and fluid, changing moment by moment.

The word used to describe the actions of the fighters in these mass battles is *ryðja*. In ancient times, this word also had the meaning of clearing away, such as clear cutting the land for farming. In modern times, the word is used for plowing a road clear of snow,[132] which gives a clear picture of the intent. This action was the goal of the warriors in a mass battle: to mow down and scatter the enemy troops.

Battles began with an exchange of missiles as the opposing sides advanced toward one another. At the Battle of Storð, King Hákon put his men in battle array against the troops of the sons of Eiríkr, and the two sides advanced and met. As they advanced, men threw their spears, then drew their swords. The king advanced in front of his standard, engaging the enemy host and cutting down men left and right.[133]

A similar story is told at the Battle of Stiklarstaðir. The two sides advanced close enough for King Óláfr to talk to Kálfr, the leader of the farmers. When no agreement could be reached, both sides shouted their battle cries and shot arrows and spears. The two sides raced forward and met in battle. Those in the front used their swords, while those in the rear threw spears or stones or axes and shot arrows, with the king in the front ranks.[134]

In some cases, both sides were drawn up in battle array, and each waited to see who would make the first move. King Haraldr was content to wait as the less-well-provisioned men of Earl Hákon suffered from cold and wet in a driving snowstorm. Haraldr's men then stood up and shouted their war cry, and Hákon's men eagerly responded by advancing directly into a trap, allowing Haraldr's troops to rush down a hill and overwhelm them.[135]

The sense one gets from reading the descriptions of mass battles is that Vikings were improvisational and fluid. They took advantage of terrain,[136] such as Þórólfr's moving his column to the edge of the forest that bordered the battlefield to use as cover. They planned and executed counterattacks,[137] such as Egill's against Earl Aðils. When fighting men saw an opportunity, they seized on and took full advantage of it.

## VIRKI

Warriors sometimes gained an advantage by fighting from a *virki*. A *virki* was a fortification—a structure, typically man made, that was intended to give a martial advantage to the warriors occupying it. The word is ancient, and

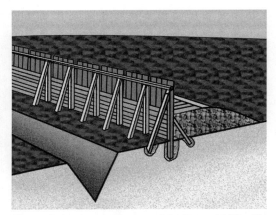

A speculative reconstruction of the *Danavirki* fortification as it existed in the early Viking age. The fortification was comprised of an earthen wall topped with a wooden palisade fence, along with a ditch in front of the barrier. Illustration: William R. Short.

common to all the Germanic languages, with the meanings of wall, stronghold, and castle.[138] Structures that seem to fit with all three translations of the word were in use in the Viking age, although the medieval stone castle was not in use in the Viking lands during this time. Rather, these structures were encountered and used to advantage by Vikings on their travels to foreign lands.

These kinds of structures were used defensively and as a base for offensive attacks. The structures were designed to be easy to attack from but difficult to attack. Fighters on the inside had a superior position for visibility and for shooting projectiles down into the enemy host while being protected by the defensive structures of the fortification. Fighters on the outside had few opportunities for attack, so their goal was to enter the fortress to level the playing field.

A wall-type *virki* is probably best represented by Danavirki, a defensive wall erected on Denmark's southern border in several phases from the eighth to the eleventh centuries.[139] The wall created a barrier at a choke point. It was built between the head of the Schlei fjord near Hedeby west to rivers and marshland, effectively blocking the southern end of Jutland

An aerial photograph of the site of the Trelleborg fortress, showing the remains of the rampart and the outlines of the buildings within the fortification. Derived from Thue C. Leibrandt, *Trelleborg*. Creative Commons.

from the rest of continental Europe. The Franks had subjugated several lands, and the relatively flat terrain between Jutland and Frankish lands made the Danish territory an easy target by land.

Each construction phase extended the wall and improved the barrier. The two earliest phases had walls made of earth, faced with wood, and topped with a wood-timber palisade.[140] In the Viking age, the walls were probably 3 m high (10 ft) and 12 m thick (39 ft), topped with a wooden palisade. A ditch outside the wall served as a moat, which was typically 1.5 m deep (5 ft) and 5 m broad (16 ft).

The literary sources paint a picture of combat at these fortifications. Earl Hákon of Norway was asked by the Danish King Haraldr to help defend Haraldr's land against Emperor Ótta from Saxland to the east. Hákon arranged for the defense of the Danavirki fortification extending across Jutland. The earl put some of his men in the strongholds outside the gates of the fortification, but most were put on top of the walls so they could be quickly moved to where they were most needed, thus blocking the emperor's advance. Other sources suggest the strength of Danavirki, telling us it was not easy to attack when guarded.[141]

The medieval castle style of *virki* arrived in Scandinavia later, after the end of the Viking era. Castles used walls of stone or wood, and later, brick, often with ramparts outside the walls to protect the urban center inside. Many of these fortifications were also called *borg*, which can mean a hill, a fortification, or a city.[142]

Another type of Scandinavian fortification is the stronghold, found in virtually every Viking land. A royal example is the so-called Trelleborg fortifications in Danish lands, typified by the find at Trelleborg.[143] Nearly identical structures are found in a small number of other locations, all seemingly placed to protect against threats arriving from the Baltic Sea. The details varied, but all consisted of a large circular rampart enclosing a settlement. The

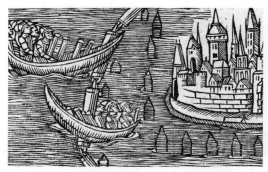

Sea barriers protecting a town. Derived from Olaus Magnus (1555).

rampart at Trelleborg is 134 m in diameter (440 ft) on the inside. The interior was divided into quarters with symmetrically placed buildings used for residences and workshops, and evidence suggests that men, women, and children lived here. Construction on all the forts began around the year 980, almost certainly by King Haraldr Gormsson. They were in use for only a short time, probably as strongpoints to impose the king's authority, and then abandoned when the political situation no longer required them, perhaps only a few years after being constructed.[144]

Kings sometimes built fortifications as an outpost in remote parts of their lands to claim the land and collect taxes from it. King Ólafr built a fortification in the south on the border with Sweden. Inside the fortification, he laid the foundation for a church, had dwellings built, provisioned the place, and lived there for the winter, controlling the movements of goods out of the district.[145]

Fortifications were built around some trading towns in Viking lands, such as at Birka and at Hedeby. These may have started as a fortified hilltop, such as Borg at Birka, where town residents could flee to safety in an attack. The ramparts that surrounded the town were probably built later, as the town prospered in the mid-tenth century. They were constructed from earth, with a wooden palisade and towers on top, and timber-lined gateways. The ramparts were as large as 8 m (26 ft) high and 25

m (82 ft) deep from outside to inside. They extended 1.3 km (0.8 mi) in a semicircle around the town, with each end connecting to the sea. The harbor was further fortified with sea barriers to limit entrance into the town by sea. These barriers took many forms in Viking lands, including piles, caissons, booms, and chains. It seems probable that submerged obstacles were placed to create barriers not visible from the surface that only locals knew about in order to limit outsiders' access to the town. Indeed, much of our knowledge about Viking ships comes from the study of ships that were likely intentionally scuttled to form a barrier.[146] As people of the sea, Vikings needed to protect themselves from dangers that arrived by sea.

The literary sources tell us of *virki* built around farms in Iceland to protect the inhabitants, sometimes by ordinary farmers in difficult times[147] and sometimes by evildoers who wanted to create a safe lair for their mob.[148]

The nature of these *virki* is unknown, but evidence of later Sturlunga-era *virki* can help inform us. The literary sources say that Snorri Sturluson had a fortification built around Reykholt high enough that men needed to use a ladder to scale it.[149] Early nineteenth-century visitors from abroad claim to have seen the remains.[150] Archaeological excavations have found a wall at the site that is more than just an ordinary enclosure wall and may be the remains of the *virki*.[151]

The literary descriptions of battles around the *virki* at a house site provide additional details. At Eyri in west Iceland, outlaws had built a fortification around the house, and at the battle at the house, both sides used projectiles, including stones, arrows, and *handskot* weapons (weapons thrown by hand). In this and other instances, men on the outside entered the fortification by jumping up, hooking their axe-head over the top of the wall, and climbing up the axe haft to enter the fortification.[152]

At the time of writing this book, the archaeological evidence for such fortifications at Viking-age house sites in Iceland is thought to

Borgarvirki, a *virki* in north Iceland. Photo: William R. Short.

have been found, but the work remains preliminary. Evidence suggests that like larger fortifications, these structures consisted of thick walls, possibly topped with a palisade. Interestingly, the site of the excavation is the Westfjords, the location of all the settlement-era *virki* mentioned in *Landnámabók*.[153]

Perhaps related to a *virki* is a *skíðgarðr*, a wooden fence enclosing a yard or a farm. In one example, it was low enough for a man to vault over, yet a *skíðgarðr* located in Baltic lands was high enough to serve as a trap, penning in Egill and his men so they could be subdued with thrusts through the fence and then captured. Even giants had a *skíðgarðr* surrounding their homes.[154]

Place-names sometimes suggest the use of a site as a *virki*, such as Borgarvirki in north Iceland. It is a natural stone bowl rising above the landscape, providing good visibility and good defense. Folk beliefs connect the site to events in *Heiðarvíga saga* and *Finnboga saga*, but neither account specifically mentions the place, so there is little that can be said definitively about its use as a fortress in the Viking age.

A Viking-age *virki* could take many forms, but one common element was a high structure intended to keep attackers on the outside and to provide a height advantage and shielding structures for the defenders on the inside. The defenders were relatively safe from attack yet in a good position to rain missiles down on the attackers. Attackers could do little but shoot missiles back at the defenders, hoping to catch one in a vulnerable moment, or else find a clever way to enter the *virki* to bring the fight to the defenders.

THE END OF THE FIGHT

The end of the battle often came when the leader fell, whether he be king or earl or landed man. Once news spread, his troops often fled the battlefield. In other cases, the leader of the army felt his situation was hopeless, gave up, and fled.[155] Typically, the victorious army pursued the fleeing men, killing all they could reach.[156]

On the one hand, there was some expectation that the enemy might flee, and the prospect was discussed before the battle began in order to plan for that outcome. Yet repeatedly, we see evidence that this behavior was thought to be cowardly. Runestones tell of leaders who died because their men fled during battle. There are examples of men about to flee, but stronger-willed men aid them and goad them into standing their ground.[157] In several instances, the implication is clear: to flee is not *drengr*. There is no *orðstírr* in fleeing. Before a battle, kings promise their men, and men promise their kings, never to flee.[158]

## AFTERMATH OF BATTLE

After the battle, the fallen were buried. After the battle at Rastarkálfr, King Hákon had the enemy dead buried in their ships in mounds. At Stiklarstaðir, the farmers had no wish to provide anything more than the minimum for the king's men. Farmers who had kinsmen among the king's men brought them to churches for a proper burial. The clearing of the battlefield of dead and wounded apparently went on for multiple days.[159] And then the farmers dispersed and went home.

*Fóstbrœðra saga* tells more about the aftermath of the battle at Stiklarstaðir.[160] Injured and wounded from both sides were either taken or found their own ways to places where medical treatment was available.[161] As they waited, wounded men on each side compared their prowess and bravery in the battle and the merits of their causes. Healers (*læknar*) performed triage on the wounded and took care of those likely to be helped with the treatments available. Healers were capable of cleaning and binding wounds, setting bones, performing simple diagnostic tests, and prescribing herbal-based medications.[162] Literary sources tell of fighters who recovered from horrific injuries, and skeletal remains show evidence of battle wounds that healed,[163] suggesting that at least in a few cases, the healers were successful in ministering to those with battle wounds.

## NAVAL BATTLES

Sea battles had many similarities with land battles but were fought on floating platforms of ships rather than on solid land. Before discussing combat at sea aboard these ships, a brief introduction to Viking ships is in order.

## INTRODUCTION TO VIKING SHIPS

Viking-age ships were more capable than other European ships in this period, and these ships were what allowed Vikings to conduct their voyages of trade, of exploration, of settlement, and of war. Viking ships could sail closer to the wind, allowing them to outsail other contemporary ships, and they drew less water, allowing them to sail in shallow seas and rivers where other ships couldn't go. They could be

sailed right up onto a sandy beach, meaning no special landing place was needed for Viking warriors or traders to disembark.

There were two broad classes of Viking ships: those intended for war and those intended for other endeavors, such as voyages for trade or exploration.

Trading ships, generally called *knörr*, were primarily powered by sail, with a few oars for maneuvering as they approached land. The *knörr* had a cargo hold amidships with half decks fore and aft. Warships, often called *langskip*, were powered by oars, supplemented by sails. Typically, a warship was longer and narrower, and drew less water than a *knörr*. Warships were optimized for speed and maneuverability.

Both kinds of ships used a single square-rigged sail. The hull was made of wood using clinker-built construction, with the strakes typically riveted together with iron rivets. The other notable feature was the steering board, the rudder located on the starboard side near the stern. The ships were open, with no sheltered space under the deck, so voyages must have been difficult by modern standards.

Ships were flexible rather than rigid. So rather than resisting rough seas, they twisted and flexed with the motion of the sea, reducing the stress on the ship. This motion gave them the appearance of a serpent or a snake moving through the water, and thus many ships were named for this movement.

A number of ships have been found, both burial ships, such as the Gokstad and Oseberg ships, and wrecks, including ships that were intentionally scuttled, such as at Skuldelev. These finds tell us about ship sizes and construction. The Skuldelev 1 was a modest oceangoing merchant ship 16 m long (52 ft), 4.8 m broad (16 ft) with a draft of 1.27 m (4.2 ft). The estimated cargo capacity is 25 tonnes (23 tons).[164]

The Hedeby 1 was a large, finely built warship of royal construction 30 m long (98 ft), 2.6 m broad (8.5 ft) with a draft of 0.75 m (2.5 ft).[165] It had spaces for about sixty rowers.[166] Likely, the crew was more than double the

A Viking warship compared to a Viking trading ship. Illustration: Andrew P. Volpe.

number of places for rowers so one man could rest or perform other duties while another rowed in his place.

The size of a ship was specified in *rúm* (rooms), the place where rowers sat between the thwarts. The *rúm* were typically about 1 m (3.3 ft) apart but were as close as 70 cm (2.3 ft) in some closely packed ships. Each *rúm* had places for two rowers, one on each side. Thus, the number of *rúm* give an indication of the length of the ship and the size of the crew.

In the literary sources, there are numerous words to describe the class of a ship, but it is hard to tease out what it is that distinguished one class from another. *Dreki* (dragon) was a large warship, such as King Óláfr Tryggvason's *Ormr inn langi* (The Long Serpent), which had places for sixty-eight rowers in thirty-four *rúm*.[167]

From the etymology of the word, a *skeið* was a swift warship. Erlingr Skjálgsson used a *skeið* for his Viking expeditions with space for sixty-four rowers in thirty-two *rúm*, carrying a crew of 240 men.[168]

The levy ships typically were *snekkja* warships, a word cognate with the English word *smack*, a coastal ship.[169] A *snekkja* ranged from twenty-six (or fewer) *rúm* up to forty *rúm*.[170] Skuldelev 5 was likely a Danish levy ship. It was a warship, well suited for coastal operations, and originally well built by a competent smith. But it was constructed from reused and repurposed materials, and then repaired again and again, rather than being scrapped, ending up being made from the parts of at least three ships. It is estimated that there were thirteen oar holes on each side, so it accommodated

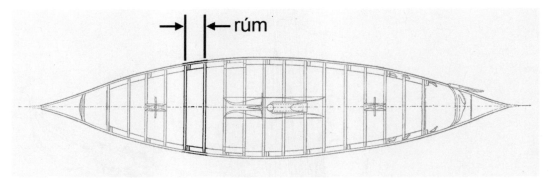

The size of a ship was specified in rúm (rooms), the place where rowers sat between the thwarts. Derived from Nicolaysen (1885).

twenty-six rower/warriors, a steersman, and a lookout,[171] but probably had a crew more than double that number. It was the smallest of the *snekkja*-class, and it was a low-prestige ship. It was well used, with many places of wear over its lifetime. Gulaþing law made it clear that maintaining the ship for the levy was a duty,[172] and one presumes that the farmers responsible for providing the ship wanted the vessel to be judged seaworthy for as long as possible to avoid the expense of having to build a new levy ship. Thus, the ship was repaired multiple times using available materials,[173] with multiple major repairs, including one such major repair just before it was intentionally scuttled at Skuldelev.

RANKS AND POSITIONS OF WARRIORS

Before naval battles, men were assigned to ranks and positions, just as before land battles. Before the battle at Mærin, the king appointed *skipstjórnir* (ship captains) and *sveitarhöfðingjar* (captains of the troops) for each ship, and he ordered each *sveit* (detachment) to a particular ship, a total of 360 men aboard his five *snekkja* ships.[174] King Haraldr directed that only men from his *hirð* be aboard his personal ship. The king's ship generally was in the center of the fleet, under his standard.[175]

In naval battles, it was customary for the hardest fighting to be near the stem at the bow, according to the literary sources.[176] Opposing ships approached each other from the front,

Disembarking from a war ship was quick, since ships could land anywhere there was a sandy beach, and warriors could be sure that the water was no more than waist deep as they jumped over the side. Dimensions of the ship's hull taken from the Hedeby 1 wreck. Illustration: William R. Short.

stem to stem. In addition, our tests of naval combat showed that the area around the stem is one of the few places where typical Viking weapons can be brought into play with minimal interference from typical ship's gear, such as rigging and benches.[177]

Thus, the king placed his best fighters forward, near the stem, where the fighting was fiercest. When King Haraldr outfitted his large *dreki*-class ship, he chose his *stafnbúar* (stem dwellers, or to use a more modern term, forecastlemen) with great care, since they carried his banner,[178] a position of great honor.

During a naval battle, the hardest fighting was near the bow, since opposing ships approached each other from the front. Illustration: Barbara Wechter.

To the aft of the *stafnbúar* the king placed his *berserkir* in the region of the forward benches, which would seem to be a less-desirable place to fight, based on our tests, because of the presence of the benches, thwarts, and other gear that was in the way. At the Battle of Hafrsfjörðr, King Haraldr had twelve *berserkir* located here aboard his own ship, just behind the best men in his *hirð*.[179]

King Óláfr's magnificent *dreki*, *Ormr inn langi*, was an extremely large and beautiful ship. His crew during the Battle of Svölðr is described in detail, with a stem man in front who carried the king's standard and with other prominent fighters near the stem. Berserks were placed behind them. More fighters were arranged along the gunwales in the forepart of the ship. Eight men were placed in each of the *hálfrúm* (half-rúm).[180] A *hálfrúm* was the space normally taken by one seated rower, suggesting that the fighting men were tightly packed. The king's *dreki* had thirty-four *rúm*,[181] implying that hundreds of warriors were packed into this space.

The literary sources suggest that the king took a position in the stern, which was raised above the deck, giving him a better view of the fighting. In some cases, the king was surrounded by a *skjaldborg*.[182] When King Magnús thought his men were not pushing the fight with enough vigor, he left his *skjaldborg* and ran forward to join in the thick of the fight.[183]

SEA BATTLE LOCATIONS

In some cases, it seems the fight took place where the two fleets met.[184] Sometimes elaborate preparations were made before a sea battle, with a location chosen to allow one side a significant hidden advantage. In one case, the fight was in a sound with a high cliff adjacent to one side of the sound. Before the battle, Önundr placed men at the top of the cliff so they could roll large stones down onto the enemy ships below during the fight. In another case, King Óláfr arranged for a fight at the mouth of a river where it entered the sea. Earlier, he had earthworks built to dam a lake above the sea that fed the river, and many tree trunks were placed below the dam in the riverbed. When King Knútr's fleet arrived, the dam was breached, and the trunks were driven down the river on the flood, damaging Knútr's ships and driving his ships out of position.[185]

## SEA BATTLE PREPARATIONS

When the battle was imminent, preparations were made. The king ordered the horn to be sounded for his ships to gather so they could be lashed together. Generally, ships in the fleet were lashed together side by side and stem to stem (and presumably stern to stern), forming a long, solid row facing the enemy fleet. In some cases, additional ships in the fleet worked independently, moving to where they were needed most to help with the fight. Saxo writes that Óðinn taught Harald this tactic.[186]

Before and during the battle, the maneuvering was done with oars, so the sail, a precious item, had likely already been stowed. The literary sources make no mention, but one wonders if the mast was lowered before a battle, thought to be a relatively easy task in a warship.[187] This move would greatly reduce the number of obstacles along the sides that a fighter would have to avoid in a battle. This conjecture is strengthened by noting that there are examples of weapons hitting thwarts, beams, and maststeps during battles,[188] but only one example of a weapon hitting the mast, which appears in a legendary saga.[189]

When arranging his ships in the fleet, the king often placed his two strongest ships and crews on either side of his own ship, in the center of the fleet. At Svölðr, King Óláfr placed the ship *Ormr inn skammi* (Short Serpent) commanded by his brother on one side, and the ship *Traninn* (The Crane) commanded by his uncles on the other side of his own ship.[190] Other fleets allied with the king were placed farther from the center. As with additional columns on land, these fleets to the side were called *fylkingararmr*.[191]

## THE SEA BATTLE BEGINS

Sea battles, like those fought on land, had a beginning, when the fleets maneuvered for posi-

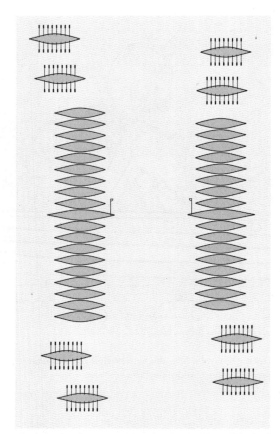

Ships in the fleet were placed side by side and lashed together forming a long, solid row facing the enemy fleet, with the king's ship in the center. Additional ships were left free to work independently. Illustration: William R. Short.

tion, a middle, when the fighting was fierce, and an end, when the losing fighters usually fled.

At Lófufjörðr, King Haraldr ordered the ships in his fleet to be lashed together. His opponent, King Sveinn, rowed his ship forward to lay against Haraldr's ship, and on either side of Sveinn were the best of the ships in his fleet. The opposing sides grappled to fasten their ships together, and the fight began.[192]

Before the battle at Árós, King Magnús's men put on their war gear and prepared their space on the ship for battle, then rowed toward the enemy, led by Earl Sveinn. Sveinn ordered his fleet to tie their ships together, and at once the battle began. Those by the stem cut at the enemy on the adjacent ship. Those behind

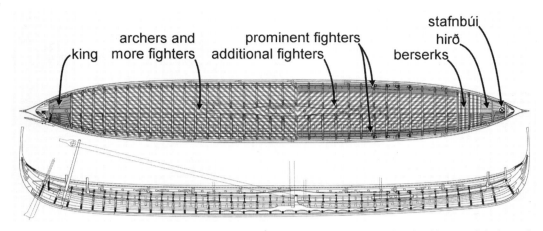

Men were arranged on board the ship, with the standard bearer at the stem, the hirð behind him, and the berserks behind them. Strong fighting men lined the gunwales in front of the mast, and archers and other projectile throwers were placed behind the mast. The king stood on the afterdeck, sometimes protected within a skjaldborg (shield castle). Drawing: Morten Gøthche. Copyright: The Viking Ship Museum, Denmark. Additions added by William R. Short.

them thrust with their *kesja*. Those farther back in the ship threw *snærisspjót* and *gaflak* and *vígörvar* (thought to be a dart-like weapon), along with stones and other improvised projectiles, as discussed in the weapons introduction chapter. Those by the mast shot arrows.[193]

THE NATURE OF NAVAL COMBAT

The goal of these fights was to clear the deck of the enemy's ship with hand-to-hand combat. As with land battles, the word used was *ryðja*, which has the sense of completely cutting down and pushing aside the obstacle. Once cleared, the ship was cut loose from adjacent ships, and the battle continued on the next ship. Men on the losing side retreated into other ships in their fleet or jumped overboard. In some battles, men stood by in boats to kill anyone jumping overboard. Eventually, the losing side cut loose as many of its ships as it could and fled.

At Árós, Magnús's men cleared the space between the mast and stem of Sveinn's ship with their cutting and their projectiles. Then Magnús and his men boarded Sveinn's ship, driving Sveinn's men back and onto other ships or overboard. Magnús cleared the deck of that ship, then another in Sveinn's fleet, and then many others. Sveinn retreated onto other ships in his fleet and fled, rowing away with a large part of his fleet.[194]

At Svölðr, King Sveinn laid his ship against the ship of King Óláfr.[195] The men in Óláfr's ship and the two ships lashed to either side threw grappling hooks (*stefnljáir*) and anchors (*akkeri*) to draw Sveinn's ship in. Óláfr's men cleared the deck of Sveinn's ship and of every other ship they could hold onto, but Sveinn and his men who escaped fled to other ships and rowed out of range.

The tide turned in the battle, and eventually only Óláfr's *dreki, Ormr inn langi*, remained of the Norwegian fleet. The battle continued with cutting weapons, spears, bow and arrow, and anything that could be thrown. Óláfr's men could not protect themselves with shields from the shower of projectiles arriving from all directions from the Danish and Swedish fleets. The men of Earl Eiríkr's ship, now laying against Óláfr's ship, leapt up onto the gunwale to give themselves more reach with their sword cuts. Many of Óláfr's men jumped overboard and sank with their weapons.

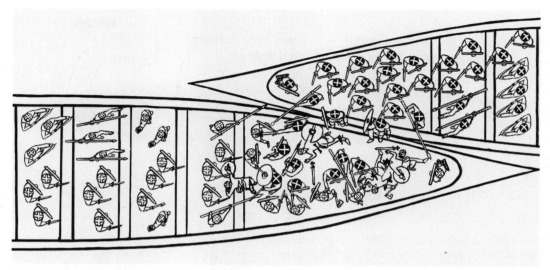

During the battle, men attempted to *ryðja* the enemy ship: to clear the deck by plowing through the enemy and cutting them down. Illustration: Barbara Wechter.

Eventually, Eiríkr and his men were able to board Óláfr's ship and work their way to the stern. The king and his men jumped overboard. Eiríkr had men in small boats surround the ship to kill any of the enemy who jumped overboard, but the king was not found.

These battles could last through the day and into the night. At the Battle at Lófufjörðr, Earl Hákon supported King Haraldr against King Sveinn. Hákon's fleet did not fasten their ships together and instead rowed to where they were most needed in the fight. In the later part of the night, Haraldr boarded Sveinn's ship and cleared it of men. When Sveinn's banner fell, all of his fleet fled. On his ships that were fastened together, his men jumped overboard, while the rest of the ships rowed away. Haraldr rowed in pursuit but made little progress because of all the thick mass of ships in the way.[196]

A similar picture of sea battles is painted in other literary sources.[197] At the end of the battle, it seems the victor took possession of any of the ships along with other booty and sailed away, claiming the lands of the defeated king.[198]

SUMMARY

It seems that Viking battles, whether they be one on one, mêlée skirmishes, or mass battles involving thousands, were more similar than different. The weapons were the same, and the use of the weapons was the same. The fighting was based on aggression and power, and the ultimate goal of the warrior was to achieve *orðstírr*.

Perhaps the most significant distinction about mass battles was the presence of a militaristic structure that had a hierarchy, with a leader issuing orders, and a combat system that used formations of warriors.

Our sources are limited, and so there are many aspects of Viking mass battles that remain hazy and speculative, ranging from the nature of the war cries, distinctive markings, and the battle standards that tied a unit together, to the nature of the formations used.

# VIKING BATTLE TACTICS

## INTRODUCTION

The Viking society was a warrior society, and a warrior cannot survive on physical capabilities and courage alone. Victory often goes to the warrior who is most clever and most tactical. Viking warriors used a number of tactics to prepare for and to fight their battles.

## ETYMOLOGY

There is no one word exactly equivalent to *tactics* in the ancient language, though *kænn* seems to come closest. It is an ancient Germanic word, cognate with the English word *keen* and having the meanings of wise, skillful, or clever.[1] In compound words, the meaning is more clear, such as *vígkænn*[2] (battle wise). One of the better examples that associates *kænn* with tactics is told in *Hákonar saga Herðubreiðs*. The king called on his man Erling skakki (the skewed), for it was said that no one from the king's team was as battle wise (*kænni*), even though other men were more intense. The king asked Erling for his advice on a battle plan proposed by another of his men, and Erling advised the king to wait until he could devise a better plan.[3] There are other words that might also describe tactics, including *brögðóttr*[4] (cunning, crafty).[5] The word is, for example, related to *bragð*, a wrestling trick, as described in the empty-hand chapter.

The US Defense Department defines tactical warfare as, "The level of warfare at which battles and engagements are planned and executed to achieve military objectives assigned to tactical units or task forces."[6] In this chapter, we will look at the tactics Vikings used to plan and achieve victory in their battles and to survive the onslaught they had to endure.

Combat tactics were thought to be a skill of the highest order. Óðinn, the all-father and highest of the gods, was a master tactician, constantly planning, plotting, and gathering intelligence, though Loki was not far behind in his hatching of schemes. Similarly, a number of heroes in the literary sources were also skilled in tactics.

## SOURCES

The literary sources and a few others teach us about Viking combative tactics. They include the *Sagas of Icelanders*, the *Kings' Sagas*, such as *Heimskringla*, and the law codes and the myths. Runestones and picture stones tell of the tactics used to kill the man in whose memory the stone was raised.[7] Archaeological finds tell us about bolt-holes, secret tunnels, and other architectural features in Viking-age houses that relate to combat. Archaeological studies of battle sites yield clues that point to the tactics used there, such as at a *vígi*, a concept discussed later in the chapter.

## PLANNING AND PLOTTING

A key to battle success is in the planning, and the literary sources are filled with examples of Vikings who made deep plans in order to outsmart their opponents and achieve their goals.

Almannagjá in Þingvellir, as the site appears today. Flosi sought this refuge during a battle to take advantage of the defensive options the ravine offered to him and his men. Photo: William R. Short.

The word *ráðagerð*[8] is used to describe this planning, a compound of the words *to make* and *plan*.[9] Additionally, there were people skilled at planning, called *ráðagerðamaðr*, which has the meaning not only of a good planner, but also a crafty planner.[10] These men seem to be valued for their clever advice. Plotters and planners included gods, kings, chieftains, and ordinary men.

Perhaps one of the foremost of these men was Snorri goði, who appears in multiple sagas crafting plans for himself and for people who came to him seeking his advice. He was said to have been better and smarter at this activity than his rivals. He made plans within plans for possible battles, having multiple options for various outcomes. He also made plans for himself and his allies to achieve their goals in noncombative affairs. For example, he used cunning and guile to trick someone into reciting a pledge of peace to end a dispute, and to mediate a settlement in order to end a feud, and to get rid of some troublesome and unwanted berserks, and to acquire his farm at a

favorable price from his dishonorable uncle. He gave good counsel to his friends, and his enemies feared his advice.[11]

An example of Snorri's crafty planning is his advice to Kári, who was the only survivor of the burning of Njáll. As Kári prepared his case against Flosi and the burners at Alþing, men from Kári's team asked Snorri what support he might give. Snorri did not offer legal help, or fighting help, but instead he offered to be Kári's back up in the battle that he foresaw coming.[12]

If Kári's team was being overwhelmed, Snorri promised his men would be in place and ready to help. If Kári was successful, Snorri predicted the Flosi would try to retreat to the safety of the ravine Almannagjá, and Snorri took on the role of making sure they could not reach the refuge. Snorri advised that then, Kári's team should kill as many of Flosi's men as possible, and Snorri would step in to stop the carnage before the compensation that would be required for those killings became overwhelming.[13]

Snorri clearly visualized the probable outcome of the legal cases: deadlock in court followed by a battle. Snorri planned his response for any of several possible outcomes for the battle, and in the case of success would monitor the results to make sure Kári and his team did not impoverish themselves.

The battle turned out as Snorri expected. When Flosi tried to retreat to Almannagjá, Snorri ordered his men to go at them with sword and spear to drive them away, back into the arms of Kári and his men, but Snorri also warned his men not to pursue them. After many of the principals were killed, Snorri stepped in to end the fight and separate the two sides.[14]

King Óláfr helgi was also a great planner. His saga mentions multiple times that he discussed and planned his schemes with his men. The saga author describes how the king listened to the discussion and advice but then made his own decision and plotted his own plans.[15]

Gods, too, are plotters and planners. In the myths, Óðinn is not described as a great warrior, a title given to Þórr, Ullr, and Týr. Yet Óðinn is the master of tactical warfare. He constantly seeks knowledge so he can have better intelligence on which to base his plans, even raising the dead to acquire knowledge.

The tales of Óðinn often revolve around his planning, plotting, and scheming for himself, for his fellow gods, and for his army of Einherjar who live and train at Valhöll. He was like a grandmaster chess player who sacrifices valuable pieces as part of a larger plan, allowing his protégés to be killed in battle so they can join him at Valhöll.[16]

He used clever ruses to steal the mead of poetry from the giants, a treasure of incomparable value. Layer upon layer of crafty planning was devised to outsmart his opponents and get past the defenses guarding the treasure.

The mead was inside a mountain, guarded by the daughter of the giant Suttungr. Óðinn, in disguise, started an argument among the workmen of the giant Baugi that resulted in their killing each other. Frantic to get the hay harvested, Baugi accepted Óðinn's offer to harvest all the hay himself in return for a sip of the mead. When the job was finished, Suttungr refused to turn over even a few drops of the mead to Óðinn, so he resorted to another ruse. He drilled a hole in the mountain, entered in the form of a snake, and slept with the giant's daughter for three nights. She then agreed to give him three sips of the mead. Óðinn consumed all the mead in three big swallows, changed into an eagle, and flew back to the gods' homeland of Ásgarðr, where he regurgitated the mead into three big cauldrons.[17] A collection of Óðinn's clever advice, suggestions, and guidance survives in the eddic poem *Hávamál*.

GATHERING INTELLIGENCE

Having more and better information than your opponent is key to any planning or plotting. Accordingly, a key aspect of Viking battle activities was gathering intelligence. If one side was better informed, it might make better plans and therefore might take the actions more likely to achieve its goals. The word for the act of gathering intelligence in the old language is *njósna* (to spy), and the people gathering the intelligence were called *njósnarmenn* (spies).[18]

The concept of being a spy differs from what we think of today. Spies came from all classes of society, from slaves to gods. The most potent gatherer of intelligence in the Viking world was Óðinn. He seeks knowledge constantly, and he has many means to obtain it. Óðinn sits in his high seat in the place called *Hliðskjálfi* from which he can see throughout all the worlds and observe the activities of all who live there.[19] Every day, Óðinn sends his ravens Huginn and Muninn out throughout the world to gather news, which they share with him when they return, whispering it into his ears.[20]

Óðinn is able to raise the dead to get information from them. He raised and preserved the severed head of Mímir, who tells him secret news from other worlds. He raised a *völva* from her grave and compelled her to tell of the upcoming death of his son, Baldr. Baldr's death presages the apocalyptic battle at Ragnarök,[21] and it seems likely that Óðinn seeks this knowledge to prepare for the battle.

Kings and farmers also gathered intelligence, and their sources and methods varied. Kings sent their men to gather intelligence before making their moves.[22] Farmers spied on kings who were trying to assert their authority over the land, or trying to convert the land to Christianity. As King Ólafr approached to force conversion, Guðbrandr dispatched 840 spies to watch his movements into the district.[23]

Traveling beggarwomen were inadvertent spies, gossiping about whom they saw and what they saw as they journeyed,[24] even visiting a specific farm if they had information that might earn them a reward from the people of that farm.[25]

Slaves, servants, and shepherds reported to their masters what they saw during the normal course of their duties, and some were sent on spying missions to neighboring farms to observe, disguising their spying behind what appeared to be a mundane visit. Sometimes, ordinary men did their own spying, traveling in disguise or pretending to be lost and asking for information that told them of the whereabouts of their enemies. And there are cases of men who can only be called professional spies, such as Njósnar-Helgi (Helgi the spy) from *Gísla Saga*,[26] discussed later.

Regardless of who did the spying, there were three main objectives: to gather good information, to avoid getting detected or caught while doing the spying, and to return and report the information.

There are many reasons for intelligence gathering in the literary sources, and nearly all of them have to do with combat: planning and preparing for the next battle action, whether it be offensive planning, such as preparing an ambush,[27] or defensive planning, such as countering an ambush.[28]

Viking-age people had to be prepared for the possibility of an armed attack at all times. In such a society, good intelligence could mean the difference between life or death. Yet the information had to be clear enough and concrete enough to be usable for planning the next action. The *njósnarmenn* had to know what information was required and how best to obtain it.

The more detailed the information gathered, the easier it was to take appropriate action. Knowing a man's location, his travel plans, and his intents made it possible to make plans against him and infer his defensive plans. At times, the information needed was as simple as if and where an ambush was planned against a man,[29] or where an ambush might be possible.[30] More information might include the number of fighters and even the identities of specific fighters at an ambush or attack.[31]

A society in which armed attack could occur at any time bred attentive men and women who were wary, suspicious, and cautious. People were always on the lookout for outsiders who might be asking questions.

In their attempt to gather intelligence, *njósnarmenn* used secrecy and deception to avoid being spotted. A spy whose identity was revealed was in jeopardy. For example, when a spy inadvertently revealed his identity to Skúta, the subject of his spying, Skúta killed the spy on the spot.[32] Additionally, a spy whose identity was revealed would destroy the element of surprise that might be essential for the plans of the man who hired the spy.

Some *njósnarmenn* went to great lengths to avoid being revealed. Disguises, theatrics, and well-crafted backstories were created to earn the trust of the one being spied on.[33]

*Njósnarmenn* might spy for an extended period to get the intelligence wanted.[34] Njósnar-Helgi was given the task of tracking down the outlaw Gísli. He spent seven years on the case, until Gísli killed him.[35] He spent long periods in Geirþjófsfjörðr and other places, where Gísli was thought to be hiding, pretending to be a traveler and, later, a wood cutter.

It appears that in Viking society, the need to be cautious and wary bordered on paranoia. One had to be vigilant against possible attacks, yet it was also a society in which hospitality to travelers was a sacred custom because of the harsh northern climate.[36] *Hávamál* teaches that one should be hospitable to a traveler:[37] give him a seat by the fire and food, dry clothing, water, and a warm welcome.[38] But at the same time, this traveler might be a spy or an enemy in disguise. Njósnar-Helgi, pretending to be a traveler, received hospitality at the farm where he thought Gísli was being hidden. The housewife was cautious, but Helgi nevertheless discovered Gísli's underground hiding place. Hosts, no doubt, kept their weapons close as they offered hospitality, just in case. And *Hávamál* warns travelers who have accepted hospitality likewise to be careful and stay finely attuned, looking and listening to inform themselves.[39]

Those who might be the target of a spy also took precautions in case spies were about. Like Gísli, they concealed themselves in hiding places or underground rooms, discussed later. They used deception and disguises and misdirection.

To avoid spies, men traveled off the main path so as not to be spotted,[40] and they traveled at times of day or at speeds that made it less likely they might be followed,[41] alert for spies.[42] When Þorkell traveled to *þing*, he wanted to hide from spying eyes the true number of supporters he was bringing with him to press his case in court. Þorkell and a small number of men took the usual route, while a much larger group of his men traveled off the main route, staying in tents that were camouflaged to hide their presence.[43] The spies working for Þorkell's opponent had no knowledge of the large number of Þorkell's men waiting just outside the *þing* site, and Þorkell's superior force quashed the case in court.

AMBUSH

The Viking way was to be clever, and a goal in any conflict was to avoid wasting manpower. An approach to reach that goal was to attack the opponent at his weakest point, where he was most vulnerable. Ambushing was a way to achieve that goal. The attacker planned to meet and attack the opponent where he was least prepared.

The ancient word for an ambush is *fyrirsát*, and the action is *sitja fyrir*. Both words are a compound of *fyrir*, meaning in the way, and *sitja*,[44] meaning to sit. The words paint a clear picture of the concept of ambushing. It involved sitting and waiting where your opponent was expected to pass.

Ambushing, like most other Viking tactics, began with information gathering. In order to plan an ambush, the attackers needed to know the target's destination, his travel route, and the timing of his travel.

Ambushing was a combative action meant to capitalize on the ambusher's strength of manpower and on the target's weakness and lack of preparation and readiness. Accordingly, the ambusher also needed to know the strength and preparedness of the target. The importance of knowing where, when, and how many is stated multiple times in the literary sources.[45]

An example of where the right information was not obtained appears in *Laxdæla saga*. Þorvaldr decided to ambush Bolli, and he arrived at the site with eighteen men. When Bolli arrived, also supported by eighteen men, Þorvaldr saw he did not have the advantage of numbers he expected, and he withdrew from the ambush with a total loss of face.[46]

The world of the Viking was one of danger and constant vigilance. This need for vigilance meant that when preparing an ambush, secrecy was of great importance to avoid alerting the target. There are many episodes where the target was warned against an upcoming ambush and used that information to prepare for the battle.[47] In some cases, that involved traveling with a larger party, or traveling more alert and prepared. In only a few cases did the target choose to avoid the ambush by taking a different route. One such traveler was Þorsteinn, who, upon seeing the glint of the ambushers' spears, told his men he had an important appointment with a farmer in a different direction and turned away.[48]

But most cases were not like Þorsteinn. Men continued to press forward toward the am-

Eyvindará, in east Iceland, where Helgi Droplaugarson was ambushed by Helgi Ásbjarnarson. Helgi D and his men were traveling down the valley (dark arrows) alongside the Eyvindará river. Helgi Á and his team waited in ambush on the hill where the photograph was taken. When the time was right, Helgi Á ran down the hill (light arrows). Helgi D wanted to go to a small hill farther down the valley to make his stand (dotted arrow) but saw that he did not have time. Instead, he turned into a ravine with a small elevation, and the fight occurred at this spot at the right edge of the photo. Photo: William R. Short.

bush, despite warnings or premonitions.[49] In some cases, upon seeing the ambush, the target sat and waited for the ambushers to arrive.[50]

Once the information about the target was obtained, the next step was to gather armed men for the ambush.[51] The choice could have complications because of conflicting loyalties. Gathering men who would agree to participate in an ambush depended on their relationships to the target and the ambusher.

The culture created men who were constantly wary and prepared but who were also passionate about trust and friendship. Men were loyal to family and friends. If a man were to break this loyalty, he would be unlikely to receive help or support in any future dealings. *Hávamál* contains several verses expressing the need for this kind of loyalty between friends.[52]

To his friend a man should be a friend
and to his friend's friend too;
but a friend no man should be
to the friend of his enemy.[53]

Families were considered to extend back many generations and so were large. At the same time, one's circle of friends might also be large. As a result, a conflict in loyalties might well arise when men were gathered for an ambush. Once again, the need for careful consideration came to the fore. If a man was asked to participate in an ambush because he was a friend, he might have distant family relations with the target and not only decline the invitation but also inform the intended target. As discussed in the mindset chapter, the foremost characteristic of a *drengr* was loyalty.

An example of this complication is described in *Laxdæla saga*. Guðrún egged on her brothers to take revenge on Kjartan by ambushing him as he rode home that day. She insisted her husband, Bolli, also participate, even though Bolli and Kjartan were foster brothers, an arrangement that at times created ties stronger than blood. Bolli at first refused to attack his kinsman, but Guðrún threatened divorce, saying Bolli was not in a position to please everyone.[54]

The size of the ambush party varied, from a few men[55] to a few dozen men.[56] In some cases, hundreds were involved.[57]

The location of the ambush was usually chosen with some care and foresight. A good location was at a choke point through which the target must pass in his travels: a river ford,[58] a narrow valley,[59] or along a path.[60] Additionally, the location was chosen based on visibility. The ambushers wanted to be able to see the target approaching.[61]

An ambush site that offered concealment to the ambushers seems to have been less important. Hiding and jumping out at the target does not seem to have been part of the ambush. There are numerous cases of the targets seeing the ambushers from afar,[62] or even of ambushers moving from their hiding place to intercept the targets.[63] Yet there are few examples of an actual hiding place offering concealment.[64]

This lack of concealment makes sense, since ambushing was not a dishonorable deed. The ambushers came at their target in plain sight. Their actions did not go unannounced, and they took responsibility for their deeds.

Once the ambushers were in place and the target was approaching, both sides took action. When the ambushers saw the target coming, they went at them, attacking to kill them with the weapons at hand.

The target often had a warning or premonition of a possible attack,[65] so they might be more alert than normal. The target often saw the ambushers from some distance and had to decide whether to stand their ground and fight or move to a superior fighting position, such as a *vígi* (discussed below), to enhance their chances of success.[66] Whatever the choices made, the two sides met and the fight began. The fight usually continued to the death of the principal on one side or another,[67] or until one side fled.[68]

After the ambush, the injured party (or their family or friends) responded in several possible ways. They could resolve the matter in court or through extrajudicial means such as a revenge attack. If the injured party was weak, they might not be able to respond in any meaningful way.

The legal procedures used to resolve an ambush are described in *Grágás*,[69] and *Brennu-Njáls saga* provides extensive detail about the court cases that followed ambushes. A killing required compensation, but some participants, due to their actions before or during the ambush, might have lost their immunity, and so their deaths did not have to be compensated. Suits and countersuits seem to have been the norm, with complex legal maneuvering.[70] Suits against men who died in the ambush were possible in order to cause them to lose their immunity retroactively, so no compensation needed to be paid. Compensation for a dead man on one side was traded off with the compensation for an equivalent dead man on the other side. Regarding the cases related to Starkaðr's ambush of Gunnar at Rangá, a point made repeatedly in the saga text is that the cases were being conducted according to law.[71]

If the ambush case was resolved out of court, revenge could be swift. After Kjartan was killed in an ambush, his brothers found and killed some of the ambushers the next day.[72]

Ambushing was just another tool in the arsenal of the Vikings. It was simple and direct, like so many other aspects of Viking society. Men gathered intelligence about the target's travels and forces, and then met him at a choke point with a larger fighting force.

One might ask why the target wasn't simply attacked at his home, where it seems more likely he could be found. The answer is that attacking a Viking man at his home was not optimal for several reasons. First, as we will see in a moment, the house provided significant protection to a man against an attack. Þórðr, when planning his ambush on Björn, stated how difficult it would be to attack Björn in his home, even though there were few men with him.[73]

Additionally, someone involved in a dispute often kept a large body of men with him in his house, above and beyond the normal residents of it. These additional men, drawn from family and friends, served to preclude such an attack.[74]

Men were wary of an attack on a home. As Flosi and the burners approached Njáll's

The exterior of the reconstructed Viking-age turf house at Eiríksstaðir in west Iceland. Eiríksstaðir was a typical, modest-sized Viking-age longhouse. Photo: William R. Short.

home, Njáll suggested people go inside where Flosi would not be able to overcome them.[75] Njáll did not foresee that Flosi would use the tactic of burning down the house.

## BURNING HOUSES

When men chose to attack another man in his home, they turned to the tactic of burning down the longhouse with the occupants inside. It was the attack called on for reliably good results. There are many examples in the literary sources.

In the *Sagas of Icelanders*, the attack was targeted and aimed at a specific person, such as Flosi's burning down Njáll's house to kill Njáll's sons.[76] In contrast, during some types of raiding, discussed in the next chapter, houses were burned indiscriminately, with the intent of destroying everything in the raiders' path.

Before discussing this tactic, it is worth pausing for a moment to review the salient features of the typical Viking-age dwelling: the longhouse.

## VIKING-AGE LONGHOUSES

Most Viking-age houses in Scandinavia were made of wood over a wood frame. However, in Iceland, houses were generally constructed with turf walls and roof over a wood frame be-

cause of the shortage of long pieces of good-quality timber for fabricating posts and beams.

The usual form of the Viking-age house was a longhouse,[77] usually 5 to 7 m broad (16 to 23 ft) and 15 to 75 m long (50 to 250 ft) The size and details varied from place to place and depending on the social position of the farmer. Rather than being a rectangle, the long walls typically bowed out along their length.

The houses were generally a single open space divided by partition walls into a few rooms intended for different purposes. Most of the house activities took place in the central room, the *skáli*, where the central firepit in the floor held a long fire for heating, light, and cooking. Often, one end room was used for food storage and preparation, and a room at the other end was for storing farm gear and possibly a byre for animals in some houses.

The wood frame was built on a stone foundation. The frame consisted of two rows of posts running the length of the house, dividing the floor space into three aisles, with a packed dirt floor. In the *skáli*, raised benches filled the two outer aisles, which were used for sleeping, sitting, and other daily activities.

The open floor plan meant privacy was unknown. Lockable bed-closets were used, but

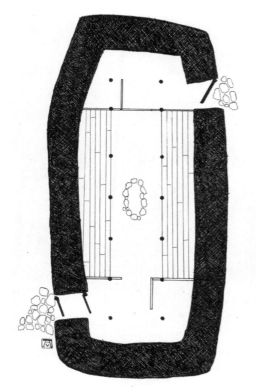

Top: Floor plan of Eiríksstaðir based on archaeological excavations. Illustration: Andrew P. Volpe. Bottom: The skáli, the main hall, of the reconstructed turf house at Eiríksstaðir. Photo: William R. Short.

Top: Speculative framing details for a turf house such as Eiríksstaðir. Illustration: Andrew P. Volpe. Bottom: A reconstruction of a Viking-age turfhouse at Stöng, showing the turf roof resting on birch stringers over the rafters. Photo: William R. Short.

probably only by the master of the house and his wife, in typical houses. Everyone else slept together on the benches.

While the roof was high, the beams that formed the frame probably were not. The space above the beams was used for open storage. An opening at the top of the roof above the firepit let out smoke. There were few doors and few windows, which typically were covered with translucent animal membrane to let in light.

The result was a home that could be dry and warm, but probably was also dark and smokey at times, with narrow passageways and obsta-

A reconstruction of a bed closet, the lockable sleeping place for the master of the household and his wife. Photo: William R. Short.

The front door of the reconstructed turf house at Stöng in south Iceland. Photo: William R. Short.

cles to passage, such as the firepit on the floor. Doors through the partition walls between rooms were likely small.

The literary sources tell of the difficulties of fighting in a longhouse, due to the poor visibility, the confined space, and the wooden framing elements that trapped weapons. Our tests, using simulated combat, suggest that, indeed, it was a difficult place in which to fight.[78] Thus it comes as no surprise that men chose to burn the occupants inside the house rather than try to fight them.

BURNING

The law codes, both Icelandic and Norwegian, state that the penalty for burning is outlawry.[79] Even to ask a man to go burn a house, regardless of the outcome, was punished with lesser outlawry.[80] Indeed, the Norwegian law codes state that house burning is *níð*.[81]

The law codes make it clear that burning was a breach of the law, yet the literary sources make it clear that it was a commonly used tac-

tic. Perhaps this discrepancy can be partially explained by the change in religion. The law codes are from the Christian era. While many old laws were maintained, there were also new laws written, more in line with the new beliefs, and the literary sources show us that burning was against Christian morals. As Flosi contemplated burning Njáll, he said both choices were bad: to turn away would lead to death, but to burn the house was a grave responsibility before God because he and his group were Christians.[82]

If the action carried such harsh penalties, why did men choose this action, especially since in virtually all the cases in the literary sources, the attackers had a superior force compared to the defenders?[83] Why not just attack men inside the house?

The literary sources suggest that burning was a choice that reduced the possibility of casualties for the attackers.[84] Not only does the defender have home-field advantage in his house, the house is difficult to attack en masse. The narrow passage of the front door prevented a mass assault and limited attackers to entering one at a time, allowing the defenders to pick them off as they entered.[85] The narrow halls and low ceiling beams of the longhouse limited fighting options and favored the defenders. Additionally, the defenders would know the hiding places and protected nooks from which they could make attacks with impunity. By setting the house ablaze from the outside, the attackers tilted the odds in their favor.

Smoldering turf. The interiors of the turf bricks are ablaze, and a turf fire is extremely difficult to extinguish once started. Photo: William R. Short.

The advantages of setting a fire to reduce casualties is stated explicitly in *Egils saga*. King Haraldr had surrounded Þórólfr's house, and he ordered the house set ablaze. He said he had no intention of fighting the men inside and losing his own men.[86]

Once the blaze was established, the options available to the defender were few. He could stay inside hoping to escape in all the chaos.[87] He could attempt to break down a wall to make an escape.[88] He could accept his fate of death and die in the flames.[89] Or he could be driven out of the house by the smoke and flames directly into the weapons of the attackers standing around the door waiting to cut down anyone who fled.[90] It was a lose-lose situation for the defenders.

Houses built from wood were easily set ablaze from the outside. When King Haraldr set Þórólfr's house ablaze in Norway, the saga mentions that it quickly became engulfed, since the wood was dry and tarred, presumably to protect it from the elements.[91]

Turf houses, on the other hand, were not so easy to ignite. Virtually the entire exterior was covered with turf, blocks of the dense root material of bog grasses. Turf is mostly organic material from the matted roots of the grasses, with some mineral material from the soil of the bog, ideally containing clay, rather than sand, to provide better structural strength to the block of turf.

In a fire, the organic materials ignite but the minerals do not, so setting the turf ablaze can be a challenge. Instead, the attackers must find a way to ignite the wood frame, which then ignites the turf. The only exposed part of the wood frame was the door to the house and the frame around it. Thus, in order to start a turf-house fire, wood or other flammable material was brought to the house,[92] piled against the door, and ignited,[93] which set fire to the wood frame. Once the door was ignited, the fire spread along the frame into the house until it ignited the turf, setting the whole inside of the house aflame. Turf burns slowly, generating heat and smoke and gases, and it is nearly impossible to extinguish. Once the turf starts burning, the house is doomed.

Once the house is ablaze, survival possibilities for the occupants become limited. There would be heat, smoke, and poisonous gases. As the beams burned and could no longer support their loads, there would be falling beams and rafters, some of them alight, along with turf and debris, making the interior of the house a confusing, frightening, and dangerous place. Additionally, the depletion of the oxygen and the creation of carbon dioxide, carbon monoxide, and poisonous gases would asphyxiate the occupants.

There was a code of conduct when it came to burning houses and the people inside them. Once the fire was set, the inhabitants who were not targeted in the fire were offered the option to leave the house safely.[94] Typically, this in-

In an attack on a house, the fight usually centered around the door, as depicted in the film *The Final Battle of Grettir the Strong.*

cluded all the women and children in the house, and often included servants. As discussed in the mindset chapter, this act of mercy was based on the code of conduct of a *drengr* to show mercy to the weak.

House burning was directed against a specific individual or group. It was meant to limit causalities to the attacker and the defender. The attackers didn't lose men while fighting the defender in a difficult battle arena: the house. The defenders who were not targeted were allowed to leave in peace.

The negotiations were conducted by the burners and the targets by calling to each other through the burning door, again showing the door to be the focal point of the situation. Fire was set at the door, and the targets attempted to extinguish the fire at the door. Both sides attacked, defended, and stood battle ready at the door, and the discussions about this dire situation took place at the door.

Naturally, people trapped in the burning longhouse looked for escape. The most direct escape route was a secret door,[95] a feature of Viking longhouses discussed later in the chapter. This method of escape from a fire is not often mentioned in the literary sources, perhaps because the attackers knew of the possibility of a secret door and looked for it and blocked it before they started the burning.[96]

The other possibility of exiting was to break through a wall of the house. As the house burned and began to fall in, openings through which men could escape might be created.[97] Men knocked down walls to escape, using whatever might be available to help them.[98]

House burning is an example of a Viking tactic that at first glance seems cruel and barbaric. Yet a closer look shows that the intent seemingly was to limit the loss of life on both sides during a violent attack.

SECRET EXITS AND ENTRANCES

The use of house burning as a tactic is only one of many reasons Vikings were wary, alert, and prepared for violent attacks, since one never knew when an attack might take place and that attack might come while one was at home. This need to be prepared affected the placement of houses: on high ground with good visibility of the surrounding countryside. Examples are found in archaeology and mentioned in the literary sources, such as the

The view of the valley from the Viking-age house at Eiríksstaðir. Houses were located on a rise so that anyone traveling through the valley toward the house could be seen well in advance of their arrival. Photo: William R. Short.

Viking-age houses at Hofstaðir, located on a slope above the river Laxá, at Eiríksstaðir, located on a slope above the river Haukadalsá, and at Hóll, on a hill in Haukadalr.[99] The need to be prepared also affected the architecture of Viking homes, which included secret exits, secret doors, escape tunnels, and places of hiding within the house. There are two broad categories of such places: tunnels and doors.

JARÐHÚS

The Old Icelandic word for these tunnels is *jarðhús*, a portmanteau of *jarð* (earth) and *hús* (house). The word has several meanings as used in the literary sources, complicating our research. It can refer either to a tunnel or to an underground room or house.[100] For a particular usage of the word, it can be hard to determine to what the word refers since often there is so little detail. Although we might speculate that a *jarðhús* in a text refers to a tunnel based on the context,[101] we dare not make the assumption, since it might be a multipurpose pit house, a storage shed, or a *fylgsni* described below.

Man-made tunnels thought to be escape tunnels are found in northern European lands from as early as 600 BCE. In Ireland, it is esti-mated that there are several thousand of these structures, dating from the ninth to the thirteenth century. Typically, the tunnel connects the living space of the house to the outside. These tunnels, also called *souterrains*, are found in smaller numbers in Scotland, the Orkneys, and the Hebrides. Few, if any, are found in Viking-age Scandinavia.[102]

These kinds of escape tunnels are also found in Iceland, but so far, all have been dated from after the Viking age. These tunnels, from the later Sturlunga era, nonetheless offer us insight into the nature of the Viking-age tunnels in Iceland described in the literary sources.

Because these tunnels were used to escape violent conflict, they were kept secret to avoid the possibility that an attacker might neutralize them, as did Hávarðr, who stationed men to watch the exits of Ljótr's tunnels before attacking. Worse yet, an attacker with knowledge of a tunnel might use it to secretly enter the house to attack the occupants. We see the degree to which tunnels were kept secret in *Reykdæla saga og Víga-Skúta*. Skúta's tunnel was known only to him and his beloved foster daughter, and to no one else in the household.[103]

Top: The interior of the escape tunnel at Keldur in south Iceland. Photo: Þór Hjaltalín. Þjms 1998. Center: Exiting a secret tunnel in west Iceland that may date from the Viking age. Photo: Reynir A. Óskarson. Bottom: The exits of the escape tunnel at Keldur, above the banks of the creek Keldnalækr. In ancient times, these exits would have been covered with vegetation to disguise them. The disguise was sufficient to prevent the tunnel from being discovered until the twentieth century. Photo: Hermann Jakob Hjartarson.

In the archaeological finds and in the literary sources, one end of these tunnels was in the living area of the house,[104] and in most cases, in the sleeping area of the house,[105] or even in the bed closet of the master of the house.[106]

Perhaps this location was chosen so the tunnel was readily accessible at the occupants' most vulnerable moments: while sleeping in bed. Perhaps it was because the bed closet of a Viking home was one of the few private places in a home, as discussed earlier, and thus one of the few places where a secret tunnel could be concealed. A tunnel entrance under their bed in the bed closet would indeed be well concealed. Perhaps the bed closet served as a kind of safe room, providing a few moments of security during an attack in which to decide whether to fight or to flee through the tunnel.

Perhaps one of the reasons so few tunnels have been found in a Viking-age context is that they were so cleverly concealed and so aggressively kept secret. An example is the tunnel found on the farm Keldur in south Iceland. The tunnel was accidentally discovered on the farm in 1932 when there was digging for a septic tank.[107] No literary source mentions this tunnel, despite the farm having been occupied since at least the tenth century and being mentioned in the *Sagas of Icelanders* and in *Sturlunga saga*.

The far end of the tunnel was usually located near running water, as is the case at Keldur.[108] In part, the exit point was chosen to hide the construction of the tunnel. As it was dug, the excavated material was moved to the stream to be carried away, hiding all traces of tunnel excavation.[109] In *Droplaugarsona saga*, a housemaid commented that the creek was so dirty that one couldn't drink from it. Ingjaldr suspected that the creek was plugged in some way and went to clear it, but in fact, Grímr had been making a tunnel and carrying the earth to the creek at night.[110]

In many of these *jarðhús* described in the literary sources, an exterior opening was covered up with vegetation to hide its presence.[111] Unfortunately, few of these examples of a *jarðhús* in the stories can be confirmed to be a tunnel, rather than some other structure, yet as the picture of the Keldur tunnel makes clear, the opening must be hidden.

Few details are known about the nature of these tunnels since few have been found. They have similar dimensions: the height and width vary between 1 and 1.5 m (3.3 – 5 ft), and the length varies between 18 and 36 m (60 – 120 ft).[112]

As this text was being written, an ongoing archaeological excavation in west Iceland has uncovered a tunnel thought to be about 100 m long (330 ft). Building a tunnel of this size must have been a massive undertaking during this period because of the limitations of the hand tools available for excavating soil. It is suspected that other such tunnels exist in Iceland, but these have not yet been confirmed or excavated.

Wooden wainscotting behind the bench covered the turf walls of a typical turfhouse. The narrow, dark air space between the wooden wainscotting and the turf wall was the skot. Although not intended as a living space, men could and did hide and move secretly in this space within the house. Photo: William R. Short.

### LAUNDYR

An alternate form of bolt-hole that would have been easier to construct in a house was a secret door. The Old Icelandic word for these doors is *laundyr*, another portmanteau combining *laun* (hidden or secret) and *dyr* (door). The etymology informs us about the intent of the door but not its nature. How it was hidden is not known, and archaeology offers few clues.

The location of a door is usually clear from the ruins of the stone foundation of a house. What is not clear is whether the door was a secret door or just a normal one. Nor is it clear how a secret door might have been concealed. It has been suggested that the secret door was covered by a layer of easily removable turf, making it hard to discern from the turf walls.

*Íslendinga saga*, set in the Sturlunga era, tells of a *roftorfsveggr*, a wall of turf that could be easily broken out for a secretive and quick escape. As the house was under attack and was starting to blaze, Skeggi told people to escape through the *roftorfsveggr* located in the privy of the house.[113]

There is another feature in Viking-age turf houses that was necessary for the integrity of the structure yet also could be used to advan-

tage in combat: the *skot*. The wood wainscotting that covered the turf walls of the interior of the house was held away from the turf to prevent the wood from rotting due to moisture. The resulting air space between the wainscotting and the turf was called the *skot*. Not a part of the normal living space, this narrow, dark passage was used to hide men and to pass through the house without being seen.[114]

### BATTLE LOCATION

The Viking-age house provided protection and an advantage to a Viking fighter. When away from his house, a warrior looked for a battle arena that might give him similar advantages in a fight. There were three main types of battle locations that Vikings used to give themselves that advantage: *fylgsni*, a hideout; *vígi*, a superior position from which to fight; and *virki*, a fortification.

### FYLGSNI

*Fylgsni*, from the verb *fela* (to hide)[115] is quite simply a hideout. It was used by a man who was being sought by others intent on harming him. Notably, hideouts were used by outlaws as a temporary stopgap and as a long-term place of concealment.

Einhamar in west Iceland, a *vígi* where Gísli Súrsson fought to his death, as depicted in the film *The Final Battle of Gísli Súrsson.*

While a multitude of *fylgsni* are mentioned in the literary sources, the variations between them are too great to allow one to draw conclusions about their nature, other than that they concealed a man. Some of the different hideouts used were a *jarðhús*,[116] a barrel,[117] an overturned boat,[118] and a covering of moss.[119]

VÍGI

The literary sources tell of a *vígi*—a place that was especially advantageous for a fight because of the tactical benefits it offered to the fighter. The word is of uncertain origin, and it does not survive in other northern languages. It is thought to be associated with a fenced-in location, or with battle gear.[120] These associations suggest that the *vígi* was advantageous less for its offensive advantages than for its defensive advantages.

Some *vígi* were man made and intended for battle, such as a fortress or *virki*.[121] Some were structures intended for more mundane use, such as a wall or enclosure that offered advantages.[122] The *vígi* was sometimes carefully planned, with man-made structures or with natural features that were scouted and modified to make the *vígi* more suitable in advance of the fight.[123] At other times, the use of a *vígi* was a spur-of-the-moment decision, finding the best ground during an ambush or surprise attack.[124]

The literary sources suggest there were several aspects that made a location suitable for a *vígi*. First, the place had a defensive advantage, restricting the enemy's attack options. It might limit possible attacks and restrict the forces that could be applied, either in numbers or in directions, such as limiting access to the back or sides of the site.

A fortification, or the top of a cliff or steep ground, or a spit of land extending into a river are examples of features that meet this requirement. Even a defile in a rockface could be a *vígi*, since it limited the attacker's options.[125]

A further aspect of being easy to defend is the presence of a narrow passage into the *vígi*, creating a choke point for enemy attempting to enter. As written earlier, Snorri goði predicted that Flosi and his men would try to enter Almannagjá, a narrow, protected ravine, should there be a battle at Alþing. During the battle that did ensue, as Flosi tried to retreat to the safety of the ravine, Snorri had his men block the narrow entrance. The saga does not make clear the features that made the ravine so defensible, but a visit today shows the narrow entrance must have played a decisive role, creating easily defensible choke points, with the ruins of Snorri's booth (*Snorrabúð*) located at the entrance to the ravine.[126]

Grettisbæli is a hideout and a *vígi* used by Grettir Ásmundarson. The hideout, located atop the smaller, darker hill in front, was desirable because it was high above the surrounding area. Photo: William R. Short.

Another desirable feature of a *vígi* is elevation above surrounding terrain, allowing the occupants an advantage when shooting any kind of projectile weapons, whether rocks, arrows, or spears. The height also allowed better visibility of the surrounding terrain and any approaching opponents. The wall of a fortress provided this kind of height advantage,[127] as did high geological features, such as a cliff[128] or a slope.[129] Even the wall of a haystack on a farm provided the height advantage needed to be considered a *vígi*.[130]

As discussed in the weapons introduction chapter, the king of Viking weapons may have been the stone, used as a projectile. A plentiful supply of stones available for throwing was another requirement for a good *vígi*.[131] There are examples of places called a good *vígi* where stones were pulled up and prepared before the battle and then thrown during the battle, with lethal results.[132] The availability of stones for throwing combined with the height of the *vígi* gave the defenders a significant advantage.

There are examples of places that are called good *vígi* that were also used as a hideout (*fylgsni*) for an outlaw or other man on the run, where he could live for an extended period.[133] Björn suggested to Grettir that he use a cave on a mountain next to the Hítará River as a *vígi*. Björn said it was high, with an easily de-fended slope below it, yet it was close to the main path. Readily available food, water, firewood, and a concealed entrance were all features of Grettir's *vígi*. He lived here for several years.

Likewise, Grettir was later advised to move to the island of Drangey because it was a good *vígi*.[134] It was an island in the fjord with cliffs rising from the sea on all sides, making a secret approach nearly impossible. Grettir and his brother lived on Drangey for three years.

VIRKI

As discussed in the mass battle chapter, a *virki* was a fortification that could range from a simple wall to an elaborate stronghold. A *virki* was another form of *vígi*.

CONCLUSIONS

Viking-age people were often involved in conflict, and they used many means to ensure themselves an advantage should it arise. These methods included fundamentals such as gathering intelligence when and where it could be found, as well as complex constructs and structures, such as escape tunnels in their homes, and fortifications.

Additionally, a man with initiative and foresight could gain the upper hand by striking when the place and time were to his advantage using an ambush.

Drangey, the island in the north of Iceland where Grettir and his brother Illugi spent the last few years of their lives. The island was a *vígi* whose sheer vertical walls out of the sea made a secret approach nearly impossible. Photo: William R. Short.

Vikings were cautious and wary, realizing the need to be tactically aware in all situations. *Hávamál* teaches the necessity of this awareness, such as the need to look around before stepping through a door.[135] That this need for awareness is stated in the first verse of *Hávamál* only stresses its importance to the people of the Viking age.

This was life in the Viking world, a place where armed attacks were possible at any time and where a wise man prepared for them.

Viking warriors used other kinds of tactics. Raiding, and the closely associated action of dueling, were at the very heart of what it meant to be a Viking. These actions were such an important part of Viking society that we have separated them into their own chapter.

# RAIDING AND DUELING

At first glance, dueling and raiding seem like very different activities. Yet both cut to the very heart of what it meant to be a Viking, and as we will see in this chapter, the lines between them are blurry. Both practices were similar in how they were carried out and in how the people doing them were perceived by the community.

ETYMOLOGY

There are a number of words in the ancient language related to dueling and raiding whose meanings are not clear in the twenty-first century, in part because the meanings of the words have changed, but also because the Old Icelandic word has entered modern English usage with a different meaning than it originally carried.

At the top of the list is the word *víkingr*, from which the English word *Viking* derives. If we are to understand what it was to be a Viking, then we must know how the ancient people understood these words and how they used these words in their runestones, genealogies, law codes, and sagas. It will require us to discard our preconceived notions of the meanings of these words lest we distort and pollute our understanding of these ancient sources. Accordingly, we start the chapter with a discussion of words, their meanings, and their derivations.

VÍKINGR

In the literary sources, the title *víkingr* (Viking) is only used in connection with those who raided or dueled. In modern popular culture, the word *Viking* conjures up solid images, but the images that most often form are based on fantasy sources rather than historical ones. The word *Viking* powerfully shapes how we moderns perceive these ancient people, and that perception is somewhat skewed. And so, we seek to distinguish between *Viking* and *víkingr*.

In the ancient tongue, a *víkingr* was a person who participated in the activity called *víking*. *Víking* might be translated as raiding or piracy, but as we will see in this chapter, there is much more to the activity than either of those English words convey.

Accordingly, when we speak of Viking people participating in this activity, we will use the ancient word *víkingr* (plural: *víkingar*) to identify them. We will use the Anglicized word *Viking* to refer generally to the northern European people in the early medieval period, as is commonly done in English-language texts, allowing this single aspect of the life of these people to stand for not only their entire society but also for the period in which they flourished: the Viking age. The Viking age is commonly taken to be the dates between the first and the last recorded major Viking raids, both in England. The year 793 is when the first raid was conducted against the Lindisfarne monastery, marking the beginning of the Viking age, and 1066 is when the last major raid was led by King Haraldr harðráði of Norway, marking the end of the Viking age. Yet Viking raids started well before 793 and continued well after 1066.

The action of going *víking* is based on the word *vík*, meaning bay or inlet.[1] It is thought that these *víkingar* sheltered in bays between their raids and piratical attacks, a practice called *liggja í víking* (laying in Viking). Laying a ship in a safe, sheltered place such as a bay was a routine precaution for any seaman while waiting, whether it be for more favorable winds or for an enticing prize to sail nearby.

And so it would seem that a *víkingr* was a man who lay in a bay (*vík*) to rob (*ræna*). It is worth reminding the reader of the distinction between robbing (*ræna*) and stealing (*stela*) discussed in the mindset chapter. *Víkingar* robbed, but they did not steal. They did not take property without the owner's knowledge. A clear example occurs in *Hrómundar þáttur halta*. Hrómundr approached some *víkingar* whom he suspected of stealing his horses and said, "It is the *víkingr's* way to gain wealth by robbing or extortion, but it is a thief's way to keep it secret."[2]

This distinction is also made in *Egils saga*, where Egill, who had been captured while on a failed raiding expedition, escaped his bonds and stole the treasure of the farmer who captured him.[3] On the way back to the ship, Egill stopped in his tracks when he realized what he had done, saying it was shameful to have stolen the treasure without the farmer's knowledge. He returned to the farmhouse to inform the farmer in typical Viking fashion: by burning the house and killing the farmer.

As we will see later in the chapter, this definition of a *víkingr* is common to both men who duel and to men who raid. Heroes,[4] villains,[5] commoners,[6] earls,[7] and kings[8] alike all went *víking*. Even landless leaders called *sækonungar* (sea kings) who commanded large fleets went raiding.[9] It is a large concept that defines many people of the Viking age.

The use of the word is ancient, and contemporary with the Viking age. Runestones mention individual *víkingar*[10] and Viking voyages,[11] and the tenth century Anglo-Saxon poem *Widsið* refers to Vikings (*wicinga*).[12]

## HERJA

Another important word related to dueling and raiding is *herja*. The English word *harrying* is derived from the word *herja*, and the meaning is the same: to make a destructive attack upon someone.[13]

The word *herja* is problematic in our studies because it is used in the context of military actions and in the context of general raiding and dueling. *Herja* is used for kings annexing lands and for *víkingar* attacking shipping lanes. Simply put, men who go *víking* (raiding) are men who *herja* (harry) and *ræna* (rob); they are called *víkingar* (Vikings).

## LAWS

The Icelandic law code *Grágás* makes clear how blurry the lines were between raiders and duelers. The law states that men who harry in the land—whether it be going to the island (a term used for a duel) or harrying in caves, fortifications, or ships—immediately forfeit their immunity.[14] They no longer had any protection under the law, and their property was seized. *Grágás* further defines harrying to be the act of taking people or people's property against their will, or to beat, bind, or wound people. The Norwegian law codes *Gulaþingslög* and *Frostaþingslög* have similar prohibitions against harrying within Norway.[15]

## FAME AND POSSESSIONS

There are even more similarities between dueling and raiding when one explores the end goals of each activity. It was expected that a young male would demonstrate to the community that he had become a man through feats requiring courage and daring, attaining for himself *frami*, *virðing*, and *orðstírr*. The kinds of feats that provided this demonstration included raiding and dueling, and the literary sources make clear the need for a young man to prove himself this way.[16]

## THE TITLE OF VÍKINGR

The fame and wealth attained from a successful harrying, whether it be raiding or dueling,

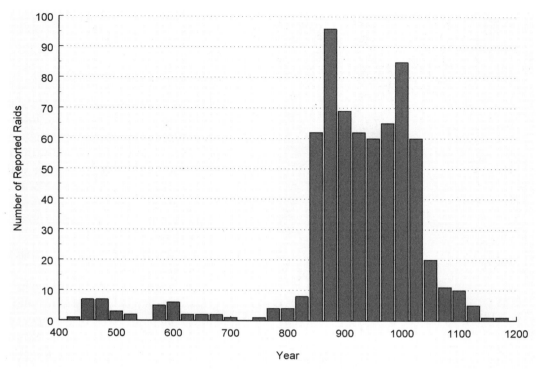

A plot of when Viking raids occurred as reported in literary sources.

could be glorious and honorable, but it also could signify something quite the opposite. Whether the title *víkingr* was honorable and prestigious or dishonorable and shameful seems to have depended on just one aspect of the harrying: was it done at home or in a far-away land?

No one likes to experience *herja* in their homes or neighborhood, and men who did such things were horrendous, despicable people.[17] They were *víkingar*.

The heroic young men who went abroad and brought back wealth and fame attained from *herja* and other daring deeds while facing life-threatening situations were glorious heroes.[18] They, too, were *víkingar*.

And so we see that *víkingr* was a name given to a man that might be either praised or despised. It was a black or white classification, with few shades of gray. What mattered was where the harrying took place. Those who harried abroad and returned home with wealth and fame were admired and called *drengr*. Those who harried at home were despised and called evil men and *níðingr*.[19]

BLURRY LINES

Raiding and dueling are so tightly interwoven in the literary sources that at times it is hard to distinguish one from another. They may even appear together on Viking-age picture stones, such as the one from Smiss that dates from the Viking age.[20] Perhaps the best approach to viewing these two subjects is similar to how they are depicted on the stone: they are so similar that they belong on the same stone, yet they are not the same picture. In the next two sections, we will discuss raiding and dueling in detail, pointing out their similarities and differences.

RAIDING

The Viking people are best remembered and most feared for their use of raiding. To give a sense of the place of raiding in society and how it was perceived, we begin this chapter with a

Raiding and dueling are both thought to be depicted on the Smiss picture stone. Derived from Christer Åhlin, *SHM 11521*. Creative Commons.

verse, composed by the poet and *víkingr* Egill Skallagrímsson when he was a child. Egill was just seven years old and had killed another boy to avenge some rough treatment during a game of *knattleikr*, the Viking ball game.

His mother was proud, saying he had the makings of a *víkingr*. Egill composed a poem, saying that when he was old enough, he should be given a warship to go raiding:

> My mother said,
> I should be bought
> a ship and beautiful oars,
> Set off with *víkingar*,
> Stand at the bow,
> Steer an expensive ship,
> Then go to harbor,
> Cut down men.[21]

This view is the popular, modern image of Viking raiders: barbaric seafarers arriving in their ships, landing, and cutting down men. There is truth to that picture, but there is much more as well.

SOURCES

We use a number of sources to obtain a clear picture of the raiding practices of *víkingar*, and the literary sources provide much of our information. The Icelandic literary sources tell of many episodes of raiding. Importantly, these depictions of raiding tell the story from several points of view: that of the raider, that of the people being raided, that of the ruler of the land being raided, and that of people who defended the land against the raiders.

*Heimskringla* tells of many raids, with many points of view, but in addition it tells of kings and earls raiding or being raided and how their raiding practices differed by being more political and more militaristic. *Jómsvíkinga saga* and *Fornkonunga saga* likewise provide details of raids and the response of kings to raiding in their lands.

Law codes, such as *Grágás* and *Gulaþingslög*, give us a good image of how raiding was perceived and how it was punished by those who were raided.

We have other early medieval Scandinavian sources that touch on the raiding practices of Vikings. Adam of Bremen, writing in the eleventh century, said those called *víkingar* (*Wichingos*) were clearly pirates.[22]

Scandinavian runestones, though terse, are contemporary records that memorialize raiders. They provide insight into the nature of the groups that went raiding and into how these adventures were perceived by the community when the *víkingar* returned home.

Literary sources from other lands, such as the *Anglo-Saxon Chronicles*, give a clear but at times distorted image of how these raiders were perceived by those unfamiliar with Vikings, their culture, and their code of conduct. Moorish sources tell of Viking raids in present-day Spain and Portugal[23] and of the Moors' admiration of the bravery of these raiders that they called *Madjus* (magicians who worshipped many gods).

The *Sea Stallion*, a replica Viking war ship based on Skuldelev 2 and operated by Vikingeskibsmuseet. Photo: Werner Karrasch. Copyright: The Viking Ship Museum, Denmark.

Place-names outside Scandinavia help indicate where the raiding happened and where the Vikings settled after raids. Place-names within Scandinavia give us clues about slaves taken from other lands during raiding, such as *Vestmannaeyjar* (Islands of the Irishmen) in Iceland, where escaped Irish slaves were run to ground.[24]

Archaeology gives us clues about where Vikings visited and about their permanent settlements in the lands where they raided, such as the towns of York and Dublin. These excavations also provide some insight into the raiding practices.

Archaeology also informs us about Viking ships, which, in many ways, made Viking raids possible. They were unique in the early medieval world, as is discussed in the mass battle chapter and expanded in this chapter. Other cultures before and during the Viking age raided, but none as successfully as Vikings, in large part because of the superiority of the Viking ships.

Experimental archaeology can tell us about the nature of Viking ships. Using replicas built according to archaeological finds, it is possible to estimate sailing capabilities, how the ships might have been rowed, and how the physical nature of the ship affected combat at sea.

Finally, genetic research informs us about the movement of people in the Viking age. For example, genetic analysis confirms what the ancient histories tell us about many Irish slaves being taken to Iceland during the settlement of that land, slaves most likely captured during raiding activities.[25]

WHAT WAS RAIDING?

Raids can be divided into three broad categories: raiding for the sake of fame and wealth, raiding with a militaristic or political intention, and piracy. These three categories blend at times, and so often we are uncertain into which category a raid falls. This fuzziness is partially due to the lack of detail in the written sources but also to the fact that raids sometimes had multiple purposes. Additionally, our modern mindset wants to force categories on that which we study, categories that may not have existed in the minds of Viking-age people.

SHIPS

As mentioned earlier, one significant factor in the success of Viking raids was the Viking ship. Since ships were already discussed in the mass

The *Ottar*, a replica Viking merchant ship based on Skuldelev 1 and operated by Vikingeskibsmuseet. Photo: Werner Karrasch. Copyright: The Viking Ship Museum, Denmark.

battle chapter, we will not rehash the material here, apart from one important point.

There were two broad categories of Viking ships: warships (*herskip*) and merchant ships (*kaupskip*). A warship was optimized for speed and maneuverability. It could sail closer to the wind than other ships, and when the wind was unfavorable, it could be rowed. The hull was optimized for speed and drew very little water, so Viking ships could sail in water unnavigable by other ships and land on any beach. A merchant ship was optimized for cargo-carrying capability. It had a deeper draft, only a few oars, and depended on the sail to power it.

Generally, each ship was used for its intended purpose, crewed by men having the skills to achieve that purpose.[26] The skill set of a raider and a trader were very different, and the literary sources are filled with episodes where these skill sets are distinguished. A clear example of this is given in *Laxdæla saga*, where Óláfr was offered a ship and crew by Gunnhildr. Óláfr said it was very important that the team be more like *hermenn* (men who harry) than *kaupmenn* (men who trade).[27]

Raiding was a seasonal activity done nearly exclusively from spring to fall.[28] Sea travel during the winter months in northern waters can be treacherous, and ice and snow can make reentry to land difficult. In winter, raiders went home or to a *friðland*, a safe haven provided by a king or earl,[29] sometimes in exchange for not raiding in that land,[30] perhaps aided by the fine gifts given by the raiders to the king.[31]

TEAMS

Raiders seem to have been drawn from all classes of society: farmers, landed men, earls, kings, good guys, and bad guys.[32] They all raided.

There seems to have been only one restriction on raiders: age. There are some references to boys being too young for raiding, such as young Egill who composed verse about his plans to raid when he was old enough.[33] Another source suggests that it was not the custom for men younger than twenty years to go *herferð* (traveling for raiding),[34] yet it also seems that the custom was occasionally ignored; boys twelve years old sailed on Viking raids.[35] Additionally, there is mention that some men were too old to go raiding.[36]

Additionally, as men grew older, they stopped raiding and settled down on their farms.[37] Perhaps they had attained enough wealth to settle comfortably, or perhaps they had earned enough *orðstírr* to be feared, making challenges to their authority less likely.

It is not clear how teams were assembled. While kings and earls already had a team of men to join them in *herja*, the literary sources suggest that other leaders gathered a team to go raiding. These teams were called *félag*, a group of men who banded together for the common good and who shared the profits of the venture. Individuals in this fellowship were called *félagi*, and the bonds between *félagi* were strong. The lost runestone of Söderby demonstrates the strength of these bonds. The inscription on the stone tells of Helgi, who was betrayed and killed by one of his *félagi*, a villainous deed and the work of a *níðingr*.[38]

The strength of the bond between *félagi* is illustrated in the laws of the Jómsvíkingar, a band of *víkingar* on the shores of the Baltic in present-day Poland. No man in the band was to flee, and all were to avenge a death as if the victim were a brother.[39]

The strength of the bond is also illustrated in an episode where a raider was unintentionally left behind after a raid.[40] When the oversight was discovered, the earl leading the raid punished the *félag* by withholding the share of the loot from the *félagi* who left the man behind.

The size of raiding parties varied. Some were only a single ship and crew, whose numbers depended on the size of the ship. When Egill raided with his friend Arinbjörn, they had three large longships and 360 men. Erlingr's raiding ship had 32 *rúm* (each with a place for two rowers to sit, one on each side), a very large ship crewed by 240 men.[41] Successful raiders might start the season with a few ships but return home with many ships, fully manned and equipped from the booty taken on their raids.[42] Raids for military purposes might have hundreds of ships in the fleet, such as King Önundr, who claimed he started his raiding season with 420 ships.[43]

LOCATIONS

The raiding locations most associated with *víkingar* in modern minds are the British Isles, but raiding was done by *víkingar* throughout Europe. Viking raids are recorded west to Greenland and east to Russia, north to Lapland and south to Africa, and everywhere in between.[44] If there was habitation near the coastline or a river with possible wealth to be gained, *víkingar* went there. Excursions deeper inland were made when kings or earls sought to demonstrate their power, but generally, raids were made close to where their ships could sail, avoiding overland travel.

Targets included trading towns,[45] villages, individual farms, churches, and monasteries.[46] Any place that might hold movable wealth located close to navigable water was vulnerable.

Between raids, *víkingar* retreated to *víkingabæli* (*bæli* means place of stay). These *víkingabæli* were places where raiders could feel comfortable harboring their ships and waiting for the next opportunity to raid.

The *víkingabæli* that are most often mentioned are the island groups *Suðureyjar* (Hebrides) off Scotland[47] and *Brenneyjar* off Gothenburg in Sweden.[48] Presumably these refuges had several elements that made them attractive: easy access to frequented shipping routes or other raiding targets, a lax political power that was unlikely to harass the raiders staying there, good hiding places from which to spring out on unsuspecting shipping, and a sheltered place to harbor the ships. The sources suggest there were trading markets and entertainment at these sites.[49]

Regardless of the nature of the raid, it seems that men gathered a team (*félag*) and sailed their longship to a site where wealth could be

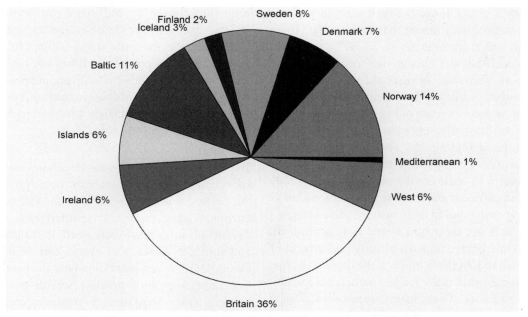

A plot of the lands raided by *víkingar* as reported in the literary sources, consolidated into ten general regions. For example, west includes lands to the west of Viking lands in continental Europe, such as Frankish lands, and Baltic includes lands to the east of Viking lands lying on the Baltic Sea.

obtained close to where their ship could sail, whether the wealth was on land or on sea. They fought, or threatened to fight, over the wealth in order to take it from its owners. Yet as mentioned earlier, there were several different categories of raiding, and next we will investigate these categories more closely.

POWER RAIDING

We have given the name power raiding to the first category of raiding because that was what it was about: demonstrating power. The intention seems to have been dominance over a people by a demonstration of power and destruction. Power raiding was more akin to a military action or a political action or even what we would refer to today as a terrorist action. In these raids, earls, kings, and their men raided other lands. It differs from the other categories of raiding in several ways.

The first difference is the intention of the raid. Power raiding had the extra ingredient of displaying power, and that extra ingredient affected the protocol of how the raid was con-

ducted. It was much more aggressive than other raiding. The raiders came unannounced and destroyed everything in their path that was of no value to them, usually because the wealth was not portable. They burned down the settlements and chased and killed those who fled. *Jómsvíkinga saga* says Haraldr's raiders rained iron and fire over the land, destroying as they went.[50]

In this time, the ruler of a land was expected to keep his people safe. If he was unable to do so, they would be less inclined to pay their taxes and tributes and more likely to be actively seeking to install another ruler who could keep them safe. For a ruler of a foreign land to cause such destruction during a raid meant two things to the people of a land: their current ruler was incapable of keeping them safe, and the foreign ruler who just inflicted the damage might be a better and safer option to act as ruler moving forward.[51] When King Haraldr was so old that he was unable to keep raiders out of his land, his leading men planned to drown

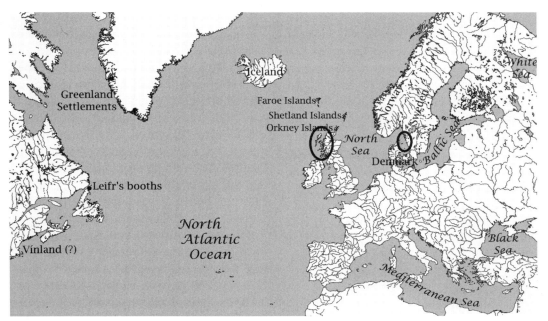

Map showing two of the *víkingabæli* most often mentioned in the literary sources: the Suðureyjar (Hebrides), and Brenneyjar off of Gothenburg in Sweden.

him in his bath so a new king could be installed. When King Buðli was feeble with age, raiders plotted to attack his lands to take them over.[52]

After this kind of destructive raid, the *herfang* (*her-* derived from harrying and *-fang* meaning capture)[53] was the spoils of the raid. It included not only valuables such as precious metals and clothing but also living beings, both animal and human. They were driven to the beach where the ship lay. Here the *strandhögg* might be delivered[54] (*strand* meaning beach and *högg* meaning blow or chop).[55] The cattle were slaughtered and brought aboard the ship for food. Humans who were desirable as either slaves or hostages were brought aboard the ship to be carried away. The suggestion is that those who were of no use to the raiders were killed there.[56]

This power raiding was very destructive to the region, making it difficult for the people who fled to safety to return and rebuild their lives. The literary sources from the foreign victims of these Viking raids describe these raids

with loathing and disgust. There are numerous such descriptions, calling on God to protect the people from the wild northern men.[57]

Alcuin wrote to King Æthelred about the raid on Lindisfarne, "never before has such terror appeared in Britain as we have now suffered from a pagan raid, nor was it thought that such an inroad from the sea could be made. Behold, the church of St. Cuthbert spattered with the blood of the priests of God, despoiled of all its ornaments." Alcuin wrote to Bishop Higbald about the same raid "when heathens desecrated God's sanctuaries, and poured the blood of saints within the compass of the altar, destroyed the house of our hope and trampled the bodies of saints in God's temple like animal dung in the street."[58]

This kind of power raid would be the practice that put fear of *víkingar* into peoples' hearts in the early medieval period. And it is this practice that forms modern people's perceptions and misconceptions about the activities of Viking raiders.

Though the activity was political, the ruler of the raiders shared the spoils with his men. The raid served to undermine the strength of the victimized rulers. In some cases, the raiding king began taxing those he raided[59] and even claimed the lands as his domain,[60] resulting in his people settling in them.[61]

## "HIGH-STAKES-POKER" RAIDING

Another type of raiding has more to do with achieving *frami, frægð, drengskapr, orðstírr,* and wealth for the individuals making up the raiding party. It is a raid by an individual and his men, rather than a raid connected to a specific ruler, though at times the lines get blurry. We call this type of raiding high-stakes-poker raiding because we believe it shares many elements with a poker game, as we will show.

Curiously, this kind of raiding is described in the literary sources only rarely in the *Sagas of Icelanders.*[62] It might be easy to dismiss this kind of raid as a literary invention, though there is a strange connection between dueling and challenge-based raiding in the law codes as well.[63]

This kind of raiding differs from power raiding in that it has an odd protocol, similar to dueling. After landing their ships and walking to the farm or other target of the raid, the raiders announced their presence. Most often, they talked directly to the head of the household. They offered him two options: hand over what the raiders wanted or fight to defend his possessions and family.

It seems strange that Viking-age parents would encourage their children to be *víkingar* if this kind of raiding is the Viking ideal, seemingly far removed from what it means to be *drengr* using our modern mindset. Perhaps our modern mindset provides us with a notion of fair play different from that of the Viking age. It seems that power trumped everything else, resulting in the sense that might equates with right, be that with physical power, power in weapon proficiency, or power in the numbers of people on your side.

We use the analogy of high-stakes poker, where might is right when the correct protocol is followed. In high-stakes poker, a player can win in one of two ways: he can have better cards than the other player, or he can pressure the other player to fold either because the money on the table is more than that player is prepared to meet or because that player thinks his opponent's cards are better than the ones he holds.

Raiding was a game of deadly violence where men forced the bet of property, women, and life itself. The Viking raider either won by having the larger force of armed men (better cards), or by causing the other players to yield and to surrender their property (fold).

Both games can be brutal. Both games can be unfair. Both games have intense levels of risk. Both games have players famed for their courage. Both games can yield immense profits. Both games are honorable and follow rules that can't be broken, lest you be deemed a *níðingr.*

It seems that these poker raids were not as destructive as the power raids. In general, nothing was burned, and no *strandhögg* was performed. These raids were about enhancing fame, honor, wealth, and good name by putting oneself to the test and by putting one's life on the line. Any wealth that was taken on the raid was shared amongst the *félag.*[64]

## PIRACY

The last form of raiding is piracy, which shared similarities with high-stakes-poker raiding, although examples of power-based piracy are also reported. The biggest difference was that instead of landing their ships and walking to a farm, the *víkingar* would wait in hiding aboard their ships for merchants or fellow *víkingar* to pass nearby. When a suitable ship was sighted by the *víkingar* to pirate, they would offer the captain of the targeted ship the option of either fighting or giving up the ship and its contents.[65]

If there were a fight, it could happen spontaneously or it could be arranged and formal, with the date and location agreed on. The fighting was done aboard the ships themselves, as with the sea battles described in the mass battle chapter. The winner took possession of all the property, including the ships. Some raiders went to sea at the beginning of the summer with only a few ships and returned home at the end of the summer with many.[66]

Sometimes no fight resulted from the piratical challenge. The crews on merchant ships were not necessarily fighters and may not have seen any possibility of a good outcome when fighting the *víkingar*.[67] In these cases, the merchants were set on land with nothing but the clothes on their backs.[68] The remainder of the property was claimed by the *víkingar*.

WEALTH AND HONOR

At the end of the raiding season, the *víkingar* returned home or to their *friðland*. They needed a safe place to winter over where there would be no reprisals for their raids. At a *friðland*, they were under the protection of a king or earl, or alternatively, there were enough other *víkingar* present to ensure safety.

If the raids were successful, *víkingar* brought home a ship full of *herfang*: precious metals, weapons, clothing, exotic foodstuffs, slaves, and other treasures. The wealth was shared among the *félagi*,[69] and at times with the earl or the king of the raiders' homeland.[70]

The leaders of these raids could become wealthy and respected men as a result of their raiding. This respect was in large part a reflection of the danger to the raider's life. Going *víking* was life threatening in multiple ways. Simply traveling at sea aboard a Viking ship held dangers from weather and other hazards at sea. The raids themselves were dangerous—fighting armed men who were not eager to give up their wealth without a fight. Additionally, many rulers set up land defenses against the raiders within their domains. These defenses took the form of levy armies, signaling systems to warn of approaching dangers,[71] and *landvarnarmenn* (land-defense men) tasked by the king with protecting his domain from raids by sea or by land.[72] Additionally, foreign *víkingar* were sometimes simply hunted down by the men of the king, who wanted to eliminate these pesky raiders and their destructive activities near his lands.[73]

VIKING RAIDS COME TO AN END

All things must come to an end, and so it was with raiding. Why did the Vikings stop raiding? The simple answer is that changes took place in European societies that made raiding less profitable and less desirable. Changes occurred not only in the Viking societies but also throughout Europe, where many of the raids took place.

One change was in the structure of Viking society. At the beginning of the Viking age, it tended to be egalitarian, with a large number of free, land-owning farmers who had the necessary means and time to engage in raiding. A ship, required for raiding, was a substantial investment, and one couldn't leave one's farm unless there were enough hired hands available to take care of the farm chores while the owner was out raiding.

By the end of the Viking age, this balance had changed. There were a small number of privileged, wealthy men and a much larger number of landless men who were tied to the land they worked in order to pay their rents and fees while supporting their families.[74] These people were not available to go raiding.

Another change was in the nature of political rule within European lands. At the beginning of the Viking age, many European lands had no central authority figures. Instead, petty kings and local chieftains were the rule in most lands.

By the end of the Viking age, most European lands had strong central authorities, including trained, standing armies capable of mounting effective defenses against Viking attacks. Generally, the *víkingar* were not trained, organized troops. While skilled at arms, their shock tactics were ineffective against trained, professional soldiers supported by the king.

Another change that occurred as a result of the Viking attacks was that some of the more desirable targets were fortified or modified, making them less susceptible to Viking raids. Walls or fortifications were built around trading towns. Monasteries erected defensive towers where valuables and people could be moved quickly in the event of a raid. Some monasteries were moved inland, away from the reach of ship-based Vikings. The island monastery at Iona was raided three times by Vikings, in the years 795, 802, and 806. Beginning in the year 807, the monastery was moved about 35 km (20 mi) inland for safety.[75]

Another change that made raiding less desirable was the conversion. The Christian church arrived in Viking lands during the Viking age. The Viking raids were not in keeping with some of the tenets of the church, so it is not a surprise that its arrival and the decline of raiding are closely tied. King Óláfr told Björn that he wanted him to give up raiding, saying, "Though you feel it suits you well, God's law is often violated."[76]

The Viking age ended when the raids stopped. The year 1066 is frequently used as a convenient marker for the end of the Viking age. At the Battle of Stamford Bridge, the Norwegian King Haraldr harðráði was repulsed and killed as he attempted to reclaim a portion of England. It was the last major Viking incursion into Europe.

The raids slowed and stopped because the times changed. It was no longer profitable or desirable to raid. Because there were fewer and fewer raids, to the rest of Europe they became not Vikings but Danes and Swedes and Norwegians and Icelanders and Greenlanders and Faroese and so on.

## DUELING

As was stated earlier, the line between raiding and dueling is blurry at times. It would not be too far-fetched to call the two activities twins. Both duelers and raiders were called *víkingr*.[77] In most cases, they both came from the sea with a group of armed men intending to take valuables (including humans) by the use of weapons, or the threat of the use of weapons. The duel was a multipurpose tool for solving issues and problems through the formal use of arms and combat.

## ETYMOLOGY

The words used for a duel in Old Norse were *hólmganga* and *einvígi*. *Hólmganga* is by far the

more frequently mentioned. It is a portmanteau of *hólmr* (a small island) and *ganga* (to go).[78] Literally, the word means going to an island. Men were challenged to go to an island to fight their duel.

*Einvígi* is also a portmanteau, of *ein* (only one or single) and *víg* (battle, but also, in legal terms, a killing), so literally, single battle.[79]

## SOURCES

As with many aspects of Viking society, the sources for dueling are limited. There are few archaeological sources for a dueling arena, at least in part because (according to literary sources) there are few traces that might be left behind that could be identified today. There is only one known picture stone that may depict dueling (see page 230).[80] Most of the picture stones of Gotland depict combat,[81] but this example is notable because the image matches the picture of dueling painted by other sources in a number of ways discussed later in the chapter.

There are a few place-names that might offer insight, but even these are problematic. The Old Norse word for duel is also the word for an island, so a place-name might be based on the landscape rather than on the events that happened there. For example, the place-name Einvígi in Arnarfjörðr in Iceland does not refer to a duel but rather the only ledge standing in the area.

We might use echoes of the past to help us form a picture of dueling, but the echoes are few and distorted. Dueling in Viking-age Scandinavia seems to have differed in significant ways from that of later medieval Europe. First, the nature of the fight itself differed, with very different rules of engagement, as is discussed later. Additionally, the later duels were enveloped in Christianity, such that the outcome of the duel was thought to have been chosen by God.[82] Viking duels were surrounded by heathenism, not only figuratively but literally as well, using heathen symbols to define the space.

Many traces of the connections between heathen beliefs and the Viking duel have been lost. *Ljósvetninga saga* makes it clear that peo-

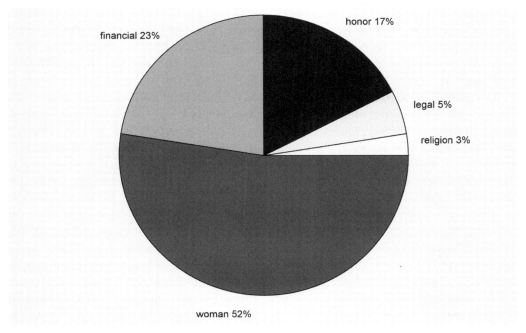

A plot of the causes of a duel as reported in the literary sources.

ple thought duels were heathen. *Kormáks saga* tells of the *tjösnur*, the pegs that hold down the cloak on which combatants fought, and of the *tjösnublót*, the heathen ritual for setting the pegs.[83] And as described in more detail later in the chapter, the setting for the duel followed heathen traditions, with bulls occasionally sacrificed by the winner at the conclusion of the duel.[84]

Another source of information is *Hednalagen* (Heathen law), thought to be a remnant of Swedish pre-Christian law that survives as a fragment in a thirteenth-century law document.[85] The text highlights the degree to which a duel was about *drengskapr*, and the loss of *drengskapr* that results from not showing up to the duel. It quotes the challenge and response spoken by the duelers for a *hólmganga*, and it teaches us about *hólmlausn*, the release from the duel discussed later in this chapter.

The word *hólmganga* does not appear to be in *Grágás*, the Icelandic law code, nor in the Norwegian law codes such as *Gulaþingslög*. That omission is a bit of a surprise. Duels were banned in Iceland and Norway only a century or so before these law codes were written down. Perhaps remnants of that old ban linger in these later law codes. *Gulaþingslög* says that if a man challenges another to combat on a *hólmr*, he loses his right to atonement, while *Grágás* bans harrying by going to a *hólmr*,[86] mentioned earlier in the chapter.

Other literary sources tell of duels, such as the *Sagas of Icelanders*, *Landnámabók*, and the myths. Additionally, Saxo tells of duels in the northern lands.

In order to understand dueling, we combine the literary sources with our force-on-force pressure testing, in which we simulate as closely as we can our ideas about dueling arenas and various dueling laws and put them to the test under the pressure of combat. The outcome of this testing, when combined with all the other sources, allows a picture to start to take form.

REASONS FOR DUELING

There are only a few kinds of issues that were solved using dueling, according to the literary evidence, falling into four broad categories:

legal matters, dishonor, fame and demonstrating a man has achieved adulthood, and financial and property gains, including gaining a woman. At times these categories overlap, and a duel described in the literary sources might fall into several of them. Additionally, we once again face the problem of our modern mindset wanting to force everything into neat categories that may not have existed in the Viking mindset.

The first of these categories is duels over legal matters. Legal issues in the Viking lands were settled via a complex set of laws and customs. Often, the winner of the case was the one with a larger group of supporters ready to fight to influence the outcome of the case. A man with fewer supporters having fewer possibilities of winning the legal case against a stronger man might instead choose to resolve the case through a duel.[87] In some Viking lands, the use of duels to resolve legal cases may have been more limited than in Iceland because of the presence of a king who might step in to adjudicate the law, as did Eiríkr when Egill challenged Berg-Önundr.[88]

Additionally, a weaker man might turn to a duel if he felt he could not enforce a legal settlement he had won in Iceland. The Icelandic state had no structure for enforcing the laws. Penalties and fines were enforced by the people involved with the case, and a weaker man might not have the power to impose the punishment. This situation is an example of might is right that seems to be a part of Viking society. Might may be right either because of an overwhelming force and numbers or because one side has a stronger fighter than the other side.

Dueling may have started as a fair way to settle legal cases in Viking lands. Rather than involving large numbers of men in a fight to influence a case, the principals on either side might choose to duel, limiting casualties to themselves. Additionally, if a court case did not go as desired, a duel was a way to follow up to get what was desired, a situation that occurs several times in *Brennu-Njáls saga* and others.[89]

Dueling was infused throughout with the concept of *drengskapr* and *orðstírr*, aspects of Viking life that towered above all else, as was discussed in the mindset chapter. When a Viking was dishonored, he had to restore his honor, preferably as soon as possible. A dishonored man was a weakened man in the society and likely to get the short end of the stick in any encounter, whether it be mercantile, legal, or societal.

Dueling was an efficient and honorable way to restore lost honor.[90] As described above, many of these honor-related duels have overlapping issues, including legal matters, spurned marriage proposals, and property disputes.

It was expected that a boy would demonstrate to the community he had become a man through feats requiring courage and daring. These feats could take the form of a duel or foreign travel for any of several reasons: trading, raiding, service to the king or to an earl, or merely adventure. Any of these adventures were opportunities for young men to prove themselves by seeing what fate had in store. A successful test brought *frami* and *orðstírr* to the young man and demonstrated he had attained his manhood. Young men who had not yet raided or dueled could not say they had proven their manhood.[91]

And so, dueling was one way for a young man to test himself and show he had become an adult. Several saga passages suggest that young men were supposed to go through a number of duels before they could be said to reach adulthood.[92]

The final category includes duels fought over finances, property, or women. At first glance, this combination might seem odd to a modern reader. Marriage in Viking society was often a business arrangement between the family of the groom and the family of the bride. It was the way wealth was passed from generation to generation and shared between families.[93] A woman with marriage prospects thus represented a valuable asset to a family. Any action that might reduce the value of that asset, as with any other asset in the family, was guarded against.

Many of the duels described in the sagas revolve around the matter of wealth: either material objects, such as livestock; property rights, such as pasture rights or fishing grounds; business deals that went wrong; or in some cases, arrangements for marriageable women.[94] This practice was sometimes called fighting for inheritance.[95]

Some of the duels over women arose when a young man and woman who thought they had an understanding about their marriage plans found those plans trumped by the bride's family. In the Viking age, although customary, it was not necessary to get the bride's approval to a match.[96] She could be betrothed by the man of the family (typically her father) without her consent. This situation sometimes led to a spurned bridegroom challenging a newly designated bridegroom to a duel over the hand of a bride.[97]

Additionally, there were men we call professional duelers who made their fortunes through dueling. They traveled from settlement to settlement, asking for the hand of a marriageable woman, along with the wealth of the woman's family. If the man of the family, whether he be the woman's father, husband, or brother, didn't yield to the dueler's demands, he was challenged to a duel.[98]

The similarities between the activities of these professional duelers and raiders are great. Both traveled, usually by sea, challenging men to fights over their wealth, with the winner taking everything. Both were called *víkingr*.

## SUMMARY OF THE DUEL

Dueling seems to have had its roots in the social structure of the Norse people in the Viking age. It gave power to an individual in a complex legal system in which the state had no power to enforce laws. It offered the possibility of resolving disputes in a manner that limited casualties to two men, rather than two families or two armies.[99] In some cases it was used as a proxy war, serving to limit casualties that resulted from the dispute, a necessity in a land with a small population.

As time passed, the view of society on the practice of dueling began to change. In part, this change may have been due to the conversion to Christianity, which looked with distaste on the connection between dueling and heathen beliefs. And it may have been due to abuses of the practice by professional duelers.

Regardless of the root cause, changes were made to dueling practices. Dueling was banned in the year 1007 by the Alþing in Iceland and in Norway around the year 1012 by Earl Eiríkr Hákonarson. *Reykdæla saga* tells us that people thought the land was cleansed when these professional duelers were dead and gone.[100]

## WHO WERE THE DUELERS?

Many kinds of people were involved with duels, but there seem to have been differences between the challengers and the challenged. The challenger, in most cases, was a professional dueler. Many of these men had such strong reputations that they were even given names that reflect their skill in dueling, such as Hólmgöngu-Bersi (Bersi the dueler), Hólmgöngu-Hrafn (Hrafn the dueler), Hólmgöngu-Starri (Starri the dueler), and Hólmgöngu-Skeggi (Skeggi the dueler).[101] Some of these professional duelers were very wealthy because of duels they had won. In the literary sources, these men are often described as bad men or berserks or *víkingar*, further demonstrating the similarity between dueling and raiding.[102]

But it was not only bad men who were duelers. Great warriors and prominent men,[103] as well as commoners,[104] issued challenges to a duel when they felt it was the best way to solve the problem at hand.

While the challengers were mostly professional duelers, the men being challenged were often the opposite. They were mostly men who possessed something that, in some way, the challenger desired. In many cases, the challenged man was not a capable fighter[105] because of advanced age, infirmities, or lack of experience. But common men,[106] great warriors,[107] kings and earls,[108] and even gods[109] were challenged to duels when the situation called for it.

It was so common for a professional dueler and *víkingr* to issue the challenge that when the tables were turned and the professional was challenged, it was thought comical. When he heard Gunnlaugr's challenge, the *víkingr* Þórormr laughed and said no one had challenged him before.[110]

ACCEPTING A DUEL

In all cases of dueling, the challenger and the challenged put their *drengskapr* at stake. A man who refused a duel or failed to show up lost all his honor. He became a *níðingr*, an object of scorn and derision. His loss of status would put him at a disadvantage in every future social interaction. As taught in *Hednalagen*,[111] the duel was about something more valuable and important in Viking society than life or death; it was about *orðstírr*.[112]

Giving in and accepting the terms of the dueler brought with it not only the loss of the disputed wealth but also the loss of face, status, and community support that went with such a decision.[113]

ISSUING THE CHALLENGE

Little can be said about the nature of making the challenge, since it seems to have varied significantly, and it is hard to find consistent narrative in the literary sources. In many cases, the challenge was spoken in the presence of and to the face of the person being challenged.[114] While in some cases the challenge was delivered in a civil manner with a handshake between the two parties,[115] in other cases the challenge was made in anger, with wicked insults and dire threats of what would happen if the challenged man did not show up.[116] Many of these insults questioned the courage and manliness of the opponent and could not go unanswered without a total loss of honor. *Egils saga* implies that witnesses needed to be present at the challenge.[117]

But in at least two cases, the challenge was passed through the grapevine.[118] A person spoke his challenge in front of witnesses, and he expected it would reach the ears of the challenged man.

The later Swedish law code *Hednalagen* specified the formula recited by the challenger and the challenged.[119]

A man uses an unutterable word to another: "You are not a man's equal and not a man at heart."

The other answers: "I am as much of a man as you."[120]

Other literary sources quote the words of the challenger, and they share similarities with those of the *Hednalagen* law code.

When the duel was accepted, the time of the duel was agreed on,[121] usually three days from the time of the challenge.[122] But the timing could range from immediately to many months in the future.[123]

PREPARATIONS FOR THE DUEL

The challenged and challenger used this time to prepare for the duel. They gathered weapons[124] and sought out magical means to gain the upper hand.[125] They might ask for assistance from the god Ullr, whom the mythological sources tell us should be called upon for a duel.[126] They gathered men to go with them to the duel site, and, if called for, they chose a shield holder, discussed later in the chapter, to assist them in the duel.

REPLACEMENT FIGHTER

If the man who was challenged doubted his ability to win the duel, he might seek a fighter to replace him.[127] It is not clear whether allowing a replacement fighter had to be agreed on by the challenger beforehand.[128] Getting a replacement dueler to take one's place in a duel was neither the most honorable approach nor was it thought to be dishonorable, depending on the opponent.[129] But there was a price to be paid.

The amount owed to the replacement dueler at the conclusion of the duel varied. In some cases, a victorious substitute expected nothing, especially if he was fighting to right a wrong or if he was stepping in for the honor of dueling.[130] Another outcome was that the substitute fighter received everything the challenger demanded when he issued the challenge.[131] Perhaps it was thought better to give the prize to an honorable man (the substitute dueler) rather than allow it to go to the bad man (the challenger).[132]

SHIELD HOLDER

We will discuss how duels were fought later in this section, but there is an aspect of the fight that must be introduced here: the presence of a shield holder. Some duels allowed shield holders, who each held and wielded the shield during the fight for his dueler, blocking the adversary's attacks and switching shields when one broke. A shield holder might have been chosen by a dueler, or he may have offered himself to take the role before a duel.

There are many examples of shield holders in the literary sources.[133] But some duelers preferred to hold their own shields, for multiple reasons. Þorsteinn turned down the earl's offer to be a shield holder, not wanting to put the earl at risk and implying there was some danger to the shield holder. The duel between Grímr and Sörkvir makes this danger clear. Grímr made the first cut to Sörkvir, which split Sörkvir's shield and cut his shield holder from shoulder to thigh. Before a duel, Eyjólfr declined a shield holder with an old saying, "One's own hand is safest," suggesting that he felt he would manage better in the duel by wielding both sword and shield himself. Yet in at least some of the duels recounted in the literary sources, a dueler who held his own shield seems to have been outside the normal procedures.[134]

To our modern mindset, the idea of a shield holder might seem bizarre, unworkable, and completely impractical. To learn more, the practice of using a shield holder was tested in our research lab.[135]

It was, indeed, a very different kind of match than our normal simulated combat, in part because it was much more of a mental challenge. Dueler and shield holder had to be alert and prepared, standing ready and unflinching as the opponent planned, possibly deceived, and then delivered his attack using full power. In some ways, it seemed to severely test the

Testing the possibility of using a shield holder in a duel using simulated combat in the Hurstwic research lab. Photo: William R. Short.

virtues of a skilled Viking fighter: courage, power, and cunning.

THE DUELING SITE: HÓLMR

When the time of the duel was arranged, so was the dueling location, the *hólmr*.[136] A *hólmr* is a small islet, usually in a bay, river, or lake.[137] Though the sources are silent about why duels were fought on an island, many theories have been proposed as to why that would be preferred.

Some suggest that an island would make it difficult for a dueler whose courage had deserted him to flee. Another theory is that an island made it harder for third parties to interfere with the duel. A third theory is that the duel was held on neutral land so if blood was spilled, it did not taint the land in some unholy way.[138] At this time, it is not possible to state definitively why an island setting was preferred.

In the literary sources, there are many islands listed on which duels took place.[139] One that is often mentioned is Öxarárhólmi in the river Öxará that bisects Þingvellir, the site of the Alþing national assembly in Iceland. Duels related to ongoing legal cases at the assembly took place on this island.[140]

Þingvellir is a geologically active site, and the landscape has changed in the centuries since

Öxarárhólmi, the dueling island at Þingvellir, as it appears today. Due to the significant geological changes at the site since the Viking age, the island today is almost certainly in a different location and of a different size than it was in the Viking age. In the photograph, the island is on the far side of the river in the foreground, and the footbridge to the island is visible in the distance on the left. Photo: William R. Short.

the Viking age. It is not clear that the island now called Öxarárhólmi is the island where the duels occurred.

### FAILING TO SHOW TO A DUEL

Not showing up to an accepted duel was an unthinkable disgrace for a Viking.[141] Duelers went to great lengths to show up to an agreed-on duel because they could not live with the shame of having failed to show up as agreed. The literary evidence paints a clear picture of how shameful this failure was and the great efforts duelers made to arrive at the agreed-on time and place.

The Swedish law code *Hednalagen* states the consequences of not showing up to a duel.[142] If the challenger did not show up, he was prohibited from ever again swearing a legal oath or from bearing witness. He was effectively banned from the legal system. If the challenged did not show up, he was declared a *níðingr*. The shame of not showing up to a duel was broadcast to the world through the use of physical symbols of *níð* that were sometimes erected when a dueler failed to show: the *níðstöng* and the *tréníð* are discussed in the mindset chapter.

One of the few valid excuses for not showing up to an agreed-on duel was the occurrence of a major, earth-shaking event, such as the death of the king.[143] From the literary sources, we see that the option of not showing up to a duel essentially did not exist for any *drengr*.

### WHO ACCOMPANIED THE DUELERS

Duelers brought with them a team of men.[144] Numbers vary, but it often was a dozen or more.[145] It seems likely that some were part of the dueler's supporters and family. Some were spectators.[146] Some were specifically chosen to travel with the dueler to the *hólmr*, perhaps to ensure the presence of reliable witnesses.

### THE DUELING ARENA

Much is uncertain about the dueling field since different literary sources provide differing and conflicting details. Many of the arenas have no description. Additionally, it seems unlikely an archaeological excavation would identify a site as having been used for dueling.

The word used is often *völlr* (field), so one presumes that men found a smooth, level area on which to stage the fight so neither had an advantage over the other. Some sagas tell of a relatively small space on which to fight, enclosed by stones,[147] or marked by cloaks laid on the ground.[148] Some were marked with strings on poles, usually made of hazel wood, in a space outside the cloak.[149]

This arrangement was used to mark sanctified places and shrines in heathen times. Strings called *vébönd* (sanctuary strings) were placed on hazel poles to mark the court at the *þing*. *Frostaþingslög* adds that it was an ancient law to mark the place of the law court in this way.[150] Other sources say battlefields were marked this way.[151] These details again show the connection between duels and heathen practices through sanctifying the dueling place with *vébönd* and hazel poles.

*Kormáks saga* has the clearest and longest description of the dueling arena, yet it remains obscure and hard to interpret.[152] A cloak was laid down 5 ells square (about 2.5 m square, or 8 ft) and pegged to the ground in a bizarre ritual. Three spaces, each a foot wide, were marked around the cloak, all of which was encircled with strings called *höslur* (hazel poles).

### HÓLMGANGA LAWS

It was the custom for the challenger to recite the *Hólmgöngulög* (the dueling laws) at this time.[153] There is a full recitation of the law recorded in *Kormáks saga*,[154] but the details contradict other literary sources. We will probably never know for certain what the laws were, whether they were consistent over place and time, or if they changed from one *hólmganga* to the next. Again, our modern mindset may be attempting to force a uniformity and consistency on the dueling regulations that may not have existed in the Viking era.

Viking-age dueling seems to have differed from the dueling practices of other cultures and from normal Viking combat. Next we will look at some of the most significant differences.

### THE FIGHT: MOVEMENT

Duels were most often conducted in a confined space: on a marked field, or on a cloak. The practice of confining the duelers served not only to contain the fight but also to prevent move-

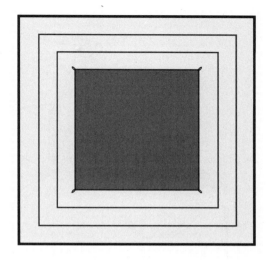

A speculative reconstruction of a dueling site of the Viking age, as described in *Kormáks saga*. A cloak (dark gray) was fastened to the ground by pegs through loops. Three equal width spaces were marked outside the cloak, and hazel poles with strings marked the outer boundary. Illustration: William R. Short.

ment away from one's opponent. It seems clear that fighters did not move during the duel. Þorkell, a great warrior, stated that in an upcoming duel, he would not move an inch. A dueler who moved during the duel was declared a *níðingr*. Perhaps the dueler's desire not to move was a way to demonstrate his resolve and courage during the ordeal. Saxo's description of a duel also suggests limited movement.[155]

### THE FIGHT: WEAPONS

This concept of no movement (or at least very limited movement) is, in some ways, supported by the weapons that were used in nearly all duels: swords[156] and shields.[157] The use of sword and shield is supported by the Smiss picture stone, thought to depict a duel that was discussed earlier in this chapter.[158] Each dueler was allowed three shields in case of breakage during the duel.[159]

There are few literary episodes that suggest other weapons were used in dueling.[160] It was so much the norm that in some episodes told in the literary sources, a sword had to be borrowed because the dueler didn't own one.

A speculative reconstruction of a Viking duel with shield holders. Illustration: Barbara Wechter.

There is even an episode where a dishonorable man wanted to borrow a sword from a reluctant and skeptical kinsman, and he told his kinsman the lie that the sword was needed for a duel to make his request more believable.[161]

We can speculate why swords and shields seemed to be the normal dueling tools. Maybe it was for the same reason that in later centuries, matched pairs of dueling pistols were chosen: to ensure that all aspects of the duel were equal. In the case of sword and shield, it also kept the distances equal so that neither dueler had an advantage. This suggests that duelers sought fair play, but it also suggests might is right if the dueler follows the rules.

One episode from the literary sources lends support to the idea of equal advantage to each fighter. A dueler accused his opponent of using a longer sword in the duel than was allowed by law, which would have given him an illegal advantage.[162]

THE FIGHT: TAKING TURNS

One might imagine a duel being a one-on-one fight in which Viking men made their stand and hacked at one another until one prevailed and the other fell, but this does not seem to have been the case. Dueling in the Viking age seems to have been a turn-based fight. The challenged man took the first swing,[163] and the challenger's shield holder (or the challenger himself if there was no shield holder) blocked the attack.[164] That led to the next turn, where the challenger attacked. Saxo also reports that in a duel, there was a definite sequence in the attacks, with a gap between each turn.[165]

This dueling system seems to be a stylized trading of blows in an organized manner. Not only is this the dueling method repeatedly mentioned in the literary sources, it is also one of the few approaches that allows a broken shield to be swapped out for a new one.[166]

This style is also one of the few ways that fighting in such a confined space would work logically. If there weren't turns, it seems the fight would be over in seconds, since the close range made it likely multiple and combination strikes would be used to make the hit, or the duelers would enter into wrestling to finish the fight. The situation is similar to that in modern-day boxing, where the boxer enters a range where he can hit his opponent without taking a step and thus rain down multiple blows, except the Viking-age dueler used a sharp sword instead of his fists. This picture does not fit Viking dueling, since there are numerous examples of duels continuing for a long time.[167]

ALTERNATIVE FORMS OF THE DUEL

In rare cases, the literary sources mention other forms of dueling. In *Egils saga* there are two examples of dueling where movement seems to have been allowed, and there were no rounds, although one of those cases might be a literary tool showing Egill's bravery and his opponent's cowardice, running backward from Egill's constant advances.[168]

Many believe that the literary sources support two distinct types of duels: the *hólmganga*, a more formal duel, and the *einvígi*, a less formal duel. Careful examination shows that in only one example is a difference between the duels noted. After being challenged, Bersi the dueler offered Kormákr the opportunity to switch from *hólmganga* to *einvígi*, saying "there is difficulty involved in a *hólmganga*, but none whatever in *einvígi*."[169]

In other examples, *hólmganga* and *einvígi* are used interchangeably to describe the same duel, suggesting they are synonyms for the same style of dueling.[170] Perhaps the words merely represent different literary styles. Perhaps it is our modern mindset attempting to impose a system of categorizing these duels that did not exist in Viking times.

Another dueling style mentioned in the literary sources is the *kerganga* (going to a tub). This turn-based duel took place in a *ker*, a large wooden tub or barrel often set in the ground in the pantry of the longhouse for storing

Top: A reconstruction of the *ker* found at Stöng, a large farm in south Iceland from the late Viking age. A *ker* is a wooden barrel partially set into the earth for the storage of dairy product at Viking-age farms. Bottom: Testing the concept of a *kerganga* (tub duel) at Hurstwic using simulated combat in an enclosure that matches the dimensions of the *ker* found at the farm at Stöng. The view is from the top looking down into the simulated *ker* at the heads of the duelers. Photos: William R. Short.

dairy products such as *skyr* or sour whey. The duelers stepped into the *ker* armed with staffs, and then the barrel was covered over. In the *kerganga* described in *Flóamanna saga*, one dueler fought with a staff one ell long (50 cm, about 20 in), while the other inexplicably used a sword.[171]

The nature of the *kerganga* was tested using simulated combat[172] in a simulated *ker* that matched the dimensions of a historical find.[173] The test showed that the combatants could not move, let alone raise a weapon to swing or to thrust in such a confined space. These results force us to question the description of the *kerganga* in the literary sources.

INGREDIENTS OF THE SUCCESSFUL DUELER
The literary sources tell us that duels were a test of three traits:

*Courage*: to show up and to stand your ground without moving, like a *drengr*.

*Cunning*: to have the ability to outsmart the opponent by being *kænn* and *brögðóttr*, as discussed in the tactics chapter. In a round-based duel in which the dueler had only one attack and his opponent was waiting for it, moves such as feinting to one target but attacking another would seem likely.[174]

*Power*: to cut with all your might when you attack. It is the ongoing theme of Viking activities and combat, and it is made evident by Saxo's description of the duel.[175] It was the force of the attacks and not their number that won glory and acclaim. The use of power is suggested by a dueler being allowed three shields in a duel to replace the ones that get smashed to bits during the fight.[176]

These three traits make up the distilled essence of Viking fighting, condensed into a space the size of the cloak laid under the duelers' feet.

DUELS THAT END IN DEATH
In the vast majority of duels, the fights ended with the death of one of the men.[177] Generally, this outcome fully resolved the dispute. The winner received whatever was at the root of the dispute, whether it be property, a woman, mer-

chandise, or favorable settlement of a legal dispute.[178] Additionally, as with raiding, it seems that the winner took the loser's possessions, including land, ships, livestock, and anything of value. This outcome is inferred in several of the examples.[179]

If the dueler was a substitute for the challenged man, it seems he received the wealth of the fallen man.[180] Sometimes he was rewarded with additional payments,[181] or even the loser's arms and armor.[182] But in other cases, the substitute declined to take any of the fallen dueler's wealth, or even any payment for his services.[183] In these cases, it seems likely the dueler stepped in for the honor of fighting a duel and for the fame that came from triumphing over a challenging or overbearing opponent. No further compensation was needed for these duelers.

DUELS THAT END BEFORE DEATH
Not all duels ended in death. Usually, a fight was called when either a dueler could no longer fight[184] (typically due to the loss of a limb)[185] or when blood was spilled onto the ground or the cloak on which the duelers stood.[186]

Sometimes the fight was ended by men who rushed between the duelers to stop it, whether because of first blood spilled or a serious wound that prevented the fight from continuing.[187]

HÓLMLAUSN
A wounded man could release himself from the duel by paying *hólmlausn* (literally, a release from the island where the duel was held). The injured dueler paid the uninjured dueler a fee to end the duel honorably.[188] The amount was agreed to in advance, and typically was three marks of silver.[189]

It is difficult to assign an equivalent value in today's dollars or even in Viking-age monetary worth, since the value of silver varied with time and place in the Viking age. Three marks would be the equivalent of twelve milk cows, a substantial sum of money. It was also the worth of a free man, according to the Icelandic law code *Grágás*. The Swedish law code *Hed-*

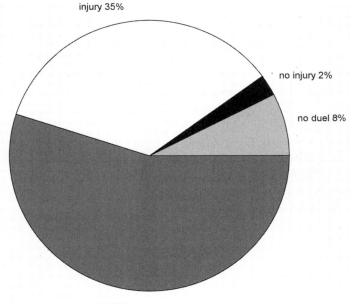

injury 35%

no injury 2%

no duel 8%

death 55%

A plot of the outcomes of the duels reported in the literary sources.

*nalagen* states that the payment is half the value of a free man.[190]

Other larger amounts are mentioned in a few examples, usually with no clear explanation of why one man might be worth more than the law allowed.[191] In one case, the challenged man asked for a larger amount because he was confident of his success and wanted to win more from the duel by specifying a larger *hólmlausn.*[192]

### OTHER ACTIVITIES AFTER THE DUEL

After the conclusion of the duel, the literary sources tell us that there were sometimes more activities. Occasionally, additional challenges were issued and more duels resulted, especially if the outcome of the original duel was not what one side or the other was expecting,[193] or if the duelers felt the outcome was not sufficiently definitive.[194] Additional challenges could come not only from the original duelers but sometimes from their shield holders.[195]

In a few cases, bulls were sacrificed by the winner at the end of the duel,[196] another example of the connections between dueling and heathen practices.

More typically, it seems that men still on their feet left the *hólmganga* arena with their *orðstírr* enhanced (or at least still intact). In one case, it seems opposing duelers even left the island on speaking terms.[197]

### SUMMARY OF DUELING

Though there remain some unknowns about the dueling practices of Vikings, and though the sources paint a strange picture to the eyes of us moderns, the actual action of the duel is clear to see. *Hólmganga* was a way for men to resolve their disputes outside the normal legal channels. This method of resolving disputes had the advantage of limiting the number of casualties, and, to a degree, offering fairness between the sides. The negative side effects include making possible the activities of professional duelers who roamed the lands challenging anyone for anything.

This highly stylized method of resolving disputes using what seems like strange and even bizarre rules to govern the duel put to extreme test the attributes and ideology of what it was to be a Viking: courage, cunning, and power.

CONCLUSION AND SUMMARY

Dueling and raiding were activities that gave a man the title of *víkingr*. It was desirable for a Viking-age boy to test himself through dueling or raiding to show he had become a man. Duels and raids both tested, at a deep and fundamental level, all of the core characteristics of a *víkingr*.

The title of *víkingr* seems to have had only two colors: black or white. The title signified something either glorious and good that you would wish your children to attain, or it signified something vile, evil, and dishonorable.

At some point in history, the word became purely negative, and the term *víkingr* became the name for all kinds of bad people. Ultimately, all Viking activities were banned by law in Iceland and Norway, according to surviving law codes, and presumably in other Viking lands as well.

# CONCLUSION

We opened this book with an introduction to Fraði, a man who was memorialized one thousand years ago by a granite stone bearing his name and the inscription telling us that he was a "terror of men" and the first among all Vikings. This book has been an exploration of Fraði and the people of his time in the northern lands, whom we collectively call Vikings.

To learn about Fraði and people like him, we turned to the scientific method, relying wherever possible on narrow sources so our understanding would not be tainted by modern material and thoughts, or by material from outside the Viking lands. We burrowed deeply into these sources, which all have violence as their main theme, creating layer upon layer of evidence to support our hypotheses and seeking the common thread running through all the evidence, rather than relying on an outlier or a single example.

Though our quest has been tightly focused on Viking combat, the same spotlight reveals the nature of Viking society. Violence permeated this society to the core: both the preparedness and readiness to use violence and the preparedness and readiness to ward against violence. This perpetual preparedness to either give or receive violence was a constant in Viking life, and it created a singular society that revolved around violence at its central axis.

One of the highest ideals in a society where violence is a constant threat is the issue of trust. Those who showed they could be trusted were *drengr*, the highest ideal to a Viking. A violent attack in accordance with law and custom could occur at the most unexpected moment, so a Viking not only needed to be prepared, he also needed to know whom he could trust: who was a *drengr*.

This was also the same society where showing hospitality to strangers in need was a sacred obligation. Travelers were invited into the home, especially in times of harsh northern weather. Those who broke these and similar obligations and ideals of trust were labeled the worst of the worst: a *níðingr* or *ódrengr*.

Vikings were also prepared to deliver violence, and they were often the perpetrators of violent attacks on others. The reasons for violence among Vikings were many, but one form of violence is at the heart of what it meant to be a Viking: the interrelated acts of dueling and raiding. We saw that only while dueling or raiding could a man be called a *víkingr*. Without this kind of pressure test, performed in a crucible of violence, there literally could be no *víkingar*: no Vikings. The violence, whether it be revenge or battle or dueling or raiding, when done in a *drengr*-like fashion, brought *orðstírr*: the state where a man's name was spoken and his deeds and accomplishments talked about.

Virtually all the deeds that brought *orðstírr* to a Viking were related to combat, and Vikings sought *orðstírr* aggressively and brutally, at least to the minds of most modern readers. Their passion for having their name known and talked about went far beyond their passion for life itself, possibly because it was more important than life itself. It was immortality, as taught in the poem *Hávamál*. The only thing that survives a man's death is his good name.

Viking combat was one of the few ways to attain this immortality, and the goal was approached directly and head on. The fighting method was without fluff, gimmicks, or complex martial techniques. Rather it was brutal, intended to get the job done. It was, at its core, about power, cunning, and daring.

Whether the conflict was one on one or a mass dynastic battle on land or at sea, the violence was delivered and was defended against in the same way, perhaps seen most clearly in isolation in their empty-handed combat of *fang*. The Viking threw down his opponent using cunning tricks, crashing him down with full power. And if that didn't end the fight, he would attain a superior ground position and use whatever tool was available to brutally kill his opponent. The Viking did what he had to do to gain *orðstírr* by defending himself or by delivering violence as long as it didn't break the code of *drengskapr*. He threw rocks at his opponent, ambushed his opponent, strangled his opponent, or burned his opponent alive inside his longhouse.

The end goal was the same: the immortality of *orðstírr*. Some Vikings managed to achieve *orðstírr*. We still talk of men like Gunnar Hámundarson, Grettir Ásmundsson, Haraldr hárfagri, and Einar þambarskelfir. We read their names and the stories of their accomplishments today, one thousand years after they lived.

And so it is with Fraði. His memorial stone proves it. His actions, whatever the specifics might have been, resulted in Fraði achieving *orðstírr* in his lifetime. This book proves his *orðstírr* lasted a long time. Today, more than

Runestone DR 216, raised in memory of Fraði, the "terror of men." Derived from Roberto Fortuna, *Tirsted-runesten*. Creative Commons.

one thousand years after his death, we still speak Fraði's name and tell of his accomplishments. He achieved his immortality.

Without an understanding of Viking combat, the path one had to travel to become a *víkingr*, there can be little understanding of Viking culture and society. We hope that through this book, the reader has gained that understanding of Viking combat and what it meant to be a Viking.

Deyr fé, deyja frændr,
deyr sjálfr it sama;
en orðstírr deyr aldregi
hveim er sér góðan getr.
—*Hávamál* v. 76

# STATISTICAL OVERVIEW OF VIKING WEAPONS

The literary sources tell of many battles involving the use of Viking weapons. We believe there is valuable information in these sources about these weapons and their use that can be teased out through statistical analyses.

In this appendix, we use statistics to learn more about how the various Viking weapons compare to one another. What targets were more likely for each weapon? How lethal was each weapon? What attacks were more typical for each weapon?

To provide quantitative answers, we turned to the *Sagas of Icelanders*. We used the sagas for this research since this source contains far more mentions of the weapons and more detailed descriptions of the use of the weapons than any other literary source. The sagas describe hundreds of armed encounters, from one-on-one disputes and duels to massive battles on land and sea. The thousands of attacks and defenses are sometimes described in great detail by authors keenly interested in combat.

To help understand weapons and weapons use described in the sagas, we created a database that we can analyze, presenting our results graphically to help us see patterns and trends.[1]

For the numerical analyses, the more than forty different kinds of weapons mentioned in the sagas were combined into a smaller number of categories. For example, all the different kinds of axes were combined into a single category, "axe." Several unknown thrusting weapons, such as *atgeirr*, *kesja*, and others that are often translated using the English word *halberd*, were combined into a single category, "halberd." Various improvised weapons, such as whale bones, stones, anvils, and the like were categorized as "other." The category "none" was created for situations where a combatant had no weapon and used empty-hand fighting.

OFFENSIVE AND DEFENSIVE USAGE

Figure A-1 shows the percentage of instances a weapon was used for an attack, while figure A-2 shows the percentage of instances a weapon was used to defend from an attack. For the plot of defensive weapons, a fighter might be armed with sword and shield, but if he blocked an attack with his shield, the instance was added only to the "shield" category. The "unspecified" category includes the situations where it is simply not possible to tell what, if any, defense was used.

TARGETS

The sagas often tell what portion of the body was targeted, and figure A-3 shows the percentage of times an area was targeted. "Head" is any attack from the neck up. "Arms" is any portion of the upper extremities. "Front" is attacks to the torso above the waist, including chest, sides, and stomach. "Back" is attacks to the back of the torso. And "legs" is any attack below the waist.

The target of the attack is broken down by weapon in figure A-4, and we begin to gain in-

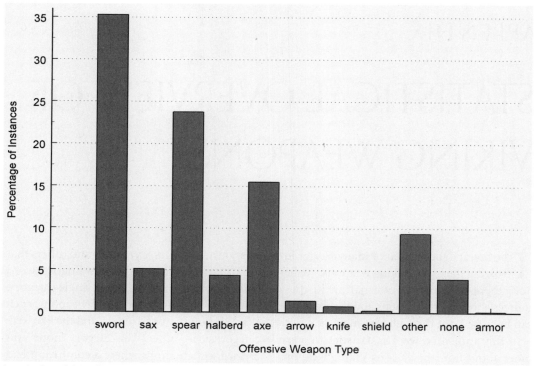

A-1. A plot of the offensive weapons used as reported in the *Sagas of Icelanders*.

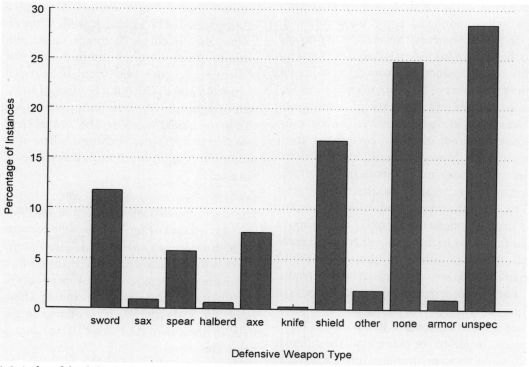

A-2. A plot of the defensive weapons used as reported in the *Sagas of Icelanders*.

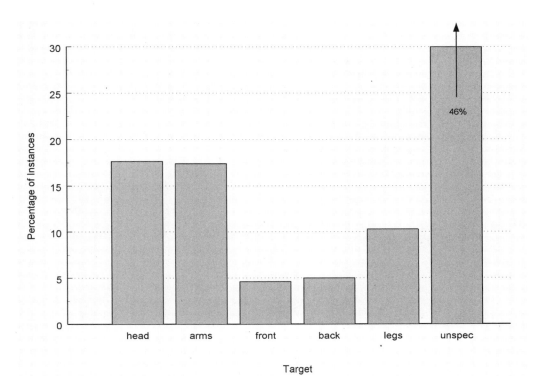

A-3. A plot of the target of the attacks reported in the *Sagas of Icelanders*.

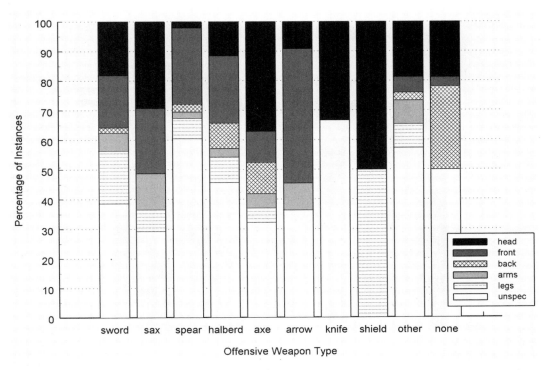

A-4. A plot of the targets of the attacks, broken down by weapon for the attacks reported in the *Sagas of Ice-landers*.

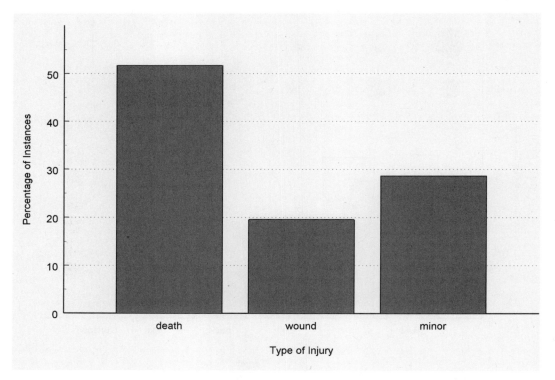

A-5. A plot of the severity of injuries resulting from attacks as reported in the *Sagas of Icelanders*.

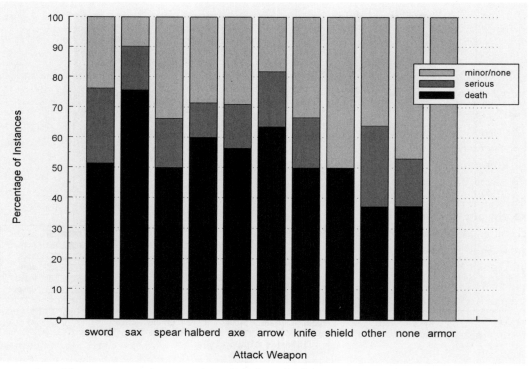

A-6. A plot of the severity of injuries resulting from attacks, broken down by attack weapon, as reported in the *Sagas of Icelanders*.

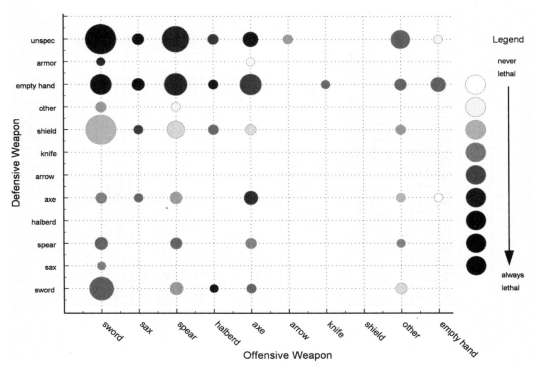

A-7. The lethality of attacks for combinations of offensive weapon and defensive weapon as reported in the *Sagas of Icelanders*. The horizontal axis shows the offensive weapon, while the vertical axis shows the defensive weapon. The size of the circle is proportional to the number of attacks for that combination of offensive and defensive weapon, and the shading of the attack is proportional to the lethality of the attack, where black is lethal in all cases, and white is not lethal in any case.

sight into how weapons were used. The individual weapons chapters detail those insights.

LETHALITY

The sagas often tell us what happened to the opponent as a consequence of an attack. These various outcomes have been grouped into three categories in our study. In some cases, the attack caused immediate death, or death shortly after the battle ended. These cases are classified as "death." In other cases, the wound was so serious that it incapacitated the man and took him out of the fight but not so serious that he died of his injuries. These cases are categorized as "wound." And in some cases, classified as "minor," the attack caused only a minor injury or no injury, and the man continued to fight. Figure A-5 shows the injuries by percentage for these three categories.

We can then break these injuries down by the weapon used in the attack that caused the injury, shown in figure A-6. It seems all the weapons, even empty hand, were capable of causing death, but some stand out as being more lethal, such as the sax.

Figure A-7 attempts to answer the question of the lethality of one weapon when used against another weapon. For example, when a sword attack was defended by a shield, how likely was the attack to cause death, on average?

In order to obtain a numerical result, we weighted the severity of the injury, with death carrying the most weight and no injury carrying the least. The use of these numerical weights allowed us to perform statistical analyses on injuries caused by one weapon against another.

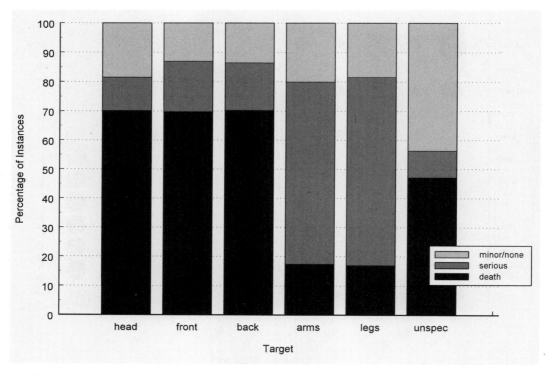

A-8. Injuries resulting from attacks, broken down by the target of the attack as reported in the *Sagas of Icelanders*.

The horizontal axis of the plot shows the offensive weapon used by the attacker, and the vertical axis shows the defensive weapon used by the defender. At the intersection of each pair of offensive and defensive weapons is a shaded circle. The size of the circle is proportional to the number of such weapons combinations reported in the sagas. A large circle represents many attacks with this combination of offensive and defensive weapons matchups, and a dot represents few or none.

The shading of the circle represents the lethality of the weapons combination to the defender. The shading varies from black (lethal in nearly every case of this weapon combination) through the grays to white (nonlethal in nearly every case).

The circles for the shield as a defense are mostly light, with some gray, suggesting the shield was an effective defense. The circles for the halberd as an offense are mostly dark, suggesting the halberd-class of weapons was effec-

tive regardless of the defense. This information helps us understand how the weapons fared one against the other.

Figure A-8 shows the injuries caused by an attack, broken down by target. Attacks to head and torso both seem to be equally effective.

KINDS OF ATTACKS

In an attack, weapons were used in various ways, such as chopping or lunging or throwing. Attacks that involved cutting or hitting or bashing were categorized as "cut." Attacks that used a thrust or a stab were categorized as "thrust." Attacks with a weapon that flew through the air were categorized as "missile." For some attacks, it is not clear how the weapon was applied to the opponent, and these are categorized as "unspecified." Figure A-9 shows the percentage of attacks that used the various types of attacks.

When these different types of attacks are broken down by weapon, as shown in figure A-10, the use of each type of weapon becomes

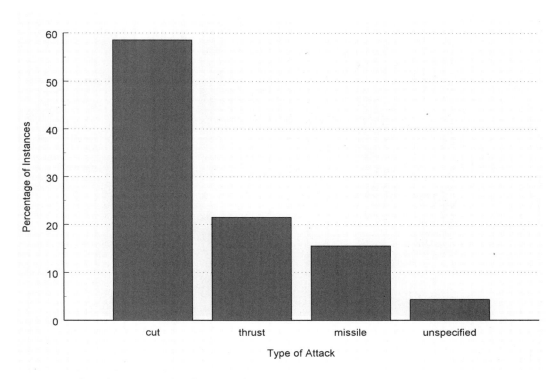

A-9. Types of attacks as reported in the *Sagas of Icelanders*.

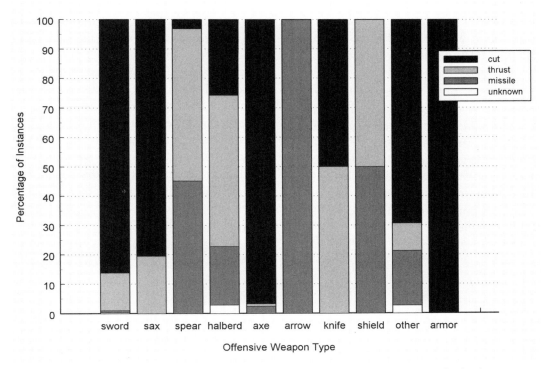

A-10. Types of attacks, broken down by the attack weapon used, as reported in the *Sagas of Icelanders*.

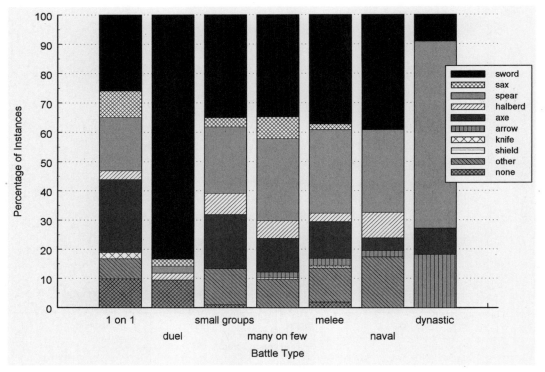

A-11. Weapons used for attacks, broken down by the type of battle, as reported in the *Sagas of Icelanders*.

more clear. Axes were used for cutting. Arrows were shot from a bow. Spears were used equally often for thrusting and for throwing.

BATTLE TYPES

The sagas described numerous types of battles, which we have placed into a small number of categories. Most of the categories are self-explanatory, such as "1-on-1." The "small groups" category includes fights with only a few men on each side, while "mêlée" fights had many men on each side. Figure A-11 shows which weapons were used in these different kinds of battles.

Again, the plot helps us understand when and how weapons were used. Duels almost always involved swords, and a few duels ended with empty-hand fighting. Naval battles used sword and spear, while dynastic land battles seemed to favor spear and arrows.

Gathering the examples from the sagas and plotting them in this manner is a tool we employ for understanding how weapons were used in the Viking age. It provides insights that we might not see based simply on reading the sagas, as we layer clue upon clue to form a picture of Viking combat.

# GLOSSARY OF NON-ENGLISH TERMS

In the book, we repeatedly utilize a number of words and phrases in Icelandic and other foreign languages because there often is no satisfactory English word that conveys the meaning of the original word as it was used in Viking times. In this glossary we use the word "unknown" to refer to weapons mentioned in literary sources for which no known archaeological examples survive. We cannot be certain of the nature of these weapons other than their general type.

PRONUNCIATION GUIDE TO OLD ICELANDIC

Icelandic has several more consonants and many more vowels than English. Additionally, the pronunciation of the words has changed from Viking times to modern times. Regardless, we would like the reader to have at least a general idea about how these words were pronounced in ancient times. Since we have no recordings of the spoken language from the Viking time, we rely on linguistic studies to create a speculative interpretation of the sound of the early language. This guide is adopted from Michael Barnes and from E. V. Gordon.[1]

| | |
|---|---|
| a | as in "father" but shorter |
| á | as in "father" |
| e | as in the French word "été" |
| é | as in the French word "été" but longer |
| i | as in "eat" |
| í | as in "eat" but shorter |
| o | as in the French word "eau" |
| ó | as in the French word "eau" but longer |
| u | as in the French word "roux" |
| ú | as in "droop" |
| y | as in the French word "rue" |
| ý | as in the French word "rue" but longer |
| æ | as in "pat" but longer |
| ø | as in the French word "feu" |
| œ | as in the French word "feu" but longer |
| ö | as in "not" |
| au | as in "now" |
| ei | as in "bay" |
| ð | like the "th" in "father" |
| þ | like the "th" in "Thor" |

The stress is always on the first syllable.

**Agnsax** (bait knife) an unknown variant of the sax

**Akkeri** anchor

**Alþing** Iceland's national governmental assembly

**Amentum** a leather throwing strap attached to a javelin used in ancient Greece

**Atgeirr** unknown spear-like weapon

**Atlatl** a rigid lever used as a spear-throwing device by numerous societies since the Stone Age

**Axlatök** (shoulder grip) a method for securing a grip using the clothing on the shoulders in wrestling

**Bakkakólfr** arrow with rounded head for practice and possibly hunting

**Beinskeyttr** (straight missile) an accurately shot missile

**Benda upp bogann** (bending the bow) to prepare the bow to shoot, either by stringing the bow or by laying on the arrow.

**Berserkr** (berserk) a strong, courageous fighter, often with supernatural capabilities

**Berserksgangr** the state of battle frenzy of a berserk

**Berskjaldaðr** unshielded; a vulnerable man

**Bíta** to bite; used to describe the cutting action of a sword

**Blámaðr** literally, a blue man, often used to describe monstrous wrestling opponents

**Blót** heathen sacrifice or ritual

**Bogastrengir** bow string

**Bogi** bow

**Bóla** shield boss

**Bolast** to fail to stand erect in modern glíma

**Bolöx** (wood axe) an unknown tool axe

**Bóndi** farmer and head of the household

**Borg** hill, fortification, city

**Bragð** a quick movement or a trick, such as a wrestling trick

**Brandr** sword blade

**Bregða** to move quickly or to draw (as a sword out of a scabbard)

**Breiðöxi** broadaxe

**Brjóta á bak aptr** a wrestling move that may refer to actually breaking the spine, as well as to a throw in which the thrower breaks the posture of his opponent's back

**Broddstöng** an unknown, spear-like weapon

**Brögðóttr** cunning, crafty

**Brókartök** (trouser grip) a method of securing a grip using the opponent's trousers.

**Brydning** modern Scandinavian term for wrestling

**Brynja** armor, mail

**Brynklungr** (mail bramble?) an unknown, spear-like weapon

**Brynstakkr** mail shirt

**Brynþvari** unknown, spear-like weapon

**Bylta** a full fall in wrestling

**Caput porci** (pig's head) the ancient Latin term for a wedge-shaped battle formation

**Döggskór** scabbard chape, a decorative protective metal or leather covering at the bottom of the scabbard

**Dönsk tunga** the Viking name for the language they spoke

**Drangr** a rocky pinnacle

**Draugr** a ghost, an animated dead man walking the earth

**Dreki** large warship

**Drengr** a person who could be trusted, the pinnacle of what Vikings aspired to

**Drengskapr** that which makes a man a *drengr*: trust infused with honor

**Eiga vígt** a legal term for having a legal right to kill

**Einhamr** (single-shape) not a shape shifter, not a berserk

**Einherjar** (those who fight alone) the elite warrior group of Óðinn made up of men slain in battle

**Einvígi** duel

**Ell** a unit of measurement about 49 cm (19 in) long

**Exi** axe

**Fang** Viking-age wrestling, as used in this book; a word with many meanings related to a catching or a holding, and includes variations such as an embrace

**Fangastakkr** a protective upper body garment for wrestling against supernatural beings

**Fanghella** a wrestling stone used for breaking the opponent's back

**Fangstaðr** an open area on the wrestler's body on which his opponent can get a hold

**Félag** a team that bands together for the common good of all for enterprises such as raiding or trading

**Félagi** member of a *félag*

**Finnbogi** Finnish bow made of multiple species of wood

**Fjaðurspjót** (feather spear) likely a spear with a head shaped like a feather

**Fjölkynngi** (multiknowledge) magic

**Fjörbaugsgarðr** the punishment known as lesser outlawry

**Fleinn** unknown, spear-like weapon; also used for an arrow with a long head

**Frægð** fame, the state of being in which a man's name was often spoken

**Frami** fame, the state of being in which a man's name was often spoken

**Francisca** an axe that was intended to be thrown, used notably in Frankish lands but in southern Norway as well

**Friðbönd** peace straps on a sword scabbard to prevent the weapon from being drawn

**Friðland** a safe haven for Vikings

**Fylgja** one's personal guardian spirit, usually in the form of an animal

**Fylgsni** hiding place, hideout

**Fylking** ranks in battle, battle formation

**Fylkingararmr** the columns to the sides, the arms of the fylking

**Fylkja hamalt** swine-array battle formation

**Fyrir** before, in front of, in the way, between oneself and one's enemy

**Fyrirrúm** thought to be the space in front of the raised afterdeck of the ship

**Fyrirsát** ambush, a compound of *fyrir*, meaning in the way, and *sitja*, meaning to sit

**Gæfa** luck

**Gaflak** an unknown, spear-like weapon sometimes used in naval battles

**Galdr** magic, derived from the phrase *to crow*

**Geirr** spear

**Gestir** men who traveled for business on behalf of the king

**Gladius** a Roman sword

**Glíma** Viking-age wrestling; in the modern era, Iceland's national sport and used as such in this book

**Goði** (pl. *goðar*) political chieftain and heathen priest

**Goðorð** the office held by the goði

**Grikkr** a leg take-down wrestling move

**Gungnir** (the swaying one) Óðinn's spear, created by blacksmith dwarves

**Hælkrókr** a heel-hook wrestling move

**Hálfrúm** (half-rúm) the space normally taken by one seated rower aboard a ship

**Hálfþynna** (half-thin axe) an unknown tool axe

**Hálstök** collar or neck hold in wrestling

**Hamalt** battle formation, as used in the ancient language; a battering ram used to break through some solid structure, as used in later centuries

**Hamast** to rage, to enter a berserk fury

**Hamr** animal shape, the skin of an animal

**Hamrammr** shape changer, berserk

**Handöxi** (hand axe) an unknown tool axe

**Handsax** (hand sax) an unknown variant of the sax

**Harðskeytr** (hard missile) a powerfully shot missile

**Háskeptr** long shaft, such as on an axe

**Haugbúi** a grave dweller, an animated dead man living in his grave mound

**Hefnd** revenge

**Heftisax** (hafted sax) an unknown variant of the sax that has some of the characteristics of a spear

**Herblástr** (war-blast) the sounding of a horn for battle

**Herfang** the spoils of a raid

**Herferð** traveling for raiding

**Herja** to harry

**Herklæðast** to dress oneself in war clothing for battle

**Herklæði** war clothing

**Herkuml** distinguishing war marks on shields and helmets to distinguish sides

**Hermenn** men who harry

**Herneskja** armor

**Herör** war arrow used to summon levy troops

**Herr** host of fighting men

**Hersir** high-ranking fighting men of the king

**Herskip** warship

**Heslistengur** (hazel poles) markers used to stake out a battleground, dueling arena, or legal court

**Hirð** the king's chosen men and bodyguards

**Hirðmaðr** a man of the hirð

**Hjálmr** helmet

**Hjörr** sword

**Hjúpr** a loose, upper-body garment

**Hlaupa** to move forward quickly, associated with running, leaping, flowing, sliding, and similar movements

**Hliðskjálfi** Óðinn's high seat from which he can see throughout all the worlds and observe the activities of all who live there

**Hnébragð** a knee trick lift and throw wrestling move

**Hnefatafl** Viking board game

**Hnéskítr** going down on one knee in a wrestling bout

**Hnykkr** a leg take-down wrestling move

**Hof** heathen temple

**Höfðingi** leader or chieftain

**Höggsax** (hewing sax) an unknown variant of the sax

**Höggspjót** cutting spear/hewings spear

**Hólmganga** duel, a portmanteau of *hólmr* (a small island) and *ganga* (to go)

**Hólmgöngulög** the dueling laws

**Hólmlausn** the fee paid by a wounded dueler to release himself from the duel

**Hólmr** a small island, the usual site for a duel

**Hornbogi** composite bow with portions made from horn

**Höslur** hazel poles used to mark battlefields and dueling arenas

**Hrafnsmerki** raven banner

**Hringabrynja** ring-mail armor

**Hryggspenna** (spanning the back) a wrestling method in which the wrestlers grasp each other around the back and from that position try to take each other down

**Hryggspennutök** a wrestling hold where wrestlers grab around each other's back

**Húnbogi** Hunnish composite bow with portions made from horn

**Húskarl** (house man) a farm hand, a servant of the king

**Hylja** to hide or to cover

**Jarðhús** a house structure that includes tunnels, underground rooms, and pit houses

**Jarl** earl

**Jötnar** giants, the agents of chaos and the enemies of the gods

**Kænn** wise, skillful, clever, also meaning tactics

**Kaupmenn** merchants

**Kaupskip** merchant ship

**Kenning** (pl: kenningar) a poetic construction where a phrase stands in for a word

**Kerganga** a tub duel in which the duelers fight enclosed in a barrel

**Kesja** unknown, spear-like weapon

**Kinnbjörg** (cheek guard) part of the helmet

**Klofbragð** a groin trick lift and throw wrestling move

**Knattleikr** the Viking ball game

**Knörr** merchant ship

**Koma í opna skjöldu** (to come upon someone in an open shield) used to describe someone who was unpleasantly surprised, typically when they were unprepared

**Krókaspjót** hooked or winged spear

**Krókör** barbed arrow

**Kviðr** abdomen

**Læknir** healer, physician

**Lamellae** an individual metal plate of lamellar armor

**Landvættir** land spirits

**Landvarnarmenn** land defensemen who protect against raiders

**Langskeptr** long-shafted (as an axe)

**Langskip** warship

**Láta kné fylgja kviði** (to let the knee follow the belly, or lower abdomen) a superior ground position in wrestling

**Laundyr** secret or hidden door

**Lausamjöðm** hip throw wrestling move

**Lausatök** (free grip) a method for securing a grip using the clothing on the shoulders in wrestling

**Leiðangur** (levy) a fully equipped reserve of fighting men

**Lendir menn** landed men, men who held land in the name of the king

**Lið** host of fighting men

**Liggja í víking** (laying in Viking) laying a ship in a safe, sheltered place such as a bay while waiting for an enticing prize to sail nearby

**Loftmjöðm** hip throw wrestling move

**Lögþing** one of four regional governmental assemblies in Norway, each with its own law codes based on customs and legislative decisions

**Lokrekkja** lockable bed closet in which the master and mistress of the house slept

**Lurkr** club-like sticks

**Lyfsteinn** healing stone, capable of healing wounds caused by its associated sword

**Mækir** sword

**Málaspjót** (inlaid spear) a decorated spear

**Merkastöng** the staff holding the battle standard

**Merki** battle standard

**Mjaðmahnykkr** hip throw wrestling move

**Mjöðm** hip throw wrestling move

**Nafnakunnigr** (name-known) to have one's name remembered, the main goal of a Viking

**Nafnfrægr** (name-famous) to have one's name remembered, the main goal of a Viking

**Nefbjörg** (nose guard) part of the helmet

**Níð** qualities that made a man *níðingr*, both his own activities, such as breach of trust, as well as curses placed on him by others

**Níðingr** a person exhibiting *níð*

**Níðingsverk** the work of a *níðingr*

**Níðstöng** a shaming pole that places *níð* on someone

**Njósna** to spy

**Njósnarmaðr** a spy

**Nornir** women of destiny who shape the lives of men

**Ódrengr** behaviors that were the opposite of *drengr*

**Óðal** hereditary land; the wealth that passed from generation to generation in a family

**Ör** arrow

**Ördrag** legal term defined by the distance of a bow shot

**Orðstírr** (word-glory) the state of having one's name mentioned and one's deeds discussed and praised

**Örlögþættir** moments of destiny in the lives of men

**Örmælir** quiver

**Örmalr** quiver

**Örskotshelgr** a legal sanctuary extending the distance of a bow shot from a place

**Öxi** axe

**Pálstafir** an unknown, spear-like weapon

**Panzari** armor in the form of a jack, a sleeveless protective jacket, sometimes described as being worn over mail

**Ráðagerð** a plan or design

**Ráðagerðamaðr** a man who is a good planner, and often a crafty planner

**Ræna** to rob, to take someone's property with his knowledge

**Ragnarök** the destiny of the gods, the enormous battle between the giants and the gods that is foretold to end in the destruction of the world

**Rani** swine-array battle formation

**Renna** to make a fast forward motion, associated with running, leaping, flowing, sliding, and similar motions

**Ríkir bændir** powerful farmers, the powerful or wealthy men of the district

**Ristarbragð** toe-trick wrestling throw involving stepping on the opponent's toes

**Rjá** to struggle, to wrestle (also spelled *hrjá*)

**Roftorfsveggr** a secret passage that can be broken through the wall out of the house

**Rúm** the space between the thwarts in a Viking ship where two rowers sat

**Rús** a term used to describe the people raiding and trading in eastern lands who may have been Vikings from lands in or near Sweden, or perhaps Slavic people from eastern Europe

**Ryðja** to clear the way

**Sækonungar** landless sea kings

**Sæmd** prestige

**Sax** a short, single-edged sword

**Scutum** a shield used by ancient Romans

**Seiðr** magic

**Sitja fyrir** ambush, a compound of *fyrir*, meaning in the way, and *sitja*, meaning to sit

**Skáli** the hall, the main room in a Viking-age longhouse

**Skálm** a tool that shares some characteristics with a sax

**Skálmöld** (age of *skálm*) a period of intense violence as stated in *Völuspá*

**Skegg** a poetic term for an axe, a beard

**Skeggexi** bearded axe

**Skeggöld** (age of *skegg*) a period of intense violence as stated in *Völuspá*

**Skeið** fast warship

**Skíðgarðr** wooden defensive fence enclosing a space, a palisade fence

**Skip** ship

**Skipreiða** ship-levies

**Skipstjórnir** ship captains

**Skjaldborg** shield castle defensive battle formation

**Skjaldmær** shield maiden, woman warrior leader

**Skjöldr** shield

**Skjóta** to shoot, such as an arrow or other projectile, but also applied to shield motion

**Skóggangr** the punishment known as full outlawry

**Skot** the passage between the turf walls and the wooden wainscotting of a longhouse, the shot of a projectile such as an arrow or a spear

**Skotbakki** archery practice range

**Smáþarmar** lower abdomen, small intestines

**Smíðaröx** (smithing axe) an unknown tool axe

**Snærisspjót** (stringed-spear) a spear thrown with the assistance of a string

**Snaghyrnd öxi** (snaghorned axe) an unknown battle-axe

**Snekkja** a smaller warship, often used by levy troops

**Sniðglíma** body drop wrestling throw

**Souterrains** underground tunnels found primarily in Ireland, and a few other European lands

**Spangabrynja** body armor of unknown nature

**Spangenhelm** helmet constructed of riveted plates

**Spjót** spear

**Spjótprika** thought to be a thin, small spear

**Stafnbúar** (stem dwellers) men at the very front of the ship in battle

**Stálhufa** (steel cap) helmet

**Stefnljáir** grappling hooks

**Stela** to steal, to take someone's property without his knowledge

**Stígandi** a constant stepping movement in modern glíma

**Strandhögg** slaughter at the shore by Viking raiders

**Sveit** detachments of troops

**Sveitarhöfðingjar** the captains of the detachments

**Sverð** sword

**Sviða** an unknown, spear-like weapon

**Svínfylking** swine-array battle formation, boar's snout formation, wedge-shaped battle formation

**Tábragð** toe-trick wrestling throw involving stepping on the opponent's toes

**Tálgöxi** an unknown tool axe thought to be an adze

**Taparöxi** (taper axe) an unknown tool axe

**Testudo** (tortoise) a battle formation used by Roman legions and recorded by Roman authors

**Þing** governmental assembly

**Þorparar** peasants

**Þræll** slave, servant, used generally for low-status people

**Tjösnublót** the heathen ritual for setting the pegs at the dueling site

**Tjösnur** the pegs that hold down the cloak on which combatants fought a duel

**Tréníð** human figures that direct *níð* on someone

**Tröll** troll, a malevolent paranormal creature taking many forms

**Tvíbyrðingr** a twofold shield, perhaps indicating layers of facing

**Tvífaldr** two-layered, used with mail

**Úlfhéðnir** berserkers wearing wolf skins

**Undir** under, underneath

**Valhöll** (hall of those slain in battle) Óðinn's hall for those slain in battle, a place to which Vikings yearned to go after death, often rendered as Valhalla in English

**Valkyrjur** Valkyrie, the choosers of the slain

**Valr** those slain in battle

**Vandræða** troublesome

**Vápntreyja** protective garment worn under mail

**Vébönd** sanctuary strings used to sanctify the dueling place with hazel poles

**Verkmenn** laborers

**Viðaröxi** (wood axe) an unknown tool axe

**Vígi** a desirable battle location due to its elevation, the availability of rocks and other missiles, and the limited access it offered to one's opponent

**Vígkænn** (battle wise) skilled in battle

**Vík** a bay or inlet, and the probable basis for the word *víkingr*

**Víkingabæli** safe places for Vikings to shelter between raids

**Víkingr** (pl. *víkingar*) raider or dueler

**Virðing** respect, a person's worth to his team

**Virki** a fortification

**Völlr** field

**Völva** (pl. *völvur*) a seeress who can foretell the future

# NOTES

### PREFACE

1. Rundata DR216, accessed Nov. 26, 2020, https://skaldic.abdn.ac.uk/db.php?id=19040&if=srdb&table=mss; Danske Runeindiskrifter, accessed Nov. 26, 2020, http://runer.ku.dk/VisGenstand.aspx?Titel=Tirsted-sten.

### METHODOLOGY

1. Alan K. Outram, "Introduction to Experimental Archaeology," *World Archaeology* 40, no. 1 (2008):1-6, accessed July 26, 2020, https://www.academia.edu/5909387/Introduction_to_experimental_archaeology.
2. Ármann Jakobsson, *The Troll Inside You* (Goleta, CA: Punctum Books, 2017).

### SOURCES

1. Bergljot Solberg, "Social Status in the Merovingian and Viking Periods in Norway from Archaeological and Historical Sources," *Norwegian Archaeological Review* 18 (1985): 246.
2. William R. Short and Hurstwic, unpublished research July 29, 2020. Based on data from Kristján Eldjárn, *Kuml og haugfé: úr heiðnum sið á Íslandi,* 2nd ed, ed. Adolf Friðriksson (Reykjavík: Mál og menning, 2000).
3. Leszek Gardela, "Entangled Worlds: Archaeologies of Ambivalence in the Viking Age" (PhD thesis, University of Aberdeen, 2012), 248-250.
4. Hildur Gestsdóttir (archaeologist, Fornleifastofnun Íslands), personal communication with the authors, Apr. 12, 2019.
5. Guðný Zoëga (bioarchaeologist, Byggðasafn Skagfirðinga), personal communication with William R. Short, Oct. 6, 2016.
6. Phillip L. Walker et al., "The Axed Man of Mosfell: Skeletal Evidence of a Viking Age Homicide and the Icelandic Sagas," in *The Bioarchaeology of Individuals: Bioarcheological Interpretations of the Human Past: Local, Regional, and Global*, ed. Ann L.W. Stodder and Ann M. Palkovich (Gainesville: University Press of Florida, 2012), 26-42.
7. Hildur Gestsdóttir, personal communication with the authors, Apr. 12, 2019.
8. William R. Short and Hurstwic, unpublished research, Apr. 21, 2019. In order to get an order-of-magnitude estimate of how many skeletal remains found from Viking-age Iceland could be expected to display battle trauma, a highly simplified model of the population of Viking-age Iceland was created based on demographic estimates. The model was used to predict the number of deaths of adult males of weapon-bearing age (between fifteen and fifty years) in the three centuries after the first settlement. The number of deaths and injuries reported in the *Sagas of Icelanders* was tabulated in Hurstwic's database of weapons and combat in the *Sagas of Icelanders*. The database was created by searching an electronic version of the sagas: *Íslendinga sögur: orðstöðulykill og texti* (Reykjavík: Mál og menning, 1998). Search terms included a wide range of words describing weapons, attacks, legal terms, and others. For each instance, the original saga text was read to gain context, and metadata created and entered into the database to categorize the success of each attack and defense. From this database, it is possible to roughly estimate the number of injuries and deaths. The sagas are unlikely to report every conflict, so this must be considered a lower bound. Combining these two results gives us an estimate of the ratio of weapons-related injuries and deaths to all deaths. When this ratio is applied to the number of graves containing human skeletal remains found in Iceland, based on information from Kristján, *Kuml og haugfé*, we see that a fraction of one of these graves could be expected to contain someone wounded or killed in battle. This result matches, within an order of magnitude, what is found and gives us confidence that

the small number of skeletal remains found with battle injuries is not too far from what we might expect based on simple models and estimates.

9. "Viking Weapons Test Cuts," Hurstwic, Mar. 16, 2012, YouTube, accessed Oct. 15, 2019, https://www.youtube.com/watch?v=juIw20z5p0c.

10. Stefán Karlsson, *The Icelandic Language*, tr. Rory McTurk (London: Viking Society for Northern Research, 2004), 9.

11. Rundata N 648, accessed Dec. 7, 2020, https://skaldic.abdn.ac.uk/db.php?id=20370&if=srdb &table=mss; Rundata N B448, accessed Dec. 7, 2020, https://skaldic.abdn.ac.uk/db.php?id=21095&if=srdb &table=mss.

12. *Gísla saga Súrssonar*, ch. 34; *Egils saga Skalla-Grímssonar*, ch. 78.

13. *Íslendingabók*, ch. 10.

14. *Eiríks saga rauða*; *Grænlendinga saga*.

15. *Eiríks saga rauða*, ch. 4.

16. Gunnar Karlsson, *The History of Iceland* (Minneapolis: University of Minnesota Press, 2000), 40.

17. Ibid., 79-82.

18. *Óláfs saga helga*, ch. 223-235.

19. *Fóstbrœðra saga*, ch. 24.

20. Rory McTurk, ed., *A Companion to Old Norse-Icelandic Literature and Culture* (Malden: Blackwell, 2005), 114-115, 431-432.

21. *Íslendinga saga*, ch. 138.

22. Ibid., ch. 138.

23. Jeffrey L. Forgeng, trans., *The Medieval Art of Swordsmanship: A Facsimile and Translation of Europe's Oldest Personal Combat Treatise Royal Armouries MS I.33* (Union City, CA: Chivalry Bookshelf, 2003).

24. *Gísla saga Súrssonar*, ch.18; *Grettis saga*, ch. 47; *Víga-Glums saga*, ch. 24.

25. Snorri Sturluson, *Heimskringla*, prologus.

26. Phillip Pulsiano, ed., *Medieval Scandinavia: An Encyclopedia*, Garland Reference Library of the Humanities, v. 934 (New York: Garland, 1993), 149.

27. McTurk, ed., *Companion*, 94.

28. *Hávamál*, v. 38.

29. Ibid., v. 1.

30. *Skáldskaparmál*, ch. 8.

31. Ibid., ch. 33.

32. *Gylfaginning*, chs. 6-8.

33. R. I. Page, "'A Most Vile People': Early English Historians on the Vikings," Dorothy Coke Memorial Lecture in Northern Studies, delivered at University College London, Mar. 19, 1986 (London: University College, 1987).

34. David N. Dumville, "Vikings in Insular Chronicling," in *The Viking World*, ed. Stefan Brink (London: Routledge, 2008), 363.

35. Anna Comnena, *The Alexiod of Anna Comnena*, tr. E. R. A. Sewter (Harmondsworth, UK: Penguin Books, 1969), bk. 2, ch. 9, 95.

36. R. I. Page, *Runes* (Berkeley: University of California Press, 1987), 49.

37. James E. Montgomery, "Ibn Fadlan and the Rusiyyah," *Journal of Arabic and Islamic Studies* 3 (2000).

38. *Laxdæla saga*, ch. 39.

39. *Reginsmál*, v. 26.

40. Joseph Stevenson, tr., *The Church Historians of England* (London: Seeleys, 1854), 2:558.

41. R. I. Page, *Chronicles of the Vikings* (Toronto: University of Toronto Press, 1995), 98.

42. Gunnar Karlsson et al. eds., *Grágás Lagasafn íslenska þjóðveldisins* (Reykjavík: Mál og menning, 1992), 266, S. 361.

43. Jón Stéfansson, "The Vikings in Spain. From Arabic (Moorish) and Spanish Sources," *Saga Book* 6 (1908–1909): 31-46.

44. Pulsiano, ed., *Medieval Scandinavia*, 567-568.

45. Saxo Grammaticus, *The History of the Danes*, ed. Hilda Ellis Davidson, tr. Peter Fisher (Cambridge, UK: D. S. Brewer, 1998), preface, 5.

46. Ibid., preface, 6.

47. Guy Halsall, *Warfare and Society in the Barbarian West, 450–900* (London: Routledge, 2003), 177; Lars Lönnroth et al., "Literature," in *The Cambridge History of Scandinavia*, ed. Knut Helle (Cambridge: Cambridge University Press, 2003), 1:503-504.

48. Alf Henrikson, *Svensk Historia* (Stockholm: Bonniers Grafiska Industrier, 1982) book 1, 114.

49. Stefan Brink, ed., *The Viking World* (London: Routledge, 2008), 27.

50. Kristján, *Kuml og haugfé*, 464-465.

51. William R. Short, *Viking Weapons and Combat Techniques* (Yardley, PA: Westholme, 2009), 171-172.

52. Richard Cleasby et al., eds., *An Icelandic-English Dictionary* (Oxford: Oxford University Press, 2003), 583, s.v. "spjót."

**CHAPTER 1: THE VIKING MINDSET**

1. Else Roesdahl and David M. Wilson, eds., *From Viking to Crusader: The Scandinavians and Europe 800–1200* (New York: Rizzoli International, 1992), cat. no. 47, 240, cat. no. 97, 252.

2. *Reginsmál* v. 25; *Hávamál*, v. 61.

3. Page, *Chronicles*, 98.

4. Laurence Larson, tr., *The Earliest Norwegian Law Being the Gulathing Law and Frostathing Law* (New York: Columbia University Press, 1935), *Gulathing Law* title 178, 137.

5. Gunnar et al., eds., *Grágás Lagasafn íslenska þjóðveldisins*, 245, K. 88.

6. Andrew Dennis et al., tr. and eds., *Laws of Early Iceland: Grágás* (Winnipeg: University of Manitoba Press, 1980), 1:258.

7. *Egils saga Skalla-Grímssonar,* ch. 46; Gunnar et al., eds., *Grágás Lagasafn íslenska þjóðveldisins,* 467-468, K. 227.

8. Rundata DR42, accessed Aug. 17, 2020, https://skaldic.abdn.ac.uk/db.php?id=18867&if=runic&table=mss; Michael P. Barnes, *Runes: a Handbook* (Woodbridge, UK: Boydell Press, 2012), 73.

9. Rundata Sö179, accessed Aug. 17, 2020, https://skaldic.abdn.ac.uk/db.php?id=15207&if=runic&table=mss; Barnes, *Runes,* 77.

10. *Egils saga Skalla-Grímssonar,* ch. 58.

11. Historiska museet SHM 25840, accessed Aug. 17, 2020, mis.historiska.se/mis/sok/fid.asp?fid=107776.

12. *Hávamál,* v. 1.

13. Adapted from Patricia Terry, tr., *Poems of the Elder Edda* (Philadelphia: University of Pennsylvania Press, 1990), "Sayings of the High One," v. 76, 21.

14. *Haralds saga Sigurðarsonar,* ch. 55; *Bjarnar saga Hítdælakappa,* ch.4; *Egils saga Skalla-Grímssonar,* ch.3; *Svarfdæla saga,* ch. 4; *Flóamanna saga,* ch. 15.

15. *Bjarnar saga Hítdælakappa,* ch. 4, ch. 10; *Egils saga Skalla-Grímssonar,* ch. 24; *Grettis saga,* ch. 82; *Gunnars saga Keldungnúpsfífls,* ch. 5; *Kormáks saga,* ch. 1; *Bósa saga og herrauðs,* ch. 3.

16. *Brennu-Njáls saga,* ch. 13, ch. 33, ch. 44, ch. 55, ch. 111, ch. 127, ch. 133; *Laxdæla saga,* ch. 21, ch. 35, ch. 37; *Vatnsdæla saga,* ch. 24, ch. 26, ch. 29, ch. 31, ch. 35.

17. *Grettis saga,* ch. 13, ch. 53; *Gunnars saga Keldugnúpsfífls,* ch. 14; *Laxdæla saga,* ch. 9; *Ásmundar saga kappabana,* ch. 9.

18. *Bósa saga og herrauðs,* ch. 7.

19. *Vatnsdæla saga,* ch. 4, ch. 7; *Heiðarvíga saga,* ch. 43; *Finnboga saga ramma,* ch. 35; *Droplaugarsona saga,* ch. 15; *Egils saga Skalla-Grímssonar,* ch. 9, *Jómsvíkinga saga,* ch. 27.

20. *Hávamál,* v. 76.

21. *Fóstbræðra saga,* ch. 8, ch. 24; *Vatnsdæla saga,* ch. 43; *Víglundar saga,* ch. 5; *Fljótsdæla saga,* ch. 10; *Jómsvíkinga saga,* ch. 4.

22. *Flóamanna saga,* ch. 15, *Haralds saga Sigurðarsonar,* ch. 55.

23. *Bjarnar saga Hítdælakappa,* ch. 3, ch. 4; *Haralds saga Sigurðarsonar,* ch. 91; *Svarfdæla saga,* ch. 4.

24. *Brennu-Njáls saga,* ch. 24, ch. 51, ch. 56, ch. 91, ch. 116; *Egils saga Skalla-Grímssonar,* ch. 25; *Grettis saga,* ch. 24; *Vatnsdæla saga,* ch. 32, ch. 45.

25. *Bjarnar saga Hítdælakappa,* ch. 4; *Brennu-Njáls saga,* ch. 88, ch. 89; *Egils saga Skalla-Grímssonar,* ch. 55, ch. 62, *Eyrbyggja saga,* ch. 25; *Svarfdæla saga,* ch. 10; *Vatnsdæla saga,* ch. 8.

26. *Brennu-Njáls saga,* ch. 20, ch. 49, ch. 95; *Eyrbyggja saga,* ch. 18; *Fljótsdæla saga,* ch. 10; *Jómsvíkinga saga,* ch. 8, *Brandkrossa þáttur,* ch. 3.

27. Maren Albertsdóttir, "Hvað felst í drengskaparheiti, hefur það til dæmis eitthvert gildi í ráðningarsam ningi?," Vísindaverfuurinn, Apr. 25, 2012, accessed Apr. 8, 2021, https://www.visindavefur.is/svar.php?id=62336.

28. Cleasby et al., eds., *Icelandic-English Dictionary,* 105, s.v. "drengr."

29. *Krákumál,* v. 23.

30. *Eyrbyggja saga,* ch. 37; *Flóamanna saga,* ch. 3; *Grettis saga,* ch. 24, ch. 57, ch. 75; *Hænsna-Þóris saga,* ch. 3; *Heiðarvíga saga,* ch. 13, ch. 17; *Laxdæla saga,* ch. 46, ch. 84; *Finnboga saga ramma,* ch. 41.

31. *Ólafs saga helga,* ch. 142; *Hálfsrekkaljóð,* v. 8; *Hervararkviða,* v. 4; *Bjarnar saga Hítdælakappa,* ch. 3, ch. 4.

32. *Flóamanna saga,* ch. 3; *Haralds saga Sigurðarsonar,* ch. 55, ch. 60, ch. 85; *Magnúss saga blinda og Haralds gilla,* ch. 5; *Heiðarvíga saga,* ch. 13.

33. *Brennu-Njáls saga,* ch. 117, ch. 118; *Egils saga Skalla-Grímssonar,* ch. 49; *Eyrbyggja saga,* ch. 29, ch. 45, ch. 58; *Finnboga saga ramma,* ch. 27, ch. 35, ch. 42; *Gísla saga Súrssonar,* ch. 35, ch. 36; *Grettis saga,* ch. 82; *Gull-Þóris saga,* ch. 13, ch. 18; *Gunnars saga Keldugnúpfífls,* ch. 4; *Heiðarvíga saga,* ch. 30; *Hrafnkels saga Freysgoða,* ch. 18; *Kjalnesinga saga,* ch. 11.

34. *Grettis saga,* ch. 19.

35. *Brennu-Njáls saga,* ch. 59; *Egils saga Skalla-Grímssonar,* ch. 84; *Hávarðar saga Ísfirðings,* ch. 9; *Heiðarvíga saga,* ch. 43; *Kjalnesinga saga,* ch. 16; *Laxdæla saga,* ch. 15.

36. *Magnúss saga blinda og Haralds gilla,* ch. 10; *Eyrbyggja saga,* ch. 26, ch. 45, ch. 58; *Finnboga saga ramma,* ch. 27, ch. 35, ch. 42; *Flóamanna saga,* ch. 18; *Gísla saga Súrssonar,* ch. 35; *Grettis saga,* ch. 82; *Gull-Þóris saga,* ch. 13, ch. 18, ch. 20; *Gunnars saga Keldugnúpfífls,* ch. 4, ch. 5; *Hallfreðar saga vandræðaskálds,* ch. 4; *Hávarðar saga Ísfirðings,* ch. 9, ch. 10; *Hrafnkels saga,* ch. 18; *Kjalnesinga saga,* ch. 11, ch. 16.

37. Rundata DR 279, accessed Aug. 20, 2020, https://skaldic.abdn.ac.uk/db.php?id=15174&if=runic&table=mss

38. *Gísla saga Súrssonar,* ch. 36.

39. *Gísla saga Súrssonar,* ch. 34; *Grettis saga,* ch. 20; *Gull-Þóris saga,* ch. 3; *Heiðarvíga saga,* ch. 30; *Króka-Refs saga,* ch. 7.

40. *Vatnsdæla saga,* ch. 2.

41. *Skáldskaparmál,* ch. 65.

42. Larson, tr., *Earliest Norwegian Law, Gulathing Law* title 299, 190-191, title 300, 191.

43. *Hænsna-Þóris saga,* ch. 17; *Harðar saga og hólmverja,* ch. 13; *Hrafnkels saga,* ch. 19; *Kjalnesinga saga,* ch. 16; *Bjarnar saga Hítdælakappa,* ch. 18.

44. *Heiðarvíga saga,* ch. 30.

45. *Fóstbræðra saga,* ch. 4; *Grettis saga,* ch. 81, ch. 82; *Gunnlaugs saga ormstunga,* ch. 11; *Heiðarvíga saga,* ch. 14; *Laxdæla saga,* ch. 87; *Reykdæla saga og Víga-Skútu,* ch. 5.

46. *Egils saga Skalla-Grímssonar,* ch. 61.

47. *Hrafns þáttur Guðrúnarsonar,* ch. 4.

48. *Laxdæla saga*, ch. 12.

49. *Egils saga Skalla-Grímssonar,* ch. 64.

50. *Grettis saga*, ch. 19, ch. 81; *Fóstbræðra saga*, ch. 4; *Gunnlaugs saga ormstungu*, ch. 12; *Magnúss saga blinda og Haralds gilla*, ch. 11; *Heiðarvíga saga*, ch. 14.

51. *Kjalnesinga saga*, ch. 5; *Laxdæla saga*, ch. 52; *Heiðarvíga saga*, ch. 30.

52. *Heiðarvíga saga*, ch. 30.

53. *Brennu-Njáls saga*, ch. 31, ch. 47, ch. 49; *Finnboga saga ramma*, ch. 35; *Hrafnkels saga*, ch. 10; *Króka-Refs saga*, ch. 12; *Ljósvetninga saga*, ch. 31; *Reykdæla saga og Víga-Skútu*, ch. 21.

54. *Brennu-Njáls saga*, ch. 8, ch. 88.

55. *Fljótsdæla saga*, ch. 19; *Gull-Þóris saga*, ch. 8; *Laxdæla saga*, ch. 40; *Reykdæla saga og Víga-Skútu*, ch. 4; *Hávarðar saga Ísfirðings*, ch. 22.

56. *Brennu-Njáls saga*, ch. 149; *Grettis saga*, ch. 38, ch. 72; *Heiðarvíga saga*, ch. 11; *Ljósventinga saga*, ch. 12.

57. *Landnámabók*, H. 268; *Þorsteins þáttur uxafóts*, ch. 1.

58. Larson, tr., *Earliest Norwegian Law, Frostathing Law* bk. 5, ch. 9, 284; Gunnar et al, *Grágás Lagasafn íslenzka þjóðveldisins*, 216, S. 277.

59. *Grettis saga*, ch. 72; *Brennu-Njáls saga*, ch. 75; *Bjarnar saga Hítdælakappa*, ch. 34.

60. *Gylfaginning*, ch. 35.

61. *Hávamál*, v. 68, v. 76.

62. *The King's Mirror*, tr. Laurence Marcellus Larson (New York: American-Scandinavian Foundation, 1917), ch. 37, 205-206; Lawrence G. Berge, "Hirðskrá 1-37, a Translation with Notes" (master's thesis, University of Wisconsin, 1968), ch. 29, 56.

63. The *Ó-* prefix negates what follows in the Old Norse language, so *ódrengur* is merely *not drengur*.

64. *Hákonar saga herðibreiðs*, ch. 12; *Magnúss saga berfætts*, ch. 25; *Ólafs saga helga*, ch. 233; *Gunnlaugs saga ormstunga*, ch. 12; *Hrafnkels saga Freysgoða*, ch. 10.

65. Rundata U954, accessed Aug 17, 2020, https://skaldic.abdn.ac.uk/db.php?id=17763&if=runic&table=mss

66. *Grettis saga*, ch. 72; *Brennu-Njáls saga*, ch. 75.

67. Gunnar et al., eds., *Grágás Lagasafn íslenska þjóðveldisins*, 281-282, K.114.

68. Peter Foote and David M. Wilson, *The Viking Achievement: The Society and Culture of Early Medieval Scandinavia* (London: Sidgwick & Jackson, 1970), 379-380; *Vatnsdæla saga*, ch. 33.

69. *Ólafs saga helga*, ch. 239; *Brennu-Njáls saga*, ch. 124; *Grettis saga*, ch. 82.

70. *Laxdæla saga*, ch. 49.

71. *Magnúss saga Erlingssonar*, ch. 12; *Egils saga Skalla-Grímssonar*, ch. 61.

72. *Brennu-Njáls saga*, ch. 146; *Skáldskaparmál*, ch. 17.

73. *Gísla saga Súrssonar*, ch. 35.

74. *Eyrbyggja saga*, ch. 45.

75. *Brennu-Njáls saga*, ch. 146.

76. Larson, tr., *Earliest Norwegian Law, Frostathing Law* bk. 4, ch. 4, 257-258.

77. Jón Jónsson (folklorist, Félag þjóðfræðinga á Íslandi), personal communication with Reynir A. Óskarson, Oct. 10, 2016.

78. Gunnar et al., eds., *Grágás Lagasafn íslenska þjóðveldisins*, 273, St 376.

79. *Brennu-Njáls saga*, ch. 44; *Víga-Glúms Saga*, ch. 18; *Þórðar Saga Hreðu*, ch. 3.

80. *Víga-Glúms saga*, ch. 18.

81. *Króka-Refs saga*, ch. 7; *Brennu-Njáls saga*, ch. 123.

82. *Fóstbræðra saga*, ch. 24; *Svarfdæla saga*, ch. 7.

83. *Þorgríms þáttur Hallsonar*; *Þorsteins þáttur skelks*, ch. 2; *Ögmundar þáttur dytts*.

84. *Skáldskaparmál*, ch. 17.

85. *Vatnsdæla saga*, ch. 33; Henrikson, *Svensk Historia*, bk. 1, 114; Foote and Wilson, *Viking Achievement*, 379-380.

86. *Þorleifs þáttr jarlaskálds*, ch. 5; Kate Heslop, "(Introduction to) Þorleifr jarlsskáld Rauðfeldarson, *Jarlsnið*," in *Poetry from the Kings' Sagas 1: From Mythical Times to c. 1035*, ed. Diana Whaley, Skaldic Poetry of the Scandinavian Middle Ages 1 (Turnhout, Belgium: Brepols, 2012), 372.

87. *Ólafs saga helga*, ch. 206.

88. *Heimskringla*, prologue.

89. *Skáldskaparmál*, G55.

90. Gunnar et al., eds., *Grágás Lagasafn íslenska þjóðveldisins*, 273-274, K. 238.

91. *Gísla saga Súrssonar*, ch. 2; *Bjarnar saga Hítdælakappa*, ch. 17.

92. *Egils saga Skallagrímssonar*, ch. 57.

93. William R. Short and Hurstwic, unpublished research, Aug. 12, 2020. A database was created by doing a search of the literary sources using keywords related to *níð*. The sources searched included *The Sagas of Icelanders, Heimskringla, Snorra edda, Eddukvæði*, law codes (*Grágás, Frostaþingslög, Gulaþingslög*), and runestones (*The Runic Dictionary*, https://skaldic.abdn.ac.uk/db.php?if=runic&table=database&view=runic). Electronic versions of the texts were searched electronically and printed versions using glossaries, concordances, and indices. For each instance of the use of a keyword, the text was read to gain context, and metadata was created and entered into the database to categorize the nature and details of the *níð*. Using this database, it was possible to create statistical summaries of *níð* as described over many literary sources.

94. *Gísla saga Súrssonar*, ch. 32.

95. William R. Short and Hurstwic, unpublished research, Aug. 12, 2020. The same database and statistical analysis based on words related to *níð* described earlier was used.

96. *Finnboga saga ramma*, ch. 20, ch. 36.

97. Larson, tr., *Earliest Norwegian Law, Frostathing Law* bk. 5, ch. 9, 284-285.

98. Gunnar et al., eds., *Grágás Lagasafn íslenska þjóðveldisins*, 214, S. 275.

99. *Þorsteins þáttur stangarhöggs*.

100. William R. Short and Hurstwic, unpublished research, Aug. 12, 2020. A similar database as described earlier was created for words related to *revenge*, which allowed for similar statistical analyses.

101. Gunnar et al., eds., *Grágás Lagasafn íslenska þjóðveldisins*, 447-448, K. 113.

102. William R. Short and Hurstwic, unpublished research, Oct. 18, 2019. In order to obtain an order-of-magnitude estimate of the number of weapon-bearing men in the same family, a statistical model was made of the population of Iceland in the Viking age, incorporating best estimates of life expectancies, birth rates, and other factors. The model results were compared to estimates of the age distribution of the population. The parameters were varied to verify that reasonable variations in the estimates did not cause gross changes in predictions. The model predicted the number of males fifteen to forty-five years old who shared the same great-great-grandparents. For simplicity, the model left out foster relations and step relations.

103. William R. Short and Hurstwic, unpublished research, Aug. 12, 2020. The same database and statistical analysis based on words related to *revenge* described earlier was used.

104. *Hrafnkels saga*, ch. 8.

105. William R. Short and Hurstwic, unpublished research, Aug. 12, 2020. The same database and statistical analysis using words related to *revenge* described earlier was used.

106. *Gunnlaugs saga ormstungu*, ch. 13.

107. *Brennu-Njáls saga*, ch. 72.

108. *Grettis saga*, ch. 15.

109. *Króka-Refs saga*, ch. 8.

110. William R. Short and Hurstwic, unpublished research, Aug. 12, 2020. The same database and statistical analysis based on words related to *revenge* described earlier was used.

111. Berge, "Hirðskrá 1-37," ch. 28, 52.

112. *Þorsteins þáttur tjaldstæðings*, ch. 3.

113. Larson, tr., *Earliest Norwegian Law, Gulathing Law* title 186, 140.

114. *Eyrbyggja saga*, ch. 44

115. *Bjarnar saga Hítdælakappa*, ch. 32.

116. *Brennu-Njáls saga*, ch. 124.

117. *Hávamál*, v. 1, v. 38.

118. ". . . með lögum skal land várt byggja, en með ólögum eyða." *Brennu-Njáls saga*, ch. 70.

119. *Haralds saga ins hárfagra*, ch. 6.

120. "Apud illos non est rex, nisi tantum lex." Adam von Bremen, *Gesta Hammaburgensis ecclesias Pontificum*, ed. Berhhard Schmeidler, Hamburgische Kirchengeschichte, 3rd ed. (Hanover: Hahn, 1917), 273, bk. 4.

121. Pulsiano, ed., *Medieval Scandinavia*, 385-386 s.v. "laws."

122. Ibid., 234-235, s.v. "Grágás."

123. Gunnar et al., eds., *Grágás Lagasafn íslenska þjóðveldisins*, 447-448, K. 113.

124. Marion Poilvez, "The Inner Exiles: Outlaws and Scapegoating Process in *Grettis saga Ásmundarson* and *Gísla saga Súrssonar*" (master's thesis, Háskóli Íslands, 2011).

125. *Reykdæla saga ok Víga-Skútu*, ch. 3.

126. Gunnar et al., eds., *Grágás Lagasafn íslenska þjóðveldisins*, 394, K. 37.

127. *Egils saga Skalla-Grímssonar*, ch. 66.

128. *Gísla saga Súrssonar*, ch. 16.

129. *Brennu-Njáls saga*, ch. 75.

130. *Hrafnkels saga*, ch. 6.

131. *Gylfaginning*, ch. 15; *Reginsmál*, v. 2; *Hamðismál*, v. 30; *Fáfnismál*, v. 11-12.

132. *Kjalnesinga saga*, ch. 8; *Laxdæla saga*, ch. 15.

133. *Kjalnesinga saga*, ch. 8.

134. *Heiðarvíga saga*, ch. 11.

135. *Helgakviða Hundingsbana I*. v. 2-3; *Orms þáttr Stórólfssonar*, ch. 5-6.

136. *Völuspá*; *Baldrs draumar*

137. *Vatnsdæla saga*, ch. 10; *Eiríks saga rauða*, ch. 4; *Landnámabók*, S. 179; *Örvar-Odds saga*, ch. 2; *Orms þáttur Stórólfssonar*, ch. 5.

138. *Eiríks saga rauða*, ch. 4.

139. *Laxdæla saga*, ch. 33; *Brennu-Njáls saga*, ch. 62.

140. *Bjarnar saga Hítdælakappa*, ch. 32.

141. *Brennu-Njáls saga*, ch. 30; *Brennu-Njáls Saga*, ch. 72.

142. *Þorsteins þáttur uxafóts*, ch. 5; *Brennu-Njáls saga*, ch. 41.

143. *Grímnismál*, v. 8-10, v. 18-26; *Gylfaginning*, ch. 20, ch. 37-40; *Helgakviða Hundingabana*, v. 38.

144. *Grímnismál*, v. 14; *Gylfaginning*, ch. 23.

145. *Skáldskaparmál*, ch. 31; *Egils saga Skalla-Grímssonar*, ch. 79; "Sonatorrek", v. 7; *Eyrbyggja saga*, ch. 54; *Friðþjófs saga ins frækna*, ch. 3.

146. Rudolf Simek, *Dictionary of Northern Mythology*, tr. Angela Hall (Cambridge, UK: D. S. Brewer, 1996), 137-138, s.v. "Hel (1)."

147. *Brennu-Njáls saga*, ch. 78.

148. *Grettis saga*, ch. 18.

149. *Eyrbyggja saga*, ch. 34, ch. 43, ch. 63; *Grettis saga*, ch. 32-35; *Flóamanna saga*, ch. 13.

150. *Landnámabók*, H. 268.

151. *Þorsteins þáttur uxafóts*, ch. 1.

152. *Ynglinga saga*, ch. 4.

153. *Gylfaginning*, ch. 15, ch. 38; *Völuspá*, v. 46; *Ynglinga saga*, ch. 4, ch. 5, ch. 7.

154. *Kormáks saga*, ch. 23; *Gull-Þóris saga*, ch. 10.

155. Saxo, *History of the Danes*, bk. 4, 111, bk. 6, 173, bk. 7, 203, bk. 7, 207.

156. *Droplaugarsona saga*, ch. 15; *Svarfdæla saga*, ch. 8-9; *Gunnlaugs saga ormstungu*, ch. 7.

157. *Laxdæla saga*, ch. 57; *Brennu-Njáls saga*, ch. 30.

158. *Fóstbræðra saga*, ch. 9; *Kormáks saga*, ch. 22.

159. *Eyrbyggja saga*, ch. 18; *Vatnsdæla saga*, ch. 19; *Ólafs saga helga*, ch. 228.

160. *Harðar saga ok Hólmverja*, ch. 22, ch. 25; *Eyrbyggja saga*, ch. 20.

161. *Hákonar saga herðibreiðs*, ch. 17.

162. *Grettis saga*, ch. 39.

163. Saxo, *History of the Danes*, bk. 7, 205.

## CHAPTER 2: EMPTY-HAND COMBAT

1. *Víga-Glúms saga*, ch. 13.

2. *Eyrbyggja saga*, ch. 10.

3. *Landnámabók*, S. 85.

4. Stiftelsen Lillehammer Museum, artifact SS-01506.

5. Helge Sognli (head of collection, Stiftelsen Lillehammer Museum), personal communication with Reynir A. Óskarson, Feb. 13, 2019.

6. Jón M. Ívarsson (historian and former chairman of Glímusamband Íslands), personal communication with Reynir A. Óskarson, May 5, 2019.

7. Guðný Zoëga (bioarchaeologist, Byggðasafn Skagfirðinga), personal communication with William R. Short, Jan. 29, 2019.

8. *Gylfaginning*, ch. 46.

9. *Magnússona saga*, ch. 21.

10. Gunnar et al., eds., *Grágás Lagasafn íslenska þjóðveldisins*, 236, K. 92.

11. Ibid., 213, K. 86.

12. Larsen, tr., *Earliest Norwegian Law, Frostathing Law*, vol. 4, ch. 18, 265-266.

13. Saxo, *History of the Danes*, bk. 3, 69.

14. Ibid., endnote 2.

15. *Bárðar saga Snæfellsás*, ch. 4; *Egils saga Skalla-Grímssonar*, ch. 40; *Finnboga saga ramma*, ch. 6; *Fóstbræðra saga*, ch. 15.

16. *Gunnlaugs saga ormstunga*, ch. 10; *Heiðarvíga saga*. ch. 11; *Kjalnesinga saga*, ch. 15; *Víga-Glúms saga*, ch. 13.

17. *Svarfdæla saga*, ch. 13; *Áns saga bogasveigis*, ch. 4; *Göngu-Hrólfs saga*, ch. 6.

18. Cleasby et al., eds., *Icelandic-English Dictionary*, 141, s.v. "fang"; Þorsteinn Einarsson, *Glima, the Icelandic Wrestling* (Reykjavík: Glímusamband Íslands, 1988), 4, accessed Feb. 12, 2019, http://www.glima.is/wp-content/uploads/2016/02/Glima-the-icelandic-wrestling-a-brief-history.pdf.

19. Cleasby et al., eds., *Icelandic-English Dictionary*, 205, s.v. "glíma."

20. M. Bennett Nichols, *Glíma: Icelandic Wrestling* (New Orleans: privately printed, 1999), 13.

21. Björn Bjarnason, *Íþróttir fornmanna á Norðurlöndum* (Reykjavík: Bókfellsútgáfan H.F., 1950), 147.

22. Þorsteinn, *Glima*, 9, accessed Feb. 12, 2019, http:// www.glima.is/wp-content/uploads/2016/02/Glima-the-icelandic-wrestling-a-brief-history.pdf

23. Ásgeir Blöndal Magnússon, *Íslensk orðsifjabók* (Reykjavík: Orðabók Háskolans, 1989), 255.

24. Cleasby et al., eds., *Icelandic-English Dictionary*, 500, s.v. "rjá," 286, s.v. "hrjá."

25. *Grettis saga*, ch. 72.

26. *Hrana saga Hrings*, ch. 8; *Þorsteins þáttur Bæjarmagns*, ch. 7; *Jökuls þáttur Búasonar*, ch. 1.

27. *Jökuls þáttur Búasonar*, ch. 2; *Hálfdánar saga Eysteinssonar*, ch. 18; *Egils saga einhenda ok Ásmundar berserkjabana*, ch, 13.

28. Glímusamband Íslands, *Glímulög* (2008), article 21, accessed Feb. 17, 2019, http://www.glima.is/wp-content/uploads/2010/01/GL%C3%8 DMUL%C3% 96G-22.feb-2008.pdf.

29. Gunnar et al., eds., *Grágás Lagasafn íslenska þjóðveldisins,* 210, K. 86.

30. *Grettis saga*, ch. 72; *Finnboga saga ramma,* ch. 37; *Hrómundar saga Gripssonar*, ch. 4.

31. *Gylfaginning*, ch. 46.

32. Glímusamband Íslands, *Glímulög*; Glímusamband Íslands, "Reglugerð um búnað glímumanna á opinberum mótum," *Regulugerðir Glímusambands Íslands* (2013):12-13, accessed Feb. 17, 2019, http://www.glima. is/wp-content/uploads/2010/01/Regluger%C3%B0ir-GL%C3%8D-1.3.jan-20131.pdf.

33. Kjartan Bergmann Guðjónsson, *Íslensk glíma og glímumenn* (Reykjavík: privately printed, 1993), 35; Stefán Jónsson, *Jóhannes á Borg: minningar glímukappans* (Reykjavík: Ægisútgafan, 1964), 109; Þorsteinn Einarsson, *Þróun glímu í íslensku þjóðlífi* (Reykjavík: Rannsóknarstofnun Kennaraháskóla Íslands, 2006), 218-219.

34. Landsbókasafn Lbs.1201, 4to. Sr. Guðmundur Einarsson; Landsbókasafn Lbs.1201, 4to. Rit Séra Þorsteinn Pálsson á Hálsi: *Fáein orð um glímur* 1861; Landsbókasafn Lbs.1201, 4to. Rit Jón Sigurðsson á Gautlöndum, 1861.

35. *Grettis saga*, ch. 72.

36. Kjartan, *Íslensk glíma og glímumenn*, 39; Glímusamband Íslands, accessed Feb. 17, 2019, http://www.glima.is/?page_id=16.

37. Glímusamband Íslands, *Regulugerðir Glímusambands Íslands* (2013): article 3.7, p. 2, accessed Feb. 17, 2019, http://www.glima.is/wp-content/uploads/2010/01/Regluger%C3%B0ir-GL%C3%8D-1.3.jan-20131.pdf.

38. Stefán Sigfússon, *Íslenzka glíman* (Reykjavík: Tímarit Hins íslenzka bókmentafélags, 1900), 137-138.

39. *Kjalnesinga saga*, ch. 15.

40. *Grettis saga*, ch. 72.

41. Glímusamband Íslands, *Regulugerðir Glímusambands Íslands* (2013): article 3.7, p. 2, accessed Feb. 17, 2019, http://www.glima.is/wp-content/uploads/2010/

01/Regluger%C3%B0ir-GL%C3%8D-1.3.jan-20131.pdf.

42. Glímusamband Íslands, "Hvað er glíma?," http://www.glima.is/?page_id=20 (accessed Feb. 12 2019).

43.Glímusamband Íslands, accessed Feb. 12, 2019, http://www.glima.is/?page_id=20; Landsbókasafn Lbs. 1201, 4to. Sr. Guðmundur Einarsson; Landsbókasafn Lbs.1201, 4to. Rit Séra Þorsteinn Pálsson á Hálsi: *Fáein orð um glímur* 1861; Landsbókasafn Lbs.1201, 4to. Rit Jón Sigurðsson á Gautlöndum, 1861.

44. Landsbókasafn Lbs.1201, 4to. Sr. Guðmundur Einarsson.

45. *Grettis saga*, ch. 35.

46. Ibid., *Grettis saga* ch. 14.

47. Björn, *Íþróttir fornmanna á Norðurlöndum*, 147; Kjartan, *Íslensk glíma og glímumenn*, 11.

48. *Glímubók* (Reykjavík: Íþróttasamband Íslands, 1916), 121; Kjartan, *Íslensk glíma og glímumenn*, 31.

49. *Magnússona saga*, ch. 21.

50. Jón Jóhannesson, *Íslendinga Saga: A History of the Old Icelandic Commonwealth*, tr. Haraldur Bessason (Winnipeg: University of Manitoba Press, 1974), 229.

51. Ibid., 278.

52. Sigurður Nordal, *Icelandic Culture*, tr. Vilhjálmur T. Bjarnar (Ithaca, NY: Cornell University Library, 1990), 289.

53. Gunnar, *History of Iceland*, 86.

54. *Hávamál*, v. 38.

55. Gunnar, *History of Iceland*, 96.

56. Ibid., 293.

57. Teresa Dröfn Freysdóttir Njarðvík (academic and author of *Runes: The Icelandic Book of Fuþark*), personal communication with Reynir A. Óskarson, Jan. 30, 2019.

58. Gunnar, *History of Iceland*, 287-289.

59. Ibid., 257.

60. Ibid., 296.

61. Wikipedia, s.v. "Beer in Iceland," accessed Mar. 2, 2019, https://en.wikipedia.org/w/index.php?title=Beer_in_Iceland&oldid=858259036.

62. Kjartan, *Íslensk glíma og glímumenn*, 35; Stefán, *Jóhannes á Borg*, 109; Þorsteinn, *Þróun glímu í íslensku þjóðlífi*, 218-219; Björk Hólm Þorsteinsdóttir and Ólafur Ingibergsson: *Íslenski þjóðbúningurinn* (Reykjavík: Ímyndir–þjóðfræði í mynd, 2012); interview with Valdimar Tryggvi Hafstein (8:40-16:30).

63. Landsbókasafn Lbs.1201, 4to. Sr. Guðmundur Einarsson; Landsbókasafn Lbs.1201, 4to. Rit Séra Þorsteinn Pálsson á Hálsi: *Fáein orð um glímur* 1861; Landsbókasafn Lbs.1201, 4to. Rit Jón Sigurðsson á Gautlöndum, 1861.

64. Stefánn, *Íslenzka glíman*, 137-138.

65. Björk and Ólafur, *Íslenski þjóðbúningurinn* (8:40-16:30).

66. Stefán, *Íslenzka glíman*, 140; Valdimar Tryggvi Hafstein, "Feeling Manly and Modern and Strong: Wrestling with Modernity," in *Kulturen der Sinne: Zugänge zur Sensualität der sozialen Welt*, ed. Karl Braun et al. (Würzburg, Germany: Verlag Königshausen & Neumann, 2017), 55-56.

67. Kjartan, *Íslensk glíma og glímumenn*, 7, 12, 39; Glímusamband Íslands, accessed Feb. 17, 2019, http://www.glima.is/?page_id=16.

68. Björn, *Íþróttir fornmanna á Norðurlöndum*, 144; Kjartan, *Íslensk glíma og glímumenn*, 16; Þorsteinn, *Þróun glímu í íslensku þjóðlífi*, 229-230.

69. *Grettis saga*, ch. 72; *Kjalnesinga saga*, ch. 18; *Áns saga bogasveigis*, ch. 4; *Egils saga einhenda ok Ásmundar berserkjabana*, ch. 6.

70. *Gylfaginning*, ch. 46.

71. *Brennu-Njáls saga*, ch. 19.

72. *Magnússona saga*, ch. 21.

73. *Finnboga saga ramma*, ch. 36.

74. *Gylfaginning*, ch. 21, ch. 46.

75. *Ólafs saga Tryggvasonar en mesta*, ch. 213.

76. *Gunnlaugs saga ormstungu*, ch. 10.

77. Landsbókasafn Lbs 2413 8vo 20v-21r.

78. Guðný Zoëga (bioarchaeologist, Byggðasafn Skagfirðinga), personal communication with William R. Short, Jan. 29, 2019.

79. *Grettis saga*, ch. 72.

80. *Víga-Glúms saga*, ch. 13; *Svarfdæla saga*, ch. 13; *Bárðar saga Snæfellsáss*, ch. 9; *Gunnlaugs saga ormstungu*, ch. 10.

81. *Laxdæla saga*, ch. 55.

82. *Bjarnar saga Hítdælakappa*, ch. 19; *Bárðar saga Snæfellsás*, ch. 20; *Finnboga saga ramma*, ch. 40; *Fóstbræðra saga*, ch. 23; *Gull-Þóris saga*, ch. 10.

83. *Egils saga Skalla-Grímsonar*, ch. 66; *Finnboga saga ramma*, ch. 11, ch. 13, ch. 37; *Grettis saga*, ch. 35, ch. 50, ch. 65, ch. 75.

84. *Bjarnar saga Hítdælakappa*, ch. 19; *Finnboga saga ramma*, ch. 11, ch. 13, ch. 37; *Fóstbræðra saga*, ch. 23; *Grettis saga*, ch. 35, ch. 50, *Göngu-Hrólfs saga*, ch. 6.

85. Cleasby et al., eds., *Icelandic-English Dictionary*, 493, s.v. "renna," 269, s.v. "hlaupa," 652, s.v. "undir."

86. *Finnboga saga ramma*, ch. 37; *Grettis saga*, ch. 35; *Bjarnar saga Hítdælakappa*, ch. 19; *Fóstbræðra saga*, ch. 23.

87. *Finnboga saga ramma*, ch. 35, ch. 37; *Grettis saga*, ch. 35; *Hávarðar saga og Ísfirðings*, ch. 2, ch. 3, ch. 21; *Göngu Hrólfs saga*, ch. 6; *Sörla saga sterka*, ch. 3; *Ármanns saga ok Þorsteins gala*, ch. 6.

88. *Svarfdæla saga*, ch. 13; *Finnboga saga ramma*, ch. 35, ch. 37; *Grettis saga*, ch. 72.

89. *Bjarnar saga Hítdælakappa*, ch. 19; *Finnboga saga ramma*, ch. 40; *Grettis saga*, ch. 50, ch. 56; *Harðar saga og Hólmaverja*, ch. 39; *Hávarðar saga og Ísfirðings*, ch. 2; *Þórðar saga hreðu*, ch. 6; *Laxdæla saga*, ch. 58.

90. *Egils saga Skalla-Grímsonar*, ch. 66; *Hávarðar saga og Ísfirðings*, ch. 21.

91. *Króka-Refs saga*, ch. 5; *Grettis saga*, ch. 72.

92. Landsbókasafn Lbs.1201, 4to. Sr. Guðmundur Einarsson.

93. Ibid.; Eggert Ólafsson, *Ferðabók Eggerts Ólafssonar og Bjarna Pálssonar um ferðir þeirra á Íslandi árin 1752–1757* (Reykjavík: Örn og Örlygur, 1981), 1:27; *Orðabók Jóns Ólafssonar úr Grunnuvík*, AM 433 fol, p. 74.

94. Eggert, *Ferðabók Eggerts Ólafssonar og Bjarna Pálssonar um ferðir þeirra á Íslandi árin 1752–1757*, 1:27.

95. *Grettis saga*, ch. 72; *Þorsteinns þáttr bæjarmagns*, ch. 7.

96. *Gunnars saga Keldugnúpsfífls*, ch. 7.

97. *Kjalnesinga saga*, ch. 15.

98. *Hálfdánar saga Eysteinssonar*, ch. 18; *Kormáks saga*, ch. 27; *Hrólfs saga Gautrekssonar*, ch. 19.

99. *Laxdæla saga*, ch. 24; *Hrómundar saga Gripssonar*, ch. 4; *Sturlaugs saga Starfsframa*, ch. 12; *Örvar-Odds saga*, ch. 20.

100. *Hrómundar saga Gripssonar*, ch. 4.

101. Stefán Jónsson, *Jóhannes á Borg: minningar glímukappans* (Reykjavík: Ægisútgafan, 1964), 117.

102. Stefán, *Íslenzka glíman*, 137.

103. *Grettis saga*, ch. 35; *Bjarnar saga Hítdælakappa*, ch. 19; *Finnboga saga ramma*, ch. 11, ch. 13, ch. 35, ch. 37; *Fóstbræðra saga*, ch. 23; *Grettis saga*, ch. 50, ch. 65; *Gunnars saga Keldugnúpsfífls*, ch. 6; *Hávarðar saga Ísfirðings*, ch. 2, ch. 3.

104. Cleasby et al., eds., *Icelandic-English Dictionary*, 141, s.v. "fang."

105. Ásgeir, *Íslensk orðsifjabók*, 75.

106. *Jökuls þáttur Búasonar*, ch. 1; *Bárðar saga Snæfellsás*, ch. 16; *Hálfdánar saga Brönufóstra*, ch. 6; *Gríms saga loðinkinna*, ch. 1.

107. *Hrana saga Hrings*, ch. 8; *Þorsteins þáttur bæjarmagns*, ch. 7; *Jökuls þáttur Búasonar*, ch. 1.

108. Kjartan, *Íslensk glíma og glímumenn*, 37; "Glímubeltin breytt til að reyna að útiloka níð," *Morgunblaðið* (Jan. 22, 1996): 26; "Glímusambandið leggur til atlögu við níðið," *Þjóðviljinn* (Jan. 16, 1966): 5, 9.

109. *Bárðar saga Snæfellsás*, ch. 9; *Finnboga saga ramma*, ch. 11; *Grettis saga*, ch. 35; *Göngu-Hrólfs saga*, ch. 33; *Orms þáttur Stórólfssonar*, ch. 9.

110. *Þorsteinns þáttr bæjarmagns*, ch. 7; *Þorsteins þáttur uxafóts*, ch. 10; *Hreiðars þáttur*, ch. 5; *Orms þáttur Stórólfssonar*, ch. 7; *Bjarnar saga Hítdælakappa*, ch. 19; *Egils saga Skalla-Grímssonar*, ch. 40; *Finnboga saga ramma*, ch. 37; *Grettis saga*, ch. 56; *Gunnars saga Keldgúnpsfífls*, ch. 1; *Jökuls þáttur Búasonar*, ch. 2; *Laxdæla saga*, ch. 55; *Göngu-Hrólfs saga*, ch. 9; *Hálfdánar saga Eysteinssonar*, ch. 17; *Sörla saga sterka*, ch. 18.

111. *Jökuls þáttur Búasonar*, ch. 2; *Hálfdánar saga Eysteinssonar*, ch. 18; *Egils saga einhenda ok Ásmundar berserkjabana*, ch. 13.

112. *Áns saga bogsveigis*, ch. 5.

113. *Króka-Refs saga*, ch. 5.

114. *Gunnlaugs saga ormstungu*, ch. 10.

115. *Hallfreðar saga vandræðaskálds*, ch. 7.

116. *Laxdæla saga*, ch. 55; *Gunnars saga Keldugnúpsfífls*, ch. 1; *Bárðar saga Snæfellsás*, ch. 16.

117. *Hávarðar saga Ísfirðings*, ch. 3; *Grettis saga*, ch. 15, ch. 35; *Finnboga saga ramma*, ch. 40; *Flóamanna saga*, ch. 13; *Hallfreðar saga vandræðaskálds*, ch. 6; *Hrana saga Hrings*, ch. 8; *Jökuls þáttur Búasonar*, ch. 2; *Laxdæla saga*, ch. 58; *Þórðar saga hreðu*, ch. 6.

118. *Hávarðar saga Ísfirðings*, ch. 3; *Bósa saga og herrauðs*, ch. 8.

119. *Finnboga saga ramma*, ch. 40; *Göngu-Hrólfs saga*, ch. 6.

120. *Hávarðar saga Ísfirðings*, ch. 2; *Grettis saga*, ch. 15; *Göngu-Hrólfs saga*, ch. 6; *Hjálmþés saga og Ölvis*, ch. 16; *Sörla saga sterka*, ch. 3, ch. 25.

121. *Bjarnar saga Hítdælakappa*, ch. 19; *Göngu-Hrólfs saga*, ch. 6; *Hjálmþés saga og Ölvis*, ch. 16.

122. *Egils saga Skalla-Grímssonar*, ch. 66; *Finnboga saga ramma*, ch. 29; *Harðar saga og Hólmverja*, ch. 39; *Hávarðar saga Ísfirðings*, ch. 21; *Jökuls þáttur Búasonar*, ch. 2; *Örvar-Odds saga*, ch. 22.

123. *Jökuls þáttur Búasonar*, ch. 2; *Bárðar saga Snæfellsás*, ch. 16; *Finnboga saga ramma*, ch. 40; *Hrana saga Hrings*, ch. 8; *Hálfdánar saga Eysteinssonar*, ch. 17.

124. *Bárðar saga Snæfellsáss*, ch. 16; Pétur Guðmann Guðmannsson (forensic examiner), personal communication with Reynir A. Óskarson, May 10, 2019. "By employing a forceful contortion and/or twist on the neck, it is possible to cause a break in the uppermost (top) neck vertebrae. The description [in the saga] where the hands are placed under the chin of the victim and the knee (which is the fulcrum) in the back seems very close. Trauma to the uppermost (top) neck vertebrae can cause deadly damage to the neck spine and swift death."

125. *Finnboga saga ramma*, ch. 35, ch. 40; *Hrana saga Hrings*, ch. 8; *Flóamanna saga*, ch. 13; *Grettis saga*, ch. 35, ch. 56; *Hallfreðar saga Vandræðaskálds*, ch. 7.

126. *Finnboga saga ramma*, ch. 35; *Grettis saga*, ch. 35; *Flóamanna saga*, ch. 13.

127. Gunnar et al., eds., *Grágás Lagasafn íslenska þjóðveldisins*, 213, K. 86.

128. *Laxdæla saga*, ch. 13; *Bárðar saga Snæfellsás*, ch. 9; *Grettis saga* ch. 39; *Víglundar saga*, ch. 4.

129. *Ljósvetninga saga*, ch. 21.

130. *Grettis saga*, ch. 39; *Gylfaginning*, ch. 48.

131. *Gylfaginning*, ch. 49.

132. *Grettis saga*, ch. 40, ch. 52.

133. *Egils saga Skalla-Grímssonar*, ch. 73; *Hallfreðar saga Vandræðaskálds*, ch. 6; *Áns saga bogsveigis*, ch. 4.

134. Gunnar et al. eds., *Grágás Lagasafn íslenska þjóðveldisins*, 211, K. 86; Larsen, tr., *Earliest Norwegian Law, Frostathing Law*, vol. 4, ch. 44, 275-276.

135. *Fóstbræðra saga*, ch. 23.

136. *Kjalnesinga saga*, ch. 15; *Gunnars saga Keldugnúpsfífls*, ch. 7, ch. 13; *Finnboga saga ramma*, ch. 16.

137. *Finnboga saga rama*, ch. 13, ch. 16; *Gunnars saga keldugnúpsfífls*, ch. 7; *Kjalnesinga saga*, ch. 15.

138. *Finnboga saga ramma*, ch. 13; *Áns saga Bogsveigis*, ch. 5; *Sturlaugs saga Starfsframa*, ch. 12.

139. *Gunnars saga Keldugnúpsfífls*, ch. 1; *Orms þáttur Stórólfssonar*, ch. 9.

140. *Brennu-Njáls saga*, ch. 145.

141. *Grettis saga*, ch. 35.

## CHAPTER 3: INTRODUCTION TO VIKING WEAPONS

1. Larsen, tr., *Earliest Norwegian Law, Gulathing Law*, title 309, 196.

2. Solberg, "Social Status," 246.

3. *Laxdæla saga*, ch. 30.

4. Ibid., *Laxdæla*, ch. 29, ch. 77.

5. *Laxdæla saga*, ch. 29; *Kormáks saga*, ch. 25; *Brennu-Njáls saga*, ch. 92; *Kormáks saga*, ch. 9.

6. *Bjarnar saga Hítdælakappa*, ch. 19; *Harðar saga og Hólmverja*, ch. 36; *Króka-Refs saga*, ch. 7.

7. *Vatnsdæla saga*, ch. 17 and *Egils saga Skalla-Grímssonar*, ch. 49; *Egils saga Skalla-Grímssonar*, ch. 25; Gunnar et al., eds., *Grágás Lagasafn íslenska þjóðveldisins*, 43, S. 49.

8. *Egils saga Skalla-Grímssonar*, ch. 38, ch. 81; *Fljótsdæla saga*, ch. 5, ch. 16, ch. 19; *Grettis saga*, ch. 19, ch. 55; *Hávarðar saga Ísfirðing*, ch. 12.

9. *Egils saga Skalla-Grímssonar*, ch. 58; *Harðar saga og Hólmverja*, ch. 15; *Reykdæla saga og Víga-Skútu*, ch. 19; *Grettis saga*, ch. 18; *Þórðar saga hreðu*, ch. 2.

10. Holger Arbman, *Birka: Untersuchungen und Studien* (Uppsala, Sweden: Almquist and Wiksell, 1943), vol. 1, Bj561, Bj581, Bj735, Bj855, Bj886; Kristján, *Kuml og haugfé*, Öndverðarnes (47), Sílastaðir (98), Grásíða (122), Ormstaðir (148).

11. Sue Brunning, *The Sword in Early Medieval Northern Europe*, Anglo-Saxon Studies 36 (Suffolk, UK: Boydell Press, 2019), 62-77; Gunnar et al., eds., *Grágás Lagasafn íslenska þjóðveldisins*, 216, S. 277.

12. *Bjarnar saga Hítdælakappa*, ch. 19; *Egils saga Skalla-Grímssonar*, ch. 62, ch. 83; *Fóstbræðra saga*, ch. 3, ch. 9, ch. 23; *Grettis saga*, ch. 62; *Hávarðar saga Ísfirðing*, ch. 14; *Kormáks saga*, ch. 9, ch. 14; *Króka-Refs saga*, ch. 8; *Laxdæla saga*, ch. 29; *Þórðar saga hreðu*, ch. 7; *Ásmundar saga kappabana*, ch. 1.

13. Kristján, *Kuml og haugfé*, 351-352.

14. Snorri Hilmarsson (author of *Um sannleiksgildi Íslendingasagna frá sjónarhóli kjötiðnaðarmannsins*), personal communication with Reynir A. Óskarson, Apr. 17, 2020.

15. Gavin Lucas, *Hofstaðir: Excavations of a Viking Age Feasting Hall in North-Eastern Iceland* (Reykjavík: Fornleifastofnun Íslands, 2009), 293-296, 307.

16. Snorri F. Hilmarsson (author of *Um sannleiksgildi Íslendingasagna frá sjónarhóli kjötiðnaðarmannsins*), personal communication with Reynir A. Óskarson, Apr. 17, 2020.

17. Lucas, *Hofstaðir*, 307.

18. Snorri F. Hilmarsson, *Um sannleiksgildi Íslendingasagna frá sjónarhóli kjötiðnaðarmannsins* (Reykjavík: Þjófur á nóttu, 1993), 15.

19. *Egils saga Skalla-Grímssonar*, ch. 19, ch. 70; *Haralds saga hárfagri*, ch. 25; *Ólafs saga Tryggvasonar*, ch. 32, ch. 39.

20. *Brennu-Njáls saga*, ch. 145; Gunnar et al., eds., *Grágás Lagasafn íslenska þjóðveldisins*, 244, K. 101.

21. *Droplaugarsona saga*, ch. 9.

22. *Brennu-Njáls saga*, ch. 44; *Finnboga saga ramma*, ch. 11.

23. *Gunnlaugs saga ormstungu*, ch. 7; *Droplaugarsona saga*, ch. 15.

24. Private collection, examined Jan. 21, 2011.

25. Guðný Zoëga (bioarchaeologist, Byggðasafn Skagfirðinga), personal communication with William R. Short, Oct. 6, 2016.

26. *Rígsþula*, v. 37.

27. Saxo, *History of the Danes*, bk. 7, 228; *King's Mirror*, ch. 37, 212.

28. *Ketil saga Hængs*, ch. 3; *Hrana saga hrings*, ch. 14; *Hálfdanar saga Eysteinssonar*, ch. 7; *Sörla þáttur eða Héðans saga ok Högna*, ch. 6.

29. Saxo, *History of the Danes*, bk. 5, 124; *Gunnars þáttur Þiðrandabana*, ch. 2.

30. *King's Mirror*, ch. 37, 212, 213.

31. *Ólafs saga Tryggvasonar*, ch. 8; *Hávarðar saga Ísfirðings*, ch. 14; *Eyrbyggja saga*, ch. 40.

32. Private collection, examined July 1, 2008.

33. Roesdahl and Wilson, eds., *Viking to Crusader*, cat. no. 222, 286.

34. Ibid., cat. no. 279, 301.

35. Jan Petersen, *De Norske Vikingesverd* (Kristiania, Norway: I Kommission Hos Jacob Dybwad, 1919).

36. R. E. Mortimer Wheeler, *London and the Vikings*, London Museum Catalogues, no. 1 (London: Lancaster House, 1927).

37. R. Ewart Oakeshott, *The Archaeology of Weapons* (London: Lutterworth Press, 1960).

38. Alfred Geibig, *Beiträge zur morphologischen Entwicklung des Schwertes im Mittelalter: eine Analyse des Fundmaterials vom ausgehenden 8. bis zum 12. Jahrhundert aus Sammlungen der Bundesrepublik Deutschland* (Neumunster, Germany: Karl Wachholtz Verlag, 1991).

39. *Reykdæla saga ok Víga-Skútu*, ch. 22.

40. *Eyrbyggja saga*, ch. 37.

41. *Hávarðar saga Ísfirðings*, ch. 10; *Hávarðar saga Ísfirðings*, ch. 4; *Víga-Glúms saga*, ch. 27; *Finnboga saga ramma*, ch. 32; *Ólafs saga Tryggvasonar*, ch. 41; *Bjarnar saga Hítdælakappa*, ch. 32; *Finnboga saga ramma*, ch. 40.

42. *Gylfaginning*, ch. 37.

43. *Brennu-Njáls saga*, ch. 63, ch. 82; *Egils saga Skalla-Grímssonar*, ch. 76; *Eyrbyggja saga*, ch. 62; *Finnboga saga ramma*, ch. 35, ch. 41; *Gísla saga Súrssonar*, ch. 36; *Heiðarvíga saga*, ch. 27; *Kjalnesinga saga*, ch. 11; *Vatnsdæla saga*, ch. 22; *Víga-Glúms saga*, ch. 11, ch. 27; *Þórðar saga hreðu*, ch. 8.

44. *Gísla saga Súrssonar*, ch. 34-35.

45. Saxo, *History of the Danes*, bk. 5, 124; *King's Mirror*, ch. 37, 213.

46. *Gísla saga Súrssonar*, ch. 20; *Finnboga saga ramma*, ch. 41; *Skáldskaparmál*, ch. 18.

47. *Egils saga Skalla-Grímssonar*, ch. 49; *Brennu-Njáls saga*, ch. 82; *Færeyjinga saga*, ch. 18, ch. 19; *Grettis saga*, ch. 4; *Gull-Þóris saga*, ch. 7; *Harðar saga og Hólmverja*, ch. 17; *Svarfdæla saga*, ch. 4; *Vatnsdæla saga*, ch. 7; *Manguss saga ins Goda*, ch. 30.

48. *Gunnars saga Keldugnúpsfífls*, ch. 7; *Svarfdæla saga*, ch. 4.

49. Saxo, *History of the Danes*, bk. 5, 125.

50. *Eyrbyggja saga*, ch. 62; *Landnámabók*, S. 168; *Hrómundar þáttr halta*, ch. 5.

51. *Egils saga Skalla-Grímssonar*, ch. 76; *Gull-Þóris saga*, ch. 14; *Hávarðar saga og Ísfirðings*, ch. 11; *Fljótsdæla saga*, ch. 5; *Laxdæla saga*, ch. 24; *Finnboga saga ramma*, ch. 35, ch. 41; *Kjalnesinga saga*, ch. 11; *Ljósvetninga saga*, ch. 24; *Víga-Glúms saga*, ch. 27.

52. *Brennu-Njáls saga*, ch. 151; *Finnboga saga ramma*, ch. 37; *Gull-Þóris saga*, ch. 13, ch. 18; *Hrafnkels saga Freysgoði*, ch. 3; *Kjalnesinga saga*, ch. 11; *Laxdæla saga*, ch. 49; *Vatnsdæla saga*, ch. 41; *Þórðar saga hreðu*, ch. 9.

53. *Haralds saga Sigurdarsonar*, ch. 92; *Encomium Emmae Reginae*, ed. and tr. Alistair Campbell (London: Royal Historical Society, 1949), bk. 2, ch. 4, 21.

54. Saxo, *History of the Danes*, bk. 2, 59.

55. *Gylfaginning*, ch. 21, ch. 42, ch. 45, ch. 48; *Þrymskviða*, v. 31-32.

56. *Svarfdæla saga*, ch. 11; *Gísla saga Súrssonar*, ch. 34.

57. Saxo, *History of the Danes*, bk. 8, 242.

58. Anthony Adams and A. G. Riggs, "A Verse Translation of Abbo of St. Germain's *Bella Parisiacae urbis*," *Journal of Medieval Latin* 14 (2004): 1-68.

59. Ibid., bk. 1, line 87, 25; bk. 1, line 207, 29.

60. Halsall, *Warfare and Society*, 177.

61. Philippe Contamine, *War in the Middle Ages*, tr. Michael Jones (Oxford: Basil Blackwell, 1984), 28.

62. *Jómsvíkinga saga*, ch. 13.

63. Rudolph Keyser et al., eds., *Konge-speilet* (Christiania, Norway: Carl C. Wener, 1848), ch. 39, 88-91, accessed Dec. 19, 2019, https://books.google.co.uk/books?id=LgtIfLwQgX4C&pg=PA133&source=gbs_toc_r&cad=3#v=onepage&q&f=false.

64. *Sverris saga*, ch. 71, ch. 130; *Magnúss saga blinda og Harald gilla*, ch. 6.

## CHAPTER 4: SAX

1. Arbman, *Birka*, 1:188-190, Bj581; 304-308, Bj834; 368-371, Bj944.

2. Charlotte Hedenstierna-Jonson, "The Birka Warrior: The Material Culture of a Martial Society" (PhD diss., Stockholm University, 2006), 56.

3. Based on a search of Arbman, *Birka*, vol. 1.

4. William R. Short and Hurstwic, unpublished research, Aug. 24, 2018. The data were collected from Astrid Daxböck, "Viking Age Weapons in Iceland," lecture, Þjóðminjasafn Íslands, Reykjavík, Sept. 30, 2008, combined with Eldjárn, *Kuml og haugfé*, and with data from Sarpur, the online museum catalog of Iceland, https://www.sarpur.is/.

5. Based on a search of the online catalog of archaeological artifacts of Universitetsmuseene, accessed Sept. 2, 2020, http://www.musit.uio.no/arkeologi/forskning/index.php.

6. William R. Short and Hurstwic, unpublished research, Aug. 24, 2018. Methodology is detailed in the appendix.

7. Berge, "Hirðskrá 1-37," 63, 64, 69; Keyser et al., *Konge-speilet*, ch. 37.

8. Cleasby et al., eds., *Icelandic-English Dictionary*, 516, s.v. "saxa."

9. *Bjarnar saga Hítdælakappa*, ch. 32; *Ólafs saga helga*, ch. 244.

10. Cleasby et al., eds., *Icelandic-English Dictionary*, 516, s.v. "sax."

11. Leslie Brown et al., eds., *Shorter Oxford English Dictionary* (Oxford: Oxford University Press, 2002), 2679, s.v. "Saxon."

12. Geoffrey of Monmouth, *Historia Regum Britanniae, A Variant Version Edited from Manuscripts*, ed. Jacob Hammer (Cambridge, MA: Mediaeval Academy of America, 1951), 118-119, accessed Oct. 3, 2019, www.medievalacademy.org/resource/resmgr/maa_books_online/hammer_0057_bkmrkdpdf.pdf.

13. Cleasby et al., eds., *Icelandic-English Dictionary*, 542, s.v. "skálm."

14. *Jökuls þáttr Búsasonar*, ch. 2; *Þorsteins þáttur uxafóts*, ch. 10.

15. *Grettis saga*, ch. 12.

16. Ibid., ch. 65; *Laxdæla saga*, ch. 48; *Haralds saga Sigurðarsonar*, ch. 80.

17. *Guðrúnarkviða II*, v. 19.

18. *Völuspá*, v. 44.

19. Gregory of Tours, *The History of the Franks*, tr. Lewis Thorpe (London: Penguin, 1974), bk. 4, ch. 51, 111.

20. *Grettis saga*, ch. 66; Björn K. Þórólfsson and Guðni Jónsson, eds., *Gísla saga Súrssonar*, Íslenzk fornrit, v. 6 (Reykjavík: Hið íslenzka fornritafélag, 1943), ch. 66, 215n3.

21. *Fóstbræðra saga*, ch. 9; *Brennu-Njáls saga*, ch. 11.

22. *Gylfaginning*, ch. 48.

23. Ibid.; *Finnboga saga ramma*, ch. 40.

24. William R. Short and Hurstwic, unpublished research, May 25, 2019. We used a replica Viking sax and a modern machete to cut brush, comparing ease of use of the tools and number of strokes required to cut through similar size branches. In all cases, the machete was the preferred tool for the task.

25. *Atlakviða*, v. 21.

26. Arbman, *Birka*, 1:188-190, Bj581.

27. Georg Schmitt, "Die Alamannen im Zollernalbkreis" (PhD diss., Johannes Gutenberg-Universität, Mainz, 2005), 33-37.

28. O. Rygh, *Norske oldsager* (Christiana, Norway: Alb. Cammermeyer, 1885), 27; William R. Short et al., "The Length of a Sax," *The Final Battle of Grettir the Strong* (Southborough, MA: Hurstwic, 2017), disc 2, ch. 10, 2:27-2:50, DVD.

29. *Grettis Saga*, ch. 82.

30. Anne Nørgård Jørgensen, *Waffen und Gräber: Typologische und chronolgische Studien zu skandinavischen Waffengräbern 520/30 bis 900 n.Chr.* (København, Denmark: Det Kongelige Nordiske Oldskriftselskab, 1999), cat. no.97, 230; William R. Short et al., "Grettir Gets His Sax," *Final Battle*, disc 1, 11:22-13:09, DVD.

31. Rygh, *Norske oldsager*, figs. 496-500; Schmitt, "Die Alamannen in Zollernalbkreis," 34; Jørgensen, *Waffen und Gräber*, 44-67.

32. William R. Short and Hurstwic, unpublished research, July 7, 2018. Methodology is detailed in the appendix.

33. Schmitt, "Die Alamannen in Zollernalbkreis," 34; Lee A. Jones (contributor to *Swords of the Viking Age*), personal communication with William R. Short, July 2, 2017.

34. William R. Short and Hurstwic, unpublished research, Aug. 10, 2017. In a simulated combat setting, a fighter first fought a round against a training partner with a dry grip and then fought a round with a slippery grip. Afterward, the fighter commented on his subjective experience. Video footage of the rounds was later reviewed to gain further insight into the situation being tested.

35. William R. Short and Hurstwic, unpublished research, July 15, 2017. For this and subsequent measurements of the impact delivered by a weapon to a target, we used a standardized procedure. To measure the response of the target to the hit, a three-axis accelerometer was attached to a target, typically a heavy bag constrained so it couldn't swing. The test subject hit to a target on the bag. We verified that during the hits, the accelerometer remained in its linear range. We verified that during the hit, the signal was sufficiently above the noise floor. Each hit was made multiple times by multiple test subjects, and the hits averaged over each instance and each test subject. We verified that the variation between hits for a given test subject and between different test subjects was small compared to the difference being tested, in this case, hits made with different slippery substances on the grip. The acceleration of all three axes of each hit was extracted from the time waveforms, windowed, and then combined and averaged in the frequency domain to minimize any errors from imperfect time alignment of the hits. All experiments were set up to be comparative measurements, such as in this case where a slippery grip was compared to a dry grip, in order to minimize any sensitivity to exact location of the accelerometer or the hits on the target. The total averaged signal level of each experimental run was compared to the nominal run to estimate the difference in the effect of the hit on the target. In this case, the hits with a bloody grip were compared to the hits with a dry grip, and the hits with a sweaty grip were compared to the hits with a dry grip.

36. Lee A. Jones (contributor to *Swords of the Viking Age*), personal communication with William R. Short, May 5, 2017.

37. *Grettis saga*, ch. 18; *Vatnsdæla saga*, ch. 3; *Þórðar Saga Hreðu*, ch. 3.

38. Arbman, *Birka*, 1:188-190, Bj581; 304-308, Bj834; 368-371, Bj944.

39. Private collection, example examined July 1, 2008, Apr. 1, 2017.

40. James Lang, *The Corpus of Anglo-Saxon Stone Sculpture*, vol. 3 (Oxford, UK: Oxford University Press, 1991), 182-184, accessed Sept. 3, 2020, http://www.ascorpus.ac.uk/catvol3.php?pageNum_urls=87.

41. Arbman, *Birka*, 1:188-190, Bj581; 368-371, Bj944.

42. Schmitt, "Die Alamannen im Zollernalbkreis," 36.

43. Quita Mould et al., *Craft, Industry and Everyday Life: Leather and Leatherworking in Anglo-Scandinavia and Medieval York* (York, UK: Council for British Archaeology, 2003), 3380-3381; Schmitt, "Die Alamannen im Zollernalbkreis," 36.

44. Arbman, *Birka*, 1:188-190, Bj581; 368-371, Bj944.

45. Mould, *Craft, Industry*, 3377-3383.

46. *Bárðar saga Snæfellsás*, ch. 20; *Brennu-Njáls saga*, ch. 120; *Grettis saga*, ch. 40, ch. 48, ch. 50, ch. 65, ch. 66, ch. 82.

47. *Fljótsdæla saga*, ch. 19; *Grettis saga*, ch. 18, ch. 55.

48. William R. Short and Hurstwic, unpublished research, Sept. 3, 2020. Physical measurements were made of a replica sword, sax, one-handed axe, and two-handed axe. From these models, a computer model was created that calculates the energy transfer between cutting tool and target at the moment of impact. The model permits the variation of parameters to estimate changes in the destructive ability of these tools for various conditions. The computer model uses a simple implementation of the interface between the hand and the grip of the weapon.

49. William R. Short and Hurstwic, unpublished research, Sept. 4, 2020. Measurements were made using hits to an instrumented target, as described in an earlier note in this chapter.

50. *Brennu-Njáls saga*, ch. 30; *Gísla saga Súrssonar*, ch. 1; *Gunnlaugs saga ormstungu*, ch. 11; *Heiðarvíga saga*, ch. 30, ch. 37; *Kormáks saga*, ch. 10; *Valla-Ljóts saga*, ch. 4.

51. *Grettis saga*, ch. 82.

52. *Vopnfirðinga saga*, ch. 7.

53. *Brennu-Njáls saga*, ch. 17, ch. 54, ch. 63; *Fóstbræðra saga*, ch. 9; *Grettis saga*, ch. 23, ch. 24, ch. 35, ch. 37, ch. 48, ch. 56, ch. 59, ch. 65, ch. 82, ch. 86; *Gull-Þóris saga*, ch. 15; *Gunnars Saga Kveldgnúpsfífls*, ch. 15; *Jökuls þáttr Búasonar*, ch. 2.

54. *Grettis saga*, ch. 65; *Gunnars Saga Kveldgnúpsfífls*, ch. 6; *Jökuls þáttr Búasonar*, ch. 2.

55. *Grettis saga*, ch. 18.

56. *Bandamanna saga*, ch. 12; *Brennu-Njáls saga*, ch. 13, ch. 19; *Fóstbræðra saga*, ch. 9; *Grettis saga*, ch. 72; *Þórðar saga herðu*, ch. 1.

57. William R. Short and Hurstwic, unpublished research, May 22, 2019. A statistical analysis was conducted using the database of weapons and their use in the *Sagas of Icelanders* described in the appendix.

58. William R. Short and Hurstwic, unpublished research, July 7, 2018. A statistical analysis was conducted using the database of weapons and their use in the *Sagas of Icelanders* described in the appendix.

59. Halsall, *Warfare and Society*, 208.

60. Larsen, tr., *Earliest Norwegian Law, Gulathing Law* title 309, 196.

61. *Grettis saga*, ch. 19, ch. 21, ch. 24.

62. *Brennu-Njáls saga*, ch. 30, ch. 71, ch. 120; *Fljótsdæla saga*, ch. 19; *Grettis saga*, ch. 19, ch. 50, ch. 86; *Vatnsdæla saga*, ch. 3; *Þórðar saga hreðu*, ch. 3.

63. Jørgensen, *Waffen und Gräber,*110-112; Patrick Ottaway, "Anglo-Scandinavian Ironwork from 16-22 Coppergate, York ," vol. 1 (PhD thesis, University of York, 1989), 167.

64. Lee A. Jones (contributor to *Swords of the Viking Age*), personal communication with William R. Short, July 2, 2019.

65. Ottaway, "Anglo-Scandinavian Ironwork," vol. 2, 1083-1086.

66. *Brennu-Njáls saga*, ch. 48; *Egils saga Skalla-Grímssonar*, ch. 44; *Eyrbyggja saga*, ch. 47; *Finnboga saga ramma*, ch. 40; *Fljótsdæla saga*, ch. 13, ch. 19; *Fóstbræðra saga*, ch. 6; *Grettis saga*, ch. 79; *Heiðarvíga saga*, ch. 33; *Reykdæla saga ok Víga-Skútu*, ch. 27.

67. *Finnboga saga ramma*, ch. 40.

68. *Eyrbyggja saga*, ch. 47; *Bandamanna saga*, ch. 12; *Finnboga saga ramma*, ch. 17, ch. 35, ch. 40; *Kormáks saga*, ch. 15.

69. *Eyrbyggja saga*, ch. 58; *Finnboga saga ramma*, ch.

17, ch. 35, ch. 40; *Fljótsdæla saga*, ch. 19; *Hallfreðar saga Vandræðaskáld*, ch. 7; *Heiðarvíga saga*, ch. 23, ch. 25, ch. 30.

70. *Bjarnar saga Hítdælakappa*, ch. 22; *Brennu-Njáls saga*, ch. 47; *Gísla saga Súrssonar* ,ch. 27; *Gull-Þóris saga*, ch. 3, ch. 4; *Hallfreðar saga Vandræðaskálds*, ch. 6; *Laxdæla saga*, ch. 20, ch. 21.

71. *Fljótsdæla saga*, ch. 19.

**CHAPTER 5: AXE**

1. *Brennu-Njáls saga*, ch. 136; *Laxdæla saga*, ch. 75; *Bjarnar saga Hítdælakappa*, ch. 19; *Eyrbyggja saga*, ch. 36; *Reykdæla saga ok Víga-Skútu*, ch. 25, ch. 27; *Vatnsdæla saga*, ch. 42; *Króka-Refs saga*, ch. 6; *Hávarðar saga Ísfirðings*, ch. 14.

2. *Svarfdæla saga*, ch. 2.

3. *Finnboga saga ramma*, ch. 24.

4. *Bjarnar saga Hítdælakappa*, ch. 19; *Vopnfirðinga saga*, ch. 2; *Harðar saga ok Hólmverja*, ch. 36.

5. *Fóstbræðra saga*, ch. 12.

6. Ibid., ch. 17, ch. 23, ch. 24; *Hallfreðar saga vandræðaskálds*, ch. 7; *Brennu-Njáls saga*, ch. 136, ch. 146; *Grettis saga*, ch. 62, ch. 79; *Hávarðar saga*, ch. 4.

7. *Brennu-Njáls saga*, ch. 99, ch. 146.

8. Norman Denny and Josephine Filmer-Sankey, *The Bayeux Tapestry* (London: Collins, 1966).

9. Comnena, *Alexiad*, bk. 2, ch. 9, 95.

10. M. J. Swanton, ed., *The Anglo-Saxon Chronicle* (London: J. M. Dent, 1996), 198.

11. Historiska museet SHM 14168, accessed Sept. 7, 2020, http://mis.historiska.se/mis/sok/fid.asp?fid=123 172&g=1.

12. Svenskt Hällristnings Forsknings Arkiv, Tanum 1:1, accessed Sept. 7, 2020, https://www.shfa.se/Bild/VisaBild.aspx?id=575&Bildtyp=v&maxWidth=550, and Tanum 12:1, accessed Sept. 7, 2020, https://www.shfa.se/Bild/VisaBild.aspx?id=23&Bildtyp=v&maxWidth=550.

13. Simek, *Dictionary of Northern Mythology,* 25-26; Historiska museet SHM8985:5, accessed Sept. 8, 2020, mis.historiska.se/mis/sok/fid.asp?fid=417801.

14. Roesdahl and Wilson, eds., *Viking to Crusader* cat. no.194, 278-279.

15. *Völuspá*, v. 44.

16. *Skáldskaparmál*, ch. 49.

17. Edith Marold, with the assistance of Vivian Busch, Jana Krüger, Ann-Dörte Kyas, and Katharina Seidel, "(Introduction to) Einarr skálaglamm Helgason, *Vellekla*," tr. from German by John Foulks, in Whaley, ed., *Poetry from the Kings' Sagas 1*, 280; Kari Ellen Gade, "(Introduction to) Halldórr ókristni, *Eiríksflokkr*," in ibid., 469; Margaret Clunies Ross, "(Introduction to) Anonymous, *Stanzas from the Fourth Grammatical Treatise*," in *Poetry from Treatises on Poetics*, ed. Kari Ellen Gade and Edith Marold, Skaldic

Poetry of the Scandinavian Middle Ages 3 (Turnhout, Belgium: Brepols, 2017), 570.

18. Cleasby et al., eds., *Icelandic-English Dictionary*, 769, s.v. "öx."

19. *Bjarnar saga Hítdælakappa*, ch. 19; *Brennu-Njáls saga*, ch. 53, ch. 109, ch. 136; *Egils saga Skalla-grímssonar*, ch. 40; *Eyrbyggja saga*, ch. 36; *Fóstbræðra saga*, ch. 24; *Grettis saga*, ch. 48, ch. 79; *Gunnlaugs saga ormstungu*, ch. 8; *Hávarðar saga Ísfirðing*, ch. 14; *Laxdæla saga*, ch. 64, ch. 75; *Reykdæla saga og Víga-Skútu*, ch. 25; *Svarfdæla saga*, ch. 2; *Vatnsdæla saga*, ch. 42; *Víga-Glúms saga*, ch. 3.

20. *Egils saga Skalla-Grímssonar*, ch. 40.

21. *Eyrbyggja saga*, ch. 40, ch. 47; *Brennu-Njáls saga*, ch. 147.

22. *Egils saga Skalla-Grímssonar*, ch. 83; *Finnboga saga ramma*, ch. 27; *Hallfreðar saga vandræðaskálds*, ch. 5, ch. 7; *Brennu-Njáls saga*, ch. 138; *Gísla saga Súrssonar*, ch. 34; *Gull-Þóris saga*, ch. 13; *Gunnars saga Keldugnúpsfifls*, ch. 4; *Laxdæla saga*, ch. 55, ch. 75; *Vatnsdæla saga*, ch. 30; *Kormáks saga*, ch. 9.

23. Roesdahl and Wilson, eds., *Viking to Crusader*, cat. no.222, 286; private collection, axe examined July 1, 2008.

24. *Fóstbræðra saga*, ch. 23.

25. James Graham-Campbell, *Viking Artifacts: A Select Catalog* (London: British Museum Publications, 1980), plate 419.

26. William R. Short and Hurstwic, unpublished research, Aug. 24, 2018. Methodology is detailed in the appendix.

27. William R. Short and Hurstwic, unpublished research, Sept. 3, 2020. Details of the model were described in chapter 4.

28. *Fóstbræðra saga*, ch. 13.

29. Petersen, *De Norske Vikingesverd*, 36-47.

30. Saxo, *History of the Danes* bk. 2, 59.

31. James Henthorn Todd, ed. and tr., *The War of the Gaedhill with the Gaill, or The Invasions of Ireland by the Danes and Other Norsemen* (London: Alexander Thjoi, 1867), 203.

32. *Egils saga Skalla-Grímssonar*, ch. 83; *Gull-Þóris saga*, ch. 14.

33. Measurements of artifacts from a private collection, Mar. 14, 2020.

34. *Brennu-Njáls saga*, ch. 146.

35. Roesdahl and Wilson, eds., *Viking to Crusader*, cat. nos. 173, 274.

36. Martin Rundkvist, *Barshalder I: A Cemetery in Grötlingbo and Fide Parishes, Gotland, Sweden, c. AD 1–1100*, Stockholm Archaeological Reports (40), 2003, Bhr 1962:11, 179.

37. Andy Helpin, "Viking Ireland 1–Weapons–The Axe," Apr. 3, 2014, YouTube, accessed Dec. 18, 2019, https://www.youtube.com/watch?v=aYDpXH4adC8.

38. Kulturhistorisk museum, C55000-126, accessed Oct. 11, 2019, http://www.unimus.no/artefacts/khm/search/?oid=573438&museumsnr=C55000&f=html.

39. Rundkvist, *Barshalder I*, 179.

40. *Bjarnar saga Hítdælakappa*, ch. 19; *Eyrbyggja saga*, ch. 37.

41. *Hávarðar saga Ísfirðings*, ch. 2.

42. *Ólafs saga helga*, ch. 143.

43. *Fóstbræðra saga*, ch. 23.

44. Ibid., ch. 12.

45. Helpin, "Viking Ireland 1."

46. Svenskt Hällristnings Forsknings Arkiv, Tanum 1:1, Tanum 12:1.

47. Denny and Filmer-Sankey, *Bayeux Tapestry*.

48. William R. Short and Hurstwic, unpublished research, July 2, 2019. In our research laboratory, we set up a time trial in which fighters were asked to hit targets at various distances and heights, some of which were moving. Accuracy and speed of each round was recorded for several test subjects. At the end of each round, subjective comments were recorded for each test subject.

49. *Brennu-Njáls saga*, ch. 39; *Eyrbyggja saga*, ch. 58.

50. *Valla-Ljóts saga*, ch. 2; *Sneglu-Halla þáttur*, ch. 10; *Brennu-Njáls saga*, ch. 11.

51. *Egils saga Skalla-Grímssonar*, ch. 38.

52. Sigurður Nordal, ed., *Egils saga Skalla-Grímssonar*, Íslenzk fornrit, v. 2 (Reykjavík: Hið íslenzka fornritafélag, 1933), 95n1.

53. Helpin, "Viking Ireland 1."

54. *Fóstbræðra saga*, ch. 24; *Harðar saga ok Hólmverja*, ch. 36.

55. Laila Kitzler Åhfelt, "Några träfynd i Sigtuna från runstenstid," *Situne Dei* (2011): 55-56.

56. *Hallfreðar saga vandræðaskálds*, ch. 6; *Grettis saga*, ch. 16.

57. *Íslendinga saga*, ch. 144.

58. *Brennu-Njáls saga*, ch. 44.

59. Ibid., ch. 11, ch. 12, ch. 92, ch. 119; *Gull-Þóris saga*, ch. 14; *Laxdæla saga*, ch. 63.

60. *Brennu-Njáls saga*, ch. 109.

61. Rundkvist, *Barshalder I*, Bhr 1936:26, 134.

62. *Fóstbræðra saga*, ch. 6, ch. 8, ch. 12; *Brennu-Njáls saga*, ch. 92, ch. 99, ch.146; *Laxdæla saga*, ch. 55, ch. 64; *Grettis saga*, ch. 12; *Eyrbyggja saga*, ch. 62.

63. *Fóstbræðra saga*, ch. 8; *Brennu-Njáls saga*, ch. 92; *Hávarðar saga Ísfirðing*, ch. 10; *Grettis saga*, ch. 16.

64. *Grettis saga*, ch. 12; *Laxdæla saga*, ch. 55; *Ólafs saga Tryggvasonar*, ch. 41.

65. *Laxdæla saga*, ch. 64; *Brennu-Njáls saga*, ch. 99.

66. *Fóstbræðra saga*, ch. 8.

67. "Axe Blow to the Head," *Viking Weapon Test Cuts*, Hurstwic, Mar. 16, 2012, YouTube, accessed Oct. 15, 2019, https://www.youtube.com/watch?v=juIw20z5p0c.

68. William R. Short and Hurstwic, unpublished research, July 6, 2018. Methodology is detailed in a note in the appendix.

69. *Hávarðar saga Ísfirðing*, ch. 4; *Egils saga Skalla-Grímssonar*, ch. 27; *Grettis saga*, ch. 16.

70. Denny and Filmer-Sankey, *Bayeux Tapestry*, scene 52a.

71. William R. Short and Hurstwic, unpublished research, Nov. 3, 2019. The computer simulation modeled the geometry of the arm and the axe, both a one-handed axe and a two-handed axe. The velocities applied were derived from high-speed video of axe cuts with replica weapons. A simple model of the hard and soft tissue of the skull was used to predict the deceleration and resulting path of the axe through the head after impact.

72. William R. Short and Hurstwic, unpublished research, Sept. 10, 2019. Measurements were made using hits to an instrumented target using steel replica weapons, as described in a note in the sax chapter.

73. *Grænlendinga þáttr*, ch. 5.

74. "Axe horn thrust to the ribs," *Viking Weapon Test Cuts*.

75. William R. Short and Hurstwic, unpublished research, Mar. 1, 2018, and unpublished research, Apr. 5, 2018. In a simulated combat setting, pairs of fighters fought rounds where one was armed with a two-handed axe and the other with the weapon or weapons of his choice. The rounds were recorded on video for later analysis, and after each round, the subjective impressions of each fighter were recorded.

76. William R. Short and Hurstwic, unpublished research, July 6, 2018. The methodology for creating and analyzing the database of weapons and weapons use in the *Sagas of Icelanders* is described in the appendix.

77. *Harðar saga og Hólmverja*, ch. 33; *Laxdæla saga*, ch. 64.

78. *Fóstbræðra saga*, ch. 24.

79. *Ólafs saga helgi*, ch. 226.

80. Jørgensen, *Waffen und Gräber*, 102-104; Schmitt, "Die Alamannen in Zollernalbkreis," 39.

81. *Egils saga Skalla-Grímssonar*, ch. 38; *Valla-Ljóts saga*, ch. 2.

82. William R. Short and Hurstwic, unpublished research, Mar. 4, 2017, June 13, 2017, and July 23, 2019. A simulated combat drill was set up in which points were awarded for hooking with the axe that permitted a successful follow-up attack, as well as for other moves being studied in this drill in order to encourage fighters to use them during the round. Test subjects selected the weapon or weapons of their choice for each round. During the round, points were scored by a referee for successfully using the move. Test subjects gave their subjective impressions after each round. In addition, video of the rounds was reviewed later. Hooking with the axe was used successfully on a number of occasions

by the test subjects. In many cases, the axe was used to control the opponent's weapon, and an attack was made with the weapon in the other hand. Test subjects often defended against an incoming attack by hooking with their axe and throwing the incoming weapon off line, which did not score points in this drill but added to the impression that hooking with the axe could be used effectively.

83. *Eyrbyggja saga*, ch. 62; *Vatnsdæla saga*, ch. 30; *Ólafs saga helga*, ch. 133.

84. *Sturlu saga*, ch. 21.

85. William R. Short and Hurstwic, unpublished research, June 13, 2017, and Dec. 28, 2017. In a simulated combat setting, pairs of fighters fought rounds where one was armed with either a one-handed or two-handed axe, and the other with the weapon or weapons of his choice. A point system was implemented in which certain moves were awarded more points if the move was successfully executed resulting in a hit during the round. The scoring encouraged fighters to try some of these moves. The rounds were scored in real time and reviewed later on video, looking both at instances where the move succeeded and where it was tried and failed. Additionally, fighters provided their subjective impressions at the end of each round.

86. *Eyrbyggja saga*, ch. 57; *Finnboga saga ramma*, ch. 34; *Gísla saga Súrssonar*, ch. 18; *Kormáks saga*, ch. 4; *Ljósvetninga saga*, ch. 4; *Þórðar saga hreðu*, ch. 9; *Ögmundar þáttur dytts*.

87. *Fóstbræðra saga*, ch. 12; *Víglundar saga*, ch. 16; *Brennu-Njáls saga*, ch. 45.

88. *Fóstbræðra saga*, ch. 3, ch. 8.

89. Denny and Filmer-Sankey, *Bayeux Tapestry*, scene 52a, scene 56.

90. William R. Short and Hurstwic, unpublished research, May 30 and July 2, 2019. In our research laboratory, we set up a time trial in which fighters were asked to hit targets at various distances and heights, some of which were moving. Accuracy and speed of each round was recorded for several test subjects. At the end of each round, subjective comments were recorded for each test subject. Additionally, in a simulated combat setting, pairs of fighters fought rounds where one was armed with axes having various haft lengths and a shield, and the other with the weapon or weapons of his choice. The rounds were recorded on video for later analysis, and after each round, the subjective impressions of each fighter were recorded.

91. *Brennu-Njáls saga*, ch. 17; *Fljótsdæla saga*, ch. 21.

92. *Eyrbyggja saga*, ch. 58.

93. *Hávarðar saga Ísfirðing*, ch. 14; *Brennu-Njáls saga*, ch. 39, ch. 128.

94. *Fóstbræðra saga*, ch. 15, ch. 24; *Ólafs saga Tryggvasonar*, ch. 32; *Hallfreðar saga vandræðaskálds*, ch. 10.

95. William R. Short and Hurstwic, unpublished research, Dec. 15, 2019. Methodology is detailed in a note in the appendix.

96. *Fóstbræðra saga*, ch. 24.

**CHAPTER 6: SWORD**

1. Examination of artifacts from a private collection, Jan. 5, 2011.

2. *Grettis saga*, ch. 17.

3. *Vatnsdæla saga*, ch. 17; *Landnámabók*, S. 179.

4. Brunning, *Sword,* 88-93.

5. Ibid., 62-77.

6. *Hávamál*, v. 38.

7. British Library, MS Stowe 944, fol.6r, accessed Sept. 14, 2020, http://www.bl.uk/manuscripts/Viewer.aspx?ref=stowe_ms_944_f006r; *Völsunga saga*, ch. 27.

8. *Laxdæla saga*, ch. 46.

9. William R. Short and Hurstwic, unpublished research, Aug. 24, 2018, and Feb. 2, 2020. The methodology for creating and analyzing the database of weapons and weapons use in the *Sagas of Icelanders* is described in the appendix.

10. *Brennu-Njáls saga*, ch. 19.

11. Petersen, *De Norske Vikingesverd*, 6; Irmelin Martens, "Indigenous and Imported Viking Age Weapons in Norway—A Problem with European Implications," *Journal of Nordic Archaeological Science* 14 (2004): 125-137.

12. Based on a search of the online catalog of archaeological artifacts of Universitetsmuseet, accessed Sept. 17, 2020, http://www.musit.uio.no/arkeologi/forskning/index.php.

13. *Ólafs saga Tryggvasonar*, ch. 109.

14. Larsen, tr., *Earliest Norwegian Law, Gulathing Law* title 309, 196.

15. Maria Herlin Karnell, ed., *Gotland's Picture Stones: Bearer of an Enigmatic Legacy* (Visby, Sweden: Gotländskt Arkiv, 2012).

16. *Gylfaginning*, ch. 27; *Skírnismál*, v. 8-9.

17. *Völuspá*, v. 50; *Gylfaginning*, ch. 51.

18. *Völsunga saga*, ch. 18; Rundata Sö 101, https://skaldic.abdn.ac.uk/db.php?id=16033&if=runic&table=mss; Universitetsmuseene C4321, accessed Sept. 14, 2020, http://www.musit.uio.no/artefacts/khm/search/?oid=4550&museumsnr=C4321&f=html.

19. Rory McTurk, "(Introduction to) Anonymous, *Krákumál*," in *Poetry in fornaldarsögur*, ed. Margaret Clunies Ross, Skaldic Poetry of the Scandinavian Middle Ages 8 (Turnhout, Belgium: Brepols, 2017), 706; Margaret Clunies Ross, "(Introduction to) Einarr skálaglamm Helgason, *Lausavísur*" in Whaley, ed., *Poetry from the Kings' Sagas 1*, 330; Edith Marold, with the assistance of Vivian Busch et al., tr. from German by John Foulks, "(Introduction to) Einarr skálaglamm Helgason, *Vellekla*," in ibid., 280; Judith Jesch, "(Intro-

duction to) R gnvaldr jarl Kali Kolsson, Lausavísur," in *Poetry from the Kings' Sagas 2: From c. 1035 to c. 1300*, ed. Kari Ellen Gade, Skaldic Poetry of the Scandinavian Middle Ages 2 (Turnhout, Belgium: Brepols, 2009), 575-609; Kari Ellen Gade, "(Introduction to) Snorri Sturluson, *Háttatal*," in *Poetry from Treatises on Poetics*, Gade and Marold, eds., Skaldic Poetry of the Scandinavian Middle Ages 3, 1094; Russell Poole, "(Introduction to) Tindr Hallkelsson, *Hákonardrápa*," in Whaley, ed., *Poetry from the Kings' Sagas 1*, 336..

20. Simek, *Dictionary of Northern Mythology*, 240-246, s.v. "Odin"; *Völuspá*, v. 24.

21. *Droplaugarsona saga*, ch. 15; *Gunnlaugs saga ormstungu*, ch. 7; *Svarfdæla saga*, ch. 8; *Gull-Þóris saga*, ch. 10.

22. *Sigrdrífumál*, v. 7; *Kormáks saga*, ch. 9.

23. Cleasby et al., eds., *Icelandic-English Dictionary*, 442, s.v. "mækir."

24. *Harðar saga og Hólmverja*, ch. 17; *Gunnars saga Keldugnúpsfífls*, ch. 7; *Ynglinga saga*, ch. 21.

25. Cleasby et al., eds., *Icelandic-English Dictionary*, 76, s.v. "brandr," 268, s.v. "hjörr."

26. Brunning, *Sword,* 84.

27. William R. Short and Hurstwic, unpublished research, Mar. 19, 2019, based on data from Ian Peirce, *Swords of the Viking Age* (Woodbridge, UK: Boydell Press, 2002), 25-143, choosing well-preserved examples.

28. William R. Short and Hurstwic, unpublished research, Feb. 6, 2020, based on data from Mikko Moilanen, *Marks of Fire, Value and Faith* (Turku, Finland: Suomen keskiajan arkeologian seura, 2015), 349-420, choosing well-preserved examples.

29. *Eyrbyggja saga*, ch. 44; *Laxdæla saga*, ch. 49.

30. *Ólafs saga Tryggvasonar*, ch. 109.

31. *Kormáks saga*, ch. 10; *Heiðarvíga saga*, ch. 30; *Gunnlaugs saga ormstungu*, ch. 11; *Gísla saga Súrssonar*, ch. 1.

32. *Kormáks saga*, ch. 10; *Heiðarvíga saga*, ch. 37.

33. Ingo Petri, "Material and Properties of VLFBERHT Swords," in *The Sword: Form and Thought*, ed. Lisa Deutscher et al. (Woodbridge: Boydell Press, 2019), 63.

34. Moilanen, *Marks*, 113-120.

35. *Kormáks saga*, ch. 9.

36. Ibid.

37. Hilda Ellis-Davidson, *The Sword in Anglo-Saxon England: Its Archaeology and Literature* (Woodridge: Boydell Press, 1962), 17.

38. Moilanen, *Marks*, 110-111.

39. Cotton Tiberius B.V., fol. 39r, accessed Jan. 29, 2020, http://www.bl.uk/manuscripts/Viewer.aspx?ref=cotton_ms_tiberius_b_v!1_f039r.

40. *Grettis saga*, ch. 17.

41. Petri, "Material," 73.

42. Alan Williams, *The Sword and the Crucible: A History of the Metallurgy of European Swords up to the 16th Century*, History of Warfare, vol. 77 (Leiden, Netherlands: Brill, 2012), 117-122.

43. Petri, "Material," 69-71, 80-86.

44. Williams, *Sword*, 117-122, 147-149.

45. Mikko Moilanen, *Marks*, 75-76.

46. Ibid., 306.

47. Ewart Oakeshott, "Introduction to the Viking Sword" in Peirce, *Swords*, 3.

48. Wikinger Museum Haithabu, no. 13018; Peirce, *Swords*, plate 6.

49. Martens, "Indigenous," 125-137; Peirce, *Swords*, 3.

50. Lee A. Jones, "Overview of Hilt & Blade Classifications," in Peirce, *Swords*, 21-24.

51. Petersen, *De Norske Vikingesverd*, 54-181.

52. Jones, "Overview," in Peirce, *Swords*, 15-24.

53. Petersen, *De Norske Vikingesverd*, 56-57.

54. William R. Short and Hurstwic, unpublished research, Mar. 19, 2019, based on data from Peirce, *Swords*, 25-143, choosing well-preserved examples.

55. Jones, "Overview," in Peirce, *Swords*, 20-21.

56. Peirce, *Swords,* 48-51.

57. Ibid., 50.

58. Arbman, *Birka*, 1:160, Bj524; 305, Bj834; Universitetsmuseene, B9015, accessed Sept. 23, 2020, http://www.musit.uio.no/artefacts/um/search/?oid=16349&museumsnr=B9015&f=html; Universitetsmuseene T5084, accessed Sept. 24, 2020, http://www.musit.uio.no/artefacts/vm/search/?oid=5314&museumsnr=T5084&f=html (accessed Sept. 24, 2020).

59. Mikko Moilanen, *Marks of Fire, Value and Faith* (Turku, Finland: Suomen keskiajan arkeologian seura, 2015), 282.

60. Arbman, *Birka*, 1:344, Bj886; 364-365, Bj942; 474, Bj1151.

61. Universitetsmuseene, C58882, accessed Aug. 24, 2020, http://www.musit.uio.no/artefacts/khm/search/?oid=1135331&museumsnr=C58882&f=html; Universitetsmuseene, C22138a, accessed Sept. 23, 2020, http://www.musit.uio.no/artefacts/khm/search/?oid=86727&museumsnr=C22138&f=html.

62. *Laxdæla saga*, ch. 29, ch. 77.

63. William R. Short and Hurstwic, unpublished research, July 15, 2017. We used our standardized procedure for measurements of the impact delivered by a weapon to a target as outlined in the sax chapter. Simulated blood and sweat were used in the tests.

64. William R. Short and Hurstwic, unpublished research, Mar. 25, 2019. Statistical analysis of well-preserved swords described in Peirce, *Swords*.

65. Petersen, *De Norske Vikingesverd*, 12.

66. Short, *Viking Weapons,* 111-112.

67. Brunning, *Sword*, 22-29.

68. William R. Short and Hurstwic, unpublished research, Mar. 25, 2019. Statistical analysis of well-preserved swords cataloged in Peirce, *Swords.*

69. William R. Short and Hurstwic, unpublished research, Feb. 6, 2020. Statistical analysis of well-preserved swords cataloged in Moilanen, *Marks.*

70. William R. Short and Hurstwic, unpublished research, Jan. 31, 2020. Eight types of replica Viking swords were used in this study from different smiths and vendors, ranging from robust training swords to museum-quality replicas of surviving swords. The swords were familiar to the test subjects, having been used for simulated combat drills over a period of years. The swords were rated for "feel" on a subjective, five-point scale. Physical measurements were made on the swords to determine the moment of inertia at the center point of the hand on the hilt, and the center of balance of the blade. The correlation between feel and moment of inertia was 0.80, while the correlation between feel and center of balance was 0.24, suggesting that the moment of inertia is a better predictor of feel than is center of balance.

71. William R. Short and Hurstwic, unpublished research, Feb. 5, 2019. We used our standardized procedure for measurements of the impact delivered by a weapon to a target outlined in the sax chapter. We compared two nominally identical replica steel swords that had masses added such that the mass of each was the same, but the center of balance of one was close to the nominal center of balance found from the analysis of the swords cataloged in Peirce, *Swords*, and the other was pushed farther out toward the blade.

72. William R. Short and Hurstwic, unpublished research, Aug. 8, 2019. In a simulated combat setting, pairs of fighters fought rounds. One fighter was given a randomly chosen sword from a set of four with nominally identical masses but with centers of balance that ranged from 15 to 31 percent of blade length. The swords were disguised so that the center of balance could not be identified by sight. The fighter had the option of fighting with sword alone or sword and shield. His opponent could choose any weapon or weapon combination he wanted. At the end of the round, fighters gave their subjective opinions of the capability of the sword they used. Video footage of the rounds was later reviewed to gain further insight into the situation being tested.

73. William R. Short and Hurstwic, unpublished research, May 9, 2017. A replica Viking sword was fitted with an accelerometer on the grip between the hilt and the swordsman's hand. A mechanical tapper repeatedly and consistently hit the edge of the sword as it moved down the length of the sword, while the acceleration delivered by the sword into the swordsman's hand was recorded. The data were analyzed in the frequency domain and plotted to yield a contour plot of vibration delivered into the swordsman's hand for hits all along the edge of the blade.

74. William R. Short and Hurstwic, unpublished research, May 18, 2017. Two replica Viking swords were measured. Each was fitted with an accelerometer on

the grip between the hilt and the swordsman's hand. A mechanical tapper consistently hit the edge of the sword, while the acceleration delivered by the sword into the swordsman's hand was recorded. The data were analyzed in the frequency domain and plotted to yield a contour plot of vibration delivered into the swordsman's hand for the hit as a function of frequency and time.

75. Kristján, *Kuml og haugfé*, 331-337.

76. Ibid., 181-184; Þjóðminjasafn Íslands number 13736/1947-154, accessed Mar. 17, 2020, https://www. sarpur.is/Adfang.aspx?AdfangID=335100.

77. Karnell, ed., *Gotland's Picture Stones*; Denny and Filmer-Sankey, *Bayeux Tapestry*, scene 9.

78. *Svarfdæla saga*, ch. 19; Birgit Arrhenius and Henry Freij, "'Pressbleck' Fragments from the East Mound in Old Uppsala Analyzed with a Laser Scanner," *Laborativ Arkeologi* 6, Stockholm University (1992): 75–110, accessed Mar. 23, 2020, https://www.archaeology.su.se/polopoly_fs/1.170010.1394448706!/menu/standard/fil e/LA6.Arrhenius%20%26%20Freij.pdf.

79. *Hallfreðar saga vandræðaskálds,* ch. 6.

80. *Harðar saga ok Hólmverja,* ch. 39.

81. *Gísla saga Súrssonar,* ch. 28; *Króka-Refs saga,* ch. 3; *Íslendinga saga,* ch. 172.

82. *Króka-Refs saga,* ch. 3.

83. *Fljótsdæla saga,* ch. 5, ch. 16; *Hávarðar saga Ísfirðing,* ch. 12.

84. William R. Short and Hurstwic, unpublished research, July 8, 2018. The methodology for creating and analyzing the database of weapons and weapons use in the *Sagas of Icelanders* is described in the appendix. Karnell, ed., *Gotland's Picture Stones*; Cleasby et al., eds., *Icelandic-English Dictionary*, 64, s.v. "bíta."

85. William R. Short and Hurstwic, unpublished research, July 6, 2018. The methodology for creating and analyzing the database of weapons and weapons use in the *Sagas of Icelanders* is described in the appendix.

86. Gail McKinnon, "Where Swords Seek to Shatter: A Study of Deliberate Trauma in the Medieval Cemeteries of St. Andrew, Fishergate, York" (master's thesis, University of Bradford, 1997).

87. "Sword Cut to a Limb," *Viking Weapon Test Cuts,* Hurstwic, Mar. 16, 2012, YouTube, accessed Oct. 15, 2019, https://www.youtube.com/watch?v=juIw20z5p 0c; "Sword Cut to the Ribs," *Viking Weapon Test Cuts,* Hurstwic, Mar. 16, 2012, YouTube, accessed Oct. 15, 2019, https://www.youtube.com/watch?v=juIw20z5p0c.

88. William R. Short and Hurstwic, unpublished research, Jan. 31, 2020. The methodology for creating and analyzing the database of weapons and weapons use in the *Sagas of Icelanders* is described in the appendix.

89. *Bjarnar saga Hítdælakappa,* ch. 32; *Brennu-Njáls saga,* ch. 63, ch. 155, ch. 158; *Finnboga saga ramma,* ch. 35, ch. 39; *Flóamanna saga,* ch. 16; *Gull-Þóris saga,* ch.

18; *Harðar saga ok Hólmverja,* ch. 38; *Þórðar saga hreðu,* ch. 9; *Ólafs saga helga,* ch. 61, ch. 118; *Haralds saga Sigurðarsonar,* ch. 94.

90. Karnell, ed., *Gotland's Picture Stones*; Swedish National Heritage Board, accessed Feb 4, 2020, http:// kmb.raa.se/cocoon/bild/show-image.html?id=1600 1000033846.

91. *Ólafs saga helga,* ch. 213; *Laxdæla saga,* ch. 30; *Haralds saga hárfagra,* ch. 40.

92. *Brennu-Njáls saga,* ch. 54.

93. Ibid., ch. 19, ch. 30.

94. William R. Short and Hurstwic, unpublished research, Jan. 31, 2020, and Sept. 3, 2020. Measurements of moment of inertia at the hand were made for a replica Viking sword, sax, spear, one-handed axe, and two-handed axe.

95. *Eyrbyggja saga,* ch. 18.

96. *Brennu-Njáls saga,* ch. 150.

97. Ibid., ch. 146.

98. *Grettis saga,* ch. 43; *Þórðar saga hreðu,* ch. 9.

99. Moilanen, *Marks*, 99-100.

100. Brunning, *Sword,* 76.

101. Joachim Meyer, *The Art of Combat: A German Martial Arts Treatise of 1570,* tr. Jeffrey L. Forgeng (London: Greenhill Books, 2006), 57-60.

102. William R. Short and Hurstwic, unpublished research, Jan. 3, 2019. We used our standardized procedure for measurements of the impact delivered by a weapon to a target as outlined in the sax chapter.

103. "Short Edge Sword Cut to a Limb," *Viking Weapon Test Cuts,* Hurstwic, Mar. 16, 2012, YouTube, accessed Oct. 15, 2019, https://www.youtube.com/watch?v= juIw20z5p0c; "Short Edge Sword Cut to the Neck," *Viking Weapon Test Cuts,* Hurstwic, Mar. 16, 2012, YouTube, accessed Oct. 15, 2019, https://www.youtube. com/watch?v=juIw20z5p0c.

104. *Óláfs saga Tryggvasonar,* ch. 109.

105. Saxo, *History of the Danes,* bk. 4, 109; Saxo Grammaticus, *Geste Danorum,* ed. Alfred Holder (Strassborg, Germany: K. J. Trubner, 1886), bk. 4, 116.

106. William R. Short and Hurstwic, unpublished research, Jan. 3, 2019. We used our standardized procedure for measurements of the impact delivered by a weapon to a target as outlined in the sax chapter. Grips tested include hammer, handshape, finger over crossguard, finger over pommel.

107. *Bjarnar saga Hítdælakappa,* ch. 18, ch. 32; *Brennu-Njáls saga,* ch. 5, ch. 30, ch. 54, ch. 150; *Droplaugarsona saga,* ch. 10; *Egils saga Skalla-Grímssonar,* ch. 58, ch. 66; *Eyrbyggja saga,* ch. 37; *Finnboga saga ramma,* ch. 27; *Fljótsdæla saga,* ch. 16; *Gísla saga Súrssonar,* ch. 34; *Grettis saga,* ch. 48; *Laxdæla saga,* ch. 55.

108. *Brennu-Njáls saga,* ch. 146; *Grettis saga,* ch. 19; *Droplaugarsona saga,* ch. 15.

109. *Kormáks saga*, ch. 14; *Fóstbræðra saga*, ch. 9; *Egils saga Skalla-Grímssonar*, ch. 66; *Hávarðar saga Ísfirðing*, ch. 21; *Göngu-Hrólfs saga*, ch. 6.

110. William R. Short and Hurstwic, unpublished research, Apr. 18, 2017. We used our standardized procedure for measurements of the impact delivered by a weapon to a target as outlined in the sax chapter.

111. William R. Short and Hurstwic, unpublished research, July 6, 2018. The methodology for creating and analyzing the database of weapons and weapons use in the *Sagas of Icelanders* is described in the appendix.

112. *Brennu-Njáls saga*, ch. 84; *Droplaugarsona saga*, ch. 13; *Egils saga Skalla-Grímssonar,* ch. 44; *Víglundar saga*, ch. 5; *Þórðar saga hreðu*, ch. 9; *Finnboga saga ramma*, ch. 35; *Ólafs saga helga*, ch. 153; *Haralds saga gráfeldar*, ch. 14; Saxo, *History of the Danes*, bk. 2, 64.

113. William R. Short and Hurstwic, unpublished research, July 6, 2018. The methodology for creating and analyzing the database of weapons and weapons use in the *Sagas of Icelanders* is described in the appendix.

114. William R. Short and Hurstwic, unpublished research, May 18, 2017. We used our standardized procedure for measurements of the impact delivered by a weapon to a target as outlined in the sax chapter.

115. *Grettis saga*, ch. 82; *Hænsna-Þóris saga*, ch. 10; *Vatnsdæla saga*, ch. 32; *Droplaugarsona saga*, ch. 4.

116. *Heiðarvíga saga*, ch. 37; *Þórarins þáttur ofsa*.

117. *Brennu-Njáls saga*, ch. 145; *Hávarðar saga Ísfirðing*, ch. 12; *Þórðar saga hreðu*, ch. 4, ch. 5.

118. *Kormáks saga*, ch. 10; *Heiðarvíga saga*, ch. 30; *Gunnlaugs saga ormstungu*, ch. 11; *Gísla saga Súrssonar*, ch. 1.

119. Moilanen, *Marks*, 99-100.

120. Study of a swords in a private collection, Jan. 8, 2011.

121. *Kormáks saga*, ch. 11.

122. Moilanen, *Marks*, 100.

123. William R. Short and Hurstwic, unpublished research, Jan. 8, 2019. In our research lab, test subjects performed combative defensive drills, using the sword as a defense, with the goal of blocking with the flat if possible, but blocking regardless. After each round, subjective comments were recorded from the test subjects. We also fought rounds of simulated combat, with both combatants using only swords and no other defensive tool. The swords were wrapped with a thin layer of tape that was abraded when struck, allowing us after each round to inspect and count where the hits were made to the sword blade to determine if the flat or edge or some combination was used for the defense. After each round, subjective comments were recorded from the two test subjects.

## CHAPTER 7: SPEAR

1. Knut Heille, ed., *The Cambridge History of Scandinavia*, vol.1 (Cambridge: Cambridge University Press, 2003), 44-45.

2. Ibid., 58.

3. Cleasby et al., eds., *Icelandic-English Dictionary*, 583, s.v. "spjót"; ibid., 196, s.v. "geirr."

4. *Helgakviða Hundingsbana II*, prose passage between v. 29-30; *Skáldskaparmál*, ch. 35; *Egils saga Skalla-Grímssonar*, ch. 79, "Sonatorrek," v. 22; Simek, *Dictionary of Northern Mythology*, 124, s.v. "Gungnir"; *Skáldskaparmál*, ch. 35; *Sigurdrífamál*, v. 17.

5. Vitlycke Museum, *The Rock Carvings at Litsleby*, 2018), accessed Mar. 11, 2020, https://www.vitlycke-museum.se/en/world-heritage-tanum/the-rock-carvings-at-litsleby/

6. *Völuspá*, v. 24; *Eyrbyggja saga*, ch. 44.

7. *Styrbjarnar þáttr Svíakappa*, ch. 2; Simek, *Dictionary of Northern Mythology*, 242, s.v. "Odin"; *Ynglinga saga*, ch. 6.

8. *Hávamál*, v. 138-139; *Gautreks saga*, ch. 7; *Víkarsbálkr*, v. 3.

9. *Ynglinga saga*, ch. 9; Simek, *Dictionary of Northern Mythology*, 102-104, s.v. "Geirahöð," "Geiravör," "Geirdriful," "Geirönul," "Geirskögull."

10. *Skáldskaparmál*, ch. 49; Kari Ellen Gade, "(Introduction to) Sturla Þórðarson, *Hákonarkviða*" in Gade, ed., *Poetry from the Kings' Sagas 2,* 699-727; McTurk, "(Introduction to) Anonymous, *Krákumál*," in Clunies, ed., *Poetry in fornaldarsögur*, 706.

11. Larsen, tr., *Earliest Norwegian Law, Gulathing Law* title 309, 196.

12. Petersen, *De Norske Vikingesverd*, 22-36.

13. L. Thålin, "En ångermanlåndsk spjutspets," in *Nordsvensk forntid: Studies in North Swedish Archaeology*, ed. H. Christianson and A Hyenstrand (Umeå, Sweden: Kungliga skytteanska samfundet, 1969), 185-196.

14. Hj. Stolpe and T. J. Arne, *Grafffältet vid Vendel* (Stockholm: K. L. Beckmans Boktryckeri, 1912), 35, accessed Nov. 4, 2019, https://babel.hathitrust.org/cgi/pt?id=njp.32101047115793&view=1up&seq=45.

15. *Laxdæla saga*, ch. 64; *Laxdæla saga*, ch. 55; *Grettis saga*, ch. 19.

16. *Grettis saga*, ch. 45.

17. Ibid., ch. 19; *Laxdæla saga*, ch. 55; *Egils saga Skalla-Grímssonar*, ch. 58.

18. Kristján, *Kuml og haugfé*, 338-344; Þjóðminjasafn Íslands Þ95-6/1995-357-368, accessed Oct. 1, 2020, https://sarpur.is/Adfang.aspx?AdfangID=1542710.

19. Universitetsmuseene C28432, accessed Mar. 3, 2021, https://www.unimus.no/portal/#/things/766d3c3e-4be4-442e-8fe6-0e474d69e128; Universitetsmuseene C19075, accessed Mar. 3, 2021, https://www.unimus.no/portal/#/photos/b0afb730-11d7-4315-9b5a-a54c1e033bca; private collection, spears examined Mar. 18, 2008, Sept. 8, 2018.

20. Lee A. Jones (contributor to *Swords of the Viking Age*), personal communication with William R. Short, Mar. 14, 2020.

21. Þjóðminjasafn Íslands 12094/1937-49, accessed Jan. 26, 2020, https://www.sarpur.is/Adfang.aspx?AdfangID=333270; Kristján, *Kuml og haugfé*, 342-343, figs.189-190.

22. Joseph Strutt, *The Sports and Pastimes of the People of England: From the Earliest Period, Including the Rural and Domestic Recreations, May Games, Mummeries, Pageants, Processions and Pompous Spectacles* (London: Methuen, 1903), 13-14.

23. *Droplaugarsona saga*, ch. 10.

24. *Grettis saga*, ch. 19.

25. *Gull-Þóris saga*, ch. 10.

26. Cleasby et al., eds., *Icelandic-English Dictionary*, 356, s.v. "krókr."

27. William R. Short and Hurstwic, unpublished research, May 14, 2019, May 11, 2017. Test subjects performed rounds of simulated combat with training partners. Test subjects used spears fitted with wings of varying sizes, and partners could choose any weapon or weapon combination of their choice. During the round, the number of uses of the spear wings was counted. After the round, subjective comments from the two fighters were recorded. Video of the rounds was studied for further insights.

28. Kristján, *Kuml og haugfé*, 343, figs. 189-192.

29. Private collection, examined Dec. 24, 2005.

30. *Gísla saga Súrssonar*, ch. 11; *Gull-Þóris saga*, ch. 4; *Laxdæla saga*, ch. 21; *Ólafs saga helga*, ch. 123.

31. Kristján, *Kuml og haugfé*, 338; Þjóðminjasafn Íslands number 1960-84, accessed Mar. 15, 2020, https://www.sarpur.is/Adfang.aspx?AdfangID=311606.

32. Cleasby et al., eds., *Icelandic-English Dictionary*, 220, s.v. "gullrekinn."

33. *Gull-Þóris saga*, ch. 8; *Hallfreðar saga vandræðaskálds*, ch. 4; *Vígu-Glúms saga*, ch. 6; *Þórðar saga hreðu*, ch. 8; *Þorsteins saga hvíta*, ch. 7; *Ólafs saga helga*, ch. 123, ch. 141, ch. 215.

34. Private collection, examined July 1, 2008.

35. Historiska museet SHM 15928, accessed Sept. 25, 2020, http://mis.historiska.se/mis/sok/fid.asp?fid=914435; Rundata G 225, accessed Sept. 25, 2020, https://rundata.info.

36. *Gísla saga Súrssonar*, ch. 6; *Króka-Refs saga*, ch. 16.

37. Karnell, ed., *Gotland's Picture Stones*; British Museum 1867,0120.1, Franks Casket, accessed Mar. 12, 2020, https://research.britishmuseum.org/research/collection_online/collection_object_details.aspx?objectId=92560&partId=1; Denny and Filmer-Sankey, *Bayeux Tapestry*, scene 56, scene 57.

38. William R. Short and Hurstwic, unpublished research, Aug. 22, 2017. We used our standardized procedure for measurements of the impact delivered by a weapon to a target as outlined in the sax chapter. We used spears fitted with nominally identical heads having shafts 1.07 m, 1.47m, and 1.98 m long (42 in, 58 in, and 78 in).

39. William R. Short and Hurstwic, unpublished research, Aug 22, 2017. Test subjects fought rounds of simulated combat. The test subjects alternated between spears with nominally the same head but with shaft lengths of 1.07 m, 1.47m, and 1.98 m (42 in, 58 in, and 78 in). Most rounds were fought with spear only, although some rounds were fought spear and shield. Their training partners were free to choose any weapon or weapon combination they wished for each round, including a spear. After the rounds, subjective comments were recorded from the combatants. Video of the rounds was reviewed to gain further insight on the capabilities and differences between the shaft lengths.

40. William R. Short and Hurstwic, unpublished research, Jan. 31, 2020, Sept. 3, 2020. The moment of inertia and its physical meaning is discussed earlier in the sword chapter.

41. Kulturhistorisk museum, Oslo C34256, accessed Nov. 8, 2019, http://www.unimus.no/arkeologi/forskning/index_katalog.php?museum=KHM&museumsnr=C34256&id=80524.

42. *Finnboga saga ramma*, ch. 31; *Fóstbræðra saga*, ch. 12; *Brennu-Njáls saga*, ch. 45, ch. 79; *Grettis saga*, ch. 66, ch. 82.

43. *Finnboga saga ramma*, ch. 32.

44. William R. Short and Hurstwic, unpublished research, Mar. 24, 2018. Combatants fought one-on-one rounds of simulated combat with weapons of their choice in a team competition event. An unintended hit to a spear cleanly severed the shaft.

45. William R. Short and Hurstwic, unpublished research, Feb. 21, 2019, Oct. 11, 2018. Test subjects cut with a sharp replica sword to a spear shaft either held in the hands or in a test stand simulating a human grip on the spear. High-speed video was used to analyze the details of the cut and the subsequent failure and breakage of the spear shaft.

46. *Vatnsdæla saga*, ch. 40; *Egils saga Skalla-Grímssonar*, ch. 53.

47. Þjóðminjasafn Íslands number 216/1865-23, accessed Mar. 15, 2020, https://www.sarpur.is/Adfang.aspx?AdfangID=329170.

48. Kulturhistorisk museum, Oslo C34256, accessed Nov. 8, 2019, http://www.unimus.no/arkeologi/forskning/index_katalog.php?museum=KHM&museumsnr=C34256&id=80524.

49. Private collection, examined Mar. 18, 2008.

50. *Grettis saga*, ch. 48; *Fljótsdæla saga*, ch. 16.

51. Universitetsmuseene C1158, http://www.musit.uio.no/artefacts/khm/search/?oid=1331&museumsnr=C1

158&f=html (accessed Oct. 1, 2020); spears from a private collection, examined Mar. 18, 2008, Sept. 8, 2018.

52. *Bjarnar saga Hítdælakappa*, ch. 18, ch. 25; *Brennu-Njáls saga*, ch. 36, ch. 45, ch. 79, ch. 84; *Egils saga Skalla-Grímssonar*, ch. 53; *Finnboga saga ramma*, ch. 27; *Grettis saga*, ch. 45, ch. 48; *Gull-Þóris saga*, ch. 8; *Hávarðar saga Ísfirðing*, ch. 9; *Þórðar saga hreðu*, ch. 7; *Þorsteins saga hvíta*, ch. 6.

53. Historiska museet SHM 13127:2, accessed Sept. 25, 2020, http://mis.historiska.se/mis/sok/fid.asp?fid=108188; Marianne Vedeler, "The Textile Interior in the Oseberg Burial Chamber," in *A Stitch in Time: Essays in Honour of Lise Bender Jørgensen* (Gothenburg, Sweden: Gothenburg University, Department of Historical Studies, 2014), 281-299.

54. Hunningestenen, Gotlands Museum GFC9286, accessed Sept 26, 2020, http://samlingarna.gotlandsmuseum.se/index.php/Detail/objects/86188.

55. Rygh, *Norske oldsager*, fig. 602.

56. *Brennu-Njáls saga*, ch. 130, ch. 157.

57. *Gull-Þóris saga*, ch. 13.

58. *Grettis saga*, ch. 19; *Eyrbyggja saga*, ch. 44.

59. William R. Short and Hurstwic, unpublished research, Aug 18, 2018. The methodology for creating and analyzing the database of weapons and weapons use in the *Sagas of Icelanders* is described in the appendix.

60. *Egils saga Skalla-Grímssonar*, ch. 53, ch. 58; *Grettis saga*, ch. 19, ch. 45, ch. 82; *Brennu-Njáls saga*, ch. 42, ch. 84, ch. 145, ch. 157; *Fóstbræðra saga*, ch. 8; *Gísla saga Súrssonar*, ch. 7, ch. 17; *Þorsteins saga hvíta*, ch. 6; *Droplaugarsona saga*, ch. 10; *Gull-Þóris saga*, ch. 8; *Harðar saga og Hólmverja*, ch. 33; *Króka-Refs saga*, ch. 16; *Laxdæla saga*, ch. 55; *Ólafs saga helga*, ch. 133.

61. *Eyrbyggja saga*, ch. 45.

62. "Spear thrust to the ribs," *Viking Weapon Test Cuts*, Hurstwic, Mar. 16, 2012, YouTube, accessed Oct. 15, 2019, https://www.youtube.com/watch?v=juIw20z5p0c.

63. *Grettis saga*, ch. 19; *Egils saga Skalla-Grímssonar*, ch. 53, ch. 70.

64. *Finnboga saga ramma*, ch. 41; *Vopnfirðinga saga*, ch. 14.

65. *Brennu-Njáls saga*, ch. 146; *Valla-Ljóts saga*, ch. 1.

66. Karnell, ed., *Gotland's Picture Stones*; Rundata Ög 181, accessed Sept. 27, 2020, https://skaldic.abdn.ac.uk/db.php?id=15695&if=srdb&table=mss.

67. Denny and Filmer-Sankey, *Bayeux Tapestry*, scene 52a, scene 52b.

68. William R. Short and Hurstwic, unpublished research, May 18, 2017. We used our standardized procedure for measurements of the impact delivered by a weapon to a target as outlined in the sax chapter.

69. William R. Short and Hurstwic, unpublished research, Mar. 14, 2019. Test subjects fought rounds of simulated combat armed with a spear or a spear and a sword. Their practice partners were free to choose any weapon or combination of weapons. After each round, subjective comments from the two fighters were recorded. Video of the rounds was studied for further insights.

70. *Völuspá*, v. 24; *Ólafs saga Tryggvasonar*, ch. 85; *King's Mirror*, ch. 37, 213.

71. *Bjarnar saga Hítdælakappa*, ch. 26, ch. 32; *Brennu-Njáls saga*, ch. 5, ch. 102, ch. 145; *Fljótsdæla saga*, ch. 12; *Gísla saga Súrssonar*, ch. 20; *Gull-Þóris saga*, ch. 15; *Hávarðar saga Ísfirðing*, ch. 11; *Króka-Refs saga*, ch. 15; *Reykdæla saga og Víga-Skútu*, ch. 11; *Valla-Ljóts saga*, ch. 7; *Þórðar saga hreðu*, ch. 9, ch. 11; *Ólafs saga helga*, ch. 123.

72. *Brennu-Njáls saga* ch. 5, ch. 30; *Egils saga Skalla-Grímssonar*, ch. 57; *Króka-Refs saga*, ch. 15; *Ólafs saga Tryggvasonar*, ch. 41.

73. *Hákonar saga Aðalsteinsfóstra*, ch. 30; *Ólafs saga helga*, ch. 112, ch. 226.

74. *Reykdæla saga ok Víga-Skútu*, ch. 11, ch. 24; *Bjarnar saga Hítdælakappa*, ch. 26.

75. *Eyrbyggja saga*, ch. 62; *Vatnsdæla saga*, ch. 30.

76. *Gísla saga Súrssonar*, ch. 20; *Fljótsdæla saga*, ch. 12; *Víglundar saga*, ch. 16; *Fljótsdæla saga*, ch. 18.

77. *Brennu-Njáls saga*, ch. 145, ch. 150; *Bjarnar saga Hítdælakappa*, ch. 32.

78. *Eyrbyggja saga*, ch. 44.

79. *Brennu-Njáls saga*, ch. 92.

80. *Reykdæla saga ok Víga-Skútu*, ch. 24.

81. Wikipedia, s.v. "Javelin throw," accessed Jan. 23, 2020, https://en.wikipedia.org/w/index.php?title=Javelin_throw&oldid=928608770.

82. William R. Short and Hurstwic, unpublished research, Aug. 31, 2019. In a public event, guests were invited to throw spears for distance on a range set up over level ground. The authors are grateful to Arms & Armor of Minneapolis for providing the spears used in this experiment. We recorded each test subject's age, own assessment of ability and experience, and distance for three throws, from the release mark to where the point hit the ground. Throws that did not hit point first were discarded. Video was shot of each throw to allow an estimate of release speed to be made for each throw.

83. William R. Short and Hurstwic, unpublished research, Sept. 11, 2019. A simple computer model of the ballistic flight of a spear was created.

84. *Ólafs saga Tryggvason*, ch. 40, ch. 107; *Ólafs saga helga*, ch. 231.

85. William R. Short and Hurstwic, unpublished research, Feb. 9, 2014. In a simulated combat situation, teams of combatants fought multiple rounds where the teams started on opposite sides of a creek, out of weapon range unless the weapons were thrown. Each team had multiple spearmen. At the end of the rounds, subjective comments from the teams of fighters were

recorded. Video of the rounds was recorded and analyzed later.

86. William R. Short and Hurstwic, unpublished research, July 8, 2018. The methodology for creating and analyzing the database of weapons and weapons use in the *Sagas of Icelanders* is described in the appendix.

87. *Eyrbyggja saga*, ch. 62; *Fljótsdæla saga*, ch. 11; *Kjalnesinga saga*, ch. 16; *Reykdæla saga og Víga-Skútu*, ch. 24; Saxo, *History of the Danes*, bk. 1, 27; *Waltharius*, ed. and tr. Abram Ring (Leuven, Belgium: Peeters, 2016), 103, lines 764-769.

88. *Fljótsdæla saga*, ch. 12.

89. Cleasby et al., eds., *Icelandic-English Dictionary*, 577, s.v. "snæri."

90. William R. Short and Hurstwic, unpublished research, July 31, 2018, July 20, 2018, July 15, 2018, May 6, 2017. We used our standardized procedure for measurements of the impact delivered by a weapon to a target as outlined in the sax chapter. Velocity measurements were made using high-speed video of the flight of the *snærisspjót* averaged over several throws by several test subjects. Accuracy was tested by throwing to a target from 10 m (33 ft) and 15 m (49 ft) distances and scoring the throws, averaged over multiple throws by multiple test subjects.

91. William R. Short and Hurstwic, unpublished research, July 31, 2018, July 20, 2018, July 15, 2018. High-speed video was recorded of the launch and of the flight of a conventional spear and several variants of a *snærisspjót*.

92. *Áns saga bogasveigis*, ch. 4.

93. Þjóðminjasafn Íslands Þ95-6/1995-357-368, accessed Oct. 1, 2020, https://sarpur.is/Adfang.aspx?AdfangID=1542710.

94. *Bjarnar saga Hítdælakappa*, ch. 32; *Hallfreðar saga vandræðaskálds*, ch. 10; *Brennu-Njáls saga*, ch. 30, ch. 54, ch. 86, ch. 129, ch. 145, ch. 150; *Gísla saga Súrssonar*, ch. 20.

95. *Brennu-Njáls saga*, ch. 77.

96. William R. Short and Hurstwic, unpublished research, Mar. 19, 2016, May 31, 2016, June 28, 2016, Sept. 3, 2016, Sept. 8, 2016, June 13, 2017. The move was tested between pairs of cooperative training partners. Once the basic skill was learned, the pressure was increased by increasing the tempo, power, and intent of the throws. Pressure was increased further by creating a drill equivalent to "spear dodgeball" in which teams armed with many spears attempted to throw and hit members of the opposite team to force them out of the game for the round. Catching and returning a spear put the thrower out of the round. Next, teams of combatants armed with spears fought rounds of simulated combat on opposite sides of a barrier that could not be easily crossed. A point system rewarded the catching and returning of spears. Lastly, teams of

combatants armed with spears and other weapons fought rounds of simulated combat on landscapes having natural barriers, such as on opposite sides of a stream that could not easily be crossed. Catching and returning a spear was encouraged. At the end of the rounds of simulated combat, subjective comments from the teams of fighters were recorded. Video of the rounds was recorded and analyzed later.

97. William R. Short and Hurstwic, unpublished research, July 8, 2018. The methodology for creating and analyzing the database of weapons and weapons use in the *Sagas of Icelanders* is described in the appendix.

98. William R. Short and Hurstwic, unpublished research, Aug. 18, 2018. The methodology for creating and analyzing the database of weapons and weapons use in the *Sagas of Icelanders* is described in the appendix.

99. William R. Short and Hurstwic, unpublished research, Jan 31, 2020; Sept. 3, 2020. The measurement of moment of inertia and the computer modeling of weapons during a cut is discussed in the sword chapter.

100. The center of percussion of a weapon or tool can be measured, but it can also be calculated using a mathematical model of the weapon. When using a model of a Viking spear, the center of percussion is calculated to be in front of the point. In practice, when measuring a physical spear, the vibration at the place where the spear is gripped that results from a hit with the spear decreases as the hit is made closer and closer to the point of the spear. But there is no minimum that rises on either side as observed on a sword, where the center of percussion is a point on the blade.

101. William R. Short and Hurstwic, unpublished research, Jan. 31, 2020; Sept. 3, 2020.

102. William R. Short and Hurstwic, unpublished research, Sept. 10, 2019, Apr. 19, 2018, Aug. 22, 2017. We used our standardized procedure for measurements of the impact delivered by a weapon to a target as outlined in the sax chapter.

103. "Sword cut to the ribs," *Viking Weapon Test Cuts*, Hurstwic, Mar. 16, 2012, YouTube, accessed Oct. 15, 2019, https://www.youtube.com/watch?v=juIw20z5p0c.

104. *Brennu-Njáls saga*, ch. 5, ch. 146; *Fóstbræðra saga*, ch. 8, ch. 12.

105. William R. Short and Hurstwic, unpublished research, July 8, 2018. The methodology for creating and analyzing the database of weapons and weapons use in the *Sagas of Icelanders* is described in the appendix.

106. *Egils saga Skalla-Grímssonar*, ch. 58.

107. *Ólafs saga Tryggvasonar*, ch. 78; *Magnúss saga góða*, ch. 30; *Haralds saga Sigurðarsonar*, ch. 72, ch. 87.

108. *Af Upplendinga konungum*, ch. 2; *Egils saga einhenda ok Ásmundar berserkjabana*, ch. 7.

109. *Sverris saga*, ch. 48.

110. *Ólafs saga helga*, ch. 213.

111. *Egils saga Skalla-Grímssonar,* ch. 53.

112. *Brennu-Njáls saga,* ch. 30.

113. Cleasby et al., eds., *Icelandic-English Dictionary,* 25-29, s.v. "at."

114. *Egils saga Skalla-Grímssonar,* ch. 58; *Egils saga einhenda ok Ásmundar berserkjabana,* ch. 7.

115. *Göngu-Hrólfs saga,* ch. 8.

116. Diana Whaley, ed., "Eindriði Einarsson, Lausavísa 1," in Whaley, ed., *Poetry from the Kings' Sagas 1,* 806; Valgerður Erna Þorvaldsdóttir, ed., "Anonymous Poems, *Brúðkaupsvísur 4,*" in Margaret Clunies Ross, ed., *Poetry on Christian Subjects,* Skaldic Poetry of the Scandinavian Middle Ages 7 (Turnhout, Belgium: Brepols, 2007), 531-532.

117. Oscar Brenner, ed., *Speculum regale,* AM 243 fol. B (München: Christian Kaiser, 1881), ch. 37, 102, accessed Nov. 10, 2019, http://www.septentrionalia.net/etexts/speculum.pdf.

118. *Göngu-Hrólfs saga,* ch. 8; *Bósa saga og herrauðs,* ch. 14.

119. *Brennu-Njáls saga,* ch. 30.

120. Ibid., ch. 63; *Landnámabók,* S. 168.

121. *Brennu-Njáls saga,* ch. 63, ch. 79; *Göngu-Hrölfs saga,* ch. 8.

122. William R. Short and Hurstwic, unpublished research, July 8, 2018. The methodology for creating and analyzing the database of weapons and weapons use in the *Sagas of Icelanders* is described in the appendix.

123. Private collection, examples examined Sept. 8, 2018.

124. *Króka-Refs saga,* ch. 8.

## CHAPTER 8: ARCHERY

1. Cleasby et al., eds., *Icelandic-English Dictionary,* 72, s.v. "bogi," s.v. "boginn."

2. Kim Hjardar and Vegard Vike, *Vikings at War,* tr. Frank Stewart (Oxford, UK: Casemate Publishers, 2016), 181-182.

3. Harm Paulsen, "Pfiel und Bogen in Haithabu," *Berichte Haithabu* 33 (1999): 95-107.

4. *Egils saga Skalla-Grímssonar,* ch. 61; *Guðrúnarkviða II,* v. 18.

5. *Rígsþula,* v. 26, v. 33; *Ragnars saga Loðbrók,* ch. 12.

6. Paulsen, "Pfiel und Bogen in Haithabu," 95-100.

7. Ibid., 125, 135.

8. *Örvar-Odds saga,* ch. 25; *Áns saga bogsveigis,* ch. 1.

9. *Magnússona saga,* ch. 21.

10. *Ólafs saga Tryggvasonar,* ch. 21, ch. 108.

11. *Örvar-Odds saga,* ch. 25.

12. *Friðþjófs saga,* ch. 4.

13. *Hávamál,* v. 85.

14. Russell Poole, "(Introduction to) Anonymous, *Liðsmannaflokkr*" in Whaley, ed., *Poetry from the Kings' Sagas 1,* 1014; Cleasby et al., eds., *Icelandic-English Dictionary,* 756, s.v. "þömb"; *Ólafs saga helga,* ch. 21.

15. *Rígsþula* v. 28; *Brennu-Njáls saga,* ch. 77.

16. *Miscellany on the life of St. Edmund,* Pierpont Morgan Library, MS M.736, fol. 14r, ca.1130, accessed Apr. 7, 2020, http://corsair.morganlibrary.org/icaimages/7/m736.014r.jpg.

17. Paulsen, "Pfiel und Bogen in Haithabu," 95-99.

18. *Brennu-Njáls saga,* ch. 89; *Örvar-Odds saga,* ch. 16; *Þorsteins saga Víkingssonar,* ch. 25.

19. *Ragnars saga Loðbrók,* ch. 5.

20. *Áns saga bogasveigis,* ch. 6.

21. *Brennu-Njáls saga,* ch. 77.

22. Ibid., ch. 19.

23. Sarpur, Sjóminjasafn Austurlands, 1992-23, accessed Oct. 26, 2020, https://www.sarpur.is/Adfang.aspx?AdfangID=1997646; Byggðasafnið Skógum, S-3221, accessed Oct. 26, 2020, https://www.sarpur.is/Adfang.aspx?AdfangID=1984189; Minjasafnið Bustarfelli, 1994-3, accessed Oct. 26, 2020, https://www.sarpur.is/Adfang.aspx?AdfangID=2102819; Byggðasafn Akranesi, 2005-18-1, accessed Oct. 26, 2020, https://www.sarpur.is/Adfang.aspx?AdfangID=1982617.

24. William R. Short and Hurstwic, unpublished research, Apr. 22, 2017. Human hair was twisted into a string and spliced into a cut bowstring. Several test subjects used the bow with a normal, unbroken string and with the repaired string to shoot for accuracy to a target. Scores were averaged over multiple shots and multiple test subjects. The energy delivered by the arrow to the target was measured using our normal test apparatus and protocol, described in a note in the sax chapter. The speed of flight of the arrow as it left the bow was measured using high-speed video. Measured speeds were averaged over multiple shots and multiple test subjects. The test was flawed by using a bow with a lighter draw weight than would be typical for the Viking age because of safety limitations in our indoor shooting range. We hope an interested reader will repeat the test with a more representative bow.

25. *Finnboga saga ramma,* ch. 8; *Laxdæla saga,* ch. 62.

26. Hjardar and Vike, *Vikings at War,* 182-183.

27. *Hervarar saga ok Heiðreks,* ch. 13.

28. Fredrik Lundström et al., "Eastern Archery in Birka's Garrison," in *The Martial Society: Aspects of Warriors, Fortifications and Social Change in Scandinavia,* ed. Lena Holmquist Olausson and Michael Olausson (Stockholm: Stockholm University, 2009), 105-116; Arbman, *Birka,* 1:463-465, Bj1125B; Hjardar and Vike, *Vikings at War,* 183; Charlotte Hedenstierna-Jonson and Lena Holmquist Olausson, *The Oriental Mounts from Birka's Garrison: An Expression of Warrior Rank and Status* (Stockholm: Almqvist & Wiksell, 2006), 66-67.

29. Lundström et al., "Eastern Archery in Birka's Garrison," 105-116; Kristján, *Kuml og haugfé,* 422-423, Þjms 329/1866-26, accessed Apr. 7, 2020, https://www.

sarpur.is/Adfang.aspx?AdfangID=340965; Short, *Viking Weapons*, 173-174.

30. Cleasby et al., eds., *Icelandic-English Dictionary*, 765-766, s.v. "ör."

31. Rygh, *Norske oldsager*, figs. 533-551.

32. Ibid.

33. Ibid., fig. 542; Arbman, *Birka*, Bj 198, vol. 1, 81, plate 12-5; Bj 754, vol. 1, 275, plate 12-6.

34. *Hákonar saga Aðalsteinsfóstra*, ch. 31; Snorri Sturluson, *Hákonar saga góða*, from *Heimskringla*, ed. Bjarni Aðalbjarnarson, Íslenzk fornrit v. 26 (Reykjavík: Hið íslenzka fornritafélag, 1951), ch. 31, 190n2.

35. Rygh, *Norske oldsager*, fig. 551.

36. Paulsen, "Pfiel und Bogen in Haithabu," 116-118.

37. *Ólafs saga helga*, ch. 21; Snorri Sturluson, *Ólafs saga helga*, ed. Bjarni Aðalbjarnarson, Íslenzk fornrit v. 27 (Reykjavík: Hið íslenzka fornritafélag, 2002), ch. 21, 27n2; Cleasby et al., eds., *Icelandic-English Dictionary*, 353, s.v. "kólfr," 555, s.v. "skot."

38. Cleasby et al., eds., *Icelandic-English Dictionary*, 353, s.v. "kólfr."

39. Larsen, tr., *Earliest Norwegian Law*, Gulathing Law title 240, 160; *Fóstbrœðra saga*, ch. 24; Paulsen, "Pfiel und Bogen in Haithabu," 111, fig. 13, no. 25, 113, fig. 14, no.1.

40. Rygh, *Norske oldsager*, fig. 545, fig. 549; Paulsen, "Pfiel und Bogen in Haithabu," fig.12-14.

41. Paulsen, "Pfiel und Bogen in Haithabu," 119-120; Dan Høj, *Bows & Arrows of the Vikings*, tr. David F. Drost et al. (Ribe, Denmark: Museum of Southwest Jutland, 2019), 95.

42. Hjardar and Vike, *Vikings at War*, 181.

43. Høj, *Bows & Arrows*, 62.

44. Paulsen, "Pfiel und Bogen in Haithabu," 118, fig. 14.8.

45. *Jómsvíkinga saga*, ch. 11.

46. Paulsen, "Pfiel und Bogen in Haithabu," 113, fig. 14; 115, fig. 14.

47. Ibid., 113, fig. 14.

48. Hjardar and Vike, *Vikings at War*, 181.

49. *Ketil saga Hœngs*, ch. 3; *Örvar-Odds saga*, ch. 11.

50. Larsen, tr., *Earliest Norwegian Law*, Gulathing Law title 309, 196.

51. *Áns saga bogsveigis*, ch. 4; *Örvar-Odds saga*, ch. 25.

52. *Örvar-Odds saga*, ch. 1.

53. Ibid., ch. 25; *Áns saga bogsveigis*, ch. 4; *Jómsvíkinga saga*, ch. 12.

54. *Örvar-Odds saga*, ch. 24.

55. Høj, *Bows & Arrows*, 54-57; *Örvar-Odds saga*, ch. 25; *Lögbók Íslendinga*, ed. Marteinn Arnoddsson (Hólar, 1709), Rekabálkr in *Jónsbók*, ch. 4, 322, accessed Oct. 15, 2020, https://ia903003.us.archive.org/25/items/LogbokIslendinga000210909v0JonsReyk/LogbokIslendinga000210909v0JonsReyk_orig.pdf.

56. Larsen, tr., *Earliest Norwegian Law*, Gulathing Law title 312, 197-198.

57. *Hákonar saga Aðalsteinsfóstra*, ch. 23; *Magnúss saga góða*, ch. 4.

58. *Ólafs saga helga*, ch. 39, ch. 94, ch. 112, ch. 120, ch. 121.

59. Larsen, tr., *Earliest Norwegian Law*, Gulathing Law title 156, 130-131.

60. *Magnúss saga blinda og Haralds gilla*, ch. 11; Jón, "Vikings in Spain," 31-46; Lundström et al., "Eastern Archery in Birka's Garrison," 109.

61. Cleasby et al., eds., *Icelandic-English Dictionary*, 409, s.v. "malr."

62. *Áns saga bogsveigis*, ch. 5; *Göngu-Hrólfs saga*, ch. 33; *Örvar-Odds saga*, ch. 1, ch. 5, ch. 11, ch. 14, ch. 16, ch. 17, ch. 20, ch. 24; *Orms þáttr Stórólfssonar*, ch. 9.

63. *Örvar-Odds saga*, ch. 3, ch. 11; *Jómsvíkinga saga*, ch. 11.

64. *Örvar-Odds saga*, ch. 1, ch. 24.

65. Denny and Filmer-Sankey, *Bayeux Tapestry*, scene 51b, scene 55, scene 56.

66. Olaus Magnus, *Historia de Gentibus Septentrionalibus* (Rome: Giovanni M. Viotto, 1555), bk. 5, ch. 29, 197, accessed Apr. 8, 2020, https://books.google.com/books?id=O9lEAAAAcAAJ&dq=inauthor%3A%22Olaus%20Magnus%22&pg=PP5#v=onepage&q&f=false.

67. Ibid., bk. 1, ch. 5, 14; bk. 20, ch. 17, 713.

68. Ibid., bk. 4, ch. 1, 130; Denny and Filmer-Sankey, *Bayeux Tapestry*, scene 51b.

69. *Brennu-Njáls saga*, ch. 72.

70. Paulsen, "Pfiel und Bogen in Haithabu," 120-121.

71. *Rígsþula*, v. 26, v. 33.

72. *Magnúss saga berfœtta*, ch. 10; *Haralds saga Sigurðarsonar*, ch. 63; *Ólafs saga Tryggvasonar*, ch. 109..

73. *Magnússona saga*, ch. 21.

74. *Sörla þáttur eða Héðans saga ok Högna*, ch. 6; *Örvar-Odds saga*, ch. 25, ch. 26.

75. *Hálfdánar saga Eysteinssonar*, ch. 7.

76. Larsen, tr., *Earliest Norwegian Law*, Gulathing Law title 309, 196; *Ólafs saga Tryggvasonar*, ch. 107; Kari Ellen Gade, "(Introduction to) Þorkell hamarskáld, *Magnússdrápa*," in Gade, ed., *Poetry from the Kings' Sagas 2*, 409-414; Russell Poole, "(Introduction to) Gunnlaugr Leifsson, *Merlínusspá I*," in Ross, ed., *Poetry in fornaldarsögur*, 38.

77. *Ólafs saga helga*, ch. 226.

78. *Brennu-Njáls saga*, ch. 19; *Hœnsa Þóris saga*, ch. 17.

79. *Skáldskaparmál*, ch. 14; *Gylfaginning*, ch. 31.

80. *Gylfaginning*, ch. 23.

81. *Ólafs saga helga*, ch. 21, ch. 82; *Magnússona saga*, ch. 21.

82. Olaus Magnus, *Historia de Gentibus Septentrionalibus*, bk. 4, ch. 12, 146.

83. Teresa Dröfn Freysdóttir Njarðvík, *Runes: The Icelandic Book of Fuþark* (Reykjavík: Icelandic Magic, 2018), 106-107.

84. Gunnar et al., eds., *Grágás Lagasafn íslenska þjóðveldisins*, 216, S. 277.

85. Þröstur Eysteinsson (director of forestry, Skógræktin), personal communication with William R. Short, Oct. 20, 2020; Skógræktin, *History of Forests in Iceland,* accessed Oct. 17, 2020, https://www.skogur.is/en/forestry/forestry-in-a-treeless-land/history-of-forests-in-iceland.

86. William R. Short and Hurstwic, unpublished research, Aug. 24, 2018. A statistical analysis was performed using data on Icelandic Viking-age weapons finds taken from Astrid Daxböck, "Viking Age Weapons in Iceland," (lecture, Þjóðminjasafn Íslands, Reykjavík, Sept. 30, 2008), and from Kristján, *Kuml og haugfé.*

87. William R. Short and Hurstwic, unpublished research, Apr. 9, 2020. A statistical analysis was performed using data compiled from Rundkvist, *Barshalder I.*

88. Hedenstierna-Jonson, "Birka Warrior," 73-75.

89. Kristján, *Kuml og haugfé,* 349.

90. *Fljótsdæla saga,* ch. 17; *Eyrbyggja saga,* ch. 45; *Hænsa-Þóris saga,* ch. 8.

91. *Hænsa-Þóris saga,* ch. 17; *Brennu-Njáls saga,* ch. 19.

92. *Brennu-Njáls saga,* ch. 77; *Hænsa-Þóris saga,* ch. 17; *Harðar saga ok Hólmverja,* ch. 31.

93. Simek, *Dictionary of Northern Mythology,* 339, s.v. "Ullr"; Rygh, *Norske oldsager,* fig. 551.

94. *Ólafs saga helga,* ch. 226; *Göngu-Hrólfs saga,* ch. 31.

95. *Hrana saga hrings,* ch. 14; *Göngu-Hrólfs saga,* ch. 31.

96. *Fornkonunga saga,* ch. 9; *Ólafs saga helga,* ch. 226.

97. *Haralds saga Sigurðarsonar,* ch. 89.

98. *Hákonar saga góða,* ch. 31.

99. *Magnúss saga berfætta,* ch. 25.

100. *Fóstbræðra saga,* ch. 24; *Fljótsdæla saga,* ch. 17.

101. *Magnúss saga blinda og Haralds gilla,* ch. 11; *Magnúss saga Erlingssonar,* ch. 40.

102. *Magnúss saga blinda og Haralds gilla,* ch. 11; *Magnúss saga Erlingssonar,* ch. 40; *Eyrbyggja saga,* ch. 62.

103. *Ólafs saga Tryggvason,* ch. 107.

104. *Fornkonunga saga,* ch. 8.

105. *Magnúss saga ins góða,* ch. 30.

106. *Ólafs saga Tryggvason,* ch. 108; *Haralds saga Sigurdarsonar,* ch. 63.

107. *Hrana saga hrings,* ch. 14; *Haralds saga Sigurðarsonar,* ch. 63; *Fornkonunga saga,* ch. 9.

108. Larsen, tr., *Earliest Norwegian Law, Gulathing Law* title 309, 196; Berge, "Hirðskrá 1-37," ch. 35, 69; *Brennu-Njáls saga,* ch. 72.

109. *Göngu-Hrólfs saga,* ch. 12; *Örvar-Odds saga,* ch. 3, ch. 11; *Göngu-Hrólfs saga,* ch. 33.

110. Lars Andersen (Viking archery researcher), personal communication with the authors, July 3, 2020.

111. *Brennu-Njáls saga,* ch. 72; *Fljótsdæla saga,* ch. 17.

112. *Ketil saga Hængs,* ch. 3; *Hrana saga hrings,* ch. 14; *Halfdánar saga,* ch. 7; *Sörla þáttur eða Héðans saga ok Högna,* ch. 6; Saxo, *History of the Danes,* bk. 5, 124.

113. *Ólafs saga helga,* ch. 21.

114. Snorri, *Ólafs saga helga,* ÍF v. 27, ch. 21, 27n2; Cleasby et al., eds., *Icelandic-English Dictionary,* 353, s.v. "kólfr."

115. *Hálfdánar saga Eysteinssonar,* ch. 7; *Örvar-Odds saga,* ch. 26.

116. *Hálfdánar saga Eysteinssonar,* ch. 7; *Göngu-Hrólfs saga,* ch.4.

117. *Ólafs saga helga,* ch. 21; *Hákonar saga Ívarssonar,* ch. 5; *Áns saga bogsveigis,* ch. 4, ch. 5; *Ólafs saga Tryggvasonar,* ch. 108.

118. Cleasby et al., eds., *Icelandic-English Dictionary,* 240, s.v. "harðr."

119. *Ólafs saga helga,* ch. 21.

120. Denny and Filmer-Sankey, *Bayeux Tapestry,* scene 56, scene 57; British Museum 1867, 0120.1

121. *Magnús saga Erlingssonar,* ch. 40; Saxo, *History of the Danes,* bk. 3, 71, bk. 8, 242.

122. *Áns saga bogasveigis,* ch. 4; *Eyrbyggja saga,* ch. 45; *Fljótsdæla saga,* ch. 17.

123. *Jómsvíkinga saga,* ch. 11.

124. *Göngu-Hrólfs saga,* ch. 31; *Hákons saga Aðalsteinsfóstra,* ch. 31; *Ólafs saga Tryggvasonar,* ch. 107; *Skáldskaparmál,* ch. 61.

125. British Museum 1867, 0120.1; Denny and Filmer-Sankey, *Bayeux Tapestry,* scene 55, scene 56.

126. Paulsen, "Pfiel und Bogen in Haithabu," 125, 135.

127. William R. Short and Hurstwic, unpublished research, Oct. 10, 2020. A simplified computer model was created based on a speculative reconstruction of the Hedeby bow and arrows.

128. *Hrana saga hrings,* ch. 14; *Göngu-Hrólfs saga,* ch. 31.

129. Cleasby et al., eds., *Icelandic-English Dictionary,* 56, s.v. "bein-skeyttr."

130. William R. Short and Hurstwic, unpublished research, Oct. 10, 2020. A simplified computer model was created based on a speculative reconstruction of the Hedeby bow and arrows.

131. Gunnar et al., eds., *Grágás Lagasafn íslenska þjóðveldisins,* 405, K. 48; 247, S. 321; 247n3.

132. *Landnámabók,* S. 348.

133. *Ólafs saga Tryggvasonar,* ch. 88, ch. 108.

134. *Magnúss saga ins góða,* ch. 30.

135. *Örvar-Odds saga,* ch. 26.

136. *Ólafs saga Tryggvasonar,* ch. 103; *Hænsa-Þóris saga,* ch. 8; *Ljósvetninga saga,* ch. 20; *Hænsa-Þóris saga,* ch. 17.

137. *Brennu-Njáls saga,* ch. 62.

138. *Göngu-Hrólfs saga,* ch. 12.

139. *Brennu-Njáls saga,* ch. 71, ch. 72.

140. *Eyrbyggja saga,* ch. 45.

141. *Fornkonunga saga,* ch. 9; *Jómsvíkinga saga,* ch. 11; *Ólafs saga Tryggvasonar,* ch. 108.

142. *Brennu-Njáls saga,* ch. 19.

143. *Áns saga bogasveigis,* ch. 7.

144. *Örvar-Odds saga*, ch. 25, ch. 26.

145. *Ólafs saga Tryggvason*, ch. 108; *Fljótsdæla saga*, ch. 17; *Áns saga bogasveigis*, ch. 4; *Yngvars saga viðförla*, ch. 6; *Þorsteins saga Víkingssonar*, ch. 23; *Örvar-Odds saga*, ch. 25; *Magnúss saga blinda og Haralds gilla*, ch. 11.

146. *Magnússona saga*, ch. 21.

147. *Ólafs saga Tryggvason*, ch. 108; *Brennu-Njáls saga*, ch. 63.

148. Rundata U855, accessed Oct. 12, 2020, https://skaldic.abdn.ac.uk/db.php?id=17665&if=srdb&table=mss; Karnell, ed., *Gotland's Picture Stones*, Klinte Hunninge I.

149. Böksta U855; British Museum 1867,0120.1; Denny and Filmer-Sankey, *Bayeux Tapestry*, scene 51b; Olaus Magnus, *Historia de Gentibus Septentrionalibus*, bk. 4, ch. 1, p. 130.

150. British Museum 1867,0120.1; Denny and Filmer-Sankey, *Bayeux Tapestry*, scene 51b; Olaus Magnus, *Historia de Gentibus Septentrionalibus*, bk. 4, ch. 1, 130.

151. Denny and Filmer-Sankey, *Bayeux Tapestry*, scene 51b; Olaus Magnus, *Historia de Gentibus Septentrionalibus*, bk. 4, ch. 1, 130.

152. British Museum 1867,0120.1; Olaus Magnus, *Historia de Gentibus Septentrionalibus*, bk. 3, ch. 7, 107.

153. William R. Short and Hurstwic, unpublished research, Mar. 6, 2021. Test subjects compared a pinch draw to a two-finger draw by shooting replica arrows from a replica bow of modest draw weight (65 lbs.). Accuracy at various ranges was recorded. The ability to shoot accurately with the low draw combined with the pinch draw was confirmed.

154. Rundata U855; British Museum 1867, 0120.1; Denny and Filmer-Sankey, *Bayeux Tapestry*, scene 51b; Olaus Magnus, *Historia de Gentibus Septentrionalibus*, bk. 4, ch. 1, p. 130.

155. "Lars Andersen: A New Level of Archery," Jan. 23, 2015, YouTube, accessed Apr. 14, 2020, https://www.youtube.com/watch?v=BEG-ly9tQGk; Lars Andersen, "Lars Andersen Reveals the Truth about the Most Viewed Archery Video Ever Made," May 18, 2020, YouTube, accessed Mar. 31, 2021, https://www.youtube.com/watch?v=i4mqt69VZ28.

## CHAPTER 9: SHIELD

1. *Brennu-Njáls saga*, ch. 63; *Fóstbræðra saga*, ch. 24; *Finnboga saga rama*, ch. 35.

2. *Ynglinga saga*, ch. 6.

3. *Svarfdæla saga*, ch. 7; *Grettis saga*, ch. 40; *Egils saga Skalla-Grímssonar*, ch. 65; *Vatnsdæla saga*, ch. 46.

4. Roesdahl and Wilson, eds., *Viking to Crusader*, cat. no. 615, 390-391.

5. *Ynglinga saga*, ch. 6; *Hávamál*, v. 82; Gunnar et al., eds., *Grágás Lagasafn íslenska þjóðveldisins*, 216, S. 277.

6. Cleasby et al., eds., *Icelandic-English Dictionary*, 553, s.v. "skjöldr."

7. *Skáldskaparmál*, ch. 21; *Völuspá*, v. 30; *Skáldskaparmál*, ch. 24; *Völuspá*, v. 47.

8. *Gylfaginning*, ch. 2, *Grímnismál*, v. 9; *Skáldskaparmál*, G55.

9. *Stjörnu-Odda draumr*, ch. 8.

10. Simek, *Dictionary of Northern Mythology*, 349, s.v. "valkyries."

11. *Brennu-Njáls saga*, ch. 63; *Áns saga bogsveigis*, ch. 4.

12. *Fóstbræðra saga*, ch. 17, ch. 24.

13. *Brennu-Njáls saga*, ch. 91; *Hrafnkells saga Freysgoða*, ch. 17; *Hávarðar saga Ísfirðings*, ch. 23; *Færeyjinga saga*, ch. 37; *Finnboga saga ramma*, ch. 41; *Eyrbyggja saga*, ch. 44.

14. *Eiríks saga rauða*, ch. 11; *Færeyjinga saga*, ch. 49; *Laxdæla saga*, ch. 21, ch. 44, ch. 77; *Þórðar saga hreðu*, ch. 7; *Ólafs saga helga*, ch. 215; *Landnámabók*, S. 168; *Hrómundar þáttur halta*, ch. 5; *Sneglu-Halla þáttur*, ch. 4.

15. *Færeyjinga saga*, ch. 49.

16. *Egils saga Skalla-Grímssonar*, ch. 84; *Saga Inga konungs og bræðra hans*, ch. 28; *Ólafs saga Tryggvasonar*, ch. 104; *Laxdæla saga*, ch. 86; *Gull-Þóris saga*, ch. 14; *Eyrbyggja saga*, ch. 13.

17. *Egils saga Skalla-Grímssonar*, ch. 81.

18. *Brennu-Njáls saga*, ch. 92.

19. *Færeyjinga saga*, ch. 49; *Saga Inga konungs og bræðra hans*, ch. 28; *Ólafs saga Tryggvasonar*, ch. 104; *Þórðar saga hreðu*, ch. 7.

20. *Ólafs saga helga*, ch. 205.

21. *Haralds saga Gráfeldar*, ch. 1; *Magnús saga Erlingsonar*, ch. 10; *Eyrbyggja saga*, ch. 44.

22. Tania Dickinson and Heinrich Härke, *Early Anglo-Saxon Shields* (London: Society of Antiquaries of London, 1992), 63.

23. A. W. Brøgger and Haakin Shetelig, *The Viking Ships: Their Ancestry and Evolution*, tr. Katherine John (Oslo: Dreyers forlag, 1951), 84.

24. Saxo, *History of the Danes*, bk. 4, 96-97.

25. *Egils saga Skalla-Grímssonar*, ch. 11, ch. 81; *Brennu-Njáls saga*, ch. 44.

26. *Finnboga saga rama*, ch. 20; *Hávarðar saga Ísfirðings*, ch. 23; *Laxdæla saga*, ch. 71, ch. 86; *Brennu-Njáls saga*, ch. 86.

27. *Landnámabók*, S. 156; *Grettis saga*, ch. 19; *Brennu-Njáls saga*, ch. 84.

28. Jonna Louis-Jensen and Tarrin Wills, eds., "Anonymous Poems, *Plácitusdrápa* 29," in Ross, ed., *Poetry on Christian Subjects*, Skaldic Poetry of the Scandinavian Middle Ages 7, 199-200; Valgerður Erna Þorvaldsdóttir, "(Introduction to) Anonymous, *Brúðkaupsvísur*," in Ross, ed., *Poetry on Christian Subjects*, Skaldic Poetry of the Scandinavian Middle Ages 7, 527-53; Margaret Clunies Ross, ed., "Bragi inn gamli Boddason, *Ragnarsdrápa* 12," in Gade and Marold, eds., *Poetry from Treatises on Poetics*, Skaldic Poetry of the Scandinavian Middle Ages 3, 46.

29. Kelsie H. Spears, "The Picture Stones of Gotland: Type C and D Stones as Death Memorials" (master's thesis, University of Houston, 2016), 84; Lärbro Tängelgårda I, SHM4373, accessed Oct. 2, 2020, mis.historiska.se/mis/sok/fid.asp?fid=108186; Ledberg stone, Rundata Ög 181, accessed Sept. 27, 2020, https://skaldic.abdn.ac.uk/db.php?id=15695&if=srdb&table=mss; Lärbro Stora Hammars I, SHM 29974, mis.historiska.se/mis/sok/fid.asp?fid=108206 (accessed Oct. 2, 2020); Stenkyrkja Lillbjärs SHM 13742, accessed Oct. 2, 2020, http://mis.historiska.se/mis/sok /fid.asp?fid=45167.

30. Vedeler, "Textile Interior," 281-299; Terry Gunnell, *The Origins of Drama in Scandinavia* (Cambridge, UK: D. S. Brewer, 1995), 61-62.

31. *Eyrbyggja saga*, ch. 19; *Þórðar saga hreðu*, ch. 12; *Heiðarvíga saga*, ch. 40; *Haralds saga Sigurðarsonar*, ch. 60; *Ólafs saga Tryggvasonar*, ch. 37, ch. 51, ch. 89; *Haralds saga hárfagra*, ch. 17; *Gylfaginning*, ch. 51; *Rígsþula*, v. 35, v. 37; *Völundarkviða*, v. 6; *Völuspá*, v. 48.

32. NTNU Vitenskapsmuseet, Trondheim: T19624, accessed July 9, 2020, http://www.unimus.no/arkeologi/forskning/index_katalog.php?museum=vm&id=32257&museumsnr=T19624.

33. N. Nicolaysen, *Langskibet fra Gokstad ved Sandefjord* (Kristiania, Norway: Alb. Cammermeyer, 1882), 62.

34. Hildur Gestsdóttir et al., "New Discoveries," *Dysnes* 12 (2017): 93-106; Þjóðminjasafn Íslands 10481/1929-17, accessed July 9, 2020, https://sarpur.is/Adfang.aspx?AdfangID=317533.

35. Arbman, *Birka*, 1:323-325, Bj 850; SHM34000, accessed July 9, 2020, mis.historiska.se/mis/sok/fid.asp?fid=573092&page=2&in=1.

36. Arbman, *Birka*, 1:267-272, Bj 750; SHM34000, accessed July 9, 2020, mis.historiska.se/mis/sok/fid.asp?fid=599634.

37. Emma Boast, "The Viking Shield in the British Isles: Changes in Use from the 8th–11th Century in England and the Isle of Man" (expanded version of master's thesis, University of York, 2017), accessed June 3, 2020, https://www.academia.edu/33540970/The_Viking_Shield_in_the_British_Isles_changes_in_use_from_the_8th_11th_Century_in_England_and_the_Isle_of_Man 116.

38. Hildur et al., "New Discoveries," 93-106.

39. Larsen, tr., *Earliest Norwegian Law, Frostathing Law*, vol. 7, ch. 15, 320; *Gulathing Law* title 309, 196.

40. Paulsen, "Pfiel und Bogen in Haithabu," 127-128; Høj, *Bows & Arrows*, 62-63.

41. Historiska museet 34000 Bj 47, accessed July 9, 2020, mis.historiska.se/mis/sok/fid.asp?fid=459711; Historiska museet 34000 Bj 535, accessed July 9, 2020, mis.historiska.se/mis/sok/fid.asp?fid=557678; Historiska museet 34000 Bj 557, accessed July 9, 2020, mis.historiska.se/mis/sok/fid.asp?fid=559209; Historiska museet 34000 Bj 606, accessed July 9, 2020, mis.historiska.se/mis/sok/fid.asp?fid=574725.

42. Gunnar et al., eds., *Grágás Lagasafn íslenska þjóðveldisins*, 151, K. 167; Larsen, tr., *Earliest Norwegian Law, Gulathing Law* title 75, 92.

43. Theophilus, *On Divers Arts: The Foremost Medieval Treatise on Painting, Glassmaking and Metalwork*, ed. and tr. John G. Hawthorne and Cyril Stanley Smith (New York: Dover, 1979), 26-27.

44. William R. Short and Hurstwic, unpublished results, July 25, 2020. Data about Viking-age shields and shield components found in Viking lands (Norway, Sweden, Denmark, Iceland, Viking-occupied England) were compiled and tabulated from archaeological reports and museum databases. Where possible, dimensions and measurements were estimated from surviving fragments and included in the dataset. This dataset allowed us to run statistical analyses on many aspects of Viking-age shields based on archaeological finds.

45. *Egils saga Skalla-Grímssonar*, ch. 53; *Göngu-Hrólfs saga*, ch. 31.

46. William R. Short and Hurstwic, unpublished results, July 25, 2020. The statistical analysis was performed using our database of Viking-age shields, described two notes above; Kirsten Christensen et al., "Trelleborgskjoldet," *Skalk* 5 (2009): 3–7.

47. Nicolaysen, *Langskibet fra Gokstad ved Sandefjord*, 62.

48. Historiska museet 34000 Bj 736, accessed July 9, 2020, mis.historiska.se/mis/sok/fid.asp?fid=477798; Historiska museet 34000 Bj 842, accessed July 9, 2020, mis.historiska.se/mis/sok/fid.asp?fid=571680.

49. Arbman, *Birka*, 1:323-325, plate 18-5b; SHM34000 Bj 850, accessed July 9, 2020, mis.historiska.se/mis/sok/fid.asp?fid=573092&page=2&in=1.

50. *Grettis saga*, ch. 40; *Valla-Ljóts saga*, ch. 4; *Kormáks saga*, ch. 8.

51. Arbman, *Birka*, 1:208-209, Bj 628, 314-316, Bj 842; Historiska museet 19802, accessed July 9, 2020, mis.historiska.se/mis/sok/fid.asp?fid=1184602.

52. Arbman, *Birka*, 1:259-261, Bj 736, plate 15.

53. Ibid., 1:259-261, Bj 736, 314-316, Bj 842; Universitetsmuseene Ts3072, accessed July 10, 2020, http://www.unimus.no/artefacts/tmu/search/?oid=3753&museumsnr=Ts3072&f=html; Universitetsmuseene Ts12156, accessed July 10, 2020, http://www.unimus.no/artefacts/tmu/search/?oid=261498&museumsnr=Ts12156&f=html.

54. Þjóðminjasafn Íslands 10481/1929-17, accessed July 10, 2020, https://www.sarpur.is/Adfang.aspx?AdfangID=317533; Arbman, *Birka*, 1:259-261, Bj 736, 289-290, Bj 798, 134-136, Bj 467, 188-190, Bj 581, 364-366, Bj 942.

55. *Waltharius*, Ring, ed. and tr., 102-105, lines 764-780, 126-127, lines 1021-1043.

56. "The Laws of King Athelstan 924-939 A.D.," in *Medieval Sourcebook: The Anglo-Saxon Dooms 560–975,* Internet History Sourcebook Project, Fordham University, accessed July 10, 2020, https://sourcebooks.fordham.edu/source/560-975dooms.asp#The%20Laws%20of%20King%20Athelstan.

57. Cleasby et al., eds., *Icelandic-English Dictionary,* 645, s.v. "tví-"; Grímr Jónsson Thorkelin, ed., *Regis Magni legum reformatoris leges Gula-Thingenses, sive, Jus commune Norvegicum cum interpretatione Lat. et Dan* (Denmark, 1817), 103; accessed July 11, 2020, https://www.google.com/books/edition/Regis_Magni_legum_reformatoris_leges_Gul/SWIPAAAAQAAJ?hl=en&gbpv=1&dq=Regis+Magni+legum+reformatoris+leges+Gula-thingenses&printsec=frontcover; R. Keyser and P. A. Munch, eds., *Norges Gamle Love Indtil 1387,* vol. 2 (Christiania, Norway: Chr. Grondahl, 1848), ch. 12, 206; Nicolaysen, *Langskibet fra Gokstad ved Sandefjord,* 33; Dickinson and Härke, *Early Anglo-Saxon Shields,* 50.

58. "*Sic ait et triplicem clieum collegit in ulnam . . .*" *Waltharius,* Ring, ed. and tr., 94-95, line 668, 100-101, line 733.

59. *Brennu-Njáls saga,* ch. 92; *Egils saga Skalla-Grímssonar,* ch. 84; *Færeyjinga saga,* ch. 37, ch. 49; *Grettis saga,* ch. 72; *Gull-Þóris saga,* ch. 12; *Heiðarvíga saga,* ch. 33; *Laxdæla saga,* ch. 84; *Völundarkviða,* v. 7.

60. Gunnar et al., eds., *Grágás Lagasafn íslenska þjóðveldisins,* 457-458, K. 115.

61. Theophilus, *On Divers Arts,* 27-29.

62. Nicolaysen, *Langskibet fra Gokstad ved Sandefjord,* 63.

63. Ibid.; Universitetsmuseene Ts12156, accessed July 10, 2020, http://www.unimus.no/artefacts/tmu/search/?oid=261498&museumsnr=Ts12156&f=html; Boast, "Viking Shield," 117, 126.

64. *Eiríks saga rauða,* ch. 11.

65. Ibid., ch. 10.

66. *Laxdæla saga,* ch. 21, ch. 44, ch. 77.

67. Thorkelin, ed., *Regis Magni legum reformatoris leges Gula-Thingenses, sive, Jus commune Norvegicum cum interpretatione Lat. et Dan.,* 103; Rundata DR202, accessed July 11, 2020, https://skaldic.abdn.ac.uk/db.php?id=19026&if=runic&table=mss; Matthew Townend, ed., "Hallvarðr háreksblesi, *Knútsdrápa 4,*" in *Poetry from Treatises on Poetics,* Gade and Marold, ed., Skaldic Poetry of the Scandinavian Middle Ages 3, 235.

68. Arbman, *Birka,* 1:344-346, Bj 886; Boast, "Viking Shield," 84, 102, 116.

69. Boast, "Viking Shield," 102, 116.

70. Arbman, *Birka,* 1:180-181, plate 19-8, Bj 561, 1:344-346, Bj 886.

71. Ibid., 1:323-325, Bj 850.

72. Universitetsmuseene C57449, accessed July 10, 2020, http://www.unimus.no/artefacts/khm/search/?oid=719873&museumsnr=C57449&f=html; Arbman, *Birka,* 1:323-325, Bj 850, 208-209, Bj 628.

73. Dickinson and Härke, *Early Anglo-Saxon Shields,* 36; Arbman, *Birka,* 1:259-261 Bj 736.

74. Nicolaysen, *Langskibet fra Gokstad ved Sandefjord,* 62-63, plate 8-7.

75. Dickinson and Härke, *Early Anglo-Saxon Shields,* 35-42.

76. *Waltharius.* Ring, ed. and tr., 106-107, lines 805-817.

77. *Valla-Ljóts saga,* ch. 4; Cleasby et al., eds., *Icelandic-English Dictionary,* 74, s.v. "bóla."

78. Rygh, *Norske oldsager,* figs. 562-565.

79. Historiska museet SHM10347:9, accessed July 14, 2020, mis.historiska.se/mis/sok/fid.asp?fid=1175889; Arbman, *Birka,* 1:208-209, Bj 628; Boast, "Viking Shield," 112-113; Kulturhistorisk museum C6032, accessed July 5, 2020, http://www.unimus.no/arkeologi/forskning/index_katalog.php?museum=khm&id=68052&museumsnr=C6032.

80. William R. Short and Hurstwic, unpublished results, July 25, 2020. The statistical analysis was performed using our database of Viking-age shields, described in an earlier note in this chapter.

81. *Waltharius,* Ring, ed. and tr., 106-107, lines 805-817.

82. William R. Short and Hurstwic, unpublished research, July 5, 2020. A computer model of a Viking shield was created that included the wooden shield plate, the iron boss, the handgrip, nails, edge clamps, adhesive, facing, and edging. The model estimated the mass of each of the components, allowing the total weight of the shield to be estimated. Material properties and dimensions of the various components could be varied to model historical (but incomplete) shields as well as hypothetical shields. The computer model was verified by modeling a modern replica shield that could be easily weighed for comparison.

83. *Brennu-Njáls saga,* ch. 44.

84. Ibid., ch. 62; *Grettis saga,* ch. 21; *Harðar saga og Hólmverja,* ch. 29; *Ólafs saga Helga,* ch. 206; *Magnúss saga góða,* ch. 26.

85. Arbman, *Birka,* 1:221-226, Bj 644.

86. *Egils saga Skalla-Grímssonar,* ch. 53, ch. 70; *Magnúss saga berfœtts,* ch. 25; *Hrafnsmál,* v. 11.

87. Karnell, ed., *Gotland's Picture Stones,* Klinte Hunninge I, Lärbo Stora Hammars I.

88. *Bjarnar saga Hítdœlakappa,* ch. 18, ch. 32; *Egils saga Skalla-Grímssonar,* ch. 84; *Finnboga saga rama,* ch. 27; *Gísla saga Súrssonar,* ch. 34; *Gull-Þóris saga,* ch. 14; *Laxdæla saga,* ch. 37, ch. 44; *Víga-Glúms saga,* ch. 19; *Hákonar saga Aðalsteinsfóstra,* ch. 28.

89. Karnell, ed., *Gotland's Picture Stones,* Lärbo Stora Hammars I, Klinte Hunninge I; Paul B. Du Chaillu, *The Viking Age: The Early History, Manners, and Customs of the Ancestors of the English-Speaking Nations,* vol. 2 (London: John Murray, 1889), 158, fig. 937;

Roesdahl and Wilson, eds., *Viking to Crusader,* cat. no. 11, 230, cat. no. 349, 317.

90. Nicolaysen, *Langskibet fra Gokstad ved Sandefjord,* 62-63.

91. *Brennu-Njáls saga,* ch. 84; *Grettis saga,* ch. 19; *Helgakviða Hjörvarðssonar,* v. 12.

92. *Landnámabók,* S. 156.

93. Ole Crumlin-Pedersen, *The Skuldelev Ships I: Topography, Archaeology, History, Conservation and Display* (Roskilde, Denmark: Viking Ship Museum, 2002), 350.

94. Ibid., 262-264.

95. Brøgger and Shetelig, *Viking Ships,* 126.

96. Crumlin-Pedersen, *Skuldelev Ships I,* 264.

97. Brøgger and Shetelig, *Viking Ships,* 165.

98. *Svarfdæla saga,* ch. 9; *Kormáks saga,* ch. 10.

99. *Brennu-Njáls saga,* ch. 130; *Völuspá,* v. 44.

100. *Egils saga Skalla-Grímssonar,* ch. 58; *Ólafs saga Tryggvasonar,* ch. 40.

101. *Færeyjinga saga,* ch. 18; *Reykdæla saga og Víga-Skútu,* ch. 13; *Ólafs saga helga,* ch. 176.

102. William R. Short and Hurstwic, unpublished research, Mar 10, 2008. Two nominally identical Viking shields were made of aspen planks (*Populus*) butted and glued together and secured with edging and a wooden handgrip. One shield was left unfaced and the other had a 1mm leather facing glued to the front surface. The shields were held in a stand that simulated a human grasp of the handgrip and struck with blows from a two-handed axe. The unfaced shield was severely compromised on the first blow and destroyed on the second blow. The faced shield was still solid and would have provided good protection to the shield holder after six blows. The subsequent blow shattered the handgrip, but the shield plate remained intact.

103. *Brennu-Njáls saga,* ch. 150; *Saga Inga konungs og bræðra hans,* ch. 6; *Skáldskaparmál,* ch. 24; *Egils saga Skalla-Grímssonar,* ch. 54; *Finnboga saga ramma,* ch. 32; *Fljótsdæla saga,* ch. 16; *Færeyjinga saga,* ch. 6; *Grettis saga,* ch. 24, ch. 40, ch. 48; *Óláfs saga helga,* ch. 176.

104. *Fóstbræðra saga,* ch. 12.

105. Cleasby et al., eds., *Icelandic-English Dictionary,* 180-182, s.v. "fyrir."

106. British Museum 1867,0120.1; Historiska museet SHM4373, accessed July 15, 2020, mis.historiska.se/mis/sok/fid.asp?fid=108186; Karnell, ed., *Gotland's Picture Stones,* Klinte Hunninge I; Lärbro Stora Hammars I, SHM 29974, accessed Oct. 2, 2020, mis.historiska.se/mis/sok/fid.asp?fid=108206.

107. *Fóstbræðra saga,* ch. 12.

108. *Gull-Þóris saga,* ch. 13; *Laxdæla saga,* ch. 55.

109. *Droplaugarsona saga,* ch. 10; *Færeyjinga saga,* ch. 18; *Víglundar saga,* ch. 16.

110. William R. Short and Hurstwic, unpublished research, Mar. 30, 2017. Test subjects fought rounds of simulated combat armed with sword and shield. A point system encouraged the use of swapping sword and shield where it made sense and could be used to advantage. After each round, subjective comments from the two fighters were recorded. Video of the rounds was studied for further insights.

111. William R. Short and Hurstwic, unpublished research, Apr. 2, 2019, June 25, 2019. The test subject was armed with sword and shield and fought rounds of simulated combat with a practice partner who was allowed a free choice of weapon or weapons. The test subject was instructed to use one of several possible shield positions for the round. After each round, subjective comments from the two fighters were recorded. Video of the rounds was studied for further insights.

112. Lärbro Stora Hammars I, SHM 29974, accessed Oct. 2, 2020, mis.historiska.se/mis/sok/fid.asp?fid=108206.

113. *Skáldskaparmál,* ch. 48.

114. *Brennu-Njáls saga,* ch. 30, ch. 72, ch. 145; *Laxdæla saga,* ch. 49; *Svarfdæla saga,* ch. 9.

115. William R. Short and Hurstwic, unpublished research, Apr. 2, 2019, June 25, 2019. Test subjects armed with sword and shield fought rounds of simulated combat with training partners who were armed with their choice of weapon or weapons. Test subjects were assigned a shield position to use for the round. After each round, subjective comments from the two fighters were recorded. Video of the rounds was studied for further insights.

116. Karnell, ed., *Gotland's Picture Stones,* Lärbro Tängelgårda I, Lärbro Stora Hammars I.

117. William R. Short and Hurstwic, unpublished research, June 27, 2019. Rounds of simulated combat were fought with pairs of combatants armed with swords and pairs of shield holders. Shield holders were assigned a shield position to use for the round so that all combinations of shield positions were tested. After each round, subjective comments from the two fighters were recorded. Video of the rounds was studied for further insights.

118. Cleasby et al., eds., *Icelandic-English Dictionary,* 77, s.v. "bregða," 552, s.v. "skjóta."

119. *Brennu-Njáls saga,* ch. 86; *Egils saga Skalla-Grímssonar,* ch. 54.

120. *Egils saga Skalla-Grímssonar,* ch. 58; *Brennu-Njáls saga,* ch. 30, ch. 54, ch. 72, ch. 77, ch. 130, ch. 145, ch. 150; *Droplaugarsona saga,* ch. 10; *Finnboga saga ramma,* ch. 35; *Færeyjinga saga,* ch. 6; *Svarfdæla saga,* ch. 9.

121. *Brennu-Njáls saga,* ch. 30, ch. 45, ch. 82.

122. *Kormáks saga,* ch. 12.

123. McTurk, ed., "Anonymous Poems, *Krákumál* 21," in Ross, ed., *Poetry in fornaldarsögur,* 760; Edith Marold, ed., "Einarr skálaglamm Helgason, *Vellekla*

22," in Whaley, ed., *Poetry from the Kings' Sagas 1*, 309; Kari Ellen Gade, ed., "Rögnvaldr jarl and Hallr Þórarinsson, *Háttalykill 5*," in Gade and Marold, eds., *Poetry from Treatises on Poetics*, 1012; Kari Ellen Gade, "(Introduction to) Snorri Sturluson, *Háttatal*," in Gade and Marold, eds., *Poetry from Treatises on Poetics*, 1094.

124. *Brennu-Njáls saga*, ch. 62; *Grettis saga*, ch. 21; *Harðar saga og Hólmverja*, ch. 29; *Ólafs saga Helga*, ch. 207; *Magnúss saga góða*, ch. 26.

125. *Fljótsdæla saga*, ch. 17; *Kjalnesinga saga*, ch. 8.

126. Þjóðminjasafn Íslands 13712/1947-130, accessed July 14, 2020, https://sarpur.is/Adfang.aspx?AdfangID=335087; Þjóðminjasafn Íslands 13738/1947-156, accessed July 14, 2020, https://sarpur.is/Adfang.aspx?AdfangID=335074.

127. Þjóðminjasafn Íslands 560-b/1868-130, accessed July 14, 2020, https://sarpur.is/Adfang.aspx?AdfangID=336554.

128. *Þórðar saga hreðu*, ch. 4.

129. *Grettis saga*, ch. 82.

130. *Brennu-Njáls saga*, ch. 99; *Eyrbyggja saga*, ch. 45; *Svarfdæla saga*, ch. 5; *Þórðar saga hreðru*, ch. 4; *Hákonar saga Aðalsteinsfóstra*, ch. 31.

131. *Gunnlaugs saga ormstunga*, ch. 11; *Kormáks saga*, ch. 10, ch. 12, ch. 14; *Reykdæla saga og Víga-Skútu*, ch. 19; *Víga-Glúms saga*, ch. 4.

132. Jónas Kristjánsson and Vésteinn Ólason, eds., *Eddukvæði II*, Íslenzk fornrit (Reykjavík: Hið íslenzka fornritfélag, 2014), 313n, line 3; *Helreið Brynhildar*, v. 9; *Haralds saga Sigurðarsonar*, ch. 89.

133. *Brennu-Njáls saga*, ch. 157; *Egils saga Skalla-Grímssonar*, ch. 22; *Ynglinga saga*, ch. 22; *Ólafs saga Tryggvasonar*, ch. 107; *Ólafs saga helga*, ch. 61, ch. 226; *Haralds saga Sigurðarsonar*, ch. 92; *Magnúss saga Berfœtts*, ch. 25; *Hákons saga herðibreiðs*, ch. 8.

134. *Ólafs saga helga*, ch. 206.

135. *Magnús saga berfœtts*, ch. 25; Cleasby et al., eds., *Icelandic-English Dictionary*, 552, s.v. "skjóta"; *Svarfdæla saga*, ch. 5.

136. *Brennu-Njáls saga*, ch. 157; *Egils saga Skalla-Grímssonar*, ch. 70; *Færeyjinga saga*, ch. 19; *Magnúss saga góða*, ch. 30.

137. *Sigurdrífamál*, prose introduction.

138. *Ólafs saga helga*, ch. 226; *Magnúss saga góða*, ch. 30.

139. *Skáldskaparmál*, ch. 49.

140. *Egils saga Skalla-Grímssonar*, ch. 70.

141. Guy Halsall, *Warfare and Society in the Barbarian West, 450–900* (London: Routledge, 2003), 177; Lars Lönnroth et al., "Literature," in *The Cambridge History of Scandinavia*, vol. 1, ed. Knut Helle (Cambridge: Cambridge University Press, 2003), 503.

142. Adams and Riggs, "Verse Translation of Abbo of St. Germain's *Bella Parisiacae urbis*," bk. 1, line 303, p. 32; Saxo, *History of the Danes*, bk. 3, 71, bk. 8, 258; William Henry Stephenson, ed., *Asser's Life of King Alfred* (Oxford: Clarendon Press, 1904), ch. 56, 45.

143. *Svarfdæla saga*, ch. 5; *Hákonar saga herðibreiðs*, ch. 8.

144. *Ólafs saga Tryggvasonar*, ch. 107.

145. *Haralds saga Sigurðarsonar*, ch. 89, ch. 92.

146. *Bjarnar saga Hítdælakappa*, ch. 32; *Brennu-Njáls saga*, ch. 92.

147. *Brennu-Njáls saga*, ch. 89; *Grettis saga*, ch. 82; *Harðar saga og Hólmverja*, ch. 17.

148. William R. Short and Hurstwic, unpublished research, Mar. 24, 2016. Test subject was armed with a sword and instructed to hit as many opponents as possible. Four to eight training partners started out of range and were instructed to close the distance and subdue him with shields, staffs, and pieces of wood. After each round, subjective comments from the fighters were recorded. Video of the rounds was studied for further insights.

149. *Grettis saga*, ch. 82.

## CHAPTER 10: ARMOR

1. *Atlakviða*, v. 7, v. 16, v. 43; *Grímnismál*, v. 9; *Grípisspá*, v. 15; *Hyndluljóð*, v. 2; *Helgakviða Hundingsbana I*, v. 15; *Helgakviða Hundingsbana II*, v. 1, v. 7; *Reginsmál*, prose following v. 14.

2. Cleasby et al., eds., *Icelandic-English Dictionary*, 266-267, s.v. "hjálmr", 304, s.v. "hylja."

3. *Finnboga saga ramma*, ch. 32; *Fljótsdæla saga*, ch. 18; *Laxdæla saga*, ch. 63; *Kristni saga*, ch. 18.

4. *Hávarðar saga Ísfirðing*, ch. 10.

5. *Bárðar saga Snæfellsáss*, ch. 18; *Haralds saga Sigurðarson*, ch. 93; *Ljósvetninga saga*, ch. 31.

6. *Gull-Þóris saga*, ch. 6; *Trójumanna saga*, ch. 22; *Hektors saga*, ch. 19.

7. *Svarfdæla saga*, ch. 25; *Víga-Glúms saga*, ch. 24; *Brennu-Njáls saga*, ch. 19; *Egils saga Skalla-Grímssonar*, ch. 12; *Ólafs saga helga*, ch. 176; *Skáldskaparmál*, ch. 49; *Stjörnu-Odda draumur*, ch. 2.

8. *Svarfdæla saga*, ch. 25; *Egils saga Skalla-Grímssonar*, ch. 53; *Fóstbræðra saga*, ch. 4, ch. 7, ch. 17; *Ólafs saga helga*, ch. 112, ch. 150.

9. Keyser et al., *Konge-speilet*, 87, ch. 38; *Þiðreks saga af Bern*, ch. 17.

10. Denny and Filmer-Sankey, *Bayeux Tapestry*, scene 49, scene 55.

11. Ibid., scene 49, scene 51a.

12. *Laxdæla saga*, ch. 63; *Grænlendinga þáttur*, ch. 5; Cleasby et al., eds., *Icelandic-English Dictionary*, 585, s.v. "spöng."

13. Hedenstierna-Jonson, "Birka Warrior," 58.

14. Peter Beatson, *Armour in Byzantium in the Early Years of the Varangian Guard, with Special Reference to Limb Defenses*, 2012, Christobel and Peter's Homepage, accessed Apr. 30, 2020, http://members.ozemail.com.au/~chrisandpeter/limb_defences/limb_defences.htm.

15. G. Arwidsson, "Armour of the Vendel period," *Acta Archaeologica* 10 (1939): 31-59.

16. Cleasby et al., eds., *Icelandic-English Dictionary*, 474, s.v. "panzari"; *Íslendinga saga*, ch. 69; Keyser et al., *Konge-speilet*, 87, ch. 38.

17. *Brennu-Njáls saga*, ch. 45.

18. Cleasby et al., eds., *Icelandic-English Dictionary*, 474, s.v. "panzari"; Einar Ól. Sveinsson, ed., *Brennu-Njáls saga*, Íslenzk fornrit v. 12 (Reykjavík: Hið íslenzka fornritafélag, 1954), ch. 45, 116n4.

19. *Ólafs saga helga*, ch. 193.

20. Cleasby et al., eds., *Icelandic-English Dictionary*, 61, s.v. "berserkr"; Snorri, *Ynglinga saga* from *Heimskringla*, ed. Bjarni Aðalbjarnarson, Íslenzk fornrit, v. 26 (Reykjavík: Hið íslenzka fornritafélag, 1951), ch. 6, 17-18n8.

21. *Grettis saga*, ch. 2.

22. *Vatnsdæla saga*, ch. 9.

23. *Grettis saga*, ch. 2; *Brennu-Njáls saga*, ch. 103; *Egils saga Skalla-Grímssonar*, ch. 9; *Eyrbyggja saga*, ch. 25; *Vatnsdæla saga*, ch. 46; *Ynglinga saga*, ch. 6.

24. "Kenning Index," *Skaldic Poetry of the Scandinavian Middle Ages*, Margaret Clunies Ross et al., accessed May 14, 2020, https://skaldic.abdn.ac.uk/db.php?if=default&table=kenning&view= .

25. *Ljósvetninga saga*, ch. 31; *Haralds saga Sigurðarsonar*, ch. 91.

26. *Skáldskaparmál*, ch. 44.

27. *Helgakviða Hörðvarðsson*, v. 28; *Helgakviða Hundingsbana I*, v. 6, v. 48; *Helgakviða Hundingsbana II*, v. 1, v. 14; *Fáfnismál*, v. 19, v. 44; *Alvíssmál*, v. 18; *Sigrdrífumál*, v. 14; *Atlakviða*, v. 3; *Grípisspá* v. 15, v. 16; *Hamðismál*, v. 25; *Atlakviða*, v. 43.

28. *Hyndluljóð*, v. 2; *Atlakviða*, v. 7, v. 16; *Helgakviða Hundingsbana I*, v. 15; *Helgakviða Hundingsbana II*, v. 7; *Guðrúnarkviða II*, v. 19.

29. *Gylfaginning*, ch. 20, ch. 51.

30. *Hákonar saga góða*, ch. 30-31; *Ólafs saga helga*, ch. 34, ch. 213; *Ólafs saga Tryggvasonar*, ch. 104; *Haralds saga Sigurðarson*, ch. 87; *Hákonar saga góða*, ch. 28.

31. *Ólafs saga helga*, ch. 29, ch. 49, ch. 61; *Haralds saga Sigurðarsonar*, ch. 87.

32. British Museum 1867, 0120.1.

33. William R. Short and Hurstwic, unpublished research, Apr. 27, 2020. The methodology for creating and analyzing the database of weapons and weapons use in the *Sagas of Icelanders* is described in the appendix.

34. Larsen, tr., *Earliest Norwegian Law, Gulathing Law* title 309, 196.

35. *Brennu-Njáls saga*, ch. 45, ch. 82, ch. 84, ch. 91, ch. 92, ch. 142; *Egils saga Skalla-Grímssonar*, ch. 45, ch. 53, ch. 60; *Grettis saga*, ch. 19, ch. 45; *Eyrbyggja saga*, ch. 44; *Finnboga saga ramma*, ch. 8, ch. 27, ch. 32; *Fljótsdæla saga*, ch. 16, ch. 18; *Fóstbrœðra saga*, ch. 19, and numerous others.

36. *Ljósvetninga saga*, ch. 31; *Reykdæla saga ok Víga-Skútu*, ch. 21; *Laxdæla saga*, ch. 37; *Grettis saga*, ch. 19; *Finnboga saga ramma*, ch. 8.

37. Vedeler, "Textile Interior," 281-299; Historiska museet SHM 4325:b, accessed Oct. 6, 2020, mis.historiska.se/mis/sok/fid.asp?fid=618349; Helle Vandkilde, "Bronze Age Voyaging and Cosmologies in the Making: The Helmets from Viksø Revisited," in *Counterpoint: Essays in Archaeology and Heritage Studies in Honour of Professor Kristian Ktistiansen*, ed. Sophie Bergerbrant and Serena Sabatini (Oxford, UK: Archaeopress, 2013), 165-177.

38. Kulturhistorish museum C27317, accessed May 1, 2020, http://www.unimus.no/arkeologi/forskning/index_katalog.php?museum=KHM&museumsnr=C27317&id=89075; Roesdahl and Wilson, eds., *Viking to Crusader,* cat. no. 108, 255.

39. Kulturhistorish museum C27317k; Hjardar and Vike, *Vikings at War,* 188.

40. Hjardar and Vike, *Vikings at War,* 188-190.

41. *Ólafs saga helga*, ch. 227; *Ólafs saga Tryggvasonar*, ch. 41.

42. *Grettis saga*, ch. 40.

43. Dominic Tweddle, "The Coppergate Helmet," *Fornvännen Journal of Swedish Antiquarian Research* 78 (1983): 109-110.

44. *Ólafs saga helga*, ch. 49; P. D. King, *Charlemagne, Translated Sources* (Lambrigg, UK: P. D. King, 1987), 266.

45. William R. Short and Hurstwic, unpublished research, May 1, 2020. A computer model of the components of the helmet was created, allowing the mass of the complete helmet to be estimated based on the dimensions of the surviving helmet fragments. The parameters could be altered to allow for mass estimates for various assumptions about the details of the complete helmet.

46. Roesdahl and Wilson, eds., *Viking to Crusader,* cat. no. 80, 247.

47. Historika Museet, SHM 13742, accessed May 4, 2020, http://mis.historiska.se/mis/sok/bild.asp?uid=17837.

48. *La Vie de saint Aubin d'Angers,* Bibliothèque nationale de France, NAL 1390, fol. 7r, accessed May 2, 2020, https://gallica.bnf.fr/ark:/12148/btv1b105157428/f27.image.

49. Kulturhistorish museum C27317; Roesdahl and Wilson, eds., *Viking to Crusader*, cat. no. 108, 255.

50. Frederik Ehlton, "Ringväv från Birkas garnison: Dokumentation, Preparering ock Analys," report, Arkeologiska forskningslaboratoriet, Stockholms universitet, 2002, 23-37.

51. Vegard Vike, *Ring Weave: A Metallographical Analysis of Ring Mail Material at the Oldsaksamlingen in Oslo* (Universitetet i Oslo, 2000), 23.

52. Peter Beatson, *Mail from the "Garrison" of Birka: A Review of Recent Research,* 2008, Christobel and Peter's Homepage, accessed May 1, 2020, http://members.oze-mail.com.au/~chrisandpeter/mail/birka_mail.htm.

53. Ehlton, "Ringväv från Birkas garnison," 16.

54. *Harðar saga ok Hólmverja,* ch. 36.

55. Cleasby et al., eds., *Icelandic-English Dictionary,* 645, s.v. "tví."

56. *Örvar-Odds saga,* ch. 14.

57. Vike, *Ring Weave,* 10-11.

58. Ehlton, "Ringväv från Birkas garnison," 15; Beatson, *Mail from the "Garrison,"* 2-3; Vike, *Ring Weave,* 23.

59. Greta Arwidsson and Gösta Berg, *The Mästermyr Find: A Viking Age Tool Chest from Gotland* (Lompoc, CA: Larson Publishing, 1999),15, 32, plate 23.

60. Matthew Marino (independent scholar), personal communication with William R. Short, May 2, 2020.

61. Hjardar and Vike, *Vikings at War,* 190; King, *Charlemagne, Translated Sources,* 266; *Sneglu-Halla þáttur,* ch. 4.

62. Nicholas Checksfield et al., "Examination and Assessment of the Wenceslaus Mail Hauberk," *Acta Militaria Mediaevalia* 7: (2012): 229-242.

63. William R. Short and Hurstwic, unpublished research, May 2, 2020. A computer model of a mail shirt was created, allowing the mass of the complete mail shirt to be estimated based on the dimensions of the surviving mail shirt fragments. The parameters could be altered to allow for mass estimates for various assumptions about the details of the complete mail shirt.

64. Ibid. The same computer model of a mail shirt was used, applied to the Gjermundbu fragments.

65. *Haralds saga Sigurðarsonar,* ch. 91; *Ljósvetninga saga,* ch. 31.

66. *Sneglu-Halla þáttur,* ch. 4.

67. *La Vie de saint Aubin d'Angers.*

68. *Ólafs saga helga,* ch. 166, ch. 228; *Hallfreðar saga vandræðaskálds,* ch. 2.

69. Tweddle, "Coppergate Helmet," 107.

70. "Sword Thrust to Butted Mail over Fabric to the Ribs," *Viking Weapon Test Cuts,* Hurstwic, Mar. 16, 2012, YouTube, accessed Oct. 15, 2019, https://www.youtube.com/watch?v=juIw20z5p0c.

71. Tweddle, "Coppergate Helmet," 107.

72. *Grettis saga,* ch. 40; Gunnar et al., eds., *Grágás Lagasafn íslenska þjóðveldisins,* 266, S. 362.

73. Denny and Filmer-Sankey, *Bayeux Tapestry,* scene 22.

74. William R. Short and Hurstwic, unpublished research, May 24, 2018, Nov. 27, 2018, Dec. 18, 2018, Mar. 5, 2019, Apr. 23, 2019. Various replica Viking helmets were tested (*spangenhelm* with nose guard, *spangenhelm* with spectacle guard, conical with nose guard, *spangenhelm* with cheek guards) using various suspension systems (leather spider suspension, sheepskin cap,

fabric cap) and various straps (single chin tie, single chin strap, yoked chin strap, no strap). As a comparison, a modern military helmet was also tested. Test subjects wore helmets while performing combative moves (running, squatting, falling to the ground and rising, spear throwing) and while fighting rounds of simulated combat with a free choice of weapons. After each test or round, subjective comments from the test subjects were recorded. Video of the tests and rounds was studied for further insights.

75. *La Vie de saint Aubin d'Angers.*

76. Denny and Filmer-Sankey, *Bayeux Tapestry,* scene 50.

77. Ibid., scene 48.

78. Brown et al., eds., *Shorter Oxford English Dictionary,* 1064, s.v. "gambeson"; Cleasby et al., eds., *Icelandic-English Dictionary,* 685, s.v. "vápn"; *Brennu-Njáls saga,* ch. 17, ch. 84; *Þorsteins þáttur Austfirðings,* ch. 1.

79. *Íslendinga saga,* ch. 5; *Hákonar saga Hákonarsonar,* ch. 238.

80. *Hirðskrá,* in Keyser and Munch, eds., *Norges Gamle Love,* ch. 35, 427.

81. *Haralds saga Sigurðarsonar,* ch. 87.

82. *Ólafs saga helga,* ch. 61, ch. 84; *Reykdæla saga ok Víga-Skútu,* ch. 21.

83. William R. Short and Hurstwic, unpublished research, May 12, 2020. Photographs of a man wearing a replica Viking tunic and of a man wearing tunic over mail over *vápntreyja* were taken and studied.

84. William R. Short and Hurstwic, unpublished research, Dec. 19, 2017, May 24, 2018. Test subjects were assessed while wearing normal training clothes, a replica mail shirt over normal training clothes, heavy *vápntreyja* over normal training clothes, mail shirt over heavy *vápntreyja* over normal training clothes, and modern training armor over normal training clothes. For some of these options, test subjects were timed and measured performing athletic activities, such as running a short dash, high jumping, and broad jumping. For all of these options, test subjects fought rounds of simulated combat. After each test or round, subjective comments from the test subjects were recorded. Video of the tests and rounds was studied for further insights.

85. William R. Short and Hurstwic, unpublished research, Dec. 22, 2016. Wool fabric with a weave similar to that thought to have been used in Viking-age clothing was hung and cuts made to it using a sharp replica sword. Tests were conducted with free-hanging fabric and with fabric draped over a heavy bag to add bulk and support to the fabric. A variety of cuts, both full power and reduced power, were made to the fabric samples. After the cuts, the fabric was studied for the damage done by the cut. Video of the cutting tests was recorded and reviewed. While powerful cuts pene-

trated the fabric, less-powerful attacks often did not. On May 12, 2019, measurements were made of the ability of various types of Viking armor to reduce the impact of the blow. The details of the measurements and results are discussed later in this chapter.

86. *Finnboga saga ramma,* ch. 32; *Bjarnar saga Hítdælakappa,* ch. 18; *Gull-Þóris saga,* ch. 13.

87. *Gull-Þóris saga,* ch. 18; *Ólafs saga Tryggvasonar,* ch. 41; *Laxdæla saga,* ch. 64.

88. *Egils saga Skalla-Grímssonar,* ch. 27; *Gunnars saga Keldugnúpsfífls,* ch. 9; *Hákonar saga góða,* ch. 31; *Ólafs saga helga,* ch. 13, ch. 227; *Haralds saga Sigurðarson,* ch. 92.

89. *Finnboga saga ramma,* ch. 32.

90. *Hákonar saga góða,* ch. 31; *Ólafs saga helga,* ch. 227; *Egils saga Skalla-Grímssonar,* ch. 27; *Gunnars saga Keldugnúpsfífls,* ch. 9.

91. William R. Short and Hurstwic, unpublished research, Jul. 25, 2017. Tests were conducted using a replica Viking sword and a replica *spangenhelm* that used a padded cap to suspend it above on the wearer's head. A measurement device consisting of a three-axis linear accelerometer and a three-axis angular velocity sensor was placed between the human test subject's skull and the padding of the helmet. Preliminary tests were performed to verify that the instrumentation was within its linear range and above its noise floor. While the test subject was standing, the helmet of the test subject was hit with a downward overhead cut from the sword. For safety sake, the cut was made using moderate power, far less intense than a full-power hit. From the angular velocity measurements, it was possible to calculate rotational acceleration of the skull.

92. William R. Short and Hurstwic, unpublished research, Dec. 18, 2018. Test subjects wore a replica *spangenhelm* with nose guard and fought rounds of simulated combat with a practice partner. For safety, test subjects wore eye protection under the helmet, and the weapons used were padded weapons or other training weapons. Test subjects were encouraged to make head and face hits if feasible. To assess the number of hits to the face that were able to get past the nose protection, subjective comments from the test subjects were recorded after each round, and video of the rounds was later studied for further insights.

93. William R. Short and Hurstwic, unpublished research, Dec. 26, 2018. A simplified computer model of a head, helmet, and sword was created and used to predict the degree of protection for various kinds of cuts. The model allowed the parameters of the helmet to be varied.

94. *Ólafs saga Tryggvasonar,* ch. 41; *Ólafs saga helga,* ch. 227.

95. *Ólafs saga helga,* ch. 61; *Hákonar saga herðibreðis,* ch. 20.

96. *Egils saga Skalla-Grímssonar,* ch. 53; *Laxdæla saga,* ch. 37; *Harðar saga ok Hólmverja,* ch. 36; *Haralds saga Sigurðarsonar,* ch. 92; *Ólafs saga Tryggvasonar,* ch. 40.

97. *Ólafs saga helga,* ch. 49.

98. Denny and Filmer-Sankey, *Bayeux Tapestry,* scene 52b, scene 53, scene 58.

99. "Sword Cut through Riveted Mail to the Neck," "Sword Cut through Riveted Mail to a Limb," *Viking Weapon Test Cuts,* Hurstwic, Mar. 16, 2012, YouTube, accessed Oct. 15, 2019, https://www.youtube.com/watch?v=juIw20z5p0c.

100. *Hallfreðar saga vandræðaskálds,* ch. 2; *Ólafs saga helga,* ch. 166; ch. 228.

101. William R. Short and Hurstwic, unpublished research, May 12, 2019. A mechanical system was created that delivered consistent, repeatable sword cuts to a human test subject at an impact level that did not cause trauma and was tolerable for the test subject. The test subject was instrumented with accelerometers directly on the skin under the impact point of the sword. The measurement system was tested to verify that the system remained in its linear range and above the noise floor. Various types of armor were put on the skin over the sensor to measure the energy transmitted by the sword cut into the tissue underneath the impact point of the blade for each type of armor. Cuts were made with a dull replica blade, since we were only interested in energy delivered and not cutting ability. Cuts were made to bare flesh, a replica wool tunic, a replica heavy *vápntreyja,* replica mail, mail over *vápntreyja,* and mail over tunic. For comparison, cuts were also made to several types of modern training armor. All the tests were made to the fleshy part of the thigh. For greater consistency, multiple cuts were measured for each type of armor and averaged in the frequency domain. For this, and indeed, for virtually all of our measurements to be valid, the system must stay in its linear region; that is, if the input is doubled, the output must likewise double. We take great pains to ensure that our system under test (including the measurement devices) are in their linear regions. If the input (the power of the sword cut) increased beyond the linear region, then the ratios measured here no longer hold. Some examples of the system being pushed outside the linear region might include blows so hard that bones break, blows so hard that the armor deforms, and blows so hard that the tissue under the blow tears or is shredded. Until this nonlinear regime is reached, the ratios should hold for any intensity of the blow.

102. *Ólafs saga Tryggvasonar,* ch. 107; ibid., ch. 112, *Haraldssona saga,* ch. 11.

103. William R. Short and Hurstwic, unpublished research, Apr. 8, 2017. Test subjects wore a replica mail shirt over replica Viking clothing. They stepped into a swimming pool and swam until they could swim no

further. Lifesaving equipment and personnel stood by in case of difficulties.

104. *Ólafs saga Tryggvasonar*, ch. 111.

**CHAPTER 11: MASS BATTLES**

1. *Heimskringla*, Prologus.
2. *Ólafs saga Tryggvasonar*, ch. 101-112.
3. Ibid., ch. 26.
4. *Ólafs saga helga*, ch. 214-229; *Fóstbræðra saga*, ch. 24.
5. Saxo, *Gesta Danorum*, 207; Saxo, *History of the Danes*, preface, 5.
6. Saxo, *Gesta Danorum*, 207; Saxo, *History of the Danes*, preface, 7.
7. *Ynglinga saga*, ch. 4; *Gylfaginning*, ch. 22; *Völuspá*, v. 21-26.
8. *Haralds saga hárfagra*, ch. 1, ch. 3.
9. Pulsiano, ed., *Medieval Scandinavia*, 267-268, s.v. "Haraldr hárfagri."
10. *Haralds saga hárfagra*, ch. 6.
11. Saxo, *History of the Danes*, bk. 7, 228; *King's Mirror*, ch. 37, 212.
12. William R. Short, *Icelanders in the Viking Age: The People of the Sagas* (Jefferson, NC: McFarland, 2009), 16.
13. "Apud illos non est rex, nisi tantum lex," Adam, *Gesta Hammaburgensis ecclesias pontificum*, bk. 4, 273,
14. Gunnar, *History of Iceland*, 52; Short, *Icelanders*, 32.
15. Jón Jóhannesson, *Íslendinga Saga: A History of the Old Icelandic Commonwealth*, tr. Haraldur Bessason (Winnipeg: University of Manitoba Press, 1974), 85.
16. Cleasby et al., eds., *Icelandic-English Dictionary*, 387, s.v. "lið," 258, s.v. "herr."
17. Ibid., 264, s.v. "hirð."
18. *Haralds saga hárfagra*, ch. 9; *Viglundar saga*, ch. 1; *Egils saga Skalla-Grímssonar*, ch. 81; *Brennu-Njáls saga*, ch. 3.
19. *Egils saga Skalla-Grímssonar*, ch. 6.
20. Saxo, *History of the Danes*, bk. 7, 228.
21. *Ketil saga Hængs*, ch. 3; *Hrana saga hrings*, ch. 14; *Halfdánar saga Eysteinssonar*, ch. 7; *Sörla þáttur eða Héðans saga ok Högna*, ch. 6.
22. Saxo, *History of the Danes*, bk. 5, 124.
23. *King's Mirror*, ch. 37, 211-213.
24. *Ólafs saga helga*, ch. 57.
25. Snorri, *Ólafs saga helga*, ÍF v. 27, ch. 57, 73n1.
26. *Ólafs saga kyrra*, ch. 4.
27. *Hákonar saga Aðalsteinsfóstra*, ch. 20.
28. Ibid.
29. The following discussion of laws regarding the king's levy is based on Larsen, tr., *Earliest Norwegian Law, Gulathing Law* titles 295-315, 188-200.
30. *Haralds saga Sigurðarsonar*, ch. 61; *Ólafs saga Tryggvasonar*, ch. 18.
31. Larsen, tr., *Earliest Norwegian Law, Gulathing Law* title 311, 196-197.
32. Ibid., *Gulathing Law* title 312, 197; Sigurður, ed., *Egils saga Skalla-Grímssonar*, ÍF v. 2, ch. 3, 9n1.

33. *Ólafs saga helga*, ch. 39.
34. Larsen, tr., *Earliest Norwegian Law, Gulathing Law* title 312, 197.
35. Cleasby et al., eds., *Icelandic-English Dictionary*, 61, s.v. "berserkr."
36. *Ynglinga saga*, ch. 6.
37. *Vatnsdæla saga*, ch. 9; *Haralds þáttr háfagra*.
38. *Grettis saga*, ch. 2; *Vatnsdæla saga*, ch. 9; *Haralds saga hárfagra*, ch. 18; *Hrafnsmál*, v. 8, v. 21.
39. *Egils saga Skalla-Grímssonar*, ch. 65; *Grettis saga*, ch. 19, ch. 40; *Vatnsdæla saga*, ch. 46; *Ásmundar saga kappabana*, ch. 4, ch. 8; *Göngu-Hrólfs saga*, ch. 30; *Hervarar saga ok Heiðreks*, ch. 3; *Hrólfs saga kraka og kappa hans*, ch. 18; *Örvar-Odds saga*, ch. 14; *Haralds saga hárfagra*, ch. 18; *Þorvalds þáttur víðförla*, ch. 4.
40. Roesdahl and Wilson, eds., *Viking to Crusader*, cat. no. 615, 390-391.
41. Cleasby et al., eds., *Icelandic-English Dictionary*, 236-237, s.v. "hamask," "hamr," and "hamramr."
42. *Bárðar saga Snæfellsáss*, ch. 5, ch. 9; *Egils saga Skalla-Grímssonar*, ch. 1, ch. 25; *Flóamanna saga*, ch. 18; *Gull-Þóris saga*, ch. 18; *Vatnsdæla saga*, ch. 42.
43. *Egils saga Skalla-Grímssonar*, ch. 27; *Göngu-Hrólfs saga*, ch. 2.
44. Cleasby et al., eds., *Icelandic-English Dictionary*, 121, s.v. "einhama."
45. *Orms þáttr Stórólfssonar*, ch. 1, ch. 3, ch.4 ; *Fljótsdæla saga*, ch. 19.
46. *Þorvalds þáttr víðförla*, ch. 4; Gunnar et al., eds., *Grágás Lagasafn íslenska þjóðveldisins*, 19, S. 18.
47. *Brennu-Njáls saga*, ch. 103; *Vatnsdæla saga*, ch. 46; *Þorvalds þáttur víðförla*, ch. 4.
48. *Gunnlaugs saga ormstungu*, ch. 7; *Svarfdæla saga*, ch. 8; *Göngu-Hrólfs saga*, ch. 2.
49. *Ynglinga saga*, ch. 6; *Egils saga einhenda ok Ásmundar berserkjabana*, ch. 8; *Gylfaginning*, ch. 49.
50. Simek, *Dictionary of Northern Mythology*, 240-246, s.v. "Odin"; "Woden id est furor." Adamus Bremensus, *Adami Gesta Hammaburgensis ecclesiae pontificum ex rècensione Lappenbergii*, ed. G. Waitz (Hanover: Hahn, 1876), bk. 4, ch. 26, 174-175.
51. *Egils saga Skalla-Grímssonar*, ch. 27; *Eyrbyggja saga*, ch. 25.
52. *Brennu-Njáls saga*, ch. 103; *Egils saga Skallagrímssonar*, ch. 9; *Vatnsdæla saga*, ch. 46; *Þorvalds þáttur víðförla*, ch. 4; Saxo, *History of the Danes*, bk. 7, 206.
53. *Egils saga Skalla-Grímssonar*, ch. 27; *Grettis saga*, ch. 2, ch. 19; *Ásmundar saga kappabana*, ch. 4; *Göngu-Hrólfs saga*, ch. 3; *Hrólfs saga Gautrekssonar*, ch. 16.
54. *Egils saga Skalla-Grímssonar*, ch. 40; *Ásmundar saga kappabana*, ch. 9.
55. *Egils saga Skalla-Grímssonar*, ch. 9; *Grettis saga*, ch. 2; *Vatnsdæla saga*, ch. 9; *Haralds saga hárfagra*, ch. 9; *Fornkonunga saga*, ch. 8; *Göngu-Hrólfs saga*, ch. 3; *Hrólfs saga Gautrekssonar*, ch. 16; *Hrólfs saga kraka og kappa hans*, ch. 16.

56. *Flóamanna saga*, ch. 15; *Grettis saga*, ch. 19; *Gunnars saga Keldugnúpsfífls*, ch. 14; *Göngu-Hrólfs saga*, ch. 8; *Hálfdánar saga Eysteinssonar*, ch. 12; *Hervarar saga ok Heiðreks*, ch. 1; *Örvar-Odds saga*, ch. 19.
57. *Þorvalds þáttur víðförla*, ch. 2.
58. *Eyrbyggja saga*, ch. 25; *Egils saga Skalla-Grímssonar*, ch. 65; *Gísla saga Súrssonar*, ch. 1; *Grettis saga*, ch. 19; *Vatnsdæla saga*, ch. 46; *Víga-Glúms saga*, ch. 6.
59. *Brennu-Njáls saga*, ch. 129; *Droplaugarsona saga*, ch. 1; *Egils saga Skalla-Grímssonar*, ch. 22; *Gull-Þóris saga*, ch. 18; *Þorsteins saga Síðu-Hallsonar*, ch. 3; *Hákonar saga herðibreiðs*, ch. 13.
60. *Gísla saga Súrssonar*, ch. 35; *Heidarvíga saga*, ch. 22.
61. Gunnar et al., eds., *Grágás Lagasafn íslenska þjóðveldisins*, 125, K. 254.
62. *Laxdæla saga*, ch. 48, ch. 60; *Brennu-Njáls saga*, ch. 91; *Kjalnesinga saga*, ch. 7; *Ljósvetninga saga*, ch. 24; *Hamðismál*, v. 2; *Af Upplendinga konungum*, ch. 2.
63. *Færeyjinga saga*, ch. 38; *Harðar saga og Hólmverja*, ch. 39.
64. Gunnar et al., eds., *Grágás Lagasafn íslenska þjóðveldisins*, 125, K. 254.
65. *Brennu-Njáls saga*, ch. 20, ch. 49, ch. 95; *Eyrbyggja saga*, ch. 18; *Fljótsdæla saga*, ch. 10; *Jómsvíkinga saga*, ch. 8.
66. *Skáldskaparmál*, ch. 65; Larsen, tr., *Earliest Norwegian Law*, *Gulathing Law* title 299, 190-191, title 300, 191.
67. *Skáldskaparmál*, ch. 3; *Gylfaginning*, ch. 46, ch. 47.
68. Cleasby et al., eds., *Icelandic-English Dictionary*, 551, s.v. "skjald-."
69. *Stjörnu-Odda draumur*, ch. 2; *Hervarar saga ok Heiðreks*, ch. 4; *Völsunga saga*, ch. 20, ch. 24; Saxo, *History of the Danes*, bk. 7, 211, 212, 225, bk. 9, 280.
70. *Fornkonunga saga*, ch. 8; *Stjörnu-Odda draumur*, ch. 2, ch. 6, ch. 8; *Hervarar saga ok Heiðreks*, ch. 4, ch. 13; *Völsunga saga*, ch. 20, ch. 29; Saxo, *History of the Danes*, bk. 7, 211, bk. 8, 238, 244.
71. *Jómsvíkinga saga*, ch. 31.
72. Viborg Museum C42194, accessed Oct. 2, 2020, https://www.kulturarv.dk/mussam/VisGenstand.action?genstandId=11247629; Valkyrien fra Hårby, Odense Bys Museer, press release, Feb. 28, 2013, accessed July 9, 2020, https://museum.odense.dk/nyheder/2013/valkyrien-fra-haarby.
73. *Stjörnu-Odda draumur*, ch. 2; *Hervarar saga ok Heiðreks*, ch. 4.
74. *Bósa saga ok Herrauðs*, ch. 2; *Völsunga saga*, ch. 9, ch. 20.
75. *Stjörnu-Odda draumur*, ch. 2; *Hervarar saga ok Heiðreks*, ch. 4; *Völsunga saga*, ch. 27, ch. 29.
76. Saxo, *History of the Danes*, bk. 7, 212.
77. Arbman, *Birka*, 1:188-190, Bj581.
78. Charlotte Hedenstierna-Jonson et al., "A Female Viking Warrior Confirmed by Genomics," *American Journal of Physical Anthropology* (2017): 1-8; Neil Price et al., "Viking Warrior Women? Reassessing Birka Chamber Grave Bj.581," *Antiquity* 93, no. 367 (Feb. 2019): 181-198.
79. Charlotte Hedenstierna-Jonson (Department of Archaeology, Uppsala universitet), personal communication with William R. Short, Mar. 12, 2019.
80. *Haralds saga Aðalsteinsfóstra*, ch. 32; *Sigurdrífumál*, prose after v. 4; *Völuspá*, v. 31; *Hákonarmál*, v. 10-11.
81. Cleasby et al., eds., *Icelandic-English Dictionary*, 676, s.v. "valr"; Ásgeir, *Íslensk orðsifjabók*, 1100, s.v. "valkyrja."
82. *Völsunga saga*, ch. 9; *Brennu-Njáls saga*, ch. 157; *Haralds saga Aðalsteinsfóstra*, ch. 32; *Skáldskaparmál*, ch. 41.
83. Rundata Ög 136, accessed Dec. 19, 2020, https://skaldic.abdn.ac.uk/db.php?id=15196&if=srdb&table=mss; Rundata Öl 1, accessed Dec. 19, 2020, https://skaldic.abdn.ac.uk/db.php?id=569&if=srdb&table=mss.
84. Rundata G 110, SHM4171, accessed Oct. 2, 2020, mis.historiska.se/mis/sok/fid.asp?fid=108203; Rundata G 268, SHM13742, accessed Oct. 2, 2020, mis.historiska.se/mis/sok/fid.asp?fid=45167; Rundata N B257, accessed Mar. 15, 2021, https://rundata.info/.
85. Roesdahl and Wilson, eds., *Viking to Crusader*, cat. no. 186, 277.
86. *Völuspá*, v. 31; *Skáldskaparmál*, ch. 2.
87. *Skáldskaparmál*, ch. 2; *Grímnismál*, v. 36.
88. *Brennu-Njáls saga*, ch. 157; *Helgakviða Hjörvarðssonar*, prose after v. 9; *Gylfaginning*, ch. 36; *Hákonarmál*, v. 1.
89. *Gylfaginning*, ch. 24; *Grímnismál*, v. 14.
90. *Skáldskaparmál*, ch. 24.
91. *Ólafs saga helga*, ch. 205.
92. Ibid., ch. 197, ch. 205.
93. *Brennu-Njáls saga*, ch. 157; *Orkneyinga saga*, ch. 109; *Hákonar saga herðibreiðs*, ch. 17, ch. 18.
94. *Ólafs saga helga*, ch. 205.
95. *Ólafs saga helga*, ch. 49; *Orkneyinga saga*, ch. 11; Denny and Filmer-Sankey, *Bayeux Tapestry*, scene 48.
96. *Ólafs saga helga*, ch. 212.
97. *Haralds saga Sigurðarsonar*, ch. 9; *Brennu-Njáls saga*, ch. 157.
98. *Haralds saga Sigurðarson*, ch. 72.
99. *Haralds saga Sigurðarson*, ch. 22.
100. *Egils saga Skalla-Grímssonar*, ch. 54.
101. *Hákonar saga góða*, ch. 25.
102. *Ólafs saga helga*, ch. 49, ch. 150, ch. 223; *Magnúss saga góða*, ch. 28; *Haralds saga Sigurðarsonar*, ch. 10, ch. 63, ch. 85; *Magnúss saga berfætts*, ch. 25; *Egils saga Skalla-Grímssonar*, ch. 22, ch. 53.
103. *Ólafs saga helga*, ch. 223.
104. Ibid., ch. 226.
105. Ibid., ch. 205.
106. Cleasby et al., eds., *Icelandic-English Dictionary*,

357-358, s.v. "kuml"; *Brennu-Njáls saga*, ch. 142; *Ólafs saga helga*, ch. 205.

107. *Ólafs saga helga*, ch. 206.

108. *Ynglinga saga*, ch. 22; *Ólafs saga Tryggvasonar*, ch.

107; *Ólafs saga helga*, ch. 61, ch. 226; *Haralds saga Sigurðarsonar*, ch. 92; *Magnúss saga Berfœtts*, ch. 25.

109. *Hákons saga herðibreiðs*, ch. 16

110. Tacitus, *Dialogus, Agricola, Germania*, tr. William Peterson (London: William Heinemann, 1914), 272-273, accessed Oct. 14, 2020, https://ryanfb.github.io/loebolus-data/L035.pdf; *King's Mirror*, ch. 37, 214.

111. Saxo, *History of the Danes*, bk. 7, 226-227.

112. Saxo, *History of the Danes*, vol.2, 122n112.

113. *Gautreks saga*, ch. 5; *Knýtlinga saga*, ch. 76; *Fornkonunga saga*, ch. 8, ch. 9.

114. Cleasby et al., eds., *Icelandic-English Dictionary*, 235, s.v. "hamalt."

115. Ibid., 483, s.v. "rani."

116. *Færeyinga saga*, ch. 19.

117. Cleasby et al., eds., *Icelandic-English Dictionary*, 235, s.v. "hamalt"; Ásgeir, *Íslensk orðsifjabók*, 303, s.v. "hamalt."

118. *Færeyinga saga*, ch. 19; Saxo, *History of the Danes*, bk. 7, 227.

119. *Fornkonunga saga*, ch. 8.

120. *Færeyinga saga*, ch.19; *Reginsmál*, v. 23.

121. Short, *Icelanders*, 199.

122. *Ólafs saga helga*, ch. 216.

123. Ibid., ch. 224; *Egils saga Skalla-Grímssonar*, ch. 54; *Gautreks saga*, ch. 5.

124. Cleasby et al., eds., *Icelandic-English Dictionary*, 384, s.v. "lendr"; *Ólafs saga helga*, ch. 224.

125. *Ólafs saga helga*, ch. 219-221, ch. 223, ch. 224.

126. Ibid., ch. 12-13; *Haralds saga Sigurðarsonar*, ch. 86; *Ólafs saga Tryggvasonar*, ch. 26.

127. *Ólafs saga Tryggvasonar*, ch. 18.

128. *Hákonar saga góða*, ch. 24; *Egils saga Skalla-Grímssonar*, ch. 52; *Fornkonunga saga*, ch. 7.

129. *Egils saga Skalla-Grímssonar*, ch. 52.

130. *Hákonar saga góða*, ch. 24.

131. *Egils saga Skalla-Grímssonar*, ch. 53.

132. Cleasby et al., eds., *Icelandic-English Dictionary*, 504-505, s.v. "ryðja"; *Eiríks saga rauða*, ch. 2; Sverrir Hólmarsson et al., *Íslensk-ensk orðabók* (Reykjavík: Iðunn, 1989), 329, s.v. "ryðja."

133. *Hákonar saga góða*, ch. 30.

134. *Ólafs saga helga*, ch. 226.

135. *Haralds saga Sigurðarsonar*, ch. 72.

136. *Egils saga Skalla-Grímssonar*, ch. 53; *Heiðarvíga saga*, ch. 27; *Ólafs saga helga*, ch. 226; *Haralds saga Sigurðarsonar*, ch. 72, ch. 85.

137. *Egils saga Skalla-Grímssonar*, ch. 53, ch. 54; *Ólafs saga helga*, ch. 226, ch. 229; *Hákonar saga góda*, ch. 31.

138. Cleasby et al., eds., *Icelandic-English Dictionary*, 710-711, s.v. "virki."

139. Else Roesdahl, *Danmarks Vikingetid* (Copenhagen: Gyldendal, 1980), 159-164.

140. Pulsiano, ed., *Medieval Scandinavia*, 120-121, s.v. "Danevirke."

141. *Ólafs saga Tryggvasonar*, ch. 26; *Jómsvíkinga saga*, ch. 7.

142. Pulsiano, ed., *Medieval Scandinavia*, 209-215, s.v. "fortification"; Cleasby et al., eds., *Icelandic-English Dictionary*, 73, s.v. "borg."

143. Roesdahl, *Danmarks Vikingetid*, 157-159.

144. Pulsiano, ed., *Medieval Scandinavia*, 214, s.v. "fortification."

145. *Magnúss saga berfœtts*, ch. 12; *Ólafs saga helga*, ch. 61.

146. Pulsiano, ed., *Medieval Scandinavia*, 209-214, s.v. "fortification"; Ole Crumlin-Pedersen and Olaf Olsen, eds., *The Skuldelev Ships I*, Ships and Boats of the North v. 4.1 (Roskilde: Viking Ship Museum, 2002), 42-46.

147. *Kormáks saga*, ch. 14; *Landnámabók* S. 168; *Hrómundar þáttur halta*, ch. 1.

148. *Eyrbyggja saga*, ch. 59; *Vatnsdæla saga*, ch. 30.

149. *Íslendinga saga*, ch. 153.

150. Ebenezer Henderson, *Iceland: or the Journal of a Residence in that Island during the Years 1814 and 1815*, vol. 2 (Edinburgh: Oliphant, Waugh and Innes, 1819), 141-142, accessed Mar. 31, 2020, https://books.google.com/books?id=5UMCAAAAYAAJ&pg=PA1&source=gbs_toc_r&cad=3#v=onepage&q&f=false.

151. Guðrún Sveinbjarnardóttir, *Reykholt: Archaeological Investigations at a High Status Farm in Western Iceland* (Reykjavík: National Museum of Iceland and Snorrastofa, 2012), 83-84.

152. *Eyrbyggja saga*, ch. 62, *Vatnsdæla saga*, ch. 30, *Ólafs saga helga*, ch. 133.

153. *Landnámabók*, S. 43, S. 151, S. 168.

154. *Egils saga Skalla-Grímssonar*, ch. 19, ch. 46; *Skirnismál*, prose after v. 10.

155. *Brennu-Njáls saga*, ch. 86; *Egils saga Skalla-Grímssonar*, ch. 53; *Magnúss saga blinda og Haralds gilla*, ch. 3.

156. *Ólafs saga helga*, ch. 229; *Hákonar saga góða*, ch. 25-26; *Egils saga Skalla-Grímssonar*, ch. 53; *Brennu-Njáls saga*, ch. 86.

157. *Svarfdæla saga*, ch. 27; *Ólafs saga helga*, ch. 226.

158. *Ólafs saga helga*, ch. 211; *Jómsvíkinga saga*, ch. 27.

159. *Hákonar saga góða*, ch. 27; *Ólafs saga helga*, ch. 235, ch. 237.

160. *Fóstbrœðra saga*, ch. 24.

161. *Ólafs saga helga*, ch. 231.

162. *Ljósvetninga saga*, ch. 24; *Þórðar saga hreðu*, ch. 7, ch. 8; *Fóstbrœðra saga*, ch. 10, ch. 23, ch. 24; *Vopnfirðinga saga*, ch. 15, ch. 18.

163. *Víga-Glúms saga*, ch. 23; G. Stroud and R.L. Kemp, *Cemeteries of St. Andrews, Fishergate*, v. 12, fasc. 2 (York: Council for British Archaeology, 1993), 232-241.

164. Crumlin-Pedersen and Olsen, eds., *Skuldelev Ships I*, 126-127, 324-325.

165. Ole Crumlin-Pedersen, *Viking-Age Ships and Shipbuilding in Hedeby/Haithabu and Schleswig*, Ships & Boats of the North, v. 2 (Roskilde, Denmark: Viking Ship Museum, 2003), 307-312.

166. Ibid., 92-93.

167. *Ólafs saga Tryggvasonar*, ch. 88.

168. Ibid., ch. 22.

169. Cleasby et al., eds., *Icelandic-English Dictionary*, 574, s.v. "snekkja."

170. Crumlin-Pedersen and Olsen, eds., *Skuldelev Ships I*, 315.

171. Ibid., 269-273, 276-278, 314.

172. Larsen, tr., *Earliest Norwegian Law, Gulathing Law* title 306, 194-195, title 310, 196.

173. Crumlin-Pedersen and Olsen, eds., *Skuldelev Ships I*, 317-319.

174. *Ólafs saga helga*, ch. 109.

175. *Haralds saga hárfagra*, ch. 9; *Ólafs saga Tryggvasonar*, ch. 40.

176. *Ólafs saga góða*, ch. 17.

177. William R. Short and Hurstwic, unpublished research, Nov. 14, 2015. Hurstwic members fought rounds of simulated combat aboard the *Sæ Hrafn*, a Viking ship replica operated by the Longship Company. After each round, subjective comments from the combatants were recorded. Video of the rounds was studied for further insights.

178. *Haralds saga hárfagra*, ch. 9.

179. *Egils saga Skalla-Grímssonar*, ch. 9.

180. *Ólafs saga Tryggvasonar*, ch. 88, ch. 94.

181. Ibid., ch. 88.

182. *Ólafs saga Tryggvasonar*, ch. 104, ch. 107; *Hákonar saga Herðibreiðs*, ch. 8.

183. *Magnúss saga góða*, ch. 30.

184. *Ólafs saga Tryggvasonar*, ch. 40, ch. 102; *Magnúss saga góða*, ch. 30.

185. *Grettis saga*, ch. 4; *Ólafs saga helga*, ch. 149-150.

186. *Haralds saga hárfagra*, ch. 11; *Ólafs saga Tryggvasonar*, ch. 103; *Haralds saga Sigurðarsonar*, ch. 63; Saxo, *History of the Danes*, bk. 7, 227.

187. Pulsiano, ed., *Medieval Scandinavia*, 578, s.v. "Ships and Shipbuilding."

188. *Brennu-Njáls saga*, ch. 30, ch. 84; *Harðar saga og Hólmverja*, ch. 17.

189. *Egils saga einhenda ok Ásmundar berserkjabana*, ch. 7.

190. *Ólafs saga Tryggvasonar*, ch. 103.

191. Ibid., ch. 40; *Jómsvíkinga saga*, ch. 31.

192. *Haralds saga Sigurðarsonar*, ch. 61, ch. 62.

193. *Magnúss saga góða*, ch. 30.

194. Ibid.

195. The following account of the battle at Svölðr is from *Ólafs saga Tryggvasonar*, ch. 105-111.

196. *Haralds saga Sigurðarsonar*, ch. 63.

197. *Jómsvíkinga saga*, ch. 31-32; *Göngu-Hrólfs saga*, ch. 8; *Bósa saga og herrauðs*, ch. 14; *Egils saga einhenda ok Ásmundar berserkjabana*, ch. 7.

198. *Ólafs saga Tryggvasonar*, ch. 113.

**CHAPTER 12: VIKING BATTLE TACTICS**

1. Cleasby et al., eds., *Icelandic-English Dictionary*, 367, s.v. "kænn."

2. *Færeyinga saga*, ch. 27; *Þorvalds þáttur víðförla*, ch. 2.

3. *Hákonar saga herðibreiðs*, ch. 5, ch. 6.

4. *Hávarðar saga Ísfirðings*, ch. 21; *Egils saga Skalla-Grímssonar*, ch. 52; *Hreiðars þáttur*, ch. 5.

5. Cleasby et al., eds., *Icelandic-English Dictionary*, 85, s.v. "brögðóttr."

6. US Department of Defense, *DOD Dictionary of Military and Associated Terms*, 2020, 212, accessed June 6, 2020, https://www.jcs.mil/Portals/36/Documents/Doctrine/pubs/dictionary.pdf.

7. Rundata U 1161, accessed June 6, 2020, https://skaldic.abdn.ac.uk/db.php?id=17971&if=srdb&table=mss; Page, *Chronicles*, 145.

8. *Egils saga Skalla-Grímssonar*, ch. 25; *Halldórs þáttur Snorrasonar hinn síðari*, ch. 3; *Bósa saga og herrauðs*, ch. 11.

9. Cleasby et al., eds., *Icelandic-English Dictionary*, 485, s.v. "ráð."

10. *Þorvalds þáttur víðförla*, ch. 2; Cleasby et al., eds., *Icelandic-English Dictionary*, 485, s.v. "ráð."

11. *Eyrbyggja saga*, ch. 28; *Brennu-Njáls saga*, ch. 139; *Heiðarvíga saga*, ch. 33-34; *Laxdæla saga*, ch. 71; *Eyrbyggja saga*, ch. 28, ch. 14, ch. 15.

12. *Brennu-Njáls saga*, ch. 139.

13. As discussed in the mindset chapter, a killing generally required compensation to be paid to the dead man's kin. Snorri realized that if Kári and his men killed too many of Flósi's supporters, the required compensation might be more than they could cover. Thus, Snorri planned to step in to stop the battle before the payments became ruinous to Kári's side.

14. *Brennu-Njáls saga*, ch. 145.

15. *Ólafs saga helga*, ch. 139, ch. 154, ch. 155, ch. 157.

16. *Gylfaginning*, ch 41; *Lokasenna*, v. 22.

17. *Skáldskaparmál*, G58.

18. Cleasby et al., eds., *Icelandic-English Dictionary*, 456, s.v. "njósna", 456, s.v. "njósn."

19. *Gylfaginning*, ch. 9.

20. Ibid., ch. 38.

21. *Ynglinga saga*, ch. 4, ch. 7; *Baldrs draumar*, v. 14.

22. *Ólafs saga helga*, ch. 152, ch. 156, ch. 166, ch. 197.

23. Ibid., ch. 38, ch. 39; ch. 112.

24. *Brennu-Njáls saga*, ch. 127.

25. Ibid., ch. 44.

26. *Laxdæla saga*, ch. 55; *Gísla saga Súrssonar*, ch. 13; *Laxdæla saga*, ch. 62; *Gísla saga Súrssonar*, ch. 22.

27. *Brennu-Njáls saga*, ch. 61; *Droplaugarsona saga*, ch. 9, ch. 10; *Egils saga Skalla-Grímssonar*, ch. 74, ch. 75; *Gull-Þóris saga*, ch. 12, ch. 15.

28. *Brennu-Njáls saga*, ch. 60, ch. 102; *Egils saga Skalla-Grímssonar*, ch. 76.

29. *Brennu-Njáls saga*, ch. 60, ch. 102; *Ólafs saga helga*, ch. 99.

30. *Droplaugarsona saga*, ch. 9, ch. 10; *Egils saga Skalla-Grímssonar*, ch. 74; *Gull-Þóris saga*, ch. 12, ch. 14; *Heiðarvíga saga*, ch. 7; *Kjalnesinga saga*, ch. 3, ch. 16; *Vopnfirðinga saga*, ch. 16.

31. *Brennu-Njáls saga*, ch. 61; *Ólafs saga Tryggvasonar*, ch. 3; *Ólafs saga helga*, ch. 74; *Magnúss saga Erlingssonar*, ch. 12; *Þórðar saga hreðu*, ch. 8.

32. *Víga-Skútu saga*, ch. 29.

33. *Egils saga Skalla-Grímssonar*, ch. 58; *Gísla saga Súrssonar*, ch. 25, ch. 31; *Harðar saga ok Hólmverja*, ch. 27; *Heiðarvíga saga*, ch. 11; *Ljósvetninga saga*, ch. 18; *Ólafs saga helga*, ch. 118.

34. *Brennu-Njáls saga*, ch. 75.

35. *Gísla saga Súrssonar*, ch. 22, ch. 34.

36. *Áns saga bogasveigis*, ch. 6.

37. *Hávamál*, v. 135-136.

38. Ibid., v. 2-4.

39. *Gísla saga Súrssonar*, ch. 25; *Hávamál*, v. 7.

40. *Brennu-Njáls saga*, ch. 150.

41. *Grettis saga*, ch. 6; *Harðar saga og Hólmverja*, ch. 32.

42. *Eyrbyggja saga*, ch. 44.

43. *Ljósvetninga saga*, ch. 10.

44. Cleasby et al., eds., *Icelandic-English Dictionary*, 180-182, s.v. "fyrir"; 530, s.v. "sitja."

45. *Bjarnar Saga Hítdælakappa*, ch. 30-31; *Brennu-Njáls saga*, ch. 61, ch. 71; *Droplaugarsona saga*, ch. 9; *Gunnars saga Keldgnúpfífls*, ch. 4; *Gull-Þóris saga*, ch. 14; *Heiðarvíga saga*, ch. 14; *Kormáks saga*, ch. 5; *Reykdæla saga ok Víga-Skútu*, ch. 29; *Vopnfirðinga saga*, ch. 16; *Þórðar saga hreðu*, ch. 8.

46. *Laxdæla saga*, ch. 84.

47. *Gull-Þóris saga*, ch. 15; *Reykdæla saga og Víga-Skútu*, ch. 29; *Víga-Glúms saga*, ch. 21; *Þórðar saga hreðu*, ch. 11.

48. *Egils saga Skalla-Grímssonar*, ch. 86.

49. *Brennu-Njáls saga*, ch. 62-63, ch. 72, ch. 102; *Egils saga Skalla-Grímssonar*, ch. 76; *Finnboga saga ramma*, ch. 37; *Gull-Þóris saga*, ch. 15; *Valla-Ljóts saga*, ch. 7; *Víglundar saga*, ch. 14; *Þórðar saga hreðu*, ch. 8, ch. 11.

50. *Hrafnkels saga*, ch. 14; *Valla-Ljóts saga*, ch. 7.

51. *Brennu-Njáls saga*, ch. 61, ch. 71; *Laxdæla saga*, ch. 84, ch. 87; *Valla-Ljóts saga*, ch. 6; *Þórðar saga hreðu*, ch. 8.

52. *Hávamál*, v. 41-44.

53. Larrington, tr., *Poetic Edda*, 20.
*Hávamál*, v. 43:

> Vin sínum
> skal maðr vinr vera,
> þeim ok þess vin;

> en óvinar síns
> skyli engi maðr
> vinar vinr vera.

54. *Laxdæla saga*, ch. 48.

55. *Bjarnar saga Hítdælakappa*, ch. 32; *Brennu-Njáls saga*, ch. 98; *Egils saga Skalla-Grímssonar*, ch. 74; *Flóamanna saga*, ch. 18; *Grettis saga*, ch. 43; *Gull-Þóris saga*, ch. 14; *Harðar saga og Hólmverja*, ch. 41; *Heiðarvíga saga*, ch. 13; *Kormáks saga*, ch. 5; *Laxdæla saga*, ch. 49; *Vatnsdæla saga*, ch. 19; *Víglundar saga*, ch. 14; *Vopnfirðinga saga*, ch. 16.

56. *Bjarnar saga Hítdælakappa*, ch. 31; *Brennu-Njáls saga*, ch. 72; *Egils saga Skalla-Grímssonar*, ch. 75; *Laxdæla saga*, ch. 84; *Reykdæla saga og Víga-Skútu*, ch. 6; *Þórðar saga hreðu*, ch. 8, ch. 11.

57. *Reykdæla saga og Víga-Skútu*, ch. 29.

58. *Brennu-Njáls saga*, ch. 72.

59. *Laxdæla saga*, ch. 49; *Kormáks saga*, ch. 5.

60. *Egils saga Skalla-Grímssonar*, ch. 75, ch. 86.

61. *Brennu-Njáls saga*, ch. 92; *Valla-Ljóts saga*, ch. 7.

62. *Brennu-Njáls saga*, ch. 72; *Gull-Þóris saga*, ch. 12; *Kormáks saga*, ch. 5; *Laxdæla saga*, ch. 49; ch. 84; *Reykdæla saga og Víga-Skútu*, ch. 29; *Þórðar saga hreðu*, ch. 9, ch. 11.

63. *Droplaugarsona saga*, ch. 10.

64. *Brennu-Njáls saga*, ch. 61, ch. 98; *Heiðarvíga saga*, ch. 13.

65. *Bjarnar saga Hítdælakappa*, ch. 18, ch. 32; *Brennu-Njáls saga*, ch. 62, ch. 72; *Droplaugarsona saga*, ch. 10; *Hrafnkels saga*, ch. 14; *Laxdæla saga*, ch. 48; *Víga-Glúms saga*, ch. 21; *Þórðar saga hreðu*, ch. 8.

66. *Bjarnar saga Hítdælakappa*, ch. 32; *Brennu-Njáls saga*, ch. 62, ch. 72; *Laxdæla saga*, ch. 49; *Þórðar saga hreðu*, ch. 8, ch. 9; *Droplaugarsona saga*, ch. 10.

67. *Bjarnar saga Hítdælakappa*, ch. 32; *Droplaugarsona saga*, ch. 10; *Laxdæla saga*, ch. 49.

68. *Brennu-Njáls saga*, ch. 63, ch. 72; *Egils saga Skalla-Grímssonar*, ch. 76.

69. Gunnar et al., eds., *Grágás Lagasafn íslenska þjóðveldisins*, 263-264, K. 108.

70. *Brennu-Njáls saga*, ch. 64-66.

71. Ibid., ch. 62-66.

72. *Laxdæla saga*, ch. 49.

73. *Bjarnar saga Hítdælakappa*, ch. 31.

74. *Grettis saga*, ch. 43.

75. *Brennu-Njáls saga*, ch. 128.

76. Ibid., ch. 129.

77. Pulsiano, ed., *Medieval Scandinavia*, 292-293, s.v. "houses"; Short, *Icelanders*, 89-102.

78. William R. Short and Hurstwic, unpublished research, Nov. 29, 2018. We created a replica of the main room of a small Viking-age longhouse, using a stand-in for the wooden framing elements that were capable of trapping weapons when hit and placing obstacles that simulated the firepit, the benches, and other im-

pediments. Practice partners fought rounds of simulated combat using the weapon or weapons of their choice, in one-on-one, one-on-two, and one-on-three situations. After each round, fighters' subjective comments were recorded. Video was shot of each round to be reviewed later.

79. Gunnar et al., eds., *Grágás Lagasafn íslenska þjóðveldisins*, 264, K. 109; Larsen, tr., *Earliest Norwegian Law, Gulathing Law* title 178, 137.

80. Gunnar et al., eds., *Grágás Lagasafn íslenska þjóðveldisins*, 264, K. 109.

81. Larsen, tr., *Earliest Norwegian Law, Gulathing Law*, title 98, 105; *Frostathing Law*, vol. 4, ch. 4, 257-258.

82. *Brennu-Njáls saga*, ch. 128.

83. *Bjarnar saga Hítdælakappa*, ch. 30; *Egils saga Skalla-Grímssonar*, ch. 12, ch. 22; *Gísla saga Súrssonar*, ch. 3; *Gull-Þóris saga*, ch. 18; *Ólafs saga helga*, ch. 169.

84. *Egils saga Skalla-Grímssonar*, ch. 22; *Þorsteins saga síðu*, ch. 3.

85. *Brennu-Njáls saga*, ch. 128.

86. *Egils saga Skalla-Grímssonar*, ch. 22.

87. *Brennu-Njáls saga*, ch. 129; *Gull-Þóris saga*, ch. 10, ch. 18.

88. *Egils saga Skalla-Grímssonar*, ch. 22; *Gísla saga Súrssonar*, ch. 3.

89. *Brennu-Njáls saga*, ch. 129.

90. *Egils saga Skalla-Grímssonar*, ch. 46; *Hákonar saga herðibreiðs*, ch. 13.

91. *Egils saga Skalla-Grímssonar*, ch. 22.

92. *Brennu-Njáls saga*, ch. 109; *Eyrbyggja saga*, ch. 31; *Hænsna-Þóris saga*, ch. 9.

93. *Brennu-Njáls saga*, ch. 129; *Gull-Þóris saga*, ch. 10, ch. 18.

94. *Brennu-Njáls saga*, ch. 129; *Droplaugarsona saga*, ch. 1; *Harðar saga ok Hólmverja*, ch. 21; *Þorsteins saga Síðu*, ch. 3; *Gull-Þóris saga*, ch. 18.

95. *Hallfreðar saga vandræðaskálds*, ch. 1; *Gísla saga (lengri gerð)*, ch. 9.

96. *Brennu-Njáls saga*, ch. 128.

97. Ibid., ch. 129.

98. *Gull-Þóris saga*, ch. 18; *Egils saga Skalla-Grímssonar*, ch. 22.

99. Lucas, *Hofstaðir*, 1-4; Guðmundur Ólafsson, *Eiríksstaðir í Haukadal: Fornleifarannsókn á skálarúst* (Reykjavík: Þjóðminjasafn Íslands, 1998), 13-15; *Gísla saga Súrssonar*, ch. 5.

100. Cleasby et al., eds., *Icelandic-English Dictionary*, 323, s.v. "jarð-hús."

101. *Reykdæla saga og Víga-Skútu*, ch. 4; *Gísla saga Súrssonar*, ch. 25; *Fljótsdæla saga*, ch. 19; *Víglundar saga*, ch. 17; *Gunnars saga Keldugnúpsfífls*, ch. 3.

102. Mark Clinton, *The Souterrains of Ireland* (Bray, Ireland: Wordwell, 2001), 95, 175-196; Þór Hjaltalín, "Íslensk jarðhús," *Árbók Hins íslenzka fornleifafélags* 101 (2010): 142; Þór Hjaltalín (archaeologist, Min-

jastofnun Íslands), personal communication with Reynir A. Óskarson, Nov. 5, 2020.

103. *Hávarðar saga Ísfirðings*, ch. 11; *Reykdæla saga og Víga-Skútu*, ch. 30; *Reykdæla saga og Víga-Skúta*, ch. 28.

104. Þór, "Íslensk jarðhús," 142; *Gísla saga Súrssonar*, ch. 23.

105. *Droplaugarsona saga*, ch. 14; *Grettis saga*, ch. 47; *Hávarðar saga Ísfirðings*, ch. 11; *Þorsteins þáttur uxafóts*, ch. 14.

106. *Reykdæla saga og Víga-Skútu*, ch. 28.

107. Þór, "Íslensk jarðhús," 155.

108. Ibid., 156; *Gísla saga Súrssonar*, ch. 23; *Droplaugarsona saga*, ch. 14.

109. *Droplaugarsona saga*, ch. 12; *Haralds saga Sigurðarsonar*, ch. 7.

110. *Droplaugarsona saga*, ch. 14.

111. *Flóamanna saga*, ch. 16; *Grænlendinga þáttur*, ch. 6; *Reykdæla saga og Víga-Skútu*, ch. 4.

112. Þór, "Íslensk jarðhús," 159, 165.

113. *Íslendinga saga*, ch. 67.

114. *Reykdæla saga og Vígu-Skútu*, ch. 27; *Flóamanna saga*, ch. 19; *Vatnsdæla saga*, ch. 44.

115. Cleasby et al., eds., *Icelandic-English Dictionary*, 179, s.v. "fylgsni."

116. *Droplaugarsona saga*, ch. 12.

117. *Brennu-Njáls saga*, ch. 88.

118. *Gunnars þáttur Þiðrandabana*, ch. 5; *Fljótsdæla saga*, ch. 19.

119. *Brennu-Njáls saga*, ch. 153.

120. Ásgeir, *Íslensk orðsifjabók*, 1133.

121. *Gull-Þóris saga*, ch. 5; *Eyrbyggja saga*, ch. 60.

122. *Eyrbyggja saga*, ch. 37.

123. *Heiðarvíga saga*, ch. 24.

124. *Gísla saga Súrssonar*, ch. 34; *Brennu-Njáls saga*, ch. 62.

125. *Hallfreðar saga vandræðaskálds*, ch. 4.

126. *Brennu-Njáls saga*, ch. 139, ch. 145; Einar, ed., *Brennu-Njáls saga*, ÍF v. 12, ch. 139, 372n3.

127. *Gull-Þóris saga*, ch. 5; *Eyrbyggja saga*, ch. 60, ch. 62.

128. *Gísla saga (styttri gerð)*, ch. 34.; *Gísla saga (lengri gerð)*, ch. 27.

129. *Eyrbyggja saga*, ch. 44.

130. Ibid., ch. 37.

131. *Þórðar saga hreðu*, ch. 8; *Eyrbyggja saga*, ch. 44.

132. *Þórðar saga hreðu*, ch. 8; *Gísla saga Súrssonar*, ch. 34-36.

133. *Grettis saga*, ch. 58.

134. Ibid., ch. 67.

135. *Hávamál*, v.1.

## CHAPTER 13: RAIDING AND DUELING

1. Cleasby et al., eds., *Icelandic-English Dictionary*, 716, s.v. "víkingr."

2. *Hrómundar þáttur halta,* ch. 3.

3. *Egils saga Skalla-Grímssonar,* ch. 46.

4. *Brennu-Njáls saga,* ch. 29.

5. *Eyrbyggja saga,* ch. 60; *Grettis saga,* ch. 4.

6. *Finnboga saga ramma,* ch. 35.

7. *Haralds saga gráfeldar,* ch. 12; *Ólafs saga Tryggvasonar,* ch. 13.

8. *Haralds saga hárfagra,* ch. 17; *Hákonar saga Aðalsteinsfóstra,* ch. 4.

9. *Ynglinga saga,* ch. 30-31; *Frá Fornjóti ok hans ættmönnum,* ch. 1, ch. 2.

10. Rundata SM10, accessed June 3, 2020, https://skaldic.abdn.ac.uk/db.php?id=16359&if=srdb&table=mss; Rundata U617, accessed June 3, 2020, https://skaldic.abdn.ac.uk/db.php?id=17439&if=srdb&table=mss; Rundata Br Barnes 1, accessed June 3, 2020, https://skaldic.abdn.ac.uk/db.php?id=21409&if=srdb&table=mss.

11. Rundata Vg61, accessed June 3, 2020, https://skaldic.abdn.ac.uk/db.php?id=16592&if=srdb&table=mss.

12. "Widsith," in *The Exeter Book: The Anglo-Saxon Poetic Records,* ed. George Philip Krapp and Elliott Van Kirk Dobbie (New York: Columbia University Press, 1936), 149-153.

13. Cleasby et al., eds., *Icelandic-English Dictionary,* 258, s.v. "herja."

14. Gunnar et al., eds., *Grágás Lagasafn íslenska þjóðveldisins,* 267, S. 365; *Grettis saga,* ch. 19.

15. Larson, tr., *Earliest Norwegian Law, Gulathing Law* title 314, 199, *Frostathing Law* vol. 7, ch. 25, 322.

16. *Vatnsdæla saga,* ch. 2; *Bjarnar saga Hítdælakappa,* ch. 3, ch. 4; *Svarfdæla saga,* ch. 4.

17. *Flóamanna saga,* ch. 15; *Grettis saga,* ch. 19; *Jómsvíkinga saga,* ch. 11.

18. *Brennu-Njáls saga,* ch. 31; *Gunnlaugs saga ormstunga,* ch. 12; *Ljósvetninga saga,* ch. 1; *Jómsvíkinga saga,* ch. 20.

19. *Landnámabók,* S. 165; Larsen, tr., *Earliest Norwegian Law, Gulathing Law* title 314, 199.

20. Historiska museet SHM 108202, accessed June 3, 2020, https://historiska.se/upptack-historien/object/108202-bildsten-av-kalksten/.

21. *Egils saga Skalla-Grímssonar,* ch. 40:

Þat mælti mín móðir,
at mér skyldi kaupa
fley ok fagrar árar
fara á brott með víkingum,
standa upp í stafni,
stýra dýrum knerri,
halda svá til hafnar,
höggva mann ok annan.

22. "Ipsi enim pyratae, quos illi Wichingos appellant." Adam, *Gesta Hammaburgensis ecclesias Pontificum,* 233, bk. 4, ch. 6.

23. Page, "'A Most Vile People'"; Jón, "Vikings in Spain," 31-46.

24. *Landnámabók,* S. 8.

25. Agnar Helgason et al., "mtDNA and the Islands of the North Atlantic: Estimating the Proportions of Norse and Gaelic Ancestry," *American Journal of Human Genetics,* 68 (2001): 723-737; *Landnámabók,* S. 6-8.

26. *Egils saga Skalla-Grímssonar,* ch. 32.

27. *Laxdæla saga,* ch. 21.

28. *Jómsvíkinga saga,* ch. 3, ch. 4, ch. 8, ch. 9, ch. 10, ch. 11, ch. 13; *Bjarnar saga Hítdælakappa,* ch. 5; *Egils saga Skalla-Grímssonar,* ch. 1, ch. 19, ch. 46-48, ch. 70; *Flóamanna saga,* ch. 2, ch. 16; *Gunnars saga Keldugnúpsfífls,* ch. 7; *Hávarðar saga Ísfirðings,* ch. 23; *Svarfdæla saga,* ch. 3, ch. 15; *Vatnsdæla saga,* ch. 7.

29. *Jómsvíkinga saga,* ch. 3, ch. 4, ch. 8, ch. 11, ch. 20; *Egils saga einhenda ok Ásmundar berserkjabana,* ch. 2.

30. *Jómsvíkinga saga,* ch. 8.

31. *Þormóðar þáttr,* ch. 2.

32. *Egils saga Skalla-Grímssonar,* ch. 1, ch. 70; *Jómsvíkinga saga,* ch. 7; *Ólafs saga Tryggvasonar,* ch. 13; *Fornkonunga saga,* ch. 3; *Flóamanna saga,* ch. 16; *Eyrbyggja saga,* ch. 59.

33. *Jómsvíkinga saga,* ch. 3, ch. 8; *Egils saga Skalla-Grímssonar,* ch. 40.

34. *Flóamanna saga,* ch. 2.

35. *Finnboga saga ramma,* ch. 35; *Ólafs saga helga,* ch. 4; *Jómsvíkinga saga,* ch. 21.

36. *Jómsvíkinga saga,* ch. 14.

37. *Flóamanna saga,* ch. 8; *Laxdæla saga,* ch. 25; *Vatnsdæla saga,* ch. 1; *Haralds saga hárfagri,* ch. 24; *Landnámabók,* S. 5, S. 112-113, S. 327; *Bósa saga og herrauðs,* ch. 2.

38. Rundata U954, accessed June 1, 2020, https://skaldic.abdn.ac.uk/db.php?id=17763&if=srdb&table=mss; Page, *Chronicles,* 145.

39. *Jómsvíkinga saga,* ch. 14.

40. *Vatnsdæla saga,* ch. 43.

41. *Egils saga Skalla-Grímssonar,* ch. 46, ch. 70; *Ólafs saga Helga,* ch. 22.

42. *Egils saga Skalla-Grímssonar,* ch. 19; *Vatnsdæla saga,* ch. 7.

43. *Ólafs saga helga,* ch. 151.

44. William R. Short and Hurstwic, unpublished research, May 21, 2020. A database of Viking raids reported in the literary sources was created, taken from the *Sagas of Icelanders, Heimskringla,* and the *Anglo-Saxon-Chronicles.* Where possible, an approximate date (to the nearest decade) and location was assigned to each raid. The data were processed to create a summary of where the raids occurred (broken down into about ten general areas) and by quarter-century.

45. R. Dozy, *Recherches sur l'histoire et la littérature del'Espagne pendant la Moyen Age,* 2nd ed., vol. 2 (Leyde, Netherlands: E. J. Brill, 1860), 282-283; *Egils saga Skalla-Grímssonar,* ch. 47.

46. *Egils saga Skalla-Grímssonar,* ch. 46, ch. 70; J. A. Giles, tr., *The Anglo-Saxon Chronicle* (London: Bell and Sons, 1914), year 793, 40, year 794, 40-41.

47. *Eyrbyggja saga,* ch. 1; *Grettis saga,* ch. 4; *Haralds saga hárfagra,* ch. 19; *Hákonar saga Aðalsteinsfóstra,* ch. 4.

48. *Egils saga Skalla-Grímssonar,* ch. 48; *Færeyinga saga,* ch. 18.

49. *Laxdæla saga,* ch. 12.

50. *Jómsvíkinga saga,* ch. 7, ch. 9, ch. 30.

51. Ibid., ch.11; *Eyrbyggja saga,* ch. 1.

52. *Fornkonunga saga,* ch. 7; *Ásmundar saga kappabana,* ch. 3.

53. Cleasby et al., eds., *Icelandic-English Dictionary,* 258-259, s.v. "herr."

54. *Jómsvíkinga saga,* ch. 22, ch. 30; *Egils saga Skalla-Grímssonar,* ch. 19, ch. 57, ch. 70; *Hrana saga Hrings,* ch. 13; *Ynglinga saga,* ch. 28, ch. 46; *Haralds saga hárfagra,* ch. 24, ch. 27; *Ólafs saga Tryggvasonar,* ch. 32, ch. 39; *Helgakviða Hundingsbana II,* prose following v. 4.

55. Cleasby et al., eds., *Icelandic-English Dictionary,* 597, s.v. "strand-högg."

56. *Ólafs saga Tryggvasonar,* ch. 39.

57. Page, "'Most Vile People'"; ". . . de gente fera Normannica nos libera . . ." *Antiphonaire de Charles le Chauvre,* BNF lat. 17436, folio 24r, accessed June 1, 2020, https://gallica.bnf.fr/ark:/12148/btv1b8426787t/f53.item.r=antiphonaire%20compiegne.

58. Kevin Crossley-Holland, tr., *The Anglo-Saxon Word: An Anthology* (Oxford: Oxford University Press, 1984), 186; Page, *Chronicles,* 79.

59. *Eyrbyggja saga,* ch. 29; *Hákonar saga Aðalsteinsfóstra,* ch. 8.

60. *Ólafs saga Tryggvasonar,* ch. 25; *Ólafs saga Helga,* ch. 96; *Fornkonunga saga,* ch. 4.

61. *Haralds saga hárfagra,* ch. 25; *Hákonar saga Aðalsteinsfóstra,* ch. 3.

62. *Flóamanna saga,* ch. 25; *Fóstbræðra saga,* ch. 4.

63. Gunnar et al., eds., *Grágás Lagasafn íslenska þjóðveldisins,* 267-268, S. 365-366.

64. *Færeyinga saga,* ch. 21; *Ólafs saga helga,* ch. 52, ch. 133.

65. *Brennu-Njáls saga,* ch. 83; *Egils saga Skalla-Grímssonar,* ch. 19; *Færeyinga saga,* ch. 18; *Gunnars saga Keldugnúpsfífls,* ch. 7; *Harðar saga og Hólmverja,* ch. 17; *Kormáks saga,* ch. 1; *Ljósvetninga saga,* ch. 29; *Svarfdæla saga,* ch. 4.

66. *Svarfdæla saga,* ch. 3; *Vatnsdæla saga,* ch. 7.

67. *Ljósvetninga saga,* ch. 29.

68. *Bjarnar saga Hítdælakappa,* ch. 7; *Egils saga Skalla-Grímssonar,* ch. 18; *Svarfdæla saga,* ch. 4.

69. *Ólafs saga helga,* ch. 52, ch. 133; *Vatnsdæla saga,* ch. 43; *Egils saga Skalla-Grímssonar,* ch. 14; *Flóamanna saga,* ch. 16.

70. *Brennu-Njáls saga,* ch. 31; *Egils saga Skalla-Grímssonar,* ch. 14; *Ólafs saga helga,* ch. 133.

71. Larsen, tr., *Earliest Norwegian Law, Gulathing Law* title 295, 188, title 311, 196-197.

72. *Jómsvíkinga saga,* ch. 7; *Egils saga Skalla-Grímssonar,* ch. 49, ch. 60; *Færeyinga saga,* ch. 19; *Ynglinga saga,* ch. 27; *Haralds saga hárfagri,* ch. 29; *Haralds saga Sigurðarsonar,* ch. 48.

73. *Jómsvíkinga saga,* ch. 11.

74. Birgit Sawyer and Peter Sawyer, *Medieval Scandinavia: From Conversion to Reformation circa 800–1500* (Minneapolis: University of Minnesota Press, 1993), 131-134.

75. James Graham-Campbell, ed., *Cultural Atlas of the Viking World* (New York: Facts on File, 1994), 148.

76. *Bjarnar saga Hítdælakappa,* ch. 9.

77. *Droplaugarsona saga,* ch. 15; *Grettis saga,* ch. 19, ch. 40; *Gull-Þóris saga,* ch. 6; *Gunnlaugs saga ormstunga,* ch. 7; *Kormáks saga,* ch. 1; *Svarfdæla saga,* ch. 4, ch. 7; *Víga-Glúms saga,* ch. 4; *Þórðar saga hreðu,* ch. 2.

78. Cleasby et al., eds., *Icelandic-English Dictionary,* 280-281, s.v. "hólm-ganga."

79. Ibid., 123, s.v. "ein-vígi."

80. Historiska museet SHM 108202, accessed Mar. 24, 2021, https://historiska.se/upptack-historien/object/108202-bildsten-av-kalksten/.

81. Kelsie Spears, "The Picture Stones of Gotland" (master's thesis, University of Houston, 2016), 69-72.

82. Jeffrey L. Forgeng (author and curator, Worcester Art Museum), personal communication with William R. Short, Sept. 26, 2019.

83. Pulsiano, ed., *Medieval Scandinavia,* 289-290, s.v. "hólm-ganga"; *Ljósvetninga saga,* ch. 30; *Kormáks saga,* ch. 10.

84. *Egils saga Skalla-Grímssonar,* ch. 66; *Kormáks saga,* ch. 22.

85. Henrikson, *Svensk Historia,* bk. 1, 113-114; Brink, ed., *Viking World,* 27.

86. *Gunnlaugs saga ormstungu,* ch. 11; Larsen, tr., *Earliest Norwegian Law, Gulathing Law* title 216, 149; Gunnar et al., eds., *Grágás Lagasafn íslenska þjóðveldisins,* 267, S. 365.

87. *Egils saga Skalla-Grímssonar,* ch. 57, ch. 66; *Ljósvetninga saga,* ch. 30.

88. *Egils saga Skalla-Grímssonar,* ch. 57.

89. *Brennu-Njáls saga,* ch. 24, ch. 56, ch. 60; *Egils saga Skalla-Grímssonar,* ch. 57.

90. *Finnboga saga ramma,* ch. 34; *Flóamanna saga,* ch. 34; *Hallfreðar saga vandræðaskálds,* ch. 4; *Kormáks saga,* ch. 21; *Vatnsdæla saga,* ch. 33; *Gunnlaugs saga ormstungu,* ch. 11; *Skáldskaparmál,* ch. 17.

91. *Vatnsdæla saga,* ch. 2; *Svarfdæla saga,* ch. 4.

92. *Fóstbræðra saga,* ch. 24; *Svarfdæla saga,* ch. 4; *Vatnsdæla saga,* ch. 2.

93. Jenny Jochens, *Women in Old Norse Society* (Ithaca, NY: Cornell University Press, 1995), 20-22; Short, *Icelanders,* 65.

94. *Droplaugarsona saga,* ch. 15; *Egils saga Skalla-*

*Grímssonar*, ch. 65; *Eyrbyggja saga*, ch. 8; *Flóamanna saga*, ch. 15, ch. 17, ch. 27, ch. 31; *Gísla saga Súrssonar*, ch. 1, ch. 2; *Grettis saga*, ch. 40; *Gull-Þóris saga*, ch. 6; *Gunnlaugs saga ormstungu*, ch. 7; *Hávarðar saga Ísfirðings*, ch. 14; *Kjalnesinga saga*, ch. 9; *Kormáks saga*, ch. 9, ch. 14; *Reykdæla saga ok Víga-skútu*, ch. 1, ch. 19; *Svarfdæla saga*, ch. 7; *Vatnsdæla saga*, ch. 46; *Víga-Glúms saga*, ch. 4; ch. 14; *Ólafs saga Tryggvasonar*, ch. 32; *Landnámabók*, S. 70, S. 86, S. 326, S. 389.

95. *Flóamanna saga*, ch. 16.

96. Short, *Icelanders*, 65-66.

97. *Víglundar saga*, ch. 6; *Gunnlaugs saga ormstunga*, ch. 11; *Kormáks saga*, ch. 9.

98. *Droplaugarsona saga*, ch. 15; *Egils saga Skalla-Grímssonar*, ch. 65; *Eyrbyggja saga*, ch. 8; *Flóamanna saga*, ch. 15, ch. 17, ch. 31; *Gísla saga Súrssonar*, ch. 1, ch. 2; *Grettis saga*, ch. 40; *Gull-Þóris saga*, ch. 6; *Gunnlaugs saga ormstungu*, ch. 7; *Kjalnesinga saga*, ch. 9; *Kormáks saga*, ch. 9; *Reykdæla saga ok Víga-skútu*, ch. 19; *Svarfdæla saga*, ch. 7; *Vatnsdæla saga*, ch. 46; *Víga-Glúms saga*, ch. 4; *Ólafs saga Tryggvasonar*, ch. 32.

99. *Bjarnar saga Hítdælakappa*, ch. 4, *Flóamanna saga*, ch. 15, ch. 17; *Egils saga einhenda ok Ásmundar berserkjabana*, ch. 4.

100. *Gunnlaugs saga ormstunga*, ch.11; Sigurður Nordal and Guðni Jónsson, eds, *Gunnlaugs saga ormstungu*, Íslenzk fornrit, v. 3 (Reykjavík: Hið íslenzka fornritafélag, 1938), lix; Guðni Jónsson, ed., *Grettis saga Ásmundarsonar*, Íslenzk fornrit, v. 7 (Reykjavík: Hið íslenzka fornritafélag, 1936), lxvii; *Reykdæla saga ok Víga-Skútu*, ch. 19.

101. *Kormáks saga*, ch. 7; *Eiríks saga rauða*, ch. 2; *Grettis saga*, ch. 70; *Gísla saga Súrssonar*, ch. 2.

102. *Droplaugarsona saga*, ch. 15; *Egils saga Skalla-Grímssonar*, ch. 65; *Eyrbyggja saga*, ch. 8; *Flóamanna saga*, ch. 15, ch. 17, ch. 27, ch. 31; *Gísla saga Súrssonar* ch. 1; *Grettis saga*, ch. 19, ch. 40; *Gull-Þóris saga*, ch. 6; *Gunnlaugs saga Ormstungu*, ch. 7; *Kormáks saga*, ch. 1; *Reykdæla saga ok Vígaskútu*, ch. 19; *Svarfdæla saga*, ch. 7; *Vatnsdæla saga*, ch. 46; *Víga-Glúms Saga*, ch. 4, ch. 5; *Landnámabók*, S. 34.

103. *Víglundar saga*, ch. 3; *Bjarnar Saga Hítdælakappa*, ch. 4; *Egils saga Skalla-Grímssonar*, ch. 57, ch. 65; *Flóamanna saga*, ch. 16, ch. 33; *Gísla saga Súrssonar*, ch. 1; *Gunnlaugs saga ormstungu*, ch. 7; *Vatnsdæla saga*, ch. 33; *Ólafs saga Tryggvasonar*, ch. 32; *Landnámabók*, S. 99.

104. *Kormáks saga* ch. 17, ch. 21; *Reykdæla saga ok Víga-Skútu* ch. 1; *Landnámabók* S. 70, S. 326.

105. *Droplaugarsona saga*, ch. 15; *Egils saga Skalla-grímssonar*, ch. 65; *Eyrbyggja saga*, ch. 8; *Flóamanna saga*, ch. 15, ch. 17, ch. 31; *Gísla saga Súrssonar*, ch. 1, ch. 2; *Grettis saga*, ch. 40; *Reykdæla saga ok Víga-Skútu*, ch. 19; *Víga-Glúms saga*, ch. 4; *Brennu-Njáls saga*, ch. 24; *Landnámabók*, S. 86.

106. *Reykdæla saga ok Víga-Skútu*, ch. 1; *Víga-Glúms Saga*, ch. 14; *Landnámabók*, S. 326; S. 389.

107. *Egils saga Skalla-Grímssonar*, ch. 65, ch. 66; *Gísla saga Súrssonar*, ch. 1; *Gunnlaugs saga ormstunga*, ch. 7; *Kjalnesinga saga*, ch. 9; *Kormáks saga*, ch. 10, ch. 21.

108. *Bjarnar Saga Hítdælakappa*, ch. 4; *Flóamanna saga*, ch. 15; *Gull-Þóris saga*, ch. 6; *Svarfdæla saga*, ch. 7.

109. *Skáldskaparmál*, ch. 17.

110. *Gunnlaugs saga ormstunga*, ch. 7.

111. Henrikson, *Svensk Historia*, bk. 1, 113-114.

112. *Egils saga Skalla-Grímssonar*, ch. 57; *Eyrbyggja saga*, ch. 8; *Flóamanna saga*, ch. 15; *Gísla saga Súrssonar*, ch. 1; *Gunnlaugs saga Ormstungu*, ch. 7.

113. *Ljósvetninga saga*, ch. 17; *Landnámabók*, S. 326; *Brennu-Njáls saga*, ch. 8.

114. *Egils saga Skalla-Grímssonar*, ch. 57, ch. 66; *Eyrbyggja saga*, ch. 8; *Grettis saga*, ch. 40; *Gunnlaugs-saga Ormstungu*, ch. 11; *Reykdæla Saga og Víga-Glúms*, ch. 1, ch. 19.

115. *Egils saga Skalla-Grímssonar*, ch. 66; *Kjalnesinga saga*, ch. 9.

116. *Flóamanna saga*, ch. 15; *Vatnsdæla saga*, ch. 33, ch. 35; *Egils saga Skalla-Grimssonar*, ch. 57.

117. *Egils saga Skalla-Grímssonar*, ch. 57.

118. *Kormáks saga*, ch. 21; *Bjarnar saga Hítdælakappa*, ch. 4.

119. Henrikson, *Svensk Historia*, bk. 1, 113-114.

120. Foote and Wilson, *Viking Achievement*, 379-380.

121. *Finnboga saga ramma*, ch. 34; *Gísla saga Súrssonar*, ch. 1, ch. 2; *Gunnlaugs saga ormstunga*, ch. 11; *Kjalnesinga saga*, ch. 9; *Kormáks saga*, ch. 9, ch. 21; *Svarfdæla saga*, ch. 7; *Vatnsdæla saga*, ch. 33.

122. *Gísla saga Súrssonar*, ch. 1, ch. 2; *Gunnlaugs saga ormstungu*, ch. 7, ch. 11; *Ljósvetninga saga*, ch. 16.

123. *Svarfdæla saga*, ch. 7; *Flóamanna saga*, ch. 33; *Gunnlaugs Saga ormstungu*, ch. 11.

124. *Gísla saga Súrssonar*, ch. 1; *Kormáks saga*, ch. 9.

125. *Kormáks saga*, ch. 22.

126. *Gylfaginning*, ch. 31.

127. *Víga-Glúms saga*, ch. 4.

128. *Bjarnar saga Hítdælakappa*, ch. 4; *Droplaugarsona saga*, ch. 15; *Flóamanna saga*, ch. 17, ch. 27; *Svarfdæla saga*, ch. 7; *Gísla saga Súrssonar*, ch. 2; *Gull-Þóris saga*, ch. 6; *Reykdæla saga og Víga-Skútu*, ch. 19.

129. *Flóamanna saga*, ch. 31; *Bjarnar saga Hítdælakappa*, ch. 4; *Gísla saga Súrssonar*, ch. 2.

130. *Bjarnar saga Hítdælakappa*, ch. 4; *Flóamanna saga*, ch. 17, ch. 27, ch. 31; *Gísla saga Súrssonar*, ch. 2.

131. *Droplaugarsona saga*, ch. 15; *Flóamanna saga*, ch. 15-16; *Svarfdæla saga*, ch. 7; *Víga-Glúms saga*, ch. 4.

132. *Svarfdæla saga*, ch. 10.

133. *Gunnlaugs saga ormstunga*, ch. 11; *Kormáks saga*, ch. 10, ch. 12.

134. *Svarfdæla saga*, ch. 9; *Gríms saga loðinkinna*, ch. 3; *Víga-Glúms saga*, ch. 4; *Gísla saga Súrssonar*, ch. 2.

135. William R. Short and Hurstwic, unpublished research, June 20, 2019; June 27, 2019. Pairs of duelers, armed with sword and shield, used simulated combat to fight rounds of duels, following the rules outlined later in the chapter. Then pairs of duelers armed with swords, accompanied by shield holders, used simulated combat to fight rounds of duels. After each round, fighters' subjective comments were recorded. Video was shot of each round to be reviewed later. In these testing sessions, a number of variants were tested: with and without shield holder, outlined above; holding the shield as outlined earlier in the shield chapter, as well as several variants of holding the shield; rounds with movement and rounds where movement was prohibited, as discussed later in this chapter; turn-based dueling as discussed later in the chapter and free-form dueling; normal shields and shields that had been secretly prepared to have a propensity to split under a blow.

136. *Gunnlaugs saga ormstungu*, ch. 11.

137. Cleasby et al., eds., *Icelandic-English Dictionary*, 280, s.v. "hólmr."

138. Foote and Wilson, *Viking Achievement*, 380.

139. *Egils saga Skalla-Grímssonar,* ch. 65; *Gísla saga Súrssonar*, ch. 1, ch. 2; *Kjalnesinga saga*, ch. 9; *Kormáks saga*, ch. 9, ch. 14; *Vatnsdæla saga*, ch. 33.

140. *Ljósvetninga saga*, ch. 16; *Gunnlaugs saga ormstunga*, ch. 11; *Landnámabók*, S. 377.

141. *Flóamanna saga*, ch. 15; *Finnboga saga ramma*, ch. 34; *Gísla saga Súrssonar*, ch. 2; *Kormáks saga*, ch. 21; *Vatnsdæla saga*, ch. 34.

142. Henrikson, *Svensk Historia*, bk. 1, 113-114; Foote and Wilson, *Viking Achievement*, 379-380.

143. *Hallfreðar saga vandræðaskálds,* ch. 10.

144. *Egils saga Skalla-Grímssonar,* ch. 65; *Flóamanna saga*, ch. 16; *Gísla saga Súrssonar*, ch. 2; *Gunnlaugs saga ormstunga*, ch. 11; *Kormáks saga*, ch. 9; *Reykdæla saga ok Víga-Skútu*, ch. 19; *Svarfdæla saga*, ch. 8; *Víga-Glúms saga*, ch. 4; *Ólafs Saga Tryggvasonar*, ch. 32.

145. *Gísla saga Súrssonar*, ch. 2; *Kormáks saga*, ch. 9; *Reykdæla saga og Víga-Skútu*, ch. 19.

146. *Kjalnesinga saga*, ch. 9; *Kormáks saga*, ch. 10.

147. *Egils saga Skalla-Grímssonar,* ch. 65.

148. *Kjalnesinga saga*, ch. 9; *Kormáks saga*, ch. 10; *Svarfdæla saga*, ch. 9.

149. *Kormáks saga*, ch. 10; *Helgakviða Hjörvarðssonar*, prose after v. 34.

150. Simek, *Dictionary of Northern Mythology*, 355, s.v. "vé"; *Egils saga Skalla-Grímssonar*, ch. 57; Larsen, tr., *Earliest Norwegian Law, Frostathing Law*, vol. 1, ch. 2, 223.

151. *Fornkonunga saga*, ch. 7; *Egils saga Skalla-Grímssonar*, ch. 52.

152. *Kormáks saga*, ch. 10.

153. *Gísla saga Súrssonar*, ch. 2; *Svarfdæla saga*, ch. 9; *Víga-Glúms saga*, ch. 4.

154. *Kormáks saga*, ch. 10.

155. *Njáls saga*, ch. 119; *Svarfdæla saga*, ch. 9; Saxo, *History of the Danes*, bk. 2, 54-55.

156. *Droplaugarsona saga*, ch. 15; *Bjarnar saga Hítdælakappa*, ch. 4; *Flóamanna saga*, ch. 17; *Gísla saga Súrssonar*, ch. 1; *Kormáks saga*, ch. 1, ch. 22, ch. 23.

157. *Egils saga Skalla-Grímssonar*, ch. 65; *Gunnlaugs saga ormstungu*, ch. 7, ch. 11; *Flóamanna saga*, ch. 16, ch. 27; *Kormáks saga*, ch. 14; *Reykdæla Saga ok Víga-Skútu*, ch. 1, ch. 19; *Svarfdæla saga*, ch. 9; *Víga-Glúms saga*, ch. 4.

158. Historiska museet SHM, 108202, accessed June 3, 2020, https://historiska.se/upptack-historien/object/108202-bildsten-av-kalksten/.

159. *Kormáks saga*, ch. 10, ch. 12; *Svarfdæla saga*, ch. 9; *Egils saga einhenda ok Ásmundar berserkjabana*, ch. 4.

160. *Flóamanna saga*, ch. 33; *Ólafs saga Tryggvasonar*, ch. 32; *Egils saga Skalla-Grímssonar*, ch. 66; *Gísla saga Súrssonar*, ch. 2.

161. *Gísla saga Súrssonar*, ch. 1; *Kormáks saga*, ch. 9; *Heiðarvíga saga*, ch. 15.

162. *Kormáks saga*, ch. 14.

163. *Flóamanna saga*, ch. 17; *Gunnlaugs saga ormstunga*, ch. 11; *Kjalnesinga saga*, ch. 9; *Kormáks saga*, ch. 10; *Svarfdæla saga*, ch. 9.

164. *Gunnlaugs saga ormstunga*, ch. 11; *Kormáks saga*, ch. 10; *Svarfdæla saga*, ch. 9; *Víga-Glúms saga*, ch. 4.

165. Saxo, *History of the Danes*, bk. 2, 54-55.

166. *Kormáks saga*, ch. 10, ch. 12; *Svarfdæla saga*, ch. 9.

167. *Svarfdæla saga*, ch. 9; *Kormáks saga*, ch. 22.

168. *Egils saga Skalla-Grímssonar,* ch. 65, ch. 66.

169. *Kormáks saga*, ch. 10

170. *Flóamanna saga*, ch. 31; *Brennu-Njáls saga*, ch. 24; *Skáldskaparmál*, ch. 17.

171. *Flóamanna saga*, ch. 17.

172. William R. Short and Hurstwic, unpublished research, Oct. 11, 2015. We used latticework to form a barrel-shaped structure we could drop over the combatants. Each was armed with a padded stick of the length mentioned in *Flóamanna saga*. Pairs of duelers fought rounds of simulated combat inside the *ker*. After each round, fighters' subjective comments were recorded. Video was shot of each round and reviewed later.

173. Guðmundur Ólafsson and Hörður Ágústsson, *The Reconstructed Medieval Farm in Þjórsárdalur* (Reykjavík: National Museum of Iceland, 2003), 13-14.

174. *Þórðar saga hreðu*, ch. 2.

175. Saxo, *History of the Danes*, bk. 2, 54-55.

176. *Svarfdæla saga*, ch. 9; *Kormáks saga*, ch. 14.

177. *Bjarnar saga Hítdælakappa*, ch. 4; *Egils saga Skalla-Grímssonar*, ch. 65, ch. 66; *Eyrbyggja saga*, ch. 8; *Flóamanna saga*, ch. 16, ch. 17, ch. 27, ch. 31, ch. 33; *Gísla saga Súrssonar*, ch. 1; *Gull-Þóris saga*, ch. 6; *Gunnlaugs*

saga ormstunga, ch. 7; *Kormáks saga*, ch. 14; *Brennu-Njáls saga*, ch. 101; *Reykdæla saga og Víga-Skútu*, ch. 19; *Landnámabók*, S. 86; S. 389; William R. Short and Hurstwic, unpublished research, Sept. 19, 2019. A database of duels reported in the literary sources including the *Sagas of Icelanders, Heimskringla*, and *Landnámabók* was compiled. Using the database, information about the outcome of duels was tabulated.

178. *Droplaugarsona saga*, ch. 15; *Egils saga Skalla-Grímssonar*, ch. 65, ch. 66; *Eyrbyggja saga*, ch. 8; *Flóamanna saga*, ch. 16; *Reykdæla saga og Víga-Skútu*, ch. 1; *Landnámabók*, S. 86, S. 389.

179. *Flóamanna saga*, ch. 16; *Ólafs saga Tryggvasonar*, ch. 32.

180. *Flóamanna saga*, ch. 15.

181. *Flóamanna saga*, ch. 17; *Droplaugarsona saga*, ch. 15.

182. *Bjarnar saga Hítdælakappa*, ch. 4.

183. *Flóamanna saga*, ch. 27; *Víga-Glúms saga*, ch. 4.

184. *Kormáks saga*, ch. 22, ch. 23.

185. *Flóamanna saga*, ch. 17; *Gísla saga Súrssonar*, ch. 2; *Kormáks saga*, ch. 1; *Víga-Glúms saga*, ch. 4.

186. *Kjalnesinga saga*, ch. 9; *Kormáks saga*, ch. 10.

187. *Kormáks saga*, ch. 10; *Gunnlaugs saga ormstunga*, ch. 11; *Kjalnesinga saga*, ch. 9.

188. Cleasby et al., eds., *Icelandic-English Dictionary*, 280-281. s.v. "hólm-lausn"; *Svarfdæla saga*, ch. 9.

189. *Svarfdæla saga*, ch. 9; *Gunnlaugs saga ormstunga*, ch. 11; *Kormáks saga*, ch. 10; *Reykdæla saga og Víga-Skútu*, ch. 1; *Víga-Glúms saga*, ch. 4.

190. Short, *Icelanders*, 126-127; Gunnar et al., eds., *Grágás Lagasafn íslenska þjóðveldisins*, 447, K. 113; Foote and Wilson, *Viking Achievement*, 379-380.

191. *Kormáks saga*, ch. 1; *Droplaugarsona saga*, ch. 15.

192. *Svarfdæla saga*, ch. 9.

193. *Gísla saga Súrssonar*, ch. 1; *Kormáks saga*, ch. 21.

194. *Gunnlaugs saga ormstunga*, ch. 11.

195. *Reykdæla saga og Víga-Skútu*, ch. 19; *Kormáks saga*, ch. 14.

196. *Egils saga Skalla-Grímssonar*, ch. 66; *Kormáks saga*, ch. 22.

197. *Kormáks saga*, ch. 10.

**APPENDIX: STATISTICAL OVERVIEW OF VIKING WEAPONS**

1. William R. Short and Hurstwic, unpublished research, July 8, 2018, and Aug. 18, 2018. The database was created by searching an electronic version of the *Sagas of Icelanders*—*Íslendinga sögur: orðstöðulykill og texti* (Reykjavík: Mál og menning, 1998). Search words included a wide range of words describing weapons, attacks, legal terms, and others. For each instance, the original saga text was read to gain context, and metadata was created and entered into the database to categorize the kinds of attacks and defenses, and which weapons were used for each attack and defense, along with information about the success of each attack and defense. From this database, it was possible to perform statistical analyses on weapons and weapons use over many thousands of mentions of such weapons and use in the sagas.

**GLOSSARY OF NON-ENGLISH TERMS**

1. Michael Barnes, *A New Introduction to Old Norse* (London: Viking Society for Northern Research, 2004), pt. 1, 8-9; E. V. Gordon, *An Introduction to Old Norse*, 2nd ed. (Oxford, UK: Clarendon Press, 1956), 266-267.

# ADDITIONAL READING

In writing this book, the authors used a wide variety of sources, as discussed in the preface and evidenced by the extensive notes for each chapter. For readers who seek more information, we encourage you to dig into the references in these notes.

Additionally, we strongly encourage all readers to seek out the primary literary sources, which, in addition to being genuinely entertaining reading, are also indispensable for understanding the Viking people, their culture, beliefs, and combat. These texts are readily accessible in the ancient languages and, generally, in good translations into modern vernacular English. Because there are so many good editions and translations, we have referenced these ancient literary sources only by title and chapter number or verse number so the readers can use the edition or translation of their choice.

For information on Viking-age artifacts, museum catalogs provide extensive details on artifacts held by museums in Nordic lands, and they are available in printed form and online. Likewise, archaeologists' reports for important excavations can be found in print and online editions.

Lastly, for those readers only just beginning their exploration of the Viking people, we provide here a short list of general Viking-related references we feel are highly accessible to non-specialist readers. Included in this list are sug-gested English translations of some of the ancient literary sources.

Anderson, Theodore M. *The Icelandic Family Saga: An Analytic Reading*. Cambridge, MA: Harvard University Press, 1967.

Ármann Jakobsson, *The Troll Inside You*. Goleta, CA: Punctum Books, 2017.

Barnes, Michael P. *Runes: A Handbook*. Woodbridge, UK: Boydell Press, 2012.

Brink, Stefan, and Neil Price, eds. *The Viking World*. London: Routledge, 2008.

Bryndís Sverrisdóttir, ed. *Reykjavík 871±2: Landnámssýningin The Settlement Exhibition*. Reykjavík: Minjasafn Reykjavíkur, 2006.

Byock, Jesse. *Viking Age Iceland*. London: Penguin, 2002.

Clover, Carol. *The Medieval Saga*. Ithaca, NY: Cornell University Press, 1982.

Crumlin-Pedersen, Ole. *Viking-Age Ships and Shipbuilding in Hedeby/Haithabu and Schleswig*. Ships and Boats of the North, vol. 2. Roskilde, Denmark: Viking Ship Museum, 2003.

Crumlin-Pedersen, Ole, and Olaf Olsen, eds. *The Skuldevev Ships I*. Ships & Boats of the North, vol. 4.1. Roskilde, Denmark: Viking Ship Museum, 2002.

Dennis, Andrew, et al., tr. and eds. *Laws of Early Iceland: Grágás*. 2 vols. Winnipeg: University of Manitoba Press, 1980 and 2000.

Foote, Peter, and David M. Wilson. *The Viking Achievement: The Society and Culture of Early Medieval Scandinavia*. London: Sedgewick & Jackson, 1970.

Gísli Sigurðsson. *The Medieval Icelandic Saga and Oral Tradition: A Discourse on Method*. Translated by Nicholas Jones. Cambridge, MA: Harvard University Press, 2004.

Gísli Sigurðsson and Vésteinn Ólason, eds. *The Manuscripts of Iceland*. Translated by Bernard Scudder. Reykjavík: Árni Magnússon Institute in Iceland, 2004.

Graham-Campbell, James. *Viking Artifacts: A Select Catalogue*. London: British Museum Publications, 1980.

Graham-Campbell, James, ed. *Cultural Atlas of the Viking World*. New York: Facts on File, 1994.

Grønlie, Siân, tr. *Íslendingabók—The Book of the Icelanders*; *Kristni saga—The Story of the Conversion*. Viking Society for Northern Research Text Series. Vol. 18. London: Viking Society for Northern Research, 2006.

Gunnar Karlsson. *The History of Iceland*. Minneapolis: University of Minnesota Press, 2000.

Haywood, John. *Encyclopaedia of the Viking Age*. New York: Thames & Hudson, 2000.

———. *The Penguin Historical Atlas of the Vikings*. London: Penguin Books, 1995.

Helle, Knut, ed. *The Cambridge History of Scandinavia*. Vol. 1. Cambridge: Cambridge University Press, 2003.

Hermann Pálsson and Paul Edwards, tr. *The Book of Settlements: Landnámabók*. Winnipeg: University of Manitoba Press, 1972.

Jochens, Jenny. *Women in Old Norse Society*. Ithaca, NY: Cornell University Press, 1995.

Jón Jóhannesson. *Íslendinga Saga: A History of the Old Icelandic Commonwealth*. Translated by Haraldur Bessason. Winnipeg: University of Manitoba Press, 1974.

Jónas Kristjánsson. *Eddas and Sagas*. Translated by Peter Foote. Reykjavík: Hið íslenska bókmenntafélag, 1997.

Jones, Gwyn. *A History of the Vikings*. 2nd ed. Oxford: Oxford University Press, 1984.

Larrington, Carolyne, tr. *The Poetic Edda*. Oxford: Oxford University Press, 2014.

Larson, Laurence, tr. *The Earliest Norwegian Law Being the Gulathing Law and Frostathing Law*. New York: Columbia University Press, 1935.

McGrail, Séan. *Ancient Boats in North-West Europe: The Archaeology of Water Transport to AD 1500*. London: Addison Wesley Longman, 1987.

McTurk, Rory, ed. *A Companion to Old Norse-Icelandic Literature and Culture*. Malden, MA: Blackwell, 2005.

Moilanen, Mikko. *Marks of Fire, Value and Faith*. Turku, Finland: Suomen keskiajan arkeologian seura, 2015.

Page, R. I. *Chronicles of the Vikings*. Toronto: University of Toronto Press, 1995.

Peirce, Ian G. *Swords of the Viking Age*. Woodbridge, UK: Boydell Press, 2002.

Pulsiano, Phillip, ed. *Medieval Scandinavia: An Encyclopedia*. Garland Reference Library of the Humanities, vol. 934. New York: Garland, 1993.

Roesdahl, Else. *The Vikings*. 2nd ed. Translated by Susan M. Margeson and Kirsten Williams. London: Penguin Books, 1998.

Roesdahl, Else, and David M. Wilson, eds. *From Viking to Crusader: The Scandinavians and Europe 800–1200*. New York: Rizzoli International, 1992.

Sawyer, Peter, ed. *The Oxford Illustrated History of the Vikings*. Oxford: Oxford University Press, 1997.

Saxo Grammaticus. *The History of the Danes*. Edited by Hilda Ellis Davidson, translated by Peter Fisher. Cambridge, UK: D. S. Brewer, 1998.

Short, William R. *Icelanders in the Viking Age: The People of the Sagas*. Jefferson, NC: McFarland, 2010.

———. *Viking Weapons and Combat Techniques*. Yardley, PA: Westholme, 2008.

Sigurður Nordal. *Icelandic Culture.* Translated by Vilhjálmur T. Bjarnar. Ithaca, NY: Cornell University Library, 1990.

Simek, Rudolf. *Dictionary of Northern Mythology.* Translated by Angela Hall. Cambridge, UK: D. S. Brewer, 1996.

Snorri Sturluson. *Edda.* Translated and edited by Anthony Faulkes. London: Everyman, 1987.

———. *Heimskringla: History of the Kings of Norway.* Translated by Lee M. Hollander. Austin: University of Texas Press, 1964.

Teresa Dröfn Freysdóttir Njarðvík. *Runes: the Icelandic Book of Fuþark.* Reykjavík: Icelandic Magic, 2019.

Vésteinn Ólason. *Dialogues with the Viking Age: Narration and Representation in the Sagas of the Icelanders.* Translated by Andrew Wawn. Reykjavík: Heimskringla, 1998.

Viðar Hreinsson, ed. *The Complete Sagas of the Icelanders.* Reykjavík: Leifur Eiríksson, 1997.

Wolf, Kirsten. *Daily Life of the Vikings.* Westport, CT: Greenwood Press, 2004.

# ACKNOWLEDGMENTS

As with any project of long duration and large scope, this book would not have been possible without the help of numerous people. This project is the culmination of a twenty-year journey, and so there are too many people who have assisted us to mention them all here. Please know that all of you are appreciated by us and have our gratitude.

At the top of the list of people to receive an accolade are those who have accepted the most punishment to make this book a reality: the people of Hurstwic, who have attained the rank of instructor. Many of the experiments detailed in these pages would not have been possible without their having generously donated their time and talents, their sweat and their blood: Matt Card, Mike Cicale, Robin Cooper, John Davis, Kristine Krakowski, Matthew Marino, Matthew Nachtrieb, and Barbara Wechter, along with the instructors in the Hurstwic affiliate groups: Michael Gelaude and Rodrigo Torres. We also thank the hundreds of Hurstwic students who willingly served as test subjects in our bizarre experiments.

A number of experts in their respective fields have served as our advisers. These people have been our sacred well of knowledge, and they selflessly allowed us to drink from their well daily. We are grateful for their advice, guidance, and setting us straight when we were on the wrong path: Lars Andersen, Ármann Guðmundsson, James Austin, Bjarki Sigurðsson, Bjarnheiður Jóhannsdóttir, Borgný Gunnarsdóttir, Dagrún Ósk Jónsdóttir, Guðmundur Stefán Sigurðsson, Guðný Zoëga, Guðvarður Már Gunnlaugsson, Halla Sigríður Steinólfsdóttir, Hildur Gestsdóttir, Hulda Björk Guðmundsdóttir, Hrönn Konráðsdóttir, Höskuldur Þorbjarnarson, Jón M. Ívarsson, Lee A. Jones, Lísabet Guðmundsdóttir, Margrét Hrönn Hallmundsdóttir, Michelle Lynn Mielnik, Stig Gunnar Myren, Ólöf Bjarnardóttir, Snorri Freyr Hilmarsson, Svana Hrönn Jóhannsdóttir, Teresa Dröfn Freysdóttir Njarðvík, Þór Hjalatín, Þórir Örn Guðmundsson, Þorleifur Geirsson, and the curators of private collections who will remain anonymous.

And special thanks to the *völva* who has the visions: Nae.

# INDEX